Lecture Notes in Artificial Intelligence 3230

Edited by J. G. Carbonell and J. Siekmann

Subseries of Lecture Notes in Computer Science

José Luis Vicedo
Patricio Martínez-Barco Rafael Muñoz
Maximiliano Saiz Noeda (Eds.)

Advances in Natural Language Processing

4th International Conference, EsTAL 2004
Alicante, Spain, October 20-22, 2004
Proceedings

Series Editors

Jaime G. Carbonell, Carnegie Mellon University, Pittsburgh, PA, USA
Jörg Siekmann, University of Saarland, Saarbrücken, Germany

Volume Editors

José Luis Vicedo
Patricio Martínez-Barco
Rafael Muñoz
Maximiliano Saiz Noeda
Universidad de Alicante
Departamento de Lenguajes y Sistemas Informáticos
Carretera de San Vicente del Raspeig
03690 San Vicente del Raspeig, Alicante, Spain
E-mail: {vicedo;patricio;rafael;max}@dlsi.ua.es

Library of Congress Control Number: 2004113295

CR Subject Classification (1998): I.2.7, F.4.2-3, I.2, H.3, I.7

ISSN 0302-9743
ISBN 3-540-23498-5 Springer Berlin Heidelberg New York

Springer is a part of Springer Science+Business Media

springeronline.com

Printed in Germany

Typesetting: Camera-ready by author, data conversion by Scientific Publishing Services, Chennai, India
Printed on acid-free paper SPIN: 11334347 06/3142 5 4 3 2 1 0

Preface

EsTAL – España for Natural Language Processing – continued on from the three previous conferences: FracTAL, held at the Université de Franch-Comté, Besançon (France) in December 1997, VexTAL, held at Venice International University, Cá Foscari (Italy), in November 1999, and PorTAL, held at the Universidade do Algarve, Faro (Portugal), in June 2002. The main goals of these conferences have been: (i) to bring together the international NLP community; (ii) to strengthen the position of local NLP research in the international NLP community; and (iii) to provide a forum for discussion of new research and applications.

EsTAL contributed to achieving these goals and increasing the already high international standing of these conferences, largely due to its Program Committee, composed of renowned researchers in the field of natural language processing and its applications. This clearly contributed to the significant number of papers submitted (72) by researchers from (18) different countries.

The scope of the conference was structured around the following main topics: (i) *computational linguistics research* (spoken and written language analysis and generation; pragmatics, discourse, semantics, syntax and morphology; lexical resources; word sense disambiguation; linguistic, mathematical, and psychological models of language; knowledge acquisition and representation; corpus-based and statistical language modelling; machine translation and translation aids; computational lexicography), and (ii) *monolingual and multilingual intelligent language processing and applications* (information retrieval, extraction and question answering; automatic summarization; document categorization; natural language interfaces; dialogue systems and evaluation of systems).

Each paper was revised by three reviewers from the Program Committee or by external referees designed by them. All those who contributed are mentioned on the following pages. The review process led to the selection of 42 papers for presentation. They have been published in this volume.

We would like to express here our thanks to all the reviewers for their quick and excellent work. We extend these thanks to our invited speakers, Walter Daelemans and Rada Mihalcea for their valuable contribution, which undoubtedly increased the interest in the conference. We are also indebted to a number of individuals for taking care of specific parts of the conference program. Specially, to Miguel Angel Varó who built and maintained all Web services for the conference.

Finally, we want to thank the University of Alicante, and, specially, the Office of the Vice-President for Extracurricular Activities (*Vicerrectorado de Extensión Universitaria*) and the Department of Software and Computing Systems (*Departamento de Lenguajes y Sistemas Informáticos*) because of their support of this conference.

October 2004 José L. Vicedo and Patricio Martinez-Barco

Preface

EsTAL – España for Natural Language Processing – continued on from the three previous conferences: FracTAL, held at the Université de Franche-Comté, Besançon (France) in December 1997, VexTAL, held at Venice International University, Cà Foscari (Italy), in November 1999, and PorTAL, held at the Universidade do Algarve, Faro (Portugal), in June 2002. The main goals of these conferences have been: (i) to bring together the international NLP community; (ii) to strengthen the position of local NLP research in the international NLP community; and (iii) to provide a forum for discussion of new research and applications.

EsTAL contributed to achieving these goals and increasing the already high international standing of these conferences, largely due to its Program Committee, composed of renowned researchers in the field of natural language processing and its applications. This clearly contributed to the significant number of papers submitted (72) by researchers from 18 different countries.

The scope of the conference was structured around the following main topics: (i) computational linguistics research (spoken and written language analysis and generation; pragmatics, discourse, semantics, syntax and morphology; lexical resources; word sense disambiguation; linguistic, mathematical, and psychological models of language; knowledge acquisition and representation; corpus-based and statistical language modelling; machine translation and translation aids; computational lexicography), and (ii) monolingual and multilingual intelligent language processing and applications (information retrieval, extraction and question answering; automatic summarization; document categorization; natural language interfaces; dialogue systems and evaluation of systems).

Each paper was revised by three reviewers from the Program Committee or by external referees designed by them. All those who contributed are mentioned on the following pages. The review process led to the selection of 42 papers for presentation, which have been published in this volume.

We would like to express here our thanks to all the reviewers for their quick and excellent work. We extend these thanks to our invited speakers, Walter Daelemans and Rada Mihalcea for their valuable contribution, which undoubtedly increased the interest in the conference. We are also indebted to a number of individuals for taking care of specific aspects of the conference organization. Specially, to Miguel Angel Varó who built and maintained all Web services for the conference.

Finally, we want to thank the University of Alicante, and, specially, the Office of the Vice-President for Extracurricular Activities (Vicerrectorado de Extensión Universitaria) and the Department of Software and Computing Systems (Departamento de Lenguajes y Sistemas Informáticos) because of their support of this conference.

October 2004 José L. Vicedo and Patricio Martínez-Barco

Organization

Program and Conference Chairs

José L. Vicedo (University of Alicante, Spain)
Patricio Martinez-Barco (University of Alicante, Spain)

Organization Chairs

Rafael Muñoz (University of Alicante, Spain)
Maximiliano Saiz (University of Alicante, Spain)

Program Committee

Alfonso Ureña (University of Jaen, Spain)
Bernardo Magnini (ITC-irst, Italy)
Dan Moldovan (University of Texas at Dallas, USA)
Elisabete Ranchhod (University of Lisbon, Portugal)
German Rigau (University of the Basque Country, Spain)
Hans Uszkoreit (Saarland University at Saarbrücken, Germany)
Henri Zingle (University of Nice, France)
Horacio Rodríguez (Technical University of Catalonia, Spain)
Horacio Saggion (University of Sheffield, UK)
Igor Melcuk (University of Montreal, Canada)
Julio Gonzalo (Universidad Nacional de Educación a Distancia (UNED), Spain)
Lidia Moreno (Polytechnical University of Valencia, Spain)
Manuel de Buenaga (European University of Madrid, Spain)
Manuel Palomar (University of Alicante, Spain)
Massimo Poesio (University of Essex, UK)
Nuno Mamede (INESC-ID Lisbon, Portugal)
Peter Greenfield (Centre Lucien Tesnière, Univ. of Franche-Comté, France)
Pierre-André Buvet (University of Paris 13, France)
Rodolfo Delmonte (University of Venice, Italy)
Ruslan Mitkov (University of Wolverhampton, UK)
Sanda Harabagiu (University of Texas at Dallas, USA)
Stephane Chaudiron (Ministry of Technology and Research, France)
Sylviane Cardey (Centre Lucien Tesnière, Univ. of Franche-Comté, France)
Victor Díaz (University of Seville, Spain)
Werner Winiwarter (University of Vienna, Austria)

Referees

Alfonso Ureña
Alicia Ageno
Ana García Serrano
Anabela Barreiro
Antonio Ferrandez
Armando Suarez
Bernardo Magnini
Carlo Strapparava
Damián López
Dan Moldovan
Diamantino Caseiro
Elisabete Ranchhod
Fernando Llopis
Finley Lacatusu
Georgiana Puscasu
German Rigau
Hans Uszkoreit
Henri Zingle
Horacio Rodríguez
Horacio Saggion
Igor Melcuk
José L. Vicedo
Juan A. Pérez-Ortiz
Julio Gonzalo
Laura Hasler
Le An Ha
Lidia Moreno
Luis Oliveira
Luisa Coheur
Manuel de Buenaga
Manuel García Vega
Manuel Palomar
María Teresa Martín
Massimo Poesio
Maximiliano Saiz Noeda
Miguel Angel García
Mijail Alexandrov
Mikel Forcada
Nuno Mamede
Olivia Sanchez
Patricio Martinez-Barco
Paul Morarescu
Paula Carvalho
Peter Greenfield
Pierre-André Buvet
Rafael Muñoz
Ramón López
Ricardo Ribeiro
Richard Evans
Rodolfo Delmonte
Ruslan Mitkov
Sanda Harabagiu
Stephane Chaudiron
Sylviane Cardey
Victor Díaz
Viktor Pekar
Werner Winiwarter
Zornitsa Kozareva

Table of Contents

Adaptive Selection of Base Classifiers in One-Against-All Learning for Large Multi-labeled Collections

Arturo Montejo Ráez[1], Luís Alfonso Ureña López[2], and Ralf Steinberger[3]

[1] European Laboratory for Nuclear Research, Geneva, Switzerland
[2] Department of Computer Science, University of Jaén, Spain
[3] European Commission, Joint Research Centre, Ispra, Italy

Abstract. In this paper we present the problem found when studying an automated text categorization system for a collection of High Energy Physics (HEP) papers, which shows a very large number of possible classes (over 1,000) with highly imbalanced distribution. The collection is introduced to the scientific community and its imbalance is studied applying a new indicator: the *inner imbalance degree*. The one-against-all approach is used to perform multi-label assignment using Support Vector Machines. Over-weighting of positive samples and S-Cut thresholding is compared to an approach to automatically select a classifier for each class from a set of candidates. We also found that it is possible to reduce computational cost of the classification task by discarding classes for which classifiers cannot be trained successfully.

1 Introduction

The automatic assignment of keywords to documents using full-text data is a subtask of *Text Categorization*, a growing area where Information Retrieval techniques and Machine Learning algorithms meet offering solutions to problems with real world collections.

We can distinguish three paradigms in text categorization: the *binary* case, the *multi-class* case and the *multi-label* case. In the binary case a sample either belongs or does not belong to one of two given classes. In the multi-class case a sample belongs to just one of a set of m classes. Finally, in the multi-label case, a sample may belong to several classes at the same time, that is, classes are *overlapped*. In binary classification a classifier is trained, by means of supervised algorithms, to assign a sample document to one of two possible sets. These sets are usually referred to as belonging (positive) or not belonging (negative) samples respectively (the one-against-all approach), or to two disjoint classes (the one-against-one approach). For these two binary classification tasks we can select among a wide range of algorithms, including Naïve Bayes, Linear Regression, Support Vector Machines (SVM) [8] and LVQ [11]. SVM has been reported to outperform the other algorithms. The binary case has been set as a base case from which the two other cases are derived. In multi-class and multi-label assignment,

J. L. Vicedo et al. (Eds.): EsTAL 2004, LNAI 3230, pp. 1–12, 2004.

the traditional approach consists of training a binary classifier for each class, and then, whenever the binary base case returns a measure of confidence on the classification, assigning either the top ranked one (multi-class assignment) or a given number of the top ranked ones (multi-label assignment). More details about these three paradigms can be found in [1]). We will refer to the ranking approach as the *battery* strategy because inter-dependency is not taken into consideration.

Another approach for multi-labeling consists of returning all those classes whose binary classifiers provide a positive answer for the sample. It has the advantage of allowing different binary classifiers for each class, since inter-class scores do not need to be coherent (since there is no ranking afterwards). Better results have been reported when applying one-against-one in multi-class classification [1], but in our multi-label case this is not an option because any class could theoretically appear together with any other class, making it difficult to establish disjoint assignments. This is the reason why one-against-all deserves our attention in the present work.

Although classification is subject to intense research (see [18]), some issues demand more attention than they have been given so far. In particular, problems relating to *multi-label* classification would require more attention. However, due to the lack of available resources (mainly multi-labeled document collections), this area advances more slowly than others. Furthermore, multi-label assignment should not simply be studied as a general multi-class problem (which itself is rather different from the binary case), but it needs to be considered as a special case with additional requirements. For instance, in multi-label cases, some classes are inter-related, the degree of imbalance is usually radically different from one class to the next and, from a performance point of view, the need of comparing a sample to every single classifier is a waste of resources.

2 The Class Imbalance Problem

Usually, multi-labeled collections make use of a wide variety of classes, resulting in an unequal distribution of classes throughout the collection and a high number of rare classes. This means not only that there is a strong imbalance between positive and negative samples, but also that some classes are used much more frequently than other classes. This phenomenon, known as the *class imbalance problem*, is especially relevant for algorithms like the C4.5 classification tree [4, 3] and margin-based classifiers like SVM [16, 20, 7].

Extensive studies have been carried out on this subject as reported by Japkowicz [7], identifying three major issues in the class imbalance problem: *concept complexity*, *training set size* and *degree of imbalance*. Concept complexity refers to the degree of "sparsity" of a certain class in the feature space (the space where document vectors are represented). This means that a hypothetical clustering algorithm acting on a class with high concept complexity would establish many small clusters for the same class. Regarding the second issue, i.e. the lack of a significantly large training sets, the only possible remedy is the usage of over-sampling when the amount of available samples is insufficient, and under-sampling techniques for classes with too many samples, e.g. just using a limited number of samples for training a SVM, by selecting those positive and negative samples that are close to each other in the feature space. The validity of these techniques is also subject to debate [4]. Finally, Japkowicz defines the degree of imbalance as an index to indicate how much a class is more represented over another, including both the degree of imbalance between classes (what we call *inter-class imbalance*) and between its positive and negative samples (what we call the *inner imbalance degree*). Unfortunately, Japkowicz defined these values for her work towards the generation of an artificial collection and rewrote them later to fit specific problems regarding fixed parameters and the C5.0 algorithm, which make them difficult to manipulate. For these reasons, we cannot reuse her equations and propose here a variant focusing on the multi-label case.

We define the *inner imbalance degree* of a certain class i as a measure of the positive samples over the total of samples:

$$i_i = |1 - 2n_i/n| \tag{1}$$

where

n is the total number of samples and
n_i is the total number of samples having the class i in their labels.

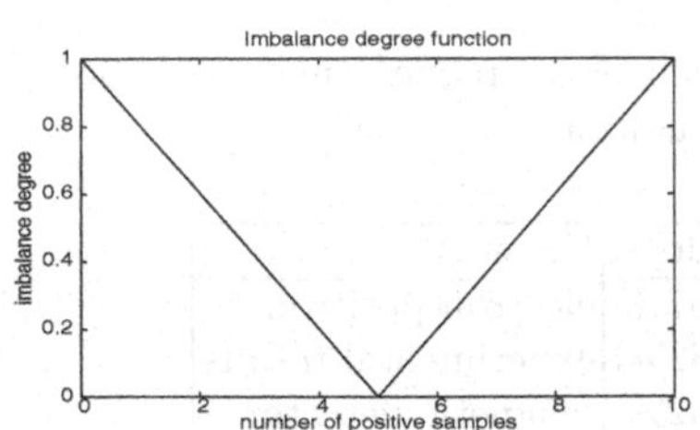

Fig. 1. The linear 'imbalance degree' function

Japkowicz' definition of imbalance degree helps in the generation of artificial distributions of documents to classes. Its value does not lie within a defined range, which makes it difficult to manipulate and compare with the degree of other classes in different partitions. The value proposed in equation 1 is zero for perfectly balanced classes, i.e. when the number of positive and negative samples are the same. It has a value of 1 when all samples are either positive or negative for that class. Its linear behavior is shown in figure 1 and, as we can see, it varies within the range [0,1].

3 The HEP Collection

A very suitable document set for multi-label categorization research is the HEP collection of preprints, available from the European Laboratory for Nuclear Research. Some experiments have been carried out using this collection ([13, 12]), and its interesting distribution of classes allows us to carry out a number of experiments and to design a new approach. An analysis of the collection has shown that there is the typical high level of imbalance among classes. If a given class is rarely represented in a collection, we can intuitively foresee a biased training that will yield classifiers with a low performance. It is clear that, if the collection were perfectly balanced, we could expect better categorization results, due to better learning.

The hep-ex partition of the HEP collection is composed of 2802 abstracts related to experimental high-energy physics that are indexed with 1093 main keywords (the categories).[1] Figure 2 shows the distribution of keywords across the collection.

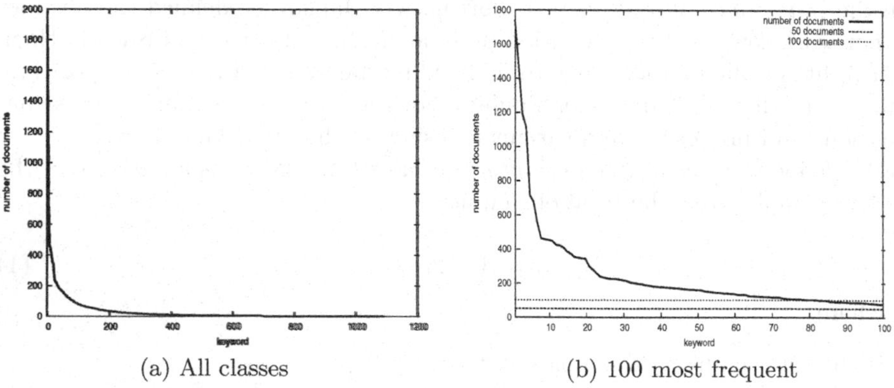

(a) All classes (b) 100 most frequent

Fig. 2. Distribution of classes across documents in the hep-ex partition

As we can see, this partition is **very** imbalanced: only 84 classes are represented by more than 100 samples and only five classes by more than 1000. The uneven use is particularly noticeable for the ten most frequent keywords: In table 1 the left column shows the number of positive samples of a keyword and the right column shows the percentage over the total of samples in the collection.

Table 1. The ten most frequent main keywords in the hep-ex partition

No. docs.	Keyword
1898 (67%)	electron positron
1739 (62%)	experimental results
1478 (52%)	magnetic detector
1190 (42%)	quark
1113 (39%)	talk
715 (25%)	Z0
676 (24%)	anti-p p
551 (19%)	neutrino
463 (16%)	W
458 (16%)	jet

We can now study this collection applying the inner imbalance degree measure defined in equation 1. The two graphs in figures 3a and 3b show the inner imbalance degree for the main keywords in the hep-ex partition. We can notice how fast

[1] We did not consider the keywords related to reaction and energy because they are based on formulae and other specific data that is not easily identifiable in the plain-text version of a paper.

the imbalance grows to a total imbalance degree of almost 1. When looking at the ten most frequent classes, we can see the effect of our degree estimation: classes 0 and 1 are more imbalanced than class 2, which gets the lowest degree of imbalance in the whole set of classes. It is due to the fact that, as shown by table 1, this class has almost the same number of positive and negative samples. From class 3 onwards, the imbalance then grows dramatically.

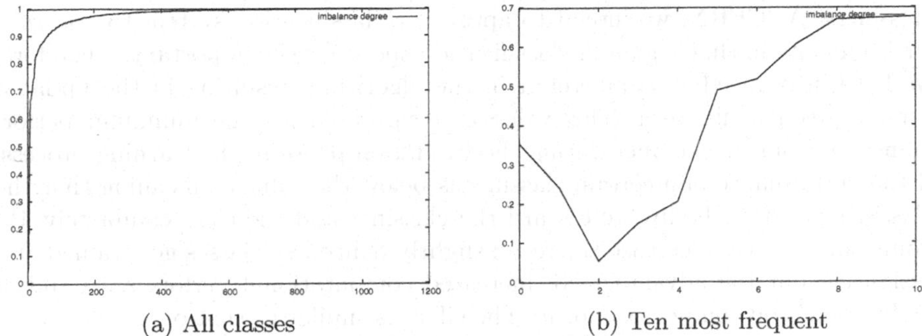

(a) All classes (b) Ten most frequent

Fig. 3. Imbalance degree of classes in the `hep-ex` partition

When training binary classifiers for these keywords, we realized that the performance decreases strongly with growing imbalance degree. To correct document distribution across classes, we can use over-sampling (or under-sampling) or tune our classifiers accordingly. For example, for SVM we can set a cost factor, by which training errors on positive samples out-weights errors on negative samples [14]. We will use this in our experiments.

4 Balance Weighting and Classifier Filtering

Some algorithms work better when, in the one-against-all approach, the number of positive samples is similar to the number of negative ones, i.e. when the class is balanced across the collection. However, multi-label collections are typically highly imbalanced. This is true for the HEP collection, but also for other known document sets like the OHSUMED medical collection used in the filtering track of TREC [5], and for the document collection of the European Institutions classified according to the EUROVOC thesaurus. This latter collection has been studied extensively for automatic indexing by Pouliquen et. al. (e.g. [2]), who exploit a variety of parameters in their attempt to determine whether some terms refer to one class or to another in the multi-labeled set.

The question now is how to deal with these collections when trying to apply binary learners that are sensitive to high imbalance degrees. We can use techniques like over-sampling and under-sampling, as pointed out earlier, but this would lead to an overload of non-informational samples in the former case, and to the loss of information in the second case. Furthermore, concept complexity has also its effects on binary classifiers. We have not paid attention to this fact since it is out of the scope of the present study, but we should consider this to be yet another drawback for collections indexed with a large number of non-balanced classes.

In our experiments we basically train a system using the battery strategy, but *(a)*, we allow tuning the binary classifier for a given class by a balance factor, and *(b)* we provide the possibility of choosing the best of a given set of binary classifiers. At CERN, we intend to apply our classification system to *real-time* environments so that a gain in classification speed is very important. Therefore, we have introduced a parameter α in the algorithm, resulting in the updated version given in figure 4. This value is a threshold for the minimum performance of a binary classifier during the validation phase in the learning process. If the performance of a certain classifier is below the value α, meaning that the classifier performs badly, we discard the classifier and the class completely. By doing this, we may decrease the recall slightly (since less classes get trained and assigned), but the advantages of increased computational performance and of higher precision compensate for it. The effect is similar to that of the *SCutFBR* proposed by Yang [21]. We never attempt to return a positive answer for rare classes. In the following, we show how this filtering saves us considering many classes without significant loss in performance.

We allow over-weighted positive samples using the actual fraction of positive samples over negative ones, that is, the weight for positive samples (w_+) is:

$$w_+ = C_- / C_+ \tag{2}$$

where

C_- is the total number of negative samples for the class
C_+ is the total number of positive samples for the class

As we can see, the more positive documents we have for a given class, the lower the over-weight is, which makes sense in order to give more weight only when few positive samples are found. This method was used by Morik et al. [14] but they did not report how much it improved the performance of the classifier over the non-weighted scheme. As we said, this w_+ factor was used in our experiments to over-weight positive samples over negative ones, i.e. the classification error on a positive sample is higher than that of a negative one.

We also considered the *S-Cut* approach. The assignation of a sample as positive can be tuned by specifying the decision border. By default it is zero, but it can be set using the S-Cut algorithm [21]. This algorithm uses as threshold the one that gives the best performance on an evaluation set. That is, once the classifier has been trained, we apply it against an evaluation set using as possible thresholds the classification values (the margin for SVM). The threshold that reported the best performance (the highest F1 in our case) will be used.

```
Input:
   a set of multi-labeled training documents D_t
   a set of validation documents D_v
   a threshold α on the evaluation measure
   a set of possible label (classes) L,
   a set of candidate binary classifiers C
Output :
   a set C' = {c_1, ..., c_k, ..., c_|L|} of trained binary classifiers
Pseudo code:
   C' = ∅
   for-each l_i in L do
      T = ∅
      for-each c_j in C do
         train-classifier(c_j, l_i, D_t)
         T = T ∪ {c_j}
      end-for-each
      c_best = best-classifier(T, D_v)
      if evaluate-classifier(c_best) > α
         C' = C' ∪ {c_best}
      end-if
   end-for-each
```

Fig. 4. The one-against-all learning algorithm with classifier filtering

5 Experiments and Results

5.1 Data Preparation

The collection consists of 2967 full-text abstracts linked to 1103 main keywords. Each abstract was processed as follows:

- Punctuation was removed
- Every character was lowercased
- Stop words were removed
- The Porter stemming algorithm [15] was applied
- Resulting stems were weighted according to the TF.IDF scheme [17]

After processing the collection in this way, we trained the system applying each strategy using the *SVM-Light*[2] package as the base binary classifier. We also filtered out classes not appearing in any document either in the training, validation or test sets, reducing the number of classes to 443.8 on average. Results are shown at the end of this section.

For the **evaluation** in experiments, *ten-fold cross validation* [9] was used in order to produce statistically relevant results that do not depend on the

[2] SVM-Light is available at `http://svmlight.joachims.org/`

partitioning of the collection into training, validation and test sets. Extensive experiments have shown that this is the best choice to get an accurate estimate. The measures computed are *precision* and *recall*. The F_1 measure (introduced by Rijsbergen [19] a long time ago) is used as an overall indicator based on the two former ones and is the reference when filtering is applied. Also *accuracy* and *error* measurements are given for later discussion. The final values are computed using macro-averaging on a per-document basis, rather than the usual micro-averaging over classes. The reason is, again, the high imbalance in the collection. If we average by class, rare classes will influence the result as much as the most frequent ones, which will not provide a good estimate of the performance of the multi-label classifier over documents. Since the goal of this system is to be used for automated classification of individual documents, we consider it to be far more useful to concentrate on these measurements for our evaluation of the system. More details about these concepts can be found in [18], [10] and [22].

5.2 Results

Table 2 shows the results of ten runs of our multi-label classifier with different configurations. The highest values of F_1 are reached when letting the system choose among fixed values for over-weighting positive samples (2, 5, 10 and 20). These are the results when applying the algorithm of figure 4 with $\alpha = 0.0$, i.e. no filtering over classifiers is done.

Table 2. Results of experiments using SVM

Experiment	Precision	Recall	F1	Accuracy	Error	% of classes covered
No weight	74.07	33.96	43.92	98.23	1.77	33.96
No weight / Scut	**74.26**	34.44	44.38	98.24	1.76	99.95
Overweight 20	51.47	**45.84**	46.50	97.71	2.29	57.32
Auto weight	58.10	44.39	48.09	97.94	2.06	58.09
Overw. 2,5,10,20 / Scut	71.74	39.92	48.47	**98.25**	**1.75**	**100.00**
Auto weight / Scut	58.03	45.30	48.56	97.89	2.11	99.82
Overweight 2	70.74	40.45	48.78	98.21	1.79	53.36
Overweight 5	64.56	43.57	49.40	98.11	1.89	57.19
Overweight 10	62.30	45.22	50.14	98.08	1.92	57.30
Overw. 2,5,10,20	65.89	44.59	**50.53**	98.17	1.83	57.53

We see that the top recall reached does not imply having more classes trained. Therefore we may want to study how we can reduce the number of classes trained to speed up the classification process without loosing too much in performance. For that purpose, we experimented with different values of α, as shown in tables 3 and 4.

Table 3. Results of experiments using multi-weighted SVM with filtering

α	0.0	0.1	0.2	0.3	0.4	0.5	0.6	0.7
Precision	65.89	70.04	70.41	70.88	71.90	71.96	71.02	67.96
Recall	44.59	44.49	43.95	42.95	40.54	36.65	31.80	23.02
F_1	50.53	**51.59**	51.32	50.77	49.21	46.11	41.70	32.83
Accuracy	98.17	98.25	98.25	98.25	98.24	98.21	98.15	98.03
Error	1.83	1.75	1.75	1.75	1.76	1.79	1.85	1.97
% classes trained	57.53	56.49	50.81	43.20	32.73	23.23	16.00	8.58

Table 4. Results of experiments using auto-weighted S-Cut thresholded SVM with filtering

α	0.0	0.1	0.2	0.3	0.4	0.5	0.6	0.7
Precision	58.03	62.47	64.84	67.45	69.47	71.19	71.14	68.24
Recall	45.30	45.04	44.83	44.24	42.76	39.59	34.43	24.88
F_1	48.56	49.93	50.47	50.75	50.27	48.37	44.10	34.76
Accuracy	97.89	98.06	98.14	98.20	98.23	98.22	98.17	98.05
Error	2.11	1.94	1.86	1.80	1.77	1.78	1.83	1.95
% classes trained	99.82	85.30	77.10	68.47	55.74	42.34	30.82	16.72

5.3 Analysis

Interesting conclusions can be drawn from the tables above. The first thing we notice is that recall is low compared to precision. This is normal if we consider the existence of rare and, therefore, difficult-to-train classes. When tuning our multi-label classifier, we see that variations in precision are more representative than for recall. The F_1 measure remains quite stable: throughout all the experiments with different configurations, the most we gain is 6.61%. However, a very important result is that, even when some configurations are able to train up to 100% of the total of classes involved (we can see how the percentage of classes successfully trained varies widely), it does not influence that much the overall performance of the classifier. We can conclude that *rare classes are not worth training*. This is the reason for the design of our filtering algorithm. Furthermore, it is not clear that S-Cut and auto-weighting strategies are so relevant for our data. As we can also notice, accuracy and error are not very sensitive to the variations of our parameters, but this is again due to imbalance: most of the classes are rare and for the most frequent ones we get high precision and recall, even with not very sophisticated configurations.

When discarding classes, we obviously gain in precision and, despite more classes not being trained, we do not lose that much in recall. The result is a better F_1 than without discarding, as shown by F1 values in 2 compared to those of tables 3 and 4. We can see how strongly we can reduce the number of classes without affecting significantly the overall performance of the multi-label classifier. Figures 5a and 5b visualize the behavior described. The bigger our α is, the more classes are discarded. From all the test runs, the best value of F_1 was

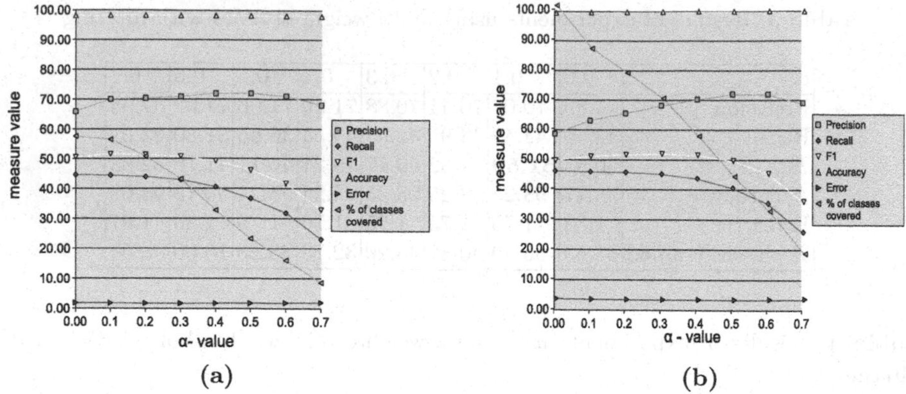

Fig. 5. Influence of filtering on (a) multi-weighted SVM and (b) auto-weighted with S-cut thresholding

obtained with an α value of 0.1 and using candidate classifiers with over-weights 2, 5, 10 and 20 for positive classes. From the graphs we can see that increasing α yields to a higher precision up to a maximum from which the threshold will be so restrictive that even good classifiers are discarding and, therefore, the precision starts to decrease accordingly. Thus, our choice of α will depend on our preference of precision over recall and our need of reducing classes for faster classification. If we are able to discard non-relevant (rarely used) classes, we can almost maintain our performance classifying against a lower number of classes.

6 Conclusions and Future Work

We have presented a new collection for multi-label indexing. The `hep-ex` partition can be obtained by contacting the authors. A calculus for measuring the imbalance degree has been proposed, along with a study of the overweight of positive classes on this collection using SVM and the application of S-Cut. The results show that this is a relevant issue, and that an imbalance study of any multi-label collection should be carried out in order to properly select the base binary classifiers. Another promising issue would be to work on other aspects of imbalance like *concept complexity* [6]. We have started investigating this topic by working with "concepts" rather than with terms in order to reduce the term space. By doing this, we would cover the main drawbacks of imbalanced collections.

Filtering by classification thresholding is very effective to reduce the number of classes involved in multi-label classification. Without forcing expensive tuning of the threshold, we propose to provide a range of α values and let the algorithm choose the classifier with the best behavior.

One of the disadvantages using the battery approach is its computational cost, since we have to launch every classifier for a sample. However, SVM is quite selective, not being trainable in many cases, discarding in this way many conflictive classes. This reduces the computation without loosing too much in performance. We have shown that, by increasing the selectivity, we can even gain significantly in precision without loosing too much in recall.

One multi-label collection issue we have not considered is inter-class dependency. In some preliminary analysis we found that the correlation among classes is relevant enough to be considered. We could actually benefit from such a correlation to speed up the classification process, by discarding those classes not correlated to the ones we have already found relevant. This relation could probably be used to fight one of the drawbacks found: our recall is very low compared to the precision. If we were able to select those classes that are highly correlated with classes assigned with high precision, we might gain in recall. This will need further investigation.

7 Acknowledgments

This work has been partially supported by Spanish Government (MCYT) with grant TIC2003-07158-C04-04.

References

1. E. L. Allwein, R. E. Schapire, and Y. Singer. Reducing multiclass to binary: A unifying approach for margin classifiers. In *Proc. 17th International Conf. on Machine Learning*, pages 9–16. Morgan Kaufmann, San Francisco, CA, 2000.
2. Bruno Pouliquen, Ralf Steinberger, and Camelia Ignat. Automatic Annotation of Multilingual Text Collections with a Conceptual Thesaurus. In A. Todirascu, editor, *Proceedings of the workshop 'Ontologies and Information Extraction' at the EuroLan Summer School 'The Semantic Web and Language Technology'(EUROLAN'2003)*, page 8 pages, Bucharest (Romania), 2003.
3. N. V. Chawla. C4.5 and imbalanced data sets: Investigating the effect of sampling method, probabilistic estimate and decision tree structure. In *Workshop on Learning from Imbalanced Datasets II, ICML*, Washington DC, 2003.
4. C. Drummond and R. C. Holte. C4.5, class imbalance, and cost sensitivity: Why under-sampling beats over-sampling. In *Workshop on Learning from Imbalanced Datasets II, ICML*, Washington DC, 2003.
5. W. Hersh, C. Buckley, T. J. Leone, and D. Hickam. Ohsumed: an interactive retrieval evaluation and new large test collection for research. In *Proceedings of the 17th annual international ACM SIGIR conference on Research and development in information retrieval*, pages 192–201. Springer-Verlag New York, Inc., 1994.
6. N. Japkowicz. Class imbalances: Are we focusing on the right issue? In *Workshop on Learning from Imbalanced Datasets II, ICML*, Washington DC, 2003.
7. N. Japkowicz and S. Stephen. The class imbalance problem: A systematic study. *Intelligent Data Analysis Journal*, 6(5), November 2002.
8. T. Joachims. Text categorization with support vector machines: learning with many relevant features. In C. Nédellec and C. Rouveirol, editors, *Proceedings of ECML-98, 10th European Conference on Machine Learning*, number 1398, pages 137–142, Chemnitz, DE, 1998. Springer Verlag, Heidelberg, DE.

9. R. Kohavi. A study of cross-validation and bootstrap for accuracy estimation and model selection. In *Proc. of the Fourteenth International Joint Conference on Artificial Intelligence*, pages 1137–1145. Morgan Kaufmann, San Mateo, CA, 1995.
10. D. D. Lewis. Evaluating Text Categorization. In *Proceedings of Speech and Natural Language Workshop*, pages 312–318. Morgan Kaufmann, 1991.
11. M. Martín-Valdivia, M. García-Vega, and L. Ureña López. LVQ for text categorization using multilingual linguistic resource. *Neurocomputing*, 55:665–679, 2003.
12. A. Montejo-Ráez. Towards conceptual indexing using automatic assignment of descriptors. Workshop in Personalization Techniques in Electronic Publishing on the Web: Trends and Perspectives, Málaga, Spain, May 2002.
13. A. Montejo-Ráez and D. Dallman. Experiences in automatic keywording of particle physics literature. *High Energy Physics Libraries Webzine*, (issue 5), November 2001. URL: http://library.cern.ch/HEPLW/5/papers/3/.
14. K. Morik, P. Brockhausen, and T. Joachims. Combining statistical learning with a knowledge-based approach - a case study in intensive care monitoring. In *Proc. 16th International Conf. on Machine Learning*, pages 268–277. Morgan Kaufmann, San Francisco, CA, 1999.
15. M. F. Porter. *An algorithm for suffix stripping*, pages 313–316. Morgan Kaufmann Publishers Inc., 1997.
16. B. Raskutti and A. Kowalczyk. Extreme re-balancing for svms: a case study. In *Workshop on Learning from Imbalanced Datasets II, ICML*, Washington DC, 2003.
17. G. Salton, A. Wong, and C. S. Yang. A Vector Space Model for Automatic Indexing. Technical Report TR74-218, Cornell University, Computer Science Department, July 1974.
18. F. Sebastiani. Machine learning in automated text categorization. *ACM Comput. Surv.*, 34(1):1–47, 2002.
19. C. J. van Rijsbergen. *Information Retrieval.* London: Butterworths, 1975. http://www.dcs.gla.ac.uk/Keith/Preface.html.
20. G. Wu and E. Y. Chang. Class-boundary alignment for imbalanced dataset learning. In *Workshop on Learning from Imbalanced Datasets II, ICML*, Washington DC, 2003.
21. Y. Yang. A study on thresholding strategies for text categorization. In W. B. Croft, D. J. Harper, D. H. Kraft, and J. Zobel, editors, *Proceedings of SIGIR-01, 24th ACM International Conference on Research and Development in Information Retrieval*, pages 137–145, New Orleans, US, 2001. ACM Press, New York, US. Describes RCut, Scut, etc.
22. Y. Yang and X. Liu. A re-examination of text categorization methods. In M. A. Hearst, F. Gey, and R. Tong, editors, *Proceedings of SIGIR-99, 22nd ACM International Conference on Research and Development in Information Retrieval*, pages 42–49, Berkeley, US, 1999. ACM Press, New York, US.

Automatic Acquisition of Transfer Rules from Translation Examples

Werner Winiwarter

Faculty of Computer Science, University of Vienna,
Liebiggasse 4, A-1010 Vienna, Austria
werner.winiwarter@univie.ac.at
http://www.ifs.univie.ac.at/~ww/

Abstract. In our research, we have developed a transfer-based machine translation architecture for the translation from Japanese into German. One main feature of the system is the fully automatic acquisition of transfer rules from translation examples by using structural matching between the parsing trees. The translation system has been implemented as part of a language learning environment with the aim to provide personalized translations for the students. In this paper we present our formalism to represent syntactic and transfer knowledge, and explain the various steps involved in acquiring and applying transfer rules.

1 Introduction

The main aim of our research is the development of a machine translation system, which produces high quality translations from Japanese into German. A second important requirement is full customization of the system because, in our opinion, there exists no "perfect" translation but only a preferred one for a certain user. Therefore, the post-editing of a translation should result in an automatic update of the translation knowledge.

Furthermore, we had to consider the two constraints that we had neither a large Japanese–German bilingual corpus nor resources to manually build a large knowledge base available. In any case, a large handcrafted knowledge base is in conflict with our need for flexible adaptation, and the insufficient data quality of today's large corpora interferes with our demand for high quality translations.

In our approach we use a transfer-based machine translation architecture (for good overviews of this topic see [1, 2, 3]). However, we learn all the transfer rules incrementally from translation examples provided by a user. For the acquisition of new transfer rules we use structural matching between the parsing trees for a Japanese–German sentence pair. To produce the input for the *acquisition component* we first compute the correct segmentation and tagging, and then transform the token lists into parsing trees. For the translation of a sentence, the *transfer component* applies the transfer rules to the Japanese parsing tree to transform it into a corresponding German parsing tree, from which we generate

J. L. Vicedo et al. (Eds.): EsTAL 2004, LNAI 3230, pp. 13–24, 2004.

a token list and surface form. In this paper we focus on the acquisition and transfer components; for a description of the other system modules we refer to [4].

We have developed the machine translation system as part of *PETRA – a Personal Embedded Translation and Reading Assistant* [5]. PETRA is a language learning environment, which assists German-speaking language students in reading and translating Japanese documents, in particular, educational texts. It is fully embedded into Microsoft Word so that the students can invoke all the features from within the text editor. The incremental improvement of the translation quality encourages a bidirectional knowledge transfer between the student and the learning environment. Besides the translation features, PETRA offers the access to the large Japanese–German dictionary WaDokuJT and a user-friendly interface to add new dictionary entries. PETRA has been implemented using Amzi! Prolog, which provides full Unicode support and an API to Visual Basic for the communication with Microsoft Word.

The rest of the paper is organized as follows. We first introduce our formalism to represent the parsing trees and transfer rules in Sect. 2 and 3 before we describe the principal steps for the acquisition and application of the transfer rules in Sect. 4 and 5.

2 Parsing Trees

The parsing trees represent the input to the acquisition component. Instead of using a fixed tree structure we decided on a more flexible and robust representation. We model a sentence as a set of constituents (represented as list in Prolog). Each constituent is a compound term of arity 1 with the constituent name as principal functor. Regarding the argument of a constituent we distinguish two different constituent types: *simple constituents* representing features or words, and *complex constituents* representing phrases as sets of subconstituents.

This representation is compact because empty optional constituents are not stored explicitly, and is not affected by the order of the different subconstituents in the arguments of complex constituents. The latter is essential for a robust and effective application of transfer rules (see Sect. 4). Figure 1 shows an example of a Japanese parsing tree. The ta-form of the main verb indicates English past tense, expressed as perfect tense in German.

For the efficient traversal, processing, and manipulation of the arguments of complex constituents we have implemented several generic predicates. In the following, we list just those predicates that are used later on in the paper:

- *find_req*$(Csub, A, Asub)$: searches for subconstituent $Csub(Asub)$ in A, fails if $Csub(\_) \notin A$;
- *replace*$(Csub, A1, Asub, A2)$: replaces $Csub(\_) \in A1$ with $Csub(Asub)$ resulting in $A2$; if $Csub(\_) \notin A1$, $Csub(Asub)$ is inserted as additional subconstituent;
- *repl_diff*$(Csub1, Csub2, A1, Asub, A2)$: same as *replace* except that also the constituent name is changed to $Csub2$;

いまのような形の本は、中世になって、はじめてあらわれた。
Das Buch in seiner heutigen Form ist im Mittelalter zum ersten Mal aufgetreten.
The book in its present form appeared in the Middle Ages for the first time.

[hew(あらわれる/ver),	head word – arawareru/verb – to appear
hwf(vta),	head word form – ta-form
pav(はじめて/adv),	predicative adverb – hajimete/adverb – for the first time
adp([hew(中世/nou),	adverbial phrase – head word – chuusei/noun – Middle Ages
php(になって/par)]),	phrase particle – ninatte/particle – in
sub([hew(本/nou),	subject – head word – hon/noun – book
anp([hew(形/nou),	attributive noun phrase – head word – katachi/noun – form
anp([hew(いま/nou)])])])]	attributive noun phrase – head word – ima/noun – present

Fig. 1. Example of Japanese parsing tree

- *split*$(A, A1, A2)$: unifies all subconstituents of $A1$ with the corresponding subconstituents in A and computes $A2 = A \setminus A1$ (used for applying transfer rules with shared variables for unification, see Sect. 3.2).

3 Transfer Rules

The transfer rules are stored as *facts* in the rule base. We have defined several *predicates* for the different types of rules. Therefore, when we talk about rules in the following, we always refer to transfer rules for machine translation in the general sense, not to logical rules in the strict sense of Prolog.

One characteristic of our transfer rules is that we can cover most translation problems with a very small number of generic abstract predicates. For some common problems we have defined some additional specialized predicates. However, all of these specialized predicates could also be expressed by using our generic predicates. We introduce them merely to increase the compactness of our rule base and the efficiency of rule application.

In the next subsections we give an overview of the different rule types along with illustrative examples. For the ease of the reader we use Roman transcription for the Japanese examples instead of the original Japanese writing.

3.1 Rules for Translating Simple Constituents

For simple context-insensitive translations at the word level, the argument of a simple constituent $A1$ is changed to $A2$ by the predicate:

$$tr\_asc(A1, A2). \tag{1}$$

Example 1. The default transfer rule to translate the Japanese noun HON (book) into the German counterpart Buch is stated as the fact:

$$tr\_asc(\text{HON}/nou, \texttt{'Buch'}/nou).$$

This general fact is then supplemented with more specific context-sensitive facts to handle different word meanings in other contexts. We have included the word category in the fact specification so that we can easily model the situation where a translation changes the word category.

Example 2. The Japanese adjectival noun ONAJI (`same`) is translated into the German adjective `gleich`:

$$tr\_asc(\text{ONAJI}/ano, \texttt{gleich}/adj).$$

More complex changes that also affect the constituent itself can be defined by using the predicate:

$$tr\_sc(C1, C2, A1, A2). \quad (2)$$

A fact for this predicate changes a simple constituent $C1(A1)$ to $C2(A2)$, i.e. constituent name and argument are replaced.

Example 3. The Japanese attributive suffix (*asf*) DAKE (`only`) is expressed as attributive adverb (*aav*) `nur` in German:

$$tr\_sc(asf, aav, \text{DAKE}/suf, \texttt{nur}/adv).$$

This predicate can also be used in situations where a Japanese word is just expressed as syntactic feature in German.

Example 4. The Japanese attributive adverb MOTTOMO (`most`) corresponds to the superlative degree of comparison (*com*) of an adjective in German:

$$tr\_sc(aav, com, \text{MOTTOMO}/adv, sup).$$

The second constituent $C2$ is not restricted to a simple constituent, it can also be a complex constituent. This way we can model translations of simple words into whole phrases.

Example 5. The Japanese predicative adverb HAJIMETE (`for the first time`) is translated into the German adverbial phrase `zum ersten Mal`:

$$tr\_sc(pav, adp, \text{HAJIMETE}/adv,$$
$$[php(\texttt{zu}/prp), det(def), num(sng), seq(\texttt{erst}/ord), hew(\texttt{'Mal'}/nou)]).$$

The adverbial phrase is specified as set of five subconstituents: phrase particle `zu`/preposition, determiner type definite, number singular, sequence `erst`/ordinal numeral, and head word `Mal`/noun. Please note that `zum` is a contraction of the preposition `zu` and the definite article `dem` for the dative case.

Finally, for modelling situations where there exist different translations for a Japanese word depending on the constituent name, we also provide a shortcut for $tr\_sc(C, C, A1, A2)$:

$$tr\_scn(C, A1, A2). \quad (3)$$

3.2 Rules for Translating Complex Constituents

Just as in the case of simple constituents, the following predicate enables the substitution of arguments for complex constituents:

$$tr\_acc(Hew, Req1, Req2). \quad (4)$$

Facts for this predicate change the argument of a complex constituent from $A1 = Req1 \cup Add$ to $A2 = Req2 \cup Add$ if $hew(Hew) \in A1$. The head word *Hew* serves as index for the fast retrieval of matching facts and the reduction of the number of facts that have to be further analyzed. The application of a transfer rule requires that the set of subconstituents in *Req*1 is included in an input constituent to replace *Req*1 by *Req*2. Besides *Req*1 any additional constituents can be included in the input, which are transferred to the output unchanged. This allows for a flexible and robust realization of the transfer module (see Sect. 5) because one rule application changes only certain aspects of a constituent whereas other aspects are translated by other rules in subsequent steps.

Example 6. The Japanese adverbial phrase CHUUSEI NINATTE (`in the Middle Ages`) is translated into the German adverbial phrase `im Mittelalter`:

$$tr\_acc(\text{CHUUSEI}/nou, [php(\text{NINATTE}/par), hew(\text{CHUUSEI}/nou)], \\ [php(\texttt{in}/prp), det(def), num(sng), hew(\texttt{'Mittelalter'}/nou)]).$$

Because *A*1 and *Req*1 are sets of constituents, the order of the subconstituents must not influence the matching of the two sets. Therefore, by applying the predicate *split* (see Sect. 2) we retrieve each element of *Req*1 in *A*1 to create a list of constituents $Req1_s$ in the same order as in *Req*1 and then try to unify the two lists. As a byproduct of this sorting process we obtain the set difference $Add = A1 \setminus Req1$ as all remaining constituents in *A*1 that were not retrieved.

Example 7. The expression JI O KAKU (literally `to write characters`) in the Japanese verb phrase KATAMEN NI JI O KAKU (`to write on one side`) is replaced by the verb `beschreiben` within the corresponding German verb phrase:

$$tr\_acc(\text{KAKU}/ver, [hew(\text{KAKU}/ver), dob([hew(\text{JI}/nou)])], [hew(\texttt{beschreiben}/ver)]).$$
$$A1 = [dob([hew(\text{JI}/nou)]), hwf(vdi), hew(\text{KAKU}/ver), \\ adp([php(\text{NI}/par), hew(\text{KATAMEN}/nou)])]$$
$$Req1_s = [hew(\text{KAKU}/ver), dob([hew(\text{JI}/nou)])]$$
$$Add = [hwf(vdi), adp([php(\text{NI}/par), hew(\text{KATAMEN}/nou)])]$$
$$A2 = [hew(\texttt{beschreiben}/ver), hwf(vdi), [adp([php(\text{NI}/par), hew(\text{KATAMEN}/nou)])]$$

The rule specifies that for any complex constituent with head word KAKU and direct object (*dob*) JI these two subconstituents are replaced by the head word `beschreiben`. In this example the input *A*1 for the application of this rule is a verb phrase with direct object JI, head word form *vdi* (verb dictionary form), head word KAKU, and adverbial phrase KATAMEN NI. $Req1_s$ is extracted from *A*1 in the correct order, leaving *Add* as list of remaining subconstituents. The result *A*2 is then formed by appending the list *Add* to *Req*2.

The expressiveness of this formalism is increased decisively by using shared variables for unification within the facts. This makes it possible to change certain parts of subconstituents and leave other parts intact. It also allows to define general rules that can be overwritten by more specific rules.

Example 8. The following rule states that a verb phrase with head word TSUNAGIAWASERU and any direct object X (`to put together from` X) is translated into a verb phrase with head word `zusammenfügen` and the prepositional object consisting of the phrase particle `aus` (`from`), number plural, determiner type indefinite, and X:

$$tr\_acc(\text{TSUNAGIAWASERU}/ver, [hew(\text{TSUNAGIAWASERU}/ver), dob(X)], [hew(\texttt{zusammenfügen}/ver), pob([php(\texttt{aus}/prp), det(ind), num(plu)|X]).$$

If this transfer rule is applied to the verb phrase PAPIRUSU O NANMAI MO TSUNAGIAWASETA (`put together from several sheets of papyrus`), we obtain:

$Req1 = [hew(\text{TSUNAGIAWASERU}/ver), dob(X)]$
$Req2 = [hew(\texttt{zusammenfügen}/ver), pob([php(\texttt{aus}/prp), det(ind), num(plu)|X]$
$A1 = [dob([hew(\text{PAPIRUSU}/nou), qua([hew(\text{MAI}/cou), php(\text{MO}/par), amo(\text{NAN}/ipr)])]), hwf(vta), hew(\text{TSUNAGIAWASERU}/ver)]$
$Req1_s = [hew(\text{TSUNAGIAWASERU}/ver), dob([hew(\text{PAPIRUSU}/nou), qua([hew(\text{MAI}/cou), php(\text{MO}/par), amo(\text{NAN}/ipr)])])]$
$Add = [hwf(vta)]$
$A2 = [hew(\texttt{zusammenfügen}/ver), pob([php(\texttt{aus}/prp), det(ind), num(plu), hew(\text{PAPIRUSU}/nou), qua([hew(\text{MAI}/cou), php(\text{MO}/par), amo(\text{NAN}/ipr)])]), hwf(vta)]$

As can be seen, the variable X is bound to the head word PAPIRUSU and the complex constituent *qua* expressing a quantity. The quantity expression (`several sheets`) consists of the head word MAI (counter for thin objects like sheets), the phrase particle MO (`also`), and the interrogative pronoun (*ipr*) NAN (`what`).

One important use of this predicate is the translation of Japanese postpositional objects into corresponding German prepositional objects because the choice of the German preposition depends in most cases on the main verb and the postposition.

As for the case of a simple constituent, we also provide a predicate to not only change the argument of a complex constituent but also the constituent name:

$$tr\_cc(C1, C2, Hew, Req1, Req2). \quad (5)$$

This changes a complex constituent $C1(A1)$ to $C2(A2)$. $A1$ is defined as union of a set of required subconstituents $Req1$ and a set of optional subconstituents Opt: $A1 = Req1 \cup Opt$. $A2$ is then computed as union of the translation $Req2$ of the required subconstituents and Opt: $A2 = Req2 \cup Opt$. Again, Hew is used to speed up the rule access. Different from the unrestricted set Add in (4), Opt

is limited to certain optional constituents, which do not change the translation of the rest of the phrase.

Example 9. The adverbial phrase KATAMEN NI (`on one side`) introduced in Example 7 is translated as predicative adjectival phrase (*pap*) with head word `einseitig` and comparison positive. An additional attributive suffix DAKE (`only`) as in KATAMEN DAKE NI is transferred unchanged to be translated in a second step as shown in Example 3:

$$tr\_cc(adp, pap, \text{KATAMEN}/nou, [php(\text{NI}/par), hew(\text{KATAMEN}/nou)], [hew(\texttt{einseitig}/adj), com(pos)]).$$
$$A1 = [php(\text{NI}/par), hew(\text{KATAMEN}/nou), asf(\text{DAKE}/suf)]$$
$$Req1_s = [php(\text{NI}/par), hew(\text{KATAMEN}/nou)]$$
$$Opt = [asf(\text{DAKE}/suf)]$$
$$A2 = [hew(\texttt{einseitig}/adj), com(pos), asf(\text{DAKE}/suf)]$$

Of course, also facts for predicate (5) can contain shared variables for unification to enable the acquisition of general transfer rules.

Example 10. The Japanese adjectival noun NITA together with a comparative phrase (*cmp*) X forms an attributive adjectival phrase (*aap*) (`being similar to` X) that is translated into a relative clause (*rcl*) with head word `ähneln` (`to resemble`) in present tense and an indirect object (*iob*) X:

$$tr\_cc(aap, rcl, \text{NITA}/ano, [hew(\text{NITA}/ano), cmp(X)], [hew(\texttt{ähneln}/ver), ten(prs), iob(X)].$$

3.3 Rules for Translating Conjunctions

German (or English) conjunctions are expressed in Japanese mainly with the help of conjunctive particles. However, the translation of a conjunctive particle often depends on the constituent name of the complex constituent in which it is included, i.e. the phrase type.

Therefore, we provide the following predicate for the definition of general transfer rules for situations where the argument $A1$ of a simple constituent is only translated to $A2$ if the constituent name of the complex constituent in which it is included equals CI:

$$tr\_sci(CI, A1, A2). \tag{6}$$

Example 11. The default transfer rule to translate the Japanese conjunctive particle TO (`and`) for combining a noun phrase with a coordinated noun phrase (*cnp*) is formulated as the fact:

$$tr\_sci(cnp, \text{TO}/par, \texttt{und}/con).$$

However, when TO is used to combine a clause with a preceding clause (*pcl*), the meaning changes to the conditional sense `wenn` (`if, when`):

$$tr\_sci(pcl, \text{TO}/par, \texttt{wenn}/con).$$

One particular characteristic of Japanese grammar is that there exist certain verb forms with conjunctional meaning to combine two clauses, e.g. the te-form. For this frequent situation we have defined the following predicate, which chooses a conjunction to insert into the preceding clause depending on the verb form and the head words of the two clauses:

$$tr\_cvf(Vf, Hew1, Hew2, Con). \quad (7)$$

This predicate is just provided for reasons of convenience and efficiency, it can also be realized with the help of predicate (4) applied to the main clause:

$$tr\_acc(Hew2, [hew(Hew2), pcl([hew(Hew1), hwf(Vf)|X])], \\ [hew(Hew2), pcl([hew(Hew1), hwf(Vf), php(Con)|X])]).$$

3.4 Rules for Translating Syntactic Features

One of the main problems with translating Japanese into German is the large discrepancy between these two languages with respect to their explicitness in expressing syntactic features at the surface level. German grammar has a complex system of declensions and conjugations to express number, gender, case, tense, mood, voice, etc. Japanese, however, is highly ambiguous regarding most of these features: it has no declension at all, does not distinguish between singular and plural, has no articles, and indicates only two tenses through conjugation. To bridge these two very different representations of linguistic knowledge, we have to find the right values for all the syntactic features required for the generation of the surface form of a German sentence.

Maybe the most difficult problem is to determine the referential properties of a Japanese noun phrase in order to generate the correct values for the syntactic features number and determiner type. In our translation model we use default values wherever possible, which are overwritten to cover special cases. To model the general situation that the determiner type and the number of a constituent with name C depend on its head word and on the head word of the constituent in which it is included, we provide the predicate:

$$tr\_dn(C, Hew1, Hew2, Det, Num). \quad (8)$$

Example 12. In the expression HIMO O TOOSU (`to thread a lace`) the direct object is an indefinite singular noun phrase:

$$tr\_dn(dob, \text{HIMO}/nou, \text{TOOSU}/ver, ind, sng).$$

As before, this rule is only a shortcut instead of writing:

$$tr\_acc(Hew2, [hew(Hew2), C([hew(Hew1)|X])], \\ [hew(Hew2), C([hew(Hew1), def(Det), num(Num)|X])]).$$

Rules of this type can again be overwritten by more specific rules. This way we can create a flexible hierarchy of rules reaching from the most general to the most specific cases. For postpositional phrases the correct number and tense is determined in parallel with the translation of the postposition whenever possible.

Syntactic features regarding verbs in verb phrases, i.e. the correct tense, voice, mood, etc., are mainly derived from the verb form. For this purpose we provide a predicate to translate a verb form into a list of syntactic features:

$$tr\_vff(Vf, FL). \tag{9}$$

Except for the tense we use default values for the syntactic features and indicate only different values to keep the German parsing tree compact. As the information derived from the conjugation of the main verb is often ambiguous, in many cases the acquisition of additional, more specific rules is necessary.

4 Acquisition of Transfer Rules

For the automatic acquisition of new transfer rules from Japanese–German sentence pairs, we first compute both parsing trees as input to the acquisition component. The acquisition algorithm traverses both syntax trees in a top-down fashion. We start the search for new rules at the sentence level before we look for corresponding subconstituents to continue the search for finer-grained transfer rules recursively. The matching algorithm performs a complete traversal of the parsing trees, i.e. rules are learnt even if they are not needed for the translation of the Japanese sentence in order to extract as much information as possible from the example.

In addition to the predicates we have already described in Sect. 2 we use the predicate *find_opt_par*($Csub, A1, A2, Asub1, Asub2$) to search for the subconstituent with name $Csub$ in $A1$ and $A2$, and retrieve the arguments of $Csub(Asub1)$ and $Csub(Asub2)$; $Asub1$=`nil` if $Csub(\_) \notin A1$, $Asub2$=`nil` if $Csub(\_) \notin A2$.

In the following we give an overview of the steps we perform to match between complex constituents. Because of space limitations, we can only present the basic principles for the most common cases. To match between two *verb phrases* we:

- derive a transfer rule of type *tr_asc* for the main verb;
- derive a transfer rule of type *tr_acc* for subconstituents of which the translation depends on the main verb, e.g. to map a postpositional object to a prepositional object, and continue the matching recursively for the two subconstituents without adpositions;
- derive transfer rules of type *tr_cc* or *tr_sc* to map Japanese subconstituents to different German subconstituents (e.g. a predicative adverb to an adverbial phrase, an adverbial phrase to a predicative adjectival phrase, etc.); if possible, matching is continued recursively for the congruent parts of the two subconstituents;
- apply *find_opt_par* to search for corresponding subconstituents for subject, direct object, preceding clause, etc., and apply matching recursively to these subconstituents;
- derive transfer rules for conjunctions and syntactic features.

To match between two *adverbial phrases* we derive a transfer rule of type *tr_acc* to translate the postposition and continue matching recursively for both phrases without adpositions. Finally, to match between two *noun phrases* we:

- derive either a default transfer rule of type *tr_asc* for the head noun or a transfer rule of type *tr_acc* for specific translations of head/modifier combinations (e.g. head noun and attributive noun phrase);
- derive transfer rules of type *tr_cc* or *tr_sc* to map Japanese subconstituents to different German subconstituents (e.g. an attributive adjectival phrase to a relative clause); if possible, matching is continued recursively;
- apply *find_opt_par* to search for corresponding subconstituents for attributive verb phrase, attributive adjectival phrase, coordinated noun phrase, etc., and apply matching recursively to these subconstituents;
- derive transfer rules for conjunctions and syntactic features.

Each rule which is not already in the rule base is validated against the existing rules to resolve any conflicts resulting from adding the new rule. This resolution is achieved by making general rules more specific. The distinction between general rules for default situations and specific rules for exceptions is drawn according to the frequency of occurrence in the collection of sentence pairs translated in the past. This way we are independent from the chronological order of analyzing new examples, i.e. the rule acquisition is not affected if an exception is learnt before a general case. Figure 2 shows the rules that are learnt from the German translation of the Japanese sentence in Fig. 1 (the syntactic features for the subject correspond with the default values so that no new rule is derived).

5 Application of Transfer Rules

The transfer component traverses the Japanese syntax tree in a top-down fashion and searches for transfer rules to be applied. We always check first whether the conditions for more specific transfer rules are satisfied before applying more general rules. As explained in Sect. 3 transfer rules can also perform only partial translations of complex constituents, leaving some parts unchanged to be transformed later on. This flexible and robust approach requires that the transfer component is able to deal with parsing trees that contain mixed representations consisting of original Japanese parts, and German parts that were already translated. This mixture gradually turns into a fully translated German parsing tree. Figure 3 shows the application of the transfer rules from Fig. 2.

As in Sect. 4, we can only highlight the basic principles of the transfer algorithm. By making use of the generic predicates to manipulate complex constituents (see Sect. 2) we have defined the predicate *tf_arg*$(C, A1, A2)$ to translate the argument $A1$ of a constituent $C(A1)$ into $A2$. For simple constituents this involves just the application of rules of type *tr_asc*, for complex constituents we perform the following principal steps: find and apply transfer rules of type *tr_acc*, transfer rules of type *tr_asc* for the head word, and transfer rules for conjunctions and syntactic features; recursively call predicates for the translation of all subconstituents.

```
[hew(あらわれる/ver), hwf(vta),                [hew(auftreten/ver), ten(per),
   pav(はじめて/adv),                             adp([hew('Mal'/nou), php(zu/prp),
   adp([hew(中世/nou),                                det(def), num(sng), seq(erst/ord)]),
      php(になって/par)]),                        adp([hew('Mittelalter'/nou), php(in/prp),
   sub([hew(本/nou),                                  det(def), num(sng)]),
      anp([hew(形/nou),                           sub([hew('Buch'/nou), det(def), num(sng),
         anp([hew(いま/nou)])])])]                    app([hew('Form'/nou), php(in/prp),
                                                        det(psv), num(sng),
                                                        aap([hew(heutig/adj), com(pos)])])])]

1. Structural matching between verb phrases
   tr_asc(あらわれる/ver, auftreten/ver).
   tr_sc(pav, adp, はじめて/adv, [php(zu/prp), det(def), seq(erst/ord), num(sng), hew('Mal'/nou)]).
   tr_vff(vta, [ten(per)]).
   2. Structural matching between adverbial phrases
      tr_acc(中世/nou, [php(になって/par), hew(中世/nou)],
         [php(in/prp), det(ind), num(sng), hew('Mittelalter'/nou)]).
      3. Structural matching between noun phrases
         tr_asc(中世/nou, 'Mittelalter'/nou).
   4. Structural matching between noun phrases
      tr_asc(本/nou, 'Buch'/nou).
      tr_cc(anp, app, 形/nou, [hew(形/nou), anp([hew(いま/nou)])],
         [php(in/prp), det(psv), num(sng), hew('Form'/nou), aap([com(pos), hew(heutig/adj)])]).
      5. Structural matching between noun phrases
         tr_asc(形/nou, 'Form'/nou).
         tr_cc(anp, aap, いま/nou, [hew(いま/nou)], [com(pos), hew(heutig/adj)]).
```

Fig. 2. Example of rule acquisition

The predicate *tf_acc*($A1, A2$) is used for finding and applying transfer rules of type *tr_acc*; if no transfer rule can be applied, the constituent is left unchanged:

$$
\begin{aligned}
&tf\_acc(A1, A2) :- find\_req(hew, A1, Hew), tr\_acc(Hew, Req1, Req2),\\
&\quad split(A1, Req1, Add), append(Req2, Add, A2).\\
&tf\_acc(A, A).
\end{aligned}
$$

The recursive call for translating a subconstituent *Csub*(*Asub*) is realized with the predicate *tf_sub*(*Csub*, $A1, A2$):

$$
\begin{aligned}
&tf\_sub(Csub, A1, A2) :- find\_req(Csub, A1, Asub), tf\_sub\_arg(Csub, Asub, A1, A2).\\
&tf\_sub(\_, A, A).
\end{aligned}
$$

and the predicate *tf_sub_arg*(*Csub*, *Asub*, $A1, A2$), which consists of several rules that either:

- find and apply a rule of type *tr_sc*: $tf\_sub\_arg(Csub, Asub, A1, A2) :- tr\_sc(Csub, Csub2, Asub, Asub2),\ repl\_diff(Csub, Csub2, A1, Asub2, A2).$
- find and apply rules of type *tr_cc* (*tf_cc* is defined in a similar way to *tf_acc*): $tf\_sub\_arg(Csub, Asub, A1, A2) :- tf\_cc(Csub, Csub2, Asub, Asub2),\ repl\_diff(Csub, Csub2, A1, Asub2, A2).$
- recursively call *tf_arg* for translating *Asub*: $tf\_sub\_arg(Csub, Asub, A1, A2) :- tf\_arg(Csub, Asub, Asub2),\ Asub \setminus{=}{=}\ Asub2,\ replace(Csub, A1, Asub2, A2).$
- otherwise leave the constituent unchanged: $tf\_sub\_arg(\_, \_, A, A).$

```
[hew(あらわれる/ver), hwf(vta), pav(はじめて/adv), adp([hew(中世/nou), php(になって/par)]),
    sub([hew(本/nou), anp([hew(形/nou), anp([hew(いま/nou)])])])]
1. tr_asc(あらわれる/ver, auftreten/ver).
  [hew(auftreten/ver), hwf(vta), pav(はじめて/adv), adp([hew(中世/nou), php(になって/par)]),
    sub([hew(本/nou), anp([hew(形/nou), anp([hew(いま/nou)])])])]
2. tr_vff(vta, [ten(per)]).
  [hew(auftreten/ver), ten(per), pav(はじめて/adv), adp([hew(中世/nou), php(になって/par)]),
    sub([hew(本/nou), anp([hew(形/nou), anp([hew(いま/nou)])])])]
3. tr_sc(pav, adp, はじめて/adv, [php(zu/prp), det(def), seq(erst/ord), num(sng), hew('Mal'/nou)]).
  [hew(auftreten/ver), ten(per), adp([php(zu/prp), det(def), seq(erst/ord), num(sng), hew('Mal'/nou)]),
    adp([hew(中世/nou), php(になって/par)]), sub([hew(本/nou), anp([hew(形/nou), anp([hew(いま/nou)])])])]
4. tr_acc(中世/nou, [php(になって/par), hew(中世/nou)], [php(in/prp), det(ind), num(sng), hew('Mittelalter'/nou)]).
  [hew(auftreten/ver), ten(per), adp([php(zu/prp), det(def), seq(erst/ord), num(sng), hew('Mal'/nou)]),
    adp([php(in/prp), det(ind), num(sng), hew('Mittelalter'/nou)]),
    sub([hew(本/nou), anp([hew(形/nou), anp([hew(いま/nou)])])])]
5. tr_asc(本/nou,'Buch'/nou).
  [hew(auftreten/ver), ten(per), adp([php(zu/prp), det(def), seq(erst/ord), num(sng), hew('Mal'/nou)]),
    adp([php(in/prp), det(ind), num(sng), hew('Mittelalter'/nou)]),
    sub([hew('Buch'/nou), det(def), num(sng), anp([hew(形/nou), anp([hew(いま/nou)])])])]
6. tr_cc(anp, app, 形/nou, [hew(形/nou), anp([hew(いま/nou)])],
      [php(in/prp), det(psv), num(sng), hew('Form'/nou), aap([com(pos), hew(heutig/adj)])]).
  [hew(auftreten/ver), ten(per), adp([php(zu/prp), det(def), seq(erst/ord), num(sng), hew('Mal'/nou)]),
    adp([php(in/prp), det(ind), num(sng), hew('Mittelalter'/nou)]),
    sub([hew('Buch'/nou), det(def), num(sng), app([php(in/prp), det(psv), num(sng), hew('Form'/nou),
      aap([hew(com(pos), heutig/adj)])])])]
```

Fig. 3. Example of rule applications

6 Conclusion

In this paper we have presented a machine translation system, which automatically learns transfer rules from translation examples by using structural matching between parsing trees. We have completed the implementation of the system and are now in the process of creating a rule base of reasonable size with the assistance of several language students from our university. So far, their feedback regarding the usefulness of PETRA for their language studies has been very positive. After we have reached a certain level of linguistic coverage, future work will concentrate on a thorough evaluation of our system.

References

1. Hutchins, J., Somers, H.: An Introduction to Machine Translation. Academic Press (1992)
2. Newton, J., ed.: Computers in Translation: A Practical Appraisal. Routledge (1992)
3. Somers, H., ed.: Computers and Translation: A Translator's Guide. John Benjamins (2003)
4. Winiwarter, W.: Incremental learning of transfer rules for customized machine translation. Proc. of the 15th Intl. Conf. on Applications of Declarative Programming and Knowledge Management, Berlin, Germany (2004) 183–192
5. Winiwarter, W.: PETRA – the personal embedded translation and reading assistant. Proc. of the InSTIL/ICALL 2004 Symposium on NLP and Speech Technologies in Advanced Language Learning Systems, Venice, Italy (2004) 111–114

Automatic Assessment of Open Ended Questions with a BLEU-Inspired Algorithm and Shallow NLP*

Enrique Alfonseca and Diana Pérez

Department of Computer Science
Universidad Autónoma de Madrid 28049 Madrid (Spain)
{Enrique.Alfonseca, Diana.Perez}@ii.uam.es

Abstract. This paper compares the accuracy of several variations of the BLEU algorithm when applied to automatically evaluating student essays. The different configurations include closed-class word removal, stemming, two baseline word-sense disambiguation procedures, and translating the texts into a simple semantic representation. We also prove empirically that the accuracy is kept when the student answers are translated automatically. Although none of the representations clearly outperform the others, some conclusions are drawn from the results.

1 Introduction

Computer-based evaluation of free-text answers has been studied since the sixties [1], and it has attracted more attention in recent years, mainly because the popularisation of e-learning courses. Most of these courses currently rely only on simple kinds of questions, such as multiple choices, fill-in-the-blanks or yes/no questions, although it has been argued that this way of assessment is not accurate enough to measure the student knowledge [2].

[3] classifies the techniques to automatically assess free-text answers in three main kinds:

- Keyword analysis, that only looks for coincident keywords or n-grams. These can be extended with the Vector Space Model and with Latent Semantic Indexing procedures [4].
- Full natural-language processing, which performs a full text parsing in order to have information about the meaning of the student's answer. This is very hard to accomplish, and systems relying on this technique cannot be easily ported across languages. On the other hand, the availability of a complete analysis of the student's essay allows them to be much more powerful. For instance, E-rater [5] produces a complete syntactic representation of the answers, and C-rater [6] evaluates whether the answers contain information related to the domain concepts and generates a fine-grained analysis of the logical relations in the text.
- Information Extraction (IE) techniques, that search the texts for some specific contents, but without doing a deep analysis. [3] describe an automatic system based on IE.

* This work has been sponsored by CICYT, project number TIC2001-0685-C02-01.

J. L. Vicedo et al. (Eds.): EsTAL 2004, LNAI 3230, pp. 25–35, 2004.

[7] provide a general overview of CAA tools.

In previous work, we have applied BLEU [8] to evaluate student answers [9, 10], with surprisingly good results, considering the simplicity of the algorithm. In this paper we focus on improving the basic BLEU algorithm with different representations of the student's text, by incorporating increasingly more complex syntactic and semantic information into our system.

The paper is organised as follows: in Section 2 we describe the variations of the original algorithm. Section 3 describes how the algorithm could be ported through languages automatically with a very slight loss in accuracy. Section 4 explains how it could be integrated inside an e-learning system. Finally, conclusions are drawn in Section 5.

2 Variations of the Scoring Algorithm

2.1 The Original BLEU Algorithm

BLEU [8] is a method originally conceived for evaluating and ranking Machine Translation systems. Using a few reference translations, it calculates an n-gram precision metric: the percentage of n-grams from the candidate translation that appear in any of the references. The procedure, in a few words, is the following:

1. For several values of N (typically from 1 to 4), calculate the percentage of n-grams from the candidate translation which appears in any of the reference texts. The frequency of each n-gram is limited to the maximum frequency with which it appears in any reference.
2. Combine the marks obtained for each value of N, as a weighted linear average.
3. Apply a brevity factor to penalise the short candidate texts (which may have many n-grams in common with the references, but may be incomplete). If the candidate is shorter than the references, this factor is calculated as the ratio between the length of the candidate text and the length of the reference which has the most similar length.

The use of several references, made by different human translators, increases the probability that the candidate translation has chosen the same words (and in the same order) as any of the references. This strength can also be considered a weakness, as this procedure is very sensitive to the choice of the reference translations.

2.2 Application in e-Learning

In the case of automatic evaluation of student answers, we can consider that the students' responses are the candidate translations, and the teacher can write a set of correct answers (with a different word choice) to be taken as references [9]. Contrary to the case of Machine Translation, where the automatic translation is expected to follow more or less rigidly the rhetorical structure of the original text, the students are free to structure their answers as they fancy, so it is to be expected a lower performance of BLEU in this case.

For evaluation purposes, we have built six different benchmark data from real exams, and an additional one with definitions obtained from Google Glossary[1]. The seven sets,

[1] http://www.google.com, writing "define:" in the query.

Table 1. Answer sets used in the evaluation. Columns indicate: set number; number of candidate texts (NC), mean length of the candidate texts (MC), number of reference texts (NR), mean length of the reference texts (MR), language (En, English; Sp, Spanish), question type (Def., definitions and descriptions; A/D, advantages and disadvantages; Y/N, Yes-No and justification of the answer), and a short description of the question

SET	NC	MC	NR	MR	Lang	Type	Description
1	38	67	4	130	En	Def.	"Operating System" defs. from "Google Glossary"
2	79	51	3	42	Sp	Def.	Exam question about Operating Systems
3	96	44	4	30	Sp	Def.	Exam question about Operating Systems
4	143	48	7	27	Sp	A/D	Exam question about Operating Systems
5	295	56	8	55	Sp	A/D	Exam question about Operating Systems
6	117	127	5	71	Sp	Y/N	Exam question about Operating Systems
7	117	166	3	186	Sp	A/D	Exam question about Operating Systems

which include more than 1000 answers altogether, are described in Table 1. All the answers were scored by hand by two different human judges, who also wrote the reference texts. The instructions they received were to score each answer in a scale between 0 and a maximum score (e.g. 1 or 10), and to write two or three reference answers for each question. We are currently transcribing other three sets corresponding to three more questions, but we still have only a few answers for each.

We have classified the ten questions in three distinct categories:

- Definitions and descriptions, e.g. *"What is an operative system?", "Describe how to encapsulate a class in C++"*.
- Advantages and disadvantages, e.g. *"Enumerate the advantages and disadvantages of the token ring algorithm"*.
- Yes/No question, e.g. *"Is RPC appropriate for a chat server? (Justify your answer)"*.

All the answers were marked manually by at least two teachers, allowing for intermediate scores if the answer was only partially correct. For instance, if the maximum score for a given question is defined as 1.5, then teachers may mark it with intermediate values, such as 0, 0.25, 0.5, 0.6, etc..

The discourse structure of the answer is different for each of these kinds. Definitions (and small descriptions) are the simplest ones. In the case of enumerations of advantages and disadvantages of something, students can structure the answer in many ways, and an Ngram-based procedure is not expected to identify mistakes such as citing something which is an advantage as a disadvantage.

2.3 Modified Brevity Penalty Factor

As discussed above, BLEU measures the n-gram precision of a candidate translation: the percentage of n-grams from the candidate that appear in the references. This metric is multiplied by a Brevity Penalty factor; otherwise, very short translations (which miss information) might get higher results than complete translations that are not fully accurate. In a way, this factor is a means to include recall intro the metric: if a candidate translation has the same length as some reference, and its precision is very high, then its recall is also expected to be high.

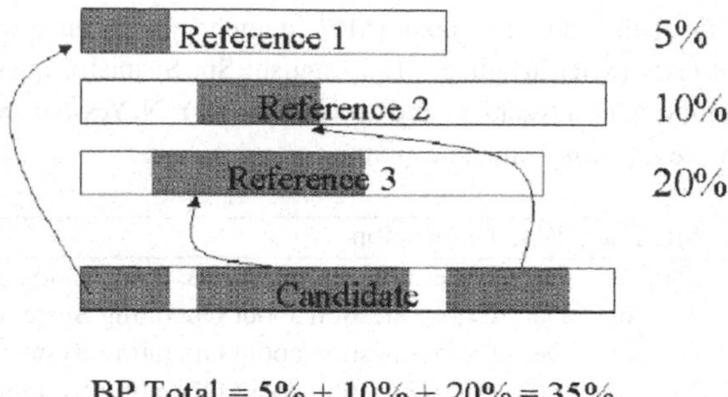

Fig. 1. Procedure for calculating the Modified Brevity Penalty factor

In contrast, ROUGE, a similar algorithm used for evaluating the output of automatic summarisation systems, only measures recall as the percentage of the n-grams in the references which appear in the candidate summary, because the purpose of a summary is to be maximally informative [11, 12]. For extract generation, in many cases precision can be taken for granted, as the summary is obtained from parts of the original document.

We argued, in previous work, that the BLEU's brevity penalty factor is not the most adequate one for CAA [9, 10]. In the case of student answers, both recall and precision should be measured, as it is important both that it contains all the required information, and that all of it is correct.

We currently encode the recall of the answer with a modified Brevity Penalty factor, that we calculate using the following procedure [10]:

1. Order the references in order of similitude to the candidate text.
2. For N from a maximum value (e.g. 10) down to 1, repeat:
   (a) For each N-gram from the candidate text that has not yet been found in any reference,
   (b) If it appears in any reference, mark the words from the N-gram as found, both in the candidate and the reference.
3. For each reference text, count the number of words that are marked, and calculate the percentage of the reference that has been found.
4. The Modified Brevity Penalty factor is the sum of all the percentage values.

Figure 1 describes how the factor is calculated. The results using this modified Brevity Penalty factor are better, statistically significant with 0.95 confidence. Surprisingly for us, the best result using this modified penalty factor was obtained just for unigrams. In automatic summarisation evaluations, unigrams have been found also to work better than n-grams in some cases [11, 12].

2.4 Extensions Proposed

There are a number of simple modifications to the original algorithm:

1. **Stemming:** to be able to match nouns and verbs inflected in different ways, e.g. *to manage* and *for managing*.

2. **Removal of Closed-Class Words.** These are usually important for finding matching N-grams for long values of N; however, in the case of unigrams, they are probably present in every kind of text and are not very informative. Given that the best correlation was obtained just for unigrams, these are not that important.
3. **Word-Sense Disambiguation.** If we were able to identify the sense intended by both the teacher and the student, then the evaluation would be more accurate. We do not have any Word-Sense Disambiguation procedure available yet, so we have tried with the following baseline methods:
   - For English, we have used the SEMCOR corpus [13] to find the most popular word sense for each of the words in WordNet, which is the sense we always take. In this case, we substitute every word w_i in the candidate and the references by the identifier of the synset such that w_i is tagged with that identifier in SEMCOR more times than with any other.
   - For Spanish, as we do not have a corpus with semantic annotations, we always choose, for every word, the first sense in the Spanish WordNet database [14].
   - For both languages, we have also tried by substituting each word by the list of the identifiers of all the synsets that contain it. In this case, we shall consider that two n-grams match if their intersection is not empty.

Figure 2 (in the next page) shows how the input text is modified before sending it to the modified BLEU algorithm. In any of these cases, the unigram co-occurrence metric is calculated after this processing. The algorithm is only modified in the last case, in which the procedure to check whether two unigrams match is not a string equality test, but a test that the set intersection is not empty.

2.5 Representing Syntactic Dependences

In order to extend the system with information about the syntactic dependences between the words in the texts, we have tried an extended version of the system in which the references and the candidate answer are analysed with a parser and next the dependences between the words are extracted. The library we have used for parsing is the `wraetlic` tools [15][2].

Figure 3 shows the dependences obtained from the candidate text from Figure 2. This can be taken as a first step in obtaining a logical representation of the text, but there are currently some limitations of our parser which do not allow us to produce a more reliable semantic analysis: it does not currently support prepositional-phrase attachment or coreference resolution.

2.6 Analysis and Discussion

Table 2 shows, for each data set and configuration of the algorithm, the results measured as the correlation between the teacher's scores and the scores produced automatically. Correlation is a metric widely used for evaluating automatic scoring systems [16, 6, 17, 7]. Given the array of scores X assigned by the teacher, and the array of scores Y assigned automatically, the correlation is defined as

[2] Available at www.ii.uam.es/~ealfon/eng/download.html

Original: Collection of programs that supervises the execution of other programs and the management of computer resources. An operating system provides an orderly input/output environment between the computer and its peripheral devices. It enables user-written programs to execute safely. An operating system standardizes the use of computer resources for the programs running under it.

Stemmed: [Collection, of, program, that, supervise, the, execution, of, other, program, and, the, management, of, computer, resource, An, operating, system, provide, an, orderly, input, environment, between, the, computer, and, its, peripheral, device, It, enable, user-written, program, to, execute, safely, An, operating, system, standardize, the, use, of, computer, resource, for, the, program, run, under, it]

Without closed-class words: [Collection, programs, supervises, execution, other, programs, management, computer, resources, operating, system, provides, orderly, input/output, environment, computer, peripheral, devices, enables, user-written, programs, execute, safely, operating, system, standardizes, use, computer, resources, programs, running]

Stemmed, no closed-class words: [Collection, program, supervise, execution, other, program, management, computer, resource, operating, system, provide, orderly, input, environment, computer, peripheral, device, enable, user-written, program, execute, safely, operating, system, standardize, use, computer, resource, program, run]

Most-common synset: [n06496793, of, n04952505, that, v01821686, the, n00842332, of, a02009316, n04952505, and, the, n00822479, of, n02625941, n11022817, An, operating, n03740670, v01736543, an, a01621495, n05924653, n11511873, between, the, n02625941, and, its, a00326901, n02712917, It, v00383376, user-written, n04952505, to, v01909959, r00152042, An, operating, n03740670, v00350806, the, n00682897, of, n02625941, n11022817, for, the, n04952505, v01433239, under, it]

Most-common synset, no closed-class words: [n06496793, n04952505, v01821686, n00842332, a02009316, n04952505, n00822479, n02625941, n11022817, operating, n03740670, v01736543, a01621495, n05924653, n11511873, n02625941, a00326901, n02712917, v00383376, user-written, n04952505, v01909959, r00152042, operating, n03740670, v00350806, n00682897, n02625941, n11022817,n04952505,v01433239]

All synsets: [[Collection], [of], [n00391804, n04952505, n04952916, n05335777, n05390435, n05427914, n05472858, n05528119], [that], [v01615271, v01821686], [the], [n00068488, n00817656, n00842332, n11140581], [of], [a02009316], [n00391804, n04952505, n04952916, n05335777, n05390435, n05427914, n05472858, n05528119], [and], [the], [n00822479, n06765853], [of], [n02625941, n07941303], [n04334536, n04749592, n11022817], ...]

All synsets, no closed-class words: [[Collection], [n00391804, n04952505, n04952916, n05335777, n05390435, n05427914, n05472858, n05528119], [v01615271, v01821686], [n00068488, n00817656, n00842332, n11140581], [a02009316], [n00391804, n04952505, n04952916, n05335777, n05390435, n05427914, n05472858, n05528119], [n00822479, n06765853], [n02625941, n07941303], [n04334536, n04749592, n11022817], ...]

Fig. 2. Modification of a candidate answer depending on the configuration of the automatic scorer. The synset identifiers in the last four cases are taken from WordNet 1.7

```
supervise([Collection], [execution, management]);
provide([Operating_System], [environment, devices]);
enable([It], [programs]);
execute([], []);
standardize([Operating_System], [use]);
run([resources], []);
user-written(program);
computer(resource);
of(programs);
of(resources);
for(programs);
under(it);
```

Fig. 3. Dependences obtained from the syntactic representation of the candidate answer

Table 2. Correlation between BLEU and the manual scores (left column), and correlations for the modified algorithm in different configurations (those from Figure 2) and, finally, the results using the syntactic dependences

Set	BLEU	Basic	stem	cc	stem-cc	WSD	WSD-cc	All	All-cc	Deps.
1	0.5886	0.5859	0.6189	0.5404	0.5821	**0.6322**	0.5952	0.2076	0.1125	0.3243
2	0.3609	0.5244	0.4832	**0.5754**	0.4797	0.4706	0.4655	0.1983	0.2968	0.2404
3	**0.3694**	0.3210	0.2364	0.3234	0.2917	0.2211	0.2844	0.1107	0.1431	0.1560
4	0.4159	0.6608	0.6590	0.6811	**0.7000**	0.6634	0.6933	0.6349	0.6702	0.4139
5	0.0209	0.1979	0.2410	0.2437	0.3013	0.2434	**0.3040**	-0.0201	0.0450	0.1884
6	0.2102	0.4027	0.3977	**0.4159**	0.4046	0.3822	0.3838	0.2607	0.3297	0.1302
7	0.4172	0.3970	0.4634	0.4326	0.4910	0.4727	**0.5261**	0.2880	0.3337	0.1726

$$correlation(X, Y) = \frac{covariance(X, Y)}{standardDev(X) \times standardDev(Y)}$$

Some observations can be drawn from these data:

- There is not any configuration that clearly outperforms the others.
- The removal of closed-class words improves the results, although it is not statistically significant.
- The rather simple Word-Sense Disambiguation procedure that we have used has attained the best results in three cases, and does not produce much loss for the remaining questions. We can take this as an indication that if we had a better algorithm these results might be better than the other configurations.
- The technique of choosing all the synsets containing a given word (with or without closed-class words) was clearly poorer than all the others.
- The metric obtained looking for coincidences of the dependences between words in the candidate answer and in the references was also inferior to the other configurations. This may be due to the fact that the dependences are only collected for some

Table 3. Correlation between BLEU and the manual scores (left column), and correlations for the modified algorithm in different configurations (those from Figure 2), using an automatic Machine Translation system

Set	BLEU	Basic	stem	cc	stem-cc	WSD	WSD-cc	All	All-cc	Deps.
1	0.5886	0.6174	0.6007	0.5663	0.5702	**0.6194**	0.5919	0.1519	0.0516	0.4081
2	0.3609	0.5330	0.4337	**0.5479**	0.5310	0.4176	0.4841	0.2276	0.2068	0.2501
3	**0.3694**	0.1660	0.1736	0.2892	0.2814	0.1734	0.3264	0.0789	0.2035	0.1210
4	0.4159	0.5937	0.6899	0.6066	0.7567	0.6998	**0.7655**	0.6008	0.6216	0.3897
5	0.0209	0.2449	0.2426	0.3213	**0.3459**	0.2358	0.3282	-0.0102	0.0220	0.0674
6	0.2102	0.3649	0.3326	0.3450	**0.3754**	0.3150	0.3586	0.1716	0.3070	0.1607
7	0.4172	0.4583	0.4635	0.4515	**0.4850**	0.4510	0.4699	0.2859	0.3452	0.1691

words because the parses are incomplete, and much information is lost using this representation.
- The correlation values obtained, although they are not high enough to be used in practical applications, are better than those obtained with other keyword-based evaluation metrics used in existing systems in combination with other techniques. Therefore, we believe that this procedure is very adequate to replace other keyword-based scoring modules in more complex evaluation environments (e.g. [5]).

3 Multilingual Evaluation

In order to check whether the evaluation system can be automatically ported across languages without the need of rewriting the reference texts, we have performed the following experiment: for each of the questions, we have translated the references manually into other language (from Spanish into English and vice versa) and we have translated the candidate texts using Altavista Babelfish[3]. Table 3 shows the results obtained.

In a real case of an e-learning application, the authors of a course would simply need to write the reference texts in their own language (e.g. Spanish). An English student would see the question translated automatically into English, would write the answer, and next the system would automatically translate it into Spanish and score it against the teacher's references. As can be seen from the results, the loss of accuracy is small; for some of the questions, the correlation in the best configuration even increases. Again, the removal of closed-class words seems to give better results, and there are two cases in which Word-Sense Disambiguation is useful.

4 Application on an On-line e-Learning System

Ideally, we would like that a student could submit the answer to a question and receive his or her score automatically. This system is not intended to substitute a teacher, but might help students in their self-study. We have built an on-line system for open-ended questions called Atenea.

[3] Available at http://world.altavista.com/

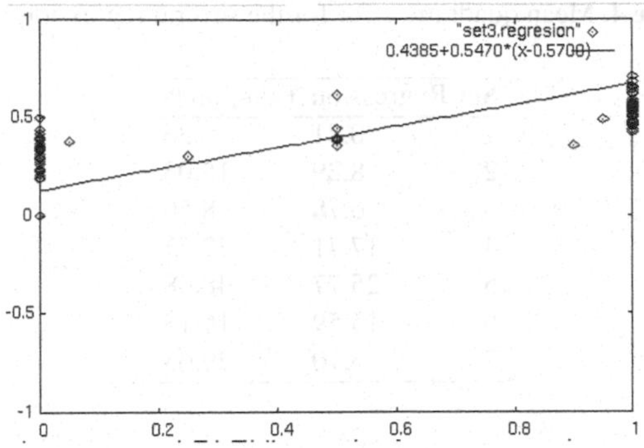

Fig. 4. Regression line between the teacher's scores and the system's scores

Given a student answer, BLEU provides a numerical score. This score needs to be put in the teacher's scale so the student can understand its meaning. For instance, Figure 4 shows the regression line for question 3. It can be seen that BLEU's scores (Y axis) are between 0 and 0.7, while the teacher marked all the answers between 0 and 1 (X axis). It is also interesting to notice that most of the teacher's scores are either 0 or 1: only a few answers received intermediate marks. In this example, if a student receives a BLEU score of 0,65, he or she would think that the answer was not very good, while the regression line indicates that that score is one of the best.

Therefore, it is necessary to translate BLEU's scores to the scale used by the teacher (e.g. between 0 and 1).

We propose the following methods:

- Evidently, if we have a set of student answers marked by a teacher, then we can calculate the regression line (as we have done in Figure 4) and use it. Given BLEU's score, we can calculate the equivalent in the teacher's score automatically. The regression line minimises the mean quadratic error.
- In same cases it may not be possible to have a set of answers manually scored. In this case, we cannot calculate the regression line, but we can estimate it in the following way:

  We take the student answers for which BLEU's scores, b_1 and b_2 are minimal and maximal, and we assume that their corresponding scores in the teacher's scale are 0 and 1 (i.e. they are the worst and the best possible answers). The estimated regression line will be the line that crosses the two points $(0, b_1)$ and $(1, b_2)$. This is only an approximation, and it has the unwanted feature that if a student produces an answer that scores best, then the remaining students will see their scores lowered down automatically, as the line will change.

Table 4 shows the mean quadratic errors produced by the regression line and the way to estimate the line unsupervisedly.

Table 4. Mean quadratic error for the several regression lines

Set	Regression	Two-points
1	0.81	6.33
2	8.29	15.03
3	6.78	8.50
4	17.41	22.73
5	25.77	48.08
6	15.59	16.13
7	5.10	29.63

5 Conclusions and Future Work

In previous work [9, 10] we described a novel application of the BLEU algorithm for evaluating student answers. We compare here several variations of the algorithm which incorporate different levels of linguistic processing of the texts: stemming, a tentative word-sense disambiguation and a shallow dependency-based representation obtained directly from a syntactic analysis. The results show that in nearly every case some of these modifications improve the original algorithm. Although no configuration clearly outperforms all the others, we can see that closed-class words removal is usually useful, and that improving the word-sense disambiguation module seems a very promising line to follow, given that a baseline procedure for WSD has been found effective for some datasets.

We also describe a feasible way in which this system might be integrated inside e-learning systems, with a little effort on behalf of the course authors, who would only be required to write a few correct answers for each of the questions. Although a set of manually corrected student answers might be desirable to minimise the mean quadratical error, there are roundabouts to omit that work. The coincident n-grams between the students' answers and the references can be useful so they can see which parts of their answers have improved their score. Finally, the characteristics of the algorithm make it very natural to be integrated in adaptive courses, in which the contents and tasks that the students must complete depend on their profiles or actions. Just by providing a different set of the reference answers (e.g. in other language, or for a different subject level), the same question can be evaluated in a suitable way depending on the student model. Furthermore, we have seen that it can be automatically ported across languages using a state-of-the-art Machine Translation system with no or small loss in accuracy.

Future work include the following lines:

- Improving the word-sense disambiguation module, and integrating it with a logical formalism of representation, so the predicates and their arguments are not words but synset identifiers.
- Study better models for estimating the regression line when the answers corrected by the teacher are not available.
- Extend the algorithm so that it is capable of discovering the internal structure of the answer. This would be desirable, for instance, when evaluating enumerations of advantages or disadvantages, where it is necessary to discover if the student is referring to one of the other.

- Explore the multilingual evaluation, to discover why is it the case that the correlation increases in some cases. A possible reason may be that the automatic translations employ a more reduced vocabulary.
- Perform a full integration of Atenea with the web-based adaptive e-learning system TANGOW [18], which has also been developed at our home university.

References

1. Page, E.B.: The use of computer in analyzing student essays. International review of education **14** (1968)
2. Whittington, D., Hunt, H.: Approaches to the computerized assessment of free text responses. In: Proceedings of the Int. CAA Conference. (1999)
3. Mitchell, T., Russell, T., Broomhead, P., Aldridge, N.: Towards robust computerised marking of free-text responses. In: Proceedings of the 6th International Computer Assisted Assessment (CAA) Conference, Loughborough, UK (2002)
4. Laham, D.: Automated content assessment of text using Latent Semantic Analysis to simulate human cognition. Ph.D. thesis, University of Colorado, Boulder (2000)
5. Burstein, J., Kukich, K., Wolff, S., Chi, L., Chodorow, M.: Enriching automated essay scoring using discourse marking. In: Proceedings of the Workshop on Discourse Relations and Discourse Marking, ACL, Montreal, Canada (1998)
6. Burstein, J., Leacock, C., Swartz, R.: Automated evaluation of essay and short answers. In: Proceedings of the Int. CAA Conference. (2001)
7. Valenti, S., Neri, F., Cucchiarelli, A.: An overview of current research on automated essay grading. Journal of I.T. Education **2** (2003) 319–330
8. Papineni, K., Roukos, S., Ward, T., Zhu, W.: Bleu: a method for automatic evaluation of machine translation (2001)
9. Pérez, D., Alfonseca, E., Rodríguez, P.: Application of the BLEU method for evaluating free-text answers in an e-learning environment. In: Proceedings of the Language Resources and Evaluation Conference (LREC-2004). (2004)
10. Pérez, D., Alfonseca, E., Rodríguez, P.: Upper bounds and extension of the BLEU algorithm applied to assessing student essays. In: IAEA-2004 Conference. (2004)
11. Lin, C.Y., Hovy, E.H.: Automatic evaluation of summaries using n-gram co-occurrence statistics. In: Proceedings of 2003 Language Technology Conference (HLT-NAACL 2003). (2003)
12. Lin, C.Y.: Rouge working note v. 1.3.1 (2004)
13. Fellbaum, C.: Analysis of a handtagging task. In: Proceedings of ANLP-97 Workshop on Tagging Text with Lexical Semantics: Why, What, and How?, Washington D.C., USA (1997)
14. Vossen, P.: EuroWordNet - A Multilingual Database with Lexical Semantic Networks. Kluwer Academic Publishers (1998)
15. Alfonseca, E.: Wraetlic user guide version 1.0 (2003)
16. Foltz, P., Laham, D., Landauer, T.: The intelligent essay assessor: Applications to educational technology. Interactive Multimedia Electronic Journal of Computer-Enhanced Learning (1999)
17. Rudner, L., Liang, T.: Automated essay scoring using bayes' theorem. In: Proceedings of the annual meeting of the National Council on Measurement in Education. (2002)
18. Carro, R.M., Pulido, E., Rodríguez, P.: Dynamic generation of adaptive internet-based courses. Journal of Network and Computer Applications **22** (1999) 249–257

Automatic Phonetic Alignment and Its Confidence Measures

Sérgio Paulo and Luís C. Oliveira

L^2F Spoken Language Systems Lab.
INESC-ID/IST,
Rua Alves Redol 9, 1000-029 Lisbon, Portugal
{spaulo,lco}@l2f.inesc-id.pt
http://www.l2f.inesc-id.pt

Abstract. In this paper we propose the use of an HMM-based phonetic aligner together with a speech-synthesis-based one to improve the accuracy of the global alignment system. We also present a phone duration-independent measure to evaluate the accuracy of the automatic annotation tools. In the second part of the paper we propose and evaluate some new confidence measures for phonetic annotation.

1 Introduction

The flourishing number of spoken language repositories has pushed speech research in multiple ways. Much of the best speech recognition systems rely on models created with very large speech databases. Research into natural prosody generation for speech synthesis is, nowadays, another important issue that uses large amounts of speech data. These repositories have allowed the development of many corpus-based speech synthesizers in the recent years, but they need to be phonetically annotated with a high level of precision. However, manual phonetic annotation is a very time-consuming task and several approaches have been taken to automate this process. Although state-of-the-art segmentation tools can achieve very accurate results, there are always some uncommon acoustic realizations or some kind of noise that can badly damage the segmentation performance for a particular file. With the increasing size of speech databases manual verification of every utterance is becoming unfeasible, thus, some confidence scores must be computed to detect possible bad segmentations within each utterance. The goal of this work is the development of a robust phonetic annotation system, with the best possible accuracy, and the development and evaluation of confidence measures for phonetic annotation process. This paper is divided into 4 sections, the section 2 describes the development of the proposed phonetic aligner. In the following section (section 3), we describe and evaluate the proposed confidence measures, and the conclusions in the last section.

J. L. Vicedo et al. (Eds.): EsTAL 2004, LNAI 3230, pp. 36–44, 2004.

2 Automatic Segmentation Approaches

Automatic phonetic annotation is composed of two major steps, the determination of the utterance phone sequence, the sequence produced by the speaker during the recording procedure, and the temporal location of the segment boundaries (phonetic alignment). Several phonetic alignment methods have been proposed, but the most widely explored techniques are based either on Hidden Markov Models (HMM) used in forced alignment mode [1] or on dynamic time alignment with synthesized speech [2]. The main reason of the superiority of two techniques is their robustness and accuracy, respectively. An HMM-based aligner consists of a finite state machine that has a set of state occupancy probabilities in each time instant and a set of inter-state transition probabilities. These probabilities are computed using some manually or automatically segmented data (training data). On the other hand, the speech-synthesis-based aligners are based on a technique used in the early days of the speech recognition. A synthetic speech signal is generated with the expected phonetic sequence, together with the segment boundaries. Then, some spectral features are computed from the recorded and the generated speech signals, and finally the Dynamic Time Warping (DTW) algorithm [3] is applied to compute the aligned path between the signals for which there is a better match between the spectral features. The reference signal segment boundaries are mapped into the recorded signal using this alignment path. A comparison between the results of HMM-based and speech-synthesis-based segmentation [4] has showed that in general (about 70% of times) the speech-synthesis-based segmentation is more accurate than the HMM-based one, however, it tends to generate few large boundary errors (when it fails it fails badly). This means that the HMM-based phonetic aligners are more reliable.

The lack of robustness of the speech-synthesis-based aligners as well as its better boundary location accuracy suggested the development of an hybrid system, a system as accurate as the speech-synthesis-based aligner and with the robustness of the hmm-based aligners.

2.1 Speech Synthesis Based Phonetic Aligners

The first conclusion taken from the usage of some commonly used speech-synthesis-based aligners is that the acoustic features does not prove to be equally good for locating the boundaries for every kind of phonetic segment. For instance, although the energy is, in general, a good feature to locate the boundary between a vowel and a stop consonant, it performed poorly on locating the boundary between two vowels. Thus, some experiments were performed with multiple acoustic features and multiple segment transitions to find the best acoustic features to locate the boundaries between each different pair of phonetic segments. This acoustic feature selection considerably increased the robustness of the resulting aligner. The reference speech signal was generated using the Festival Speech Synthesis System [5] using a Portuguese voice recorded at our lab. A detailed description of this work can be found in [6].

2.2 HMM Based Phonetic Aligners

Once the speech-synthesis-based aligner was built with a good enough robustness, it was used to generate the training data for the HMM-based aligner. Given the amount of available training data, context-independent models were chosen for the task. Figure 1 shows the different phone topologies. The upper one is used for all phonetic segment but the silence, semi-vowels and shwa. The central topology is used to represent segments with short durations like the semi-vowels and shwa, by allowing a skip between and first and last states. The silence model is the lower one. In this case a transition from the first state to the last as well as another one from the last to the first state can be observed, this can be used to model very large variations on the duration of the silences in the speech database. Each model states consists of a set of eight gaussian mixtures. The adopted features were the Mel-Frequency Cepstrum Coefficients, their first and second order differences and the energy and its first and second differences. Each frame is spaced by 5-miliseconds , with a 20-milisecond long window. The training of the model was preformed by using the HTK toolkit.

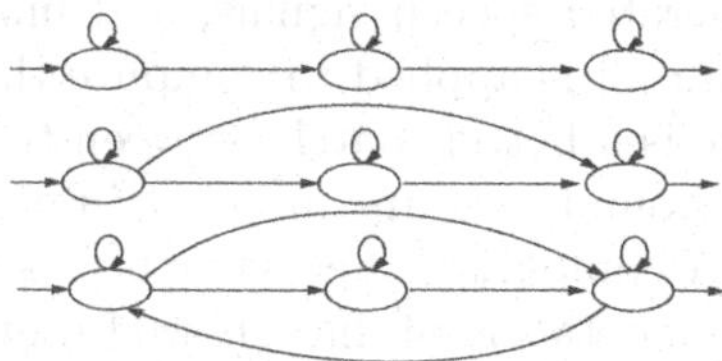

Fig. 1. Three HMM topologies were used for the different kinds of phonetic segments. The upper one is the general model, the central topology in used for semi-vowels and shwa, and the last one for the silence

2.3 Segment Boundary Refinement

As expected, using the HMM-based aligner, a more robust segmentation was obtained. The next step was to use our speech-synthesis-based aligner to refine the location of the segment boundaries.

2.4 Segmentation Results

Two of the most common approaches to evaluate the segmentations' accuracy is to compute of the phonetic segment percentage that have boundary location errors less than a given tolerance (often 20 ms), or the root mean square error of the boundary locations. Although these can be good predictors for aligners' accuracy, it is clear that an error of about 20 ms in a 25-ms long segment is much more serious that the same error in a 150-ms long segment. In the first case the segment frames are almost always badly assigned. This way, a phone-based duration-independent measure is proposed to evaluate the aligners' accuracy, that is to determine the percentage of well assigned frames, within the segment. We will call it the *Overlap Rate* (*OvR*). Fig. 2 illustrates the computation of this measure. Given a segment, a reference segmentation (RefSeg), and the segmentation to be evaluated(AutoSeg), OvR is the ratio between the number of frames that belong to that segment in both the segmentations ($Common\_Dur$ in the fig. 2) and the number of frames that belong to the segment in one segmentation, at least(Dur_max if the fig. 2). The following equation illustrates the computation of OvR:

$$OvR = \frac{Common\_Dur}{Dur\_max} = \frac{Common\_Dur}{Dur\_ref + Dur\_auto - Common\_Dur} \quad (1)$$

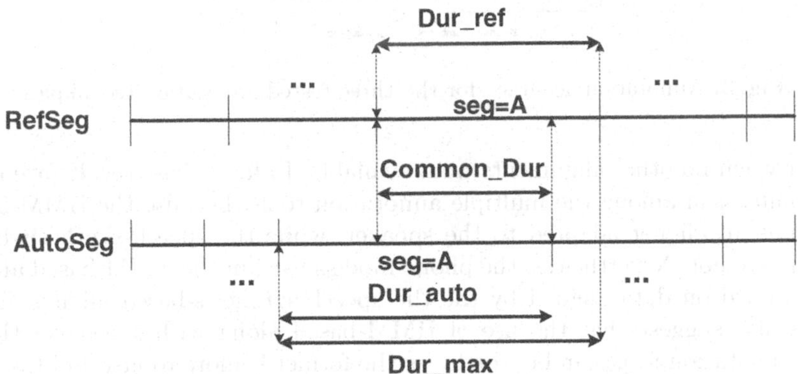

Fig. 2. Graphical representation of the quantities involved in the computation of the Overlap Rate

Regarding the equation 1, one can realize that if, for example, a phone duration in the reference segmentation differs considerably from its duration in the other segmentation, the OvR quantity takes a very small value. Let X be the Dur_ref, Y the Dur_auto and z the $Common\_Dur$ of Fig. 2, and suppose $X \leq Y$, thus:

$$0 \leq OvR = \frac{z}{X + Y - z} \leq \frac{X}{Y} \quad (2)$$

since the number of common frames (z) is at most the same as the minimum number of frames in the two annotations of the given segment. This way, one can conclude that this measure is duration independent, and is able to produce a more reliable evaluation of the annotation accuracy.

Figure 3, shows the accuracy of the three developed annotation tools. The x-axis is the percentage of incorrectly assigned frames ($(1-OvR)\cdot 100\%$) and the y-axis is the percentage of phones that has a percentage of incorrectly assigned frames lower than the value given in the x-axis. The solid line represents the accuracy of the HMM-based aligner, the dashed line is the accuracy of the speech-synthesis-based aligner when it is used to refine the results of the HMM-based aligner. The dotted line represents the accuracy of the speech-synthesis-based

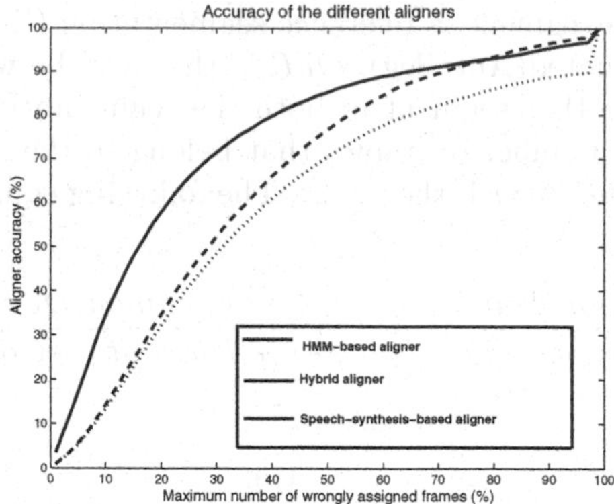

Fig. 3. Annotation accuracy for the three tested annotation techniques

aligner when no other alignments were available. In fact, these results are not a fair comparison among the multiple annotation tools, because the HMM-based aligner is an aligner adapted to the speaker, while the speech-synthesis-based aligners are not. Nevertheless, the phone models used in the HMM-based aligner were trained on data aligned by the the speech-synthesis-based aligner. These results also suggest that the use of HMM-based along with speech-synthesis-based annotation tools can be worthy as the former is more robust and the later is more accurate.

3 Confidence Scores

In this section we propose some phone-based confidence scores for detecting misalignments in the utterance. The goal is to locate regions of the speech signal where the alignment method may have failed and that could benefit from human intervention.

3.1 The Chosen Features

The alignment process provides a set of features that can be used as indicators of annotation mismatch. This set of features is described below.

- DTW mean distance: mean distance between the features of the recorded signal frames and the synthesized speech signal over the alignment path for a given phone;
- DTW variance: variance of the mean distance between the features of the recorded signal frames and the synthesized speech signal over the alignment path for a given phone;
- DTW minimal distance: minimal distance between the features of the recorded signal frames and the synthesized speech signal over the alignment path for a given phone;

- DTW maximal distance: maximal distance between the features of the recorded signal frames and the synthesized speech signal over the alignment path for a given phone;
- HMM mean distance: mean distance between the features of the recorded signal frames and the phone model;
- HMM variance: variance of the distance between the features of the recorded signal frames and the phone model;
- HMM minimal distance: minimal distance between the features of the recorded signal frames and phone model;
- HMM maximal distance: maximal distance between the features of the recorded signal frames and phone model

Each segment of the database is associated with a vector of features that will be used to predict a confidence score for the alignment of that phone. To provide some context we decided to include not only the feature vector of the current phone but also the feature vectors of the previous and following segments.

We were now in the condition of performing the evaluation the reliability of the different techniques that we propose to detect annotation problems.

Three different approaches will be evaluated: Classification and Regression Trees (CART), Artificial Neural Networks (ANN) and Hidden Markov Models (HMM).

3.2 Definition of Bad Alignment

A boundary between good and bad alignment is hard to define. Some researchers assume that boundary errors larger than 10 miliseconds must be considered misalignments, while others are more tolerant. As we explained before, the effect of the error in the location of the boundaries may be different from segment to segment, depending on its duration. Thus, we will use the duration-independent feature proposed before to computed the accuracy of annotation tools: we will assume that a misalignment occurs when $OvR \leq 0.75$.

3.3 Classification and Regression Trees

To train a regression tree we have used the *Wagon* program, that is part of Edinburgh Speech Tools[7]. This program can be used to build both classification and regression trees, but in this problem it was used as a regression tool to predict the values of the OvR based on the former features. We used a training set with 28000 segments and a test set with 10000 segments.

Since the leafs of the tree are the average value of OvR and its variance, assuming a gaussian distribution in the leafs, we can compute the probability of the having OvR with a value lower than the threshold defined in the previous subsection. Let μ and σ be the average value of OvR and its standard deviation, respectively, in a given leaf of the tree. Then, the probability of misalignment is given by:

$$P(OvR \leq 0.75|\mu,\sigma) = \frac{1}{\sqrt{2\cdot\pi\cdot\sigma^2}} \int_0^{0.75} e^{-\frac{(x-\mu)^2}{2\cdot\sigma^2}}\,dx \qquad (3)$$

We than had to apply a threshold to the resulting probability. By varying these threshold we obtained a Precision/Recall curve represented as a dotted line in Fig. 4.

3.4 Artificial Neural Networks

Using a neural network simulator developed at our lab, and the same feature vectors used in the previous experiment, we trained a binary classifier, which computes the probability of misalignment for each segment. As we did in the trainning of the regression tree, we had to apply a threshold to the outputs of the neural network. The variation of this threshold created the lower dashed line of Fig. 4.

3.5 Hidden Markov Models

Two one-state models were created for each phonetic segment. A model for aligned segments, and a model for the misaligned ones. Since the amount of training data were not large enough to build context dependent models, we had to choose a context-independent approach. However, we took into account the influence of the different contexts in the models in some extent by using four gaussian mixtures in each state. Each model was based on the feature vectors described in 3.1. After model training, we performed a forced alignment between the feature vector sequences and the model pairs trained for each phonetic segment. This experiment allowed us to find values for precision and recall for each phonetic segment. We depict the experiment results based on phone groups (Vowels, Liquids, Nasals, Plosives, Fricatives, Semi-Vowels and the Silence), which is enough to show that the precision and recall values can vary largely with the phone types in analysis.

Table 1. Best feature pairs for the multiple phonetic segment class transitions

Class	Precision(%)	Recall(%)
Vowels	73.2	69.8
Liquids	48.6	64.0
Nasals	82.0	67.7
Plosives	78.7	72.4
Fricatives	88.0	69.0
Semi-Vowels	44.9	67.5
Silence	97.3	87.8

Based on the previously trained models, we computed a score($HmmSore$) for each segment to precision-recall curves, like we did for CART and ANN. This score was calculated using equation 4.

$$HmmScore = \frac{P(x = Al|Model_{Al})}{P(x = Al|Model_{Al}) + P(x = Misal|Model_{Misal})} \quad (4)$$

where $P(x = Al|Model_{Al})$ is the probability that segment x is aligned given the model of aligned phones for that segment and $P(x = Misal|Model_{Misal}))$ is the probability that segment x is misaligned given its model of misaligned phones. The score values are between 0 and 1. We computed the upper curve of Fig. 4 by imposing different thresholds to the score, like we had already done for the two other approaches. It is important to point out that in this case we are detecting the **aligned** segments rather than **misaligned** ones.

3.6 Results

The results depicted in Fig. 4 suggest the HMM approach outperforms all others by far. The other two approaches are very similar, for some applications one should choose CARTs, for others one should choose ANNs.

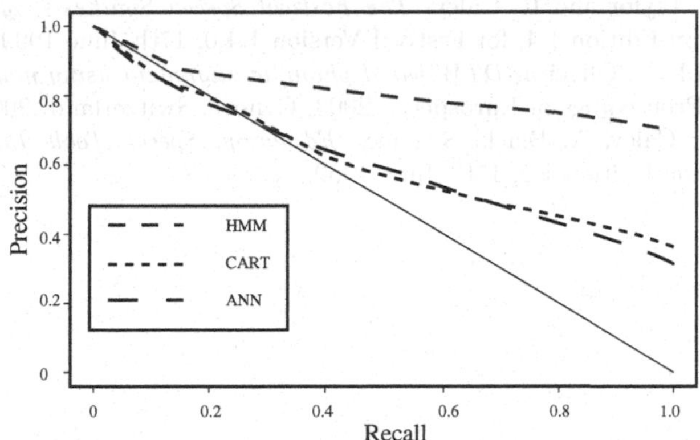

Fig. 4. Plot of precision and recall of the proposed confidence measures

4 Conclusions

In the first part of the paper, we have explored the advantages of using an HMM-based aligner together with an aligner based on speech-synthesis, and we showed the increase of the accuracy of the combined system, and a new measure of alignment accuracy was proposed. In the second part of the paper we proposed and evaluated three new approaches to compute confidence measures for phonetic annotation. In this part we realized that the approach using HMMs is largely the best one.

5 Acknowledgements

The authors would like to thank M. Céu Viana and H. Moniz for providing the manually aligned reference corpus. This work is part of Sérgio Paulo's PhD

Thesis sponsored by a Portuguese Foundation for Science and Technology (FCT) scholarship. INESC-ID Lisboa had support from the POSI Program.

References

1. D. Caseiro, H. Meinedo, A. Serralheiro, I. Trancoso and J. Neto, *Spoken Book alignment using WFST* HLT 2002 Human Language Technology Conference.
2. F. Malfrère and T. Dutoit, *High-Quality Speech Synthesis for Phonetic Speech Segmentation.* In Proceedings of Eurospeech'97, Rhodes, Greece, 1997.
3. Sakoe H. and Chiba,*Dynamic programing algorithm optimization for spoken word recognition.* IEEE Trans. on ASSP, 26(1):43-49, 1978.
4. J. Kominek and A. Black, *Evaluating and correcting phoneme segmentation for unit selection synthesis.* In Proceedings of Eurospeech'2003, Geneve, Switzerland, 2003.
5. A. Black, P. Taylor and R. Caley, *The Festival Speech Synthesis System.* System documentation Edition 1.4, for Festival Version 1.4.0, 17th June 1999.
6. S. Paulo and L. C. Oliveira, *DTW-based phonetic alignment using multiple acoustic features.* In Proceedings of Eurospeech'2003, Geneve, Switzerland, 2003.
7. P. Taylor R. Caley, A. Black, S. King, *Edinburgh Speech Tools Library* System Documentation Edition 1.2, 15th June 1999.

Automatic Spelling Correction in Galician*

M. Vilares[1], J. Otero[1], F.M. Barcala[2], and E. Domínguez[2]

[1] Department of Computer Science, University of Vigo
Campus As Lagoas s/n, 32004 Ourense, Spain
{vilares,jop}@uvigo.es

[2] Ramón Piñeiro Research Center for Humanities
Estrada Santiago-Noia, Km. 3, A Barcia, 15896 Santiago de Compostela, Spain
{fbarcala,edomin}@cirp.es

Abstract. We describe a proposal on spelling correction intended to be applied on Galician, a Romance language. Our aim is to put into evidence the flexibility of a novelty technique that provides a quality equivalent to global strategies, but with a significantly minor computational cost. To do it, we take advantage of the grammatical background present in the recognizer, which allows us to dynamically gather information to the right and to the left of the point at which the recognition halts in a word, as long as this information could be considered as relevant for the repair process. The experimental tests prove the validity of our approach in relation to previous ones, focusing on both performance and costs.

1 Introduction

Galician belongs to the group of Latin languages, with influence of peoples living here before the Roman colonization, as well as contributions from other languages subsequent to the breaking-up of this empire. Long time relegated to informal usage, it has managed to survive well into the 20th century until it was once again granted the status of official language for Galicia, together with Spanish. Although there several dialects exist, it has been recently standardized and, as a consequence, there is a pressing need for tools in order to permit a correct linguistic treatment. A main point of interest is the development of efficient error repair tools, in particular for spelling correction purposes.

In this context, the state of the art focuses on global techniques based on the consideration of error thresholds to reduce the number of repair alternatives, a technique often dependent on the recognizer. So, Oflazer [5] introduces a *cut-off distance* that can be performed efficiently by maintaining a matrix [2] which help the system to determine when a partial repair will not yield any result by providing non-decreasing repair paths. In order to save this maintaining, Savary [6] embeds the distance in the repair algorithm, although this allows to partial corrections may be reached several times with different intermediate

* Research partially supported by the Spanish Government under projects TIC2000-0370-C02-01 and HP2002-0081, and the Autonomous Government of Galicia under projects PGIDIT03SIN30501PR and PGIDIT02SIN01E.

J. L. Vicedo et al. (Eds.): EsTAL 2004, LNAI 3230, pp. 45–57, 2004.

distances; which is not time-efficient for error threshold values bigger than one. Anyway, these pruning techniques are strongly conditioned by the estimation of the repair region and their effectiveness is relative in global approaches.

In contrast to global algorithms, that expend equal effort on all parts of the word, also on those containing no errors; we introduce regional repairs avoiding to examine the entire word. This is of importance since Galician is an inflectional language with a great variety of morphological processes, and a non-global strategy could drastically reduce the costs. In effect, work underway focusing on word processing, the descriptive model is a regular grammar (RG) and the operational one is a finite automaton (FA). At this point, repairs on RG's are explored breadth-wise; whilst the number of states in the associated finite automaton (FA) is massive. So, a complex morphology impacts both time and space bounds, that can even become exponential; which justifies our approach.

2 The Error Repair Model

Our aim is to parse a word $w_{1..n} = w_1 \ldots w_n$ according to a RG $\mathcal{G} = (N, \Sigma, P, S)$. We denote by w_0 (resp. w_{n+1}) the position in the string, $w_{1..n}$, previous to w_1 (resp. following w_n). We generate from $\mathcal{G}$ a *numbered minimal acyclic finite automaton* for the language $\mathcal{L}(\mathcal{G})$. In practice, we choose a device [4] generated by GALENA [3]. A FA is a 5-tuple $\mathcal{A} = (\mathcal{Q}, \Sigma, \delta, q_0, \mathcal{Q}_f)$ where: $\mathcal{Q}$ is the set of states, Σ the set of input symbols, δ is a function of $\mathcal{Q} \times \Sigma$ into $2^{\mathcal{Q}}$ defining the transitions of the automaton, q_0 the initial state and $\mathcal{Q}_f$ the set of final states. We denote $\delta(q, a)$ by $q.a$, and we say that $\mathcal{A}$ is *deterministic* iff $| q.a | \leq 1$, $\forall q \in \mathcal{Q}$, $a \in \Sigma$. The notation is transitive, $q.w_{1..n}$ denotes the state $(\overset{n}{\ldots} (q.w_1) \overset{n-1}{\ldots}).w_n$. As a consequence, w is *accepted* iff $q_0.w \in \mathcal{Q}_f$, that is, the *language accepted by* $\mathcal{A}$ is defined as $\mathcal{L}(\mathcal{A}) = \{w, \text{ such that } q_0.w \in \mathcal{Q}_f\}$. A FA is *acyclic* when the underlying graph it is. We define a *path in the* FA as a sequence of states $\{q_1, \ldots, q_n\}$, such that $\forall i \in \{1, \ldots, n-1\}$, $\exists a_i \in \Sigma$, $q_i.a_i = q_{i+1}$. In order to reduce the memory requirements, we apply a minimization process [1]. Two FA's are *equivalent* iff they recognize the same language. Two states, p and q, are *equivalent* iff the FA with p as initial state, and the one that starts in q recognize the same language. An FA is *minimal* iff no pair in $\mathcal{Q}$ is equivalent.

2.1 The Dynamic Programming Frame

Although the standard recognition process is deterministic, the repair one could introduce non-determinism by exploring alternatives associated to possibly more than one recovery strategy. So, in order to get polynomial complexity, we avoid duplicating intermediate computations in the repair of $w_{1..n} \in \Sigma^+$, storing them in a table $\mathcal{I}$ of *items*, $\mathcal{I} = \{[q, i], \ q \in \mathcal{Q}, \ i \in [1, n+1]\}$, where $[q, i]$ looks for the suffix $w_{i..n}$ to be analyzed from $q \in \mathcal{Q}$.

We describe our proposal using *parsing schemata* [7], a triple $\langle \mathcal{I}, \mathcal{H}, \mathcal{D} \rangle$, with $\mathcal{H} = \{[a, i], \ a = w_i\}$ an initial set of items called *hypothesis* that encodes the word to be recognized[1], and $\mathcal{D}$ a set of *deduction steps* that allow to derive items from previous ones. These are of the form $\{\eta_1, \ldots, \eta_k \vdash \xi \,/ conds\}$, meaning that if all antecedents η_i are present and the conditions *conds* are satisfied, then the consequent ξ is generated. In our case, $\mathcal{D} = \mathcal{D}^{\text{Init}} \cup \mathcal{D}^{\text{Shift}}$, where:

$$\mathcal{D}^{\text{Init}} = \{\vdash [q_0, 1]\} \qquad \mathcal{D}^{\text{Shift}} = \{[p, i] \vdash [q, i+1] \,/ \exists [a, i] \in \mathcal{H},\ q = p.a\}$$

The recognition associates a set of items S_p^w, called *itemset*, to each $p \in \mathcal{Q}$; and applies these deduction steps until no new application is possible. The word is recognized iff a *final item* $[q_f, n+1]$, $q_f \in \mathcal{Q}_f$ has been generated. We can assume, without lost of generality, that $\mathcal{Q}_f = \{q_f\}$, and that exists an only transition from (resp. to) q_0 (resp. q_f). To get this, we augment the FA with two states becoming the new initial and final states, and relied to the original ones through empty transitions, our only concession to the notion of minimal FA.

2.2 The Formalization

Let's assume that we deal with the first error in a word $w_{1..n} \in \Sigma^+$. We extend the item structure, $[p, i, e]$, where now e is the error counter accumulated in the recognition of w at position w_i in state p. We talk about the *point of error*, w_i, as the point at which the difference between what was intended and what actually appears in the word occurs, that is, $q_0.w_{1..i-1} = q$ and $q.w_i \notin \mathcal{Q}$. The next step is to locate the origin of the error, limiting the impact on the analyzed prefix to the context close to the point of error, in order to save the computational effort.

Since we work with acyclic FAs, we can introduce a simple order in $\mathcal{Q}$ by defining $p < q$ iff exists a path $\rho = \{p, \ldots, q\}$; and we say that q_s (resp. q_d) is a *source* (resp. *drain*) for ρ iff $\exists a \in \Sigma,\ q_s.a = p$ (resp. $q.a = q_d$). In this manner, the pair (q_s, q_d) defines a *region* $\mathcal{R}_{q_s}^{q_d}$ iff $\forall \rho$, source$(\rho) = q_s$, we have that drain$(\rho) = q_d$ and $|\ \{\forall \rho,\ \text{source}(\rho) = q_s\}\ | > 1$. So, we can talk about *paths*$(\mathcal{R}_{q_s}^{q_d})$ to refer the set $\{\rho / \text{source}(\rho) = q_s,\ \text{drain}(\rho) = q_d\}$ and, given $q \in \mathcal{Q}$, we say that $q \in \mathcal{R}_{q_s}^{q_d}$ iff $\exists \rho \in \text{paths}(\mathcal{R}_{q_s}^{q_d})$, $q \in \rho$. We also consider $\mathcal{A}$ as global region. So, any state, with the exception of q_0 and q_f, is included in a region. This provides a criterion to place around a state in the underlying graph a zone for which any change applied on it has no effect over its context. So, we say that $\mathcal{R}_{q_s}^{q_d}$ is the *minimal region in $\mathcal{A}$ containing* $p \in \mathcal{Q}$ iff it verifies that $q_s \geq p_s$ (resp. $q_d \leq p_d$), $\forall \mathcal{R}_{p_s}^{p_d} \ni p$, and we denote it as $\mathcal{M}(p)$.

We are now ready to characterize the point at which the recognizer detects that there is an error and calls the repair algorithm. We say that w_i is *point of detection* associated to a point of error w_j iff $\exists q_d > q_0.w_{1..j}$, $\mathcal{M}(q_0.w_{1..j}) = \mathcal{R}_{q_0.w_{1..i}}^{q_d}$, that we denote by *detection*$(w_j) = w_i$. We then talk about $\mathcal{R}_{q_0.w_{1..i}}^{q_d}$ as the *region defining the point of detection* w_i. The error is located in the left recognition context, given by the closest source. However, we also need to locate it from an operational viewpoint, as an item in the process. We say that $[q, j] \in S_q^w$ is an *error item* iff $q_0.w_{j-1} = q$; and we say that $[p, i] \in S_p^w$ is a *detection item* associated to w_j iff $q_0.w_{i-1} = p$.

[1] A word $w_{1\ldots n} \in \Sigma^+$, $n \geq 1$ is represented by $\{[w_1, 1],\ [w_2, 2],\ \ldots\ ,\ [w_n, n]\}$.

Once we have identified the beginning of the repair region, we introduce a *modification* to $w_{1..n} \in \Sigma^+$, $M(w)$, as a series of edit operations, $\{E_i\}_{i=1}^n$, in which each E_i is applied to w_i and possibly consists of a sequences of insertions before w_i, replacement or deletion of w_i, or transposition with w_{i+1}. This topological structure can be used to restrict the notion of modification, looking for conditions that guarantee the ability to recover the error. So, given $x_{1..m}$ a prefix in $\mathcal{L}(\mathcal{A})$, and $w \in \Sigma^+$, such that xw is not a prefix in $\mathcal{L}(\mathcal{A})$, we define a *repair of w following x* as $M(w)$, so that:

(1) $\mathcal{M}(q_0.x_{1..m}) = \mathcal{R}_{q_s}^{q_d}$ (the minimal region including the point of error, $x_{1..m}$)
(2) $\exists\{q_0.x_{1..i} = q_s.x_i, \ldots, q_s.x_{i..m}.M(w)\} \in \text{paths}(\mathcal{R}_{q_s}^{q_d})$

denoted by *repair*(x, w), and $\mathcal{R}_{q_s}^{q_d}$ by *scope*(M). We can now organize this concept around a point of error, $y_i \in y_{1..n}$, in order to take into account all possible repair alternatives. So, we define the *set of repairs for y_i*, as *repair*$(y_i) = \{xM(w) \in \text{repair}(x, w)/w_1 = \text{detection}(y_i)\}$.

Later, we focus on filter out undesirable repairs, introducing criteria to select those with minimal cost. For each $a, b \in \Sigma$ we assume insert, $I(a)$; delete, $D(a)$, replace, $R(a, b)$, and transpose, $T(a, b)$, costs. The *cost of a modification* $M(w_{1..n})$ is given by *cost*$(M(w_{1..n})) = \Sigma_{j \in J_\dashv} I(a_j) + \Sigma_{i=1}^n (\Sigma_{j \in J_i} I(a_j) + D(w_i) + R(w_i, b) + T(w_i, w_{i+1}))$, where $\{a_j,\ j \in J_i\}$ is the set of insertions applied before w_i; $w_{n+1} = \dashv$ the end of the input and $T_{w_n,\dashv} = 0$. From this, we define the set of *regional repairs* for $y_i \in y_{1..n}$, a point of error, as

$$\text{regional}(y_i) = \{xM(w) \in \text{repair}(y_i) \Big/ \begin{array}{l} \text{cost}(M) \leq \text{cost}(M'),\ \forall M' \in \text{repair}(x, w) \\ \text{cost}(M) = \min_{L \in \text{repair}(y_i)} \{\text{cost}(L)\} \end{array} \}$$

Before to deal with cascaded errors, precipitated by previous erroneous repairs, it is necessary to establish the relationship between recovery processes. So, given w_i and w_j points of error, $j > i$, we define the set of *viable repairs* for w_i in w_j as $\text{viable}(w_i, w_j) = \{xM(y) \in \text{regional}(w_i)/xM(y) \ldots w_j \text{ prefix for } \mathcal{L}(\mathcal{A})\}$. Repairs in *viable*$(w_i, w_j)$ are the only ones capable of ensuring the recognition in $w_{i..j}$ and, therefore, the only possible at the origin of cascaded errors. In this sense, we say that a point of error w_k, $k > j$ is a *point of error precipitated by w_j* iff $\forall xM(y) \in \text{viable}(w_j, w_k)$, $\exists \mathcal{R}_{q_0.w_{1..i}}^{q_d}$ defining $w_i = \text{detection}(w_j)$, such that $\text{scope}(M) \subset \mathcal{R}_{q_0.w_{1..i}}^{q_d}$. This implies that w_k is precipitated by w_j when the region defining the point of detection for w_k summarizes all viable repairs for w_j in w_k. That is, the information compiled from those repairs has not been sufficient to give continuity to a process locating the new error in a region containing the precedent ones and, as a consequence, depending on these. We then conclude that the origin of the current error could be a wrong study of past ones.

2.3 The Algorithm

Most authors appeal to global methods to avoid distortions due to unsafe error location [5, 6]; but our proposal applies a dynamic estimation of the repair region, guided by the linguistic knowledge present in the underlying FA. Formally, we extend the item structure, $[p, i, e]$, where now e is the error counter accumulated in the recognition of w at position w_i in state p.

Once located the point of error, we apply all possible transitions beginning at its point of detection, which corresponds to the following deduction steps in error mode, $\mathcal{D}_{\text{error}} = \mathcal{D}_{\text{error}}^{\text{Shift}} \cup \mathcal{D}_{\text{error}}^{\text{Insert}} \cup \mathcal{D}_{\text{error}}^{\text{Delete}} \cup \mathcal{D}_{\text{error}}^{\text{Replace}} \cup \mathcal{D}_{\text{error}}^{\text{Transpose}}$:

$$\mathcal{D}_{\text{error}}^{\text{Shift}} = \{[p,i,e] \vdash [q,i+1,e],\ \exists [a,i] \in \mathcal{H},\ q = p.a\}$$

$$\mathcal{D}_{\text{error}}^{\text{Insert}} = \{[p,i,e] \vdash [p,i+1,e+I(a)],\ \nexists\, p.a\}$$

$$\mathcal{D}_{\text{error}}^{\text{Delete}} = \{[p,i,e] \vdash [q,i-1,e+D(w_i)] \Big/ \begin{array}{l} \mathcal{M}(q_0.w_{1..j}) = \mathcal{R}_{q_s}^{q_d} \\ p.w_i = q_d \in \mathcal{R}_{q_s}^{q_d} \textbf{or } q = q_d \end{array}\}$$

$$\mathcal{D}_{\text{error}}^{\text{Replace}} = \{[p,i,e] \vdash [q,i+1,e+R(w_i,a)], \Big/ \begin{array}{l} \mathcal{M}(q_0.w_{1..j}) = \mathcal{R}_{q_s}^{q_d} \\ p.a = q \in \mathcal{R}_{q_s}^{q_d} \textbf{ or } q = q_d \end{array}\}$$

$$\mathcal{D}_{\text{error}}^{\text{Transpose}} = \{[p,i,e] \vdash [q,i+2,e+T(w_i,w_{i+1})] \Big/ \begin{array}{l} \mathcal{M}(q_0.w_{1..j}) = \mathcal{R}_{q_s}^{q_d} \\ p.w_i.w_{i+1} = q \in \mathcal{R}_{q_s}^{q_d} \textbf{ or } q = q_d \end{array}\}$$

where $w_{1..j}$ looks for the current point of error. Observe that, in any case, the error hypotheses apply on transitions behind the repair region. The process continues until a repair covers the repair region.

In the case of dealing with an error which is not the first one in the word, it could condition a previous repair. This arises when we realize that we come back to a detection item for which some recognition branch includes a previous recovery process. The algorithm re-takes the error counters, adding the cost of new error hypotheses to profit from the experience gained from previous repairs. This permits us to deduce that if w_l is a point of error precipitated by w_k, then:

$$q_0.w_{1..i} < q_0.w_{1..j},\ \mathcal{M}(q_0.w_l) = \mathcal{R}_{q_0.w_{1..i}}^{q_d},\ w_j = y_1,\ xM(y) \in \text{viable}(w_k, w_l)$$

which proves that the state associated to the point of detection in a cascaded error is minor that the one associated to the source of the scope in the repairs precipitating it. So, the minimal possible scope of a repair for the cascaded error includes any scope of the previous ones, that is,

$$\max\{\mathit{scope}(M),\ M \in \text{viable}(w_k, w_l)\} \subset \max\{\mathit{scope}(\tilde{M}),\ \tilde{M} \in \text{regional}(w_l)\}$$

This allows us to get an asymptotic behavior close to global repair methods, ensuring a quality comparable to those, but at cost of a local one in practice.

3 An Overview on Galician

Although Galician is a non-agglutinative language, it shows a great variety of morphological processes. The most outstanding features are found in verbs, with a highly complex conjugation paradigm, including ten simple tenses. If we add the present imperative with two forms, not conjugated infinitive, gerund and participle. Then 65 inflected forms are possible for each verb. In addition, irregularities are present in both stems and endings. So, very common verbs, such as `facer` (*to do*), have up to five different stems: `fac-er`, `fag-o`, `fa-s`, `fac-emos`, `fix-en`. Approximately 30% of Galician verbs are irregular. We have implemented 42 groups of irregular verbs. Verbs also include enclitic pronouns producing changes in the stem due to the presence of accents: deu (*gave*), déullelo (*he/she gave it to them*).

In Galician the unstressed pronouns are usually suffixed and, moreover, pronouns can be easily drawn together and they can also be contracted (lle + o = llo), as in the case of váitemello buscar (*go and fetch it for him (do it for me)*). It is also very common to use what we call a *solidarity pronoun*, in order to let the listeners be participant in the action. Therefore, we have even implemented forms with four enclitic pronouns, like perdéuchellevolo (*he had lost it to him*). Here, the pronouns che and vos are solidarity pronouns and they are used to implicate the interlocutor in the facts that are being told. None of them has a translation into English, because this language lacks these kinds of pronouns. So, the analysis has to segment the word and return five tokens.

There exist highly irregular verbs that cannot be classified in any irregular model, such as ir (*to go*) or ser (*to be*); and other verbs include gaps in which some forms are missing or simply not used. For instance, meteorological verbs such as chover (*to rain*) are conjugated only in third singular person. Finally, verbs can present duplicate past participles, like impreso and imprimido (*printed*).

This complexity extends to gender inflection, with words with only one gender as home (*man*) and muller (*woman*), and words with the same form for both genders as azul (*blue*). We also have a lot of models for words with separate masculine and feminine forms: autor, autora (*author*); xefe, xefa (*boss*); poeta, poetisa (*poet*); rei, raiña (*king*) or actor, actriz (*actor*). We have implemented 33 variation groups for gender.

We can also refer to number inflection, with words only being presented in singular form, such as luns (*monday*), and others where only the plural form is correct, as matemáticas (*mathematics*). The construction of different forms does not involve as many variants as is the case for gender, but we can also consider a certain number of models: roxo, roxos (*red*); luz, luces (*light*); animal, animais (*animal*); inglés, ingleses (*English*); azul, azuis (*blue*) or funil, funís (*funnel*). We have implemented 13 variation groups for number.

4 The System at Work

Our aim is to validate our proposal comparing it with global ones, an objective criterion to measure the quality of a repair algorithm since the point of reference is a technique that guarantees the best quality for a given error metric when all contextual information is available. We choose to work with a lexicon for Galician built from GALENA [3], which includes 304.331 different words, to illustrate this aspect. The lexicon is recognized by a FA containing 16.837 states connected by 43.446 transitions, whose entity we consider sufficient for our purposes.

4.1 The Operational Testing Frame

From this lexicon, we select a representative sample of morphological errors to its practical evaluation. This can be easily verified from Fig. 1, that shows the similar distribution of both the original lexicon and the running sample, in terms of lengths of the words to deal with. In each length-category, errors have been randomly generated in a number and position in the input string that are shown in Fig. 2. This is of importance since, as the authors claim, the performance of previous proposals depend on these factors, which has no practical sense. No other dependencies have been detected at morphological level and, therefore, they have not been considered.

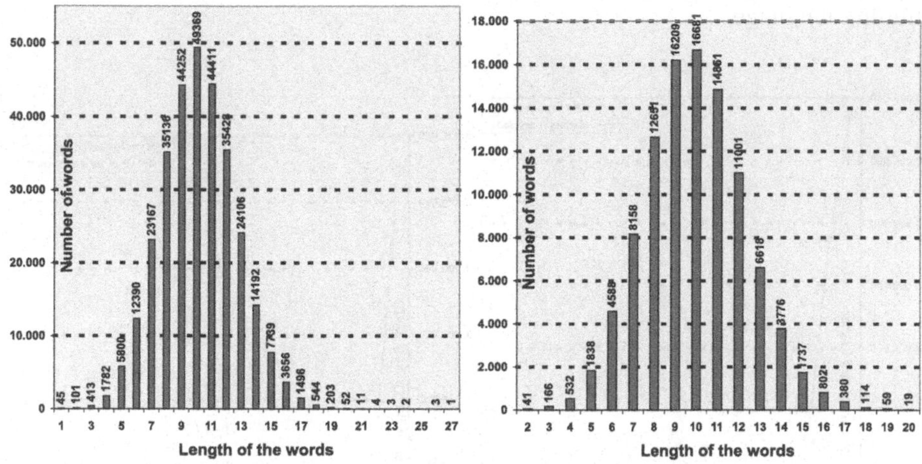

Fig. 1. Statistics on the general and error lexicons

In this context, our testing framework seems to be well balanced, from both viewpoints operational and linguistic. It remains to decide what repair algorithms will be tested. We compare our proposal with the Savary's global approach [6], an evolution of the Oflazer's algorithm [5] and, in the best of our knowledge, the most efficient method of error-tolerant look-up in finite-state dictionaries. The comparison has been done from three viewpoints: the size of the repair region considered, the computational cost and the repair quality.

4.2 The Error Repair Region

We focus on the evolution of this region in relation to the location of the point of error, in opposition to static strategies associated to global repair approaches. To illustrate it, we take as running example the FA represented in Fig. 3, which recognizes the following words in Galician: *"chourizo"* (sausage), *"cohabitante"* (a person who cohabit with another one), *"coherente"* (coherent) and *"cooperase"* (you cooperated). We consider as input string the erroneous one *"coharizo"*, resulting from transpose *"h"* with *"o"* in *"chourizo"* (sausage), and replace the character *"u"* by *"a"*. We shall describe the behavior from both viewpoints, the Savary's [6] algorithm and our proposal, proving that in the worst case, when precipitated errors are present, our proposal can re-take the repair process to recover the system from errors in cascade.

In this context, the recognition comes to an halt on state q_9, for which $\mathcal{M}(q_9) = \mathcal{R}_{q_6}^{q_{22}}$ and no transition is possible on *"r"*. So, our approach locates the error at q_6 and applies from it the error hypotheses looking for the minor editing distance in a repair allowing to reach the state q_{22}. In this case, there are two possible regional repairs consisting on first replace *"a"* by *"e"* and later insert an *"e"* after *"r"* (resp. replace *"i"* by *"e"*), to obtain the modification on the entire input string *"coherezo"* (resp. *"cohereizo"*), which is not a word in our running language.

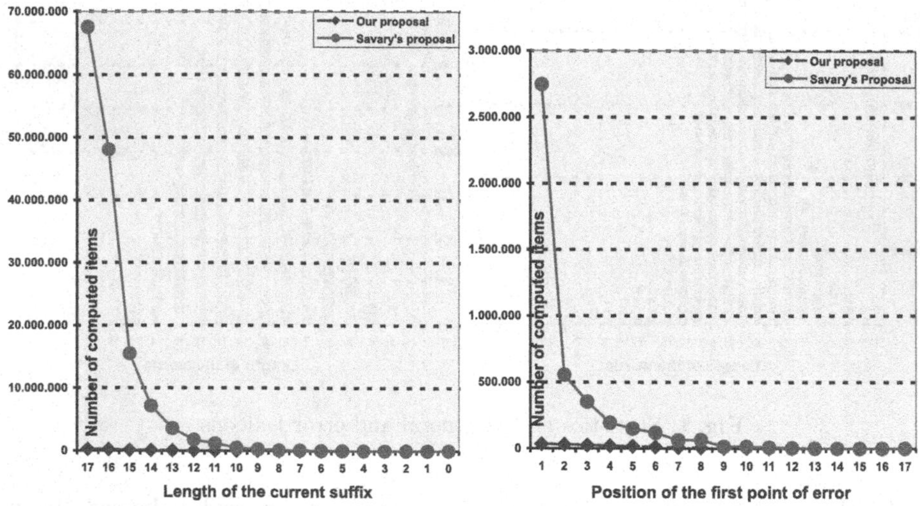

Fig. 2. Number of items generated in error mode

As a consequence, although we return to the standard recognition in q_{22}, the next input character is now *"i"* (resp. *"z"*), for which no transition is possible and we come back to error mode on the region $\mathcal{M}(q_{22}) = \mathcal{R}_{q_4}^{q_{24}}$ including $\mathcal{M}(q_9) = \mathcal{R}_{q_6}^{q_{22}}$. We then interpret that the current error is precipitated by the previous one, possibly of type in cascade. As result, none of the regional repairs generated allow us to re-take the standard recognition beyond the state q_{24}. At this point, $\mathcal{M}(q_{24}) = \mathcal{R}_{q_2}^{q_{25}}$ becomes the new region, and the only regional repair is now defined as the transposition of the *"h"* with *"o"*, and the substitution of *"a"* by *"u"*; which agrees with the global repair proposed by Savary, although the repair region is not the total one as is the case for that algorithm. This repair finally allows the acceptance by the FA.

The repair process described is interesting for two reasons. First, it puts into evidence that we do not need to extend the repair region to the entire FA in order to get the least-cost correction and, secondly, the risk of errors in cascade can be efficiently solved in the context of non-global approaches. Finally, in the worst case, our running example clearly illustrate the convergence of our regional strategy towards the global one from both viewpoints, the computational cost and the quality of the correction.

4.3 The Computational Cost

These practical results are compiled in Fig. 2, using as unity to measure the computational effort the concept of item previously defined. We here consider two complementary approaches illustrating the dependence on both the position of the first point of error in the word and the length of the suffix from it. So, in any case, we are sure to take into account the degree of penetration in the FA at that point, which determines the effectiveness of the repair strategy. In effect, working on regional methods, the penetration determines the number of regions in the FA including the point of error and, as a consequence, the possibility to consider a non-global resolution.

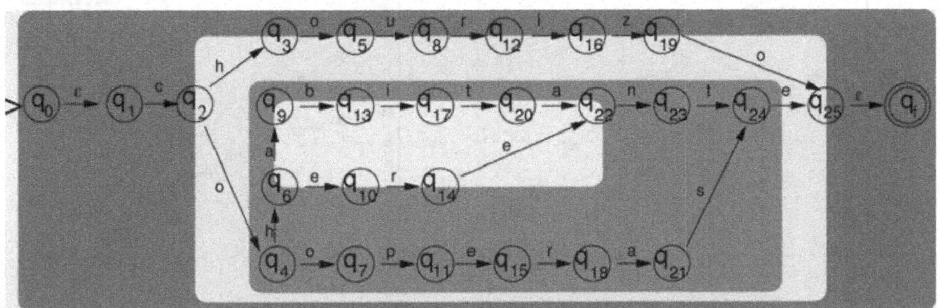

Fig. 3. The concept of region in error repair

In order to clearly show the detail of the tests on errors located at the end of the word, which is not easy to observe from the decimal scale of Fig. 2, we include in Fig. 4 the same results using a logarithmic scale. So, both graphics perfectly illustrate our contribution, in terms of computational effort saved, from two viewpoints which are of interest in real systems: First, our proposal shows in practice a linear-like behavior, in opposite to the Savary's one that seems to be of exponential type. In particular, this translates in an essential property in industrial applications, the independence of the the time of response on the initial conditions for the repair process. Second, in any case, the number of computations is significantly reduced when we apply our regional criterion.

4.4 The Performance

However, statistics on computational cost only provide a partial view of the repair process that must also take into account data related to the performance from both the user's and the system's viewpoint. In order to get this, we have introduced the following two measures, for a given word, w, containing an error:

$$performance(w) = \frac{useful\ items}{total\ items} \qquad recall(w) = \frac{proposed\ corrections}{total\ corrections}$$

that we complement with a global measure on the *precision* of the error repair approach in each case, that is, the rate reflecting when the algorithm provides the correction attended by the user. We use the term *useful items* to refer to the number of generated items that finally contribute to obtain a repair, and *total items* to refer to the number of these structures generated during the process. We denote by *proposed corrections* the number of corrections provided by the algorithm, and by *total corrections* the number of possible ones, absolutely.

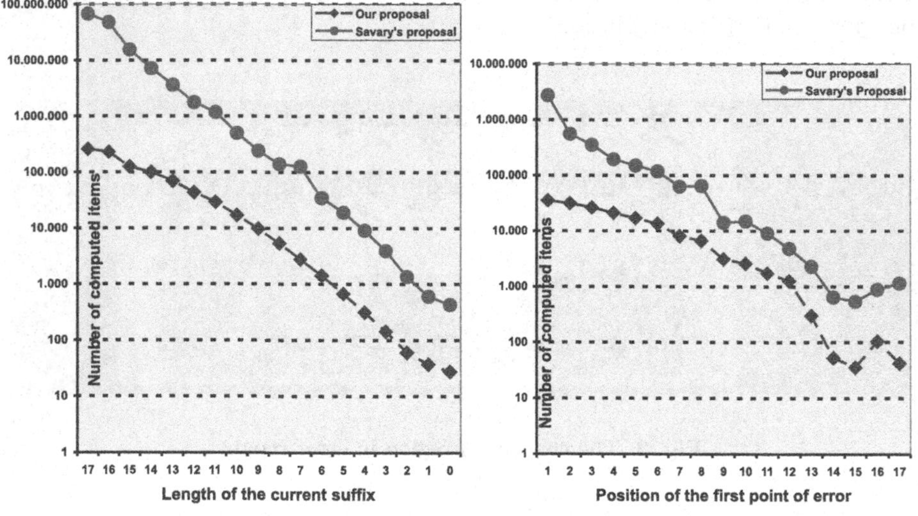

Fig. 4. Number of items generated in error mode. Logarithmic scale

These results are shown in Fig. 5, illustrating some interesting aspects in relation with the asymptotic behavior we want to put into evidence in the regional approach. So, considering the running example, the performance in our case is not only better than Savary's; but the existing difference between them increases with the location of the first point of error. Intuitively this is due to the fact that closer is this point to the beginning of the word and greater is the number of useless items generated in error mode, a simple consequence of the higher availability of different repair paths in the FA when we are working in a region close to q_0. In effect, given that the concept of region is associated to the definition of corresponding source and drain points, this implies that this kind of regions are often equivalent to the total one since the disposition of these regions is always concentric. At this point, regional and repair approaches apply the same error hypotheses not only on a same region, but also from close states given that, in any case, one of the starting points for these hypotheses would be q_0 or a state close to it. That is, in the worst case, both algorithms converge.

The same reasoning could be considered in relation to points of error associated to a state in the recognition that is close to q_f, in order to estimate the repair region. However, in this case, the number of items generated is greater for the global technique, which is due to the fact that the morphology of the language often results on the generation of regions which concentrate near of q_f, a simple consequence of the common derivative mechanisms applied on suffixes defining gender, number or verbal conjugation groups. So, it is possible to find a regional repair just implicating some error hypotheses from the state associated to the point of error or from the associated detection point and, although this regional repair could be different of the global one; its computational cost would be usually minor.

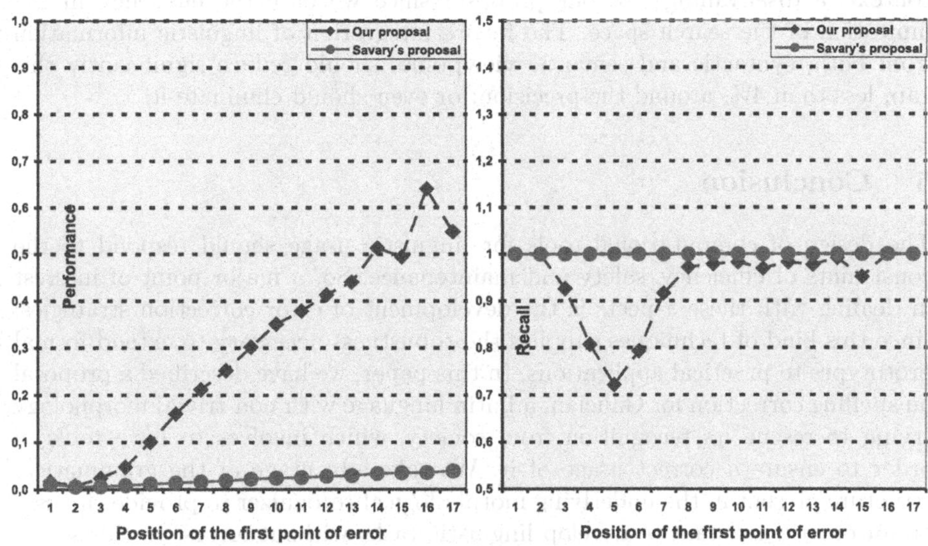

Fig. 5. Performance and recall results

A similar behavior can be observed with respect to the recall relation. Here, Savary's algorithm shows a constant graph since the approach applied is global and, as consequence, the set of corrections provided is always the entire one for a fixed error counter. In our proposal, the results prove that the recall is smaller than for Savary's, which illustrates the gain in computational efficiency in opposite to the global method. Related to the convergence between regional and global approaches, we must again search around points of detection close to the beginning of the word, which often also implies repair regions be equivalent to the total one and repairs starting around of q_0, such as is illustrated in Fig. 5.

However, in opposite to the case of performance, we remark that for recall the convergence between global and regional proposals seems also extend to processes where the point of error is associated to states close to q_f, that is, when this point is located near of the end of the word. To understand this, it is sufficient to take into account that we are not now computing the number of items generated in the repair, but the number of corrections finally proposed. So, given that closer to the end of the word we are and smaller is the number of alternatives for a repair process, both global and regional approaches converge also towards the right of the graph for recall.

Finally, the regional (resp. the global) approach provided as correction the word from which the error was randomly included in a 77% (resp. 81%) of the cases. Although this could be interpreted as a justification to use global methods, it is necessary to remember that we are now only taking into account morphological information, which has an impact in the precision for a regional approach, but not for a global one that always provide all the repair alternatives without exclusion. So, the precision represents, in an exclusively morphological context, a disadvantage for our proposal since we base the efficiency in the limitation of the search space. The future integration of linguistic information from both, syntactic and semantic viewpoints should reduce significantly this gap, less than 4%, around the precision; or even should eliminate it.

5 Conclusion

The design of computational tools for linguistic usage should respond to the constraints of efficiency, safety and maintenance. So, a major point of interest in dealing with these aspects is the development of error correction strategies, since this kind of techniques supplies the robustness necessary to extend formal prototypes to practical applications. In this paper, we have described a proposal on spelling correction for Galician, a Latin language with non-trivial morphology trying to rescue its recognition from society, which involves to have tools in order to ensure a correct usage of it. We take advantage of the grammatical structure present in the underlying morphological recognizer to provide the user an automatic assistant to develop linguistic tasks without errors. In this sense, our work represents an initial approach to the problem, but preliminary results seem to be promising and the formalism well adapted to deal with more complex problems such as the consideration of additional linguistic knowledge.

References

1. J. Daciuk, S. Mihov, B.W. Watson, and R.E. Watson. Incremental construction of minimal acyclic finite-state automata. *Computational Linguistics*, 26(1):3–16, 2000.
2. M. W. Du and S.C. Chang. A model and a fast algorithm for multiple errors spelling correction. *Acta Informatica*, 29(3):281–302, June 1992.

3. J. Graña, F.M. Barcala, and M.A. Alonso. Compilation methods of minimal acyclic automata for large dictionaries. *Lecture Notes in Computer Science*, 2494:135–148, 2002.
4. C.L. Lucchesi and T. Kowaltowski. Applications of finite automata representing large vocabularies. *Software-Practice and Experience*, 23(1):15–30, January 1993.
5. K. Oflazer. Error-tolerant finite-state recognition with applications to morphological analysis and spelling correction. *Computational Linguistics*, 22(1):73–89, 1996.
6. A. Savary. Typographical nearest-neighbor search in a finite-state lexicon and its application to spelling correction. *Lecture Notes in Computer Science*, 2494:251–260, 2001.
7. K. Sikkel. *Parsing Schemata.* PhD thesis, Univ. of Twente, The Netherlands, 1993.

Baseline Methods for Automatic Disambiguation of Abbreviations in Jewish Law Documents

Yaakov HaCohen-Kerner[1], Ariel Kass[1], and Ariel Peretz[1]

[1] Department of Computer Sciences, Jerusalem College of Technology (Machon Lev)
21 Havaad Haleumi St., P.O.B. 16031, 91160 Jerusalem, Israel
{kerner, akass, arielp}@jct.ac.il

Abstract. In many languages, abbreviations are widely used either in writing or talking. However, abbreviations are likely to be ambiguous. Therefore, there is a need for disambiguation. That is, abbreviations should be expanded correctly. Disambiguation of abbreviations is critical for correct understanding not only for the abbreviations themselves but also for the whole text. Little research has been done concerning disambiguation of abbreviations for documents in English and Latin. Nothing has been done for the Hebrew language. In this ongoing work, we investigate a basic model, which expands abbreviations contained in Jewish Law Documents written in Hebrew. This model has been implemented in a prototype system. Currently, experimental results show that abbreviations are expanded correctly in a rate of almost 60%.

1 Introduction

Abbreviations have long been adopted by languages and are widely used either in writing or in talking. However, they are not always defined and in many cases they are ambiguous. Many authors create their own sets of abbreviations. Some abbreviations are specific to certain aspects of a language such as Science, Press (newspapers, television, etc.) or Slang. Correct disambiguation of abbreviations may affect the proper understanding of the whole text. In general, for any given abbreviation this process is composed of the following two main steps: (1) finding all possible extensions and (2) selecting the most correct extension.

Research concerning disambiguation of abbreviations for documents in English and Latin has yet to mature and is only investigated in minimal domains (section 2.1). Research of this subject is completely absent for the Hebrew language. In Hebrew, the task of disambiguation of abbreviations is critical due to the following reasons:

Hebrew is very rich in its vocabulary of abbreviations. The number of Hebrew abbreviations is about 17,000, relatively high comparing to 40,000 lexical entries in the Hebrew language. Various kinds of Hebrew texts contain a high frequency of abbreviations. For example, Jewish texts, scientific texts, texts in professional domains such as: computer sciences, economics, medicine and military.

People who learn Hebrew in general, immigrants, children and people who need to read and learn documents related to a new domain (e.g., a specific professional domain) in particular, a lot of help. Many times they do not know what are the

J. L. Vicedo et al. (Eds.): EsTAL 2004, LNAI 3230, pp. 58–69, 2004.

possible extensions or part of them and they cannot find the most correct extension. Therefore, they experience great difficulty understanding the meaning of the running text.

In this paper, we present the current state of our ongoing work. We develop six different basic methods and combinations of them for abbreviation disambiguation in Hebrew. The first three methods focused on unique characteristics of each abbreviation, e.g.: common words, prefixes and suffixes. The next two methods are statistical methods based on general grammar and literary knowledge of Hebrew. The final method uses the numerical value (Gematria) of the abbreviation.

This paper is organized as follows. Section 2 gives background concerning disambiguation of abbreviations, previous systems dealing with automatic disambiguation of abbreviations and the Hebrew language. Section 3 describes the proposed baseline methods for disambiguation of Hebrew abbreviations. Section 4 presents the experiments we have carried out. Section 5 discusses hard cases of abbreviations that our basic methods are not able to disambiguate, gives an example for such a hard case and proposes future methods for solving them. Section 6 concludes and proposes future directions for research. The Appendix contains the Hebrew Transliteration Table.

2 Background

Abbreviation is a letter or group of letters, which is a shortened form of a word or a sequence of words. The word or sequence of words is called a *long form* of an abbreviation. Abbreviation disambiguation means to choose the correct long form while depending on its context.

Abbreviations are very common and are widely used either in writing or in talking. However, they are not always defined and in many cases they are ambiguous. Disambiguation of abbreviations is critical for correct understanding not only for abbreviations themselves but for the whole text.

Initialism is an abbreviation formed by using the first letters, or initials, of a series of words, e.g., "AA" or "ABC". There are some that make a distinction between regular initialisms and an acronym. An *Acronym* exists when the letters form a pronounceable word, like “ASCII”, while initialisms are pronounced by sounding out each letter, like “CDC” ("see dee see"). In this article we will make no distinction between these concepts and refer to them both as initialisms.

In English, there are several forms for abbreviations and initialisms. For example:

- Uppercase-Uppercase (e.g., AA is an abbreviation for the following extensions: Alcoholics Anonymous, American Airlines, Automobile Association, Anti-aircraft, Argentinum Astrum, Alcoa (stock symbol))
- Uppercase-lowercase (e.g.: Au means Australia or Austria or Gold)
- lowercase-lowercase (e.g.: au that means atomic units)
- Usage of periods and space (e.g.: DC., D.C, D.C., D. C.)

Additional examples for ambiguous initialisms and their extensions can be obtained from [15].

2.1 Previous Automatic Disambiguation of Abbreviations

Little research has been done in the domain of abbreviation disambiguation. An automatic abbreviation dictionary, called S-RAD, has been created automatically for biomedicine by Adar [1]. Statistical studies concerning abbreviations in general and three-letter abbreviations in particular in medical texts are presented in [10] and [9], respectively.

An automatic system that disambiguates abbreviations in medical abstracts was developed by YU et. al. [16]. Their system uses a machine learning technique called Support Vector Machines (SVM). SVM is a supervised machine-learning technique proposed by Cortes and Vapnik [4]. This method optimizes the error rate on the training data set, the ability of the model for prediction, and the ability depends on concept VC-dimension. The SVM is applied in various research domains such as word sense disambiguation [3] and text classification [8]. In addition, their method uses the One Sense per Discourse Hypothesis, which was introduced by Gale et. al. [5]. They reported that 94% occurrences of ambiguous words from the same discourse have the same meaning. For abbreviation, analogically, when considering its sense as its long form, we can observe and assume that when an abbreviation has different occurrences within a medical abstract, all of the occurrences have the same long form. Experiments show that their method achieves an accuracy of about 84% for selecting the most correct long form for a given abbreviation.

Another working system has been constructed by Rydberg-Cox [11]. This system disambiguates abbreviations in early modern texts written in Latin. The system uses a three-step algorithm for a given abbreviation. The first two steps identify all possible expansions for this abbreviation. In the first stage, they use a Latin morphological analyzer in order to parse every possible expansion. In the second stage, they search a database of known inflected forms of Latin literature for other possible expansions. In the final stage, they use three relatively simple metrics to select the best possible expansion: (1) expansions discovered using the Latin morphological analyzer are preferred to those discovered using the search in a database of known inflected forms, (2) frequency tables for expanded forms in their corpus and (3) search a database of collocations to determine whether the current context is similar to other contexts where possible expansions of the abbreviation occur in their corpus. In preliminary tests in a small corpus, they report accurate expansions for most abbreviations. They plan to develop better statistical metrics for the third step and to test their algorithm on a larger corpus.

However, nothing has been done concerning automatic abbreviation disambiguation for Hebrew. Abbreviations in Hebrew are widely used and many of them are ambiguous. In the next sub-section, we will discuss various aspects of Hebrew and abbreviations in Hebrew.

2.2 The Hebrew Language

Hebrew is a Semitic language. It uses the Hebrew alphabet and it is written from right to left. Hebrew words in general and Hebrew verbs in particular are based on three (sometimes four) basic letters, which create the word's stem. The stem of a Hebrew verb is called *pl*[1,2] (פעל, "verb"). The first letter of the stem *p* (פ) is called *pe hapoal*; the second letter of the stem (ע) is called *ayin hapoal* and the third letter of the stem *l* (ל) is called *lamed hapoal*. The names of the letters are especially important for the verbs' declensions according to the suitable verb types.

Except for the word's stem, there are several other components, which create the word's declensions:

Conjugations: The Hebrew language contains seven conjugations that include the verb's stem. The conjugations add different meanings to the stem such as: active, passive, cause, etc. For example the stem *hrs* (הרס, "destroy") in one conjugation hrs means destroy but in another conjugation *nhrs* (נהרס, "being destroyed").

Verb types: The Hebrew language contains several verb types. Each verb type is a group of stems that their verbs are acting the same form in different tenses and different conjugations. There is a difference in the declensions of the stem in different verb types. In English, in order to change the tense, there is a need to add only one or two letters as suffixes. However, In Hebrew, for each verb type there is a different way that the word changes following the tense.

To demonstrate, we choose two verbs in past tense of different verb types: (1) *ktv* (כתב, "wrote") of the *shlemim* verb type (strong verbs - all three letters of the stem are apparent), and (2) the word *nfl* (נפל, "fell") of the *hasrey_pay_*noon verb type (where the first letter of the stem is the letter n and in several declensions of the stem this letter is omitted). When we use the future tense, the word *ktv* (כתב, "wrote") will change to *ykhtv* (יכתב, "will write") while the second word nfl will change to *ypl* (יפל, "will fall") which does not include the letter n. Therefore, in order to find the right declensions for a certain stem, it is necessary to know from which verb type the stem come from.

Subject: Usually, in English we add the subject as a separate word before the verb. For example: I ate, you ate; where the verb change is minimal if at all. However, in Hebrew the subject does not have to be a separated word and it can appear as a suffix.

Prepositions: Unlike English, which has unique words dedicated to expressing relations between objects (e.g.: at, in, from), Hebrew has 8 prepositions that can be written as a concatenated letter at the beginning of the word. Each letter expresses another relation. For example: (1) the meaning of the letter *v* (ו) at the beginning of word is identical to the meaning of the word "and" in English. For example, the Hebrew word *v't'* (ואתה) means "and you"; (2) the meaning of the letter *l* (ל) at the beginning of word is similar to the English word "to". For instance, the Hebrew word *lysr'l* (לישראל) means "to Israel".

Belonging: In English, there are some unique words that indicate belonging (e.g.: my, his, her). This phenomenon exists also in Hebrew. In addition, there are several suffixes that can be concatenated at the end of the word for that purpose. The meaning of the letter *y* (י) at the end of word is identical to the meaning of the word "my" in English. For example, the Hebrew word *ty* (עטי) has the same meaning as the English words "my pen".

Object: In English, there are some unique words that indicate the object in the sentence, such as: him, her, and them. This is also the case in Hebrew. In addition,

[1] See Appendix for the Hebrew Transliteration Table.

[2] Each Hebrew word is presented in three forms: (1) transliteration of the Hebrew letters written in italics, (2) the Hebrew letters, and (3) its translation into English in quotes.

there are several letters that can be concatenated at the end of the word for that purpose. The letter *v* (ו) at the end of a word has the same meaning as the word him in English. For example, the Hebrew word *r'ytyv* (ראיתיו) has the same meaning as the English words "I saw him".

Terminal letters: In Hebrew, there are five letters: *m* (מ), *n* (נ), *ts* (צ), *p* (פ), *kh* (כ) which are written differently when they appear at the end of word: *m* (ם), *n* (ן), *ts* (ץ), *p* (ף), *kh* (ך) respectively. For example, the verb *ysn* (ישן, "he slept") and the verb *ysnty* (ישנתי, "I slept"). The two verbs have the same stem *ysn*, but the last letter of the stem is written differently in each one of the verbs.

In Hebrew, it is impossible to find the declensions of a certain stem without an exact morphological analysis based on the features mentioned above. The English language is richer in its vocabulary than Hebrew (the English language has about 40,000 stems while Hebrew has only about 4,000 and the number of lexical entries in the English dictionary is 150,000 compared with only 40,000 in the Hebrew dictionary), but the Hebrew language is richer in its morphology forms. For example, the single Hebrew word *vlkhsykhuhu* (ולכשיכוהו) is translated into the following sequence of six English words: "and when they will hit him". In comparison to the Hebrew verb, which undergoes a few changes, the English verb stays the same.

In Hebrew, there are up to seven thousand declensions for only one stem, while in English there are only a few declensions. For example, the English word eat has only four declensions (eats, eating, eaten and ate). The relevant Hebrew stem *'khl* (אכל, "eat") has thousands of declensions. Ten of them are presented below: (1) *'khlty* (אכלתי, "I ate"), (2) 'khlt (אכלת, "you ate"), (3) *'khlnv* (אכלנו, "we ate"), (4) *'khvl* (אוכל, "he eats"), (5) *'khvlym* (אוכלים, "they eat"), (6) *'tkhl* (תאכל, " she will eat"), (7) *l'khvl* (לאכל, "to eat"), (8) *'khltyv* (אכלתיו, "I ate it"), (9) *v'khlty* (ואכלתי, "and I ate") and (10) *ks'khlt* (כשאכלת, "when you ate").

For more detailed discussions of Hebrew grammar from the viewpoint of computer science, refer to [13]. For Hebrew grammar, refer either to [6, 12] in English or to [15] in Hebrew.

Gematria (Numerology). Numerology is an arcane study of the purported mystical relationship between numbers and the character or action of physical objects and living things. Numerology and numerological divination was popular among early mathematicians such as Pythagoras.

These methods derived from the basic need of keeping count. This system was widely used in Mesopotamia. In this case, numerical values were assigned to the characters in their syllabary, and the numerical values of names were computed. The Greeks decided to adopt this method and called it isopsephia.

In this system, the first letter of the alphabet is used as the numeral One, the second letter as Two and so on, until the ninth letter is assigned to Nine. Then you start on the Tens, assigning the 10th letter to Ten, the 11th letter to 20, and so on, until you reach the 18th letter which is assigned to 90. Then, you count in hundreds. The 19th letter is used as a symbol for 100, the 20th letter for 200 and so until you reach the 27th letter and the number 900. This system has since been in wide use in several common languages: Hebrew, Greek, Arabic and Chinese. The Greek alphabet has only 24 letters, so it uses three ancient characters, Digamma or Fau, Qoppa and Tsampi which had dropped out of use as letters as the numerals 6, 90 and 900. The Arabic alphabet has 28 characters, one of which (Ghain) is used as a symbol for 1000.

The system of Hebrew numerals is called Gematria. Gematria is the calculation of the numerical equivalence of letters, words or phrases. Thus, gaining insight into interrelation of different concepts and exploring the interrelationship between words and ideas. There are more than ten ways to calculate equivalence of individual letters in Gematria. We used one of the most common methods: Absolute Value - also known as Normative Value. Each letter is given the value of its accepted numerical equivalent: א (alef, the first letter) equals 1, ב (beit, the second letter) equals 2, and so on. The tenth letter, י (yud) is numerically equivalent to 10, and successive letters equal 20, 30, 40, and so on. The letter ק (kuf) near the end of the alphabet, equals 100; and the last letter, ת (tav) equals 400.

In this reckoning, the letters ך (final chaf), ם (final mem), ן (final nun), ף (final pei), and ץ (final tzadik) which are the "final forms" of the letters כ (chaf), מ (mem), נ (nun), פ (pei), and צ (tzadik), used when these letters conclude a word, generally are given the same numerical equivalent of the standard form of the letter.

This system is used nowadays mainly for specifying the days and years of the Hebrew calendar as well as chapter and page numbers.

2.3 Abbreviations in Hebrew

In Hebrew, there are about 17,000 common abbreviations, not including unique professional abbreviations [2]. About 35% of them are ambiguous. That is, about 6000 abbreviations have more than one possible extension for each abbreviation. Every Hebrew abbreviation contains quotation marks between the two last letters of the abbreviation.

An example of an extremely ambiguous abbreviation is אא (א"א, "AA"). This abbreviation has 110 possible long forms [2]. Ten of them are presented below: (1) (אמר אברהם, "Abraham said"), (2) (אי אפשר, "not possible"), (3) (אשת איש, "married woman"), (4) (אבות אבותינו, "our fore fathers"), (5) (אבי אבי , "my father's father"), (6) (אם אבי , "my father's mother"), (7) (אין אוכלים, "eating disallowed"), (8) (אין אומרים, "saying disallowed"), (9) (אם אומרים, "if said") and (10) (אתה אומר, "you say").

3 Baseline Methods for Abbreviation Disambiguation in Hebrew

In this section, we introduce the baseline methods we use for abbreviation disambiguation in Hebrew. Our methods only disambiguate abbreviations with sequences of words as their long forms. Our methods are classified into two kinds: the first set of methods is based on research of our corpus. This research focused on unique characteristics of each abbreviation and unique characteristics of the Hebrew language. For instance: prefixes, suffixes, common words which appear in the vicinity of the abbreviation and numerical value of the abbreviation.

The second set of methods is composed of statistical methods based on general grammar and literary knowledge of Hebrew, e.g.: context related words that may appear in the vicinity of the abbreviation and probability of disambiguation solution based on the field of discussion in the context. Currently, we have not addressed semantic methods dealing with the meaning of abbreviations, words and sentences.

So far, the above sets of methods have produced six baseline methods. The first four methods belong to the first set and the two last methods belong to the second set. The definition of these methods is as follows:

1) Word Before (WB): this method tries to conclude the proper disambiguation long form based on the word that appears immediately before the abbreviation in the sentence. The credibility of this method is based on the assumption that certain words may appear before the abbreviation a considerable amount of times based on literal and syntax relationships in Hebrew. Many words may be uniquely related to a single abbreviation. For example in the following Hebrew sentence: "והמלאכות המותרות לכתחילה ע"י א"י מותר גם על ידו" – the abbreviation *'y* (א"י) may be interpreted as (אינו יהודי, "non Jew") or (ארץ ישראל, "land of Israel"). Based on the word before *y* (ע"י, "performed by") we can understand that the sentence refers to a person performing an action. Therefore, the correct solution would be "non Jew".

2) Word After (WA): this method tries to conclude the proper disambiguation solution based on the word that appears immediately after the abbreviation in the sentence. The credibility of this method is based on the assumption that certain words may appear after the abbreviation a considerable amount of times based on literal and syntax relationships in Hebrew. Many words may be uniquely related to a single abbreviation. For example in the following Hebrew sentence: "והנה כ"ז מיירי לעניין לשאת התיק של הבתי עינים..." – the abbreviation *kz* (כ"ז) may be interpreted as (כל זה, "all this") or 27 (the numerical value of the Hebrew characters כ & ז). Based on the word after *myyry* (מיירי, "is discussed") we can understand that the sentence is trying to explain to us which cases are discussed. Therefore, the correct disambiguation would be 'all this'.

3) Prefixes (PR): this method tries to conclude the proper disambiguation solution based on the prefixes added to the abbreviation (Section 2.2). The credibility of this method is based on knowledge of syntax rules in Hebrew, which in certain cases impose specific prefixes to be added. Many prefixes may be uniquely related to a single abbreviation. For example in the following Hebrew sentence: "ויש אוסרים וכנ"ל בסי"א" – the abbreviation *y'* (י"א) may be interpreted as (יש אומרים, "some say") or 11 (numerical value of the Hebrew characters י & א). The prefix letter *s* (ס) adds the word *syf* (סעיף, "paragraph") before the abbreviation. Therefore, the paragraph number is the correct solution, i.e. 11. There is no meaning to the second long form.

4) Numerical Value - Gematria (GM): this method tries to conclude the proper disambiguation solution based on the numerical value of the abbreviation. In essence, every abbreviation has a numerical value solution. For example in the following Hebrew sentence: "וכדלקמן בסימן רס"ג סי"ז ע"ש הטעם במ"ב" – the abbreviation *rsg* (רס"ג) may be interpreted as (רבי סעדיה גאון, "a Jewish Scholar") or 273 (the numerical value of this abbreviation). This method will choose 273 as the disambiguation solution.

5) Most Common Extension in the Text (CT): this method tries to conclude the proper disambiguation solution based on the statistical frequency of each solution in the context of the text file. For example in the following Hebrew sentence: "עכ"פ איסורא מיהא איכא לכו"ע וע"י א"י מותר" – the abbreviation *'y* (א"י) may be interpreted as (אינו יהודי, "non Jew") or (ארץ ישראל, "land of Israel"). The most common long form in the context of the discussed text file is (אינו יהודי, "non Jew") and is therefore the disambiguation solution.

6) Most Common Extension in the Language (CL): this method tries to conclude the proper disambiguation solution based on the statistical frequency of each solution in the Hebrew language. For example in the following Hebrew sentence: "ודע דמ"מ סעודה זו אינה חובה עליו" – the abbreviation *mm* (מ"מ) may be interpreted as (מכל מקום, "anyhow") or (מאמר מרדכי, "a name of a Jewish law book") or (מגיד משנה, "another name of a Jewish law book"). The most common long form in the Hebrew language is (מכל מקום, "anyhow") and is therefore the disambiguation solution.

4 Experiments

We have constructed a relatively small corpus, taken from [7]. This corpus discusses Jewish laws referring to Saturday. It contains about 19,000 Hebrew words including about 1500 abbreviations of them 557 are ambiguous. Each abbreviation has, on average, 2.3 possible long forms. We used each of the above baseline methods independently to detect and disambiguate abbreviations that have more than two longs forms. Table 1 shows the results of our six methods acting independently on ambiguous abbreviations, regarding correct disambiguation: count and percentage.

Table 1. Summarization of the results for the methods acting independently

#	Method	Correct Disambiguation	
		#	%
1	WB	235	42.2
2	WA	245	44
3	PR	253	45.4
4	GM	48	8.7
5	CT	320	57.5
6	CL	239	42.9

The best baseline method: CT presents a rate of about 57.5%. This means that the statistical frequencies of the long forms contained in the text file is the best method.

We also combined the above baseline methods to work concurrently. The number of combinations tested was 57 (there are 15 possibilities to combine 2 methods together, 20 possibilities to combine 3 methods together, 15 possibilities to combine 4 methods together, 6 possibilities to combine 5 methods together and an 1 experiment was done using all 6 baseline methods at once).

In these experiments, each baseline method returned the abbreviation disambiguation solution best suited to the method. Each solution was given equal weight in the consideration of the final solution. When a decision was needed between 2 equally possible solutions, the first of the solutions to appear in the solution possibility set was chosen. Table 2 shows the results of our methods working in different combinations on ambiguous abbreviations, regarding correct disambiguation: count and percentage.

Table 2. Summarization of the results for combinations of methods acting together

#	Method	Correct Disambiguations #	%
1	PR-WB-WA-CT	327	58.7
2	PR-WB-WA-CT-CL	324	58.1
3	PR-WB-WA-CT-CL-GM	322	57.9
4	CT-GM	306	55.1
5	CL-CT	295	53
6	PR-WB-CL	293	52.6
7	PR-CL	286	51.3

The best combination of baseline methods: PR-WB-WA-CT presents a rate of almost 60%. The CL method - the statistical frequencies known in the Hebrew language – and the GM method – the numerical value of the abbreviation - are the only methods that are not included in the combination of the methods. It might be a supporting evidence that the most important methods to disambiguate correctly are based on internal-file information such as the CT method and all the first three methods that discuss one word before, one word after and prefixes. It may also support the claim that Gematria should not receive equal weight since it only has potential to have a real meaning when the letters of the abbreviation are written in descending value and not in any kind of abbreviation.

5 Hard Cases

Analyzing the results from the above experiments led us to understand what the hard cases that we could not solve were. A very potent characteristic of these cases was the semantic context of the initialisms. Since our current methods are static, we could not correctly disambiguate this kind of initialism.

An example of such a case is given with two subsequent sentences:
Sentence A: "שאלתי את א"א אודות הטיול מחר" (I questioned A"A about the trip tomorrow)
Sentence B: "ענתה היא לי שהטיול בוטל" (She answered me that the trip was canceled)

Let us Assume that the two most suitable solutions for the abbreviation '' (א"א, A"A) in Sentence A are extensions # 5 & 6 mentioned in the last paragraph on Section 2. That is, the potential solutions are: (1) (אבי אבי, "my father's father") or (2) (אם אבי, "my father's mother"). We can clearly conclude that the correct solution is the second one - "my father's mother", since the second sentence tells us that the questioned person in the first sentence is a female. This is clearly a semantic understanding of the sentences and it is based on multiple sentence diagnostics.

Our research does not include this type of natural language understanding, but we may develop additional methods and their combinations, which will help solve many hard cases.

We also propose a dynamic method that will be implemented and tested in the near future. This method uses static technical analysis to help indirectly solve part of these hard cases. After applying the above six static methods on all the initialisms in the text, we extract all the "sure thing" cases (ambiguous abbreviations with 100% certainty of disambiguation solution) based on these methods' analysis. We then add to a result file, created for each pair consisted of an initialism and a specific potential solution, all the words in the sentence in which the initialism occurs in (not including 'stop-words'). With each solution we enlarge our word collection file. After the entire file is analyzed once, we then reiterate through all the "unsure" cases (2 or more disambiguation solutions are equally possible) in the text. We examine the sentence that contains the initialism and count the amount of words from the sentence that appear in each of the word collection files for each solution. The solution with the highest number of common words in the examined sentence is selected.

This method is truthful to the language characteristic of reoccurring words in the vicinity of others. This method also adds a dynamic dimension to our research and may give different results for different texts based on the "sure thing" cases of the text.

6 Conclusions, Summary and Future Work

Our basic system is the first to disambiguate abbreviations for Hebrew text-files. It presents a rate of about 58.5% using the best baseline method: CT. This means that the statistical frequencies regarding the context of the text file forms the best independent method.

The best combination of baseline methods presents a rate of about 60%. The methods in this combination are based on internal-file information: CT and the methods that discuss one word before, one word after and prefixes.

Future directions for research are: (1) Finding new baseline methods and combining between these and previous baseline methods, (2) Enlarging the different text file types and further research of new abbreviations, (3) Using learning techniques in order to find the best weighted combinations of methods and (4) Elaborating the model for abbreviation disambiguation for various kinds of Hebrew documents.

References

1. Adar, E.: S-RAD: A Simple and Robust Abbreviation Dictionary. Technical Report. HP Laboratories (2002)
2. Ashkenazi, S., Jarden, D.: Ozar Rashe Tevot: Thesaurus of Hebrew Abbreviations (in Hebrew). Kiryat Sefere LTD., Jerusalem (1994)
3. Cabezas, C., Resnik, P., Stevens, J.: Supervised Sense Tagging using Support Vector Machines. Proceedings of the Second International Workshop on Evaluating Word Sense Disambiguation Systems (SENSEVAL-2), Toulouse, France (2001)
4. Cortes, C., Vapnik, V.: Support-Vector Networks. Machine Learning 20 (1995) 273-297
5. Gale, W.A., Church, K.W., Yarowsky, D.: One Sense Per Discourse. Proceedings of the ARPA Workshop on Speech and Natural Language Processing (1992) 233-237
6. Glinert, L., Gilinert, L.: Hebrew – An Essential Grammar. Routledge, London (1994)
7. HaCohen, Rabbi Y. M.: Mishnah Berurah.Vol. 3, Pisgah Foundation, Jerusalem (1993)
8. Joachims, T.: Learning to Classify Text using Support Vector Machines. Kluwer Academic Publishers (2001)

9. Liu, H., Aronson, A. R., Friedman, C.: A Study of Abbreviations in MEDLINE Abstracts. Proc AMIA Symp. (2002) 464-468
10. Liu, H., Lussier, Y. A., Friedman, C.: A Study of Abbreviations in the UMLS. Proc AMIA Symp. (2001) 393-397
11. Rydberg-Cox, J. A.: Automatic Disambiguation of Latin Abbreviations in Early Modern Texts for Humanities Digital Libraries. International Conference on Digital Libraries, Proceedings of the third ACM/IEEE-CS joint conference on Digital libraries, IEEE Computer Society (2003) 372-373
12. Wartski, I.: Hebrew Grammar and Explanatory Notes. The Linguaphone Institute, London (1900)
13. Wintner, S. Hebrew Computational Linguistics: Past and Future. Artificial Intelligence Review, 21:2 (2003) 113-138
14. WordiQ. http://www.wordiq.com/ (2003)
15. Yelin, D.: Dikduk HaLason HaIvrit (Hebrew Grammar, in Hebrew), Jerusalem (1970)
16. Yu, Z., Tsuruoka, Y., Tsujii, J.: Automatic Resolution of Ambiguous Abbreviations in Biomedical Texts using Support Vector Machines and One Sense Per Discourse Hypothesis. SIGIR'03 Workshop on Text Analysis and Search for Bioinformatics (2003) 57-62

Appendix

The Hebrew Transliteration Table presented below, which has been used in this paper, is taken from the web site of the Princeton university library (http://infoshare1.princeton.edu/katmandu/hebrew/trheb.html).

Consonants

Vernacular	*Romanization*
א	ʼ (alif) *or disregarded*
בּ	b
ב	v (*in Yiddish,* b)
ג	g
ד	d
ה	h
ו	v *(only if a consonant)*
וו	v *(only if a consonant)*
ז	z
ח	ḥ
ט	ṭ
י	y *(only if a consonant)*
כּ final ךּ	k
כ final ך	kh
ל	l
מ final ם	m
נ final ן	n
ס	s
ע	ʻ (ayin)
פּ final ףּ	p
פ final ף	f
צ final ץ	ts
ק	ḳ
ר	r
שׁ	sh
שׂ	ś
תּ	t
ת	t (*in Yiddish* s̀)

Vowels

Hebrew	*Romanization*
ַ	A
ָ	a *or* o´
ֶ	E
ֵ	E
ִ	I
ֹ	O
ֻ	U
ֶי	E
ַי	Ai
ֵי	E
ִי	I
וֹ	O
וּ	U
ְ	e *or* *disregarded*
ֲ	A
ֱ	E
ֳ	O

Bayes Decision Rules and Confidence Measures for Statistical Machine Translation

Nicola Ueffing and Hermann Ney

Lehrstuhl für Informatik VI - Computer Science Department
RWTH Aachen University
Ahornstrasse 55
52056 Aachen, Germany
{ueffing,ney}@cs.rwth-aachen.de

Abstract. In this paper, we re-visit the foundations of the statistical approach to machine translation and study two forms of the Bayes decision rule: the common rule for minimizing the number of string errors and a novel rule for minimizing the number of symbol errors. The Bayes decision rule for minimizing the number of string errors is widely used, but its justification is rarely questioned.

We study the relationship between the Bayes decision rule, the underlying error measure, and word confidence measures for machine translation. The derived confidence measures are tested on the output of a state-of-the-art statistical machine translation system. Experimental comparison with existing confidence measures is presented on a translation task consisting of technical manuals.

1 Introduction

The statistical approach to machine translation (MT) has found widespread use. There are three ingredients to any statistical approach to MT, namely the Bayes decision rule, the probability models (trigram language model, HMM, ...) and the training criterion (maximum likelihood, mutual information, ...).

The topic of this paper is to examine the differences between string error (or *sentence* error) and symbol error (or *word* error) and their implications for the Bayes decision rule. The error measure is referred to as loss function in statistical decision theory. We will present a closed representation of different word error measures for MT. For these different word error measures, we will derive the posterior risk. This will lead to the definition of several confidence measures at the word level for MT output.

Related Work: For the task of MT, statistical approaches were proposed at the beginning of the nineties [3] and found widespread use in the last years [12, 14]. To the best of our knowledge, the 'standard' version of the Bayes decision rule, which minimizes the number of sentence errors, is used in virtually all approaches to statistical machine translation (SMT). There are only a few research groups that do not take this type of decision rule for granted.

J. L. Vicedo et al. (Eds.): EsTAL 2004, LNAI 3230, pp. 70–81, 2004.

In [8], an approach to SMT was presented that minimized the posterior risk for different error measures. Rescoring was performed on 1,000-best lists produced by an SMT system. In [11], a sort of error related or discriminative training was used, but the decision rule as such was not affected. In other research areas, e.g. in speech recognition, there exist a few publications that consider the word error instead of the sentence error for taking decisions [6].

2 Bayes Decision Rule for Minimum Error Rate

2.1 The Bayes Posterior Risk

Knowing that any task in natural language processing (NLP) is a difficult one, we want to keep the number of wrong decisions as small as possible. To classify an observation vector y into one out of several classes c, we resort to the so-called statistical decision theory and try to minimize the posterior *risk* $R(c|y)$ in taking a decision. The posterior risk is defined as

$$R(c|y) = \sum_{\tilde{c}} Pr(\tilde{c}|y) \cdot L[c, \tilde{c}] \ ,$$

where $L[c, \tilde{c}]$ is the so-called *loss function* or *error measure*, i.e. the loss we incur in making decision $\tilde{c}$ when the true class is c. The resulting decision rule is known as *Bayes decision rule* [4]:

$$y \rightarrow \hat{c} \ = \ \arg\min_{c} R(c|y) \ = \ \arg\min_{c} \left\{ \sum_{\tilde{c}} Pr(\tilde{c}|y) \cdot L[c, \tilde{c}] \right\} \ .$$

In the following, we will consider two specific forms of the error measure, $L[c, \tilde{c}]$. The first will be the measure for *sentence* errors, which is the typical loss function used in virtually all statistical approaches. The second is the measure for *word* errors, which is the more appropriate measure for machine translation and also speech recognition.

In NLP tasks such as Part-of-Speech tagging, where we do not have the alignment problem, the optimal decision is the following: compute the Bayes posterior probability and accept if the probability is greater or equal to 0.5. We omit the proof here. Following this, we formulate the Bayes decision rule for two different word error measures in MT. From those we can derive word confidence measures for MT according to which the words in MT output can be either accepted as correct translations or rejected.

2.2 Sentence Error

For machine translation, the starting point is the observed sequence of words $y = f_1^J = f_1...f_J$, i.e. the sequence of words in the source language which has to be translated into a target language sequence $c = e_1^I = e_1...e_I$.

The first error measure we consider is the sentence error: two target language sentences are considered to be identical only when the words in each position are identical (which naturally requires the same length I). In this case, the error measure between two strings e_1^I and $\tilde{e}_1^{\tilde{I}}$ is:

$$L[e_1^I, \tilde{e}_1^{\tilde{I}}] = 1 - \delta(I, \tilde{I}) \cdot \prod_{i=1}^{I} \delta(e_i, \tilde{e}_i) \ ,$$

with the Kronecker delta $\delta(.,.)$. In other words, the errors are counted at the *string* (or sentence) level and not at the level of single symbols (or words). Inserting this cost function into the Bayes risk (see Section 2.1), we obtain the following form of *Bayes decision rule for minimum sentence error*:

$$\begin{aligned} f_1^J \to (\hat{I}, \hat{e}_1^{\hat{I}}) &= \arg\max_{I, e_1^I} \{Pr(I, e_1^I | f_1^J)\} \\ &= \arg\max_{I, e_1^I} \{Pr(I, e_1^I, f_1^J)\} \ . \end{aligned} \tag{1}$$

This is the starting point for virtually all statistical approaches in machine translation. However, this decision rule is only optimal when we consider *sentence* error. In practice, however, the empirical errors are counted at the *word* level. This inconsistency of decision rule and error measure is rarely addressed in the literature.

2.3 Word Error

Instead of the *sentence* error rate, we can also consider the error rate of *symbols* or single *words*. In the MT research community, there exist several different error measures that are based on the word error. We will investigate the *word error rate (WER)* and the *position independent word error rate (PER)*.

The symbol sequences in Figure 1 illustrate the differences between the two error measures WER and PER: Comparing the strings 'ABCBD' and 'ABBCE', WER yields an error of 2, whereas the PER error is 1.

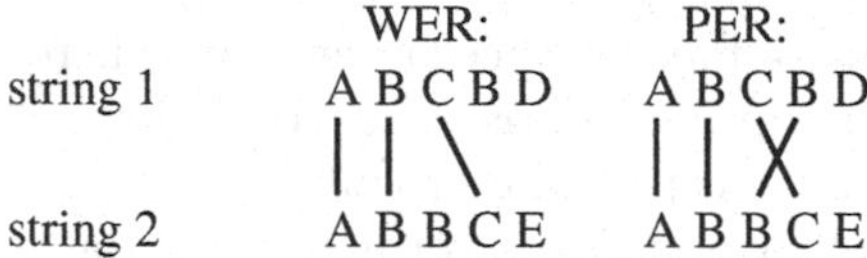

Fig. 1. Example of the two symbol error measures WER and PER: The string 'ABCBD' is compared to 'ABBCE'

For NLP tasks where there is no variance in the string length (such as Part-of-Speech tagging), the integration of the symbol error measure into Bayes decision rule yields that a maximization of the posterior probability for each position i has to be performed [10]. In machine translation, we need a method for accounting for differences in sentence length or word order between the two strings under consideration, e.g. the Levenshtein alignment (cf. WER).

- **WER** (word error rate): The word error rate is based on the Levenshtein distance [9]. It is computed as the minimum number of substitution, insertion, and deletion operations that have to be performed to convert the generated sentence into the reference sentence. For two sentences e_1^I and $\tilde{e}_1^{\tilde{I}}$, the Levenshtein alignment is denoted by $\mathcal{L}(e_1^I, \tilde{e}_1^{\tilde{I}})$; for a word e_i, the Levenshtein aligned word in $\tilde{e}_1^{\tilde{I}}$ is denoted by $\mathcal{L}_i(e_1^I, \tilde{e}_1^{\tilde{I}})$ for $i = 1, \ldots, I$.

  In order to keep the presentation simple, we only consider substitutions and deletions of words in e_1^I and omit insertions in $\tilde{e}_1^{\tilde{I}}$. The error measure is defined by

$$L[e_1^I, \tilde{e}_1^{\tilde{I}}] = \sum_{i=1}^{I} \left[1 - \delta(e_i, \mathcal{L}_i(e_1^I, \tilde{e}_1^{\tilde{I}}))\right] .$$

  This yields the posterior risk

$$\begin{aligned} R(I, e_1^I | f_1^J) &= \sum_{\tilde{I}, \tilde{e}_1^{\tilde{I}}} Pr(\tilde{I}, \tilde{e}_1^{\tilde{I}} | f_1^J) \cdot \sum_{i=1}^{I} \left[1 - \delta(e_i, \mathcal{L}_i(e_1^I, \tilde{e}_1^{\tilde{I}}))\right] \\ &= \sum_{i=1}^{I} \left(1 - \sum_{\tilde{I}, \tilde{e}_1^{\tilde{I}} : \mathcal{L}_i(e_1^I, \tilde{e}_1^{\tilde{I}}) = e_i} Pr(\tilde{I}, \tilde{e}_1^{\tilde{I}} | f_1^J)\right) . \end{aligned}$$

  In Section 3.2 we will see that this is related to the word posterior probabilities introduced in [15]. The *Bayes decision rule for minimum WER* is obtained by minimizing the risk.
- **PER** (position independent word error rate): A shortcoming of the WER is the fact that it does not allow for movement of words or blocks. The word order of two target sentences can be different even though they are both correct translations. In order to overcome this problem, the position independent word error rate compares the words in the two sentences *without* taking the word order into account. Words that have no matching counterparts are counted as substitution errors, missing words are deletion and additional words are insertion errors. The PER is always lower than or equal to the WER.

  To obtain a closed-form solution of the PER, we consider for each word $e = 1 \ldots E$ in the target vocabulary the number n_e of occurrences in sentence e_1^I, i.e. $n_e = \sum_{i=1}^{I} \delta(e_i, e)$. The number of occurrences of word e in sentence $\tilde{e}_1^{\tilde{I}}$ is denoted by $\tilde{n}_e$, respectively. The error can then be expressed as

$$L[e_1^I, \tilde{e}_1^{\tilde{I}}] = \max(I, \tilde{I}) - \sum_{e} \min(n_e, \tilde{n}_e) .$$

  Thus, the error measure depends only on the two sets of counts $n_1^E := n_1 \ldots n_e \ldots n_E$ and $\tilde{n}_1^E := \tilde{n}_1 \ldots \tilde{n}_e \ldots \tilde{n}_E$. The integration of this error measure into the posterior risk yields [16]

$$R(n_1^E|f_1^J) = \frac{1}{2}\sum_e \sum_{\tilde{n}_e} |n_e - \tilde{n}_e| \cdot Pr_e(\tilde{n}_e|f_1^J) + \frac{1}{2}\sum_{\tilde{I}} |I - \tilde{I}| \cdot Pr(\tilde{I}|f_1^J) \quad (2)$$

where $Pr_e(n_e|f_1^J)$ is the posterior probability of the count n_e of word e.

3 Confidence Measures for Machine Translation

3.1 Introduction

In many applications of machine translation, a method for labeling the generated words as either correct or incorrect is needed. To this purpose, each word in the generated target sentence is assigned a so-called confidence measure. This confidence measure can be used e.g. in interactive systems to report possible errors to the user or to propose translations only when they are likely to be correct.

Confidence measures have been extensively studied for speech recognition, but are not well known in other areas. Only recently have researchers started to investigate confidence measures for machine translation [1, 2, 5, 15].

We apply word confidence measures in MT as follows: For a given translation produced by an MT system, we calculate the confidence of each generated word and compare it to a threshold. All words whose confidence is above this threshold are tagged as correct and all others are tagged as incorrect translations. As stated before, this approach is related to the minimization of the expected number of *word* errors instead of sentence errors.

In this section, we will shortly review some of the word confidence measures that have proven most effective, and show their connection with the Bayes risk as derived in Section 2.1. In addition, we will introduce new confidence measures and give an experimental comparison of the different methods.

3.2 Word Posterior Probabilities

In [15], different variants of word posterior probabilities which are applied as word confidence measures are proposed. We study three types of confidence measures:

Target Position: One of the approaches to word posterior probabilities presented in [15] can be stated as follows: the posterior probability $p_i(e|f_1^J, \hat{I}, \hat{e}_1^{\hat{I}} \backslash \hat{e}_i)$ expresses the probability that the target word e occurs in position i (given the other words in the target sentence $\hat{e}_1^{\hat{I}} \backslash \hat{e}_i$). In Section 2.3, we saw that the (modified) word error measure WER directly leads to this word posterior probability. Thus, we study this word confidence measure here.

The word posterior probability can be calculated over an N-best list of alternative translations that is generated by an SMT system. We determine all sentences that contain the word e in position i (or a target position Levenshtein aligned to i) and sum their probabilities, i.e.

$$p_i(e|f_1^J, \hat{I}, \hat{e}_1^{\hat{I}} \setminus \hat{e}_i) = \frac{p_i(e, f_1^J, \hat{I}, \hat{e}_1^{\hat{I}} \setminus \hat{e}_i)}{\sum_{e'} p_i(e', f_1^J, \hat{I}, \hat{e}_1^{\hat{I}} \setminus \hat{e}_i)} ,$$

where $$p_i(e, f_1^J, \hat{I}, \hat{e}_1^{\hat{I}} \setminus \hat{e}_i) = \sum_{\tilde{I}, \tilde{e}_1^{\tilde{I}} : \mathcal{L}_i(\hat{e}_1^{\hat{I}}, \tilde{e}_1^{\tilde{I}}) = e} p(\tilde{I}, \tilde{e}_1^{\tilde{I}}, f_1^J) \ . \quad (3)$$

This probability depends on the target words $\hat{e}_1^{\hat{I}} \setminus \hat{e}_i$ in the generated string, because it is based on the Levenshtein alignment $\mathcal{L}_i(\hat{e}_1^{\hat{I}}, \tilde{e}_1^{\tilde{I}})$.

Average Target Position: Due to the reordering of words which takes place in translation, the same target word may appear in different positions in the generated translations. The word posterior probabilities based on target positions presented above partially compensate for this effect by determining the Levenshtein alignment over the N-best list. Nevertheless, this cannot handle all reordering within the sentence that may occur. Therefore, we also introduce a new version of word posterior probabilities that determines the *average* over all posterior probabilities based on target positions:

$$p_{\text{avg}}(e|f_1^J) = \frac{p_{\text{avg}}(e, f_1^J)}{\sum_{e'} p_{\text{avg}}(e', f_1^J)} , \quad p_{\text{avg}}(e, f_1^J) = \frac{1}{I^*} \sum_{\tilde{I} \geq i, \ \tilde{e}_1^{\tilde{I}} : \tilde{e}_i = e} p(\tilde{I}, \tilde{e}_1^{\tilde{I}}, f_1^J) \quad (4)$$

where I^* is the maximum of all generated sentence lengths. The idea is to determine the probability of word e occurring in a generated sentence at all - without regarding a fixed target position. Note that here no Levenshtein alignment is performed, because the variation in sentence positions is accounted for through the computation of the arithmetic mean.

Word Count: In addition to the word posterior probabilities described above, we also implemented a new variant that can be derived from Eq. 2 (Sec. 2.3), taking the counts of the words in the generated sentence into account, i.e. we determine the probability of target word e occurring in the sentence n_e times:

$$p_e(n_e|f_1^J) = \frac{p_e(n_e, f_1^J)}{\sum_{n_e'} p_e(n_e', f_1^J)} ,$$

where $$p_e(n_e, f_1^J) = \sum_{\tilde{n}_1^E : \tilde{n}_e = n_e} p(\tilde{n}_1^E, f_1^J) = \sum_{\tilde{I}, \tilde{e}_1^{\tilde{I}} : \tilde{n}_e = n_e} p(\tilde{I}, \tilde{e}_1^{\tilde{I}}, f_1^J) \ . \quad (5)$$

Implementation: As already stated above, the word posterior probabilities can be calculated over N-best lists generated by an SMT system. Thus, the sum over all possible target sentences $\tilde{e}_1^{\tilde{I}}$ is carried out over the alternatives contained in the N-best list. If the list is long enough, this approximation is not harmful. In our experiments, we used 1,000-best lists.[1]

Since the true probability distribution $Pr(I, e_1^I, f_1^J)$ is unknown, we replace it by a *model distribution* $p(I, e_1^I, f_1^J)$. This model distribution is the one from the SMT baseline system (see Section 4.2).

3.3 IBM-1

We implemented another type of confidence measure that determines the translation probability of the target word e averaged over the source sentence words according to Model 1 introduced by IBM in [3]. We determine the probability according to the formula[2]

$$p_{\text{IBM}-1}(e|f_1^J) = \frac{p_{\text{IBM}-1}(e, f_1^J)}{\sum_{e'} p_{\text{IBM}-1}(e', f_1^J)}, \quad p_{\text{IBM}-1}(e, f_1^J) = \frac{1}{J+1} \sum_{j=0}^{J} p(e|f_j) \quad (6)$$

where f_0 is the 'empty' source word [3]. The probabilities $p(e|f_j)$ are word based lexicon probabilities, i.e. they express the probability that e is a translation of the source word f_j.

Investigations on the use of the IBM-1 model for word confidence measures showed promising results [1, 2]. Thus, we apply this method here in order to compare it to the other types of confidence measures.

4 Results

4.1 Task and Corpus

The experiments are performed on a French-English corpus consisting of technical manuals of devices such as printers. This corpus is compiled within the European project TransType2 [13] which aims at developing computer aided MT systems that apply statistical techniques. For the corpus statistics see Table 1.

4.2 Experimental Setting

As basis for our experiments, we created 1,000-best lists of alternative translations using a state-of-the-art SMT system. The system we applied is the so-called alignment template system as described in [12]. The key elements of this approach are pairs of source and target language phrases together with an alignment between the words within the phrases.

---

1 In the area of speech recognition, much shorter lists are used [7]. The justification is that the probabilities of the hypotheses which are lower in the list are so small that they do not have any effect on the calculation of the word posterior probabilities. Nevertheless, we use longer N-best lists here to be on the safe side.

2 Note that this probability is different from the one calculated in [1]; it is normalized over all target words e'. Nevertheless, both measures perform similarly well.

Table 1. Statistics of the training, development and test set

		French	English
Training	Sentences	52 844	
	Words + Punctuation Marks	691 983	633 770
Vocabulary	Size	14 831	13 201
	Singletons	4 257	3 592
Develop	Sentences	994	
	Words	11 731	10 903
Test	Sentences	984	
	Words	11 800	11 177

This system – like virtually all state-of-the-art SMT systems – applies the Bayes decision rule in Eq. 1, i.e. it takes the decision based on *sentence* error.

4.3 Word Error Measures

It is not intuitively clear how to classify words in MT output as correct or incorrect when comparing the translation to one or several references. In the experiments presented here, we applied WER and PER for determining which words in a translation hypothesis are correct. Thus, we can study the effect of the word posterior probabilities derived from the error measures in Section 2.3 on the error measures they are derived from.

These error measures behave significantly different with regard to the percentage of words that are labeled as correct. WER is more pessimistic than PER and labels 58% of the words in the develop and test corpus as correct, whereas PER labels 66% as correct.

4.4 Evaluation Metrics

After computing the confidence measure, each generated word is tagged as either *correct* or *false*, depending on whether its confidence exceeds the tagging threshold that has been optimized on the development set beforehand. The performance of the confidence measure is evaluated using three different metrics:

- **CAR** (**C**onfidence **A**ccuracy **R**ate): The CAR is defined as the number of correctly assigned tags divided by the total number of generated words in the translation. The baseline CAR is given by the number of correct words in the generated translation, divided by the number of generated words. The CAR strongly depends on the tagging threshold. Therefore, the tagging threshold is adjusted on a development corpus *distinct* from the test set.
- **ROC** (**R**eceiver **O**perating **C**haracteristic curve) [4]: The ROC curve plots the *correct rejection rate* versus *correct acceptance rate* for different values of the tagging threshold. The correct rejection rate is the number of incorrectly translated words that have been tagged as wrong, divided by the total number of incorrectly translated words. The correct acceptance rate is the ratio of correctly translated words that have been tagged as correct. These two

rates depend on each other: If one of them is restricted by a lower bound, the other one cannot be restricted. The further the ROC curve lies away from the diagonal, the better the performance of the confidence measure.

- **AROC** (**A**rea under **ROC** curve): This value specifies twice the size of the area between the ROC curve and the diagonal; it ranges from 0 to 1. The higher this value, the better the confidence measure discriminates.

4.5 Experimental Results

We studied the performance of the word confidence measures described in Sections 3.2 and 3.3. The results are given in Tables 2 and 3. For both the word error measure PER as well as WER, the best performance in terms of CAR is achieved by the IBM-1 based word confidence measure.

Table 2. CAR [%] and AROC [%] on the test corpus. The error counting is based on PER (see Sec. 4.3)

	CAR	AROC
Baseline	64.4	-
averaged target position (Eq. 4)	64.8	6.6
target position (Eq. 3)	67.2	28.3
word counts (Eq. 5)	68.1	29.8
IBM-1 (Eq. 6)	71.6	21.5

Table 3. CAR [%] and AROC [%] on the test corpus. The error counting is based on WER (see Sec. 4.3)

	CAR	AROC
Baseline	55.9	-
averaged target position (Eq. 4)	59.3	9.1
target position (Eq. 3)	64.1	26.4
word counts (Eq. 5)	62.0	20.8
IBM-1 (Eq. 6)	66.3	18.7

When comparing the CAR for the word posterior probabilities given in Eqs. 3,4,5 and the IBM-1 based confidence measure, it is surprising that the latter performs significantly better (with regard to both word error measures WER and PER). The IBM-1 model is a very simple translation model which does not produce high quality translations when applied in translation. Thus it was interesting to see that it discriminates so well between good and bad translations. Moreover, this method relies only on one target hypothesis (and the source sentence), whereas the word posterior probabilities take the whole space of possible translations (represented by the N-best list) into account.

In contrast to the good performance in CAR, the IBM-1 based confidence measure yields a much lower AROC value than two of the other measures. Looking at the ROC curve[3] in Figure 2 we find the reason for this: there is a small area on the left part of the curve where the IBM-1 model based confidence measure actually discriminates better than all of the other confidence measures. Nevertheless, the overall performance of the word posterior probabilities based on target positions and of those based on the word count are better than that of the IBM-1 based confidence measure.

We assume that the better performance of the IBM-1 based confidence measure is due to the fact that the involved lexicon probabilities do not depend on the specific N-best lists, but on a translation model that is trained on the whole training corpus. Thus, they are more exact and do not rely on an approximation as introduced by the Levenshtein alignment (cf. Eq. 3). Moreover, the tagging threshold can be estimated very reliably, because it will be the same for the develop and the test corpus. In order to verify this assumption, we analyzed the CAR on the develop corpus. This is used for the optimization of the tagging threshold. Thus, if the other measures indeed discriminate as well as or better than the IBM-1 based confidence measure, their CAR should be higher for the optimized threshold. Table 4 presents these experiments. We see that indeed the word posterior probabilities based on target positions and those based on word counts have a high accuracy rate and show a performance similar to (or better than) that of the IBM-1 based confidence measure.

Table 4. Comparative experiment: CAR [%] on the develop set (threshold optimized). Results for error counting based on PER and WER (see Sec. 4.3)

	word error measure	
	WER	PER
Baseline	60.5	67.1
averaged target position (Eq. 4)	62.1	67.5
word counts (Eq. 5)	67.3	72.1
target position (Eq. 3)	**69.0**	71.3
IBM-1 (Eq. 6)	67.8	**72.5**

5 Outlook

We saw in the derivation from Bayes risk that word posterior probabilities are closely related to *word* error rate minimization. Moreover, we found that they show a state-of-the-art performance as confidence measures on the word level. Therefore, we plan to apply them directly in the machine translation process and study their impact on translation quality. One possible approach would be

[3] We only present the ROC curve for the word error measure PER here. The curve for WER looks very similar.

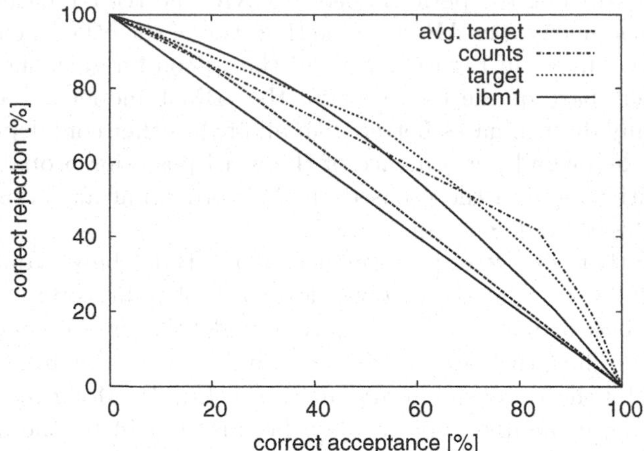

Fig. 2. ROC curve on the test set. The error counting is based on PER (see Sec. 4.3)

to combine them with the sentence error based decision rule that is widely used for rescoring N-best lists.

6 Conclusion

In this work, we have taken first steps towards studying the relationship between Bayes decision rule and confidence measures. We have presented two forms of Bayes decision rule for statistical machine translation: the well-known and widely-applied rule for minimizing sentence error, and one novel approach that aims at minimizing word error. We have investigated the relation between two different word error measures and word confidence measures for SMT that can be directly derived from Bayes risk.

This approach lead to a theoretical motivation for the target position based confidence measures as proposed in [15]. In addition, we derived new confidence measures that reduced the baseline error in discriminating between correct and incorrect words in MT output by a quarter. Other studies report similar reductions for Chinese–English translation [1, 2].

Acknowledgement

This work was partly supported by the RTD project TransType2 (IST–2001–32091) funded by the European Commission.

References

1. Blatz, J., Fitzgerald, E., Foster, G., Gandrabur, S., Goutte, C., Kulesza, A., Sanchis, A., Ueffing, N.: Confidence Estimation for Machine Translation. Final report of the JHU/CLSP Summer Workshop. (2003) `http://www.clsp.jhu.edu/ws2003/groups/estimate/`

2. Blatz, J., Fitzgerald, E., Foster, G., Gandrabur, S., Goutte, C., Kulesza, A., Sanchis, A., Ueffing, N.: Confidence Estimation for Machine Translation. Proc. 20th Int. Conf. on Computational Linguistics (COLING). (2004)
3. Brown, P. F., Della Pietra, S. A., Della Pietra, V. J., Mercer, R. L.: The Mathematics of Statistical Machine Translation: Parameter Estimation. Computational Linguistics, Vol. 19 (2). (1993) 263–311.
4. Duda, R. O., Hart, P. E., Stork, D. G. Pattern classification. John Wiley & Sons, New York (2001)
5. Gandrabur, S., Foster, G.: Confidence Estimation for Text Prediction. Proc. Conf. on Natural Language Learning (CoNLL). Edmonton, Canada (2003) 95–102
6. Goel, V.,Byrne, W.: Minimum Bayes-Risk Automatic Speech Recognition. In: W. Chou and B. H. Juang (eds.): Pattern Recognition in Speech and Language Processing. CRC Press (2003)
7. Komatani, K., Kawahara, T.: Flexible Mixed-Initiative Dialogue Management using Concept-Level Confidence Measures of Speech Recognizer Output. Proc. 18th Int. Conf. on Computational Linguistics (COLING). Saarbrücken, Germany (2000) 467–473
8. Kumar, S., Byrne, W.: Minimum Bayes-Risk Decoding for Statistical Machine Translation. Human Language Technology conference/North American chapter of the Association for Computational Linguistics annual meeting (HLT/NAACL). Boston, MA (2004)
9. Levenshtein, V. I.: Binary Codes Capable of Correcting Deletions, Insertions and Reversals. Soviet Physics Doklady, Vol. 10 (8) (1966) 707-710
10. Ney, H., Popović, M., Sündermann, D.: Error Measures and Bayes Decision Rules Revisited with Applications to POS Tagging. Proc. Conf. on Empirical Methods for Natural Language Processing (EMNLP). Barcelona, Spain (2004)
11. Och, F. J.: Minimum Error Rate Training for Statistical Machine Translation. Proc. 41th Annual Meeting of the Assoc. for Computational Linguistics (ACL). Sapporo, Japan (2003)
12. Och, F. J., Ney, H.: The alignment template approach to statistical machine translation. *To appear in* Computational Linguistics (2004)
13. TransType2 – Computer Assisted Translation. RTD project TransType2 (IST–2001–32091) funded by the European Commission. `http://tt2.sema.es/`
14. Vogel, S., Zhang, Y., Huang, F., Tribble, A., Venugopal, A., Zhao, B., Waibel, A.: The CMU Statistical Machine Translation System. Proc. MT Summit IX. New Orleans, LA (2003)
15. Ueffing, N., Macherey, K., Ney, H.: Confidence Measures for Statistical Machine Translation. Proc. MT Summit IX. New Orleans, LA (2003) 394–401
16. Ueffing, N., Ney, H.: Confidence Measures for SMT and Bayes Decision Rule. Unpublished results. RWTH Aachen University, Computer Science Department (2004)

Character Identification in Children Stories

Nuno Mamede and Pedro Chaleira

L²F - Spoken Language Systems Lab
INESC-ID Lisboa / IST, R. Alves Redol 9, 1000-029 Lisboa, Portugal
{Nuno.Mamede, Pedro.Chaleira}@l2f.inesc-id.pt
http://www.l2f.inesc.pt

Abstract. The automatic identification of direct and indirect discourses and the association of each "direct" utterance with its author are research topics that begin to be explored in Natural Language Processing.

We developed the DID system that when applied to children stories starts by classifying the utterances that belong to the narrator (indirect discourse) and those belonging to the characters taking part in the story (direct discourse). Afterword, DID tries to associate each direct discourse utterance with the character(s) in the story.

This automation can be advantageous, namely when it is necessary to tag the stories that should be handled by an automatic story teller.

1 Introduction

Children stories have some intrinsic magic that captures the attention of any reader. This magic is transmitted by intervening characters and by the narrator that contributes to the comprehension and emphasis of the fables. Inherent to this theme emerges the direct and indirect discourse apprehension by the human reader that corresponds to characters and narrator, respectively.

The automatic identification of speakers in children's stories is a necessary step for the comprehension of the story, namely when it is necessary to tag the stories that should be handled by an automatic story teller. After knowing which portions of the story should be read by which speaker, it is possible to choose the appropriate voices for synthesizing the story characters [5], to choose the appropriate character representation and animate it in a story teller [1].

This work deals with the identification of the character (the narrator may be considered another character, for this purpose) that is responsible for each story utterance. The result is expressed in a final document with tags associated with each character.

For example, consider the following excerpt of a story[1]:

```
They arrived at the lake. The boy waved to them, smiling.
Come, it is really good!
```

[1] Although some examples are in english, our system only handles portuguese texts.

J. L. Vicedo et al. (Eds.): EsTAL 2004, LNAI 3230, pp. 82–90, 2004.

Our system identifies the text associated with each character of the story:

```
<person name=narrator>
   They arrived at the lake. The boy waved to them, smiling.
</person>
<person name =boy>
   Come, it is really good
</person>
```

Our approach consists of two basic stages: (i) identification of the utterances that belong to the narrator and the utterances that are said by a character, and (ii) association of each character utterance wit a specific story character. The first stage is described in Section 2 and the second stage is described in Section 3.

2 Direct/Indirect Discourse Identification

2.1 Pre-processing

In order to apply DID it is necessary to resort to Smorph [6], a morphological analyzer, and PasMo [4], which divides the text into paragraphs and transforms word tags. Thus, the story texts are first submitted to Smorph and then PasMo, which produces XML documents.

2.2 Solution

We started by collecting a set of children stories, all of them written by Portuguese authors. These dorpora was divided into a training set (the first eleven stories of Table 1), and a test set (the last four stories of the same table). After hand inspecting the training set, we extracted twelve heuristics:

H1 A dash at the beginning of a paragraph identifies a direct discourse;
H2 A paragraph mark after a colon suggests the paragraph corresponds to a character (direct discourse);
H3 If a paragraph has a question mark at the end then it, probably, belongs to a character;
H4 The exclamation mark at the end of a paragraph identifies a direct discourse, with some probability. This heuristic follows the reasoning of H3;
H5 The personal or possessive pronouns in the 1st or 2nd person indicate that we are in the presence of a direct discourse;
H6 Verbs in past tense, present, future or imperfect tense are characteristics of direct discourse because they are verbs directed to characters;
H7 The usage of inverted commas can indicate the speech of a character, but generally it is the narrator imitating the character and not the character speaking about himself/herself;
H8 The usage of tense adverbs (tomorrow, today, yesterday, etc.) can identify a direct discourse;
H9 If next to a direct discourse there is a short text between dashes, then the next text excerpt probably belongs to a character;

H10 The imperfect tense verbs that can be expressed in the same way for a character and for a narrator just lead to a direct discourse when there is a personal pronoun corresponding to a character;
H11 In the phrase, if there is a text excerpt between two dashes where a declarative verb exists (declare, say, ask, etc.) in the third person, then we can say that a character expresses the text excerpt appearing before the left dash;
H12 The use of interjections identifies a direct discourse because only characters use them.

The input of DID is PasMo's output. DID analyses the text paragraph by paragraph. Heuristics are then applied to each one. After processing the whole text, DID returns an XML document, in VHML format [2], that contains all the identified discourses accordingly to the tags supported by this language.

DID followed the Theory of Confirmation to get the degree of trust with which identified direct discourse: the user can define the trust to associate with each heuristic and also the value of its threshold, which defines the limit between success and failure. Thus, we can say that DID works like an expert system.

However, DID first results made us improve these heuristics, namely:

- H3 and H4 have different trust values deppending on the position of the mark on the paragraph. If there is a question or exclamation mark in the middle of a paragraph, the trust value is lower. When the mark is at the end of the paragraph the trust value is higher. So, these heuristics have two trust values.
- H5 and H6 have been combined, because DID's input has many ambiguities.
- H7 revealed to be a neutral heuristic so it was removed.

Final results can be seen in Table 1

Table 1. Performance of direct/indirect discourse separation

Story	Correct	Incorrect	Success rate
1 - O Gato das Botas	28	0	100%
2 - O Macaco do Rabo Cortado	48	0	100%
3 - O Capuchinho Vermelho	41	1	97%
4 - Os Trs Porquinhos	28	1	96%
5 - Lisboa 2050	147	6	96%
6 - A Branca de Neve	43	2	95%
7 - Ideias do Canrio	41	2	95%
8 - Anita no Hospital	102	11	90%
9 - Os Cinco e as Passagens Secretas	131	19	87%
10 - A Bela e o Monstro	31	6	83%
11 - O Bando dos Quatro: A Torre Maldita (Chap. 1)	70	40	63%
12 - Pinquio	43	1	97%
13 - O estratagema do amor	147	11	93%
14 - O rei	81	9	90%
15 - Aduzinda e Zulmiro a magia da adolescncia	95	12	88%

2.3 Evaluation

In order to check the capabilities of DID system, we developed a new system: DID-Verify, which is responsible for the comparison between DID's output and the idealized result. This comparison verifies whether discourses were well identified by DID and also shows the number of times that each heuristic was applied.

After analyzing the results obtained with the training set, we can easily infer that the best results are obtained for the children stories (e.g. O Gato das Botas, O Macaco do Rabo Cortado), what can be explained by the fact that characters are mainly identified by Heuristic 1. The worst result is obtained with the story O Bando dos Quatro, because here the narrator is also a character of the story, leading to an ambiguous agent: sometimes speaking like a narrator and others like a character. DID is not prepared to treat this ambiguity. Two children stories achieved 100% successful results, confirming the good performance of DID as a tagger for a Story Teller System under development by other researchers of our research institute. The result obtained for the story Lisboa 2050 must be heightened because this story has a large number of discourses and DID performs a 96% successful result! Summarizing the results, DID obtains an average of 89% of success showing that the results are similar to the projected objectives.

Analyzing the test set, all the results surpass 80% of success with an average of 92%. That is very reasonable for a set of texts that was not used to train the DID system. This result also shows that DID has a fine performance in different types of stories.

Examining the results obtained by DID-Verify with the test set, we obtained the 2, which shows the performance of each heuristic. Here we conclude that Heuristic 1 is the most applied, identifying a larger number of discourses correctly. Heuristic 5 and Heuristic 6 also lead to good results. Heuristic 2 never fails but was only applied six times. Heuristic 4 is the one that leads to more mistakes, because the exclamation mark is many times used in narration discourses. Generally, all the heuristics have a high success rate.

Table 2. Analysis of the correctness of each heuristic

Heuristic	N Successes	N Failures	Success rate
H1	188	2	98.9%
H2	6	0	100%
H3	59	1	98.3%
H4	37	3	92.5%
H5	81	2	97.6%
H6	70	1	98.6%
H8	7	1	87.5%
H12	17	1	94.4%

3 Character Identification

3.1 VHML Changes

Sometimes, it is not clear, even for humans, which is the character that must be associated with a given utterance. To allow the representation of this king of ambiguity, and to avoid the repetition of utterances whenever an utterance is simultaneously said by multiple characters, we made small changes to the VHML language. Namely, we introduced the concept of speaker:

```
<!ELEMENT vhml (paragraph|p|person|references|speaker|mark)+>
<!ELEMENT speaker ((personname|colective)+,person)>
<!ELEMENT colective (personname,personname+)>
<!ELEMENT personname (#PCDATA)>
```

The following example represents an ambiguity: Text..." must be associated either with a group of characters (`Character1`, `Character2` and `Character3`) or with `Character4`:

```
<speaker>
   <personname>Group1</personname>
   <colective>
      <personname>Character1</personname>
      <personname>Character2</personname>
      <personname>Character3</personname>
   </colective>
   <personname>Character4</personname>
   <person>
      <p>Text...</p>
   <person>
</speaker>
```

3.2 Pre-processing

The text is processed by a shallow parsing module – SuSAna – that performs efficient analysis over unrestricted text. The module recognizes, not only the boundaries, but also the internal structure and syntactic category of syntactic constituents [3]. It is used to identify the nucleus of the noun phrases.

A *single noun phrase* (SNP), is a noun phrase containing either a proper noun or an article followed by a noun phrase.

We *only* considered as declarative the following verbs: *acrescentar*, *acudir*, *adicionar*, *afirmar*, *anunciar*, *aparecer*, *argumentar*, *atalhar*, *atirar*, *avisar*, *chamar*, *comunicar*, *confessar*, *continuar*, *concluir*, *declarar*, *dizer*, *exclamar*, *explicar*, *expor*, *fazer*, *gritar*, *interromper*, *manifestar*, *meter*, *noticiar*, *observar*, *ordenar*, *pensar*, *perguntar*, *publicitar*, *redarguir*, *repetir*, *replicar*, *resmungar*, *responder*, *retorquir*, *rosnar*, *ser*.

The system knows the characters that are referred in each story, which is expressed in a XML file with the following format:

```
<characters>
   <newcharacter>
      <name>Character name</name>
      <gender>male, female or neutral<gender>
      <cardinality>singular or plural</cardinality>
      <alterntivename>
         <name>Alternative name 1</name>
         <name>Alternative name 2</name>
```

```
        <name>Alternative name 3</name>
      </alternativename>
    </newcharater>
     .
     .
     .
</characters>
```

3.3 Solution

From the hand inspection of the training set (the first eleven stories of Table 1), we extracted five rules. They are not called heuristics to avoid confusions with direct/indirect heuristics, already presented.

Rule 1 If the first sentence of the indirect discourse (imediately following a direct discourse) contains a declarative verb (3rd person) that appears before the first SNP, and the SNP is a valid character name, then that name is the responsible for the previous direct discourse utterance.

Example, from the corpora:
– *Mas no vo conseguir - disse a Ana, inesperadamente.*

Rule 2 If in a direct discourse, any sentence belonging to a previous (search is performed from the direct discourse to the beginning of the document) indirect discourse, the word that precedes a SN containing a character name is a declarative verb on the 3rd person, then the noun of that SN refers the character responsible for the direct discourse.

Example:
E mais uma vez apareceu o lobo mau:
– *TOC! TOC! TOC!*

Rule 3 If in a direct discourse, any sentence belonging to a previous (search is performed from the direct discourse to the beginning of the document) direct discourse starts with a SN containing a character name, then the noun of that SN refers the character responsible for the present direct discourse.

Example:
E eis que a menina bate porta...
– *Av, sou eu. Tenho aqui uma pequena prenda para si...*

Rule 4 If the direct discourse itself contains (search is performed from the beginning to the end of the direct discourse) either a SN containing a character name preceded by a verb on present, 1st or 3rd person, or a SN containing a character name imediately preceded by the verb "chamar" in the present, reflexive 1st person, then the noun of that SN refers the character responsible for the present direct discourse.

Example:
Uma rapariga loira e bonita apresentou-se:
– *Sou a Sofia e vou tratar da sua viagem. Que filme que quer ver?*

Rule 5 If in a direct discourse, any sentence belonging to a previous (search is performed from the direct discourse to the beginning of the document) direct discourse has a SN containing a character name, not preceded by a declarative verb, or imediately followed by a punctuation mark, then the noun of that SN refers the character responsible for the present direct discourse.

Example:
- *At que enfim que te encontro, Anita! Procurei-te por todo o lado. Tenho uma carta para ti.*
- *Uma carta? Para mim?*

3.4 Evaluation

The evaluation process compares the noun included in the selected NP with the names described in the file that contains the enumeration of all story characters. If the noun is either included (a string operation) in the correct name of the character, or is included in any of the alternate names, we consider it a correct identification. Sometimes, it may lead to a "soft" evaluation, since the name *porquinho* is considered a correct identification of any of the following characters: *porquinho mais velho*, *porquinho do meio*, and *porquinho mais novo*.

The first step was the independent evaluation of each rule, see Table 3. Then we trained a decision tree (CART) to identify the rule that is able to predict the character responsible for each direct utterance. To train the decision tree, we used as features:

1 parameter containing the rule with the correct result;

5 parameters containing the information about the use of each rule: 0 means the rule did not trigger, 1 that the rule did trigger;

10 parameters containing the agreement between rules: 0 means that at least one of the rules did not trigger, 1 the rules agree, and 2 the rules did not agree.

The performance of the decision tree after training was as is depicted in Table 4: 84.8% of correct answers on the training corpus (145 correct answers out of 171), and 65.7% of correct answers on the test corpus (23 correct out of 35). Table 5 contains the confusion matrix after the training.

3.5 Discussion

First of all, the performance achieved is very good, considering that these are the first results, and there is place for improving every stage of the chain processing. One can also conclude that both corpus are small, and the test corpus is not ???????, since it does not contain elements of class 4 (R4 should be applied) and class 5 (R5 should be applied).

The rules, when they decide to trigger, produce good results, but either they should be active more often (68% of direct discourses are not associated with any character), or other rules are missing. R4 and R5 should be revised, since they are triggered only 1%.

After a more detailed evaluation of the errors in both corpora we concluded that: (i) only twice a part-of-speech tagger is the culprit; (ii) the incorrect identification of

Table 3. Results of DID measured by DID-Verify

Story	DD #	Rule 1 App %	Rule 1 Succ %	Rule 2 App %	Rule 2 Succ %	Rule 3 App %	Rule 3 Succ %	Rule 4 App %	Rule 4 Succ %	Rule 5 App %	Rule 5 Succ %
1	7	42.8	100	42.8	100	14.3	100	0	—	0	—
2	28	14.3	100	14.3	0	32.1	88.9	0	—	0	—
3	20	5	—	0	—	30	66.7	0	—	0	—
4	15	6.6	100	13.3	100	20	66.7	30	100	0	—
5	91	4.4	100	6.6	50	18.7	52.9	2.2	100	3.3	100
6	13	7.7	100	15.4	50	30.8	75	0	—	0	—
7	36	0	—	0	—	2.8	100	0	—	0.0	100
8	66	7.5	100	9.1	66.7	22.7	40	1.5	100	1.5	100
9	76	46	100	48.7	75.7	3.9	66.7	0	—	1.3	100
10	9	0	—	0	—	22.2	50	0	—	0	—
11	62	6.5	100	8.1	40	8.1	40	0	—	4.8	0.0
Sum	**423**	**13.7**	**98.3**	**15.6**	**65.2**	**15.6**	**59.1**	**1.4**	**100**	**2.1**	**66.7**
12	15	13.3	100	20	33.3	0	—	0	—	0	—
13	104	2.9	100	4.8	80	1	100	0	—	0	—
14	38	5.3	100	5.3	50	7.9	—	0	—	0	—
15	59	6.8	50	6.8	50	23.7	57.1	0	—	0	—
Sum	**216**	**5.1**	**81.8**	**6.5**	**57.1**	**8.3**	**50**	**0**	**—**	**0**	**—**

Table 4. Performance of the Decision Tree on Identifying the Character of each Direct Utterance

	Recall	**Precision**
Training Corpus	34.3%	84.8%
Test Corpus	10.6%	65.7%

Table 5. Confusion Matrix of the Decision Tree on Identifying the Character of each Direct Utterance

Training corpus	**–**	**R1**	**R2**	**R3**	**R4**	**R5**	**Sum**	**Succ**
–	0	1	11	11	0	2	25	0%
R1	0	57	0	0	0	0	57	100%
R2	0	0	42	0	0	0	42	100%
R3	0	0	1	36	0	0	37	97.3%
R4	0	0	0	0	5	0	5	100%
R5	0	0	0	0	0	5	5	100%
Sum	0	58	54	47	5	7	171	83.3%

Test corpus	**–**	**R1**	**R2**	**R3**	**R4**	**R5**	**Sum**	**Succ**
–	0	0	5	6	0	0	11	0%
R1	0	9	0	0	0	0	9	100%
R2	0	0	7	0	0	0	7	100%
R3	0	1	0	7	0	0	8	87.5%
R4	0	0	0	0	0	0	0	100%
R5	0	0	0	0	0	0	0	100%
Sum	0	10	12	13	0	0	35	68.6%

direct/indirect discourse is responsible for 13 mistakes (rule R1-1, R2-2, R3-7 and R5-3); (iii) The shallow parser did not identify a NP and, consequently, R3 failed to identify the correct character 4 times; and the decision tree has made an incorrect choice 24 times.

4 Future Work

We have made good progress on children story interpretation/marking, but, since it is a complex and heterogeneous problem, a lot of work remains to be done, namely:

- to increment the size and variety of both corpora;
- to define associations of words and expressions to help identify some type of story characters;
- to use a morphossyntatic disambiguator to handle the ambiguous word classifications;
- to improve the automatic text segmentation in sentences ;
- to define a set of verbs that cannot be expressed by a narrator;
- to identify relations (ownership and creation) between objects and characters;
- to identify the family relations between characters;
- to introduce in the processing chain a new module to identify the characters taking part in a story, which is, for the moment, given by the user;
- to use anaphora to help identifying characters referred by pronouns;
- to implement and evaluate a new rule: whenever two consecutive direct utterances are associated with different characters, and until the next indirect utterance, consider the identified characters alternate in the enclosed direct discourses;
- to include propositional and adjective attachments in the noun phrases, to enable a better identification of the story characters;
- to identify the subject and complements of each sentence, which will enable a better redesign/performance of rules R2 and R3;
- to develop new modules to identify the gesture and emotions as well as the environment where each scene takes place.

Acknowledgments

The Direct/Indirect Discourse Identification task must be credited to Diogo Barbosa and Ricardo Costa, while their stay at L^2F in 2002.

References

1. A. Silva, M. Vala, A. Paiva, Papous: The Virtual Storyteller, Intelligent Virtual Agents, 3rd International Workshop, Madrid, Spain, 171181, Springer-Verlag LNAI 2190 (2001).
2. C. Gustavson, L. Strindlund, W. Emma, S. Beard, H. Quoc, A. Marriot, J. Stallo, VHML Working Draft v0.2 (2001).
3. F. Batista, Nuno Mamede, SuSAna: Mdulo Multifuncional da Anlise Sintctica de Superfcie, in Proc. Multilingual Information Access and Natural Language Processing Workshop (IBERAMIA 2002), Sevilla, Spain, 29-37 (2002).
4. J. Paulo, M. Correia, N. Mamede, C. Hagge: Using Morphological, Syntactical and Statistical Information for Automatic Term Acquisition", in Proceedings of the PorTAL - Portugal for Natural Language Processing, Faro, Portugal, Springer-Verlag, 219-227 (2002).
5. J. Zhang, A. Black, R. Sproat, Identifying Speakers in Children's Stories for Speech Synthesis, Eurospeech 2003, Geneva, Switzerland (2003).
6. S. Ait-Mokhtar: L'analyse prsyntaxique en une tape. Thse de Doctorat, Universit Blaise Pascal, GRIL, Clermont-Derrand (1998).

Comparison and Evaluation of Two Approaches of a Multilayered QA System Applied to Temporality*

E. Saquete, R. Muñoz, P. Martínez-Barco, and J.L. Vicedo

Grupo de investigación del Procesamiento del Lenguaje y Sistemas de Información
Departamento de Lenguajes y Sistemas Informáticos. Universidad de Alicante, Alicante, Spain
{stela,rafael,patricio,vicedo}@dlsi.ua.es

Abstract. This paper compares two approaches to a multilayered Question Answering (QA) architecture suitable for enhancing current QA capabilities with the possibility of processing complex questions. That is, questions whose answer needs to be gathered from pieces of factual information that is scattered in different documents. Specifically, we have designed a layer oriented to process the different types of temporal questions. In the first approach, complex temporal questions are decomposed into simple questions, according to the temporal relations expressed in the original question. In the same way, the answers of each resulting simple question are recomposed, fulfilling the temporal restrictions of the original complex question. In the second approach, temporal information is added to the sub-questions before being processed. Evaluation results show that the second approach outperforms the first one in a 30%.

1 Introduction

Question Answering can be defined as the answering by computers to precise or arbitrary questions formulated by users. There are different types of questions that achieves to answer. Current QA systems are mainly focused on the treatment of factual questions, but these systems are not so efficient if the questions are complex, that is, questions composed by more than one event interrelated by temporal signals, like after, before, etc... The task of answering this type of questions is called Temporal Question Answering.

Temporal QA is not a trivial task due to the complexity temporal questions can achieve, and it is not only useful when dealing with complex questions, but also when the questions contain any kind of temporal expression that needs to be solved before being able to answer the question. For example, for the question "Who was president of Spain two years ago?", it will be necessary to solve the temporal expression "two years ago" first and then use that information in order

* This paper has been supported by the Spanish government, projects FIT-150500-2002-244, FIT-150500-2002-416, TIC-2003-07158-C04-01 and TIC2000-0664-C02-02.

J. L. Vicedo et al. (Eds.): EsTAL 2004, LNAI 3230, pp. 91–102, 2004.

to answer the question by a current QA system. It seems necessary to emphasize the system described in Breck et al.[1] as the only one that also uses implicit temporal expression recognition for QA purposes by applying the temporal tagger developed by Mani and Wilson [2]. However, questions referring to the temporal properties of the entities being questioned and the relative ordering of events mentioned in the questions are beyond the scope of current QA systems:

- "Who was spokesman of the Soviet Embassy in Baghdad *during* the invasion of Kuwait?"

This work presents a QA system that achieves to answer complex temporal questions. This proposal tries to imitate human's behavior when solving this type of questions. For example, a human that wants to answer the question: *"Who was spokesman of the Soviet Embassy in Baghdad during the invasion of Kuwait?"* would follow this process:

1. First, he would decompose the example complex question into two simple ones: *"Who was spokesman of the Soviet Embassy in Baghdad?"* and *"When did the invasion of Kuwait occur?"*.
2. He would look for all the possible answers to the first simple question: *"Who was spokesman of the Soviet Embassy in Baghdad?"*.
3. After that, he would look for the answer to the second simple question: *"When did the invasion of Kuwait occur?"*
4. Finally, he would give as final answer one of the answers for the first question (if there is any), whose associated date is included within the period of dates corresponding to the answer of the second question. That is, he would obtain the final answer by recomposing the respective answers to each simple question through the temporal signal in the original question (*during*).

Or this process:

1. First, he would decompose the example complex question into two simple ones: *"Who was spokesman of the Soviet Embassy in Baghdad?"* and *"When did the invasion of Kuwait occur?"*.
2. He would look for the answer to the second simple question which is asking for a date: *"When did the invasion of Kuwait occur?"*.
3. After that, first question could be rewritten as: *"Who was spokesman of the Soviet Embassy in Baghdad in August 1990?"*
4. Finally, he would give as final answer one of the answers for this question (if there is any), but in this case, the searching of the answer is more exactly because only the answers of the first question included in that period of time are obtained. (*in August 1990* is part of the first question now).

Therefore, the treatment of complex question is basically based on the decomposition of these questions into simple ones that can be resolved using conventional QA systems. Answers to simple questions are used to build the answer to the original question. Our proposal to solve the problem is based on a multilayered architecture that allows the processing of the questions with temporal features. In addition, two proposals for the resolution of this problem have been developed with the objective of determining which one is better.

The paper has been structured in the following way: first of all, section 2 presents our proposal of a taxonomy for temporal questions. Section 3 describes the two approaches to our general architecture of a temporal QA system. Finally, in section 4, the evaluation of the system and some conclusions are shown.

2 Proposal of a Temporal Questions Taxonomy

Before explaining how to answer temporal questions, it is necessary to classify them, since the way to solve them will be different in each case. Our classification distinguishes first between simple questions and complex questions and was deeply presented in Saquete et al. [6]. We will consider as simple those questions that can be solved directly by a current General Purpose QA system, since they are formed by a single event. On the other hand, we will consider as complex those questions that are formed by more than one event related by a temporal signal which establishes an order relation between these events.

Simple Temporal Questions:

Type 1: Single event temporal questions without temporal expression (TE). They are resolved by a QA System directly without pre or postprocessing of the question. Example: *"When did Jordan close the port of Aqaba to Kuwait?"*

*Type 2: Single event temporal questions with temporal expression.*The temporal expressions needs to be recognized, resolved and annotated. Example: *"Who won the 1988 New Hampshire republican primary?"*

Complex Temporal Questions:

Type 3: Multiple events temporal questions with temporal expression. Questions that contain two or more events, related by a temporal signal, and a temporal expression. Example: *"What did George Bush do after the U.N. Security Council ordered a global embargo on trade with Iraq in August 90?"*

Type 4: Multiple events temporal questions without temporal expression. Questions that consist of two or more events, related by a temporal signal. Example: *"What happened to world oil prices after the Iraqi annexation of Kuwait?"*.

3 Multilayered Question-Answering System Architecture

Current QA system architecture does not allow to process complex questions. That is, questions whose answer needs to be gathered from pieces of factual information that is scattered in a document or through different documents. In order to be able to process these complex questions, we propose a multilayered architecture. This architecture [5] increases the functionality of the current QA systems, allowing us to solve any type of temporal questions. Complex questions have in common the necessity of an additional processing of the question in order to be solved. Our proposal to deal with these types of more complex questions is to superpose an additional processing layer, one by each type, to a current

General Purpose QA system, as it is shown in Figure 1. This layer will perform the following steps:

- the decomposition of the question into simple events to generate simple questions or sub-questions (with or without adding extra temporal information to the question) and the ordering of the sub-questions,
- sending simple questions to a current General Purpose QA system,
- receiving the answers to the simple questions from the current General Purpose QA system,
- the filtering and comparison between sub-answers to build the final complex answer.

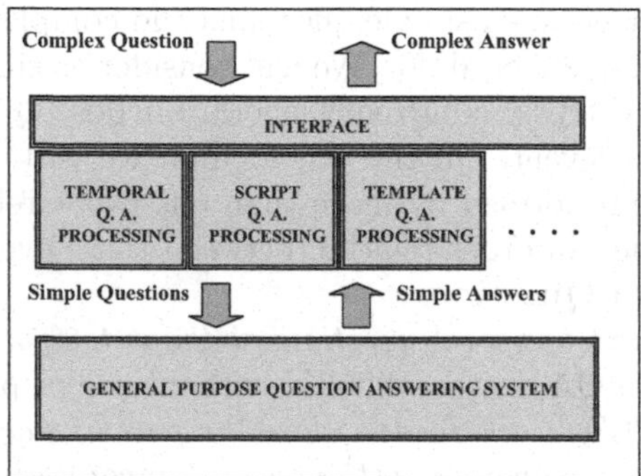

Fig. 1. Multilayered Architecture of a QA

Next, we present two approaches of how a layer is able to process temporal questions according to the taxonomy shown in section 2. The second approach is based on the first one, but tries to resolve some problems observed in the evaluation.

3.1 First Approach of Architecture of a Temporal Question Answering System

The main components of the first approach of a Temporal Question Answering System are (See Figure 2): Question Decomposition Unit, General purpose QA system and Answer Recomposition Unit.

These components work all together in order to obtain a final answer. The Question Decomposition Unit and the Answer Recomposition Unit are the units that conform the Temporal QA layer which process the temporal questions, before and after using a General Purpose QA system.

- *The Question Decomposition Unit* is a preprocessing unit which performs three main tasks. First of all, the recognition and resolution of temporal expressions in the question is done. Secondly, regarding the taxonomy of the questions shown in section 2, there are different types of questions and every

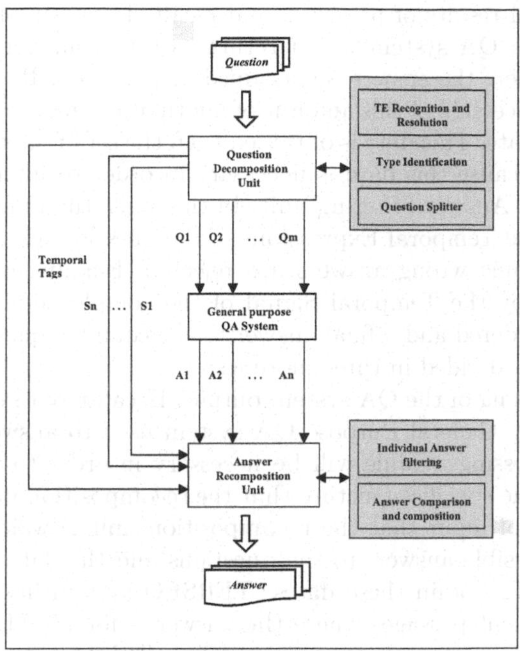

Fig. 2. Temporal Question Answering System (1st approach)

type has to be treated in a different way from the others. For this reason, type identification needs to be done. After that, complex questions, that are Type 3 and 4, are split into simple ones. These simple questions are the input of a General Purpose Question-Answering system. For example, the question *"Where did Bill Clinton study before going to Oxford University?"*, is divided into two sub-questions that are related through the temporal signal *before*:

- Q1: Where did Bill Clinton study?
- Q2: When did *Bill Clinton* go to Oxford University?

– *A General Purpose Question Answering System.* Simple factual questions generated are processed by a General Purpose QA system. Any QA system could be used here. We have used a general QA system that is available on the Internet: the IO Question Answering system[1]. The only condition is to know the kind of output returned by the system in order to adapt the layer interface. For the example above, a current QA system returns the following answers:
  - Q1 Answers: Georgetown University (1964-68) // Oxford University (1968-70) // Yale Law School (1970-73)
  - Q2 Answer: 1968

– *The Answer Recomposition Unit* is the last stage in the process. The complex questions were divided by the Decomposition Unit into simple ones

[1] http://www.ionaut.com:8400/

with successful results of precision and recall. These simple questions were processed by a QA system which returns a set of answer and passages of documents where the answer is contained. The Answer Recomposition Unit needs a preprocessing of this amount of information in order to relate the answers with a date. This date is obtained from the set of passages related with the answer because this date is necessary in order to filter the answers by the Individual Answer Filtering unit. In this unit, the temporal constraints imposed by the Temporal Expressions of the question are applied to all the answer and some wrong answers are rejected. Finally, using the ordering key imposed by the Temporal Signal of the complex questions, the single answers are ordered and a final answer to the complex question is obtained. This process is divided in three modules:

- Preprocessing of the QA system output: Because our system is independent of the General Purpose QA system used to answer the questions, a preprocessing module will be necessary in order to format these answers to the specific structure that the recomposition unit is waiting for. The kind of input that the recomposition unit is waiting is a file with all the possible answers to the questions and the dates related to these answers. To obtain these dates, TERSEO system has been applied to the document passages where the answer is found. TERSEO system is used to recognize, annotate and resolve all the temporal expressions in the passages so that it is possible to obtain a date of occurrence of the event the system is asking about. The system looks for the event in the document and obtains the date related to this event. Once the answer and the date of the answer are obtained, the recomposition can be done.
- Individual Answer Filtering: All the possible answers given by the General Purpose QA system are the input of the Individual Answer Filtering. For the sub-questions with a temporal expression, it selects only those answers that satisfy the temporal constraints obtained by the TE Recognition and Resolution Unit as temporal tags. Only those answers that fulfill the constraints go to the Answer Comparison and Composition module, and
- Answer Comparison and Composition: Finally, once the answers are filtered, using the signals and the ordering key implied by these signals, the results for every sub-question are compared by the Comparison and Composition Unit.

This unit has as input the set of individual answers and the temporal tags and signals related with the question, information that is needed to obtain the final answer. Temporal signals denote the relationship between the dates of the events that they relate. Assuming that *F1* is the date related to the first event in the question and *F2* is the date related to the second event, the signal will establish a certain order between these events, which is called *ordering key*. An example of some ordering keys are shown in Table 1.

Table 1. Example of signals and ordering keys

SIGNAL	ORDERING KEY
After	F1 > F2
Before	F1 < F2
During	F2(begin) <= F1 <= F2(end)
From F2 to F3	F2 <= F1 <= F3
On / in	F1 = F2
While	F2(begin) <= F1 <= F2(end)
At the time of	F1 = F2
Since	F1 > F2

3.2 Evaluation of the System with the First Approach

For this evaluation, we chose the TERQAS question corpus [4], [3] that consists of 124 complex temporal questions. This set of questions was split by the Question Decomposition Unit into simple questions. The answers to these simple questions were obtained by a General Purpose QA system[2] and they were recomposed by the Recomposition unit. The results for every approach have been compared with the results obtained by a General Purpose QA system and can be classified in three main groups:

Table 2. Evaluation of the system with the first approach

Questions	TOTAL	BETTER RESULTS	EQUAL RESULTS	WORST RESULTS
Type 1	47	-	47 (100%)	-
Type 2	59	36 (61%)	23 (39%)	-
Type 3	3	-	3 (100%)	-
Type 4	15	6 (40%)	8 (54%)	1 (6%)
All Questions	124	42 (34%)	81 (65%)	1 (0.8%)

- The results are the same in both systems. That is because:
  - The QA system does not give back any answer for that question and therefore the TQA system does not give back anything either. There are 47 questions of that kind and the type of questions more affected are Type 1 and Type 2.
  - The TQA system returns the same answers as the QA system does. This it is exclusively the case of Type 1 questions since our system does not

[2] http://www.ionaut.com:8400/

make any type of processing on those questions. There are 34 questions of this kind in our set.
- Our system obtains better results than the QA system. There are four different situations:
  - The TQA system does not give back any answer because, although QA system gives back a set of answers, none of them fulfill the temporal constraints imposed by the question and therefore none of these answer is the correct answer. This would be considered a success on our system. There are 12 questions of this kind, and 11 of them are questions of Type 2.
  - The QA system does not give back any answer and nevertheless, when splitting the question in simple ones and later reconstructing the answer, the TQA system is able to give an answer to the complex question. There is only 1 question of this kind.
  - The QA system returns wrong answers, nevertheless, when filtering the Temporal Expressions and splitting the question, more temporal information is obtained and the TQA system is able to answer properly to the complex question. There is only 1 question of this type.
  - The QA system returns a set of answers, but without considering the temporal information and the TQA is able to filter those answers and giving back just those that fulfill the temporal restrictions. Therefore, in this case, the TQA is answering better than the QA system.There are 28 questions of this type and they are questions of Type 2 and Type 4.
- Our system obtains worst results than the QA system
  - The QA system is able to answer but the TQA is not. That is because, when the complex question is divided into two simple ones, there are some keywords in the second questions that are not being used to ask for the first question and these keywords may be useful to find any answer. For example, in the question *"Who was Secretary of Defense during the Gulf War?"*, the system looks for the keywords: *"Secretary of Defense"* and *"Gulf War"* and returns answers like *"Colin Powell"*, *"George Bush"*, *"Dick Cheney"*. But, using the TQA system, the question is divided into two simple questions: *"Who was Secretary of Defense?"* and *"When did the Gulf Was occur?"*. When the first question is processed the results are not good because the information given by the keyword *"Gulf War"* is missed. However, there is only 1 question with this problem.

The results of this study are shown in Table 2. As a conclusion, it could be said that our system is improving a General Purpose QA system in the 34% of the questions and it works worst only in less that 1% of the questions.

3.3 Second Approach of Architecture of a Temporal Question Answering System

After the evaluation of the first approach, it can be observed that when splitting complex questions into two independent sub-questions, some information necessary to answer the complex questions can be lost. For example, for the question

"Who was Secretary of Defense during the Gulf War?", instead of dividing the question in: *"Who was Secretary of Defense?"* and *"When was the Gulf War?"*, the search will be far better if the second question, that refers to a date, is solved and, after that, the first question is transformed adding this temporal data obtained to it: *"Who was Secretary of Defense in 1991?"* . Using this approach, questions that were not answered first by lack of information could be solved now. In addition, this approach makes a more exhaustive filtering of the results than the first one, since there are more resolute temporal information before formulating the question to a current QA system.

In order to be able to evaluate this new solution, a new intermediate unit that makes the transformation of the first question using the answer of second is added to the first approach. In addition, this unit is in charge to transform the possible implicit temporal expressions that can appear in the questions as well (See Figure 3).

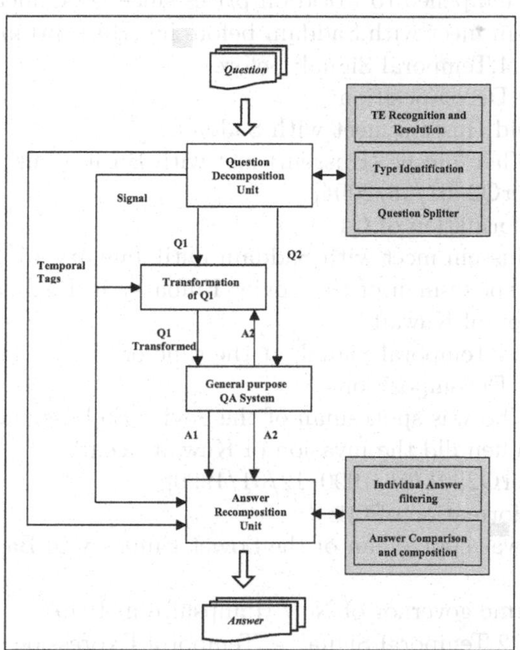

Fig. 3. Temporal Question Answering System (2nd approach)

- *The Q1 Transformation Unit.* This unit is only useful when we are dealing with Type 3 or 4 questions, that are complex questions that need to be divided in two for being answered and Type 2 questions that have a temporal expression in the question. There are two possible transformations of the first question:

  - Temporal expressions of the question are transformed into dates or concrete ranges and this transformed question goes through the General Purpose QA system.
  - The second sub-question, which is a When question, is answered by the General Purpose QA system, and the answer of this second question, which is a date or period is added to the first question. Now, the answer of the transformed question is obtained by the QA system.
- *Example of transformations*
  - What happened to world oil prices after the Iraqi "annexation" of Kuwait?
    1. Type: 4,Temporal Signal: after
       Initial Decomposition:
       Q1: What happened to world oil prices?
       Q2: When did the Iraqi "annexation" of Kuwait occur?
    2. AnswerQ2:[01/01/1991–12/31/1991]
    3. Transformation of Q1:
       What happened to world oil prices since December 31,1991?
  - Did Hussein meet with Saddam before he (Hussein) met with Bush?
    1. Type: 4,Temporal Signal: before
       Initial Decomposition:
       Q1: Did Hussein meet with Saddam?
       Q2: When did he (Hussein) met with Bush occur?
    2. AnswerQ2:[01/15/2004]
    3. Transformation of Q1:
       Did Hussein meet with Saddam until January 15, 2004?
  - Who was spokesman of the Soviet Embassy in Baghdad at the time of the invasion of Kuwait?
    1. Type: 4,Temporal Signal: at the time of
       Initial Decomposition:
       Q1: Who was spokesman of the Soviet Embassy in Baghdad?
       Q2: When did the invasion of Kuwait occur?
    2. AnswerQ2:[01/01/1990–12/31/1990]
    3. Transformation of Q1:
       Who was spokesman of the Soviet Embassy in Baghdad between in 1990?
  - Who became governor of New Hampshire in 1949?
    1. Type: 2,Temporal Signal: -, Temporal Expression: in 1949
    2. Transformation of Q1:
       Who became governor of New Hampshire from January 01,1949 to December 31,1949?

3.4 Evaluation of the System with the First Approach

In this evaluation, two kinds of results are shown:

- In one hand, which questions have a smaller and more precise set of answers than in the first approach but still correct.

Table 3. Evaluation of the system with the second approach (NQ = Number of Questions and AA = Average of Answers)

	TOTAL	BEST RESULTS 1st APPROACH		BEST RESULTS 2nd APPROACH		IMPROVEMENT (%)	
		NQ	AA	NQ	AA	NQ(%)	AA(%)
Type 1	47	-	-	-	-	-	-
Type 2	59	36	2.8	9	1.6	25%	57%
Type 3	3	-	-	-	-	-	-
Type 4	15	6	6	4	2	67%	33%
All Questions	124	42	2.83	13	1.6	30%	56%

– On the other hand, we have calculated the average number of answers of this question corpus for the first approach and for the second with the objective of determining if this set is reduced.

After evaluating this new approach and comparing the results with first one, the following results are observed:

– There are the same number of questions in which the TQA system answered the same as the QA system in both approaches.
– Nevertheless, 13 of those questions in which the TQA system was better than the QA system have been improved, because the new set of answers for these questions are much more precise and filtered. The set of answers is smaller but in every case the correct answer belongs to this new set of answers. Therefore, the possibility of obtaining an erroneous answer for that question is now reduced with this new approach.
    • There are 9 questions of Type 2 that have better answers for this approach due to the previous resolution of the temporal expression before asking the General Purpose QA system. In average, for the first approach there are 2.8 answers per question and with the second approach there are 1.6 answers and the correct one is in this group of questions.
    • There are 4 questions of Type 4 that have better answers because the answer of the second sub-question is being used to reformulate the first question before asking the QA system. That gives extra information to the QA system and that is why the results are much better. Moreover, in average, there are 6 answers for question in the first approach and this number is reduced to 2 in the second approach.

The results of this evaluation are shown in Table 3. This table, in the first column, contains the total amount of questions in the question corpus divided by each type. The second column refers to the number of questions that were better in the first approach compared to the QA system and the number of answers as average per question. The third columns shows the number of these questions that were much better in the second approach than in the first one and the number of answers as average per question, and finally, in the fourth column, a percentage of improvement of the second approach compared with the first one is presented.

4 Conclusions

This paper presents a new and intuitive method for answering complex temporal questions using an embedded factual-based QA system. This method is based on a proposal for the decomposition of temporal questions where complex questions are divided into simpler ones by means of the detection of temporal signals. The TERSEO system, a temporal information extraction system, has been used to detect and resolve temporal expressions in questions and answers.

This work proposes a multilayered architecture that enables to solve complex questions by enhancing current QA capabilities. Two approaches have been presented. The first one is based on the decomposition of complex questions into simpler ones and the second one, apart from the decomposition, reformulates the sub-questions adding temporal information to them.

As a conclusion, the evaluation shows an improvement of the first approach of the TQA system of 34% compared with a current QA system. Besides, the second approach of the system is a 30% better that the first one. Moreover, the number of answers for every question has been reduced, in the second approach, more than a 50%, and in this reduction of answers, the correct answer was still in the set.

In future, our work is directed to fine tune this system and increase system capabilities in order to be able to process more kinds of complex questions.

References

1. E. Breck, J. Burger, L. Ferro, W. Greiff, M. Light, I. Mani, and J. Rennie. Another sys called quanda. In *Ninth Text REtrieval Conference*, volume 500-249 of *NIST Special Publication*, pages 369–378, Gaithersburg, USA, nov 2000. National Institute of Standards and Technology.
2. I. Mani and G. Wilson. Robust temporal processing of news. In ACL, editor, *Proceedings of the 38th Meeting of the Association of Computational Linguistics (ACL 2000)*, Hong Kong, October 2000.
3. J. Pustejovsky. Terqas:time and event recognition for question answering systems. `http://time2002.org/`, 2002.
4. D. Radev and B. Sundheim. Using timeml in question answering. `http://www.cs.brandeis.edu/ ~jamesp/ arda/ time/ documentation/ TimeML-use-in-qa-v1.0.pdf`, 2002.
5. E. Saquete, P. Martínez-Barco, R. Muñoz, and J.L. Vicedo. Multilayered question answering system applied to temporality evaluation. In SEPLN, editor, *XX Congreso de la SEPLN*, Barcelona, España, July 2004.
6. E. Saquete, P. Martínez-Barco, R. Muñoz, and J.L. Vicedo. Splitting complex temporal questions for question answering systems. In ACL, editor, *42nd Annual Meeting of the Association for Computational Linguistics*, Barcelona, España, July 2004.

The Contents and Structure of the Context Base, and Its Application

Yusuke Takahashi, Ichiro Kobayashi, Michiaki Iwazume, Noriko Ito, and Michio Sugeno

Laboratory for Language-Based Intelligent Systems,
Brain Science Institute, RIKEN
2-1 Wako, Hirosawa, Saitama, 351-0198 Japan
{tkhsysk, iwazume, itoh, msgn}@brain.riken.jp
Faculty of Sciences, Ochanomizu University
2-1-1 Otsuka, Bunkyo-ku, Tokyo, 112-8610, Japan
koba@is.ocha.ac.jp

Abstract. The objective of this paper is to show the text processing, especially text generation using the contextual features. For a computer system to operate everyday language the context which surrounds language use must be considered and this is one of the reasons why we adopt Systemic Functional Linguistics. In this paper we introduce the database for text processing system called "the Semiotic Base", which contains "the Context Base" as the model of the context and show how this system works in the text processing, especially in the text planning and generation.

1 Introduction

We have developed a computational model of language in context. As a basic theory, we adopt Systemic Functional Linguistics (SFL) [1] that aims at describing the system of language comprehensively and provides a unified way of modeling language in context. In this section we illustrate the conception of Everyday Language Computing and SFL.

1.1 Everyday Language Computing

We propose the paradigm shift from the information processing with numbers and formal symbolic logic to that with our everyday or commonsense use of language. In this project of "Everyday Language Computing", the role language plays in human intelligence is regarded as important. On the basis of this conception our project aims at realizing language-based intelligent systems on computers in which the human language is embedded. In this project we have adopted SFL as the model of language to be embedded in the system, and have constructed the Semiotic Base, a database for text processing system using SFL, having developed the systems using this database [2, 3, 4, 5, 6].

J. L. Vicedo et al. (Eds.): EsTAL 2004, LNAI 3230, pp. 103–114, 2004.

1.2 Systemic Functional Linguistics

SFL is regarded as functionalism in terms of linguistics. According to Matthiessen [7], SFL regards language as a resource for communication rather than a set of rules. As such, the main characteristics of linguistic text are the followings: stratification, metafunction and instantiation.

A text can be stratified into four strata: context, meaning, wording (lexicogrammar: grammar and lexis) and expression. Context is realized into the meaning of the text, the meaning is realized into the wording of the text and the wording is realized into the expression of the text.

According to Halliday the language has three metafunctions: ideational, interpersonal and textual. Ideational metafunction corresponds to the functions by which to constitute events expressed in language and to show the logical conjunction of them. Interpersonal metafunction corresponds to the functions by which to show the social relationship between the interactants. Textual metafunction correspond to the functions by which to make the text coherent and appropriate to the context in which it is produced. In addition context is divided into three values: Field (the social activity done in the interaction), Tenor (the social relationship between the interactants) and Mode (the nature of media used in the interaction), and they roughly correspond to ideational, interpersonal and textual metafunctions respectively.

A language can be seen as a cline of instantiation. A text is an instance of language in context at one extreme of the cline. Language as a whole system is the potential at the other. A set of texts using the same linguistic resources constitutes a text type. The resources used in the texts can be regarded as a register of the text type. We can place these text type and register somewhere in the middle of the cline.

1.3 The Semiotic Base

In this section we introduce the overall contents and structure of the Semiotic Base, a computational model based on SFL.

The main components of the Semiotic Base are the Context Base, the Meaning Base, the Wording Base and the Expression Base. Each database describes contextual or linguistic features to characterize the system of language and relations among the features within a base as well as those between other bases.

The Context Base characterizes context by Field, Tenor and Mode. Once these variables are determined, the context is specified as instances of Situation Types. Furthrer the way of developing a text in each Situation Type is described as a Generic structure. In addition to the main bases the Semiotic Base includes Concept Repository, General Dictionary and Situation-Specific Dictionary.

2 Contents of the Context Base

In this chapter we show the contents and structure, and data structure of the Context Base.

We have built a prototype system equipped with the Semiotic Base with the Context Base. This system is made in order for ordinary people to operate a computer with their everyday use of language. They, as users, can talk with a client secretary in the computer and create a document such as invitation card or manage the e-mail by asking the secretary to do so.

2.1 Contents of the Context Base

The Context Base consists of the following contents: databases of Field, Tenor and Mode, a database of situation types with generic structure. Further, it is supplemented with the Machine Readable Dictionaries (the Concept Repository and the Situation Specific Dictionary), the Knowledge Base and the Corpus Base as shown in Fig. 1.

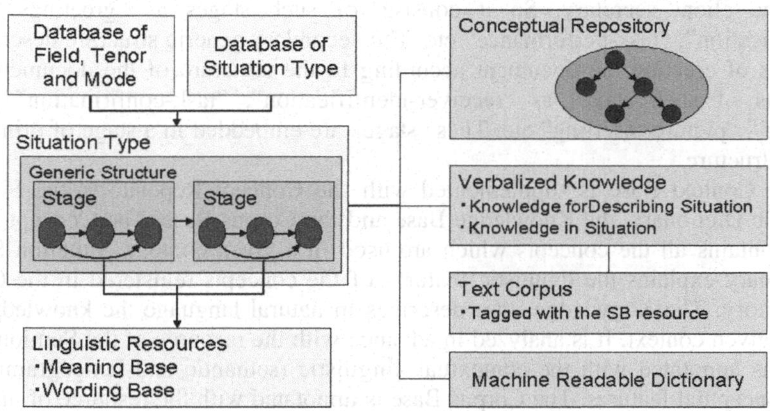

Fig. 1. Contents of the Context Base

The values of Field, Tenor and Mode characterize a situation type. We made a prototype model of context with these situation types.

This situation type is divided into two: the primary situation type and the secondary situation type[1]. In our prototype system we must consider two types of situation. One is the situation in which a computer user and a client secretary are talking each other in order to create a document with the word processor. This situation is realized into a dialogue between the two interactants. We call it primary situation type. The other is a sub-situation appearing in the document and so on. In this situation, the user invites people to a party, sends summer greetings to people and so on. This type of sub-situation appears within the primary situation type. We call it secondary situation type. Both situation types are tagged with the values of Field, Tenor and Mode.

In the prototype system we adopt the viewpoint that the document realizing the secondary situation type (such as a summer greetings) is produced through the dialogue between the user and the secretary realizing the primary situation type. This is why we embed the secondary situation type in the primary situation type.

---

1 Some systemic functional linguists say that a context of situation can be divided into two: first-order and second-order ones [7]. This conception seems similar to ours. However these two kinds of context reflect different aspects of the same context and both of them are realized into the same text. On the other hand, our primary and secondary situation types imply different contexts and are realized into different text: a dialogue between the interactants and a document to be created through the dialogue respectively.

Generic structure describes the development of the text surrounded by the given context. According to SFL, a text or an interaction develops through some steps called "stages" towards the goal. So, generic structure consists of some stages with transition which are necessary or optional to deal with for the text in the given context. Each stage further contains some moves in the interaction and the information of the move transition. Each move has the information of the possible speech-function in the interactants' utterance.

According to the situation types divided into two, the Context Base accommodates the primary generic structure and the secondary generic structure. The primary generic structure describes the development of the dialogue between the computer user and the client secretary. So it consists of such stages as "greetings", "task-identification", "task-performance" etc. The secondary generic structure describes the process of creating the document according to the structure of the document. So it consists of such stages as "receiver-identification", "task-confirmation", "body-editing", "picture-inserting" etc. These stages are embedded in a stage of primary generic structure.

The Context Base is supplemented with the Concept Repository, the Situation-Specific Dictionary, the Knowledge Base and the Corpus Base. The Concept Repository contains all the concepts which are used in a given context. Situation Specific Dictionary explains the linguistic features of the concepts registered in the Concept Repository. The Knowledge Base describes in natural language the knowledge used in the given context. It is analyzed in advance with the resource of the Semiotic Base, i.e. it is annotated with the contextual, linguistic (semantic and lexicogrammatical) and conceptual features. The Corpus Base is annotated with the resource of the Semiotic Base just as the Knowledge Base. The difference between the Knowledge Base and the Corpus Base is that while the Knowledge Base has the standard form, the Corpus Base doesn't.

2.2 Data Structure

The data of a situation type consists of the followings: ID of the situation, The features of Field, Tenor and Mode, upper situation types, embedded situation type, list of the Knowledge for Describing Situation (KDS), Concept Repository of the situation type and generic structure.

Upper situation type describes the data of situation types in order to show the position of the given situation type. Embedded situation type shows what situation type is embedded in the given situation type. It implies that the embedded situation type is the second situation type while the embedding situation type is the primary situation type in a given interaction.

The list of the KDS shows what kind of knowledge is deployed in the given situation type. Each KDS is given its unique ID and is used by calling their ID when needed.

Generic structure consists of ID of the generic structure and the list of the possible stages. A stage consists of the ID of the stage and the list of possible moves in it. A move consists of ID of the move, polarity of the move, the structure of the move, the list of the moves to which it is possible to transit.

As for the move structure, it is shown as a conceptual frame of speech function and speech content. The speech function implies the interpersonal meaning the speaker conveys to the hearer and roughly corresponds to the "illocutionary act" in Speech

Act Theory. The speech function concept has the slots of speaker, hearer and content and the value of the content slot is the concept of the speech content, which implies the ideational meaning of the given move.

3 Text Generation

We have made a computational model of text processing using the Semiotic Base. We focus on text generation hereafter. For the algorithm of text understanding, see [5].

It is often the case that we cannot continue conversation without contextual knowledge. The following is the dialogue between a secretary and a client, where a client, computer user, asks a secretary agent to create a document. In this case A must take into account the contextual feature so that A could ask B again in utterance 3 whether or not s/he wishes to change the passage according to the addressee of the greeting card. In this case A must know that the nature of both B's friends and colleagues: the social hierarchy and distance between A and his/her friends or colleagues.

(1) A: syotyuu-mimai-o donata-ni okuri-masu-ka?
summer-greeting-card-Acc. who-Dat. send-polite-question
Who do you send the greeting cards?

(2) B: yuujinn-to kaisya-no dooryoo desu.
friends-and company-Gen colleague is
To the friends and colleagues of my company.

(3) A: syotyuu-mimai-no bunmen-o kae-masu-ka?
summer-greeting-card-Gen passage-Acc change-polite-question
Do you change the passage of the card?

Linguistically generation is the inverse process of understanding. In generation we transform the linguistic system or potential into the linguistic instance. Selecting some conceptual features characterizing what to say, we realize these features as a text using linguistic resources.

3.1 Text Planning: Determining What to Say

Text planning is the process of deciding the content which is to be generated. At this step, the algorithm begins with checking the conceptual analysis of user's utterance. Then, the current move is checked with reference to the Stage Base and the values of context are investigated. At the next the candidates of the content of generation are picked up from the Stage Base and the most appropriate one is chosen.

The content to be generated is given by an instance conceptual frame selected in the Stage Base. Taking the above utterance (3) as an example in the sequel, we will show the process of planning the content as a speech content and generating the text string. Fig. 2 shows the stage "receiver-identification" with four moves concerning the dialogue between a secretary and a client.

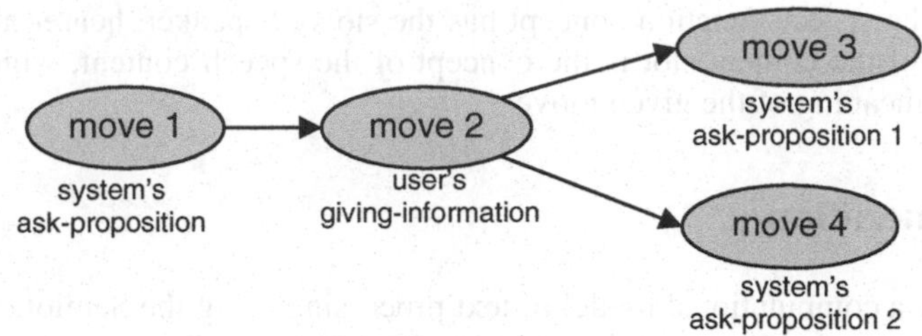

Fig. 2. Moves and Their Transition in a Stage: the Case of "Receiver-Identification"

In this figure the moves 1 and 2 correspond to the utterance 1 and 2, respectively. In each move of the Stage Base concerning the system's utterance, there is written a prototype of a conceptual frame to express a speech content. Suppose that we are at the move 2. The Utterance 2 of the user at the move 2 is found, by the conceptual analysis in the understanding model, to have the conceptual frame as shown in Fig. 3.

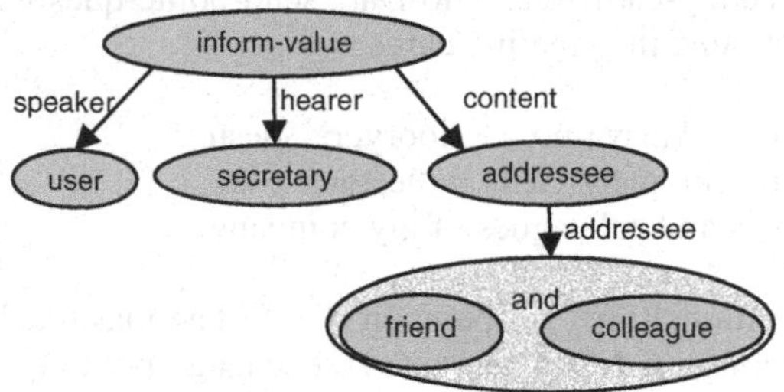

Fig. 3. Conceptual Frame of Utterance 2

Now we go to the next move. If there are plural move candidates after the move 2, we determine which move is the most appropriate. In this case, there are two candidates: the move 3 and the move 4. Fig. 4 shows two different speech contents for the secretary corresponding to the move 3 and the move 4.

The next move is specified in the Stage Base and the way of determining the next move differs according to the stage or move to be dealt with. In this case, the move candidates are move 3 and move 4. These in the moves 3 and 4 can be read "Do you change the passage of the summer greetings card?" and "Is it OK that the passages of the cards are the same?" respectively.

In order to determine the speech content for the utterance 3, we use the contextual features concerning Tenor and situational knowledge in the Context Base. According to the conceptual frame of the utterance 2, there are two tenors as addresses: friend and colleagues, and their social hierarchy and distance is found to be rather large. The situational knowledge concerning the content or style of a card says that the content may differ according to the social distance of addressees. As a result the speech content in the move 3 is selected to generate the utterance 3.

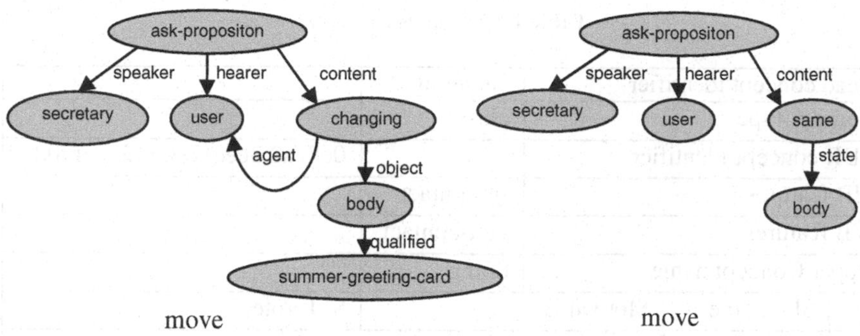

Fig. 4. Conceptual Frame of Utterance 3 and 4

In this case the move candidate is determined according to the difference of Tenor between the user and the addressee. Here we search for the KDS. The KDS used is as follows:

<colleague> is <superior> to <user> in terms of <social hierarchy>
<friend> is <equal> to <user> in terms of <social hierarchy>
<colleague> is <distant> to <user> in terms of <social distance>
<friend> is <close> to <user> in terms of <social distance>

From these KDSs we determine the next move by identifying the TenorValue, which shows the difference of Tenor between the friends and the colleagues with the following rules:

If the TenorValue is <large>, then set the CurrentMove to move3.
If the TenorValue is <medium>, then set the CurrentMove to move4.
If the TenorValue is <small>, then set the CurrentMove to move4.

By these rules and identified TenorValue we determine the next move. In this case TenorValue is decided as <large> and move 3 is selected as the next move.

3.2 Text Generation: Determining How to Say

After determining the content of generation, we generate the text string from the instance conceptual frame determined.

First, we search for the Concept Repository to find a concept item corresponding to the concept "changing" in the conceptual frame for the utterance 3. From the corresponding item shown in Table 1, we obtain the semantic feature of the Process "changing" and Participants and Circumstances, where Process implies "verbs", for instance, doing something in terms of SFL, Participants are like subject and object taking part in Process, and circumstances are like means and location for Process. In this example, referring to the term "changing" in the Concept Repository, we can find the semantic feature "fg-contact" of Process "changing" and further we can obtain the SFL roles of Participants, "Actor" for agent and "Goal" for object. In this case there is no Circumstance with this Process. Fig. 5 illustrates this process.

Table 1. Concept Repository

Head concept identifier		changing	
Concept type		class	
EDR concept identifier			0e87a2 3ceec7 3cf4fc 3cf90d
MB features		fg-contact	
WB features		mat-contact	
Upper Concept name		doing	
	Slot name	Slot value	SFL role
1	agent	agent	Actor
2	object	domain-concept	Goal

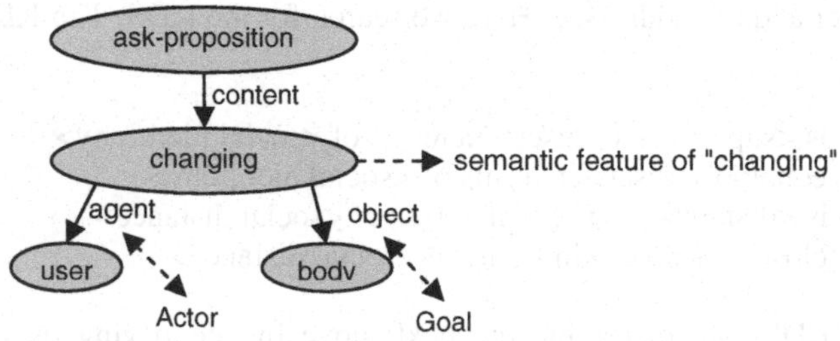

Fig. 5. Correspondences of Concepts with Semantic Roles

At the step we obtain the followings:

changing → semantic feature of "changing"
agent → Actor
object → Goal

Next, we obtain the lexicogrammatical feature corresponding to the semantic feature obtained at the last step, and case markers and the word order. At this step we obtain the lexicogrammatical feature of the Wording Base from the realization statement attached to the corresponding semantic feature obtained at the last step in the Meaning Base. Then, we refer to the realization statement (the linguistic constraint attached to the feature in the database) to the Wording Base and looks up the constraints about the case markers and the word order.

In this example we find the lexicogrammatical feature "mat-contact" in the Wording Base from the realization statement attached to the semantic feature "fg-contact" in the Meaning Base. Then, referring to the realization statement corresponding to the obtained feature "mat-contact", we can find the case markers and word order. Fig. 6 illustrates this process.

The result of this step is as follows:

semantic feature of "changing" → lexicogrammatical feature of "changing"
Actor → ga (nominal case marker)
Goal → o (accusative case marker)
The word order： [user (Actor)-ga body (Goal)-o changing]

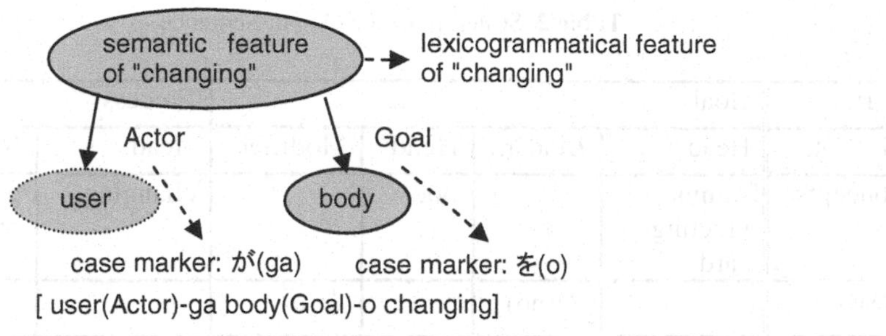

Fig. 6. Case Markers and Word Order

Further we follow some lexicogrammatical constraints, if any: ellipsis, thematization, for instance. In this example a system network in the Wording Base says that Japanese subject which takes the role of Actor and which is marked with nominal case should become theme in the clause and this type of theme should be elliptical by default. So, the part of "user" is deleted and we do not deal with this part any longer.

Next we determine the fine structure of the Process and Participants. So far the rough structure of the text string has been determined, but the details of the text string, especially the internal structures of each Participant, Circumstance or Process remain unspecified. At this step, we relate the grammatical categories, concepts and, if possible, lexical items to the participants, circumstances or process.

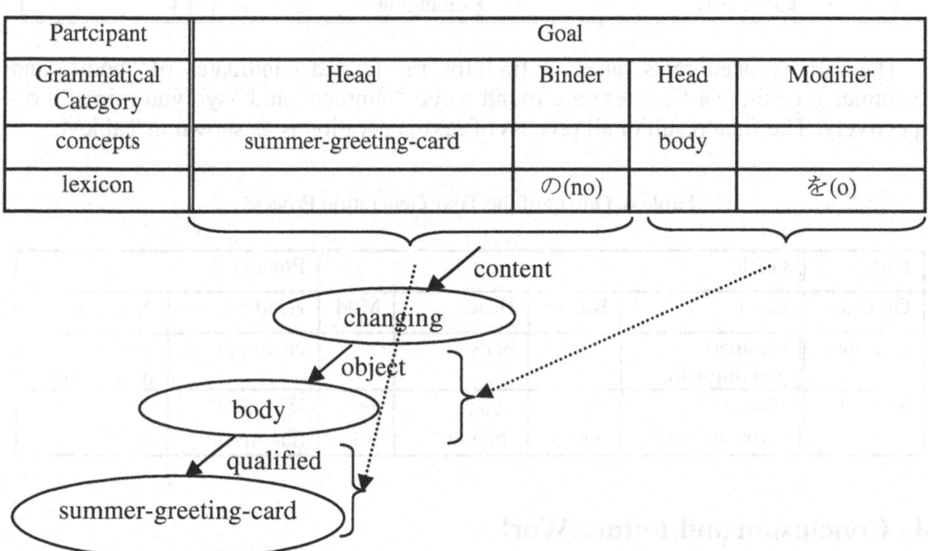

Partcipant	Goal			
Grammatical Category	Head	Binder	Head	Modifier
concepts	summer-greeting-card		body	
lexicon		の(no)		を(o)

Fig. 7. Relation of Participant "Goal" to Grammatical Categories and Concept Instance

The last step is the lexical selection. At this step, we look up the most appropriate exical items of concept instance in the Situation-Specific Dictionary. We first search for the candidates of the lexical item referring to concept labels and situation types

Table 2. Structure of the Output Sentence

Part.	Goal				Process	
Gr. Cat.	Head	Binder	Head	Modifier	Head	Negotiator
concepts	summer-greeting-card		body		changing	ask-proposition
lexicon		の(no)		を(o)		か(ka)

described in the Situation Specific Dictionary. Then, we select the most appropriate candidate with the frequency information in the Situation-Specific Dictionary.

For example, as for "changing", the result of searching for the candidates of lexical item is shown below in Table 3. From the candidates, we choose the most frequent item "kae-masu".

Table 3. Lexical Items for "Changing"

Index	Conceptual label	frequency
改めます(aratame-masu)	changing	0.2
変更します (henkoo-simasu)	changing	0.3
変えます (kae-masu)	changing	0.5

The same procedure is taken to find for the lexical candidates of "body" and "summer-greeting-card". These are found to be "bunmen" and "syotyuu-mimai", respectively. The final result of all process of text generation is as shown in Table 4.

Table 4. Output of the Text Generation Process

Part.	Goal				Process	
Gr. Cat.	Head	Binder	Head	Mod	Head	Negotiator
concepts	summer-greeting-card		body		changing	ask-proposition
lexicon	招待状 (syootai-zyoo)	の (no)	文面 (bunmen)	を (o)	変えます (kae-masu)	か (ka)

4 Conclusion and Future Works

In this paper, after explaining the basic conceptions of Everyday Language Computing and SFL, we showed the contents and overall structure of the Context Base as a subcomponent of the Semiotic Base. Then we showed how the Context Base works in text generation. The Semiotic Base is context sensitive due to the Context Base. The Context Base uses the contextual features in term of SFL comprehensively and explicitly. The supplemental components such as MRDs, the Knowledge Base and the

Corpus Base make the Context Base work effectively in the text processing. We have already implemented the prototype system by which a user can operate word processor with his/her everyday use of language [6]. In this system, the Concept Repository for creating document contains about 200 class concepts and the number of them is expected to expand.

There are some previous works on text generation adopting SFL. Among them, for example, COMMUNAL [8] and Multex [9] considers the contextual feature. COMMUNAL is sensitive to Tenor and Mode, which enables the generator to deal with some linguistic variations for the same content of generation. However, it still does not deal with the contextual features comprehensively and does not have semantic stratum as the Semiotic Base has. Multex considers both the contextual and semantic contents in terms of SFL. However, the contextual features of this system are limited to the level of situation types in terms of SFL. The Semiotic Base is more comprehensive than this in that it considers the values itself of Field, Tenor and Mode, and generic structures.

We still have several works to do. Among them, it is the most significant theoretically how to link from the Context Base to other components of the Semiotic Base. The bridge between the Context Base and the Meaning Base/the Wording Base is now Concept Repository and Situation-Specific Dictionary: the linguistic realizations of a given situation are shown as the concepts and their linguistic representation as the supplement of the main database. But ideally the linguistic realization of context should be indicated in the system network in the Context Base just as the lexicogrammatical realizations of the semantic features are indicated in the realization statements in the Meaning Base. We are now investigating how to show the linguistic realization of a given context directly in the Context Base.

It is also an important issue how to deal with the situational knowledge such as KDS. We have compiled situational knowledge them manually and the amount of the compiled knowledge is extremely small relative to deal with all possible actions in the given context. We must compile the situational knowledge further. At the same time we must consider what kind of knowledge is really needed in the given context so that we may avoid explosion.

As for the application to text generation, the problem of input specification is the most significant. Our present model starts from a conceptual frame as the content of generation by which the meaning features are assigned. What is a trigger to this selection process? How is the content of generation formed and expressed? We have to identify the input for selecting meaning features, a sort of intention, together with its representation for the computational model of generation.

References

1. Halliday, M.A.K. and Matthiessen, C. M. I. M.: Construing Experience through Meaning: A Language-based Approach to Cognition. Cassell, London New York (1999)
2. Kobayashi, I. and Sugeno, M.: Toward Everyday Language Computing –Computing from a Viewpoint of Linguistic Theory-. Journal of Advanced Computational Intelligence, Vol. 1 No.1 (1997) 1-8
3. Sugimoto, T., Ito, N., Fujishiro, H. and Sugeno. M.: Dialogue Management with the Semiotic Base: A Systemic Functional Linguistic Approach. 1st International Conference on Soft Computing and Intelligent Systems (2002)

4. Iwazume, M., Kobayashi, I., Sugimoto, T. Iwashita, S. Takahashi, Y. Ito, N. and Sugeno, M.: Everyday Language Computing-Toward Language-based Computational Environment. Transactions of the Japanese Society for Artificial Intelligence, Vol18, Vol.1 (2003) 45-56 (in Japanese)
5. Ito, N., Sugimoto, T. and Sugeno, M.: A systemic-functional approach to Japanese text understanding. 5th International Conference on Intelligent Text Processing and Computational Linguistics (CICLing 2004), Seoul (2004) 26-37
6. Ito, N., Sugimoto, T., Iwashita, S., Michiaki, I., Takahashi, Y., Kobayashi, I. and Sugeno, M.: Everyday Language Application Systems with the Semiotic Base (Part 2), The18th Conference of Japanese Society for Artificial Intelligence, Kanazawa (2004) 2C1-05 (in Japanese)
7. Matthiessen, C. Lexicogrammatical Cartography: English Systems. International Language Sciences Publishers, Tokyo (1995)
8. Fawcett, R.P. Tucker, G.H. and Lin, Y.Q.: How a systemic functional grammar works: the roles of realization in realization. In: Horacek, H. and Zock, M. (ed.): New Concepts in Natural Language Generation: Planning, Realization and Systems, Pinters, London and New York (1993) 114-186
9. Matthiessen, C., Zeng, L., Cross, M., Kobayashi, I., Teruya, K. and Wu, C.: The Multex generator and its environment: application and development. The 9th International Workshop on Natural Language Generation (INLG-98), Niagara-on-the-Lake (1998) 228-237

Developing a Minimalist Parser for Free Word Order Languages with Discontinuous Constituency

Asad B. Sayeed and Stan Szpakowicz

School of Information Technology and Engineering
University of Ottawa, 800 King Edward Avenue
Ottawa, Ontario, Canada K1N 6N5
{asayeed@mbl.ca,szpak@site.uottawa.ca}

Abstract. We propose a parser based on ideas from the Minimalist Programme. The parser supports free word order languages and simulates a human listener who necessarily begins sentence analysis before all the words in the sentence have become available. We first sketch the problems that free word order languages pose. Next we discuss an existing framework for minimalist parsing, and show how it is difficult to make it work for free word order languages and simulate realistic syntactic conditions. We briefly describe a formalism and a parsing algorithm that elegantly overcome these difficulties, and we illustrate them with detailed examples from Latin, a language whose word order freedom causes it to exhibit seemingly difficult discontinuous noun phrase situations.

1 Introduction

The Minimalist Programme as described by Chomsky and others [6] seeks to provide an explanation for the existence of the capacity of language in humans. Syntax merits particular attention in this programme, as it is syntax that mediates the interactions between the requirements of articulation and those of meaning. Minimalism characterizes syntax as the simplest possible mapping between semantics and phonology. It seeks to define the terms of simplicity and determine the structures and processes required to satisfy these terms.

That the object of investigation is syntax suggests that it is possible to extract a formal and computable model of syntactic processes from minimalist investigations. Doubly so, as the concept of economy in minimalism can be said to correspond to computational complexity.

In this paper, we look at the problem of developing a minimalist account of parsing. We turn our attention in particular to free word order phenomena in Latin and to simulating a realistic human parser given that people do not have a complete sentence before they begin processing. We first give background on free word order phenomena and on minimalist parsing. Next we discuss a formalism that performs free word order parsing in such a realistic manner. We show two complete parses of representative sentences to demonstrate the algorithm, one

J. L. Vicedo et al. (Eds.): EsTAL 2004, LNAI 3230, pp. 115–126, 2004.

of which is a case of discontinuous constituency, a special challenge for parsing languages such as Latin.

2 Background

2.1 Latin and Free Word Order

Principle-based parsing of free word order languages has been considered for a long time—see, for example, [1]—but not much in the context of the Minimalist Programme. We propose a minimalist parser and illustrate its operation with Latin, a language that exhibits high word order freedom. For example,

pater	laetus	amat	filium	laetum
father-Nom	happy-Nom	loves-3Sg	son-Acc	happy-Acc

'The happy father loves the happy son.'

For a simple sentence such as this, in theory all $5! = 120$ permutations should be grammatical. We briefly discuss in section 4 whether this is really the case. This is not true of Latin sentences in which function words must be fixed in place.

It is often remarked that these word orders, though semantically equivalent, differ in pragmatic import (focus, topic, emphasis, and so on). Existing elaborate accounts of contextual effects on Latin word order [3] are rarely sufficiently formal for parser development, and do not help a parser designed to extract information from a single sentence out of context. It should still be possible to extract the propositional content without having to refer to the context; hence, we need an algorithm that will parse all 120 orders as though there were no real differences between any of them. After all, people can extract information from sentences out of context.

2.2 Derivational Minimalism

[4] defines a minimalist grammar as $G = (V, Cat, Lex, F)$. V is a set of "non-syntactic features" (phonetic and semantic representations), Cat is a set of "syntactic features," Lex is the lexicon ("a set of expressions built from V and Cat"), and F is "a set of partial functions from tuples of expressions to expressions"—that is, structure-building operations such as MOVE and MERGE. MERGE, a binary operation, composes words and trees into trees. MOVE removes and reattaches subtrees; these manipulations are performed in order to *check* features. Checking ensures, among other things, that words receive required complements. Stabler characterizes checking as the cancellation of corresponding syntactic features on the participant lexical items, but requires that features be checked in a fixed order.

[5] proposes a minimalist recognizer that uses a CKY-like algorithm to determine membership in $L(G)$. Limiting access to features to a particular order may not work for free word order languages, where words can often appear in any order. Either duplicate lexical entires must proliferate to handle all cases, or

Stabler's specification requirements of lexical entries must be relaxed. We choose the latter path.

Stabler's CKY inference rules do not themselves directly specify the order in which items are to be MERGEd and MOVEd into tree structures. This apparent nondeterminism is less significant if the feature order is fixed. Since we propose a relaxation of the ordering constraint for free word order languages, the nondeterminism will necessarily be amplified.

This dovetails with a practical goal. In free word order languages, semantically connected words can appear far apart in a sentence. In *pater amat filium laetum laetus*, *pater* and *laetus* must be merged at some point in a noun-adjective relationship. But *pater* is the subject of *amat*. In order to simulate a human listener, the parser would have to MERGE *pater* and *amat* first, despite that *pater* and *laetus* form one NP; the human listener would hear and make the connection between *pater* and *amat* first.

Consequently, we propose a parser that simulates a human listener by limiting at each step in a derivation what words are accessible to ("have been heard by") the parser and by defining the precedence of the operators in a way that fully extracts the syntactic and semantic content of the known words before receiving further words. We develop a formalism to allow this while providing the flexibility needed for free word order languages. This formalism, illustrated later by examples, reflects many of the ideas of Stabler's formalism, but is otherwise independent.

3 The Parser

3.1 Lexicalized Grammatical Formalism

We briefly describe enough of the lexicon structure to assist in understanding the subsequent parsing examples. A lexical entry has the form

$$\alpha : \Gamma$$

α is a word's phonetic or orthographic representation as required. Γ is a set of feature structures, henceforth called "feature sets."[1] Γ contains feature paths, described below. But more fundamental are the feature bundles from which feature paths are constructed.

Feature bundles are required given the fact that highly inflected languages often compress several features into a single morpheme. Feature bundles provide the means to check them simultaneously. A feature bundle is represented as follows:

[1] There is a third, hidden entity here: the semantic representation of α. We leave it implied that parsing operations perform semantic composition; the formal specification of this is left for future work, but it can be specified in the lambda calculus as in [2] or via theta roles, and so on. Nevertheless, this paper is ultimately directed towards laying the syntactic groundwork for the extraction of semantic content from free word order sentences.

$$\beta(\tau_1 : \phi_1, \ldots, \tau_n : \phi_n) : \delta, n \geq 1$$

β is the feature checking status. It can be `unchecked` (`unch`), `UNCHECKED` (`UNCH`), `checked` (`ch`), `CHECKED` (`CH`), `unchecked-adjoin` (`unch+`), `checked-adjoin` (`ch+`). When feature bundles are checked against one another, β can change. The examples will illustrate the relation between feature checking status symbols during the checking.

Each τ is a feature type. It can be one of such things as case, gender, number, and so on. Each ϕ is a feature value such as Nom (nominative), Sg (singular), and so on. The correspondence between feature types and features is required for the unification aspect of the checking operation, again demonstrated in the examples.

δ is direction. An item ι carrying the feature bundle can only check the bundle with a bundle on another item to the δ of ι. δ can be *left* or *right*, and δ is omitted when the direction does not matter (a frequent situation in free word order languages).

A feature path has the form:

$$\pi \rightarrow \Gamma$$

π is a feature bundle and Γ is a feature set. A feature path makes Γ inaccessible for checking until π has been checked. Γ can be empty, in which case the $\rightarrow$ is not written.

A feature set is simply an unordered list of unique feature paths: $\{\eta, \ldots\}$. These sets allow each η to be checked independently of the others. In our representation of lexicon entries, we leave out the braces if there is only one η.

3.2 Data Structures and Operations

A parse (also known as a derivation) consists of a number of steps. Each step is of the form:

$$\Phi \mid \Psi$$

Ψ is the queue of incoming words. It is used to simulate the speaker of a sentence. The removal of words is restricted to the left end of the queue. A word is shifted onto the right end of Φ, given conditions described below. Shifting is equivalent to "hearing" or "reading" the next word of a sentence. Φ is a list, the processing buffer. It is a list of trees whereon the parser's operations are performed. The initial state of a parse has an empty Φ, and the final successful state has an empty Ψ and a single tree in Φ without any unchecked features. A parse fails when Ψ is empty, Φ has multiple trees or unchecked feature bundles, and no operations are possible.

Tree nodes are like lexicon entries, maybe with some features checked. The form is $[\alpha\ \Gamma]$ if it is the node with word α closest to the root, or α if it is a lower node. A single node is also a tree.

At each step, the parser can perform one of three operations: MOVE a node on a tree to a higher position on the same tree, MERGE two adjacent trees, or shift a word from the input queue to the processing buffer in the form of a node with the corresponding features from the lexicon.

MERGE and MOVE are well known in the minimalist literature, but for parsing we present them a little differently. Their operation is illustrated in the subsequent examples. In this parser, MERGE finds the first[2] two compatible trees from the processing buffer with roots α and β, and replaces them with a tree with either α or β as the root and the original trees as subtrees. MOVE finds a position α in a tree (including the possible future sister of the root node) that commands[3] a compatible subtree; the subtree is replaced by a trace at its original position and merged with the item at its new position. Adjunct movement and specifier movement are possible. Our examples only show adjunct movement. MOVE acts on the first tree for which this condition exists.

There are locality conditions for MERGE and MOVE. For MERGE, the trees must be adjacent in the processing buffer. For MOVE, the targeted tree positions must be the ones as close as possible to the root.

Compatibility is determined by feature checking. It relies on unification and unifiability tests. Sometimes checking succeeds without changing the checking status of its participants, because further checking may be required. These aspects of checking are also described in the examples.

At every step, MOVE is always considered before MERGE. This is to minimize the number of feature-compatible pairs of movement candidates within the trees in the processing buffer. If no movement is available in any tree, the parser looks for adjacent candidates to MERGE, starting from left to right. If neither MERGE nor MOVE is possible, a new word is shifted from the input queue.

3.3 Examples of Parsing

Here is the initial lexicon:

```
pater: unch(case:Nom, num:Sg, gnd:Masc)
filium: unch(case:Acc, num:Sg, gnd:Masc)
amat: {UNCH(case:Nom, num:Sg), UNCH(case:Acc)}
laetus: unch+(case:Nom, num:Sg, gnd:Masc)
laetum: unch+(case:Acc, num:Sg, gnd:Masc)
```

Inflection in Latin is often ambiguous. More entries for *laetum* would exist in a realistic lexicon. As disambiguation is not in the scope of this paper, we assume that the only entries in the lexicon are those useful for our examples.

Example #1: *pater laetus filium amat laetum.* This example illustrates the basic machinery of the parser, but it also demonstrates how the parser handles the discontinuous constituency of phrases, in this case noun phrases. *filium laetum* ("the happy son") is split across the verb. We begin with an empty processing buffer:

[2] We scan from the left. Since the trees closer to the left end of Φ tend to have their features already checked, processing usually affects recently shifted items more.

[3] Node ξ *commands* node ζ if ξ's sister dominates ζ.

```
| pater laetus filium amat laetum
```

pater and *laetus* are shifted into the buffer one by one. They are "heard"; the lexicon is consulted and the relevant features are attached to them. (For the sake of brevity, we will combine multiple steps, particularly when a word is heard and some MERGE happens immediately as a result.)

```
[pater unch(case:Nom, num:Sg, gnd:Masc)]
[laetus unch+(case:Nom, num:Sg, gnd:Masc)]
| filium amat laetum
```

laetus adjoins to *pater*. There is no unifiability conflict between the features of both words. If a conflict had occurred, there would be no MERGE. The lack of conflict here indicates that the adjunction is valid. Thus, the feature on the adjective is marked as checked. Since adjunction is optional, and further adjunctions are theoretically possible, the feature on the noun is not checked yet.

```
([pater unch(case:Nom, num:Sg, gnd:Masc)]
    pater
    [laetus ch+(case:Nom, num:Sg, gnd:Masc)])
| filium amat laetum
```

We shift *filium* into the buffer. *filium* cannot be absorbed by the *pater* tree. So we shift *amat*. Their nodes look as follows:

```
[filium unch(case:Acc, num:Sg, gnd:Masc)]
[amat {UNCH(case:Nom, num:Sg), UNCH(case:Acc)}]
```

Can anything be merged? Yes, *filium* checks a feature bundle on *amat* that was the one looking for another compatible bundle in order to project to the root of the new tree. When *filium*'s feature bundle checks with the corresponding bundle on *amat*, several things occur:

1. *amat*'s feature bundle's status changes from `UNCH` to `CH`, and *filium*'s bundle's status changes from `unch` to `ch`.
2. *amat* projects: a new tree is formed with *amat* and its features at the root. This is specified in the feature bundle: the capitalized form indicates that *amat* is looking for a constituent to fill one of its semantic roles.
3. *amat*'s feature bundle is unified with that of *filium* and replaced with the unification result; in other words, it acquires *filium*'s gender. *filium* does not gain any features, as its bundle is not replaced with the unification result. Only the projecting item *amat* is altered, as it now dominates a tree containing *filium* as a constituent. The non-projecting item becomes a subtree, inaccessible for MERGE at the root and thus not needing to reflect anything about *amat*.

Table 1 describes the interactions between feature bundle checking status types. In all four cases, only the item containing bundle 2 projects and forms the root of the new tree. A unifiability test occurs in each checking operation, but replacement with the unification result happens only in the feature checked on the projecting item (bundle 2) in the first case. No combinations other than these are valid for checking. The relation only allows us to check `unch` with `UNCH` feature bundles, since `UNCH` bundles indicate that their bearers project; there must be exactly one projecting object in any MERGE or MOVE. `unch+` check with `CH` feature bundles, because their `CH` (and feature-compatible) status will have resulted from a merge with an item that can accept the adjunct in question. `unch+` check with any compatible `unch` or `ch` feature bundles, as this indicates that the target of adjunction has been reached. We consider this analysis of checking relations to be exhaustive, but we save the rigorous elimination of other combinations for future work.

Table 1. Checking status interactions

Bundle 1	**Bundle 2**	after checking:	**Bundle 1**	**Bundle 2**	**Replace bundle 2 with unif. result?**
unch	UNCH		ch	CH	Y
unch+	CH		unch+	CH	N
unch+	unch		ch+	unch	N
unch+	ch		ch+	ch	N

Here is the result of the MERGE of *filium* and *amat* (to save space, we omit the *pater* tree):

```
([amat {UNCH(case:Nom, num:Sg),
            CH(case:Acc, num:Sg, gnd:Masc)}]
     [filium ch(case:Acc, num:Sg, gnd:Masc)]
     amat)
| laetum
```

MERGE occurs at the roots of trees. It treats each tree as an encapsulated object and does not *search* for places within trees to put objects. In more complicated sentences, searching would require more involved criteria to determine whether a particular attachment is valid. For the sake of minimality, we have developed a process that does not require such criteria, but only local interaction at a surface level. In doing so, we preserve our locality requirements.

The only attachments to trees that are valid are those that are advertised at the root. MOVE within trees takes care of remaining checkable features given criteria of minimality described above.

Now, *pater* is adjacent to *amat* and can thus MERGE with it, checking the appropriate bundle.

```
([amat {CH(case:Nom, num:Sg, gnd:Masc),
            CH(case:Acc, num:Sg, gnd:Masc)}]
     ([pater ch(case:Nom, num:Sg, gnd:Masc)]
          pater
          [laetus ch+(case:Nom, num:Sg, gnd:Masc)])
     (amat
          [filium ch(case:Acc, num:Sg, gnd:Masc)]
          amat)  )
| laetum
```

In the processing buffer, no more features can be checked. The system needs to process *laetum*. It moves in and presents a problem:

```
[laetum unch+(case:Acc, num:Sg, gnd:Masc)] |
```

To what can *laetum* attach? We have defined the merge operation so that it cannot search inside a tree—it must operate on objects in the buffer. Fortunately, the rules we have defined allow an item with an adjunct feature bundle to be merged with another item with a `ch` projecting feature bundle if both bundles can be correctly unified. The adjunct feature remains `unch` until movement causes a non-projecting non-adjunct feature to be checked with it.

```
([amat {CH(case:Nom, num:Sg, gnd:Masc),
           CH(case:Acc, num:Sg, gnd:Masc)}]
     (amat
          ([pater ch(case:Nom, num:Sg, gnd:Masc)]
               pater
               [laetus ch+(case:Nom, num:Sg, gnd:Masc)])
          (amat
               [filium ch(case:Acc, num:Sg, gnd:Masc)]
               amat)  )
     [laetum unch+(case:Acc, num:Sg, gnd:Masc)]) |
```

The rules for movement seek out the highest two positions on the tree that can be checked with one another. *filium* and *laetum* are precisely that. *filium* is copied, checked, and merged with *laetum*. For the sake of convention, we mark the original position of *filium* with a trace (<*filium*>).

```
([amat {CH(case:Nom, num:Sg, gnd:Masc),
           CH(case:Acc, num:Sg, gnd:Masc)}]
     (amat
          ([pater ch(case:Nom, num:Sg, gnd:Masc)]
               pater
               [laetus ch+(case:Nom, num:Sg, gnd:Masc)])
          (amat
               <filium>
               amat)  )
     ([filium ch(case:Acc, num:Sg, gnd:Masc)]
          filium
          [laetum ch+(case:Acc, num:Sg, gnd:Masc)])  ) |
```

filium dominates because *laetum* is only an adjunct. All features are now checked, and the parse is complete.

Example #2: *pater laetus a filio laeto amatur.* This sentence is in the passive voice, included to demonstrate the need for feature paths. Passives in Latin are very similar to passives in English. *a filio laeto* is similar to an agent *by*-phrase. This requires new lexicon entries for all the words except for *pater* and *laetus.* The additional entries:

```
a: UNCH(case:Abl):right --> unch(by:0)
filio: unch(case:Abl, num:Sg, gnd:Masc)
laeto: unch+(case:Abl, num:Sg, gnd:Masc)
amatur: {UNCH(case:Nom, num:Sg, gnd:Masc), UNCH(by:0)}
```

The *by*-feature is similar to Niyogi's [2] solution for *by*-phrases in English. 0 is there as a place-holder, since the *by*-feature does not have multiple values; it is either present or absent. We also use 0 to indicate that the feature *must* be present in order for the feature bundle to be unifiable with a corresponding `UNCH` feature bundle. *a* is a preposition in Latin with other uses (like *by* in English); making it necessarily attach to a verb as the deliverer of an agent requires a special feature.

The *by*-feature is the second element along a feature path. Before *a* can be merged with a verb, it must first be merged with a complement in the ablative case. This complement is directionally specified (to the right of *a*).

Let us begin:

```
| pater laetus a filio laeto amatur
```

pater and *laetus* are each shifted to the processing buffer. They adjoin:

```
([pater unch(case:Nom, num:Sg, gnd:Masc)]
      pater
      [laetus ch+(case:Nom, num:Sg, gnd:Masc)])
| a filio laeto amatur
```

a and *filio* enter; *filio* is a noun in the ablative case and can be checked against *a*. (We will henceforth omit the *pater* tree until it becomes necessary.)

```
([a CH(case:Abl, num:Sg, gnd:Masc):right --> unch(by:0)]
      a
      [filio ch(case:Abl, num:Sg, gnd:Masc)])
| laeto amatur
```

filio checks the case feature on *a* immediately. There will be an adjective that needs to adjoin to *filio*, but it has not yet been heard; meanwhile, the system has a preposition and a noun immediately ready to work with. The mechanism of unification allows *a* to advertise the requirements of *filio* for future adjunction. There is no reason for the system to wait for an adjective, as it obviously cannot know about it until it has been heard. The noun does not need an adjective and only permits one if one is available.

As before, *laeto* is absorbed and attached to *a*.

```
([a CH(case:Abl, num:Sg, gnd:Masc):right --> unch(by:0)]
      (a
            a
            [filio ch(case:Abl, num:Sg, gnd:Masc)])
      [laeto unch+(case:Abl, num:Sg, gnd:Masc)])
| amatur
```

This adjunction occurs because unification and replacement have caused *a* to carry the advertisement for a `Sg`, `Masc` adjunct in its now-`CH` feature that previously only specified ablative case.

MOVE connects *filio* and *laeto*, leaving <*filio*>:

```
([a CH(case:Abl, num:Sg, gnd:Masc):right --> unch(by:0)]
      (a
            a
            <filio>)
      ([filio ch(case:Abl, gnd:Masc, num:Sg)]
            filio
            [laeto ch+(case:Abl, num:Sg, gnd:Masc)])  )
| amatur
```

The buffer now contains two trees (remember the *pater* tree). Neither of their roots have any features that can be checked against one another. *amatur* is heard:

```
[amatur {UNCH(case:Nom, num:Sg, gnd:Masc), UNCH(by:0)}] |
```

The case feature was checked on *a*, so the *by*-feature is available for checking with the verb. Recall that a MERGE in the processing buffer only occurs between adjacent elements. In the next step *amatur* can only merge with *a*.

```
([amatur {UNCH(case:Nom, num:Sg, gnd:Masc),
          CH(by:0, case:Abl, num:Sg, gnd:Masc)}]
    ([a CH(case:Abl, num:Sg, gnd:Masc):right --> ch(by:0)]
        (a
            a
            <filio>)
        ([filio ch(case:Abl, gnd:Masc, num:Sg)]
            filio
            [laeto ch+(case:Abl, num:Sg, gnd:Masc)]) )
    amatur) |
```

The *by*-feature on *amatur* has been unified with all the features on the feature path of *a*, required in case the order had been *pater laetus amatur a filio laeto*. In that situation, *a filio* would have been merged with *amatur* before *laeto* would be heard, since *laeto* is an adjunct. This mechanism ensures that permission for the attachment of an adjunct to *filio* is exposed at the root of the tree dominated by *amatur*. Here it is not an issue, but the operator covers this possibility.

Merging with *pater* (which we now reintroduce) is the next and final step:

```
([amatur {UNCH(case:Nom, num:Sg, gnd:Masc),
         CH(by:0, case:Abl, num:Sg, gnd:Masc)}]
    ([pater unch(case:Nom, num:Sg, gnd:Masc)]
        pater
        [laetus ch+(case:Nom, num:Sg, gnd:Masc)])
    (amatur
        ([a CH(case:Abl, num:Sg, gnd:Masc):right --> ch(by:0)]
            (a
                a
                <filio>)
            ([filio ch(case:Abl, gnd:Masc, num:Sg)]
                filio
                [laeto ch+(case:Abl, num:Sg, gnd:Masc)]) )
        amatur) ) |
```

4 Conclusions and Future Work

Through examples, we have presented an algorithm and formal framework for the parsing of free word order languages given certain limitations: highly constrained operations with strong locality conditions (MOVE and MERGE), no attempts at simulating nondeterminism (such as lookahead), and a limitation on the availability of the words in the sentence over time (the input queue simulates a listener processing a sentence as words arrive). Under these limitations, we demonstrated the algorithm for a sentence with a discontinuous noun phrase and one in the passive voice.

The precedence of operations serves to connect shifted items semantically as soon as possible, though we do not fix the semantic representation; whenever

MERGE and MOVE are performed, we assume that a more complete semantic representation of the sentence is achieved. We will seek compositional semantic formalisms that can handle the flexibility of our syntactic formalism.

The algorithm favours MOVE to ensure that all features in the current set of trees in the processing buffer are exhausted. This precludes multiple pairs of compatible subtrees, since that can only happen when MERGE joins a new item to a tree without exhausting the available movement candidates.

This has the effect of creating a "shortest move condition," which [5] enforces by only allowing one instance of a pair of compatible features in a tree. Multiple compatible pairs can only arise when a movement frees a feature set along a feature path, and the feature bundles in the feature set are each compatible with different commanded subtrees. The highest commanded subtree moves first, since it is the first found in a search from the tree root. This exception is required by the mechanisms we use to handle free word order languages, which Stabler does not consider. We conjecture that this may only appear in practice if there are actual adjunct attachment ambiguities.

The locality of MERGE (adjacent items only) precludes search for every possible pair of movement candidates on the list. MERGE's precedence over shifting and locality together have the effect of forcing MERGE of the most recently shifted items first, since they bring in new unchecked features. (This fits the intuition that semantic connections are the easiest among the most recently heard items). Shifting last prevents occurrences of multiple compatible candidates for merging.

We will thoroughly demonstrate these claims in forthcoming work; here, we trust the reader's intuition that the definitions of these operations do prevent most ambiguous syntactic states, barring those caused by attachment or lexical ambiguities with semantic effect.

Feature paths are used to force checking certain feature bundles in certain orders, usually so that a word's complements can be found before it is absorbed into a tree. Feature sets allow the opposite; free word order languages let most features be checked in any order. Unification and unifiability tests provide sufficient flexibility for split phrases by allowing dominating nodes to advertise outstanding requirements of their descendants.

A less general version of this parsing algorithm, written in Prolog and designed specifically for these example sentences, showed that 90 of the 120 permutations of *pater laetus amat filium laetum* can be parsed. *filium laetus laetum amat pater* typifies the remaining 30, in that the adjective *laetum* cannot be absorbed by *amat*, since *amat* has not yet merged with *filium*; the 30 all have similar situations caused by the adjacency condition we impose on merging. These sentences are a subset of those exhibiting discontinuous constituency.

In a further experiment, we allowed implied subjects (for example, omitting *pater* is grammatical in Latin in example #1). This reduced the number of unparsable sentences to 16. *pater* was still in all the sentences, but in the 14 that became parsable, *laetus* and *pater* were originally obstructed from merging. We lifted the obstruction by allowing *laetus* to merge with *amat* first. Without implied subjects, *laetus* acted as an obstacle in the same way as *laetum*; it ceased to be an obstacle after we introduced implied subjects.

Though we are able to parse most of the sentences in this constrained environment (and thus most examples of discontinuous constituency), we are working on determining how to minimally weaken the contraints or complexify the algorithm in order to handle the remaining 16 orders. But before deciding how to modify the system, we need to determine how many of these orders are actually valid in real Latin, and thus whether modifications to the system are really justified. We have embarked on a corpus study to determine whether these orders were actually plausible in classical Latin; a corpus study is necessitated by the lack of native speakers. We work with material generously provided by the Perseus Project (`http://www.perseus.tufts.edu/`).

This paper discusses the parser as an algorithm. In our pilot implementation, we simulated the checking relations between the Latin words that we used to experiment with the algorithm. We are now implementing the full parser in SWI Prolog using Michael Covington's GULP package to provide the unification logic. We will also seek a way to convert existing comprehensive lexica into a form usable by our parser, both for Latin and for other languages.

Work in minimalist generation and parsing has, thus far, mostly stayed within the limits of theoretical linguistics. A parser with the properties that we propose would help broaden the scope of the study of minimalist parsing to more realistic, complex linguistic phenomena. It could take this parsing philosophy toward practical applications. An example is speech analysis, where it would be advantageous to have a parsing algorithm that recognizes the need to make syntactic, and thus semantic, links as soon as a word enters the system.

References

1. Michael B. Kashket. Parsing Warlpiri—a free word order challenge. In Robert C. Berwick, Steven P. Abney, and Carol Tenny, editors, *Principle-Based Parsing: Computation and Psycholinguistics*. Kluwer, Dordrecht, 1991.
2. Sourabh Niyogi. A minimalist interpetation of verb subcategorization. International Workshop on Parsing Technologies (IWPT-2001), 2001.
3. Harm Pinkster. *Latin Syntax and Semantics*. Routeledge, New York, 1990. Translated by Hotze Mulder.
4. Edward P. Stabler. Derivational minimalism. In C. Rétoré, editor, *Logical Aspects of Computational Linguistics*, volume 1328 of *Lecture Notes in Artificial Intelligence*. Springer-Verlag, 1997.
5. Edward P. Stabler. Minimalist grammars and recognition. In Christian Rohrer, Antje Roßdeutscher, and Hans Kamp, editors, *Linguistic Form and its Computation*. CSLI Publications, Stanford, 2001.
6. Juan Uriagereka. *Rhyme and Reason: An Introduction to Minimalist Syntax*. MIT Press, Cambridge, Mass., 1998.

Developing Competitive HMM PoS Taggers Using Small Training Corpora*

Muntsa Padró and Lluís Padró

TALP Research Center
Universitat Politècnica de Catalunya
{mpadro,padro}@lsi.upc.es

Abstract. This paper presents a study aiming to find out the best strategy to develop a fast and accurate HMM tagger when only a limited amount of training material is available. This is a crucial factor when dealing with languages for which small annotated material is not easily available.

First, we develop some experiments in English, using WSJ corpus as a test-bench to establish the differences caused by the use of large or a small train set. Then, we port the results to develop an accurate Spanish PoS tagger using a limited amount of training data.

Different configurations of a HMM tagger are studied. Namely, trigram and 4-gram models are tested, as well as different smoothing techniques. The performance of each configuration depending on the size of the training corpus is tested in order to determine the most appropriate setting to develop HMM PoS taggers for languages with reduced amount of corpus available.

1 Introduction

PoS Tagging is a need for most of Natural Language applications such as Sumarization, Machine Translation, Dialogue systems, etc. and the basis of many higher level NLP processing tasks. It is also used to obtain annotated corpora combining automatic tagging with human supervision. These corpora may be used for linguistic research, to build better taggers, or as statistical evidence for many other language-processing related goals.

PoS tagging has been largely studied and many systems developed. There are some statistical implementations [5, 6, 11, 13, 12, 1] and some knowledge-based taggers (finite-state, rule-based, memory based) [8, 2, 7]. There are also some systems that combine different implementations with a voting procedure.

This work presents a thorough study aiming to establish which is the most appropiate way to train a HMM PoS tagger when dealing with languages with a limited amount of training corpora. To do so, we compare different smoothing techniques and different order HMMs.

Experiments are performed to determine the performance of the best configuration when the tagger is trained with a large English corpus (1 million words from WSJ),

* This research has been partially supported by the European Comission (Meaning, IST-2001-34460) and by the Catalan Government Research Department (DURSI).

J. L. Vicedo et al. (Eds.): EsTAL 2004, LNAI 3230, pp. 127–136, 2004.

and comparing the results with those for a training corpus ten times smaller. Then, the experiments for the small train corpus are repeated in another language (Spanish), validating the conclusions. The tested HMM configurations vary on the order of the model (3 and 4 order HMMs are tested) and in the smoothing technique (Lidstone's law *vs.* Linear Interpolation) used to estimate model parameters.

Section 2 presents the theoretical basis of a HMM and the different smoothing techniques used in this work. Section 3 shows the realized experiments and the obtained results. Section 4 states some conclusions and further work.

2 Hidden Markov Models

We will be using Hidden Markov Models Part-of-Speech taggers of order three and four. Depending on the order of the model, the states represent pairs or triples of tags, and obviously, the number of parameters to estimate varies largely. As the states are pairs or triples of tags, the possible number of states are the possible combinations of all the tags in groups of two or three. Table 1 shows the number of tags for each language and the consequent number of potential states. This number is very large but there are many states that will never be observed. The emmited symbols are words, which we estimated to be about 100,000 for English and 1,000,000 for Spanish.

Table 1. Number of potential tags and states for English and Spanish with both models

	English	Spanish
Number of tags	47	67
Number of potential states in a 3-gram HMM	2,209	4,489
Number of potential states in a 4-gram HMM	103,823	300,763

The parameters of such models are initial state probabilities, state transition probabilities and emission probabilities. That is:

$$\pi_i = P(q_1 = s_i)$$

is the probability that a sequence starts at state s_i,

$$a_{ij} = P(q_{t+1} = s_j | q_t = s_i)$$

is the transition probability from state i to state j (i.e. trigram probability $P(t_3|t_1t_2)$ in a 3rd order model, or 4-gram probability $P(t_4|t_1t_2t_3)$ in a 4-gram HMM), and

$$b_i(k) = P(w_k|s_i)$$

is the emission probability of the symbol w_k from state s_i.

In the PoS task model, the emitted symbols are the observed words and the observed sequence is a complete sentence. Given a sentence, we want to choose the most likely sequence of states (i.e. PoS tags) that generated it. This is computed using the Viterbi algorithm [14].

2.1 Parameter Estimation

The simplest way to estimate the HMM parameters is Maximum Likelihood Estimation (MLE), which consists in computing observation relative frequencies:

$$P_{MLE}(x) = \frac{count(x)}{N}$$

$$P_{MLE}(x|y) = \frac{count(x,y)}{count(x)}$$

For the case of the HMM we have to compute this probability estimation for each initial state, transition or emission in the training data:

$$\pi_i = \frac{count(s_i(t=0))}{count(sentences)}$$

$$a_{ij} = \frac{count(s_i \to s_j)}{count(s_i)}$$

$$b_i(k) = \frac{count(s_i, w_k)}{count(s_i)}$$

where $count(s_i(t=0))$ is the number of times that s_i is visited as an initial state, $count(sentences)$ is the number of sentences, $count(s_i \to s_j)$ is the count of the transitions from state s_i to s_j, $count(s_i)$ is the number of visits to state s_i and $count(s_i, w_k)$ is the number of times that symbol w_k is emmited from state s_i.

Actually, computing $b_i(k)$ in this way is quite difficult because the number of occurrences of a single word will be too small to provide enough statistical evidence, so Bayes rule is used to compute $b_i(k)$ as:

$$b_i(k) = P(w_k|s_i) = \frac{P(s_i|w_k)P(w_k)}{P(s_i)}$$

where:

$$P(s_i) = \frac{count(s_i)}{count(words)}; \quad P(w_k) = \frac{count(w_k)}{count(words)}$$

being $count(words)$ the number of words in the training corpus.

Since $P(s_i|w_k)$ would also require lots of data to be properly estimated, we approximate it as $P(t|w_k)$, where t is the last tag in the n-gram corresponding to the state. Similarly, $P(s_i)$ is approximated as $P(t)$.

2.2 Smoothing

MLE is usually a bad estimator for NLP purposes, since data tends to be sparse[1]. This leads to zero probabilities being assigned to unseen events, causing troubles when multiplying probabilities.

[1] Following Zipf's law: a word's frequency is inversely proportional to its rank order.

To solve this sparseness problem it is necessary to look for estimators that assign a part of the probability mass to the unseen events. To do so, there are many different smoothing techniques, all of them consisting of decreasing the probability assigned to the seen events and distributing the remaining mass among the unseen events. In this work two smoothing methods are compared: Lidstone's law and Linear Interpolation.

Laplace and Lidstone's Law. The oldest smoothing technique is Laplace's law [9], that consists in adding one to all the observations. That means that all the unseen events will have their probability computed as if they had appeared once in the training data. Since one observation for each event (seen or unseen) is added, the number of different possible observations (B) has to be added to the number of real observations (N), in order to maintain the probability normalised.

$$P_{La}(x) = \frac{count(x+1)}{N+B}$$

However, if the space is large and very sparse –and thus the number of possible events (B) may be similar to (or even larger than) the number of observed events– Laplace's law gives them too much probability mass.

A possible alternative is Lidstone's law (see [10] for a detailed explanation on these and other smoothing techniques) which generalises Laplace's and allows to add an arbitrary value to unseen events. So, for a relatively large number of unseen events, we can choose to add values lower than 1. For a relatively small number of unseen events, we may choose 1, or even larger values, if we have a large number of observations (N).

$$P_{Ld}(x) = \frac{count(x)+\lambda}{N+B\lambda} \qquad \lambda > 0$$

To use Laplace's or Lidstone's laws in a HMM-based tagger we have to smooth all probabilities involved in the model:

$$\pi_i = \frac{count(s_i(t=0)) + \lambda_\pi}{count(sentences) + B_{tag}\lambda_\pi}$$

$$a_{ij} = \frac{count(s_i \to s_j) + \lambda_A}{count(s_i) + B_{tag}\lambda_A}$$

$$P(s_i) = \frac{count(s_i) + \lambda_s}{count(words) + B_{tag}\lambda_s}$$

$$P(w_k) = \frac{count(w_k) + \lambda_w}{count(words) + B_w\lambda_w}$$

where B_{tag} is the number of possible tags and B_w is the number of words in the vocabulary (obviously, we can only approximate this quantity).

Since there are different counts involved in each probability, we have to consider different λ values for each formula. In the case of Laplace's law, all λ are set to 1, but when using Lidstone's, we want to determine which is the best set of λ, and how they vary depending on the train set size, as discussed in section 3.1.

Linear Interpolation. A more sophisticated smoothing technique consists of linearly combine the estimations for different order n-grams:

$$P_{li}(t_3|t_1t_2) = c_1P(t_3) + c_2P(t_3|t_2) + c_3P(t_3|t_1t_2)$$
$$P_{li}(t_4|t_1t_2t_3) = c_1P(t_4) + c_2P(t_4|t_3) + c_3P(t_4|t_2t_3) + c_4P(t_4|t_1t_2t_3)$$

where $\sum_i c_i = 1$ to normalise the probability. Although the values for c_i can be determined in many different ways, in this work they are estimated by deleted interpolation as described in [1]. This technique assumes that the c_i values don't depend on the particular n-gram and computes the weights depending on the counts for each i-gram involved in the interpolation.

3 Experiments and Results

The main purpose of this work is to study the behaviour of different configurations for a HMM-based PoS tagger, in order to determine the best choice to develop taggers for languages with scarce annotated corpora available.

First, we will explore different configurations when a large amount of training corpus is available. The experiments will be performed on English, using 1.1 million words from the Wall Street Journal corpus. Then, the same configurations will be explored when the training set is reduced to 100,000 words.

Later, the behaviour on the reduced train set will be validated on a manually developed 100,000 word corpus for Spanish [4].

The tested configurations vary on the order of the used HMM (trigram or 4-gram), and on the smoothing applied (Lidstone's law or Linear Interpolation).

All the experiments are done using ten fold cross-validation. In each fold, 90% of the corpus is used to train the tagger and the rest to test it.

In the following sections, we present the behaviour of the different HMM configurations for English, both with a large and a small corpus. After, we repeat the tests using a small corpus for Spanish.

3.1 Applying Lidstone's Law

As it has been explained in section 1, when Lidstone's law is used in a HMM tagger, there are four λ values to consider. Changing these values significantly affects the precision of the system.

Thus, before comparing this smoothing technique with another, we have to select the set of λ that yields the best tagger performance. After performing some experiments, we observed that λ_A is the only parameter that significantly affects the behaviour of the system. Modifying the other three values didn't change the system precision in a significant way. So λ_π, λ_s, and λ_w were set to some values determined as follows:

- λ_π is the assigned count for unobserved initial states. Since initial states depend only on the tag of the first word in the sentence, and the tag set we are using is quite reduced (about 40 tags), we may consider that in a 1,000,000 word corpus, at least one sentence will start with each tag. So, we will count one occurrence for unseen

events (i.e. we are using $\lambda_\pi = 1$, Laplace's law, for this case). When the corpus is ten times smaller, we will use a proportional rate of occurrence ($\lambda_\pi = 0.1$).
- λ_s is the count assigned to the unseen states. Since we approximate $P(s_i)$ by $P(t)$ (see section 2.1), the possible events are the number of tags in the tag set, and we can reason as above, assuming at least one occurrence of each tag in a 1,000,000 word corpus (again, Laplace's law, $\lambda_s = 1$), and a proportional value for the small corpus ($\lambda_s = 0.1$)
- λ_w is the count assigned to the unseen words. Obviously, enforcing that each possible word will appear at least once would take too many probability mass out of seen events (English vocabulary is about 100,000 forms, which would represent 10% of a 1 million word corpus), so we adopt a more conservative value: $\lambda_w = 0.1$ for the large corpus, and the proportional value $\lambda_w = 0.01$ for the small one.

After setting these three λ values, we have to select the best value for λ_A. To diminish the risk of getting local maxima, we will repeatedly use hill-climbing with different starting values and step lengths ($\Delta\lambda$), and choose the value that produces better results.

In table 2 the results of this hill-climbing algorithm using the whole English corpus (1 million of words) are presented. Table 3 show the same results for the 100.000 words English corpus.

Table 2. Precision obtained applying hill-climbing on the complete English corpus

		Trigram HMM			4-gram HMM		
Initial	$\Delta\lambda$	Initial	Final		Initial	Final	
λ_A		precision	precision	λ_A	precision	precision	λ_A
0.05	0.01	96.98	97.00	0.22	96.72	96.88	0.28
0.05	0.005	96.98	96.99	0.085	96.72	96.81	0.125
0.5	0.1	97.008	97.009	0.6	96.91	96.93	1.0
0.5	0.05	97.008	97.009	0.4	96.91	96.93	0.95
1.0	0.5	97.00	**97.01**	0.5	96.93	**96.94**	1.5
1.0	0.1	97.00	**97.01**	0.6	96.93	96.93	1.0

Table 3. Precision obtained applying hill-climbing on the reduced English corpus

		Trigram HMM			4-gram HMM		
Initial	$\Delta\lambda$	Initial	Final		Initial	Final	
λ_A		precision	precision	λ_A	precision	precision	λ_A
0.05	0.01	96.56	96.63	0.09	95.79	96.30	0.33
0.05	0.005	96.56	96.63	0.1	95.79	96.20	0.2
0.5	0.1	96.69	96.69	0.5	96.36	96.43	0.8
0.5	0.05	96.69	96.69	0.5	96.36	96.43	0.75
1.0	0.5	96.70	96.70	1.0	96.44	**96.51**	3.5
1.0	0.1	96.70	**96.71**	0.9	96.44	96.46	1.2

As it was expected, when using a small corpus the precision falls, specially when a 4-gram HMM is used, since the evidence to estimate the model is insufficient. This point is discussed in section 3.3.

These results show that the value selected for λ_A is an important factor when using this smoothing technique. As can be seen in table 3, the precision of the tagger varies up 0.7% depending on the value used for λ_A.

After performing the hill climbing search, we choose the λ_A that gives better results in each case, as the optimal parameter to use with this smoothing technique. So, for the whole corpus using a Trigram HMM, λ_A is set to 0.6 and the tagger yields a precision of 97.01%, while if we use a 4-gram HMM, $\lambda_A = 1.5$ leads to a precision of 96.94%. When the experiments are performed over the reduced corpus, the best results are obtained with $\lambda_A = 0.9$ for a trigram HMM (96.71%) and with $\lambda_A = 3.5$ for a 4-gram model (96.51%).

3.2 Applying Linear Interpolation

The performance of the taggers when using Linear Interpolation to smooth the probability estimations has been also tested. In this case, the coefficients c_i are found via the deleted interpolation algorithm (see section 2.2).

When using Linear Interpolation, the precision obtained by the system with the whole corpus is 97.00% with a trigram HMM, and 97.02% with a 4-gram HMM. For the reduced corpus the precision falls slightly and we obtain 96.84% for the trigram model and 96.71% for the 4-gram HMM.

The results obtained using Linear Interpolation and a trigram model should reproduce those reported by [1], where the maximum precision reached by the system on WSJ is 96.7%. In our case we obtain a higher precision because we are assuming the nonexistence of unknown words (i.e. the dictionary contains all possible tags for all words appearing in the test set. Obviously, word-tag frequency information from the test corpus is not used when computing $P(s_i|w_k)$).

3.3 Best Configuration for English

Best results obtained for each HMM tagger configuration are summarized in table 4. Results are given both for the large and small corpus.

Comparing the results for the two smoothing methods used with different order models, we can draw the following conclusions:

- In general, Linear Interpolation produces taggers with higher precision than using Lidstone's law.
- For the case of the large corpus, the results are not significantly different for any combination of n-gram order and smoothing technique. While for the reduced corpus it is clearly better to use a trigram model than a 4-gram HMM, and Linear Interpolation yields slightly better results.
- Using Linear Interpolation has the benefit that the involved coefficients are computed using the training data via deleted interpolation, while for Lidstone's law the precision is very dependent on the λ_A value, which has to be costly optimised (e.g. via hill-climbing).

Table 4. Obtained results for all HMM PoS tagger configurations using large and small sections of WSJ corpus

1,1 Mword English corpus

	Lidstone's law	Linear Interpolation
trigram	97.01%	97.00%
4-gram	96.94%	**97.02%**

100 Kword English corpus

	Lidstone's law	Linear Interpolation
trigram	96.71%	**96.84%**
4-gram	95.51%	96.71%

3.4 Behaviour in Spanish

The same experiments performed for English were performed with a Spanish corpus (CLiC-TALP Corpus[2]) which has about 100,000 words. This corpus is manually validated so, although it is small, it is more accurately tagged than WSJ.

In this case the tagger relies on FreeLing morphological analyser [3] instead of using a dictionary built from the corpus. Nevertheless, the situation is comparable to the English experiments above: Since the corpus and the morphological analyser have been hand-developed and cross-checked, they are mutually consistent, and so we don't have to care about unknown words in the test corpus.

Applying Lidstone's Law. In the same way than for the English corpus, a hill-climbing search is performed to study the influence of λ_A value in the precision of the system. The λ_π, λ_s and λ_w values are fixed to the same values used for the reduced WSJ.

Table 5. Precision obtained with the hill-climbing algorithm on the Spanish corpus

		Trigram HMM			4-gram HMM		
Initial	$\Delta\lambda$	Initial	Final		Initial	Final	
λ_A		precision	precision	λ_A	precision	precision	λ_A
0.05	0.01	96.54	96.68	0.18	95.49	96.00	0.35
0.05	0.005	96.54	96.58	0.065	95.49	95.82	0.15
0.5	0.1	96.79	96.80	0.5	96.06	96.16	1.6
0.5	0.05	96.79	96.81	0.55	96.06	96.14	1.05
1.0	0.5	96.80	**96.85**	1.5	96.14	**96.22**	2.5
1.0	0.1	96.80	96.84	1.1	96.14	96.16	1.6

Table 5 shows the results of these experiments. The best λ_A for the trigram HMM is $\lambda_A = 1.5$, yielding a precision of 96.85%. The best value for a 4-gram model is $\lambda_A = 2.5$, which produces a precision of 96.22%

[2] More information in `http://www.lsi.upc.es/~nlp/`

Applying Linear Interpolation. The coefficients for Linear Interpolation are computed for Spanish in the same way than for English (section 3.2). The precision of the obtained taggers is 96.90% for the trigram HMM and 96.73% for the 4-gram model.

Best Configuration for Spanish. Results for Spanish are –as it may be expected– similar to those obtained with the reduced English corpus. Again, working with a trigram HMM gives higher precision than working with a 4-gram one, for both smoothing techniques, and using Linear Interpolation gives a slightly better results than using Lidstone's law. Table 6 summarizes the obtained results for both smoothing methods.

Table 6. Obtained results for all HMM PoS tagger configurations using Spanish 100 Kwords corpus

100 Kword Spanish corpus

	Lidstone's law	Linear Interpolation
trigram	96.85%	**96.90%**
4-gram	96.22%	96.73%

Nevertheless, some important remarks can be extracted from these results:

- Competitive HMM taggers may be build using relatively small train sets, which is interesting for languages lacking large resources.
- The best results are obtained using trigram models and Linear Interpolation.
- Lidstone's law may be used as an alternative smoothing technique, but if λ_A is not tuned, results are likely to be significantly lower.

4 Conclusions and Further Work

We have studied how competitive HMM-based PoS taggers can be developed using relatively small training corpus.

Results point out that accurate taggers can be build provided the appropriate smoothing techniques are used. Between both techniques studied here, in general the one that gives a higher precision is Linear Interpolation but Lidstone's law can reach, in many cases, similar precision rates if a search is performed through the parameter space to find the most appropriate λ_A.

The model proposed in [1] (trigram tagger, Linear Interpolation smoothing) is not only the more suitable for big training corpus but also it gives the best results for limited amounts of training data.

The use of four-gram models may result in a slight increase in precision when using large corpus. Nevertheless, the gain is probably not worth the increase in complexity and size of the model.

Further work to be performed includes dealing with unknown words, and study their influence on the taggers developed on small corpus. Also, we plan to port the same experiments to other languages (namely, Catalan) to further validate the conclusions of this paper.

References

1. Brants, T.: Tnt - a statistical part- of-speech tagger. In: Proceedings of the 6th Conference on Applied Natural Language Processing, ANLP, ACL (2000)
2. Brill, E.: A Corpus–based Approach to Language Learning. PhD thesis, Department of Computer and Information Science, University of Pennsylvania (1993) http://www.cs.jhu.edu/~brill/acadpubs.html.
3. Carreras, X., Chao, I., Padró, L., Padró, M.: Freeling: An open-source suite of language analyzers. In: Proceedings of the 4th International Conference on Language Resources and Evaluation (LREC'04), Lisbon, Portugal (2004)
4. Civit, M.: Criterios de etiquetación y desambiguación morfosintáctica de corpus en español. PhD thesis, Linguistics Department, Universitat de Barcelona (2003)
5. Church, K.W.: A stochastic parts program and noun phrase parser for unrestricted text. In: Proceedings of the 1st Conference on Applied Natural Language Processing, ANLP, ACL (1988) 136–143
6. Cutting, D., Kupiec, J., Pedersen, J.O., Sibun, P.: A practical part–of–speech tagger. In: Proceedings of the 3rd Conference on Applied Natural Language Processing, ANLP, ACL (1992) 133–140
7. Daelemans, W., Zavrel, J., Berck, P., Gillis, S.: Mbt: A memory–based part–of–speech tagger generator. In: Proceedings of the 4th Workshop on Very Large Corpora, Copenhagen, Denmark (1996) 14–27
8. Karlsson, F.: Constraint grammar as a framework for parsing running text. In: Proceedings of 13th International Conference on Computational Linguistics, COLING, Helsinki, Finland (1990) 168–173
9. Laplace, P.S.m.: Philosophical Essay on Probabilities. Springer-Verlag (1995)
10. Manning, C.D., Schütze, H.: Foundations of Statistical Natural Language Processing. The MIT Press (1998)
11. Merialdo, B.: Tagging english text with a probabilistic model. Computational Linguistics **20** (1994) 155–171
12. Ratnaparkhi, A.: A maximum entropy part–of–speech tagger. In: Proceedings of the 1st Conference on Empirical Methods in Natural Language Processing, EMNLP. (1996)
13. Schmid, H.: Improvements in part–of–speech tagging with an application to german. In: Proceedings of the EACL SIGDAT Workshop, Dublin, Ireland (1995)
14. Viterbi, A.J.: Error bounds for convolutional codes and an asymptotically optimal decoding algorithm. IEEE Transactions on Information Theory (1967) 260–269

Exploring the Use of Target-Language Information to Train the Part-of-Speech Tagger of Machine Translation Systems*

Felipe Sánchez-Martínez, Juan Antonio Pérez-Ortiz, and Mikel L. Forcada

Departament de Llenguatges i Sistemes Informàtics
Universitat d'Alacant
E-03071 Alacant, Spain

Abstract. When automatically translating between related languages, one of the main sources of machine translation errors is the incorrect resolution of part-of-speech (PoS) ambiguities. Hidden Markov models (HMM) are the standard statistical approach to try to properly resolve such ambiguities. The usual training algorithms collect statistics from source-language texts in order to adjust the parameters of the HMM, but if the HMM is to be embedded in a machine translation system, target-language information may also prove valuable. We study how to use a target-language model (in addition to source-language texts) to improve the tagging and translation performance of a statistical PoS tagger of an otherwise rule-based, shallow-transfer machine translation engine, although other architectures may be considered as well. The method may also be used to customize the machine translation engine to a particular target language, text type, or subject, or to statistically "retune" it after introducing new transfer rules.

1 Introduction

One of the main sources of errors in machine translation (MT) systems between related languages is the incorrect resolution of part-of-speech (PoS) ambiguities. Hidden Markov models (HMMs) [9] are the standard statistical approach [3] to automatic PoS tagging. Typically the training of this kind of taggers has been carried out from source-language (SL) untagged corpora (see below) using the Baum-Welch algorithm [9].

But target-language (TL) texts may also be taken into account in order to improve the performance of these PoS taggers, specially as to the resulting translation quality, an aspect not faced by training algorithms which use information from SL only. We propose a training method for HMMs which considers the likelihood in the TL of the translation of each of the multiple disambiguations

* Work funded by the Spanish Government through grants TIC2003-08681-C02-01 and BES-2004-4711. We thank Rafael C. Carrasco for useful comments on this work. We also thank Geoffrey Sampson (University of Sussex, England) for his Simple Good-Turing implementation.

J. L. Vicedo et al. (Eds.): EsTAL 2004, LNAI 3230, pp. 137–148, 2004.

of a source text which can be produced depending on how its PoS ambiguity is resolved. To achieve this goal, these steps are followed: first, the SL text is segmented; then, the set of all possible disambiguations for each segment is generated; after that, each disambiguation is translated into TL; next, a TL statistical model is used to compute the likelihood of each translated disambiguation of the segment; and, finally, these likelihoods are used to adjust the parameters of the SL HMM: the higher the likelihood, the higher the probability of the original SL tag sequence in the model being trained. Rules for text segmentation must be carefully chosen so that the resulting segments are treated independently by the rest of the modules in the MT system.

One of the main obstacles to overcome is the presence of *free rides*, that is, an ambiguous SL word which is translated into the same TL word for every possible disambiguation; therefore, the ambiguity remains intact in the TL and no TL information can be used for disambiguation purposes. This is specially harmful in the case of related languages, where free rides are very common.

Most current MT systems follow the *indirect* or *transfer* approach [5, ch. 4]: SL text is analysed and converted into an intermediate representation which becomes the basis for generating the corresponding TL text. Analysis modules usually include a PoS tagger for the SL. Our method for training PoS taggers may be applied, in principle, to any variant of an indirect architecture which uses or may use a HMM-based PoS tagger. In particular, a MT system using a classical *morphological transfer* architecture will be considered in the experiments.

We will refer to a text as *unambiguously tagged* or just *tagged* when each occurrence of each word (ambiguous or not) has been assigned the correct PoS tag. An *ambiguously tagged text* or *untagged* text corpus is one in which all words are assigned (using a morphological analyser) the set of possible PoS tags independently of context; in this case, ambiguous and unknown words would receive more than one PoS tag (unknown words, that is, words not found in the lexicon, are usually assigned the set of *open* categories, that is, categories which are likely to grow by new words of the language: nouns, verbs, adjectives, adverbs and proper nouns). Words receiving the same set of PoS tags are said to belong to the same *ambiguity class* [3]; for example, the words *tailor* and *book* both belong to the ambiguity class {noun, verb}.

The paper is organized as follows. Section 2 presents the basics of HMM use in disambiguation tasks and discusses existing methods for PoS tagger training; section 3 describes our proposal for HMM training and the TL model used in this paper; section 4 introduces the translation engine and shows the main results of the experiments; finally, in sections 5 and 6 we discuss the results and outline future work to be done.

2 Part-of-Speech Tagging

When a HMM is used for lexical disambiguation purposes in the *ambiguity class mode* (in which each input word is replaced by its corresponding ambiguity class) each HMM state is made to correspond to a different PoS tag and the set of observable items consists of all possible ambiguity classes [3]. Building a PoS tagger based on HMMs for the SL in a MT system usually implies:

1. *Designing or adopting a reduced tagset* (set of PoS) which groups the finer tags delivered by the morphological analyser into a smaller set of coarse tags adequate to the translation task (for example, singular feminine nouns and plural feminine nouns may be grouped under a single "noun" tag). Additionally, the number of different lexical probabilities in the HMM is usually drastically reduced by grouping words in ambiguity classes.
2. *Estimating proper HMM parameters*, that is, finding adequate values of the parameters of the model. Existing methods may be grouped according to the kind of corpus they use as input: *supervised* methods require *unambiguously tagged texts* (see the introduction); *unsupervised* methods are able to extract information from *ambiguously tagged texts*, that is, from sequences of ambiguity classes.

   On the one hand, estimating parameters from an unambiguously tagged corpus is usually the best way to improve performance, but unambiguously tagged corpora are expensive to obtain and require costly human supervision. A supervised method counts the number of occurrences in the corpus of certain tag sequences (usually bigrams) and uses this information to determine the values of the parameters of the HMM. On the other hand, for the unsupervised approach no analytical method is known, and existing methods, such as the Baum-Welch algorithm [9], are only guaranteed to reach local (not global) maxima of the expectation.

   Some estimation methods, like those using statistics from unambiguously tagged corpus, may be used in isolation or as an initialization algorithm for further reestimation via the Baum-Welch method. In other cases, simple estimation methods are exclusively considered for initialization purposes. A good initialization can significantly improve the final performance of a Baum-Welch-trained PoS tagger, although it will not completely avoid the risk of convergence at local maxima.

   The new method presented in the following section requires only ambiguously tagged SL texts and raw TL texts (needed to compute a TL model); it may, in principle, be used as a complete training method by itself, although it may as well be considered for initialization purposes.

3 Target-Language-Based Training

This section gives mathematical details on how to train a SL HMM using information from the TL.

Let S be the whole SL corpus, s be a (possibly ambiguous) segment from S, g_i a sequence of tags resulting from one of the possible disambiguation choices in s, $\tau(g_i, s)$ the translation of g_i in the TL, and $p_{\text{TL}}(\tau(g_i, s))$ the likelihood of $\tau(g_i, s)$ in some TL model. We will call each g_i a *path* since it describes a unique state path in the HMM and write $g_i \in T(s)$ to show that g_i is a possible disambiguation of the words in s. Now, the likelihood of path g_i from segment s may be estimated as:

$$p(g_i|s) = \frac{p(g_i|\tau(g_i,s))\, p_{\mathrm{TL}}(\tau(g_i,s))}{\sum_{g_j \in T(s)} p(g_j|\tau(g_j,s))\, p_{\mathrm{TL}}(\tau(g_j,s))} \quad (1)$$

where the term $p(g_i|\tau(g_i,s))$ is the conditional probability of g_i given translation $\tau(g_i,s)$. That is, the likelihood of path g_i in source segment s is made proportional to the TL likelihood of its translation $\tau(g_i,s)$, but needs to be corrected by a weight $p(g_i|\tau(g_i,s))$, because more than one g_i may contribute to the same $\tau(g_i,s)$.

The fact that more than one path in segment s, say g_i and g_j, can produce the same translation in TL (that is, $\tau(g_i,s) = \tau(g_j,s)$ with $i \neq j$) does not imply that $p(g_i|\tau(g_i,s)) = p(g_j|\tau(g_j,s))$. Indeed, the real probabilities of paths are in principle unknown (note that their computation is the main goal of the training method). In the absence of such information, the contributions of each path will be approximated in this paper to be equally likely:

$$p(g_i|\tau(g_i,s)) = \frac{1}{\mathrm{card}\left(\{g_j \in T(s) : \tau(g_j,s) = \tau(g_i,s)\}\right)} \quad (2)$$

Now, we describe how to obtain the parameters of the HMM from the estimated likelihood of each path in each segment, $p(g_i|s)$, which will be treated as a fractional count. An estimate of tag pair occurrence frequency based on $p(g_i|s)$ is:

$$\tilde{n}(\gamma_i\gamma_j) \cong \sum_{s\in S} \sum_{g_i \in T(s)} C_{s,g_i}(\gamma_i,\gamma_j)\, p(g_i|s) \quad (3)$$

where $C_{s,g_i}(\gamma_i,\gamma_j)$ is the number of times tag γ_i is followed by tag γ_j in path g_i of segment s. Therefore, the HMM parameter $a_{\gamma_i\gamma_j}$ corresponding to the transition probability from the state associated with tag γ_i to the state associated with tag γ_j [9, 3] can be computed as follows:

$$a_{\gamma_i\gamma_j} = \frac{\tilde{n}(\gamma_i\gamma_j)}{\sum_{\gamma_k \in \Gamma} \tilde{n}(\gamma_i\gamma_k)} \quad (4)$$

where Γ is the tagset, that is, the set of all PoS tags.

In order to calculate emission probabilities, the number of times an ambiguity class is emitted by a given tag is approximated by means of:

$$\tilde{n}(\sigma,\gamma) \cong \sum_{s\in S} \sum_{g_i \in T(s)} C_{s,g_i}(\sigma,\gamma)\, p(g_i|s) \quad (5)$$

where $C_{s,g_i}(\sigma,\gamma)$ is the number of times ambiguity class σ is emitted by tag γ in path g_i of segment s. Therefore, the HMM parameter $b_{\gamma_i\sigma}$ corresponding to the emission probability of ambiguity class σ from the state associated with γ_i is computed as:

$$b_{\gamma_i\sigma} = \frac{\tilde{n}(\sigma,\gamma_i)}{\sum_{\sigma' : \gamma_i \in \sigma'} \tilde{n}(\sigma',\gamma_i)} \quad (6)$$

Source language	Target language	$p(g_i\|s)$
$s \equiv$ y la para si $\{\texttt{CNJ}\}$ $\left\{\begin{matrix}\texttt{ART}\\ \texttt{PRN}\end{matrix}\right\}$ $\left\{\begin{matrix}\texttt{VB}\\ \texttt{PR}\end{matrix}\right\}$ $\{\texttt{CNJ}\}$	$\tau(g_1, s) \equiv$ i la per a si $g_1 \equiv$ CNJ ART PR CNJ	0.0001
	$\tau(g_2, s) \equiv$ i la para si $g_2 \equiv$ CNJ ART VB CNJ	0.4999
	$\tau(g_3, s) \equiv$ i la per a si $g_3 \equiv$ CNJ PRN PR CNJ	0.0001
	$\tau(g_4, s) \equiv$ i la para si $g_4 \equiv$ CNJ PRN VB CNJ	0.4999

Fig. 1. Example of an ambiguous SL (Spanish) text segment, paths and translations (into Catalan) resulting from each possible disambiguation, and normalized estimated likelihood for each path translation. The second source-language word (*la*) is a free ride, as can be observed in the corresponding translation into target language

Notice that when training from unambiguously tagged texts the expressions used to compute transition and emission probabilities are analogous to previous equations, but in this case $p(g_i|s) = 1$ in (3) and (5) as only one path is possible in a tagged corpus segment; therefore, (3) and (5) would not be approximate anymore, but exact. Figure 1 shows an example of the application of the method.

SL text segmentation must be carefully designed so that two words which get joint treatment in some stage of processing of the MT system are not associated to different segments. This would result in incorrect sequences in TL (for example, if two words involved in a word reordering rule are assigned to different segments) and, as a consequence of that, in wrong likelihood estimations. In general, HMMs can be trained by breaking the corpus into segments whose first and last word are unambiguous, since unambiguous words reveal or *unhide* the hidden state of the HMM [3, sect. 3.4]. Adequate strategies for ensuring segment independence depend on the particular translation system (we will describe in section 4 the strategy used in our experiments).

3.1 Target-Language Model

A classical trigram model of TL surface forms (SF, lexical units as they appear in original texts) is considered for this paper, although it may be worth studying some other language models. The trigram model is obtained in an unsupervised manner from a 1 822 067-word TL corpus taken from Catalan newspapers.

In order to avoid unseen trigrams to give zero probability for every text segment containing them, probabilities are smoothed via a form of deleted interpolation [6]. The smoothed trigram probabilities consist of a linear combination of trigram, bigram and unigram probabilities, and the successive linear abstraction approximation [1] is used to compute the corresponding coefficients. Since in the case of unseen words the resulting smoothed trigram probability is still zero, unigram probabilities are smoothed as well using the Good-Turing method [4].

When evaluating path likelihoods, if text segmentation is correctly performed so that segments are independent (as already mentioned), a good estimate of

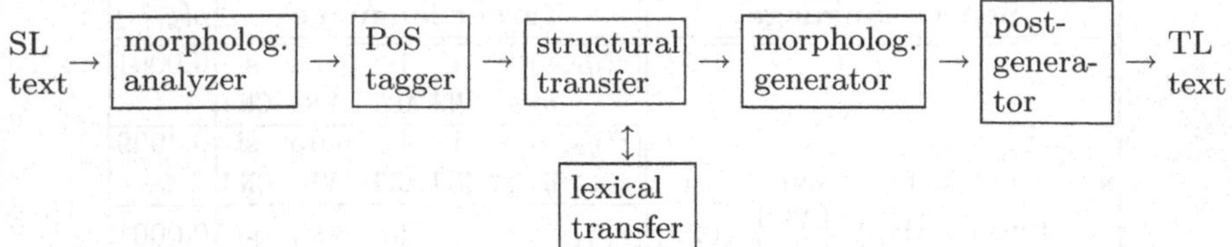

Fig. 2. Main modules of the transfer machine translation system (see section 4.1) used in the experiments

trigram probabilities for a given path can be performed considering all possible translations of the two words preceding the current segment and the two first words of the following one. This local approach can be safely used because a complete trigram likelihood evaluation for the whole corpus would multiply the likelihood by the same factor[1] for every possible path of the segment and, therefore, it would not affect the normalized likelihood estimated for each path of a segment in eq. (1).

Finally, notice that computing likelihoods as trigram probability products causes (as in most statistical MT approaches) shorter translations to receive higher scores than larger ones.

4 Experiments

4.1 Machine Translation Engine

Since our training algorithm assumes the existence of a MT system (most likely, the system in which the resulting PoS tagger will be embedded) in order to produce texts from which statistics about TL will be collected, we briefly introduce the system used in the experiments, although almost any other architecture (with a HMM-based PoS tagger) may also be suitable for the algorithm.

We used the publicly accessible Spanish–Catalan (two related languages) MT system interNOSTRUM [2], which basically follows the (morphological) transfer architecture shown in figure 2:

- A *morphological analyser* tokenizes the text in surface forms (SF) and delivers, for each SF, one or more lexical forms (LF) consisting of *lemma*, *lexical category* and morphological inflection information.
- A *PoS tagger* (categorial disambiguator) chooses, using a hidden Markov model (HMM), one of the LFs corresponding to an ambiguous SF.
- A *lexical transfer* module reads each SL LF and delivers the corresponding TL LF.

[1] This factor results from the contribution of trigrams which do not include words in the current segment.

- A *structural transfer* module (parallel to the lexical transfer) uses a finite-state chunker to detect patterns of LFs which need to be processed for word reordering, agreement, etc.
- A *morphological generator* delivers a TL SF for each TL LF, by suitably inflecting it.
- A *postgenerator* performs some orthographical operations such as contractions.

4.2 Text Segmentation

An adequate strategy for SL text segmentation is necessary. Besides the general rules mentioned in section 3, in our setup it must be ensured that all words in every pattern transformed by the structural transfer belong to the same segment.

The strategy followed in this paper is segmenting at nonambiguous words whose PoS tag is not present in any structural transfer rule or at nonambiguous words appearing in rules not applicable in the current context. In addition, an exception is being taken into account: no segmentation is performed at words which start a multiword unit that could be processed by the postgenerator (for example, *de* followed by *los*, which usually translates as *dels* in Catalan). Unknown words are also treated as segmentation points, since the *lexical transfer* has no bilingual information for them and no *structural transfer* rule is activated at all.

4.3 Results

We study both PoS tagging performance and translation performance after training the PoS tagger for Spanish. The Spanish corpus is divided into segments as described in 4.2. For each segment, all possible translations into TL (Catalan) according to every possible combination of disambiguations are considered. The likelihoods of these translations are computed through a Catalan trigram model and then normalized and transferred to the transition matrix and emission matrix of the HMM as described in section 3. The whole process is unsupervised: no unambiguously tagged text is needed.

The tagset used by the Spanish PoS disambiguator consists of 82 coarse tags (69 single-word and 13 multi-word tags for contractions, verbs with clitic pronouns, etc.) grouping the 1 917 fine tags (386 single-word and 1 531 multiword tags) generated by the morphological analyser. The number of observed ambiguity classes is 249. In addition, a few words such as *para* (preposition or verb), *que* (conjunction or relative), *como* (preposition, relative or verb) and *más/menos* (adverb or adjective) are assigned special hidden states, and consequently special ambiguity classes, in a similar manner to that described in [8].

For comparison purposes, a HMM-based PoS tagger was trained from ambiguously tagged SL corpora following a classical approach, that is, initializing the parameters of the HMM by means of Kupiec's method [7] and using the Baum-Welch algorithm to reestimate the model; a 1 000 000-word ambiguous corpus was used for training. The resulting PoS tagger was tested after each iteration and the one giving an error rate which did not improve in the subse-

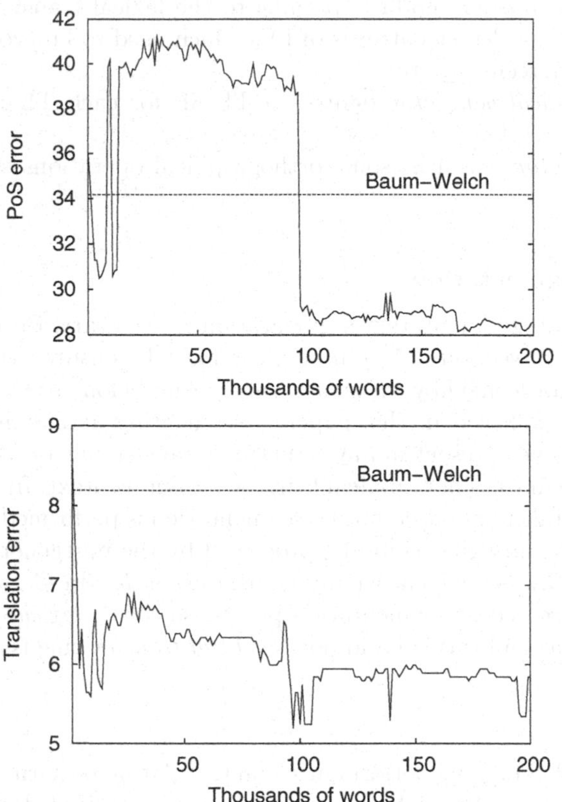

Fig. 3. PoS tagging error rate (top) and translation error rate (bottom). The Baum-Welch error rate after training with a 1 000 000-word corpus is given as well. PoS tagging error rate is expressed as the percentage of incorrect tags assigned to *ambiguous words* (including unknown words). Translation errors are expressed as the percentage of words that need to be post-edited due to mistaggings

quent 3 iterations was chosen for evaluation; proceeding in this way, we prevent the algorithm from stopping if a better PoS tagger can still be obtained. Moreover, another HMM was trained from an unambiguously tagged 20 000-word SL corpus and used as a reference of the best attainable results.

A set of disjoint SL corpora with 200 000 words each was considered for evaluating the proposed method and the resulting performance was recorded at every 1 000 words. Figure 3 shows the evolution of the PoS tagging error rate and the translation error rate for one representative corpus (the rest of the corpora behave in a similar way); Baum-Welch results are reported there as well. PoS tagging errors in figure 3 are expressed as the percentage of incorrect tags assigned to *ambiguous words* (including unknown words), not as the overall percentage of correct tags (over ambiguous and nonambiguous words); translation errors, however, do not consider unknown words and are expressed as the percentage of words that need to be corrected or inserted because of wrongly tagged words when post-editing the translation (in some cases, a wrongly tagged word implies correcting more than one TL word because of single words translating into multiword units or because of actions of the structural transfer or the postgenerator which would not have been performed if the word had been correctly tagged or vice versa).

The PoS tagging error is evaluated using an independent 8 031-word unambiguously tagged Spanish corpus. The percentage of ambiguous words (according to the lexicon) is 26.71% and the percentage of unknown words is 1.95%. For translation evaluation, an 8 035-word Spanish corpus and the corresponding human-corrected machine translation into Catalan are used.

The tagging error rate obtained with the PoS tagger trained from a *nonambiguous* corpus (obtained in a supervised manner) is 10.35% and the translation error rate is 2.60%; these figures can be used as a reference for the best possible results.

As can shown in figure 3, sudden oscillations causing the PoS tagging error to change around 10% occur in just one step. This behaviour is due to free rides (very common in the case of related languages like Spanish and Catalan): since free rides give the same translation regardless of disambiguation choices, the TL trigram model can not be used to distinguish among them and, consequently, paths involving free rides receive the same weight when estimating the parameters of the PoS tagger.

The most common free rides in Spanish-Catalan translation are the Spanish words *la*, *las* and *los* that belong to the same ambiguity class formed by article and proclitic pronoun. In the evaluation corpus these three words are 22.98% of the ambiguous words. Nevertheless, it may be argued that free rides should not affect the translation error rate; however, they do. This is because depending on the tag choice the *structural transfer* performs changes (gender agreement, for example) or the *postgenerator* performs contractions; in these cases, these words are not free rides, but the number of times they occur is not enough for the TL trigram model to capture their influence and make the system more stable. In the next subsection, a way of addressing this undesirable effect of free rides is explored.

4.4 Reducing the Impact of Free Rides

The problem of free rides may be partially solved if linguistic information is used to forbid some impossible tag bigrams so that paths containing *forbidden bigrams* are ignored. The previous experiments were repeated introducing this new approach and results are discussed here.

A HMM-based PoS tagger trained via the Baum-Welch algorithm is used again for comparison purposes, but using the information from forbidden bigrams as follows: forbidden bigrams are transferred into the HMM parameters by introducing zero values in the transition matrix after Kupiec's initialization but before training. The Baum-Welch algorithm naturally preserves these zeroes during the reestimation process.

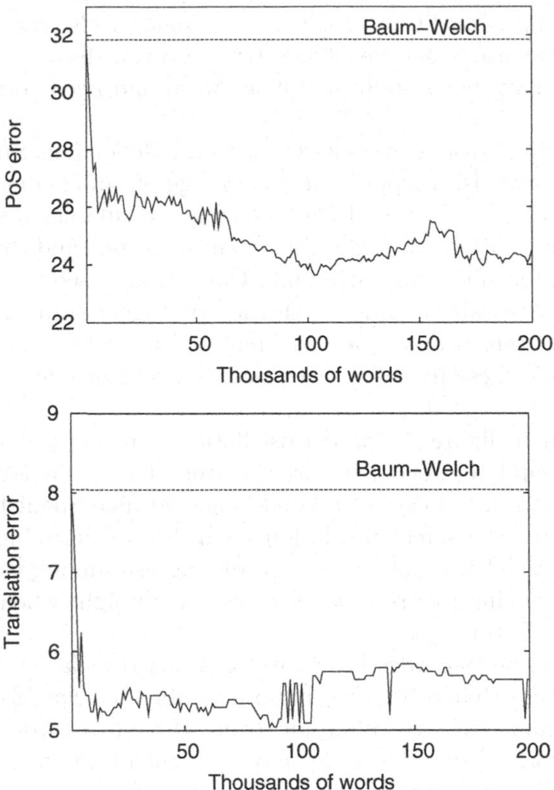

Fig. 4. PoS tagging error rate (top) and translation error rate (bottom) when rules to forbid impossible bigrams are considered (compare with figure 3). The Baum-Welch error rate after training with a 1 000 000-word corpus is given as well. PoS tagging error rate is expressed as the percentage of incorrect tags assigned to *ambiguous words* (including unknown words). Translation errors are expressed as the percentage of words that need to be corrected (post-edited) due to mistaggings

The number of forbidden bigrams (independently collected by a linguist) is 218; the more statistically important are *article* before *verb in personal form*, *proclitic pronoun* followed by words which are not *proclitic pronouns* or *verbs in personal form*, and *article* before *proclitic pronoun*.

As can be seen in figure 4 (compare with figure 3 where the same corpus is considered), sudden oscillations decrease and the PoS tagging error rate is significantly lower than that obtained without forbidden bigrams. Smaller sudden oscillations still happen due to other free rides (for example, *que*, *conjunction* or *relative pronoun*) not in the set of forbidden bigrams but with a secondary presence in Spanish corpora.

Concerning execution time, the new method needs higher training time than the Baum-Welch algorithm because of the enormous number of translations and path likelihoods that need to be explicitly considered (remember, however, that the time necessary for processing ambiguous texts after training is independent of the algorithm being used for estimating the parameters of the HMM). With the example corpus the original algorithm takes up to 44 hours in a typical desktop computer, and around 16 hours when forbidden bigrams are introduced. The number of paths n_p and, consequently, the number of segment translations grows exponentially with segment length l and can be approximated by $n_p \approx 1.46^l$.

5 Discussion

It has been shown that training HMM-based PoS taggers using unsupervised information from TL texts is relatively easy. Moreover, both tagging and translation errors lie between those produced by classical unsupervised models using Baum-Welch estimation and those attained with a supervised solution based on nonambiguous texts.

The presence of free rides —very common when translation involves closely-related languages like Spanish and Catalan (both coming from Latin and more related than other Romance languages)— makes the algorithm behave unstably due to the kind of TL model used in the experiments (superficial form trigrams). This problem may be partially overcome by using a small amount of linguistic information (forbidden bigrams) which can be obtained in most cases much more easily than the hand-tagged corpora needed for supervised training.

Since our goal is to produce PoS taggers to be embedded in MT systems, we can focus on translation error and conclude that, despite the fact that the tagging error rate starts with higher values than the one obtained with a Baum-Welch-trained tagger, the final translation error is around 2% smaller. Our method significantly reduces the tagging error when compared with other training methods using ambiguously tagged SL texts.

The training method described in this paper produces a PoS tagger which is in tune not only with SL but also with the TL of the translation engine. This makes it suitable for training PoS taggers to be embedded in MT systems. The method may also be used to customize the MT engine to a particular text type or subject or to statistically "retune" it after introducing new transfer rules in the MT system.

6 Future Work

We plan to study other TL models. One of the most interesting alternatives in the case of a bidirectional MT system is to consider another HMM as TL model. In this way, the two HMMs used as PoS taggers in a bidirectional MT system could be trained simultaneously from scratch by initializing one of them (with Kupiec's method, for example) and using it as TL model to estimate the parameters of the other one through our training algorithm. After that, roles could be interchanged so that the last HMM being trained is now used as TL model, and so on until convergence. The process may be seen as a kind of bootstrapping: the PoS tagger for one of the languages is initialized in a simple way and both HMMs alternate either as TL model or as adjustable one.

A different line of research will study the improvement of the estimation in eq. (2). A better estimation for $p(g_i|\tau(g_i, s))$ might reduce the impact of free rides without considering linguistic information. One possible approach is to query the model currently being estimated about this probability.

Finally, another line of work will focus on time complexity reduction. On the one hand, we propose to introduce new forbidden tag bigrams to reduce even more the number of translations to be computed. On the other hand, other strategies may prove valuable like, for example, using the model being estimated to calculate approximate likelihoods which make it possible to consider only the k best paths for translation.

References

1. T. Brants and C. Samuelsson. Tagging the Teleman corpus. In *Proceedings of the 10th Nordic Conference of Computational Linguistics*, Helsinki, Finland, 1995.
2. R. Canals-Marote, et al. The Spanish-Catalan machine translation system interNOSTRUM. In *Proceedings of MT Summit VIII, Machine Translation in the Information Age*, pages 73–76, 2001.
3. D. Cutting, J. Kupiec, J. Pedersen, and P. Sibun. A practical part-of-speech tagger. In *Third Conference on Applied Natural Language Processing. Association for Computational Linguistics. Proceedings of the Conference.*, pages 133–140, 1992.
4. W. Gale and G. Sampson. Good-Turing smoothing without tears. *Journal of Quantitative Linguistics*, 2(3), 1995.
5. W.J. Hutchins and H.L. Somers. *An Introduction to Machine Translation.* Academic Press, London, 1992.
6. F. Jelinek. *Statistical Methods for Speech Recognition.* The MIT Press, Cambridge, Massachusetts, 1997.
7. J. Kupiec. Robust part-of-speech tagging using a hidden Markov model. *Computer Speech and Language*, 6(3):225–242, 1992.
8. F. Pla and A. Molina. Improving part-of-speech tagging using lexicalized HMMs. *Journal of Natural Language Engineering*, 10(2):167–189, 2004.
9. L. R. Rabiner. A tutorial on hidden Markov models and selected applications in speech recognition. *Proceedings of the IEEE*, 77(2):257–286, 1989.

Expressive Power and Consistency Properties of State-of-the-Art Natural Language Parsers

Gabriel Infante-Lopez and Maarten de Rijke

Informatics Institute, University of Amsterdam
Kruislaan 403, 1098 SJ Amsterdam, The Netherlands
{infante,mdr}@science.uva.nl

Abstract. We define Probabilistic Constrained W-grammars (PCW-grammars), a two-level formalism capable of capturing grammatical frameworks used in two state of the art parsers, namely bilexical grammars and stochastic tree substitution grammars. We provide embeddings of these parser formalisms into PCW-grammars, which allows us to derive properties about their expressive power and consistency, and relations between the formalisms studied.

1 Introduction

State of the art statistical natural language parsers, e.g., [1, 3, 4] are procedures for extracting the syntactic structure hidden in natural language sentences. Usually, statistical parsers have two clearly identifiable main components. One has to do with the nature of the set of syntactic analyses that the parser can provide. It is usually defined using a grammatical framework, such as probabilistic context free grammars (PCFGs), bilexical grammars, etc. The second component concerns the way in which the different parts in the grammatical formalism are learned. For example, PCFGs can be read from tree-banks and their probabilities estimated using maximum likelihood [11].

Clearly, the grammatical framework underlying a parser is a key component in the overall definition of the parser which determines important characteristics of the parser, either directly or indirectly. Among others, the grammatical framework defines the set of languages the parser can potentially deal with, a lower bound on the parser's complexity, and the type of items that should be learned by the second component mentioned above. Hence, a thorough understanding of the grammatical framework on which a parser is based provides a great deal of information about the parser itself. We are particularly interested in the following properties: (1) The expressive power of a grammar formalism. (2) Conditions under which the probability distribution defined over the set of possible syntactic analyses is consistent: if this is the case, the probabilities associated with an analysis can be used as meaningful probabilistic indicators both for further stages of processing [11] and for evaluation [7]. (3) The relation to other grammatical frameworks; this provides insights about the assumptions made by the various frameworks.

J. L. Vicedo et al. (Eds.): EsTAL 2004, LNAI 3230, pp. 149–160, 2004.

Since building a parser is a time consuming process, formal properties of the underlying grammatical framework are not always a priority. Also, comparisons between parser models are usually based on experimental evidence. In order to establish formal properties of parsers and to facilitate the comparison of parsers, we believe that a unifying grammatical framework, of which different parsers' grammars can be obtained as instances, is instrumental. Our main contribution in this paper is the introduction of a grammatical framework capable of capturing state of the art grammatical formalisms. Our framework is based on so-called W-grammars, due originally to Van Wijngaarden [13]. We constrain W-grammars to obtain CW-grammars, which are more suitable for statistical natural language parsing than W-grammars. PCW-grammars extend CW-grammars with probabilities. In this paper we provide embeddings of bilexical grammars [5] and stochastic tree substitution grammars [1] into PCW-grammars, and we use these embeddings to derive results on expressive power, consistency, and relations with other grammatical formalisms. Due to lack of space, embeddings of further grammatical formalisms have had to be omitted.

In Section 2 we present our grammatical framework and establish results on expressive power and conditions for inducing consistent distributions. In Section 3 we capture the models mentioned above in our framework, and derive consequences of the embeddings. In Section 4 we conclude.

2 Grammatical Framework

In this section we describe the grammatical framework we will be working with. We introduce constrained W-grammars, then present a probabilistic version, and also introduce technical notions needed in later sections.

2.1 Constrained W-Grammars

A *constrained W-grammar* (*CW-grammar*) is a 6-tuple $(V, NT, T, S, \xrightarrow{m}, \xrightarrow{s})$ such that:

- V is a set of symbols called *variables.* Elements in V are denoted with calligraphic characters, e.g., $\mathcal{A}, \mathcal{B}, \mathcal{C}$.
- NT is a set of symbols called *non-terminals*; elements in NT are denoted with upper-case letters, e.g., X, Y, Z.
- T is a set of symbols called *terminals*, denoted with lower-case letters, e.g.: a, b, c, such that V, T and NT are pairwise disjoint.
- S is an element of NT called *starting symbol.*
- $\xrightarrow{m}$ is a finite binary relation defined on $(V \cup NT \cup T)^*$ such that if $x \xrightarrow{m} y$, then $x \in V$. The elements of $\xrightarrow{m}$ are called *meta-rules.*
- $\xrightarrow{s}$ is a finite binary relation on $(V \cup NT \cup T)^*$ such that if $r \xrightarrow{s} s$ then $r \in NT$, $s \neq \epsilon$ and s does not have any variable appearing more than once. The elements of $\xrightarrow{s}$ are called *pseudo-rules.*

CW-grammars differ from Van Wijngaarden's original W-grammars in that pseudo-rules have been constrained. The original W-grammars allow pseudo-rules to have variables on the left-hand side as well as repeated variables on both the right- and left-hand side. The constrained version defined above yields a dramatic reduction in the expressive power of W-grammars, but, as we will see below, at the same time it allows us to capture state of the art parsers.

CW-Grammars are rewriting devices, and as such they consist of rewriting rules. They differ from the usual rewriting systems in that the rewriting rules do not exist a-priori. Using pseudo-rules and meta-rules one builds 'real' rules that can be used in the rewriting process. The rewriting rules produced are denoted by $\stackrel{w}{\Longrightarrow}$. These rules are built by first selecting a pseudo-rule, and then using meta-rules for instantiating all the variables the pseudo-rule might contain.

For example, let $W = (V, NT, T, S, \stackrel{m}{\longrightarrow}, \stackrel{s}{\longrightarrow})$ be a CW-grammar where $V = \{\mathcal{ADJ}\}$, $NT = \{S, \mathit{Adj}, \mathit{Noun}\}$, $T = \{\mathit{ball}, \mathit{big}, \mathit{fat}, \mathit{red}, \mathit{green}, \ldots\}$, while $\stackrel{m}{\longrightarrow}$ and $\stackrel{s}{\longrightarrow}$ are given by the following table:

meta-rules	pseudo-rules
$\mathcal{ADJ} \stackrel{m}{\longrightarrow} \mathcal{ADJ}\,\mathit{Adj}$	$S \stackrel{s}{\longrightarrow} \mathcal{ADJ}\,\mathit{Noun}$
$\mathcal{ADJ} \stackrel{m}{\longrightarrow} \mathit{Adj}$	$\mathit{Adj} \stackrel{s}{\longrightarrow} \mathit{big}$
	$\mathit{Noun} \stackrel{s}{\longrightarrow} \mathit{ball}$

Suppose now that we want to build the rule $\mathcal{S} \stackrel{w}{\Longrightarrow} \mathit{Adj}\ \mathit{Adj}\ \mathit{Noun}$. We take the pseudo-rule $\mathcal{S} \stackrel{s}{\longrightarrow} \mathcal{ADJ}\ \mathit{Noun}$ and instantiate the variable $\mathcal{ADJ}$ with *Adj Adj* to get the desired rule. The rules defined by W have the following shape: $\mathcal{S} \stackrel{w}{\Longrightarrow} \mathit{Adj}^*\ \mathit{Noun}$. Trees for this grammar are flat, with a main node S and all the adjectives in it as daughters; see Figure 1.

The *string language* $L(W)$ generated by a CW-grammar W is the set $\{\beta \in T^+ : S \stackrel{w\,*}{\Longrightarrow} \beta\}$. In words, a string β belongs to the language $L(W)$ if there is a way to instantiate rules $\stackrel{w}{\Longrightarrow}$ that derive β from S. A *W-tree* yielding a string l is defined as the $\stackrel{w}{\Longrightarrow}$ derivation producing l. A W-tree 'pictures' the rules (i.e., pseudo-rules + variable instantiations) that have been used for deriving a string; Figure 1(a) shows an example. The way in which a rule has been obtained from pseudo-rules or the way in which its variables have been instantiated remains hidden. The *tree language* generated by a CW-grammar W is the set $T(G)$ defined by all W-trees generated by W yielding a string in $L(G)$.

Theorem 1. *CW-Grammars are weakly equivalent to context-free grammars.*

Proof. Let $W = (V, NT, T, S, \stackrel{m}{\longrightarrow}, \stackrel{s}{\longrightarrow})$ be a CW-grammar. Let $G_W = (NT', T', S', R')$ be a context-free grammar defined as follows (to avoid confusion we denote the rules in R by $\rightarrow$): $NT' = (V \cup NT)$; $T' = T$; S' is the starting symbol in W; and $X \rightarrow \alpha \in R$ iff $X \stackrel{m}{\longrightarrow} \alpha$ or $X \stackrel{s}{\longrightarrow} \alpha$. It can be shown that G_W is well-defined and generates the same language as W.

Given a CW-grammar W, the *context-free grammar underlying* W, notation $\mathit{CFG}(W)$, is the grammar G_W defined in the proof of Theorem 1. In Figure 1 we show a derivation in W and the corresponding one in $\mathit{CFG}(W)$.

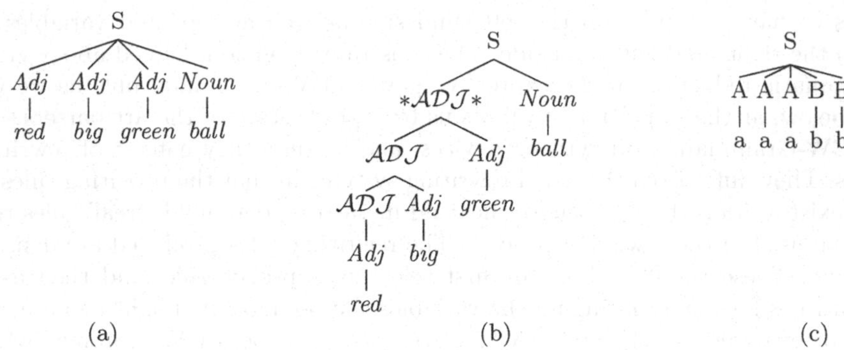

Fig. 1. (a) A tree generated by W. (b) The same tree with meta-rule derivations made visible. (c) A derivation tree for the string "*aaabb*"

Lemma 1. *Let W be a CW-grammar and let $G = CFG(W)$. For every τ in $T(G)$ there is a unique tree $v \in T(W)$ such that v is the product of hiding all meta derivations in τ.*

Proof. We sketch the proof using Figure 1. Suppose we want to derive the W-tree corresponding to the tree in Figure 1(a) from the one in Figure 1(b). Besides the G-tree we need to know which rules in G are meta-rules in W and which non-terminals in G are variables in W. To obtain a W-tree from a G-tree we replace all variables in CFG-rules (corresponding to pseudo-rules) by the yield of the CFG-derivation (corresponding to a meta-derivation). To illustrate this idea, consider the yield *red big green* below the variable $*\mathcal{ADJ}*$ in Figure 1(b): 'hide' the meta-derivation producing it, thus obtaining the tree in Figure 1(a), the W-tree. Since such a replacement procedure is uniquely defined, for every tree in $T(G)$ there is a unique way to hide meta-derivations, consequently for every G-tree there is a unique W-tree, as desired.

Next, we give an example to show that CW-grammars are *not* strongly equivalent to context-free grammars. In other words, trees generated by CW-grammars are different from trees generated by context-free grammars.

Example 1. Let $W = (V, NT, T, S, \xrightarrow{m\,*}, \xrightarrow{s\,*})$ a CW-grammar with $V = \{\mathcal{A}, \mathcal{B}, \mathcal{S}\}$, $NT = \{A, B\}$, $T = \{a, b\}$, $\xrightarrow{m} = \{\mathcal{A} \xrightarrow{m} \mathcal{A}A,\ \mathcal{A} \xrightarrow{m} A,\ \mathcal{B} \xrightarrow{m} \mathcal{B}B,\ \mathcal{B} \xrightarrow{m} B\}$, and $\xrightarrow{s} = \{A \xrightarrow{s} a,\ B \xrightarrow{s} b,\ \mathcal{S} \xrightarrow{s} \mathcal{A}\mathcal{B}\}$.

The grammar W generates the language $\{a^*b^*\}$ through instantiations of the variables A and B to strings in A^* and B^* respectively. The derivation $\overset{w}{\Longrightarrow}$ for a string *aaabb* is as follows: $S \overset{w}{\Longrightarrow} AAABB \overset{w}{\Longrightarrow} aAABB \overset{w}{\Longrightarrow} aaABB \overset{w}{\Longrightarrow} aaaBB \overset{w}{\Longrightarrow} aaabB \overset{w\,*}{\Longrightarrow} aaabb$. The tree representing this derivation (Figure 1(c)) has only one internal level (labeled $AAABB$), and its leaves form the accepted string. Observe that no CFG can generate the kind of flat structures displayed in Figure 1(c) since any context-free grammar producing the same language as W will have more than one intermediate level in its derivation trees.

2.2 Probabilistic CW-Grammars

Probabilistic CW-grammars (PCW-grammars, for short) are CW-grammars in which the rules are augmented with a probability value, such that the probabilities belonging to rules sharing the same left-hand side sum up to one. More formally, in a probabilistic CW-grammar $(V, NT, S, \xrightarrow{m}, \xrightarrow{s})$ we have that

- $\sum_{x \xrightarrow{m}_p y} p = 1$ for all meta-rules $x \xrightarrow{m}_p y$ having x in the left-hand side.
- $\sum_{x \xrightarrow{s}_p y} p = 1$ for all pseudo-rules $x \xrightarrow{s}_p y$ having x in the left-hand side.

Next, we need to define how we assign probabilities to derivations, rules, and trees. To start with derivations, if $\alpha' \xrightarrow{m\ *} \alpha$ then there are $\alpha_1, \ldots, \alpha_k$ such that $\alpha_i \xrightarrow{m} \alpha_{i+1}$, $\alpha_1 = \alpha'$ and $\alpha_k = \alpha$. We define the probability $P(\alpha' \xrightarrow{m\ *} \alpha)$ of a derivation $\alpha' \xrightarrow{m\ *} \alpha$ to be $\prod_{i=1}^{k-1} P(\alpha_i \xrightarrow{m} \alpha_{i+1})$.

Now, let $X \overset{w}{\Longrightarrow} \alpha$ be a rule. The probability $P(X \overset{w}{\Longrightarrow} \alpha)$ is defined as the product of $P(\alpha' \xrightarrow{m\ *} \alpha)$ and $\sum_{\alpha' \in A} P(X \xrightarrow{s} \alpha')$, where

$$A = \{\alpha' \in (V \cup NT \cup T)^+ : X \xrightarrow{s} \alpha', \alpha' \xrightarrow{m\ *} \alpha\}.$$

I.e., the probability of a 'real' rule is the sum of the probabilities of all meta derivations producing it.

The *probability of a tree* is defined as the product of the probabilities of the rules making up the tree, while the *probability of a string* $\alpha \in T^+$ is defined as the sum of the probabilities assigned to all trees yielding α.

Theorem 2. *Let W be a CW-grammar, let G be CFG(W), and let W' be a PCW-grammar that extends W by assigning probability values to all rules in W. There is a way to extend G into a PCFG G' such that W' and G' assigning the same probability mass to all strings in the language accepted by G (which coincides with the language accepted by W).*

Proof. Let $G = (NT', T', S', R')$ be a PCFG with NT', T', S' as defined in the proof of Theorem 1 and R' such that $X \to \alpha \in R$ iff $X \xrightarrow{m} \alpha$ or $X \xrightarrow{s} \alpha$. Note that a $\overset{w}{\Longrightarrow}$ derivation τ might be the product of many different derivations using rules in R' (G-derivations for short); call this set $D(\tau)$. From the definitions it is clear that $p(\tau) = \sum_{v \in D(\tau)} p(v)$. To prove the theorem we need to show (1) that for τ and τ' two different $\overset{w}{\Longrightarrow}$ derivations of the string α, it holds that $D(\tau) \cap D(\tau') = \emptyset$, and (2) that for every G-derivation v there is a $\overset{w}{\Longrightarrow}$ derivation τ such that $v \in D(\tau)$. Both results follow from Lemma 1.

For a given PCW-grammar W, the PCFG defined in the proof of Theorem 2 is called *the PCFG underlying W*. As an immediate consequence of the construction of the PCFG given in Theorem 2 we get that a PCW-grammar is *consistent* iff its underlying PCFG is consistent.

2.3 Learning CW-Grammars from Tree-Banks

PCW-grammars are induced from tree-banks in almost the same way as PCFGs are. The main difference is that the former require an explicit decision on the nature of the hidden derivations. As we will see below, the two different approaches to natural language parsing that we present in this paper differ substantially in the assumptions they make in this respect.

2.4 Some Further Technical Notions

Below we will use PCW-grammars to "capture" models underlying a number of state of the art parsers. The following will prove useful. Let F and G be two grammars with tree languages $T(G)$ and $T(F)$ and languages $L(F)$ and $L(G)$, respectively. Then, F is *f-equivalent* to G if $L(F) = L(G)$ and there is a bijective function $f : T(F) \to T(G)$. Given two grammatical formalisms A and B, we say that A is *f-transformable* to B, if for every grammar F in A there is a grammar G in B such that F is f-equivalent to G.

3 Capturing State of the Art Parsers

In this section we use PCW-grammars to capture the models underlying two state of the art parsers.

3.1 Bilexical Grammars

Bilexical grammar [4, 5] is a formalism in which lexical items, such as verbs and their arguments, can have idiosyncratic selectional influences on each other. They can be used for describing bilexical approaches to dependency and phrase-structure grammars, and a slight modification yields link grammars.

Background. A *split unweighted bilexical grammar* B is a 3-tuple $(W, \{r_w\}_{w \in W}, \{l_w\}_{w \in W})$ where:

- W is a set, called the (terminal) *vocabulary*, which contains a distinguished symbol ROOT
- For each word $w \in W$, a pair of regular grammars l_w and r_w, having starting symbols S_{l_w} and S_{r_w}, respectively. Each grammar accepts some regular subset of W^*.

A *dependency tree* is a tree whose nodes (internal and external) are labeled with words from W; the root is labeled with the symbol ROOT. The children ('dependents') of a node are ordered with respect to each other and the node itself, so that the node has both *left children* that precede it and *right children* that follow it. A dependency tree T is *grammatical* if for every word token w that appears in the tree, l_w accepts the (possibly empty) sequence of w's left children (from right to left), and r_w accepts the sequence of w's right children (from left to right). *Weighted bilexical grammars* are like unweighted bilexical grammars but all of their automata assign weights to the strings they generate. Lemma 2 implies that weighted bilexical grammars are a subset of PCW-grammars.

Bilexical Grammars as CW-Grammars. With every bilexical grammar B we associate a CW-grammar W_B as follows.

Definition 1. Let $B = (W, \{l_w\}_{w \in L}, \{r_w\}_{w \in L})$ be a split bilexical grammar. Let $W_B = (V, NT, T, S, \xrightarrow{m}, \xrightarrow{s})$ be the CW-grammar defined as follows:

- The set of variables V is given by the set of starting symbols S_{l_w} and S_{r_w} from regular grammars l_w and r_w respectively, and w in W.
- The set of non-terminals NT is some set in 1-1-correspondence with W, e.g., it can be defined as $NT = \{w' : w \in W\}$.
- The set of terminals T is the set of words W.
- The set of meta-rules is given by the union of $\{w' \xrightarrow{m} w : w \in W\}$ and the rules in all of the right and left regular grammars in B.
- The set of pseudo-rules is given by $X' \xrightarrow{s} S_{\overline{l}_w} x S_{r_w}$ where $\overline{l}_w$ denotes the regular expression inverting (reading backwards) all strings in $L(l_w)$.

Below, we establish the (weak) equivalence between a bilexical grammar B and its CW-grammar counterpart W_B. The idea is that the set of meta-rules, producing derivations that would remain hidden in the tree, are used for simulating the regular automata. Pseudo-rules are used as a nexus between a hidden derivation and a visible one: For each word w in the alphabet, we define a pseudo-rule having w as a terminal, and two variables S_{l_w} and S_{r_w} marking the left and right dependents, respectively. These variables correspond to the starting symbols for the left and right automata l_w and r_w, respectively. Instantiating the pseudo-rule associated to w would use a left and a right derivation using the left and the right automata, respectively, via meta-rules. The whole derivation remains hidden in the $\stackrel{w}{\Longrightarrow}$ derivation, as in bilexical grammars.

Lemma 2. *Bilexical grammars are f-transformable to CW-grammars.*

Proof. We have to give a function $f : T(B) \to T(W_B)$, where B is a bilexical grammar and W_B the grammar defined in Definition 1, such that f is invertible. A bilexical tree yielding the string $s = w_1, \ldots, w_n$ can be described as a sequence $u_1, \ldots, u_n$ of 3-tuples $\langle \alpha_i, w_i, \beta_i \rangle$ such that l_{w_i} accepts α_i and r_{w_i} accepts β. The desired function f transforms a dependency tree in a W-tree by transforming the sequence of tuples into a $\stackrel{w}{\Longrightarrow}$ derivation. We define f as $f(\langle \alpha, w_i, \beta \rangle) = W_i \stackrel{w}{\Longrightarrow} \alpha w_i \beta$. The rule corresponding to $\langle \alpha, w_i, \beta \rangle$ is the one produced by using the pseudo rule $W_i' \xrightarrow{s} S_{\overline{l}_w} x S_{r_w}$ and instantiating $S_{\overline{l}_w}$ and S_{r_w} with α and β respectively. Since the sequence of tuples forms a dependency tree, the sequence of W-rules builds up a correct W-tree.

Expressive Power and Consistency. By Lemma 2 bilexical grammars are weakly equivalent to context-free grammars. Moreover, the idea behind Example 1 can be used to prove that bilexical grammars are not strongly equivalent to CFGs. Briefly, bilexical grammars can create flat structures of the kind produced by the grammar in Example 1; such structures cannot be produced by CFGs.

As a consequence of Lemma 2, learning bilexical grammars is equivalent to learning PCW-grammars, which, in turn, is equivalent to learning the PCFGs underlying the PCW-grammars. Eisner [4] assumed that all hidden derivations were produced by Markov chains. Under the PCW-paradigm, his methodology is equivalent to transforming all trees in the training material by making all their hidden derivations visible, and inducing the underlying PCFG from the transformed trees. Variables in the equivalent PCW-grammar are defined according to the level degree of the Markov chain (we assume that the reader is familiar with Markov models and Markov chains [11]). In particular, if the Markov chain used is of degree one, variables are in one-to-one correspondence with the set of words, and the consistency result follows from the fact that inducing a degree one Markov chain in a bilexical grammar is the same as inducing the underlying PCFG in the equivalent PCW-grammar using maximum likelihood, plus the fact that using maximum likelihood estimation for inducing PCFGs produces consistent grammars [2, 8].

3.2 Stochastic Tree Substitution Grammars

Data-oriented parsing (DOP) is a memory-based approach to syntactic parsing. The basic idea is to use the subtrees from a syntactically annotated corpus directly as a stochastic grammar. The DOP-1 model [1] was the first version of DOP, and most later versions of DOP are variations on it. The underlying grammatical formalism is stochastic tree substitution grammars (STSG), which is the grammatical formalism we capture here.

Background. The model itself is extremely simple and can be described as follows: for every sentence in a parsed training corpus, extract every subtree. Then we use these trees to form an stochastic tree substitution grammar. Formally, a *stochastic tree-substitution grammar* (STSG) G is a 5-tuple $\langle V_N, V_T, S, R, P\rangle$ where

- V_N is a finite set of nonterminal symbols.
- V_T is a finite set of terminal symbols.
- $S \in V_N$ is the distinguished symbol.
- R is a finite set of elementary trees whose top nodes and interior nodes are labeled by nonterminal symbols and whose yield nodes are labeled by terminal or nonterminal symbols.
- P is a function which assigns to every elementary tree $t \in R$ a probability $P(t)$. For a tree t with a root node symbol $root(t) = \alpha$, $P(t)$ is interpreted as the probability of substituting t on a node α. We require, therefore, for a given α that $\sum_{\{t:root(t)=\alpha\}} = 1$ and that $0 < P(t) \leq 1$ (where t's root node symbol is α).

If t_1 and t_2 are elementary trees such that the leftmost non-terminal frontier node symbol of t_1 is equal to the root node symbol of t_2, then $t_1 \circ t_2$ is the tree that results from substituting t_2 in this leftmost non-terminal frontier node symbol in t_1. The partial function $\circ$ is called *leftmost substitution* or simply *substitution*. Trees are derived using left most substitution.

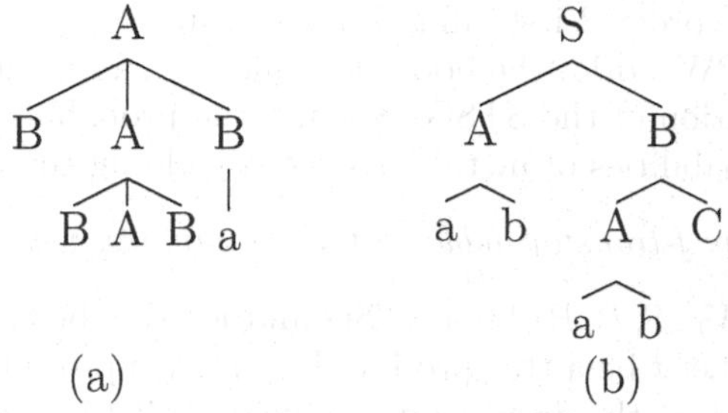

Fig. 2. (a) A derivation tree (b) An elementary tree

STSGs as CW-Grammars. STSGs are not quite context-free grammars. The main difference, and the hardest to capture in a CFG-like setting, is the way in which probabilities are computed for a given tree. The probability of a tree is given by the sum of the probabilities of all derivations producing it. CW-grammars offer a similar mechanism: the probability of the body of a rule is the sum of the probabilities of all meta-derivations producing it. The idea of the equivalence is to associate to every tree produced by a STSG a 'real' rule of the PCW-grammar in such a way that the body of the rule codifies the whole tree.

To implement this idea, we need to code up trees as strings. The simplest way to achieve this is to visit the nodes in a depth first left to right order and for each inner node use the applied production, while for the leaves we type the symbol itself if the symbol is a terminal and a primed version of it if the symbol is a non-terminal. For example, the derivation describing the tree in Figure 2(a) is $(A, BAB)B'(A, BAB)B'A'B'(B, a)a$.

The first step in capturing STSGs is to build rules capturing elementary trees using the notation just introduced. Specifically, let t be an elementary tree belonging to a STSG. Let S be its root and α its string representation. The CF-like rule $S' \to \alpha$ is called the *elementary rule* of t. Elementary rules store all information about the elementary tree. They have primed non-terminals where a substitution can be carried out. E.g., if t is the elementary tree pictured in Figure 2(b), its elementary rule is $S' \to (A, B)(A, ab)ab(B, AC)(A, ab)abC'$. Note the primed version of C in the frontier of the derivation.

Definition 2. Let $H = (V_N, V_T, S, R, P)$ be a STSG. Let $W_H = (V, NT, T, S', \xrightarrow{m}, \xrightarrow{s})$ be the following CW-grammar.

- V is the primed version of V_T.
- (A, α) is in NT iff $(A, \alpha) \to \epsilon$ appears in some elementary tree.
- T is exactly as V_T.
- S' is a new symbol.
- The set of meta-rules is built by transforming each elementary tree to its corresponding elementary rule.
- The set of pseudo-rules is given by $(A, \alpha) \xrightarrow{s} \epsilon$ if $A \to \alpha$ appears in a elementary tree, plus rules $S' \xrightarrow{s} S$.

Two remarks are in order. First, all generative capacity is encoded in the set of meta-rules. In the CW-world, the body of a rule (i.e., an instantiated pseudo-rule) encodes a derivation of the STSG. Second, the probability of a 'real' rule is the sum of the probabilities of meta-derivations yielding the rule's body.

Lemma 3. *STSGs are f-transformable to CW-grammars, with f invertible.*

Proof. Let $H = (V_N, V_T, S, R, P)$ be a STSG and let W_H be the CW-grammar given in Definition 2. Let t be a tree produced by H. We prove the lemma using induction on the length of the derivation producing t. If t has length 1, there is an elementary tree t_1 such that S is the root node and yields α, which implies that there is a meta-rule obtained from the elementary rule corresponding to the elementary tree t_1. The relation is one-to-one as, by definition, meta-rules are in one-to-one correspondence with elementary trees.

Suppose the lemma is true for derivation lengths less than or equal to n. Suppose t is generated by a derivation of length $n + 1$. Assume there are trees t_1, t_2 with $t_1 \circ t_2 = t$. By definition there is a unique meta-rule r_1 corresponding with t_1 and by inductive hypothesis there is a unique derivation for t_2.

Corollary 1. *Let $H = (V_N, V_T, S, R, P)$ be an STSG, and let W_H be the CW-grammar given in Definition 2. There is a one-to-one correspondence between derivations in H and W_H.*

Lemma 4. *Let $H = (V_N, V_T, S, R, P)$ be an STSG, and let W_H be the CW-grammar given in Definition 2. Both grammars assign the same probability mass to trees related through the one-to-one mapping described in Lemma 1.*

Proof. A tree has a characteristic W-rule, defined by its shape. Moreover probability of a W-rule, according to the definition of PCW-grammars, is given by the sum of the probabilities of all derivations producing the rule's body, i.e., all STSG derivations producing the same tree. As a consequence, a particular STSG tree, identified from the body of the corresponding W-rule, has the same probability assigned by the equivalent CW-Grammar.

Expressive Power and Consistency. By Corollary 3, STSGs are weakly equivalent to context-free grammars. The consistency of an STSG depends on the methodology used for computing the probabilities assigned to its elementary trees. DOP-1 is one particular approach to computing these probabilities. Under the DOP-1 perspective, a tree t contributes all its possible subtrees to a new tree-bank from which the probabilities of elementary trees are computed. Probabilities of an elementary tree are computed using maximum likelihood. Since the events in the new tree-bank are not independently distributed, the resulting probabilities are inconsistent and biased [9]. Solutions taking into account the dependence between trees in the resulting tree-banks have been suggested [12].

Even though consistency conditions cannot be derived for the DOP-1 estimation procedure given that it does not attempt to learn the underlying PCFG, our formalism suggests that probabilities should be computed differently from the way it is done in DOP-1. By our embedding, a tree t in the tree-bank corresponds to the body of a pseudo-rule instantiated through meta-derivations; t is the final "string" and does not have any information on the derivation that took place. But viewing t as a final string changes the problem definition! Now, we have as input a set of elementary rules and a set of accepted trees. The problem is to compute probabilities for these rules: an unsupervised problem that can be solved using any unsupervised technique. The consistency of the resulting STSG depends on the consistency properties of the unsupervised method.

4 Discussion and Conclusion

We introduced probabilistic constrained W-grammars, a grammatical framework capable of capturing a number of models underlying state of the art parsers. We established expressive power properties for two formalisms (bilexical grammars, and stochastic tree substitution grammars) together with some conditions under which the inferred grammars are consistent. We should point out that, despite their similarities, there is a fundamental difference between PCW-grammars and PCFGs, and this is the two-level mechanism of the former formalism. This mechanism allows us to capture two state of the art natural language parsers, which cannot be done using standard PCFGs only.

We showed that, from a formal perspective, STSGs and bilexical grammars share certain similarities. Bilexical grammars suppose that rule bodies are obtained by collapsing hidden derivations. That is, for Eisner, a rule body is a regular expression. Similarly, Bod's STSGs take this idea to the extreme by taking the whole sentence to be the yield of a hidden derivation. PCW-grammars naturally suggest different levels of abstraction; in [6] we have shown that these levels can be used to reduce the size of grammars induced from tree-banks, and, hence, to optimize parsing procedures.

From a theoretical point of view, the concept of f-transformable grammars, which we use heavily in our proofs, is a very powerful one that relaxes the known equivalence notions between grammars. Since arbitrary functions f can be defined between arbitrary tree languages and CFG-like trees, they can be used to map other formalisms to context-free trees. Examples include Collins' first model (based on Markov rules) [3], Tree Adjoining Grammars [10] or Categorial Grammars [14]. As part of our future research, we aim to capture further grammatical formalisms, and to characterize the nature of the functions f used to achieve this.

Acknowledgments

Both authors were supported by the Netherlands Organization for Scientific Research (NWO) under project number 220-80-001. In addition, Maarten de Rijke was also supported by grants from NWO, under project numbers 365-20-005, 612.069.006, 612.000.106, 612.000.207, and 612.066.302.

References

1. R. Bod. *Beyond Grammar—An Experience-Based Theory of Language*. Cambridge University Press, Cambridge, England, 1999.
2. Z. Chi and S. Geman. Estimation of probabilistic context-free grammars. *Computational Linguistics*, 24(2):299–305, 1998.
3. M. Collins. Three generative, lexicalized models for statistical parsing. In *Proc. ACL'97 and EACL'97*, pages 16–23, Madrid, Spain, 1997.
4. J. Eisner. Three new probabilistic models for dependency parsing: An exploration. In *Proceedings of COLING-96*, pages 340–245, Copenhagen, Denmark, 1996.
5. J. Eisner. Bilexical grammars and their cubic-time parsing algorithms. In H. Bunt and A. Nijholt, editors, *Advances in Probabilistic and Other Parsing Technologies*, pages 29–62. Kluwer Academic Publishers, October 2000.
6. G. Infante-Lopez and M. de Rijke. Alternative approaches for generating bodies of grammar rules. In *Proc. ACL'04*, Barcelona, Spain, 2004.
7. G. Infante-Lopez and M. de Rijke. Comparing the ambiguity reduction abilities of probabilistic context-free grammars. In *Proc. of LREC'04*, 2004.
8. S. Joan-Andreu and J.-M. Benedí. Consistency of stochastic context-free grammars from probabilistic estimation based on growth transformations. *IEEE Transactions on Pattern Analysis and Machine Intelligence*, 19(9):1052–1055, 1997.
9. M. Johnson. The DOP estimation method is biased and inconsistent. *Computational Linguistics*, 28(1):71–76, 2002.
10. A.K. Joshi. Tree Adjoining Grammars: How much context sensitivity is required to provide a reasonable structural description. In I. Karttunen D. Dowty and A. Zwicky, editors, *Natural Language Parsing*, pages 206–250, Cambridge, U.K., 1985. Cambridge University Press.
11. C. Manning and H. Schütze. *Foundations of Statistical Natural Language Processing*. The MIT Press, Cambridge, MA, 1999.
12. K. Sima'an and L. Buratto. Backoff parameter estimation for the DOP model. In *Proc. of ECML*, 2003.
13. A. van Wijngaarden. Orthogonal design and description of a formal language. Technical Report MR76, Mathematisch Centrum., Amsterdam, 1965.
14. M. Wood. *Categorial Grammars*. Routledge., London, 1993.

An Independent Domain Dialogue System Through a Service Manager*

Márcio Mourão, Renato Cassaca, and Nuno Mamede

L^{2}F - Spoken Language Systems Lab
INESC-ID Lisboa / IST, R. Alves Redol 9, 1000-029 Lisboa, Portugal
{Marcio.Mourao, Renato.Cassaca, Nuno.Mamede}@l2f.inesc-id.pt
http://www.l2f.inesc-id.pt

Abstract. Building a generalized platform for having dialogues is a hard problem in the topic of dialogue systems. The problem becomes still more difficult if there is the possibility of having a conversation about more than one domain at the same time. To help solving this problem, we have built a component that deals with everything related to the domains. In this paper, we describe this component, named Service Manager, and explain what and how it passes all the information that a dialogue manager needs to conduct a dialogue.

1 Introduction

Only recently Spoken Dialogue Systems (SDS) started emerging as a practical alternative for a conversational computer interface, mainly due to the progress in the technology of speech recognition and understanding[1]. Building a generalized platform for having dialogues is a hard problem. Our main goal is to have a system easely adaptable to new dialogue domains, without changing any code or structures that lie behind the system[2].

When we turned our efforts to implement a natural language dialog system, we selected an architecture that could satisfy the requirements of adaptability to different domains. Our dialog system follows the TRIPS architecture, and consists of four main modules: Interpretation Manager (IM), Discourse Context (DC), Behavioural Agent (BA), and Generation Manager (GM)[3].

Faced with a multiplicity of possible dialogues, we restricted our manager to task-oriented dialogues in order to reduce the information acquisition needs. For each domain, it is necessary to define the actions available to the user. The dialog manager's task is to determine the action intended by the user and request the information needed to perform it.

We use frames to represent both the domain and the information collected during the interaction with the users [4]. Each domain handled by the dialogue system is internally represented by a frame, which is composed by slots and rules. Slots define domain data relationships, and rules define the system behaviour. Rules are composed by operators (logical, conditional, and relational) and by functions.

To keep the filling of the frame slots consistent, it is necessary to indicate the set of values with which a slot can be instantiated. To avoid invalid combination of values, we

* This research has been partially supported by Fundação para a Ciência e Tecnologia under project number POSI/PLP/41319/2001 (POSI and FEDER).

J. L. Vicedo et al. (Eds.): EsTAL 2004, LNAI 3230, pp. 161–171, 2004.

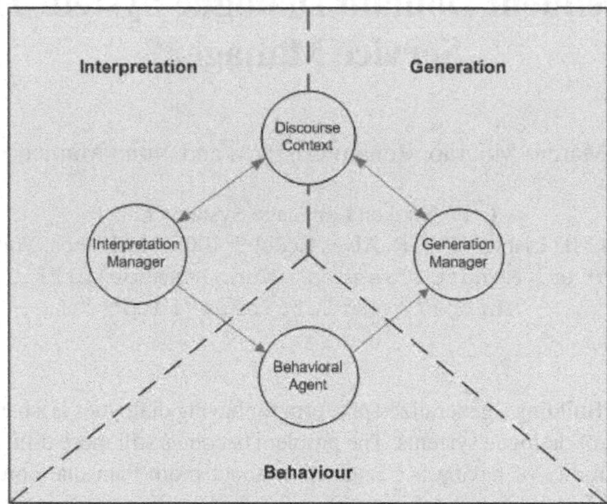

Fig. 1. Architecture of the Dialogue Manager

have defined a meta-language to express the constraints that must be satisfied. So, each frame definition includes a set of recognition rules, used to identify the objects that come with an user utterance and to specify the set of values that each slot may hold; a set of validation rules, to express a set of domain restrictions, i.e., invalid combination of slot values; and classification rules, used to specify the actions that must be performed when some conditions are satisfied, i.e., the valid combinations of values. This approach has the advantage of making the dialogue control independent of the domain.

We have designed a Service Manager (SM) as the interface between the spoken dialogue platform and a set of heterogeneous devices. The role of the SM is to provide the dialogue manager with everything that is related to a domain, which includes representation, access restrictions and, most important of all, dialogue independence. More than one device can be part of a single domain. The SM module determines what can a user really do or execute in a task oriented dialogue system, that is, the services. Inside a domain, a set of services is grouped in one or more states. The services returned by the SM to the dialogue manager will be restricted to the current state, not allowing users doing things that they are not supposed to do, like turning on the lights when the lights are already turned on.

Our spoken dialog platform has been used to produce a spoken dialog system called "house of the future", and it is also being used on a demonstration system, accessible by telephone, where people can ask for weather conditions, stock hold information, bus trip information and cinema schedules.

This paper is divided into six sections. The next section describes the Dialogue Manager, and its actual four main components. Section three describes Service Manager, and its main role to achieve dialogue domain independence. In section four we present a dialogue example, showing the fluxes between the dialogue manager and the Service Manager. Next to last, we describe our real experience in the implementation of our dialogue system in controlling parts of the "house of the future". Finally, we present some concluding remarks and future work.

2 Dialogue Manager

Our Dialogue Manager is composed by four main modules: (i) Interpretation Manager; (ii) Discourse Context; (iii) Behavioral Agent; and (iv) Generation Manager;

The Interpretation Manager (IM) receives a set of speech acts and generates the correspondent interpretations and discourse obligations[5][6][7]. Interpretations are frame instantiations that represent possible combinations of speech acts and the meaning associated to each object it contains[1]. To select the most promising interpretation two scores are computed. The recognition score to evaluate the rule requirements already accomplished, and the answer score, a measure of the consistency of the data already provided by the user. A more detailed description of this process can be found in [8].

The Discourse Context (DC) manages all knowledge about the discourse, including the discourse stack, turn-taking information, and discourse obligations.

The Behavioral Agent (BA) enables the system to be mixed-initiative: regardless of what the user says, the BA has its own priorities and intentions. When a new speech act includes objects belonging to a domain that is not being considered, the BA assumes the user wants to introduce a new dialog topic: the old topic is put on hold, and priority is given to the new topic. Whenever the system recognizes that the user is changing domains, it first verifies if some previous conversation has already taken place.

The Generation Manager (GA) is a very important component in a dialog manager. To communicate with the user, it has to transform the system intentions in natural language utterances. It receives discourse obligations from the Behavioral Agent, and transforms them into text, using template files. Each domain has a unique template file. The Generation Manager uses another template file to produce questions that are not domain specific. For example, domain desambiguation questions, used to decide proceeding a dialogue between two or more distinct domains, or to clarify questions, are defined in this file.

3 Service Manager

We designed the Service Manager (SM) as the interface between the spoken dialogue platform and a set of heterogeneous domains[2]. A domain is a representation of a set of devices that share the same description. This description is composed by slots and rules. Slots define domain data relationships, and rules define the system behaviour. A rule or service represents an user possible action. The spoken dialogue platform has been applied to several different types of devices. They are splitted into two big sets: (i) in a home environment; and (ii) on a database retrieval, see Figure 2. In the first, based on X10 and IRDA protocols, we control a wide range of home devices, such as, lights, air conditioning, hi-fi, and TV. We can extend the application to include any infra-red controllable device or whose control functions may be programmed by the X10 protocol. The second type of application, information retrieval via voice from remote databases, has been tested with weather information, cinema schedules and bus trip information. This type of application can easily be extended to other domains.

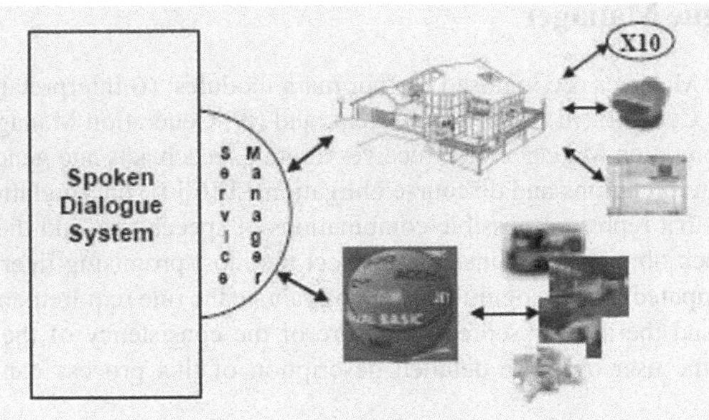

Fig. 2. Interaction with the Service Manager

3.1 Interface Operations

The Service Manager component of the Spoken Dialogue System provides the following main set of operations:

- Domain Description Insertion: this operation inserts a new domain in the Service Manager. It receives as argument a path to a file that contains a XML description of a domain. After the completion of this operation, a Service Manager internal representation of the domain is maintained, for future requests.
- Objects Recognition: to become possible the construction of interpretations and discourse obligations by the Interpretation Manager, an identification of every speech utterance object is crutial. Whenever this identification is needed, this operation will be invoked, using as arguments: (i) a list with the name of all objects to be recognized; and (ii) the current user. This operation returns a list with the description of the identified objects. Objects belonging to domains where the current user does not have access are not checked. If an object is not recognized, the name of the object will be returned without a description.
- Domain Services Return: a service represents an user possible action. This operation returns the set of services associated with the specified domain(s). In a task oriented dialogue system, these services are used to determine the system behavior: an answer or the execution of a procedure. The operation receives as arguments: (i) the domains; and (ii) the current user. It is possible to ask for all domain services, or ask for services from specific domains. The current user is used to check if the user has access to the services.
- Execution of Services: this operation allows for execution of services that belong to a domain in the Service Manager. More than one service can be ordered to be executed at the same time.

The use of the Service Manager with these operations provides the following features:

- A dialogue independent component that offers all the information related with domains. The Service Manager becomes the only "door" by which the SDS components gets information about a domain.

- There is no mixture between the linguistic parts of the SDS and information about the domains.
- Because information about the domains is concentrated, it is more easier to define layers of reasoning using that information and extract knowledge from it.
- As we are working with different types of devices there was the need to define an abstract representation to create an uniform characterization of domains. The definition of this abstract description allows for an equal treatment of the domains.
- A new domain is more easily introduced.

3.2 Architecture

Figure 3 shows the service manager architecture. It is composed by five modules: (i) Service Manager Galaxy Server; (ii) Device Manager; (iii) Access Manager; (iv) Object Recognition Manager; and (v) Device Proxy.

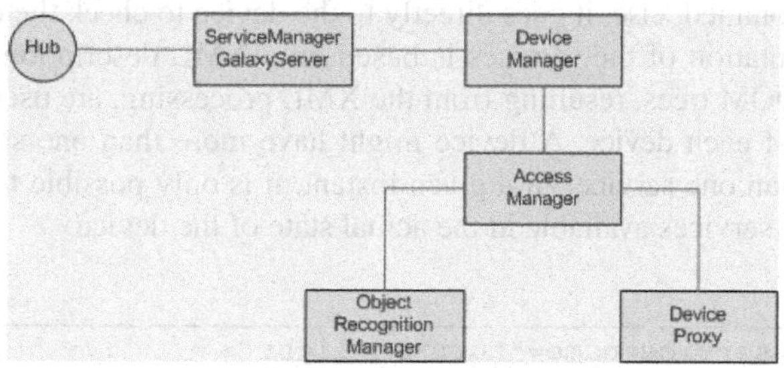

Fig. 3. Service Manager Architecture

The Service Manager Galaxy Server defines the interface of the service manager. So, it is the unique point of communication from where all requests and responses are made. All the operations in the interface that were explained before are defined here. This module follows a design pattern named "facade". This pattern provides a simplified, standardized interface to a large set of objects. This avoids the problem of having to reference many different, complicated interfaces to each object of that set.

The Device Manager is the service manager main module. It is the business layer of the architecture. It has the main methods by which the service manager works, including the ones that deal with the service requests.

The Access Manager component main function is to serve as a filter. This filter is applied for all requests of services. It restricts the available services to the current user. For doing that, this module manages a device restrictions file, and checks whether or not that user has permission to access to specific devices.

The Object Recognition Manager component is responsible for the identification of all objects. This component manages the XML description object files for each domain available in the system. Figure 4 shows part of a lights domain recognition objects file. Two actions are available, turn-on and turn-off. This means that these two objects are identified as being actions in the lights domain.

```
<objects>
 <action>
  <item> turn-on </item>
  <item> turn-off </item>
 </action>
</objects>
```

Fig. 4. Part of a recognition objects file

The Device Proxy module keeps the connection to the real device (the one that implements services). For some devices, it is impossible to obtain its state directly from it. For example, it is difficult to check if a televison is turn-on or turn-off. Most part of the televisions do not have sensors to do this job. By this reason, this module is also capable of creating and managing a device state. This device state can be changed only when a service is executed. The system only uses this capability when no state from the device can be obtained, else, it goes directly to the device to check the current state.

The representation of the services is based on a XML description, validated by a generic DTD. DOM trees, resulting from the XML processing, are used as the internal representation of each device. A device might have more than one state. A state can include more than one service. At a given instant, it is only possible to have access to the hierarchy of services available in the actual state of the device.

```
<service name="turn-on-light">
 <label>Turns on the bedroom light</label>
 <params>
  <param action value="turn-on"></param>
  <or>
   <param action value="turn-on"></param>
   <param zone></param>
  </or>
 </params>
 <execute>
  <name>turn-on</name>
  <success>on</sucess>
  <failure/>
 </execute>
</service>
```

Fig. 5. Description of a service

Figure 5 contains a description of a service. It is only part of a large set of services of a domotic domain we have implemented. It shows a description of a service that is used to turn on the lights of two different zones of a house. Nested to the XML tag "params", there are explicit the preconditions for the service execution. By default, the logical operator "and" is used. In this case, there are two possible ways of executing a service: (i) provide only an action with value equals to "turn-on". This means that a user can only say "turn-on" to the system to turn the lights on; (ii) provide an action with value equals to "turn-on", and the zone where the user wants to act.

The tag named "execute" defines the behavior for the execution of the service. The tag "name" indicates the function code name that is executed when the service is selected. The tag "sucess" indicates the new state of the device. This new state: "on", does not include, naturally, the "turn-on-light" service, but it includes a "turn-off-light" service. Theoretically, if we turn on a light we cannot turn on the same light again, but we are able to turning it off.

The SM can also restrict the access of certain users to the services. There are three types of devices: (i) public, (ii) private, and (iii) restricted devices. The public devices are available for all users. Whenever the SM looks for services, these ones are immediately considered. The private devices are only avaliable for those users that have gained privilege access, and therefore, have inserted a key or password in the system. The restricted devices are even more specific than the private ones. They demand particular users, and no one else can access those devices besides them. Figure 6 shows part of a file defining the access information related to three devices. The first device named "Future House Bedroom Light Controller", is declared public, so everyone has access to it. Underneath is a private device named Future House Bedroom TV Controller, meaning that users who want to play with the TV controller must have privilege access. At the bottom is a restricted device. In this case, only the user named "marcio" can access the device.

```
<device hashcode="589654695" type="public">
 <name>Future House Bedroom Light Controller</name>
 <first_access>1083357587921</first_access>
 <last_access>1084211071109</last_access>
 <users/>
</device>
<device hashcode="614235759" type="private">
 <name>Future House Bedroom TV Controller</name>
 <first_access>1084204657484</first_access>
 <last_access>1084204716140</last_access>
 <users/>
</device>
<device hashcode="614235761" type="restricted">
 <name>Future House Bedroom Glass Controller</name>
 <first_access>1084206473546</first_access>
 <last_access>1084211071109</last_access>
 <users>
  <user>marcio</user>
 </users>
</device>
```

Fig. 6. Device restriction file content example

3.3 Addition of a New Domain

To add a new dialogue domain, it is necessary to: (i) define a description of the domain in XML. This description includes the new services, see figure 5; (ii) define the implementation code that will real execute the services. This is a kind of device driver; (iii) define a file in XML with the identification of the domain objects. This file will be used to make the recognition of the objects, see Figure 4. (iv) Define a template file in XML of the system domain utterances. The Generation Manager module makes use of this file, but it is currently loaded by the Generation Manager and not requested to the Service Manager. Figure 7 shows some utterances used by the dialogue system in the lights domain. The tag "requestslot" is used to ask for a specific slot value. When an action must be fullfilled, one of the three utterances inside the scope of the tag "action" is ramdomly choosed. If the system wants to ask for a zone to act, the utterance nested to tag "zone" is sent to user with "`[$action]`" being actually replaced for an action previously provided by the user.

```
<requestslot>
 <action>
  <utt> Do you wish to turn-on or turn-off the light? </utt>
  <utt> What are your intentions?You want the lights on or off?
  </utt>
  <utt> Do you wish to raise or diminish the light intensity?
  </utt>
 </action>
 <zone>
  <utt> What light do you want to [$action]? </utt>
 </zone>
</requestslot>
```

Fig. 7. Part of a template system utterances file

4 Dialogue Flow Example

In this section we present a small example of how our dialogue system works, including some of the messages interchanged between the components. This example makes the assumption that the dialogue system controls the lights and the television of a home division. The system can turn on and turn off the lights as well as the television. The difficulty is extended because there exists two independent light zones, where the user can apply the light operations. It is possible to apply operations to one zone independent of the other. For example, turn-on the lights of the A zone and after, turn-off the lights of the B zone.

1. **The user starts by saying "turn-on".** The Interpretation Manager (IM) component receives the speech act associated with this phrase. To build the interpretations, the IM needs to know what it means in the available domains.

2. **The IM requests Service Manager (SM) to give information about the "turn-on" object.** The SM grasps the available and accessible user domains and searches a database for the object with that information.
3. **The SM responds to the IM.** The response gives the characteristics of the object to the IM. In this case, the object is recognized in two different domains. The word is an action that belongs to the lights domain and to the television domain.

   We should note that at any time, what is recognized or not, is totally dependent on SM. So, if for some reason, we decide to pull out the lights device from the domain, turning it inaccessible, the next time recognition is made, the answer would be positive, but only for the television domain.
4. **The IM creates two interpretations.** Because the object was recognized in two different domains, the IM creates a Discourse Obligation (DO) accordingly. In this case, the IM creates a Domain Desambiguation DO.
5. **The IM sends the DO created to the Behavioral Agent (BA).**
6. **The BA selects this DO as the next system action, and sends it to the Generation Manager (GM).**
7. **The GM uses the domain independent template file to generate a desambiguation question.** In this case the system generates a question like: "What do you pretend to turn-on, the lights or the tv?". We should note that the system uses a single independent domain template file to generate all the desambiguation questions. In this one, "turn-on" is the intendent action and, "lights", or "tv", are the domain names associated with the Service Manager.

   Lets suppose the user says that he wants to turn on the lights. In other words, the user answer was "the light". With this answer, the desambiguation is over, and IM will deal with only one interpretation.
8. **IM requests SM for services associated with the light domain.** IM needs to know now how to proceed the dialog. To do that, IM requests SM information about all the services associated with that particular domain.
9. **SM processes the IM request.** SM retrieves information about all services associated with the particular domain. As said before, these services define the behavior of the system, and constitutes what can be done by the Dialogue Manager. We are assuming that the user has the necessary privileges to access these services.
10. **The SM returns a response to IM.**
11. **The IM processes the SM answer.** The SM has found at least two services for the light domain: (i) the turn on; and (ii) the turn off service. But because the user has already said that he wants to turn on the lights (the Discourse Context provides this information), only this service is considered.
12. **IM creates a DO for execution of the service.**

5 House of the Future

We recently extended the demo room at our lab to the project known as "Casa do Futuro". This project consists of a house where are installed some of the latest technology inovations in smart-house. We have installed our system in the main bedroom. In this division there is: (i) one big tv with split screen capabilities; (ii) two independent light zones; and (iii) a glass with the ability to change its state to opaque or lucid. It was not possible to obtain the current state of the television and of the glass. No feedback directly from these devices could then be used. For that reason, except for the lights where we could obtain their intensity, the current state of the television and of the glass was maintained in the Service Manager, and updated by the execution of operations on the device.

Besides the integration of the recognition and synthesis technologies with the spoken dialogue system, we also developed an animated character with lypsinc capability[9]. So, whenever a visitor wants to control a device, he calls our virtual buttler, and he appears on the tv set, waiting for any order, and giving feedback when something happens.

6 Concluding Remarks

The work reported in this paper results from an integration of several components being developed in our lab. This system is the result of a collaborative effort between people working in the different technologies, and it became a common platform where the different components can be associated to produce multiple applications.

The Service Manager (SM) was developed to provide an unique point of contact with the dialogue domain(s). The SM can be modified with the ignorance of the dialogue manager, only reflecting the modifications when a request is made. We achieved independence of the dialogue manager relative to the domains, and we can introduce new domains without having to modify the dialogue manager behavior. Currently, the system utterances template file used by the the dialogue system is loaded in the Generation Manager module. Because this is an activity that envolves domain knowledge, the SM should also provide to the Dialogue Manager information about generation activities. This remains future work in the SM development.

The system has been used in the "house of the future" to control three devices. This work made also use of speech recognition and an animated character. It is also being used on a demonstration system, accessible by telephone, where people can ask for weather conditions, stock hold information, bus trip information and cinema schedules.

We expect to conduct a more formal evaluation of our system in order to quantify the user satisfaction.

References

1. M. McTear, "Spoken Dialogue Technology: Enabling the Conversational User Interface", in ACM Computing Surveys, pp. 1-85 (2002).
2. J. Neto, N. Mamede, R. Cassaca, L. Oliveira, The Development of a Multi-purpose Spoken Dialogue System, EUROSPEECH'2003 - 8th European Conference on Speech Communication and Technology, (2003).
3. J. Allen, G. Ferguson, A. Stent: An architecture for more realistic conversational systems, in Proc. of Intelligent User Interfaces (IUI-01), Santa Fe, NM, Jan, 14-17 (2001).
4. P. Madeira, M. Mourão, N. Mamede: STAR FRAMES - A step ahead in the design of conversational systems capable of handling multiple domains, ICEIS, Angers, France (2003).
5. D.R.Traum: Speech Acts for Dialogue Agents. UMIACS, Univ. of Maryland, pp. 17-30 (1999).

6. J. Kreutel, C. Matheson: Modelling Questions and Assertions in Dialogue Using Obligations, 3rd Workshop on the Semantics and Pragmatics of Dialogue. Univ. of Amsterdam (1999).
7. D. R. Traum, J. F. Allen: Discourse Obligations in Dialogue Processing, in Proc. of the 32nd Annual Meeting of the Association for Computational Linguistics, pp. 1-8 (1994).
8. M. Mourão, P. Madeira, N. Mamede, "Interpretations and Discourse Obligations in a Dialog System", in Proc.Propor 2003, Faro, Portugal, pp. 197-200 (2003). Springer-Verlag Berlin Heidelberg 2003.
9. M. Viveiros, "Cara Falante - Uma interface visual para um sistema de diálogo falado", Graduation Thesis, IST, Work in progress.

Information Retrieval in Digital Theses Based on Natural Language Processing Tools

Rocío Abascal, Béatrice Rumpler, and Jean-Marie Pinon

INSA of Lyon – LIRIS
7 Avenue J. Capelle Bât 502 – Blaise Pascal
F69621 Villeurbanne cedex, France
{Rocio.Abascal, Beatrice.Rumpler}@insa-lyon.fr

Abstract. Search performance can be greatly improved by describing data using Natural Language Processing (NLP) tools to create new metadata and domain ontologies. A methodology is presented to use domain specific knowledge to improve user request. This knowledge is based on concepts, extracted from the document itself, used as *"semantic metadata tags"* in order to annotate XML documents. We present the process followed to define and to add new XML semantic metadata into the digital library of scientific theses. Using these new metadata, an ontology is also constructed by following a methodology. Effective retrieval information is obtained by using an intelligent system based on XML semantic metadata and domain ontology.

1 Introduction

Internet has developed digital libraries that make available a great amount of digital information. Search engines work to provide this information to the user. Although there have been substantial advances to structure information, users must still evaluate the pertinence of documents presented by the web. Generally, to evaluate the pertinence, users read several fragments of the documents rather than the complete documents. It is fastidious to read and then to evaluate several entire documents, that is why many pertinent documents are always unknown by users. Our objective is to propose a solution to enable a better access to pertinent documents or fragments of documents in digital libraries.

The project of INSA of Lyon called CITHER (consultation of entire text versions of theses) concerns the online publishing of scientific theses. We encountered the same difficulties to find pertinent information in the CITHER system as in other digital libraries. During a search session, it is impossible to extract the pertinent contents of several theses. To evaluate the pertinence of a thesis, users must read the entire document. Furthermore, a document may be too long for a quick evaluation.

A promising way to solve this problem is to use metadata to *"annotate"* the documents and to describe their content in a better way. In our proposal, we have decided to extract the concepts that best describe the theses and to use them as metadata like *"semantic tags"*. Of course, manual extraction of concepts is a time-consuming, so we use Natural Processing Language (NLP) tools for automating the extraction of concepts to overcome these limitations.

Another promising way is to use an ontology based on concepts used as *"semantic tags"*. An ontology is the description of concepts and their relationships. In our

J. L. Vicedo et al. (Eds.): EsTAL 2004, LNAI 3230, pp. 172–182, 2004.

approach, the construction of an ontology from digital theses is proposed by following a methodology.

In our context, which is a digital library that publishes scientific theses, the addition of new semantic information into documents is intended to improve information retrieval. In order to insert new semantic information into digital theses, we have used a tool able to extract concepts from a given document. Section 3.1 describes how we have chosen this tool, and then we present the annotation system.

One of the causes of non-pertinent retrieval comes from the difficulty to describe with the appropriate words the users' needs. Therefore, queries are often too broad or too specific to cover relevant information. So, our approach is based on the search of annotated theses by using an ontology to expand user requests and to give the possibility to select between pertinent documents. The ontology is composed by the terms of a domain, which become, in our proposition, *"semantic tags"* used to annotate theses (Section 3). In addition, the ontology is composed by the identification of relationships between concepts. The identification of relationships among concepts and the methodology followed to construct our ontology are described in Section 4. This methodology is based on two steps: (1) the ontology capture step (Section 4.1) and (2) the ontology coding step (Section 4.2). In Section 5, we present the intelligent system designed to access to pertinent information by using our ontology. The conclusion and further research are proposed at the end.

2 Background

The terms are linguistic representations of concepts in a particular subject field [6]. Consequently, applications in automatic extraction of concepts, called terms in many cases, include specialized dictionary constructions, human and machine translations, indexing in books and digital libraries [6].

The ontology of the University Michigan Digital Library (UMDL) [23] delineates the process of publications using six formal concepts: *"conception"*, *"expression"*, *"manifestation"*, *"materialization"*, *"digitization"* and *"instance"*. Each of these concepts is related to other concept by using: *"has"*, *"of"*, *"kind-of"* or *"extends"* relationships.

An ontology in the domain of the digital library is presented in [19]. This ontology named ScholOnto is an ontology-based digital library server to support scholarly interpretation and discourse. It enables researchers to describe and debate via a semantic network the contributions a document makes, and its relationship to the literature. As a result, by using this ontology, researchers will no longer need to make claims about the contributions of documents (e.g. *"this is a new theory"*, *"this is a new model"*, *"this is a new notation"*, etc), or contest its relationships to other documents and ideas (e.g. *"it applies"*, *"it extends"*, *"it predicts"*, *"it refutes"*, etc).

Some of the methods used to specify ontologies in digital library projects include vocabularies and cataloguing codes such as Machine Readable Cataloguing (MARC). Other projects are based on the use of thesauri and classifications to describe different components of a document such as the title, the name of the author, etc. Thus, semantic relationships among concepts are defined by using broader and related terms in thesauri [4].

3 Methodology Used to Annotate Theses

In large document collections, such as digital libraries, it is very important to use mechanisms able to select the pertinent information. The use of *"keywords"* to represent documents is a promising way to manipulate information and to classify pertinent or non-pertinent documents contained in digital libraries.

Annotation is the process of adding semantic markups to documents, but determining which concepts are tied to a document is not an easy task. To address this problem, several methods are proposed to extract concepts from a given document. In the field of NLP tools for the extraction of concepts we consider two main approaches: *"key phrase assignment"* and *"key phrase extraction"* [24].

By the term *"key phrase"*, we mean a phrase composed by two or more words that describes, in a general way, the content of the document. *"Key phrases"* can be seen as *"key concepts"* able to classify documents into categories.

A *"key phrase assignment"* uses a controlled vocabulary to select concepts or phrases that describes, in a general way, the document. Instead, the *"key phrase extraction"* selects the concepts from the document itself.

Our approach takes a document as input and generates automatically a list of concepts as output. This work could be called *"key phrase generation"* or *"concept generation"*. However, the NLP tool used in our work performs *"concept extraction"* which means that the extracted concepts always appear in the body of the input document.

3.1 A Natural Language Processing Tool to Extract Concepts

In order to choose one tool able to extract the higher number of pertinent concepts, we have analyzed four tools: (1) TerminologyExtractor of Chamblon Systems Inc., (2) Xerox Terminology Suite of Xerox, (3) Nomino of Nomino Technologies and (4) Copernic Summarizer of NRC.

To evaluate the output list generated by each tool, we have compared each list with a list composed by concepts generated manually. The measure of performance and the method followed for scoring concepts, as well as the results that show that Nomino is the most interesting tool for our approach, are described in [1].

Therefore, in our work we use Nomino to automatically extract concepts from documents. Nomino is a search engine distributed by Nomino Technologies [16]. It adopts a morphosyntactic approach and uses a morphological analyzer that makes *"stemming"*. *"Stemming"*, means that the prefix and the suffix are removed to make a simple word. Nomino applies empirical criteria to filter the noise associated to the extracted concepts. These criteria include frequency and category, as well as stop lists.

Nomino produces two types of interactive index containing all the concepts that most accurately summarize the content of a given document. One of the indexes created is very general. However, the other one contains concepts that are based on two principles: the *"gain to express"* and the *"gain to reach"*. The *"gain to express"* classifies the concepts according to their location in the given document. For example, if a paragraph is only concerned with one concept then this concept will be classified as important. The *"gain to reach"* classifies the concepts according to the frequency of appearance. If a word is very rare then it will be selected as important. For example, if in a given document we have the phrase *"computer software"* and the phrase *"developing computer software"*. Then the second phrase will be selected as the most important because it is more complete for describing one activity. On the other hand, if the frequency of *"computer software"* is higher than *"developing computer software"*, then both phrases will appear in the concepts list created by Nomino.

3.2 The Annotation Tool

Since manual annotation can be time consuming and open to error, we have developed a tool to easily add metadata into documents by making selections from one base of concepts.

To use the concepts that were extracted by the index of Nomino, we have proposed a tool to *"annotate"* documents [1]. The task consists in adding new metadata into the thesis while the PhD student is writing it. We do not consider the writing process using LaTeX since many of the theses found in the CITHER project were not written using LaTeX. The student adds the new metadata based on (1) the base of concepts, (2) the Nomino evaluation and (3) the personal tags. The new metadata are characterized by using a particular symbol. So, after the student has inserted the metadata and the thesis is completed the tool allows the identification of the semantic markups. Usually when the paragraph containing the symbol inserted (which contains the concept) is identified, it is embedded by a simple tag such as *"<concept-name>"* and *"</concept-name>"* at the end. This annotation scheme allows us the management of Nomino concepts as well as the indexation and extraction of pertinent paragraphs from the document according to specific search criteria. During a search session, the system focuses on semantic markups, the XML tags, in order to retrieve the pertinent paragraph(s).

The following features characterize our annotation tool:

- The PhD student uses the annotation tool at anytime during the writing process of the thesis.
- Nomino reads the selection of the student (parts of the thesis) and proposes concepts to the student. The student can accept, deny or complete the Nomino's proposition.
- The concepts proposed to the user can be: concepts extracted from the document itself (by using Nomino) or concepts usually used in all the theses (e.g. *"model"*, *"architecture"*).
- The validated concepts are integrated into the thesis as metadata tags. These new tags will be exploited during a search session.

The next Figure, (Fig. 1) presents the general structure of our annotation tool.

We have made another study in order to improve the annotation tool. In the next section (Section 4), we describe this work, which concerns the construction of an ontology able to expand the requests and categorize the documents.

4 Methodology Used to Construct the Domain Ontology

Gruber has defined an ontology as *"an explicit specification of a conceptualization"*. A conceptualization is defined by concepts and other entities that are presumed to exist in some area of interest and the relationships that hold among them [11]. An ontology in the artificial intelligence community means the construction of knowledge models [11], [13], [18], [20] which specify concepts, their attributes and

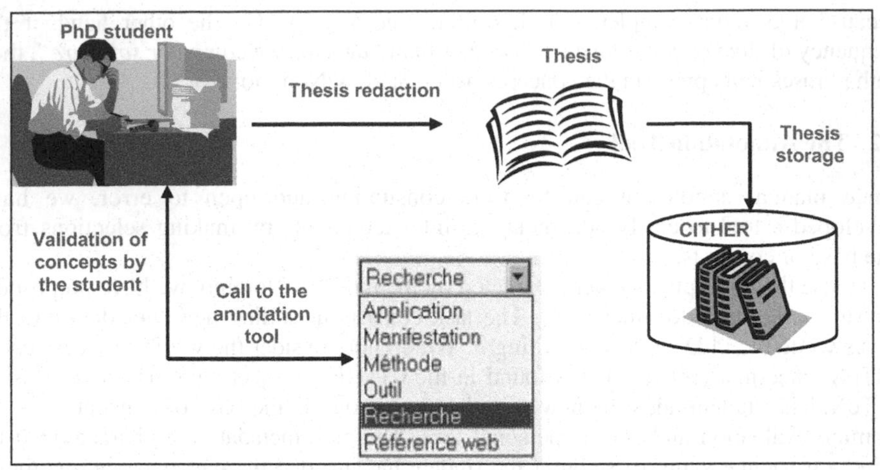

Fig. 1. General structure of the annotation tool

inter-relationships. A knowledge model is a specification of a domain that focuses on concepts, relationships and reasoning steps characterizing the phenomenon under investigation.

Our ontology is composed of two elements: the *"domain concepts"* and the *"relationships"* among them. The *"domain concepts"* are words or groups of words that are used to characterize a specific field. The *"relationships"* among these concepts are characterized by associative and hierarchic type.

Two main approaches can be chosen when building an ontology. The first one relies on a *"top-down method"*. Someone may use an existing ontology and specify or generalize it to create another one. The second way to build an ontology is by using a *"bottom-up method"*. This method consists in extracting from the appropriate documents all the concepts and relations among concepts to compose an ontology. We believe that this last method is accurate to our case because it does not exist yet an ontology tied to our domain. This method relies on two main steps: the (1) extraction of domain concepts (Section 4.1.1) and (2) the identification of relationships among these domain concepts (Section 4.1.2).

Various methodologies exist to guide the theoretical approach chosen, and numerous tools for building an ontology are available. The problem is that these procedures have not merged into popular development styles or protocols, and tools have not yet matured to the degree one expects in other software practices. Examples of methodologies followed to build an ontology are described in [2], [12], [21]. In general, the following steps can define the methodology used to build our ontology: (1) the *"ontology capture"* step and (2) the *"ontology coding"* step. The *"ontology capture"* step consists in the identification of concepts and relationships. The *"ontology coding"* step consists in the definition of concepts and relationships in a formal language. These two steps will be described in the following paragraphs in order to present the construction of our ontology.

4.1 The Ontology Capture Step

The ontology capture step consists in designing the overall conceptual structure of the domain. This will likely involve identifying the main concrete concepts of the domain (Section 4.1.1) and their properties, and identifying relationships among concepts (Section 4.1.2).

4.1.1 Concept Extraction

This section reports on our methodology used to define concepts that describe the content of theses. The backbone of our ontology is a hierarchy of concepts that have been extracted from the theses themselves.

Concepts of the ontology are used to automatically categorize documents to allow a thematic access to documents. The problem of retrieving concepts and their structure comes from the use of tools able to retrieve concepts. As described in Section 2, we have used Nomino to extract our concepts. Given a document or a group of documents, Nomino constructs a specific index, which contains phrases composed of two or more words that are supposed to define the field. These concepts are called CNU (Complex Noun Units); they are series of structured terms composed by nominal groups or prepositional groups [8]. We used these CNU as a starting point to construct our ontology.

The use of NLP tools, like Nomino, often produces *"errors"* that have to be corrected by a specialist of the domain. Some of these *"errors"* include phrases that are not really concepts or phrases that do not really describe the document. These *"errors"* are further described by [3]. The *"errors"* found in our work, by using Nomino, were generally about the kind of: (1) verbs frequently used (e.g. *"called"*), (2) abbreviations of names (e.g. *"J.L. Morrison"*.), (3) names of people, cities, etc., (e.g. *"France community"*), and also (4) phrases composed by CNU concepts which describe the actual situation of the document (*"next chapter"*, *"next phase of the development"*). The corpus used to construct the ontology was composed of scientific documents. At this time we have only worked with a sample composed by six theses of the computer science field. This corpus represents different applications of the computer science field. We have worked only with these six theses because we have noticed that using theses of the computer science field the augmentation of concepts is very little especially when we have new theses. For example, the Table 1 shows that there is a tendency to use the same concepts. For example, when we have 12 theses there are not new concepts.

Although, in the Table 1 we have an augmentation of concepts only in the row of 7 theses. This is because in our work we are focus in the concepts that, in general, often appear in almost all the theses. Also, Nomino does not considers the concepts that are used all the time in a document, this means that if a word is used very often is probably a "common" word and not a concept. Although, by using Nomino we have obtained 1,007 concepts. We obtained concepts like: "information research", "information system", "research system", "remote training", "abstract ontology", "logical model" etc. However, some concepts are not pertinent and a human expert must evaluate them. After the evaluation we have selected only 688 concepts.

The next step to construct the ontology is to define the relationships among concepts. In the next paragraph, we will describe the process used to find relationships by using Nomino's concepts as input. These concepts are proposed to the PhD student while the redaction process takes place.

Table 1. Comparison of the concepts extracted for the set of theses when adding a new thesis to the corpus. The numbers of the first column are the number of theses in which the concepts agree

# of theses where the concepts agree	Initial corpus	Initial corpus + new thesis
1	14784	13878
2	1141	1016
3	303	234
4	115	78
5	43	33
6	24	16
7	8	10
8	4	4
9	4	2
10	2	1
11	1	0
12	0	0

4.1.2 Identification of Semantic Relationships

With regard to the acquisition of semantic relationships, there are several approaches for acquiring semantic information. Once concepts have been retrieved, by using Nomino, they must be structured. One of the best-used techniques to discover relationships among concepts relies on the number of co-occurrences. This technique identifies concepts that often occur together in documents.

There are different techniques used to identify relationships among concepts. These techniques are based on contexts of their co-occurrences. The idea is that two similar concepts do not necessarily occur together, but can occur in similar contexts.

A first method based on this principle is described in [7]. This method defines a context and determines which concepts or terms, from a predefined list, often occurs in similar contexts. The terms from the predefined list are called *"target words"* and the ones appearing in the same context are known as *"context words"*. Each *"context word"* is weighed according to the dependency that exists among the given target and with other context words.

A second method relying on this idea of similarity between contexts of concepts' occurrences is described in [9]. This method, which uses syntactical information, considers the concepts themselves, mainly noun phrases and linking words composing these concepts, based on the similarity of their syntactical contexts.

In our approach, we used a NLP tool able to extract relationships among concepts. This tool is named LIKES (Linguistic and Knowledge Engineering Station) [17]. LIKES, based on statistical principles, is a computational linguistic station with certain functions able to build terminologies and ontologies.

The concepts extracted by Nomino have been paired up in order to find relationships between them. Thus, we have manually paired all the concepts. These pairs have also been compared in the opposite way. For example, the pair *"knowledge / language"* has also been evaluated as *"language / knowledge"*. Identifying relationships with LIKES takes a long time to process the corpus and to visualize the possible relationships. Furthermore, the relationships found have to be evaluated by a human expert.

LIKES allows the representation of relationships in order to find similar relationships in other pairs of concepts. Examples of phrases that contained some relationships between the concept pair *"knowledge / language"* are the following (we have kept the same sentence structure in English as in French language):

- *Knowledge* is represented by all the *Languages*;
- *Knowledge* is represented by some *Languages*;
- *Knowledge* is represented in all the *Languages*.

We can notice in this example that the relation *"Is represented"* is in evidence.

In the ontology-coding step we are going to explain how relationships identified by LIKES are used to model a formal ontology.

4.2 The Ontology-Coding Step

Uschold [22] defines *"coding"* as the explicit representation of the captured conceptualization in a formal language.

In order to represent concepts and their relationships we have chosen the tool named Protégé-2000. Protégé-2000 is a knowledge-engineering tool that enables developers to create ontologies and knowledge bases [5], [10], [14], [15].

So, we have used Protégé-2000 to model the concepts extracted by Nomino and the relationships among concepts identified by LIKES. Now, we have an ontology of the computer science field composed by 3194 concepts.

5 Effective Retrieval Information

Most of search engines use simple keywords connected by logical operators to make queries. In our context, we have developed a domain ontology and we have inserted new metadata into the digital theses. Nowadays, we are working on the implementation of a prototype able to improve the query process. This prototype will provide several improvements in information retrieval processes:

- Terms used in the user's request will be transformed into concepts;
- It will be easier to navigate between concepts;
- Information obtained will be more precise to the users' needs.

The terms used in the user's request will be transformed by the use of the ontology. Often, when a user proposes a query, the terms are ambiguous and frequently different from those used in the documents. So, we are conceiving an intelligent system able to expand the users' requests with the concepts contained in the documents. The intelligent system will propose new concepts or synonyms to expand the user's query. These candidate concepts will be first selected from the ontology. In way to expand the users request, new concepts and logical operators are studied. Moreover, a thesaurus will be used to complete the ontology. User will accept or deny the system suggestion.

Once the request is defined, the system will find pertinent information, included in the theses, by using semantic metadata. Then the paragraphs containing the pertinent information will be displayed. Users will be able to select the most pertinent paragraph(s) before reading the complete document(s).

The following features characterize our proposal for an intelligent access (Fig. 2):

- User input will be done via an HTML page.
- Parsing will be used to determine the sentence composition of the user's request.
- The ontology will allow the selection of new concepts to expand the request.
- The new query will be sent to the database in order to retrieve fragments or complete theses. In this step, the query will be based on the semantic metadata contained in the theses (see Fig. 1).
- The end user will get the results via the HTML page.
- User will be able to retrieve the entire thesis if there exist satisfaction with the results.

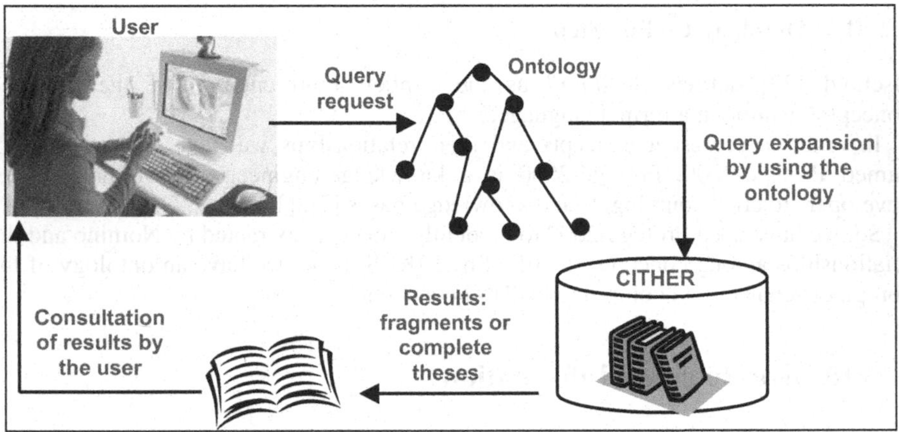

Fig. 2. General structure of the proposed model to expand the user query requests

In general, given a search term, the ontology will propose closer terms to significantly enrich the request of the user.

6 Conclusion and Further Research

We have presented an approach to improve document retrieval by using NLP tools based on the semantic content of digital theses. Our approach has a double advantage: first, it can entirely exploit the content of digital theses by using semantic annotations and second, it can provide new alternatives to the users' requests.

Ontologies can be used to support the growth of a new kind of digital library, implemented as a distributed intelligent system [23]. In consequence, an ontology can be used to deduce characteristics of content being searched, and to identify appropriated and available operations in order to access or manipulate content in other ways.

We have constructed an ontology by following a logical methodology. As long as there are no tools able to automatically construct ontologies from documents, the process carried out by using NLP tools will continue to require the help of human experts. The extraction of relationships by hand is very complex and with the use of NLP tools there are still some concepts whose relationships have to be instantiated by the human expert.

It is evident that there are still some needs in the ontology construction domain. The construction of our ontology is only the first step towards making available the pertinent information in the digital library.

Currently, we are developing a prototype to access to the pertinent information. To retrieve this information, the prototype will be based on the new semantic metadata tags. These tags are the ones added by the PhD student while the writing process of the thesis takes place. The retrieval of information will be also based on the ontology concepts in order to expand query requests during a search session. Our prototype will propose different keywords to the user. Requests will be completed during the research of theses.

Further research should investigate the use of dictionaries or thesauri in digital libraries to detect similar and non-identical concepts. The use of synonyms to complete our ontology could be another attempt.

References

1. R. Abascal, B. Rumpler, and J-M Pinon. An analysis of tools for an automatic extraction of concept in documents for a better knowledge management. In Proceedings of 2003 IRMA International Conference, Philadelphia Pennsylvania, May 2003.
2. M. Blazquez, M. Fernandez, J-M Garcia-Pinar, and A. Gomez-Perez. Building Ontologies at the Knowledge Level using the Ontology Design Environment. In B.R. Gaines and M.A. Musen, editors, Proceedings of the 11th Banff Knowledge Acquisition for Knowledge-based Systems workshop, KAW'98. SRDG Publications, Department of Computer Science, University of Calgary, 1998.
3. A. Condamines and J. Rebeyrolle. Construction d'une Base de Connaissances Terminologiques à partir de Textes: Expérimentation et Definition d'une Méthode. In Journées Ingénierie des Connaissances et Apprentissage Automatique (JICAA'97), Roscoff, France, 191-206, 1997.
4. Y. Ding and S. Foo. Ontology Research and Development. Part 1 – A Review of Ontology Generation. Journal of Information Science, 28(2), 2002.
5. H. Eriksson, E. Berglund, and P. Nevalainen. Using Knowledge Engineering Support for a Java Documentation Viewer. In ACM Press, editor, Proceedings of the 14th International Conference on Software Engineering and Knowledge Engineering, 57-64, Ischia, Italy, 2002.
6. K. Frantzi and S. Ananiadou. Automatic term recognition using contextual clues. In Third DELOS Workshop. Cross-Language Information Retrieval. Zurich 5-7 March, 1997.
7. Susan Gauch, Jianying Wang, and Satya Mahesh Rachakonda. A corpus analysis approach for automatic query expansion and its extension to multiple databases. ACM Transactions on Information Systems, 17(3):250, 1999.
8. J. Golebiowska. SAMOVAR - Knowledge Capitalization in the Automobile Industry Aided by Ontologies. In Proceedings of the 12th International Conference on Knowledge Engineering and Knowledge Management (EKAW 2000), Juan-les-Pins, France, October 2000.
9. Gregory Grefenstette. Explorations in Automatic Thesaurus Discovery. Kluwer Academic Publishers, 1994.
10. W. Grosso, H. Eriksson, R. Fergerson, J. Gennari, S. Tu, and M. Musen. Knowledge Modeling at the Millennium: The Design and Evolution of Protégé. In Proceedings of the 12th International Workshop on Knowledge Acquisition, Modeling and Management (KAW'99).
11. T. R. Gruber. A translation approach to portable ontology specifications. Knowledge Acquisition, 5(2):199-220, June 1993.

12. Knowledge Based Systems Inc. The IDEF5 Ontology Description Capture Method Overview. Technical report, KBSI, Texas, 1994.
13. E. Motta. Reusable Components for Knowledge Modelling. In IOS Press, Amsterdam, NL, 1999.
14. M. A. Musen, R. W. Fergerson, W. Grosso, N. F. Noy, M. Crubezy, and J. H. Gennari. Component-Based Support for Building Knowledge-Acquisition Systems. In Proceedings of the Conference on Intelligent Information Processing IPP 2000 of the International Federation for Information Processing World Computer Congress (WCC 2000), Beijing, 2000.
15. N. Noy, R. Fergerson, and M. Musen. The knowledge model of Protégé-2000: Combining interoperability and flexibility. In Proceedings of EKAW'2000, 2000.
16. P. Plante, L. Dumas, and A. Plante. Nomino version 4.2.22. http://www.nominotechnologies.com, 2001.
17. F. Rousselot and P. Frath. Terminologie et Intelligence Artificielle. Traits d'Union, G.Kleiber and N. Le Queler, dir., Presses Universitaires de Caen, 181-192, 2002.
18. W. Schuler and J. Smith. Author's Argumentation Assistant (AAA): A Hypertext-Based Authoring Tool for Argumentative Texts. In Proceedings of the ECHT'90: European Conference on Hypertext: Argumentation, Design and Knowledge Acquisition, 137-151, Cambridge, Cambridge University Press, 1990.
19. Simon Buckingham Shum, John Domingue, and Enrico Motta. Scholarly Discourse as Computable Structure. In OHS-6/SC-2, 120-128, 2000.
20. Simon Buckingham Shum, Enrico Motta, and John Domingue. ScholOnto: an ontology-based digital library server for research documents and discourse. International Journal on Digital Libraries, 3(3):237-248, August/Sept 2000.
21. M. Uschold and M. Gruninger. Ontologies: Principles, Methods and Applications. Knowledge Engineering Review, 11(2), 1996.
22. M. Uschold and M. King. Towards a Methodology for Building Ontologies. In Workshop on Basic Ontological Issues in Knowledge Sharing held in conjunction with IJCAI-95, 1995.
23. P.Weinstein. Seed Ontologies: Growing Digital Libraries as Distributed, Intelligent Systems. In Proceedings of the Second International ACM Digital Library Conference, Philadelphia, PA, USA, July 1997.
24. H. Ian Witten, G. W. Paynter, E. Frank, C. Gutwin, and C. G. Nevill-Manning. KEA: Practical Automatic Keyphrase Extraction. In ACM DL, 254-255, 1999.

Integrating Conceptual Density with WordNet Domains and CALD Glosses for Noun Sense Disambiguation

Davide Buscaldi[1,2], Paolo Rosso[2], and Francesco Masulli[3]

[1] Dipartimento di Informatica e Scienze dell'Informazione (DISI), Università di Genova, Italy
buscaldi@disi.unige.it

[2] Dpto. de Sistemas Informáticos y Computación (DSIC), Universidad Politecnica de Valencia, Spain
prosso@dsic.upv.es

[3] INFM - Genova and Dipartimento di Informatica, Università di Pisa, Italy
masulli@disi.unige.it

Abstract. The lack of large, semantically annotated corpora is one of the main drawbacks of Word Sense Disambiguation systems. Unsupervised systems do not need such corpora and rely on the information of the WordNet ontology. In order to improve their performance, the use of other lexical resources need to be investigated. This paper describes the effort to integrate the Conceptual Density approach with sources of lexical information different from WordNet, particularly the WordNet Domains and the Cambridge Advanced Learner's Dictionary. Unfortunately, enriching WordNet glosses with samples of another lexical resource did not provide the expected results.

1 Introduction

The lack of large, semantically annotated corpora is one of the main drawbacks of supervised Word Sense Disambiguation(*WSD*) approaches. Our unsupervised approach does not need such corpora: it relies only on the WordNet (*WN*) lexical resource, and it is based on *Conceptual Density* and the frequency of WordNet senses[7]. Conceptual Density *(CD)* is a measure of the correlation among the sense of a given word and its context. The foundation of this measure is the *Conceptual Distance*, defined as the length of the shortest path which connects two concepts in a hierarchical semantic net.

Our approach gave good results, in terms of precision, for the disambiguation of nouns over SemCor (81.55% with a context window of only two nouns, compared with the MFU-baseline of 75.55%), and in the recent all-words task in the Senseval-3 (73.40%, compared with the MFU-baseline of 69.08%) [2]. Unfortunately, although the precision achieved by our system is above that of the baseline, we still need to improve the recall, since there are nouns, whose senses

J. L. Vicedo et al. (Eds.): EsTAL 2004, LNAI 3230, pp. 183–194, 2004.

are close in meaning, that are left undisambiguated by our system. We investigated the use of other lexical resources, the *WordNet Domains*[1] [5] and the Cambridge Advanced Learner's Dictionary[2] (*CALD*) to improve our approach.

2 Combining Conceptual Density and Frequency

In our approach the noun sense disambiguation is carried out by means of the formula presented in [7]. This formula has been derived from the original Conceptual Density formula described in [1]:

$$CD(c,m) = \frac{\sum_{i=0}^{m-1} nhyp^i}{\sum_{i=0}^{h-1} nhyp^i} \tag{1}$$

where c is the synset at the top of subhierarchy, m the number of word senses falling within a subhierarchy, h the height of the subhierarchy, and $nhyp$ the averaged number of hyponyms for each node (synset) in the subhierarchy. The numerator expresses the expected area for a subhierarchy containing m marks (word senses), whereas the divisor is the actual area.

Due to the fact that the averaged number of hyponyms for each node in WN2.0 (the version we used) is greater than in WN1.4 (the version which was used originally by Agirre and Rigau), we decided to consider only the *relevant* part of the subhierarchy determined by the synset paths (from c to an ending node) of the senses of both the word to be disambiguated and its context, and not the portion of subhierarchy constituted by the synsets that do not belong to the synset paths. The base formula takes into account the M number of relevant synsets, corresponding to the *marks* m in Formula 1 ($|M|$=$|m|$, even if we determine the subhierarchies before adding such marks instead of vice versa like in [1]), divided by the total number nh of synsets of the subhierarchy.

$$baseCD(M, nh) = M/nh \tag{2}$$

The original formula and the above one do not take into account sense frecuency. It is possible that both formulas select subhierarchies with a low frequency related sense. In some cases this would be a wrong election. This pushed us to modify the CD formula by including also the information about frequency contained in WN:

$$CD(M, nh, f) = M^{\alpha}(M/nh)^{\log f} \tag{3}$$

where M is the number of relevant synsets, α is a constant (the best results were obtained over the SemCor corpus with α near to 0.10), and f is an integer representing the frequency of the subhierarchy-related sense in WN (1 means the most frequent, 2 the second most frequent, etc.). This means that the first sense of the word (i.e., the most frequent) gets at least a density of 1 and one of the

[1] Istituto per la Ricerca Scientifica e Tecnologica, Trento, Italy.
[2] http://dictionary.cambridge.org/

less frequent senses will be chosen only if it will exceed the density of the first sense. The M^{α} factor was introduced to give more weigth to those subhierarchies with a greater number of relevant synsets, when the same density is obtained among many subhierarchies.

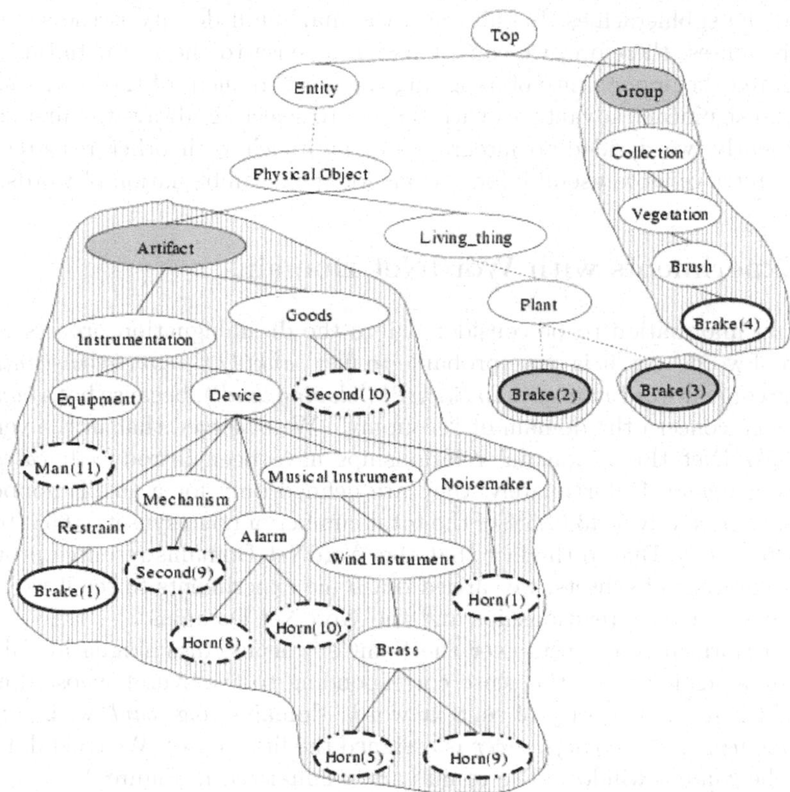

Fig. 1. Subhierarchies resulting from the disambiguation of *brake* with the context words {*horn, man, second*}. Example extracted from the Senseval-3 english-all-words test corpus ($M_1 = 9$, $nh_1 = 21$, $M_2 = M_3 = nh_2 = nh_3 = 1$ $M_4 = 1$, $nh_4 = 5$, where M_i and nh_i indicates, respectively, the M and nh values for the i-th sense)

In Figure 1 are shown the resulting WordNet subhierarchies from the disambiguation of *brake* with the context words {*horn, man, second*} from the sentence: "Brakes howled and a horn blared furiously, but the man would have been hit if Phil hadn't called out to him a second before", extracted from the all-words test corpus of Senseval-3. The areas of subhierarchies are drawn with a dashed background, the root of subhierarchies are the darker nodes, while the nodes corresponding to the synsets of the word to disambiguate and those of the context words are drawn with a thicker border. Four subhierarchies have been identified, one for each sense of *brake*. The senses of the context words falling outside of these subhierarchies are not taken into account. The resulting

CDs are, for each subhierarchy, respectively: $9^{0.10} * (9/21)^{\log 1} = 1.27$, 1, 1 and $1^{0.10} * (1/5)^{\log 4} = 0.07$; therefore, the first one is selected and the first sense is assigned to *brake*.

Nouns are left undisambiguated when different senses are close in meaning, like the senses 2 and 3 of *brake* in the previous example, and no context senses fall into the subhieracheis. In this case, the maximum density is the same (1) for more senses, therefore, we cannot assign a sense to the word. Initially, we investigated the opportunity of assigning the most frequent of those senses, but it gave no significant advantages with respect to selecting always the first sense. Consequently, we decided to integrate our approach with other resources, in order to retrieve more useful informations for the disambiguation of words.

3 Experiments with WordNet Domains

An useful information to be considered into the disambiguation process is the domain of words: e.g. it is more probable to find *bank(1)* (*'financial institution'*) with the context word *money* than *bank(2)* (*'sloping land'*), because both *bank(1)* and *money* concern the domain of "economy". We observed that in the version 2.0 of WordNet three 'domain' relationships have been introduced: *category*, *usage* and *region*. Unfortunately, they are defined only for a small number of synsets: respectively 3643 (4.5% of the total number of noun synsets), 653 (0.8%) and 1146 (1.4%). Due to the fact that the WordNet Domains resource provides a wider coverage of synsets, we carried out some experiments to see if we could exploit both the new relationships and the WordNet Domains.

We performed some tests over the SemCor corpus, disambiguating all the words by assigning them the sense corresponding to the synset whose domain is matched by the majority of context words' domains (e.g. *bank* with context words *money, stock, savings, river* is assigned the first sense). We tried different size of the context window. The results are summarized in Figure 2.

The very low recall, even with large context windows, and the smaller precision, obtained by using the domains relationship in WN2.0 with respect to the WordNet Domains resource, suggested us to rely only on the latter for further experiments. Since WordNet Domains has been developed on the version 1.6 of WordNet, it has been necessary to map the synsets from the older version to the the last version. This has been done in a fully automated way, by using the WordNet mappings for nouns and verbs, and by checking the similarity of synset terms and glosses for adjectives and adverbs. Some domains have also been assigned by hand in some cases, when necessary.

Thereafter, additional weights (*Mutual Domain Weights, MDWs*) have been added to the densities of the subhierarchies corresponding to those senses having the same domain of context nouns' senses. Each weight is proportional to the frequency of such senses, and is calculated in the following way:

$$MDW(w_f, c_{ij}) = \begin{cases} 0 & \text{if } Dom(w_f) \neq Dom(c_{ij}) \\ 1/f * 1/j & \text{if } Dom(w_f) = Dom(c_{ij}) \end{cases} \tag{4}$$

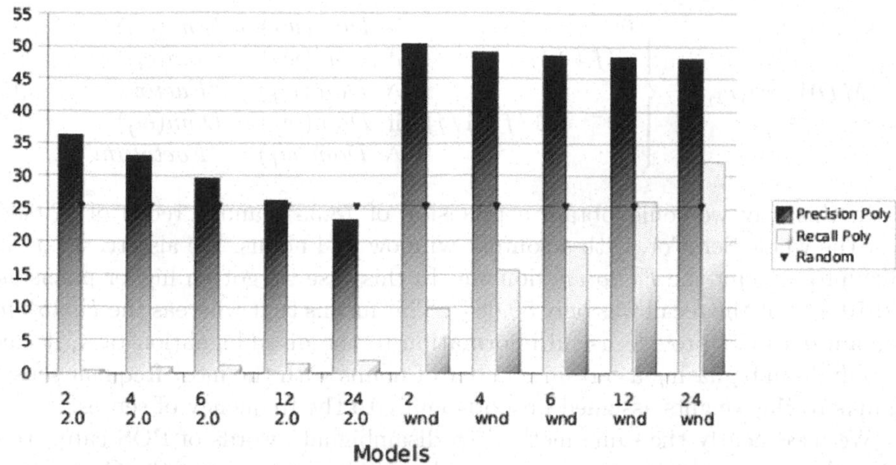

Fig. 2. Confrontation between WN2.0 domains relationships (2.0 columns) and WordNet domains (wnd columns) with different window sizes over polysemic nouns in the SemCor corpus. Precision and recall are given as percentages

where f is an integer representing the frequency of the sense of the word to be disambiguated, j gives the same information for the i-th context word, $Dom(x) : Synsets \longrightarrow Domains$ is the function returning the domain(s) corresponding to synset x, w_f and c_{ij} are, respectively, the synsets corresponding to the f-th sense of the word to be disambiguated and the j-th sense of the i-th context word.

E.g. if the word to be disambiguated (w) is *doctor*, we obtain $Dom(w_1) =$ "*Medicine*" and $Dom(w_4) =$ "*School*". Therefore, if the context word (c_i) is *university*, for which $Dom(c_{i3}) =$ "*School*", the resulting weight for *doctor(4)* and *university(3)* is $1/4 * 1/3$. Therefore, after the inclusion of MDWs, the formula (3) becomes as follows:

$$CD(M, nh, w, f, C) = M^{\alpha}(M/nh)^{\log f} + \sum_{i=0}^{|C|} \sum_{j=1}^{k} MDW(w_f, c_{ij}) \qquad (5)$$

where C is the vector of context words, k is the number of senses of the context word c_i, and c_{ij} is the synset corresponding to the j-th sense of the context word c_i.

With the introduction of MDWs, however, we did not obtain the desired improvements (70.79% in precision and 67.91% for recall, below the MFU baseline of 75.5% for both measures). The reason is that many of the correspondances in domains are found for the domain *Factotum*, that is too generic and, consequently, it does not provide any useful information about the correlation of two word senses. Our solution was to reduce by a 10 factor the relevance of the *Factotum* domain, with the formula(4) modified as follows:

$$MDW(w_f, c_{ij}) = \begin{cases} 0 & \text{if } Dom(w_f) \neq Dom(c_{ij}) \\ 1/f * 1/j & \text{if } Dom(w_f) = Dom(c_{ij}) \\ & \wedge\ Dom(w_f) \neq \text{“}Factotum\text{”} \\ 10^{-1} * (1/f * 1/j) & \text{if } Dom(w_f) = Dom(c_{ij}) \\ & \wedge\ Dom(w_f) = \text{“}Factotum\text{”} \end{cases} \quad (6)$$

In this way we could obtain a precision of 78.33% and a recall of 62.60% over the whole SemCor, with a context window of 4 nouns. We also tried not to take into account the *Factotum* domain. In this case we got an higher precision (80.70%), but the recall was only 59.08%. This means that whereas the *Factotum* domain does not provide useful information to the disambiguation task, it can help in disambiguating a certain number of nouns with the most frequent sense, thanks to the weights assigned proportionally to the frequency of senses.

We used nearly the same method to disambiguate words of POS categories other than nouns. In these cases we could not take into account the Conceptual Density. For the following reasons: first of all, in WordNet there is not a hierarchy for adjectives and adverbs. With regard to verbs, the hierarchy is too shallow to be used efficiently. Moreover, since the disambiguation is performed one sentence at a time, in most cases only one verb for each sentence can be found (with the consequence that no density can be computed).

The sense disambiguation of an adjective is performed only on the basis of the domain weights and the context, constituted by the *Closest Noun (CN)*, i.e., the noun the adjective is referring to (e.g. in *"family of musical instruments"* the CN of *musical* is *instruments*). Given one of its senses, we extract the synsets obtained by the *antonymy*, *similar_to*, *pertainymy* and *attribute* relationships. For each of them, we calculate the MDW with respect to the senses of the context noun. The weight assigned to the adjective sense is the average between these MDWs. The selected sense is the one having the maximum average weight.

In order to achieve the maximum coverage, the *Factotum* domain has been also taken into account to calculate the MDWs between adjective senses and context noun senses. However, due to the fact that in many cases this domain does not provide a useful information, the weights resulting from a *Factotum* domain are reduced by a 0.1 factor. E.g. suppose to disambiguate the adjective *academic* referring to the noun *credit*. Both *academic(1)* and *credit(6)* belong to the domain *School*. Furthermore, the *Factotum* domain contains the senses 1 4 and 7 of *credit*, and senses 2 and 3 of *academic*. The extra synsets obtained by means of the WN relationships are: *academia(1):Sociology*, pertainym of sense 1; *theoretical(3):Factotum* and *applied(2):Factotum*, similar and antonym of sense 2; *scholarly(1):Factotum* and *unscholarly(1):Factotum*, similar and antonym of sense 3. Since there are no senses of *credit* in the *Sociology* domain, *academia(1)* is not taken into account. Therefore, the resulting weights for *academic* are:
$1 * 1/6 = 0.16$ for sense 1;
$0.1 * (1/2 + 1/2 * 1/4 + 1/2 * 1/7 + [1/2 * 1/3 + 1/2 * 1/2])/5 \simeq 0.02$ for sense 2;
$0.1 * (1/3 + 1/3 * 1/4 + 1/3 * 1/7 + [1/3 * 1 + 1/3 * 1])/5 \simeq 0.02$ for sense 3.

The weights resulting from the extra synsets are represented within square brackets. Since the maximum weight is obtained for the first sense, this is the sense assigned to *academic*.

We tried to use the same idea to improve the results for the noun sense disambiguation task: if in the sentence *"family of musical instruments" musical* has a closer link to *instruments* than to *family*, it is also true that *instruments* has a close link to *musical*. This kind of link is also easy to be found, since in English adjectives always come before the noun they are referring to. Therefore, we investigated the utility of choosing only the *Closest Adjective* (CA) in the context for calculating MDWs for nouns, in a similar way to what we did for adjectives. Our experiments show that the precision and the recall values differ slightly from the base results obtained without domains.

Table 1. Comparison among approaches to noun sense disambiguation making use of WordNet Domains. The results are obtained over the whole SemCor with a context window size of 4 words (in all cases but the CA and the MFU ones)

	MFU	no WND	WND	WND (CA)
Precision	75.55%	80.70%	78.33%	80.45%
Recall	75.55%	59.07%	62.60%	59.42%
Coverage	100%	73.20%	79.91%	73.86%

The same experiments carried out over the Senseval-3 corpus showed a more significative difference between the CA technique and the other ones. Moreover, in this case the precision is even higher than the one obtained without taking into account the WordNet domains.

Table 2. Comparison among approaches to noun sense disambiguation making use of WordNet Domains. The results are obtained over the Senseval-3 All-Words Task corpus with a context window size of 4 words (in all cases but the CA and the MFU ones)

	MFU	no WND	WND	WND (CA)
Precision	69.08%	73.40%	65.39%	74.30%
Recall	69.08%	51.81%	58.28%	52.69%
Coverage	100%	70.58%	89.13%	70.91%

We tried to limit the search of the closest adjective for the noun only to the immediately preceding word or to the two preceding words, but results differ only of a 0.1 – 0.2% (Tables 3 and 4) from those obtained without doing such distinction.

The results are very similar, since the approaches differ for a few hundreds nouns, as it can be observed from the coverage values (the corpus is made up of more than 70000 nouns).

Table 3. Comparison among approaches to noun sense disambiguation searching backwards in context for the closest adjective without restrictions, only within 2 words before the noun, and just the word before. The results are obtained over the whole SemCor

	unrestricted	2 words	1 word
Precision	80.45%	80.55%	80.57%
Recall	59.42%	59.32%	59.27%
Coverage	73.86%	73.64%	73.56%

Table 4. Comparison among approaches to noun sense disambiguation searching backwards in context for the closest adjective without restrictions, only within 2 words before the noun, and only the word before. The results are obtained over the whole Senseval-3 All-Words Task corpus

	unrestricted	2 words	1 word
Precision	74.30%	74.41%	74.49%
Recall	52.69%	52.57%	52.68%
Coverage	70.91%	70.58%	70.80%

The results obtained over the Senseval-3 All-Words Task corpus confirm that the precision of the CA approach can be slightly improved by considering adjectives with a stronger tie (i.e., closer) to the noun to disambiguate.

Another approach we evaluated was to add weights to subhierarchies only when nouns were left undisambiguated by the use of the "clean" CD formula (3). In other words, to include the sum in formula (5) only when CD and frequency are not able to disambiguate the noun. Unfortunately, the results are approximately the same of those in Tables 3 and 4, and, therefore, they are not worth mentioning.

The sense disambiguation of a verb is done nearly in the same way than for adjectives, but taking into consideration only the MDWs with the verb's senses and the context words (i.e., in the example above, if we had to disambiguate a verb instead of an adjective, the weights within the square brackets would not have been considered). In the Senseval-3 all-words and gloss disambiguation tasks the two context words were the noun before and after the verb, whereas in the lexical sample task the context words were four (two before and two after the verb), without regard to their POS category. This has been done in order to improve the recall in the latter task, whose test corpus is made up mostly by verbs, since our experiments carried out over the SemCor corpus showed that considering only the noun preceding and following the verb allows for achieving a better precision, while the recall is higher when the 4-word context is used. However, our results over verbs are still far from the most-frequent baseline. The sense disambiguation of adverbs (in every task) is carried out in the same way of the disambiguation of verbs for the lexical sample task.

4 Experiments with Glosses

Glosses have been used in the past as a resource for Word Sense Disambiguation by Lesk[4] and many other researchers. Usually WordNet glosses are composed of two parts:

- *definition* part;
- *sample* part.

E.g. the gloss of *light(7)* is: *used of vowels or syllables; pronounced with little or no stress; "a syllable that ends in a short vowel is a light syllable"; "a weak stress on the second syllable"*; the definition part in this case is *used of vowels or syllables; pronounced with littel or no stress*, while the sample part is *"a syllable that ends in a short vowel is a light syllable"; "a weak stress on the second syllable.*

We carried out some experiments over the WordNet glosses in order to understand which of these portions is more important to the task of Word Sense Disambiguation. Initially, we defined *Gloss Weights* (*GWs*) similarly to MDWs. Each GW is calculated as follows:

$$GW(w_f, c_i) = \begin{cases} 0 & \text{if } c_i \notin Gl(w_f) \\ 0.3 & \text{if } c_i \in Gl(w_f) \end{cases} \tag{7}$$

where c_i is the i-th word of the context, w_f is the f-th sense of the word to be disambiguated, and $Gl(x)$ is the function returning the set of words being in the gloss of the synset x without stopwords. E.g. $Gl(light_7)$={*used, vowels, syllables, pronounced, little, stress, syllable, ends, short, vowel, light, weak, stress, second*}.

The GWs are added to the formula(3) as an alternative to MDWs:

$$CD(M, nh, w, f, C) = M^{\alpha}(M/nh)^{\log f} + \sum_{i=0}^{|C|} GW(w_f, c_i) \tag{8}$$

where C is the vector of context words, and c_i is the i-th word of the context.

We initially used a weight of 0.5, considering as a good matching the fact that two context words were found in a gloss, but subsequently we obtained better results with a weight of 0.3 (i.e., at least three context words are needed to be found in a gloss to obtain a density close to 1). Two other Gloss Weights were defined, each making use of a different Gl function: GW_d, which, by using $Gl_d(x)$, returns the set of words in the definition part of the gloss of the synset x; and GW_s, which uses $Gl_s(x)$ to return the set of words in the sample part.

The obtained results show that disambiguation carried out by considering only the sample portion of WordNet glosses is more precise than working on the whole gloss and/or the definitions. This has been observed also in the experiments conducted over the Senseval-3 All-Words Task corpus (Table 5). Therefore, we looked for another machine-readable resource in order to expand the sample portions of WordNet glosses. We decided to use the Cambridge Advanced Learner's Dictionary (CALD), since it is one of the few available on-line, and its

Table 5. Results obtained over the whole SemCor and Senseval-3 All-Words Task corpora, with a window size of 4 nouns, by using whole glosses or their separate parts, and Gloss Weights of 0.3

SemCor	precision	recall
Whole gloss	79.31	60.22
Definition only (GW_d)	79.85	59.52
Samples only (GW_s)	80.12	59.96
Senseval-3 AWT		
Whole gloss	73.75	52.14
Definition only (GW_d)	73.98	51.81
Samples only (GW_s)	74.06	52.03

HTML pages are organized in a format that allows to easily retrieve information about the POS of a word, its definition, and the sample parts of glosses.

The heuristics we use to retrieve a CALD gloss corresponding to a WordNet's one compares its synset terms and the definition parts of the gloss. For each synset in WordNet, we search in CALD the synset's words, and then select the resulting entries as candidate glosses. If more than the 40% of the definition part of the WordNet gloss is found in one of the CALD definition parts of candidate glosses, then the corresponding sample part is added to the WordNet gloss.

E.g. for the WordNet synset *coherence, coherency, cohesion, cohesiveness, (the state of cohering or sticking together)*, we search in the CALD web page for: *coherence*, *coherency*, *cohesion*, *cohesiveness*, obtaining respectively 1, 0 and 1 entries (one is missing since the CALD returns the same entry for *cohesion* and *cohesiveness*). A matching greater than 40% is found only within the CALD definition of *coherence*: "the quality of cohering or being coherent". Since this definition shares 4 words (over 7) with the WN gloss (the, of, cohering, or), the resulting matching is $4/7 = 54\%$, with the result that the following sample sentence is added to the WordNet gloss: "There was no coherence between the first and the second half of the film". A drawback of this heuristics is that stopwords are taken into account in the calculation of similarity between glosses. This may be useful when they keep the same order and position in both definitions, like in the previous example, but in most cases they are actually adding noise into the disambiguation process. Therefore, we will need to determine a better way to check the matching of gloss definitions.

In WordNet 2.0 there are 8195 noun glosses with samples. With our heuristics, we found 7416 totally new sample sentences, raising the total number of sample sentences from 8195 to 15611. Moreover, new sample sentences were added to 2483 already existing samples. We used these "expanded" glosses to carry out some Word Sense Disambiguation tests over the SemCor and the Senseval-3 All-Words Task corpora. The results are shown in Table 6.

The experiments have been carried out initially looking for all the context words in the expanded gloss of the word to be disambiguated. Thereafter, due to the poor results obtained, we used only those samples which contained its context nouns. Finally, we tried to select the gloss in a more precise way by

Table 6. Results obtained using the glosses expanded with CALD samples over the whole SemCor and Senseval-3 AWT corpora. The window size was of 4 words

SemCor	precision	recall
All context words	73.84	67.07
Only context nouns	79.78	59.76
Context nouns and word to be disambiguated	78.97	59.58
Senseval-3 AWT		
Only context nouns	64.72	48.73

using only those containing the word to be disambiguated itself together with the context nouns. With respect to the Senseval-3 All-Words Task, we performed the test only with the context nouns, which gave the best results over the SemCor. Whereas for the SemCor corpus we obtained results comparable with those in Table5, for the Senseval-3 AWT we observed a precision decrease of about 10%.

The reason of these poor results is that many of the added glosses were "off-topic", like: *"The Chinese anthem was played after the Union Jack was lowered in Hong Kong for the last time."*, that has been added for the synset *jack,(an electrical device consisting of a connector socket designed for the insertion of a plug)*. Therefore, we tried to improve the quality of the added samples by setting an higher threshold (70%) for the matching of the WordNet and CALD definitions, and by selecting only those glosses sharing at least a (non stopword) lemma with the defintion part of the gloss to be expanded. In this case, only 264 sample sentences were added, a number not relevant with respect to the total number of gloss samples in WordNet (8195 samples over 79688 glosses). Even if a more precise study over the threshold parameter could be done, we suspect that it could be really difficult to select gloss samples from different lexical resources, since in each resource can be different the way definitions are given. Therefore, the heuristics we used, inspired by the one used for the mapping of different versions of WordNet, cannot be applied between different lexical resources.

5 Conclusions and Further Work

The experiments with the WordNet Domains show that using this resource allows for improving recall without losing too much in precision, although the conditions when this can be done are very few. This is mostly due to the small number of correspondances that can be found for domains different than "Factotum". We observed that a better precision can be obtained for the gloss approach if we consider only the sample part of WordNet glosses. Therefore, we tried to add further gloss samples from the Cambridge Advanced Learner's online Dictionary. However, due to the poor results obtained, we decided not to integrate in our approach also the CALD glosses, until we will not be able to add gloss samples in an appropriate way. Maybe it could be worthwhile to investigate the possibility of selecting the gloss samples by disambiguating glosses and find a matching between concepts. The use of other resources such as the Roget's Thesaurus or the Oxford Advanced Learner's Dictionary will be also investigated. At the moment, we are also investigating the possibility to use the web as a knowledge source for WSD [3], by using an approach inspired by [6].

Acknowledgments

This work was supported by the CIAO SENSO MCYT Spain-Italy (HI 2002-0140), the R2D2 CICYT (TIC2003-07158-C04-03) and the ICT for EU-India Cross-Cultural Dissemination (ALA/95/23/2003/077-054) projects.

References

1. Agirre, E. and Rigau, G.: A proposal for Word Sense Disambiguation using Conceptual Distance. In: Proceedings of the International Conference on Recent Advances in NLP. RANLP-2000, Tzhigov Chark, Bulgaria, (2000).
2. Buscaldi, D., Rosso,P., Masulli,F.: The upv-unige-CIAOSENSO WSD System. Senseval-3 Workshop, ACL - Association of Computational Linguistics. Barcelona, Spain (2004) (in press).
3. Gonzalo, J., Verdejo, F., Chugar, I.: The Web as a Resource for WSD. In: 1st MEANING workshop, Spain (2003).
4. Lesk, M.: Automatic Sense Disambiguation using Machine Readable Dictionaries: How to tell a Pine Cone from an Ice Cream Cone. In: Proceedings of SIGDOC'86, U.S.A. (1986)
5. Magnini, B. and Cavaglià, G.: Integrating Subject Field Codes into WordNet. In: Proceedings of LREC-2000, Second International Conference on Language Resources and Evaluation. (2000) 1413–1418.
6. Mihalcea, R., Moldovan, D.I.: A Method for Word Sense Disambiguation of Unrestricted Text. In: Proceedings of the 37th Annual Meeting of the Association for Computational Linguistics (ACL-99). Maryland, NY, U.S.A. (1999)
7. Rosso, P., Masulli, F., Buscaldi, D., Pla, F., Molina, A.: Automatic Noun Disambiguation. Lecture Notes in Computer Science, Vol. 2588. Springer-Verlag (2003) 273–276

Intertwining Deep Syntactic Processing and Named Entity Detection

Caroline Brun and Caroline Hagège

Xerox Research Centre Europe
6, Chemin de Maupertuis
38210 Meylan France
{Caroline.Brun,Caroline.Hagege}@xrce.xerox.com

Abstract. In this paper, we present a robust incremental architecture for natural language processing centered around syntactic analysis but allowing at the same time the description of specialized modules, like named entity recognition. We show that the flexibility of our approach allows us to intertwine general and specific processing, which has a mutual improvement effect on their respective results: for example, syntactic analysis clearly benefits from named entity recognition as a pre-processing step, but named entity recognition can also take advantage of deep syntactic information.

1 Introduction

The robust system presented in this article performs deep syntactic analysis associated with the detection and categorization of named entities that are present in texts. This system is robust as it takes any kind of text as input and always gives an output in a short time (about 2000 words/second). At the same time, we show that robustness is not synonymous with shallowness, as our system is able to handle fine-grained syntactic phenomena (like control and raising). Furthermore, our system is flexible enough to enable the integration of specialized modules, as we did for named entity recognition. We first describe our system, then focus on the entity recognition module we developed and show how it is integrated in the general processing chain. We then give some examples of the benefit of having these two modules developed together: syntactic analysis benefits from named entity recognition and the task of named entity recognition benefits from a fine-grained syntactic analysis. Finally we conclude by giving some hints of our future work.

2 Description of Our System

2.1 Robust and Deep Syntactic Analysis Using XIP

IP (erox Incremental Parser) (see Aït et al.[2]) is the tool we use to perform robust and deep syntactic analysis. Deep syntactic analysis consists for us in the

J. L. Vicedo et al. (Eds.): EsTAL 2004, LNAI 3230, pp. 195–206, 2004.

construction of a set of syntactic relations from an input text. Although dependency grammars (see Mel'cuk [12] and Tesnière [16]) inspired us, we prefer calling the syntactic output of our system syntactic relations as we do not obey principles like projectivity and we take liberties with the above-mentioned syntactic paradigms. These relations[1] link lexical units of the input text and/or more complex syntactic domains that are constructed during the processing (mainly chunks, see Abney [1])). These relations are labelled, when possible, with deep syntactic functions. More precisely, we try to link a predicate (verbal or nominal) with what we call its deep subject, its deep object, and modifiers. When the deep subjects and deep objects are not found, the general syntactic relations are still available. For instance, for the sentence *The escheat law cannot be enforced now because it is almost impossible to locate such property, Daniel declared.*, the parser produces the following relations:

```
DETD(law,The)                     MOD_POST_INFINIT(impossible,locate)
MOD_PRE(law,escheat)              MOD_PRE(impossible,almost)
NUCL_VLINK_MODAL(cannot,be)       EMBED_INFINIT(locate,is)
NUCL_VLINK_PASSIVE(be,enforced)   OBJ-N(locate,property)
OBJ-N(enforced,law)               MOD_PRE(property,such)
TIME(enforced,now)                SUBJ-N(declared,Daniel)
EMBED(is,enforced)                MAIN(declared)
NUCL_SUBJCOMPL(is,impossible)     SUBJ-N(is,it)
```

It is important to notice that, in this example, the passive form *The escheat law cannot be enforced* has been recognized as such and then normalized, as we obtain the relation *OBJ-N(enforce,law).*

We now briefly explain below how these relations are obtained.

XIP and General Syntactic Analysis. IP is a tool that integrates different steps of NLP, namely: tokenization, POS tagging (combination of HMM and hand-made rules), chunking and the extraction of syntactic relations. Chunking is not compulsory for the syntactic relation extraction, but we decided to apply this first stage of processing in order to find the boundaries of non-recursive phrases. This preliminary analysis will then facilitate the latter processing stage (See Giguet's work [6] for more detailed indications of the interest of finding chunks in order to ease the extraction of dependencies).

A chunking rule can be expressed in two ways:

- by *sequence rules* which define a list of categories;
- by *ID (immediate dominance) rules* defining sets of categories that are combined with LP (linear precedence) constraints.

In both cases, contextual information can be given.

For instance, the following sequence rule (in which no specific context is given) expresses that a Nominal Chunk (NP) starts with a lexical unit bearing

[1] We consider binary and more generally n-ary relations.

the feature det:+ (i.e. is a determiner), can be followed by 0 or more adjectives which are followed by a lexical unit having the feature noun:+

```
NP = ?[det:+], (adj)*, ?[noun:+] .
```

This rule could also have been expressed by the following ID rule and LP constraints[2].

```
NP -> ?[noun:+], ?[det:+], (adj)* .
[det:+] < [adj:+]
[adj:+] < [noun:+]
```

In our approach, after chunking is performed, the system calculates syntactic relations through what we call deduction rules. These rules apply on a chunk tree (that can be completely flat if no chunks have been previously calculated) and consist in three parts: **context**, **condition** and **extraction**.

Context is a regular expression on chunk tree nodes that has to match with a syntactic construction.

Condition is a boolean condition on dependencies, on linear order between nodes of the chunk tree, or on a comparison of features associated with nodes.

Extraction corresponds to a list of dependencies to be created if the contextual description matches and the condition is true.

For instance, the following rule establishes a *SUBJ* relation between the head of a nominal chunk and a finite verb:

```
| NP{?*,#1[last:+]},  ?*[verb:~],  VP{?*, #2[last:+]}|
if (~SUBJ(#2,#1))
SUBJ(#2,#1).
```

The first line of the rule correspond to context and describe a nominal chunk in which the last element is assigned to the variable #1, followed by any thing but a verb, followed by a verbal chunk in which the last element is assigned to the variable #2. The second line checks wether a *SUBJ* relation exists between the lexical nodes corresponding to the variable #2 (the verb) and #1 (the head of the nominal chunk). The test is true if the *SUBJ* relation does not exist. If both context and condition are verified, then a relation *SUBJ* is created between the verb and the noun (last line).

An important feature is that our parser always provides a unique analysis (it is deterministic), this analysis being potentially underspecified.

XIP and Deep Syntactic Analysis. Together with surface syntactic relations handled by a general English grammar, we calculate more sophisticated and complex relations using derivational morphology properties, deep syntactic properties (subject and object of infinitives in the context of control verbs), and some limited lexical semantic coding (Levin's verb class alternations). These deep syntactic relations correspond roughly to the agent-experiencer roles that

[2] The symbol < expresses linear precedence.

is subsumed by the *SUBJ-N* relation and to the patient-theme role subsumed by the *OBJ-N* relation. Not only verbs bear these relations but also deverbal nouns with their corresponding arguments (for more details on deep syntactic analysis using IP see Hagge and Roux[7]).

For instance the following rule establishes that the surface subject of a verb in passive form is in fact the deep object of this verb while the surface object of this verb corresponds to the deep subject.

```
if ( SUBJ(#1[passive:+],#2) & OBJ(#1,#3) )
    SUBJ-N(#1,#3),
    OBJ-N(#1,#2) .
```

At the end of the deep syntactic analysis stage, deep syntactic relations together with surface syntactic relations are available.

2.2 A Basic System for Named Entity Categorization

Named entity recognition and categorization is a fundamental task for a wide variety of natural language processing applications, such as question answering, information management, text mining and business intelligence, lexical acquisition, etc. Therefore, the NLP community shows a great interest concerning this issue. For example, the MUC conferences defined a task of named entity recognition using annotated corpora, and enabled the comparison of different methods for the task (see Sekine and Eryguchi[14] for an interesting state of the art of the different methodologies, and Poibeau [13] for an analysis of the evaluation criteria). More recently, the ACE [3] project (Automatic Content Extraction) has a specific task concerning named entities as well.

This task is also a useful step towards achieving fined-grained syntactic and semantic analysis. For these reasons, it seemed useful to integrate such functionality into the IP parser. Moreover, the overall parsing process should benefit from the integration of this module.

The system we built for named entity categorization focuses on the following predefined classes:

- percentages, e.g. *10 , 10 per cent*
- dates, e.g. *March 4, 1991*, and temporal expressions, e.g. *Tuesday*
- expressions denoting an amount of money, e.g. *$26 billion*
- locations, e.g. *West Bank*, *Mount Everest*
- person names e.g. *President Saddam Hussein*, *Jacques Chirac*, *Edward III of England*
- organizations e.g. *British Aiways*, *Bang Olufsen*, *Bank of Brazil*
- events e.g. *World War II*, *America s Cup*
- legal documents *Warsaw Pact*, *Maastricht Treaty*

This list is non-exhaustive, but corresponds to the most common types of entities generally recognized by dedicated systems. This "basic" system is built

[3] http://www.ldc.upenn.edu/Projects/ACE/intro.html

within the IP parser presented above, on top of a part-of-speech tagger. This system is purely rule-based. It consists in a set of ordered local rules that use lexical information combined with contextual information about part-of-speech, lemma forms and lexical features. These rules detect the sequence of words involved in the entity and assign a feature (loc, org, etc.) to the top node of the sequence, which is a noun in most of the cases. In the incremental parsing process, these rules are applied in the pre-syntactic component, before the chunking and dependency rules, therefore no syntax is used at this stage. For example, the following rule is used to detect and categorize organization names consisting in a sequence of nouns starting with a capital letter (feature *cap*) and finishing with a typical organisation marker like *Ltd.*, *Corp*, *Inc.*, etc. These markers bear the feature *orgEnd* within the lexicon.

```
noun[org=+] -> noun+[cap=+],noun[orgEnd=+]
```

The rule enables the detection of the organization name in the following example:

<ORG>Apple Computer Inc. </ORG> said its chief financial officer, Fred Anderson, will retire june 1.

At this stage of the processing, one can already use contextual information in these rules. This is illustrated on the following rule:

```
noun[person=+] = noun[cap=+] |part, noun[famtie=+]|
```

This rule transforms (overriding sign =) a noun starting with a capital letter in a person name, when it is followed by an element of category part (s) and by a noun bearing the feature *famtie*, like *brother*, *mother*, etc. It enables the detection of the person name in the following example, *They were ying to Miami for a bash hosted by <PERS>Graf</PERS> s brother.*

These rules are combined with a propagation system integrated into the parser, that allows subparts of the entities to be marked, and then allows new occurrences of these subparts to be categorized when encountered later on in the text. For example if the word *Washington*, which is ambiguous between a person name and a city name, is encountered in some part of the text in the string *George Washington*, then the system tags all remaining occurrences of *Washington* as a person, using feature propagation on this entity part. This functionality is also very useful when proper nouns are truncated, which is very common for (business) organisation names:

<ORG>Allied Supermarkets Inc</ORG> said it filed with the Securities and Exchange Commission ... <ORG>Allied</ORG> named Drexel Burnham Lambert Inc and Donaldson, Lufkin and Jenrette Securities Corp as co-underwriters of both offerings.

At the current stage of development, the basic system contains about 300 local grammar rules for entity detection.

Since the entity recognition system is embedded in a syntactic parser, the corresponding rules have been built in order to maintain a high precision, which attempt to prevent any deterioration of the parsing results. We have conducted a preliminary evaluation on a short corpus (about 500 sentences) from the Reuters news agency, on the location, person, and organisation named entities. It led to 90.2% precision and 75.5% recall.

2.3 Complete Architecture

The complete architecture of the parsing system, including entity processing is shown on figure 1. Parsing and named entity categorization can interact one with another (bold arrows).

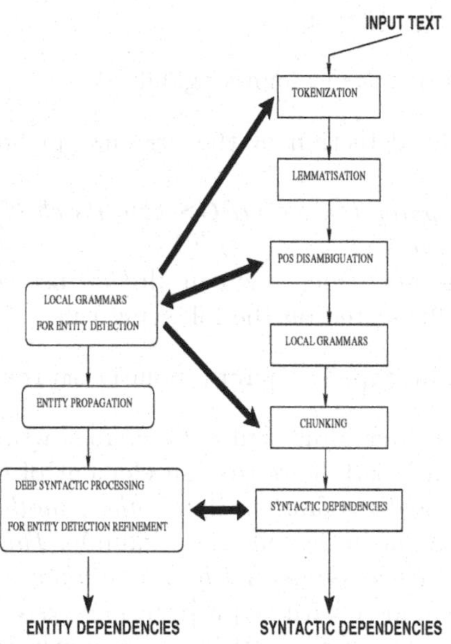

Fig. 1. Architecture of the System

3 Parsing and Entity Categorization as Interleaved Processes

3.1 Syntax and Entities

As presented before, our entity recognition system is embedded in our syntactic parser. Apart from being a useful task by itself, entity recognition improves the overall quality of the parsing output.

Entities for Better Tokenization. The first straightforward improvement concerns tokenization problems. Treating numbers, dates, monetary expressions, etc., as syntactic units avoids many word segmentation problems, since these expressions are often formed with punctuation signs that could be misinterpreted at a deeper syntactic level. Consider the following sentence:

George Unzelman, president of HyOx, Inc., said these proposals "will place pressure on small refining operations and promote further industry consolidation."

Analysing *HyOx, Inc.* as a unit (organization), allows the nominal apposition of *George Unzelman* to be delimited properly: the interpretation of the commas needs to be different when it marks the boundaries of a nominal apposition or when it is employed within an organisation name. This is what is reflected by our incremental multi-layer analysis.

Entities and POS Tagging. Still in pre-syntactic processing, at the level of POS disambiguation, the previous detection of entities can enable to avoid POS tagging errors that will have then consequences in the rest of processing. Take for instance the following example *Seat and Porsche had fewer registrations in July 1996.* Having *Seat* detected as an organization prevents it being interpreted as a verb which will have important consequences in the syntactic processing.

Entities and Syntactic Analysis. More interestingly, another kind of improvement concerns syntactic analysis directly. In fact, entity categorization gives some semantic information that can benefit the syntactic analysis. We can take a concrete case that represents one of the difficult points in the syntactic processing, namely the treatment of coordination.

Consider for instance the two following utterances where geographical entities are marked up with <LOC> and organizations with <ORG>:

He will be replaced by Eliahu Ben-Elissar, a former Israeli envoy to <LOC> Egypt < /LOC> and <LOC> Jordan < /LOC>

and

He will be replaced by Eliahu Ben-Elissar, a former Israeli envoy to <LOC> Egypt < /LOC> and <ORG> Likud party < /ORG> politician.

In the first example, the fact that *Jordan* and *Egypt* are both geographical entities enables us to consider that they are coordinated together. In the contrary, in the second example, as *politician* is not of the same type than *Egypt*, we will prefer to coordinate it with the name *envoy.*

Entities : A Step Towards Semantics. Finally, when an entity name is dependent on a governor, knowing the semantic type of the entity can help determining the kind of relationship that exists between the entity and its governor. It can help the labelling of semantic-oriented relations. Take the following example:

They met in Baghdad.

- Knowing that *Baghdad* is marked up as a geographical entity,

- having the syntactic relation *MODIFIER* between *met* and *Baghdad* where *met* is the governor and *Baghdad* a dependent,

- and knowing that *Baghdad* is introduced by the preposition *in* enables the MODIFIER syntactic relation to be further specified as a LOCALIZATION relation.

3.2 Entities and Deep Syntax

Entity Metonymy. Recently, the ACE project had focused on *Entity Detection and Tracking*, *Relation Detection and Characterization* and *Event Detection and Characterization*. In the context of this project, a particular emphasis is placed on named entity metonymy, namely the fact that a given entity may have different "senses", and therefore should be categorized differently according to the context. For instance, the word *China* can be marked as a geographical entity (LOC), but when used in the following context: *"China on Wednesday called on Japan to acknowledge its wartime past..."*, it is obvious that *China* should not be considered as a geographical unit but as a human organization. In a similar way, the word *Rolex* in *"If you are a real Rolex lover like I am, purchase the book"* should not be typed as an organization (Swiss watch designer company) but as a common noun (watches made by the Rolex company). This phenomenon is distinct from "basic ambiguity", as for *Washington*, which is either a location or a person. Therefore ACE focuses on semantic analysis whereas previous project in the same line, like MUC, focussed on linguistic analysis.

In this context, Maynard et al.[11] show how they adapt their "standard" entity detection system to the ACE requirement, in a very efficient way, taking advantage of the modularity of the GATE architecture. However, the adaptation of the system to take into account the phenomena of metonymy is not described. Furthermore, in the work described by Maynard et al., parsing is not one of the stages in the processing chain.

Along these lines, we decided to do an experiment on the contribution of deep syntactic parsing to named entity metonymy detection, making use of the flexibility of our architecture.

The system of named entity extraction we presented above can be enriched and improved using the results of robust deep syntactic processing with some limited lexical semantic coding. As claimed in McDonald[10], richer contextual information is necessary for high accuracy, and in our case this richer information consists in deep parsing results combined with lexical knowledge.

The enrichment, provided by an independent module, can be applied to any kind of named entity extraction system (rule-based in our case but it could also be used on top of a learning system or a mixed approach). This enables better semantic categorization of entities and also the discovery of named entities that are not easily detectable within a restricted context. Moreover, this information will allow entity categorization to be overridden or more precisely specified when some strings that could denote entity names are used as common nouns (e.g. *"I drive an Alfa Romeo"* where *Alfa Romeo* is here an artefact, i.e. a car of brand Alfa Romeo). To a certain extent, the task we want to perform is similar to Word Sense Disambiguation (see for example Ide and Veronis[8]), in the context of named entity categorization: we use prototypical information about subcategorization frames to disambiguate named entities.

In the following subsections we describe our module for the refinement of semantic categorization of named entities, which is based on deep syntactic processing.

This deep syntactic processing produces a normalized syntactic analysis (taking advantage of morphological properties of words and of a minimal lexical semantic information). At the end of the analysis process, the labeling of previously detected entities is refined. Some categories attached to entities that have been detected may be overridden by others or simply discarded. Moreover, it is important to observe that our methodology improves entity detection for other kind of problems:

- It helps characterize highly ambiguous entities, since they are syntactically related to words which bear some semantic features (e.g. "<PERS> Turner </PERS> says..." vs. "<LOC> Turner </LOC> is located in the hills of Western Maine")
- It enables entities to be typed even when gazette er information is missing (e.g. "<ORG> DELFMEMS </ORG> will be a new company created in 2004").

It is important to notice that we do not follow the ACE guidelines (ACE[5]) exactly, in particular for the Geopolitical entities (GPE, i.e. "composite entities comprised of a population, a government, a physical location and a nation"), for which we have a less fine-grained tagset. Indeed, we do not keep the distinction between:

- *France signed a treaty with Germany last week* : GPE with role ORG;
- *France likes to eat cheese* : GPE with role PERS;
- *The world leaders meet in France yesterday* : GPE with role LOC;
- *France produces better wine than New Jersey*: GPE with role GPE;

Since for us, an organisation is a basically a group of people, we simply aim to distinguish the location sense of GPE from the other senses, which we consider as organization.

Moreover, our system focuses on proper noun categorization: it won't attempt to spot common noun like *the house painters*, as in ACE.

How Deep Syntax Can Help. The contextual rules of the entity recognition module described above enable us to catch and categorize named entities with reasonable precision. In this section we show how deep syntax can help and improve the named entity recognition task in the following ways:

- refine a rough but correct categorization done in a previous step,
- detect some entities that have not been detected previously,
- override an incorrect entity categorization that has been previously made.

As said before, our system can extract deep syntactic relations between predicates and their arguments. Having some information about selectional restriction of predicates appearing in the text thus enables us to check and possibly correct the tagging of named entities which are arguments of these predicates. In this paper, what especially interests us is the *SUBJ-N* relation that links a predicate to its normalized subject. If a predicate denotes an activity that is typically performed by human beings, then we can be sure that the normalized subject of this predicate has to bear a human feature. Having this in mind, when entities are found to be involved in a *SUBJ-N* dependency with a predicate that expresses a human activity, then we know that this entity cannot be a product or or a location but something that denotes one or a group of human beings. This enables the refinement of named entity tags found in a previous step or possibly the detection of some entities that have not been previously detected because of a lack of context. For instance in the example *China declared* ... as *declared* is typically a verb whose deep subject is a human or a group of human beings, we can easily that the *LOC* interpretation for the entity *China* is not correct and that *China* is here an organisation.

Furthermore, simple syntactic contexts can be clues to override erroneous named entity categorization. For instance in the example *He won the race with his Mitsubishi*, as we have a possessive *his* determining the word *Mitsubishi*, it is very unlikely that *Mitsubishi* has the status of a company name and hence is not a named entity even if starting with upper-case and present in some gazetteer.

The limited lexical coding that we performed in order to refine our named entity categorization module consists mostly in the categorization of a set of verbs expecting a human (or at least a living) being or a group of human beings as normalized subject.

As much as possible, we use pre-defined semantic verb classes, such as Levin's classes (see Levin [9]). Interesting classes that we found in Levin are the following:

- "Learn verbs", for instance *learn, memorize, study*, etc.
- "Social interaction verbs", for instance *agree, argue, struggle, debate*, etc.
- "Communication verbs", for instance *dictate, write, recite, telephone*, etc.
- "Ingestion verbs", for instance *eat, gobble, swallow, devour*, etc.
- "Killing verbs", for instance *murder, massacre, poison, strangle*, etc.

Together with these significant Levin classes, we also use verbs that introduce indirect speech which were already marked in our system, as they possess specific syntactic properties (inversion of the subject for instance). This class of verb was extracted from the COMLE lexicon [4] and consists in verbs like *say, declare, utter*, etc.

We give below an example of a IP rule showing that if we find that the deep subject of a verb of human activity is tagged as a named entity denoting a location, then, we retract this interpretation and we type this entity as a person or human organisation (PERS_OR_ORG unary relation).

```
if (  SUBJ-N(#1[human_activ],#2) & ^LOCATION(#2) )
        PERS_OR_ORG(#2)
```

The next section shows that this limited and straighforward classification, even if modest, refines some of the entity categorization performed by the general system.

3.3 About Evaluation

In this section we describe a small experiment we performed in order to evaluate the impact of deep syntactic analysis on the named entity detection and categorization task.

In this experiment, the challenge is different than what we expect from the general named entity detection system. We want to be able to distinguish here when an entity like *China* denotes a place and when it denotes an organization (see ACE and GPE distinctions above). Once again, we use a small corpus of about 500 sentences and annotate it manually, taking metonymy into account.

Results we obtained with the general entity detection system on the refined catogories set are the following:

- Precision : 81 %
- Recall : 75 %

Using deep syntax and the limited lexical information we mentionned above, we obtained the following results:

- Precision : 85 %
- Recall : 74 %

These results show that with a minimal effort in lexical coding and with the use of only two kinds of grammatical relations (namely deep-subject and possessive), precision increases. We expect that a deeper study on the impact of syntactic properties on entity categorization will enable us to go further in that direction.

4 Conclusions and Future Work

In this paper, we present a robust architecture for deep syntactic analysis, enriched by a named entity detection module. Named entity detection is often seen as an independent NLP task, but we show that a syntactic parser can benefit from it as a pre-processing step. Moreover, since recent trends in named entity categorization focus on semantic analysis (e.g. metonymy), we think that deep syntactic information is necessary to bridge the gap between a linguistic analysis and a deeper semantic analysis of named entities. We thus propose a system that interleaves parsing and entity detection. First results are encouraging, and we plan to pursue our work with a deeper linguistic study of the syntactic information needed to improve our system.

In addition to that, we think that Word Sense Disambiguation is a task that should make the most of entity categorization. We developed previously a rule-based Word Sense Disambiguation system of which one the main components is our syntactic parser (Brun and Segond[3]). Since the integration of named entity categorization results is handled directly by our architecture, it could be worthwhile to evaluate the consequences on the Word Sense Disambiguation task.

References

1. Abney S. Parsing by Chunks. In *Robert Berwick, Steven Abney and Carol Tenny (eds.). Principle-Based Parsing,* Kluwer Academic Publishers (1991).
2. Aït-Mokhtar S., Chanod J-P and Roux C. Robustness beyond shallowness: incremental dependency parsing. Special issue of the NLE Journal (2002).
3. Brun C., Segond F. Semantic encoding of electronic documents. In *International Journal of Corpus Linguistic, vol. 6, no 1, 2001.*
4. Grishman R., Macleod C., Meyers A. COMLEX: building a computational lexicon. In *Proceedings of the 15th International Conference on Computational Linguistics* (1994).
5. EDT Guidelines for English V4.2.6. In *ACE Current Annotation Effort: http://www.ldc.upenn.edu/Projects/Ace/Annotation.*
6. Giguet E. Mthodes pour l'analyse automatique de structures formelles sur documents multilingues. Thse de Doctorat en Informatique de l'Universit de Caen. (1998)
7. Hagge C., Roux C. Entre syntaxe et smantique: Normalisation de l'analyse syntaxique en vue de l'amlioration de l'extraction d'information partir de textes. In *Actes de TALN 2003, Batz-sur-Mer, France.* (2003)
8. Ide N., Veronis J. Introduction to the Special Issue on Word Sense Disambiguation: The State of the Art In *Computational Linguistics, vol. 24, no 1, 1998.*
9. Levin B. English Verb Classes and Alternations - A Preliminary Investigation. The University of Chicago Press (1993).
10. MacDonald. Internal and External Evidence in the Identification and Semantic Categorization of Proper Names. In *B. Boguraev and J.Pustejovsky editors, Corpus Processing For Lexical Acquisition, pp 21-29, Mit Press.*
11. Maynard D., Bontcheva K., Cunningham H. Towards a semantic extraction of named entity recognition. In *Proceedings of RANLP 2003, Borovets, Bulgaria. (2003).*
12. Mel'cuk I. Dependency Syntax. State University of New York, Albany, (1988)
13. Poibeau, Thierry.: Deconstructing Harry, une valuation des systmes de reprage d'entits nommes. In *Revue de la socit d'lectronique, d'lectricit et de traitement de l'information, 2001.*
14. Sekine S., Eryguchi Y. Japanese Named Entity Extraction and Evaluation - Analysis of Results. In *Proceedings of Coling'2000,Saarbrucken, Germany, pp. 25-30.*
15. Sekine S., Kiyoshi S., Chikashi N. Extended Named Entity Hierarchy. In *Proceedings of LREC2002, Las Palmas, Spain, 2002.*
16. Tesnière L. Eléments de syntaxe structurale. Editions Klincksieck, Deuxième édition revue et corrigée Paris (1969)

Language Understanding Using n-multigram Models*

Lluís Hurtado, Encarna Segarra, Fernando García, and Emilio Sanchis

Departament de Sistemes Informàtics i Computació (DSIC),
Universitat Politècnica de València (UPV),
Camí de Vera s/n, 46022 València, Spain
{lhurtado,esegarra,fgarcia,esanchis}@dsic.upv.es

Abstract. In this work, we present an approach to language understanding using corpus-based and statistical language models based on multigrams. Assuming that we can assign meanings to segments of words, the *n-multigram* modelization is a good approach to model sequences of segments that have semantic information associated to them. This approach has been applied to the task of speech understanding in the framework of a dialogue system that answers queries about train timetables in Spanish. Some experimental results are also reported.

1 Introduction

Nowadays, the use of automatic learning techniques for Language Modelling is quite extensive in the field of Human Language Technologies. A good example of this can be found in the development of Spoken Dialogue systems. Very important components of these systems, such as the Language Model of the speech recognition component, the Language Model of the understanding component and the dialogue structure, can be modelled by corpus-based and statistical finite-state models. This is the case of the widely used n-gram models [1][2].

An n-gram model assigns a probability to a word depending on the previous n-1 words observed in the recent history of that word in the sentence. In these models, the word is the selected linguistic unit for the language modelization, and the recent history considered for the model always has the same length. Over the last few years, there has been an increasing interest in statistical language models which try to take into account the dependencies among a variable number of words; that is, stochastic models in which the probability associated to a word depends on the occurrence of a variable number of words in its recent history. This is the case of the grammar-based approaches [3][4][5], in which models take into account variable-length dependencies by conditioning the probability of each word with a context of variable length. In contrast, in segment-based approaches such as multigrams [6][7][8], sentences are structured into variable-length segments, and probabilities are assigned to segments instead of words. In other words, multigram approaches to language modelling take segments of

* Work partially funded by *CICYT* under project TIC2002-04103-C03-03, Spain.

J. L. Vicedo et al. (Eds.): EsTAL 2004, LNAI 3230, pp. 207–219, 2004.

words as basic units; these models try to naturally model the fact that there are certain concatenations of words that occur very frequently. These segments could constitute one of the following: relevant linguistic units; syntactic or semantic units; or a concatenation of words, which works well from the language modelling point of view (independently of the linguistic relevance of the segments).

Language Understanding systems have many applications in several areas of Natural Language Processing. Typical applications are train or plane travel information retrieval, car navigation systems or information desks. In the last few years, many efforts have been made in the development of natural language dialog systems which allow us to extract information from databases. The interaction with the machine to obtain this kind of information requires some dialog turns. In these turns, the user and the system interchange information in order to achieve the objective: the answer to a query made by the user. Each turn (a sequence of natural language sentences) of the user must be understood by the system. Therefore, an acceptable behavior of the understanding component of the system is essential to the correct performance of the whole dialog system.

Language understanding can be seen as a transduction process from sentences to a representation of their meaning. Frequently, this semantic representation consists of sequences of concepts (semantic units). Multigram models have been applied to language modeling tasks [6][8]; however, as the multigram approach is based on considering a sentence as a sequence of variable-length segments of words, it could be interesting to apply this methodology to language understanding.

In this work, we propose the application of multigram models to language understanding. In this proposal, we associate semantic units to segments, and we modelize the concatenation of semantic units as well as the association of segments of words to each semantic unit. This approach has been applied to the understanding process in the BASURDE dialog system [9]. The BASURDE system answers telephone queries about railway timetables in Spanish.

This paper is organized as follows: in Section 2, the concept of *n-multigram* is described. In Section 3, the task of language understanding is presented and in Section 4, the application of *n-multigram* to language understanding is proposed. In Section 5, the two grammatical inference techniques used in the experiments are illustrated. Finally, results of the application of the *n-multigram* models to a task of language understanding and some concluding remarks are presented.

2 The *n-multigram* Model

Let W be a vocabulary of words, and let $w = w_1\, w_2\, w_3\, w_4$ be a sentence defined on this vocabulary, where $w_i \in W, i = 1, \ldots, 4$. From a multigram framework point of view, the sentence w has the set of all possible segmentations of the sentence associated to it. Let S be this set of segmentations for w. If we use the symbol # to express the concatenation of words which constitutes the same segment, S is as follows:

$$S = \left\{ \begin{array}{ll} w_1\ w_2\ w_3\ w_4, & w_1\ w_2\ w_3\#w_4, \\ w_1\ w_2\#w_3\ w_4, & w_1\#w_2\ w_3\ w_4, \\ w_1\ w_2\#w_3\#w_4, & w_1\#w_2\ w_3\#w_4, \\ w_1\#w_2\#w_3\ w_4, & w_1\#w_2\#w_3\#w_4 \end{array} \right\}$$

From a multigram language model point of view, the likelihood of a sentence is computed by summing up the likelihood values of all possible segmentations of the sentence into segments [6] [8]; let w be a sentence, and let S be the set of all segmentations of w. The likelihood of the sentence $\mathcal{L}(w)$ given a multigram language model is:

$$\mathcal{L}(w) = \sum_{s \in S} \mathcal{L}(w,\, s) \tag{1}$$

where, $\mathcal{L}(w,\, s)$ is the likelihood of the sentence w given the segmentation s.

The likelihood of any particular segmentation depends on the model assumed to describe the dependencies between the segments. The most usual approach, called *n-multigram* [8], assumes that the likelihood of a segment depends on the n-1 segments that precede it. This approach can be seen as an extension of n-gram models of words to n-gram models of segments. Therefore, the likelihood of a segmentation is:

$$\mathcal{L}(w,\, s) = \prod_{\tau} p(s_{(\tau)} | s_{(\tau-n+1)} \cdots s_{(\tau-1)}) \tag{2}$$

where $s_{(\tau)}$ represents the τ-th segment in the segmentation s.

Due to the high number of parameters to estimate, it is convenient to define classes of segments. The formula presented above becomes:

$$\mathcal{L}(w,\, s) = \prod_{\tau} p\left(C_{q(s_{(\tau)})} | C_{q(s_{(\tau-n+1)})} \cdots C_{q(s_{(\tau-1)})}\right) p\left(s_{(\tau)} | C_{q(s_{(\tau)})}\right) \tag{3}$$

where q is a function that assigns a class to each segment (it is generally assumed that a segment is associated to only one class); $C_{q(s_i)}$ is the class assigned to the segment s_i; and $p\left(s_i | C_{q(s_i)}\right)$ is the probability of the segment s_i in its class.

Thus, an *n-multigram* model based on classes of segments is completely defined by: the probability distribution of sequences of classes, and the classification function q.

As we mentioned above, to obtain the likelihood of a sentence $\mathcal{L}(w)$, all the possible segmentations have to be taken into account. It can be computed as follows:

$$\mathcal{L}(w) = \alpha(|w|) \tag{4}$$

where $\alpha(t)$ is the likelihood of $w_1 \cdots w_t$, that is, the prefix of w of length t. Considering that the number of words in the segments is limited by l, we can define $\alpha(t)$ as:

$$\alpha(t) = \sum_{i=1}^{l} \alpha_i(t) \tag{5}$$

where $\alpha_i(t)$ is the likelihood of the sentence $w_1 \cdots w_t$ which only takes into account those segmentations whose last segment is composed by i words. This value can be calculated as:

$$\alpha_i(t) = \begin{cases} 1 & : \quad t = 0 \wedge i = 1 \\ \sum_{r=1}^{\min(l,t-i)} \alpha_r(t-i) \cdot p(w_{t-i+1}^{t} | w_{t-i-r+1}^{t-i}) & : 1 \le t \le |w| \wedge 1 \le i \le l \end{cases} \quad (6)$$

In the case of considering classes of segments (and assuming that each segment has only been associated to a class), (6) can be calculated by:

$$\alpha_i(t) = \begin{cases} 1 & : \quad t = 0 \wedge i = 1 \\ \sum_{r=1}^{\min(l,t-i)} \alpha_r(t-i) \cdot p(w_{t-i+1}^{t} | C_{q(w_{t-i+1}^{t})}) \cdot \\ \quad p(C_{q(w_{t-i+1}^{t})} | C_{q(w_{t-i-r+1}^{t-i})}) & : 1 \le t \le |w| \wedge 1 \le i \le l \end{cases} \quad (7)$$

where $C_{q(w_{m-i}^{m})}$ is the class associated to the segment $w_{m-i}\#\ldots\#w_m$ by the function q, and $p(w_{m-i}^{m} | C_{q(w_{m-i}^{m})})$ is the probability that this segment belongs to the category $C_{q(w_{m-i}^{m})}$.

3 Language Understanding

A language understanding system can be viewed as a transducer in which natural language sentences are the input and their corresponding semantic representation (frames) are the output. In [10], an approach for the development of language understanding systems that is based on automatic learning techniques has been presented. In this approach, the process of translation is divided into two phases: the first phase transduces the input sentence into a semantic sentence (a sequence of semantic units) which is defined in a sequential Intermediate Semantic Language (ISL). The second phase transduces the semantic sentence into its corresponding frames. Automatic learning techniques are applied in the first phase, and the second phase is performed by a simple rule-based system.

As the ISL sentences are sequential with the input language, we can perform a segmentation of the input sentence into a number of intervals which is equal to the number of semantic units in the corresponding semantic sentence. Let W be the vocabulary of the task (set of words), and let V be the alphabet of semantic units; each sentence $w \in W^*$ has a pair (u,v) associated to it, where v is a sequence of semantic units and u is a sequence of segments of words. That is, $v = v_1 v_2 \ldots v_n, v_i \in V, i = 1, \ldots, n \quad u = u_1 u_2 \ldots u_n, u_i = w_{i_1} w_{i_2} \ldots w_{i_{|u_i|}},$ $w_{i_j} \in W, i = 1, \ldots, n, j = 1, \ldots, |u_i|$.

For example, in the BASURDE corpus, the sentence "me podría decir los horarios de trenes para Barcelona" (*can you tell me the railway timetables to*

Barcelona), whose translation in ISL could be *consulta <hora_salida> marcador_destino ciudad_destino* (*query <depart_time> destination_marker destination_city*), has the following pair associated to it, which is the output of the first phase of our understanding approach.

$$(u,v)=(u_1u_2u_3u_4, v_1v_2v_3v_4) \text{ where:}$$

Spanish		English	
u_1: me podría decir	v_1: consulta	u_1: can you tell me	v_1: query
u_2: los horarios de trenes	v_2: <hora_salida>	u_2: the railway timetables	v_2: <departure_time>
u_3: para	v_3: marcador_destino	u_3: to	v_3: destination_marker
u_4: Barcelona	v_4: ciudad_destino	u_4: Barcelona	v_4: destination_city

The output for the second phase is the following frame:

(DEPART_TIME)
DESTINATION_CITY: Barcelona

4 Applying *n-multigram* Models to Language Understanding

The first phase of our language understanding approach, that is, the semantic segmentation of a sentence w, consists of dividing the sentence into a sequence of segments ($u = u_1u_2 \ldots u_n$) and associating a semantic unit $v_i \in V$ to each segment u_i. Due to the fact that the multigram approach considers sentences as sequences of segments of variable length, it seems especially appropriate for the semantic segmentation problem. In order to apply *n-multigrams* to language understanding, the following considerations must be taken into account:

- The training corpus consists of a set of segmented and semantically labelled sentences.
- The classes of segments are the semantic vocabulary V, which is obtained from the definition of the ISL for the understanding task.
- A segment could be assigned to several classes, so the classification function q must be adapted in order to provide a membership probability for each segment in each class.

4.1 Learning the Semantic *n-multigram* Model

In an *n-multigram* model, there are two kind of probability distributions that have to be estimated: a) the language model for the sequences of classes of segments and b) the membership probability of segments in classes.

The probability distribution (a) is estimated as an n-gram model of classes of segments from the sequences of semantic units $v = v_1v_2 \ldots v_n, v_i \in V, i = 1, \ldots, n$ of the training set.

A language model is learnt from the set of segments of words u_i of the training set associated to each class. These language models provide the membership probability of segments in classes (b). We have explored some approaches to automatically obtain these language models. In particular, we used n-gram models, the Prefix-Tree Acceptor (PTA)[1] estimated from the training set, and two Grammatical Inference (GI) techniques (MGGI and ECGI) which are described in section 5.

We define a function of segment classification $q : \Sigma^* \rightarrow 2^V$

$$q(s) = \{v_1, \ldots, v_{|q(s)|}\}, \quad \forall v_i \in V \tag{8}$$

where $q(s)$ is the set of all the classes such as $p(s \mid v_i) > 0$.

4.2 The Semantic Segmentation

Once the model that represents the sequences of semantic units and the probability distributions of membership for each class are learnt, the process to obtain the likelihood α is obtained through:

$$\alpha = \sum_{i=1}^{l} \sum_{v \in q(w_{t-i+1}^{t})} \alpha_i^v(t) \tag{9}$$

This formula (9) is an adaptation of (5) for the case of permitting the assignation of more than one class to each segment. $\alpha(t)$ represents the accumulated likelihood taking into account all the segmentations for the t first words of the sentence $(w_1 \ldots w_t)$. And $\alpha_i^v(t)$ represents the likelihood of all the segmentations of the t first words, taking into account only those that end with a segment assigned to the class v and that have length i. It is calculated as follows:

$$\alpha_i^v(t) = \begin{cases} 1 & : \quad t = 0 \wedge i = 1 \\ 0 & : \quad t = 0 \wedge i > 1 \\ \sum_{r=1}^{l} p(w_{t-i+1}^{t} | v) \cdot \sum_{v' \in q(w_{t-i-r+1}^{t-i})} \alpha_r^{v'}(t-i) \cdot p(v|v') & : 1 \leq t \leq |w| \wedge 1 \leq i \leq l \end{cases} \tag{10}$$

The segmentation of maximum likelihood in terms of semantic units is obtained by using the Viterbi algorithm. Let $w = w_1 w_2 \cdots w_{|w|}$ be the sentence to analyze. The best segmentation is given by:

$$(u, v) = \underset{s \in S,\, q(s_\tau)}{\operatorname{argmax}} \ \mathcal{L}(w, s) \tag{11}$$

where S is the set of all segmentations of w, and $q(s_\tau)$ is the set of all classes that can be assigned to the τ-th segment of the segmentation s.

5 The Two GI Techniques: The MGGI Methodology and the ECGI Algorithm

As we mentioned above, we used two Grammatical Inference techniques in order to obtain the language models which represent the membership probability of

[1] The finite state automaton that only accepts the strings in the training set.

segments in classes. These techniques are the Morphic Generator Grammatical Inference (MGGI) methodology [11][12] and the Error Correcting Grammatical Inference (ECGI) algorithm [13][14]. In this section, we briefly describe these two GI techniques.

5.1 MGGI

The Morphic Generator Grammatical Inference (MGGI) methodology is a grammatical inference technique that allows us to obtain a certain variety of regular languages. The application of this methodology implies the definition of a renaming function, that is, each symbol of each input sample is renamed following a given function g. Different definitions of the function g will produce different models (stochastic regular automata).

Let R be a sample over the alphabet Σ. Let Σ' be a finite alphabet. Let h be a letter-to-letter morphism, $h : \Sigma'^* \rightarrow \Sigma^*$, and g a renaming function, $g : R \rightarrow \Sigma'^*$. The Regular Language, L, generated by the MGGI-inferred grammar, G, is related to R through the expression: $L = h(l(g(R)))$, where $l(g(R))$ is inferred from $g(R)$ through the 2-Testable in the Strict Sense (2-TSS) inference algorithm [15].

Next, we describe the MGGI methodology through an example. In order to better explain its performance, we show the 2-TSS model estimated from a training set and the finite automaton estimated through the MGGI methodology from the same training set:

Let $\Sigma = \{a, b\}$ be an alphabet and let $R = \{aabaa,\ abba,\ abbbba,\ aabbbba\}$ be a training set over Σ.

a) 2-Testable in the Strict Sense inference algorithm (its stochastic version is equivalent to bigrams):

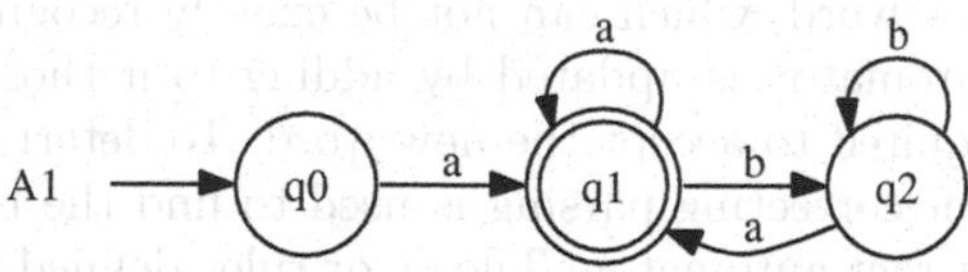

Fig. 1. The finite automaton inferred from R by the 2-Testable in the Strict Sense algorithm

The language accepted by the automaton of Figure 1 is: $L(A1) = a + a(b + a)^*a$. That is, the strings in $L(A1)$ begin and end with the symbol a and contain any segment over the alphabet Σ. For example, $a \in L(A1)$, $aaa \in L(A1)$, $ababa \in L(A1)$, $abbba \in L(A1)$, etc.

b) MGGI algorithm:

The renaming function $g : \Sigma^* \rightarrow \Sigma'^*$ is defined in this example as the relative position, considering that each string is divided into 2 intervals. This definition allows distinguishing between the first and the second parts of the strings.

$$g(R) = \{a_1a_1b_1a_2a_2,\ a_1b_1b_2a_2,\ a_1b_1b_1b_2b_2a_2,\ a_1a_1b_1b_1b_2b_2a_2\}$$

The language accepted by the automaton in Figure 2 is: $L(A2) = a^+b^+a^+$. That is, the strings in $L(A2)$ contain a sequence of 1 or more symbols a, followed

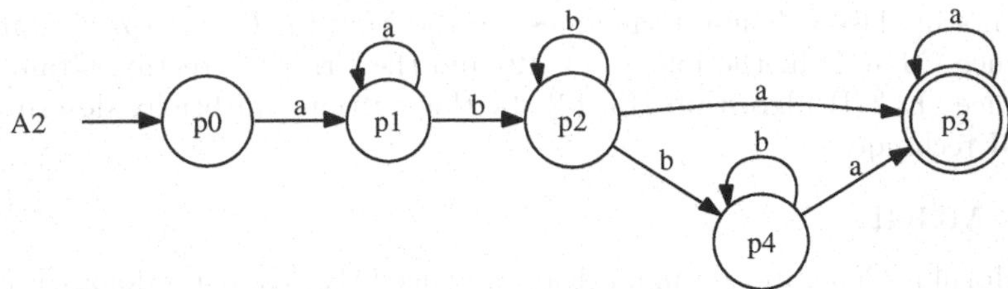

Fig. 2. The finite automaton inferred from R by MGGI algorithm, with a relative position renaming function

by a sequence of 1 or more symbols b, and followed by a sequence of 1 or more symbols a. For example $abbba \in L(A2)$ but $a \notin L(A2)$, $aaa \notin L(A2)$ and $ababa \notin L(A2)$. As can be observed from this example, the language inferred by the MGGI methodology is more similar to the strings in the training set than those inferred by the 2-TSS algorithm.

There is another interesting feature of the MGGI methodology. Given a task (a language to modelize), we can choose an adequate definition of a renaming function g. Different definitions of this function produce different models.

5.2 ECGI

The ECGI algorithm is a Grammatical Inference algorithm that infers a finite-state model in an incremental way and is based on an error correcting parsing. The ECGI builds a finite-state automaton through the following incremental procedure: initially, a trivial automaton is built from the first training word. Then, for every new word, which can not be exactly recognized by the current automaton, the automaton is updated by adding to it those states and transitions which are required to accept the new word. To determine such states and transitions, an error correcting parsing is used to find the best path for the input word in the current automaton. The error rules defined for the analysis are: substitution, insertion and deletion of symbols. This way, the error correcting parsing finds the word in the current inferred language which is closest to the new word, according to the Levenshtein distance. To generate an automaton which is free of loops and circuits, some heuristic restrictions are imposed in the process of adding new states and transitions. Thus, the inference procedure attempts to model the duration and the position of the substructures that appear in the training data. Figure 3 shows the inference process of the ECGI algorithm using the same training set of the examples in Figures 1 and 2.

6 Experimental Results

In order to evaluate the performance of the *n-multigram* models in a language understanding task, a set of experiments was conducted on the BASURDE [9] [10] dialog system, which answers queries about train timetables by telephone in

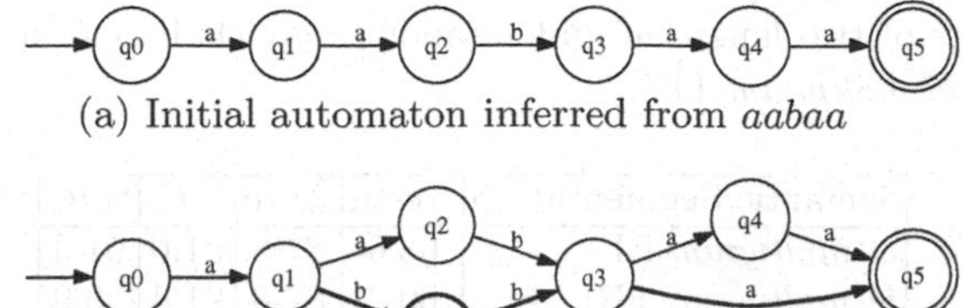

(a) Initial automaton inferred from *aabaa*

(b) Automaton after analyzing the string *abba*. A substitution rule and a deletion rule have been applied to accept this string. A new state, q_6, and some transitions have been added.

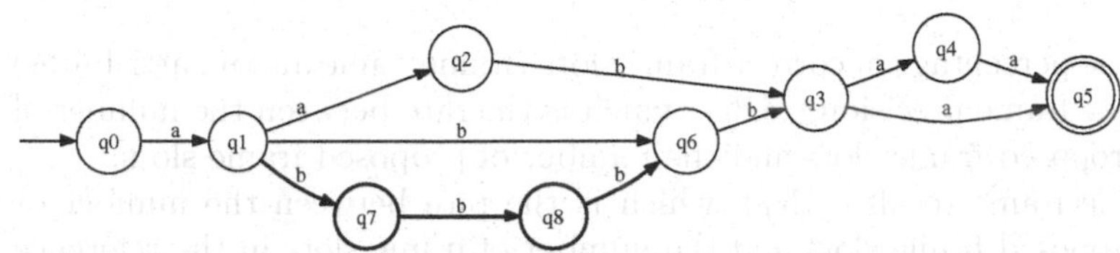

(c) Automaton after analyzing the string *abbbba*. Two insertion rules have been used. Two new states, q_7 and q_8, and some transitions have been added.

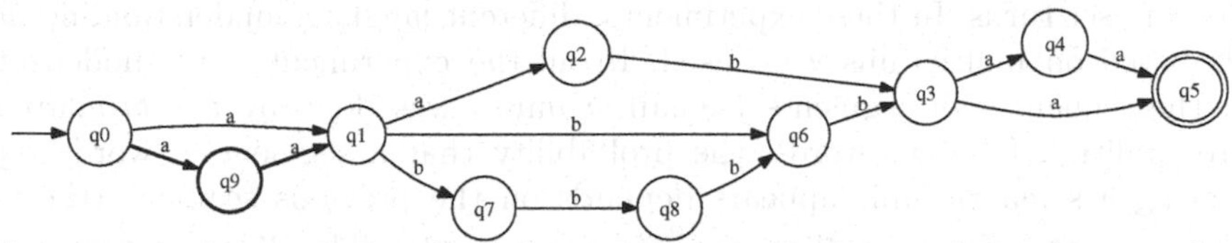

(d) Automaton after analyzing the string *aabbbba*. An insertion rule has been used. A new state, q_9, and some transitions have been added.

Fig. 3. The inference process of the ECGI algorithm using R

Spanish. The corpus consisted of a set of 215 dialogs, obtained through a Wizard of Oz technique [16]. These dialogs contained 1,440 user turns, with 14,902 words and a vocabulary of 637 different words. A cross-validation procedure was used to evaluate the performance of our language understanding models. To this end, the experimental set was randomly split into five subsets of 288 turns. Our experiment consisted of five trials, each of which had a different combination of one subset taken from the five subsets as the test set, with the remaining 1,168 turns being used as the training set.

We defined several measures to evaluate the accuracy of the strategy in both phases of the understanding process:

- The percentage of correct sequences of semantic units (%cssu).
- The percentage of correct semantic units (%csu).
- The semantic precision ($\%P_s$), which is the rate between the number of correct proposed semantic units and the number of proposed semantic units.
- The semantic recall ($\%R_s$), which is the rate between the number of correct proposed semantic units and the number of semantic units in the reference.
- The percentage of correct frames (%cf), which is the percentage of resulting frames that are exactly the same as the corresponding reference frame.

Table 1. Results of two language understanding models based on *bi-multigrams*: *bi-multigram*-BI y *bi-multigram*-TRI

Semantic Segmentation	%cssu	%csu	$\%P_s$	$\%R_s$
bi-multigram-BI	68.6	87.8	91.0	91.3
bi-multigram-TRI	69.2	87.8	91.4	90.9
Frame Transduction	%cf	%cfs	$\%P_f$	$\%R_f$
bi-multigram-BI	78.5	85.7	88.9	91.3
bi-multigram-TRI	79.0	86.1	89.6	91.0

- The percentage of correct frame slots (frame name and its attributes) (%cfs).
- The frame precision ($\%P_f$), which is the rate between the number of correct proposed frame slots and the number of proposed frame slots.
- The frame recall ($\%R_f$), which is the rate between the number of correct proposed frame slots and the number of frame slots in the reference.

A first set of experiments was performed using the orthographic transcription of user turns. In these experiments, different language understanding models based on multigrams were used. In all the experiments, the modelization of the sequences of segments (semantic units) was done by the *bi-multigram* probabilities. In other words, the probability that a segment of words representing a semantic unit appears depends on the previous segment (the term $p\left(C_{q(s_{(\tau)})}|C_{q(s_{(\tau-n+1)})}\cdots C_{q(s_{(\tau-1)})}\right)$ in formula (3)). The difference among the experiments consisted in which classification function (of the segments in classes) was chosen (the term $p\left(s_{(\tau)}|C_{q(s_{(\tau)})}\right)$ in formula (3)). Table 1 shows the results obtained using bigrams and trigrams of words to assign membership probabilities of the segments to each class.

Table 2 shows the results obtained by using the PTA, the MGGI and the ECGI techniques (described in section 5). These techniques obtain stochastic automata that represent the segments of words that can be associated to each class. These automata represent a modelization of the training samples and supply the membership probabilities associated to the segments. In order to increase the coverage of these models, we used a smoothing method for stochastic finite automata, which was recently proposed in [17].

These results for all techniques are similar. Nevertheless, the models obtained by GI techniques slightly outperform the n-gram models; this could be explained by the fact that the GI techniques better represent the structure of the segments of the training set.

In order to study the performance of the proposed models in real situations, we also performed a second set of experiments using the recognized utterances supplied by a speech recognizer from the same set of dialogs. The recognizer [9] used Hidden Markov Models as acoustic models and bigrams as the language model; its Word Accuracy for the BASURDE corpus was 80.7%. In these

Table 2. Results for the language understanding models: *bi-multigram*-PTA, *bi-multigram*-MGGI and *bi-multigram*-ECGI

Semantic Segmentation	%cssu	%csu	$\%P_s$	$\%R_s$
bi-multigram-PTA	69.0	88.0	91.5	91.1
bi-multigram-MGGI	69.3	88.3	91.6	91.3
bi-multigram-ECGI	68.9	88.3	91.4	91.8
Frame transduction	%cf	%cfs	$\%P_f$	$\%R_f$
bi-multigram-PTA	78.5	86.0	89.3	91.0
bi-multigram-MGGI	79.0	86.3	89.6	91.4
bi-multigram-ECGI	80.0	87.2	90.1	92.5

Table 3. Results for the understanding models based on *bi-multigrams*, with different models of membership probabilities, using the output of the recognizer

Semantic Segmentation	%cssu	%csu	$\%P_s$	$\%R_s$
bi-multigram-BI	44.3	74.3	81.6	82.5
bi-multigram-TRI	44.3	74.4	82.1	82.0
bi-multigram-AP	44.3	74.4	81.7	82.4
bi-multigram-MGGI	44.4	74.6	81.8	82.7
bi-multigram-ECGI	44.7	74.9	81.9	83.2
Frame Transduction	%cf	%cfs	$\%P_f$	$\%R_f$
bi-multigram-BI	54.9	69.6	77.6	81.7
bi-multigram-TRI	55.0	69.8	78.1	81.4
bi-multigram-AP	55.0	69.3	77.5	81.5
bi-multigram-MGGI	55.4	70.1	78.1	81.8
bi-multigram-ECGI	56.4	70.8	78.7	82.5

experiments, the models were the same as before; that is, they were estimated from the orthographic transcription of the sentences, but the test was done with the recognized sentences. Table 3 shows the results for the recognized dialogs, using the same understanding models based on *bi-multigrams* as in the previous experiments (Tables 1 and 2).

The results show a generalized reduction in the performance of the understanding system, if we compare them with those corresponding to transcribed utterances. This reduction is especially significant (over 20%) for %cssu and %cf. They respectively measure the percentage of sentences that are segmented perfectly and the percentage of sentences that are perfectly translated to their corresponding frames. Although less than 42% of the sentences are correctly recognized, the understanding system, *bi-multigram*-ECGI, is able to correctly understand 56% of the sentences. As far as recall and precision, the reduction is much lower, around 10% in most cases. The best model was the *bi-multigram*-ECGI. It obtained a Precision (P_f) and a Recall (R_f) of 78.7% and 82.5%, respectively, at frame level.

7 Conclusions

We have presented an approach to language understanding that is based on multigrams. In our language understanding system, segments of words represent semantic information. Therefore, considering a language modelization based on variable length segments is an appropriate approach. We have proposed different methods to assign segments to semantic units and we have applied our language understanding system based on multigrams to a dialog task. Our results are similar to those obtained by other approaches [10] and show that the proposed methodology is appropriate for the task. This modelization has the advantage that different models can be used to represent the segments associated to the semantic units; even different modelizations can be applied to different semantic units.

We think that the understanding system could be improved by adding information about the relevant keywords for each class in the classification function. It would also be interesting to develop techniques to automatically obtain the set of classes of segments, that is the set of semantic units, which in our system are manually defined.

References

1. Bahl, L., Jelinek, F., Mercer, R.: A maximum likelihood approach to continuous speech recognition. IEEE Trans. on **PAMI-5** (1983) 179–190
2. Clarkson, P., Rosenfeld, R.: Statistical language modeling using the CMU-cambridge toolkit. In: Proc. Eurospeech, Rhodes, Greece (1997) 2707–2710
3. Bonafonte, A., Mariño, J.B.: Language modeling using X-grams. In: Proc. of ICSLP, Philadelphia, PA (1996) 394–397
4. Bonafonte, A., Mariño, J.B.: Using X-Gram For Efficient Speech Recognition. In: Proc. of ICSLP, Sydney, Australia (1998)
5. Riccardi, G., Pieraccini, R., Bocchieri, E.: Stochastic automata for language modelling. Computer Speech and Language **10** (1996) 265–293
6. Deligne, S., Bimbot, F.: Language modeling by variable length sequences: theoretical formulation and evaluation of multigram. In: Proc. of ICASSP (1995) 169–172
7. Deligne, S., Bimbot, F.: Inference of variable-length acoustic units for continuous speech recognition. In: Proc. ICASSP, Munich, Germany (1997) 1731–1734
8. Deligne, S., Sagisaka, Y.: Statistical language modeling with a class-based n-multigram. Computer Speech and Language **14** (2000)
9. Bonafonte, A., et al: Desarrollo de un sistema de diálogo oral en dominios restringidos. In: I Jornadas en Tecnología del Habla, Sevilla (Spain). (2000)
10. Segarra, E., Sanchis, E., García, F., Hurtado, L.: Extracting semantic information through automatic learning techniques. IJPRAI **16** (2002) 301–307
11. García, P., Segarra, E., Vidal, E., Galiano, I.: On the use of the Morphic Generator Grammatical Inference (MGGI) Methodology in automatic speech recognition. IJPRAI **4(4)** (1990)
12. Segarra, E., Hurtado, L.: Construction of Language Models using Morfic Generator Grammatical Inference MGGI Methodology. In: Proc. of Eurospeech, Rhodes, Greece (1997) 2695–2698

13. Prieto, N., Vidal, E.: Learning language models through the ECGI method. Speech Communication (1992)
14. Prieto, N., Sanchis, E., Palmero, L.: Continuous speech understanding based on automatic learning of acoustic and semantic models. In: Proc. of ICSLP (1994) 2175–2178
15. García, P., Vidal, E.: Inference of k-testable languages in the strict sense and application to syntactic pattern recognition. IEEE Trans. on **PAMI-12** (1990) 920–925
16. Fraser, N.M., Gilbert, G.N.: Simulating speech systems. Computer Speech and Languages **5** (1991) 81–99
17. Segarra, E., et al: Achieving full coverage of automatically learnt finite-state language models. In: Proc. of EACL, Budapest (2003) 135–142

Multi-label Text Classification Using Multinomial Models*

David Vilar[1], María José Castro[2], and Emilio Sanchis[2]

[1] Lehrstuhl für Informatik VI,
Computer Science Department,
RWTH Aachen University,
D-52056 Aachen (Germany),
vilar@cs.rwth-aachen.de

[2] Departament de Sistemes Informàtics i Computació,
Universitat Politècnica de València,
E-46022 València, Spain,
{mcastro,esanchis}@dsic.upv.es

Abstract. Traditional approaches to pattern recognition tasks normally consider only the unilabel classification problem, that is, each observation (both in the training and test sets) has one unique class label associated to it. Yet in many real-world tasks this is only a rough approximation, as one sample can be labeled with a set of classes and thus techniques for the more general multi-label problem have to be explored. In this paper we review the techniques presented in our previous work and discuss its application to the field of text classification, using the multinomial (Naive Bayes) classifier. Results are presented on the Reuters-21578 dataset, and our proposed approach obtains satisfying results.

1 Introduction

Traditional approaches to pattern recognition tasks normally consider only the unilabel classification problem, that is, each observation (both in the training and test sets) has one unique class label associated to it. Yet in many real-world tasks this is only a rough approximation, as one sample can be labeled with a set of classes and thus techniques for the more general multi-label problem have to be explored. In particular, for multi-labeled documents, text classification is the problem of assigning a text document into one or more topic categories or classes [1]. There are many ways to deal with this problem. Most of them involve learning a number of different binary classifiers and use the outputs of those classifiers to determine the label or labels of a new sample[2]. We explore this approach using a multinomial (Naive Bayes) classifier and results are presented on the Reuters-21578 dataset. Furthermore, we explore the result that using an accumulated posterior probability approach to multi-label text classification performs favorably compared to the more standard binary approach to multi-label classification.

* This work has been partially supported by the Spanish CICYT under contracts TIC2002-04103-C03-03 and TIC2003-07158-C04-03.

J. L. Vicedo et al. (Eds.): EsTAL 2004, LNAI 3230, pp. 220–230, 2004.

The methods we discuss in this paper were applied to the classification phase of a dialogue system using neural networks [3], but the simplicity of the methods allows us to easily extend the same ideas to other application areas and other types of classifiers, such as the multinomial Naive Bayes classifier considered in this work for text classification.

2 Unilabel and Multi-label Classification Problems

Unilabel classification problems involve finding a definition for an unknown function $k^\star(\boldsymbol{x})$ whose range is a discrete set containing $|\mathcal{C}|$ values (i.e., $|\mathcal{C}|$ "classes" of the set of classes $\mathcal{C} = \{c^{(1)}, c^{(2)}, \ldots, c^{(|\mathcal{C}|)}\}$). The definition is acquired by studying collections of training samples of the form

$$\{(\boldsymbol{x}_n, c_n)\}_{n=1}^{N}, \quad c_n \in \mathcal{C}, \tag{1}$$

where $\boldsymbol{x}_n$ is the n-th sample and c_n is its corresponding class label.

For example, in handwritten digit recognition, the function $k^\star$ maps each handwritten digit to one of $|\mathcal{C}| = 10$ classes. The Bayes decision rule for minimizing the probability of error is to assign the class with maximum a posteriori probability to the sample $\boldsymbol{x}$:

$$k^\star(\boldsymbol{x}) = \operatorname*{argmax}_{k \in \mathcal{C}} \Pr(k|\boldsymbol{x}). \tag{2}$$

In contrast to the unilabel classification problem, in other real-world learning tasks the unknown function $k^\star$ can take more than one value from the set of classes $\mathcal{C}$. For example, in many important document classification tasks, like the Reuters-21578 corpus we will consider in Section 4, documents may each be associated with multiple class labels [1,4]. In this case, the training set is composed of pairs of the form

$$\{(\boldsymbol{x}_n, C_n)\}_{n=1}^{N}, \quad C_n \subseteq \mathcal{C}. \tag{3}$$

Note that the unilabel classification problem is a special case in which $|C_n| = 1$ for all samples.

There are two common approaches to this problem of classification of objects associated with multiple class labels. The first is to use specialized solutions like the accumulated posterior probability approach described in the next section. The second is to build a binary classifier for each class as explained afterwards.

Note that in certain practical situations, the amount of possible multiple labels is limited due to the nature of the task and this can lead to a simplification of the problem. For instance, if we know that the only possible appearing multiple labels can be $\{c^{(i)}, c^{(j)}\}$ and $\{c^{(i)}, c^{(k)}\}$ we do not need to consider all the possible combinations of the initial labels. In such situations we can handle this task as an unilabel classification problem with the extended set of labels $\hat{\mathcal{C}}$ defined as a subset of $\mathcal{P}(\mathcal{C})$. The question whether this method can be reliably used is highly task-dependent.

2.1 Accumulated Posterior Probability

In a traditional (unilabel) classification system, given an estimation of the a posteriori probabilities $\Pr(k|\boldsymbol{x})$, we can think of a classification as "better estimated" if the probability of the destination class is above some threshold (i.e., the classification of a sample

$\boldsymbol{x}$ as belonging to class k is better estimated if $\Pr(k|\boldsymbol{x}) = 0.9$ than if it is only 0.4). A generalization of this principle can be applied to the multi-label classification problem.

We can consider that we have correctly classified a sample only if the *sum* of the a posteriori probabilities of the assigned classes is above some threshold $\mathcal{T}$. Let us define this concept more formally. Suppose we have an ordering (permutation) $\{k^{(1)}, k^{(2)}, \ldots, k^{(|\mathcal{C}|)}\}$ of the set $\mathcal{C}$ for a sample $\boldsymbol{x}$, such that

$$\Pr(k^{(i)}|\boldsymbol{x}) \geq \Pr(k^{(i+1)}|\boldsymbol{x}) \quad \forall 1 \leq i < |\mathcal{C}| . \tag{4}$$

We define the *accumulated posterior probability* for the sample $\boldsymbol{x}$ as

$$\Pr_j(\boldsymbol{x}) = \sum_{i=1}^{j} \Pr(k^{(i)}|\boldsymbol{x}) \qquad 1 \leq j \leq |\mathcal{C}| . \tag{5}$$

Using the above equation, we classify the sample $\boldsymbol{x}$ in n classes, being n the smallest number such that

$$\Pr_n(\boldsymbol{x}) \geq \mathcal{T}, \tag{6}$$

where the threshold $\mathcal{T}$ must also be learned automatically in the training process. Then, the set of classification labels for the sample $\boldsymbol{x}$ is simply

$$K^\star(\boldsymbol{x}) = \{k^{(1)}, \ldots, k^{(n)}\} . \tag{7}$$

2.2 Binary Classifiers

Another possibility is to treat each class as a separate binary classification problem (as in [5, 6, 7]). Each such problem answers the question, whether a sample should be assigned to a particular class or not.

For $C \subseteq \mathcal{C}$, let us define $C[c]$ for $c \in \mathcal{C}$ to be:

$$C[c] = \begin{cases} \textsf{true}, & \text{if } c \in C ; \\ \textsf{false}, & \text{if } c \notin C . \end{cases} \tag{8}$$

A natural reduction of the multi-label classification problem is to map each multi-labeled sample $(\boldsymbol{x}, C)$ to $|\mathcal{C}|$ binary-labeled samples of the form $(\langle \boldsymbol{x}, c\rangle, C[c])$ for all $c \in \mathcal{C}$; that is, each sample is formally a pair, $\langle \boldsymbol{x}, c\rangle$, and the associated binary label, $C[c]$. In other words, we can think of each observed class set C as specifying $|\mathcal{C}|$ binary labels (depending on whether a class c is or not included in C), and we can then apply unilabel classification to this new problem. For instance, if a given training pair $(\boldsymbol{x}, C)$ is labeled with the classes $c^{(i)}$ and $c^{(j)}$, $(\boldsymbol{x}, \{c^{(i)}, c^{(j)}\})$, then $|\mathcal{C}|$ binary-labeled samples are defined as $(\langle \boldsymbol{x}, c^{(i)}\rangle, \textsf{true})$, $(\langle \boldsymbol{x}, c^{(j)}\rangle, \textsf{true})$ and $(\langle \boldsymbol{x}, c\rangle, \textsf{false})$ for the rest of classes $c \in \mathcal{C}$.

Then a set of binary classifiers is trained, one for each class. The ith classifier is trained to discriminate between the ith class and the rest of the classes and the resulting classification rule is

$$K^\star(\boldsymbol{x}) = \{k \in \mathcal{C} \mid \Pr(k|\boldsymbol{x}) \geq \mathcal{T}\} , \tag{9}$$

being $\mathcal{T}$ a threshold which must also be learned. Note that in the standard binary classification problem $\mathcal{T} = 0.5$, but experiments have shown that better results are obtained if we allow the more general formulation of equation (9). We can also allow more generalization by estimating one different threshold $\mathcal{T}_c$ for each class, but this would mean an increased number of parameters to estimate and the approach with only one threshold often works well in practice.

3 The Multinomial Model

As application of the multi-label classification rules we will consider a text classification task, where each document will be assigned a W-dimensional vector of word counts, where W is the size of the vocabulary. This representation is known as "bag-of-words". As classification model we use the *Naive Bayes* text classifier in its *multinomial* event model instantiation [8]. In this model, we make the assumption that the probability of each event (word occurrence) is independent of the word's context and position in the document it appears, and thus the chosen representation is justified. Given the representation of a document by its counts $\boldsymbol{x} = (x_1, \ldots, x_W)^t$ the class-conditional probability is given by the multinomial distribution

$$p(\boldsymbol{x}|c) = p(x_+|c)p(\boldsymbol{x}|c, x_+) = p(x_+|c)\frac{x_+!}{\prod_w x_w!}\prod_w p(w|c, x_+)^{x_w} , \qquad (10)$$

where $w = 1, \ldots, W$ denotes the word variable, $x_+ = \sum_w x_w$ is the length of document $\boldsymbol{x}$, and $p(w|c, x_+)$ are the parameters of the distribution, with the restriction

$$\sum_w p(w|c, x_+) = 1 \quad \forall c, x_+ . \qquad (11)$$

In order to reduce the number of parameters to estimate we assume that the distribution parameters are independent of the length x_+ and thus $p(w|c, x_+) = p(w|c)$, and that the length distribution is independent of the class c, so (10) becomes

$$p(\boldsymbol{x}|c) = p(x_+)\frac{x_+!}{\prod_w x_w!}\prod_w p(w|c)^{x_w} . \qquad (12)$$

Applying Bayes rule we obtain the unilabel classification rule

$$\begin{aligned} k^\star(\boldsymbol{x}) &= \operatorname*{argmax}_{c \in \mathcal{C}}\{p(c|\boldsymbol{x})\} \\ &= \operatorname*{argmax}_{c \in \mathcal{C}}\{\log p(c)p(\boldsymbol{x}|c)\} \\ &= \operatorname*{argmax}_{c \in \mathcal{C}}\left\{\log p(c) + \sum_w x_w \log p(w|c)\right\} . \end{aligned} \qquad (13)$$

The multi-label classification rules can be adapted accordingly.

To estimate the prior probabilities $p(c)$ of the class and the parameters $p(w|c)$ we apply the maximum-likelihood method. In the training phase we replicate the multi-labeled samples, that is, we transform the training set $\{(x_n, C_n)\}_{n=1}^N, C_n \subseteq \mathcal{C}$ into the the "unilabel" training set

$$\mathcal{M}\left(\{(\boldsymbol{x}_n, C_n)\}_{n=1}^N\right) = \bigcup_{n=1}^{N} \bigcup_{c \in C_n} \{(\boldsymbol{x}_n, c)\} \\ =: \{(\tilde{\boldsymbol{x}}_n, \tilde{c}_n)\}_{n=1}^{\tilde{N}} . \tag{14}$$

The log-likelihood function of this training set is then

$$\log \mathcal{L}(\{p(c)\}, \{p(w|c)\}) = \sum_{n=1}^{\tilde{N}} \left(\log p(c_n) + \sum_w \tilde{x}_{nw} \log p(w|\tilde{c}_n) \right. \\ \left. + \operatorname{const}(\{p(c)\}, \{p(w|c)\}) \right) . \tag{15}$$

Using Lagrange multipliers we maximize this function under the constrains

$$\sum_c p(c) = 1 \quad \text{and} \quad \sum_w p(w|c) = 1, \quad \forall 1 \leq c \leq |\mathcal{C}| . \tag{16}$$

The resulting estimators[1] are the relative frequencies

$$\hat{p}(c) = \frac{N_c}{\tilde{N}} \tag{17}$$

and

$$\hat{p}(w|c) = \frac{N_{cw}}{\sum_{w'} N_{cw'}} , \tag{18}$$

where $N_c = \sum_n \delta(\tilde{c}_n, c)$ is the number of documents of class c and similarly $N_{cw} = \sum_n \delta(\tilde{c}_n, c)\tilde{x}_{nw}$ is the total number of occurrences of word w in all the documents of class c. In this equations $\delta(\cdot, \cdot)$ denotes the Kronecker delta function, which is equal to one if its both arguments are equal and zero otherwise.

3.1 Smoothing

Parameter smoothing is required to counteract the effect of statistical variability of the training data, particularly when the number of parameters to estimate is relatively large in comparison with the amount of available data. As smoothing method we will use *unigram interpolation* [9].

The base of this method is known as *absolute discounting* and it consists of gaining "free" probability mass from the seen events by discounting a small constant b to every (positive) word count. The idea behind this model is to leave the high counts virtually unchanged, with the justification that for a corpus of approximately the same size, the counts will not differ much, and we can consider the "average" value, using a non-integer discounting. The gained probability mass for each class c is

$$M_c = \frac{b \cdot \left|\{w' : N_{cw'} > 0\}\right|}{\sum_{w'} N_{cw'}} , \tag{19}$$

[1] We will denote parameter estimations with the hat ($\hat{\cdot}$) symbol.

and is distributed in accordance to a *generalized distribution*, in our case, the *unigram distribution*

$$p(w) = \frac{\sum_c N_{cw}}{\sum_{w'} \sum_c N_{cw'}} . \tag{20}$$

The final estimation thus becomes

$$\hat{p}(w|c) = \max\left\{0, \frac{N_{cw} - b}{\sum_{w'} N_{cw'}}\right\} + p(w) M_c . \tag{21}$$

The selection of the discounting parameter b is crucial for the performance of the classifier. A possible way to estimate it is using the so called *leaving-one-out* technique. This can be considered as an extension of the cross-validation method [10, 11]. The main idea is to split the N observations (documents) of the training corpus into $N-1$ observations that serve as training part and only 1 observation, the so called hold-out part, that will constitute the simulated training test. This process is repeated N times in such a way that every observation eventually constitutes the hold-out set. The main advantage of this method is that each observation is used for both the training and the hold-out part and thus we achieve and efficient exploitation of the given data. For the actual parameter estimation we again use maximum likelihood. For further details the reader is referred to [12].

No closed form solution for the estimation of b using leaving-one-out can be given. Nevertheless, an interval for the value of this parameter can be explicitly calculated as

$$\frac{n_1}{n_1 + 2n_2 + \sum_{r \geq 3} n_r} < b < \frac{n_1}{n_1 + 2n_2} . \tag{22}$$

where $n_r = \sum_w \delta(\sum_c N_{cw}, r)$ is the number of words that have been seen exactly r times in the training set. Since in general leaving-one-out tends to underestimate the effect of unseen events we choose to use the upper bound as the leaving-one-out estimate

$$\hat{b}_{\text{l1o}} \cong \frac{n_1}{n_1 + n_2} . \tag{23}$$

3.2 A Note About Implementation

On the actual implementation of the multinomial classifier we can not directly compute the probabilities as given in equation (12) due to underflows in the computation of the exponentiation of the multinomial parameters[2]. In the unilabel classification tasks (and therefore in the extension to binary classifiers) we avoid this problem by using the joint probability in the maximization (see eq. (13)), but for the accumulated posterior probability approach we have to work with real posterior probabilities in order to handle the threshold in a correct way. A possibility to compute this probabilities in a numerically stable way is to introduce a maximum operation in Bayes rule

$$p(c|\boldsymbol{x}) = \frac{\dfrac{p(\boldsymbol{x}, c)}{\max_{c''} p(\boldsymbol{x}, c'')}}{\displaystyle\sum_{c'} \frac{p(\boldsymbol{x}, c')}{\max_{c''} p(\boldsymbol{x}, c'')}} , \tag{24}$$

[2] Note that the multinomial coefficient cancels when applying Bayes rule.

and then introduce a logarithm and an exponentiation function that allow us to compute the probabilities in a reliable way

$$p(c|\boldsymbol{x}) = \frac{\exp\left(\log p(\boldsymbol{x}, c) - \max_{c''} \log p(\boldsymbol{x}, c'')\right)}{\sum_{c'} \exp\left(\log p(\boldsymbol{x}, c') - \max_{c''} \log p(\boldsymbol{x}, c'')\right)} . \tag{25}$$

4 Experimental Results

4.1 The Dataset

As corpus for our experiments we use the Reuters-21578, a collection of articles appeared in the Reuters newswire in 1987. More precisely we use the Modified Apte Split as described in the original corpus, consisting of a training set of 9 603 documents and a test set of 3 299 documents (the remaining 8 676 are not used). Although this partition originally intended to restrict the set of used documents to those with one or more well defined class labels (topics as they are called in the documentation), problems with an exact definition of what was exactly meant with 'topic' results in documents without associated class labels appearing both in the training and the test set. Statistics of the corpus are shown in Table 1.

Table 1. Statistics for the Reuters-21578 dataset

	Number of documents			
	Total	**No label**	**Unilabel**	**Multi-Label**
Training	9 603	1 828 (19.0%)	6 552 (68.3%)	1223 (12.7%)
Test	3 299	280 (8.5%)	2 581 (78.2%)	438 (13.3%)

In spite of the explanation given in the "README" file accompanying the dataset, we feel that the presence of unlabeled documents in the corpus is not adequate, as they seem to be the result of an incorrect labelling, and therefore should be eliminated of the test set. We report results with the whole set, however, in order to better compare our results with other researches. On the other hand, the presence of such documents in the training set does provide some useful information and can be considered as a "real life" situation, where only a subset of the available data has been labeled. In our case we use the unlabeled documents as an aid to better estimate the smoothing parameters, but can also be used in a more powerful way [7]. This will be the subject of further research.

For the accumulated posterior probability approach, the presence of unlabeled samples in the test set represents immediately a classification error, as the definition of the approach requires that at least one label to be detected. One possibility to avoid this problem could be to include a "`<no_class>`" label, trained with the unlabeled samples in the training set and being mutually exclusive with the other classes. This seems however an ad hoc solution that does not generalize well so we decided not to

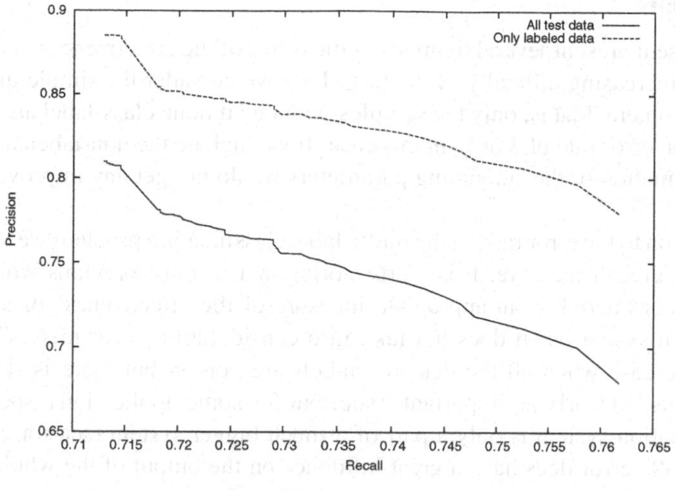

(a) Accumulated Posterior Probability

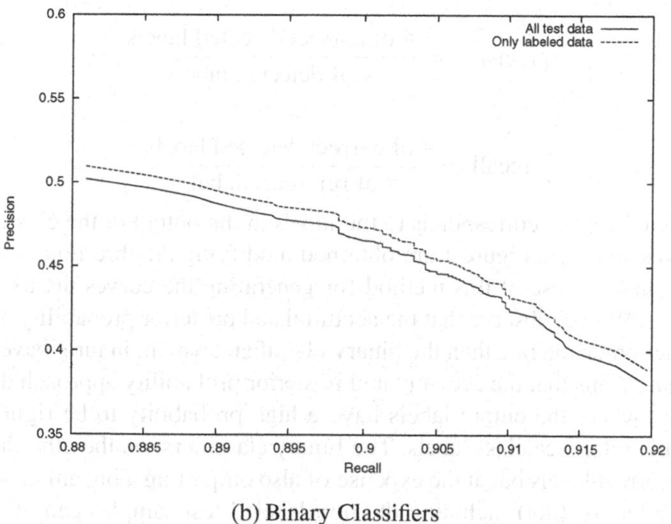

(b) Binary Classifiers

Fig. 1. Precision and recall curves for the Reuters-21578 dataset. Note the different scaling of the axis

apply it. On the other hand, the binary classifiers can handle the case of unlabeled samples in a natural way, if none of the posterior probabilities lies above the predefined threshold.[3]

[3] In the "normal" case where each sample should be labeled, we could choose the class with highest probability as the one unique label if no probability is higher than the threshold.

4.2 Results

We will present present several figures as a measures of the effectiveness of our methods in order of increasing difficulty of the task. First we consider the simple unilabel classification problem, that is, only the samples with one unique class-label are considered. We obtain an error rate of 8.56% in this case. If we include the non-labeled samples for a better estimation of the smoothing parameters we do not get any improvement in the error rate.

In addition to the error rate, in the multi-label classification problem we also consider the precision/recall measure. It is worth noting that in most previous work, the error rate is not considered as an appropiate measure of the effectiveness of a multi-label classification system, as it does not take into consideration "near misses", that is for example the case when all the detected labels are correct but there is still one label missing. This is clearly an important issue, but for some applications, specially when the classification system is only a part of a much bigger system (see for example [3]) such a "small" error does have a great influence on the output of the whole system, as it propagates into the subsequent constituents. Therefore we feel that the true error rate should also be included in such a study.

In the case of multi-label classification, precision is defined as

$$\text{precision} = \frac{\text{\# of correct detected labels}}{\text{\# of detected labels}} \tag{26}$$

and recall as

$$\text{recall} = \frac{\text{\# of correct detected labels}}{\text{\# of reference labels}} \tag{27}$$

where "detected labels" corresponds to the labels in the output of the classifier.

The curves shown in Figure 1 are obtained modifying the threshold $\mathcal{T}$ in the range $(0, 1)$. Note that because of this method for generating the curves the axis ranges are quite different. We can observe that the accumulated posterior probability approach has a much higher precision rate than the binary classifiers, which, in turn, have a higher recall rate. That means that the accumulated posterior probability approach does a "safe" classification, where the output labels have a high probability to be right, but it does not find all the reference class labels. The binary classifiers, on the other hand, do find most of the correct labels but at the expense of also outputting a big amount of incorrect labels. The effect of (not) including the non labeled test samples can also be seen in the curves. As expected, the performance of the accumulated posterior probability approach increases when leaving this samples out. In the case of the binary classifiers, the difference is not as big, but better results are still obtained when using only the labeled data.

It is also interesting to observe the evolution of the error rate when varying the threshold value. For the multi-label problem, for a sample to be correctly classified, the whole set of reference labels must be detected. That is, the number of detected labels must be the same in the reference and the output of the classifier (and obviously the labels also have to be the same). This a rather strict measure, but one must consider that in many systems the classification is only one step in a chain of processes and we are interested in the exact performance of the classifier [3]. The error rate is showed in

Figure 2. Note that this curves show the error rate on the *test set* in order to analyze the behavior of the classification methods. For a real-world classification system we should choose an appropriate threshold value (for example by using a validation set) and then use this value in order to obtain a figure for the error rate.

We see that when considering the error rate, the accumulated posterior probability approach performs much better than the binary classifiers. For this approach the threshold does not have a great influence on the error rate unless we use high values, where an increase of the number of class labels the classifier has to include for reaching the threshold produces an increase of the error rate. Somehow surprisingly, for binary classifiers, the best results are obtained for low threshold values. This is probably due to the unclean division between the classes defined in every binary subproblem, that leads to an incorrect parameter estimation. Taking into account the correlation between the classes may help to alleviate the problem.

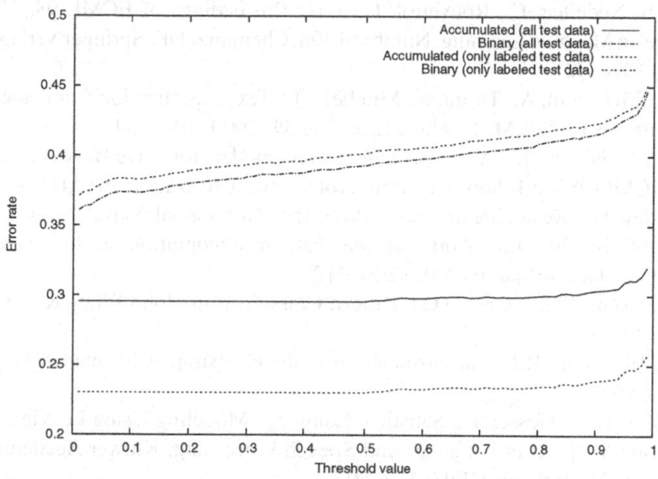

Fig. 2. Error rate for the two multi-label methods

5 Conclusions

In this paper we have discussed some possibilities to handle the multi-label classification problem. The methods are quite general and can be applied to a wide range of statistical classifiers. Results on text classification with the Reuters-21578 corpus have been presented, where the accumulated posterior probability approach performs better that the most widely used binary classifiers.

However, in these approaches we did not take the relation between the different classes into account. Modeling this information may provide a better estimation of the parameters and better results can be expected. For the Reuters-21578 corpus in particular, a better exploitation of the unlabeled data can also lead to an improvement in performance.

References

1. McCallum, A.K.: Multi-Label Text Classification with a Mixture Model Trained by EM. In: NIPS99. (1999)
2. Sebastiani, F.: Machine learning in automated text categorization. ACM Comput. Surv. **34** (2002) 1–47
3. Castro, M.J., Vilar, D., Sanchis, E., Aibar, P.: Uniclass and Multiclass Connectionist Classification of Dialogue Acts. In Sanfeliu, A., Ruiz-Shulcloper, J., eds.: Progress in Pattern Recognition, Speech and Image Analysis. 8 th Iberoamerican Congress on Pattern Recognition (CIARP 2003). Volume 2905 of Lecture Notes in Computer Science. Springer (2003) 266–273
4. Schapire, R.E., Singer, Y.: Boostexter: A boosting-based system for text categorization. Machine Learning **39** (2000) 135–168
5. Yang, Y.: An evaluation of statistical approaches to text categorization. Information Retrieval **1** (1999) 69–90
6. Joachims, T.: Text categorization with Support Vector Machines: Learning with many relevant features. In Nédellec, C., Rouveirol, C., eds.: Proceedings of ECML-98, 10th European Conference on Machine Learning. Number 1398, Chemnitz, DE, Springer Verlag, Heidelberg, DE (1998) 137–142
7. Nigam, K., McCalum, A., Thrun, S., Mitchell, T.: Text classification from labeled and unlabeled documents using EM. Machine Learning **39** (2000) 103–134
8. McCallum, A., Nigam, K.: A comparison of event models for naive Bayes text classification. In: AAAI/ICML-98 Workshop on Learning for Text Categorization, AAAI Press (1998) 41–48
9. Juan, A., Ney, H.: Reversing and Smoothing the Multinomial Naive Bayes Text Classifier. In: Proc. of the 2nd Int. Workshop on Pattern Recognition in Information Systems (PRIS 2002), Alacant (Spain) (2002) 200–212
10. Duda, R.O., Hart, P.E., Stork, D.G.: Pattern Classification. John Wiley & Sons, New York, NY, USA (2001)
11. Efron, B., Tibshirani, R.J.: An Introduction to the Bootstrap. Chapman & Hall, New York, NY, USA (1993)
12. Ney, H., Martin, S., Wessel, F.: Satistical Language Modeling Using Leaving-One-Out. In: Corpus-based Methods in Language and Speech Proceesing. Kluwer Academic Publishers, Dordrecht, the Netherlands (1997) 174–207

A Multi-use Incremental Syntax-Semantic Interface*

Luísa Coheur[1], Nuno Mamede[2], and Gabriel G. Bès[3]

[1] L^{2}F INESC-ID / GRIL, Lisboa, Portugal
Luisa.Coheur@l2f.inesc-id.pt
[2] L^{2}F INESC-ID / IST, Lisboa, Portugal
Nuno.Mamede@inesc-id.pt
[3] GRIL / Univ. Blaise-Pascal, Clermont-Ferrand, France
Gabriel.Bes@univ-bpclermont.fr

Abstract. AsdeCopas is a module designed to interface syntax and semantics. It is based on self-contained, hierarchically organised semantic rules and outputs formulas in a flat language. This paper extends a previous definition of semantic rules and describes two applications of AsdeCopas, namely in question interpretation and in semantic disambiguation.

1 Introduction

In 1997, and in order to allow Natural Language access to a database of tourist resources, a linguistically motivated system called Edite [13, 23, 14] was created. Edite had a traditional syntax-semantic interface, where semantic rules were associated with syntactic rules and the semantic analysis was made by a bottom-up parser. Edite had a fast development, but it soon became saturated, mainly due to the dependency between syntactic and semantic rules. This experiment made us change our approach and invest in a more robust methodology. We found in the 5P Paradigm [4, 16, 5] the background we were looking for. The syntax-semantic interface presented in this paper reflects the effort of adapting to 5P demands.

Firstly, our syntax-semantic interface builds a dependency structure from a surface analysis [10]. Then, a module called AsdeCopas [8, 9, 11], based on incremental, hierarchically organised semantic rules, generates logical formulas. Although, logical formulas generation was AsdeCopas original goal, it can also execute other tasks. In this paper we show how it can be used in question interpretation and in semantic disambiguation.

This paper is organised as follows: in section 2 we present some related work; in section 3 we describe our interface, focussing on the semantic rules and AsdeCopas; in sections 4 and 5 we detach the mentioned applications. Final remarks and future directions can be found in section 6.

* This paper was supported by FCT (Fundação para a Ciência e Tecnologia) and by Project POSI/PLP/41319/2001 (FEDER).

J. L. Vicedo et al. (Eds.): EsTAL 2004, LNAI 3230, pp. 231–242, 2004.

2 Related Work

Syntax-semantic interfaces, as the ones presented in [3] and [18] are largely spread. These interfaces are based on semantic rules associated with syntactic rules and typically semantic analysis is executed in a bottom-up analysis. On the contrary, syntax-semantic interfaces based on dependencies are not so easy to find. [21] is an answer extraction system that executes a syntax-semantic interface over dependencies. According to [20], the current version of ExtrAns uses either Link Grammar [15] or the Conexor FDG parser [17] to generate dependencies. Then, different algorithms are implemented over each one of the dependency structures. In the first case, the logical-form is constructed by a top-down procedure, starting in the head of the main dependency and following dependencies. The algorithm is prepared to deal with a certain type of dependencies, and whenever an unexpected link appears, a special recovery treatment is applied. When describing the algorithm, the authors say that most of these steps "... become very complex, sometimes involving recursive applications of the algorithm" and also that "specific particularities of the dependency structures returned by Link Grammar add complexity to this process" [20]. In the second case, that is, after the Conexor FDG parsing, the bottom up parser used has three stages. In the first one (introspection) possible underspecified predicates are associated with each word. Object predicates introduce their own arguments, but other predicates remain incomplete until the second stage (extrospection). During extrospection, arguments are filled by looking at the relation between each word and its head. Sometimes dummy arguments need to be assigned when the algorithm faces disconnected dependency structures. A third stage (re-interpretation) is needed to re-analyse some logical constructs. According to the authors, the algorithm cannot produce the correct argument structure for long distance dependencies.

In our proposal, semantic rules are set apart from the algorithm. As so, the algorithm is independent from the dependency structures. As semantic rules are sensitive for the (possibly non-local) syntactic context, long distance dependencies cause no problem and we are able to make semantic rules return precise semantic values that depend on the context. Moreover, each semantic rule contains all the necessary information to calculate the corresponding formulas. As a result, all words, independently from their category, are mapped into formulas in one step. Additionally, there is no need to recursively apply the algorithm. Finally, semantic rules are organised in a hierarchy. Therefore, instead of creating dummy arguments when disconnected dependency structures are found, default rules are triggered in these situations.

3 Our Proposal

3.1 The Syntax-Semantic Interface

The whole syntax-semantic interface is integrated in a system called Javali [7]. It has three modules:

- Algas and Ogre, that generate dependency structures from a surface analysis [10] (from now on we call "graphs" to these dependency structures);
- AsdeCopas, that takes the graph as input and performs several tasks such as enriching the graph by adding labels to its arrows; calculating semantic values; generating logical forms, etc.

Each graph node contains: (i) a word; (ii) the word's category; (iii) the word's position in the text; (iv) extra information about the word (this field might be empty).

Each graph arc maintains information about: (i) the position and the category associated with the source node; (ii) the position and the category associated with the target node; (iii) the arrow label (possibly undefined)[1].

As an example, given the question *Quais os hotéis com piscina de Lisboa?* (*Which are the hotels with a swimming pool from Lisbon?*), the following graph is obtained, where the interrogative pronoun (qu) *Quais*, arrows the common noun (cn) *hotéis*, which is also the target of the article *os*, the proper noun (pn) *Lisboa* and the cn *piscina*. Moreover, the cn *hotéis* arrows itself and can be seen as the head of the question. Both prepositions (prep) *com* and *de* arrow the heads of the prepositional phrases they introduce, respectively, *piscina* and *Lisboa*:

```
node('Quais', qu, 9, _), arc(qu, 9, cn, 11, _),
node('os', artd_p, 10, _), arc(artd_p, 10, cn, 11, _),
node('hotéis', cn, 11, _), arc(cn, 11, cn, 11, _),
node('com', prep, 12, _), arc(prep, 12, cn, 13, _),
node('piscina', cn, 13, _), arc(cn, 13, cn, 11,  _),
node('de', prep, 14, _), arc(prep, 14, pn, 15, _),
node('Lisboa', pn, 15, _), arc(pn, 15, cn, 11, _).
```

3.2 Semantic Rules

Incrementability and Specificity. Aït-Mokhtar [2] defines an incremental rule as "a self-contained operation, whose result depends on the set of contextual restrictions stated in the rule itself. [...] If a sub-string matches the contextual restrictions, the corresponding operation applies without later backtracking". Our semantic rules were designed having this property in mind. As a result, each semantic rule is divided into three parts:

- the element or elements to transform;
- the context of the elements to transform (it can be seen as a set of conditions that, being verified, indicate that the rule can be applied);
- the output (specified by a set of functions that will transform the elements according to the chosen representation).

[1] Within our applications, dependencies are unlabelled, and go from dependents to the head. The motivation behind these structures came from the 5P Paradigm.

Moreover, we assume the following:

- if an element appears either as an element to transform or as part of the rule context, the semantic rule has access to all the semantic information of that element. That is, it knows its variables, handles, associated predicates, unspecified semantic values, and so on;
- the function that perform the transformation can only use information from elements defined as elements to transform or that appear in the rule's context.

As a result, semantic rules are similar to the rules used in [1] and they can also be seen as incremental rules as previously defined.

Additionally, semantic rules are organised in a subsumption hierarchy. Therefore, if a set of rules can be applied, only the rules that do not subsume other rules – that is the most specific rules – are triggered. This allows to add new, more specific information to the system without having to rewrite general rules.

Syntax. Let W be a set of words, C a set of category labels, D a set of arrow labels and P a set of variables denoting positions. The symbol "_" is used to represent an underspecified value. Consider the following definitions:

- Element: $\mathsf{elem}(w, c, p)$ is an element, where: (i) $w \in \{\_\} \cup \mathsf{W}$; (ii) $c \in \{\_\} \cup \mathsf{C}$; (iii) $p \in \mathsf{P}$.
- Arrow: $\mathsf{arrow}(w_1, c_1, p_1, w_2, c_2, p_2, d, l)$ is an arrow, and $\mathsf{no\_arrow}(w_1, c_1, p_1, w_2, c_2, p_2, d, l)$ a non existing arrow where: (i) w_1, $w_2 \in \{\_\} \cup \mathsf{W}$; (ii) c_1, $c_2 \in \mathsf{C}$ (c_1 and c_2 are, respectively, the arrow source and target); (iii) $p_1, p_2 \in \mathsf{P}$; (iv) $d \in \{\_\} \cup \{\mathrm{L}, \mathrm{R}\}$ (d is the arrow orientation: L if it goes from right to left, R from left to right); (v) $l \in \{\_\} \cup \mathsf{D}$ (l is a possibly undefined arrow label).
- Semantic Rule: $[\mathrm{R}_i]\ \Sigma : \Theta \mapsto \Gamma$ is a semantic rule where: (i) Σ is a possibly empty set of elements (the elements to operate on); (ii) Θ is a possible empty set of existing and non existing arrows (the rule's context); (iii) Γ is a set of transformation functions, that vary according to the chosen representation language.

Semantic rules presented here are an extension of semantic rules presented in [11], where there is no position associated with elements and arrows have no words in its arguments. By associating (variables over) positions to elements, there is no need to use indexes to distinguish two different objects with the same category. Introducing words in the arrows arguments allows to define more precise semantic rules.

Extra constraints over semantic rules syntax can be found in [8, 9].

For now, and because of the applications from sections 4 and 5, we introduce the following transformation functions: (i) $sem(\mathrm{X}_1)$: returns the (default) predicate of the element in position X_1; (ii) var: returns a variable associtated with the element in position X_1.

Hierarchy of Rules. In the following, we define the subsumption relation between semantic rules. This relation establishes the hierarchy of rules and it is based on the subsumption relation between categories (notice that, although we use labels to represent categories, each category is a set of attribute/value pairs organised in a subsumption hierarchy). Due to the syntactic extensions of semantic rules, the hierarchy relation defined below is also an extension of the hierarchy relation presented in [11].

- Element subsumption: Given $e_1 = \mathsf{elem}(w_1, c_1, p_1)$ and $e_2 = \mathsf{elem}(w_2, c_2, p_2)$ from Σ, e_1 subsumes e_2 ($e_1 \sqsubseteq_e e_2$) iff (i) $c_1 \sqsubseteq c_2$; (ii) $(w_1 \neq \_) \Rightarrow (w_2 = w_1)$.
- Arrow subsumption: Given $a_1 = \mathsf{arrow}(w_1, c_1, p_1, w_2, c_2, p_2, d_1, l_1)$ and $a_2 = \mathsf{arrow}(w_3, c_3, p_3, w_4, c_4, p_4, d_2, l_2)$ from Θ, a_1 subsumes a_2 ($a_1 \sqsubseteq_a a_2$) iff (i) $(w_1 \neq \_) \Rightarrow (w_3 = w_1)$; (ii) $(w_2 \neq \_) \Rightarrow (w_4 = w_2)$; (iii) $c_1 \sqsubseteq c_3 \wedge c_2 \sqsubseteq c_4$; (iv) $(d_1 \neq \_) \Rightarrow (d_2 = d_1)$; (v) $(l_1 \neq \_) \Rightarrow (l_2 = l_1)$.
- Subsumption of non existing arrows: Given $a_1 = \mathsf{no\_arrow}(w_1, c_1, p_1, w_2, c_2, p_2, d_1, l_1)$ and $a_2 = \mathsf{no\_arrow}(w_3, c_3, p_3, w_4, c_4, p_4, d_2, l_2)$ from Θ, a_1 subsumes a_2 ($a_1 \sqsubseteq_a a_2$) iff (i) $(w_1 \neq \_) \Rightarrow (w_3 = w_1)$; (ii) $(w_2 \neq \_) \Rightarrow (w_4 = w_2)$; (iii) $c_1 \sqsubseteq c_3 \wedge c_2 \sqsubseteq c_4$; (iv) $(d_1 \neq \_) \Rightarrow (d_2 = d_1)$; (v) $(l_1 \neq \_) \Rightarrow (l_2 = l_1)$.
- Rule subsumption: Given two semantic rules $\mathrm{R}_1 = (\Sigma_1, \Theta_1, \Gamma_1)$ and $\mathrm{R}_2 = (\Sigma_2, \Theta_2, \Gamma_2)$, R_1 subsumes R_2 ($\mathrm{R}_1 \sqsubseteq_r \mathrm{R}_2$) iff (i) $(\forall\, e_1 \in \Sigma_1)(\exists\, e_2 \in \Sigma_2)(e_1 \sqsubseteq_e e_2)$; (ii) $(\forall\, a_1 \in \Theta_1)(\exists\, a_2 \in \Theta_2)(a_1 \sqsubseteq_a a_2)$.

If R_1 subsumes R_2, R_2 is said to be more specific than R_1. If both rules can apply, only the most specific one does so.

3.3 AsdeCopas

AsdeCopas is implemented in Prolog. It goes through each graph node and: (i) identifies the rules that can be applied; (ii) chooses the most specific rules; (iii) triggers the most specific rules (notice that at each step more than one rule can be triggered).

Within AsdeCopas we detach the following:

- The order of rule's application is not relevant as results remain the same, independently from the order of rule's application;
- AsdeCopas controls variable generation as instead of randomly generating variables, each variable is indexed by the position that the related word occupies in the text. By this we guarantee that each semantic rules "knows" the variables associated with each element to transform or appearing in the context[2].

As an example of AsdeCopas output, see the representation obtained for the question *Quais os hotéis com piscina de Lisboa?*.

---

[2] Although we have not yet used this possibility, this control of variables should allow us to run different semantic processes at different times and merge the results at the end.

```
R10:   ?x11, R1:    hotéis(x11), R7:    com(x11, x13)
R1:    piscina(x13), R7:    de(x11, x15), R2:    NAME(x15, Lisboa)
```

In the next section we detach the rules responsible for this result.

4 Task 1: Question Interpretation

In Task 1 AsdeCopas is used to generate logical forms from questions. Quantification is ignored.

4.1 Semantic Rules

In the following we present a simplified set of the semantic rules that we use in this task. Namely, we present rules associated with names, adjectives and interrogative pronouns. These rules illustrate how logical forms are constructed.

Let us assume that the representation of a cn is a unary formula. For example, the cn *praia* (*beach*) originates the formula `praia(x)`. The next rule calculates the cn representation. Notice that this rule applies independently from the arrowing context of the cn.

$[\mathrm{R}_1]\ \mathsf{elem}(\_, \mathsf{cn}, \mathrm{X}_1) : \emptyset \mapsto \mathit{sem}(\mathrm{X}_1)(\mathit{var}(\mathrm{X}_1))$

Consider now a pn. Each pn originates a binary formula, with predicate `NAME` as suggested in [18]. The first argument is the variable of the named entity and the second argument is its name. The variable used for the named entity depends if the pn arrows a verb (v) or a cn, because we want *O Ritz tem piscina?* (*Does Ritz have a swimming pool?*) to be represented as `NAME(x, Ritz), tem(e,x,y), piscina(y))` and *O hotel Ritz tem piscina?* (*Does Ritz hotel have a swimming pool?*) as `hotel(x), NAME(x,Ritz), tem(e,x,y), piscina(y)`.

The following rules cover both situations. R_2 is a generic rule and R_3 is more specific and is subsumed by R_2.

$[\mathrm{R}_2]\ \mathsf{elem}(\_, \mathsf{pn}, \mathrm{X}_1) : \emptyset \mapsto \mathrm{NAME}(\mathit{var}(\mathrm{X}_1), \mathit{sem}(\mathrm{X}_1))$

$[\mathrm{R}_3]\ \mathsf{elem}(\_, \mathsf{pn}, \mathrm{X}_1) : \{\mathsf{arrow}(\_, \mathsf{pn}, \mathrm{X}_1, \_, \mathsf{cn}, \mathrm{X}_2, \_, \_),$
$\mathsf{no\_arrow}(\_, \mathsf{prep}, \mathrm{X}_3, \_, \mathsf{pn}, \mathrm{X}_1, \mathrm{R}, \_)\} \mapsto \{\mathrm{NAME}(\mathit{var}(\mathrm{X}_2), \mathit{sem}(\mathrm{X}_1))\}$

Consider now the rules for adjectives (adj). We assume that an adjective may originate either a unary formula or a binary formula with predicate `AM` (as suggested in [18]). The first representation is the default representation; the second representation is used when the adj arrows a noun n (either cn or a pn). The followings rules cover these cases (and R_5 is subsumed by R_4).

$[R_4]$ elem(_, adj, X_1) : $\emptyset \mapsto sem(X_1)(var(X_1))$

$[R_5]$ elem(_, adj, X_1):
{arrow(_, adj, X_1, _, n, X_2, _, _), no_arrow(_, prep, X_3, _, adj, X_1, R, _)} $\mapsto$
$\{AM(var(X_2), var(X_1)), sem(X_1)(var(X_1))\}$

By applying these rules, the adj *nudista* (*nudist*) in *praia para nudistas* (*beach for nudists*) is transformed into `nudista(x)` and the adj *bonita* (*beautiful*) from *A praia bonita* (*The beautiful beach*) in `AM(x, y), bonita(y)`, where `x` is the variable associated with *praia*.

Consider now the rule for prepositions. We assume, as usual, that a preposition results in a binary formula, where the first argument is the head of the phrase to which the prepositional phrase is attached, and the second the target of the preposition's arrow. The first argument can be an event (rule R_6) or an entity (rule R_7). The following rule

$[R_6]$ elem(_, prep, X_1) : {arrow(_, prep, X_1, _, n, X_2, R, _),
arrow(_, n, X_2, _, n, X_3, _, _)} $\mapsto \{sem(X_1)(var(X_3), var(X_2))\}$

transforms the preposition from *hotel de Lisboa* (*hotel from Lisbon*) into `prep(x, y)`, where `x` is the variable associated with *hotel* and `y` with *Lisboa*. The next rule covers the verbs situation:

$[R_7]$ elem(_, prep, X_1) : {arrow(_, prep, X_1, _, n, X_2, R, _),
arrow(_, n, X_2, _, v, X_3, _, _)} $\mapsto \{sem(X_1)(var(X_3), var(X_2))\}$

This rule creates the formula `para(e, x)` from the phrase *... vai para Lisboa?* (*... goes to Lisbon*), where `e` is the event associated with the verb `vai` and `x` with *Lisboa*.

In order to represent the interrogative pronouns *quem*, *qual*, *quais* and *que...* (labelled qu), we use the formula `?x`, where `x` is a variable representing the objects we are asking for.

$[R_8]$ elem(_, qu, X_1) : {arrow(_, qu, X_1, _, n, X_2, R, _)} $\mapsto \{?var(X_2)\}$

With rule R_8, the qu from *Que hotéis ...* results in the formula `?x`, where x is the variable associated with *hotéis*.

4.2 Paraphrases

A special effort was made in this task to solve some paraphrasic relations. As an example, both phrases *Quais os hotéis que têm piscina?* (*Which are the hotels with a swimming pool?*) and *Em que hotéis há piscina?* (*In which hotels is there a swimming pool?*), result in a formula (similar) to:

```
?x, hotéis(x), tem(e, x, y), piscina(y)
```

Notice that in order to reach this result, we only looked into the particular syntactic conditions that make verb *haver* behave as the verb `ter`.

4.3 Evaluation

Consider that:

- a "system representation" (SR) is the set of formulas that the system suggests as a represention of the question;
- a "correct representation" (CR) is the set of formulas representing a question, where the exact number of expected predicates are produced, and variables are in the correct places.

For example, being given the question *Quais os roteiros pedestres sinalizados em Lisboa?* (*Which are the signalised footways in Lisbon?*), its CR is:

```
?x759 , roteiros(x759), AM(x759, x760), pedestres(x760)
AM(x759, x761), sinalizados(x761)
em(x759, x763), NAME(x763, Lisboa)
```

Nevertheless, as the word *sinalizados* was not understood by the system, it generates the following SR:

```
?x759, roteiros(x759), AM(x759, x760), pedestres(x760)
em(x759, x763), NAME(x763, Lisboa)
```

From system Edite we inherited a corpus of 680 non-treated questions about tourist resources. A first evaluation made over 30 question is presented in [11]. In that evaluation AsdeCopas input was a set of graphs that did not necessarily represent the correct analysis. Moreover, as in previous steps several graphs were associated with each question, each question had more than one graph associated and consequently, each question had more that one SR. In that evaluation we obtained a precison of 19% and a recall of 77%. Nevertheless, in that evaluation, as incorrect graphs were accepted, we were not really evaluating AsdeCopas, but the whole system. Besides, we did not measure the distance between the obtained SR and the CR, which can be a extremelly useful evaluation. For instance, in the previous example, most of the information from the CR is in the SR.

As so, we propose here a new evaluation where the correct graph is chosed, and new metrics are used. Notice that if only one graph is associated with each question, as we admit underspecified semantic values, with the actual set of semantic rules, only one (underspecified) SR is obtained. Consider that: (i) SF is a formula, such that SF $\in$ SR (system formula); (ii) CF is a formula, such that CF $\in$ SR $\cap$ CR (correct formula); (iii) NCF is the number of (correct) formulas within a CR (number of (correct) formulas in a correct representation).

We use the following metrics for each SR: (i) precision: number of CF/number of SF; (ii) recall: number of CF/NCF.

In an evalution over 50 questions, we obtained 45 SR such that precision = recall = 100%. The remaining 5 SR, were evaluated according with the previous presented metrics and results are the following:

From these results we can conclude that the SR is very close to the CR. That is, even if we are not able to calculate the exact result, we can calculate a set of formulas that are very similar with the wanted results.

Table 1. Evaluation results

Question number	Precision	Recall
23	0,86	1
28	0,85	0,85
37	1	0,92
40	1	0,8
42	0,86	0,75

5 Task 2: Semantic Disambiguation

5.1 The Problem

As the majority of the words, the word *qualquer* (roughly, *any*) can take several semantic values. Sometimes the syntactic context allows to choose the correct semantic value, sometimes only semantic information lead to the correct value, sometimes the correct semantic values is impossible to calculate.

In this task, we try to identify subsets of the set of the semantic values that *qualquer* might take, by analysing its syntactic context. Semantic rules, as defined in 3.2, will be used in this task.

Additionally, as other quantifiers can also take the same semantic values of *qualquer*, we also try to identify these values and the associated syntactic contexts. The following examples illustrate the difficulty of the task.

(1) *O David não conhece qualquer livro do Tolkien.*
(*David doesn't know any book from Tolkien.*)

This sentence is equivalent to

(2) *O David desconhece qualquer livro do Tolkien*[3].

Nevertheless, (1) is also equivalent to

(3) *O David não conhece nenhum livro do Tolkien.*

but (2) is not equivalent to

(4) **O David desconhece nenhum livro do Tolkien.*

which is not grammatical. To complicate, (1), (2) and (3) are equivalent to

(5) *O David desconhece todos os livro do Tolkien.*

But not to:

(6) *O David não conhece todos os livro do Tolkien*[4].

because (1), (2), (3) and (5) are true only if David does not know all the Tolkien books, and (6) is true if David does not know one book from Tolkien. Moreover, (1), (2), (3) e (5) are equivalent to:

(7) *O David não conhece livro algum do Tolkien.*

---

[3] Notice that this sentence could also be interpreted as if David only knew one book from Tolkien.

[4] Comparing (1) and (6), *todos* and *qualquer*, that seems to have the same meaning, have different values in the same syntactic context.

5.2 Semantic Values

In the following examples we show some of the semantic values that *qualquer* can take (see [19] for a detailed discussion about the multiple interpretations of *qualquer*):

- In *Qualquer cão gosta de ossos* (*All dogs like bones*) it has an universal value (`univ`);
- In *Ele tem qualquer problema* (*There is some problem with him*) it has an existential value (`exist`);
- In *Ele é um jornalista qualquer* (*He is an insignificant journalist*) it is an adjective, and it means something like "with no relevant characteristics in the class denoted by the noun it qualifies". We will denote this semantic value as `indiscriminate`;
- In *Ele não é um jornalista qualquer* (*He is not an insignificant journalist*) it has the same `indiscriminate` value.

5.3 Semantic Rules

In this section we show the kind of rules we have in [6] and [9], where we try to go as far as possible in the disambiguation process of *qualquer*, *algum* (*some*), *todos* (*all*) and *nenhum* (*none*), by using its syntactic context. First let us define a default rule. The default semantic value, can be an underspecified value [22] representing all of the semantic values, or a default value. For example, the universal value since it is the most common. Let us opt for the universal default value and write the default rule:

$[\mathrm{R}_1]$ {elem(*qualquer*, qt, X_1)} : $\emptyset \mapsto$ {*sem*(X_1) = `univ`}

Assuming that on the right of the main verb, in the scope of negation, *qualquer* takes the value `indiscriminate`, the following rule allows to choose the correct value for *qualquer* in that context:

$[\mathrm{R}_2]$ {elem(*qualquer*, qt, X_1)}: {arrow(*qualquer*, qt, X_1, _, n, X_2, L, _), arrow(_, n, X_2, _, v, X_3, L, _), arrow(_, neg, X_4, _, v, X_3, R, _)} $\mapsto$ {*sem*(qt) = `indiscriminate`}

R_2 is more specific than rule R_1, thus it is applied in these particular conditions. In order to disambiguate, or at least to limit semantic values, other semantic rules would have to be added.

To conclude this section, notice that a traditional syntax-semantic interface, operating in a bottom-up process is not able to execute this task. Considering that on the right of a main verb in the scope of negation, *qualquer* takes the `indiscriminate` semantic value. Typically, in a bottom-up parsing (Figure 1) we will not be able to discard unnecessary values, as in point (1), when finally we have the whole vision of the subtree, the semantic rule will not take into consideration the negation inside V.

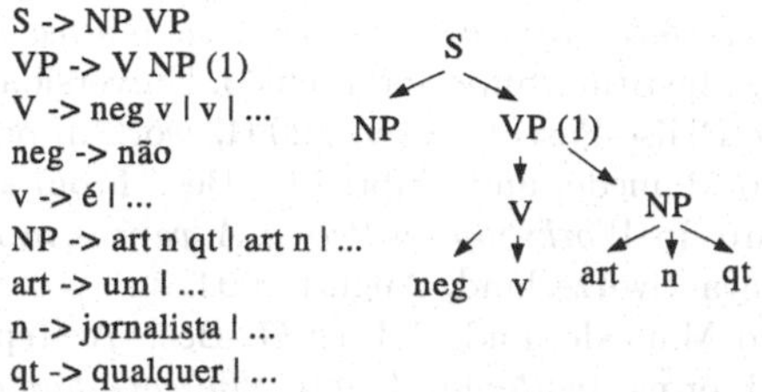

Fig. 1. Grammar and *qualquer* example

6 Conclusions

We presented AsdeCopas a multi-task module based on incremental rules, hierarchically organized and we apply it to question interpretation and semantic desambiguation.

In the present time, we are using AsdeCopas to map Portuguese statements into Minimal Recursion Semantics [12]. Quantification is being carefully studied in this task that had a preliminar presentation in [11].

References

1. Salah Aït-Mokhtar and Jean-Pierre Chanod. Incremental finite-state parsing. In *Proceedings 5th Conference on Applied Natural Language Processing (ANLP-97)*, Washington DC, 1997.
2. Salah Aït-Mokhtar, Jean-Pierre Chanod, and Claude Roux. Robustness beyound shallowness: incremental deep parsing. *Natural Language Engineering*, pages 121–144, 2002.
3. James Allen. *Natural Language Understanding (second edition).* The Benjamin Cummings Publishing Company, Inc, 1995.
4. Gabriel G. Bès. La phrase verbal noyau en français. In *Recherches sur le français parlé*, volume 15, pages 273–358. Université de Provence, France, 1999.
5. Gabriel G. Bès and Caroline Hagège. Properties in 5P. Technical report, GRIL, Université Blaise-Pascal, Clermont-Ferrand, France, November 2001.
6. Luísa Coheur. A situação do "qualquer" em qualquer situação. Technical Report RT/004/03-CDIL, L^2F-Laboratório de Sistemas de Língua Falada, Inesc-id, Lisboa, Portugal, Março 2003.
7. Luísa Coheur, Fernando Batista, and Joana Paulo. JaVaLI!: understanding real questions. In *EUROLAN 2003 student workshop: Applied Natural Language Processing, possible applications for the Semantic Web*, Bucharest, Romania, July 2003.
8. Luísa Coheur, Nuno Mamede, and Gabriel G. Bés. ASdeCopas: a syntactic-semantic interface. In Fernando Moura Pires and Salvador Abreu, editors, *Progress in Artificial Intelligence: 11th Portuguese Conference on Artificial Intelligence, EPIA 2003*, volume 2902 / 2003 of *Lecture Notes in Artificial Inteligence*, Beja, Portugal, Dezembro 2003. Springer-Verlag.

9. Luísa Coheur. *A interface entre a sintaxe e a semântica no quadro das línguas naturais*. PhD thesis, Instituto Superior Técnico, Universidade Técnica de Lisboa, Portugal, Université Blaise-Pascal, France, 2004. work in progress.
10. Luísa Coheur, Nuno Mamede, and Gabriel G. Bès. From a surface analysis to a dependency structure. In *Workshop on Recent Advances in Dependency Grammar (Coling 2004)*, Geneva, Switzerland, August 2004.
11. Luísa Coheur, Nuno Mamede, and Gabriel G. Bès. A step towards incremental generation of logical forms. In *Romand 2004: 3rd workshop on RObust Methods in Analysis of Natural Language Data (Coling 2004)*, Geneva, Switzerland, August 2004.
12. Ann Copestake, Dan Flickinger, Carl Pollard, and Ivan A. Sag. Minimal recursion semantics: An introduction. *L&C*, 1(3):1–47, 2001.
13. Luísa Marques da Silva. Edite, um sistema de acesso a base de dados em linguagem natural, análise morfológica, sintáctica e semântica. Master's thesis, Instituto Superior Técnico, Universidade Técnica de Lisboa, Portugal, 1997.
14. Luísa Marques da Silva, Nuno Mamede, and David Matos. Edite - um sistema de acesso a uma base de dados em linguagem natural. In *Workshop sobre taggers para o português*, pages 20–33, Lisboa, Portugal, 1997. Instituto de Linguística Teórica e Computacional.
15. Dennis Grinberg, John Lafferty, and Daniel Sleator. A robust parsing algorithm for link grammars. Technical Report CMU-CS-TR-95-125, School of Computer Science, Carnegie Mellon University, Pittsburgh, August 1995.
16. Caroline Hagège. *Analyse Syntatic Automatique du Portugais*. PhD thesis, Université Blaise Pascal, Clermont-Ferrand, France, 2000.
17. Timo Järvinen and Pasi Tapanainen. A dependency parser for english. Technical Report TR-1, Department of Linguistics, University of Helsinki, Helsinki, 1997.
18. Daniel Jurafsky and James Martin. *Speech and Language Processing*, chapter 15. Prentice Hall, 2000.
19. Telmo Móia. *Aspectos da Semântica do Operador Qualquer (Cadernos de Semântica n° 5)*. Faculdade de Letras da Universidade de Lisboa, 1992.
20. Diego Mollá and Ben Hutchinson. Dependency-based semantic interpretation for answer extraction. In *Proceedings of the Australasian NLP Workshop (ANLP'02)*, Canberra, 2002.
21. Diego Mollá, Rolf Schwitter, Fabio Rinaldi, James Dowdall, and Michael Hess. Extrans: Extracting answers from technical texts. *IEEE Intelligent Systems*, 18(4), July/August 2003.
22. M. Poesio. Ambiguity, underspecification and discourse interpretation. In R. A. Muskens H. Bunt and G. Rentier (eds.), editors, *Proceedings of the First International Workshop on Computational Semantics*, pages 151–160. "ITK, Tilburg University", 1994.
23. Paulo Reis, J. Matias, and Nuno Mamede. Edite - a natural language interface to databases: a new dimension for an old approach. In *Proceedings of the Fourth International Conference on Information and Communication Technology in Tourism (ENTER'97)*, pages 317–326, Edinburgh, Escócia, 1997. Springer-Verlag, Berlin, Germany.

Multiword Expression Translation Using Generative Dependency Grammar

Stefan Diaconescu

SOFTWIN Str. Fabrica de Glucoza Nr. 5, Sect.2, 020331 Bucharest, ROMANIA
sdiaconescu@softwin.ro

Abstract. The Multi-word Expressions (MWE) treatment is a very difficult problem for the Natural Language Processing in general and for Machine Translation in particular. This is true because each word of a MWE can have a specific meaning but the expression can have a totally different meaning both in source and in target language of a translation. The things are complicated also by the fact that the source expression can appear in the source text under a very different form from its form in a bilingual MWE dictionary (it can have some inflections) and, most of all, it can have some extensions (some MWE words can have associated new words that do not belong to the MWE). The paper show how this kind of problems can be treated and solved using Generative Dependency Grammar with Features.

1 Introduction

The translation problem of Multiword Expressions (MWE) is one of the most difficult problems of machine translation and even human translation. As [15] says, the MWE are "a pain in the neck of natural language processing (NLP)". There are many types of MWE classified on different criteria [15] [5]. MWE appear under different names and interpretations: collocations, compound words, co-occurrences, idioms, fixed syntagmas, lexical solidarities, phraseologisms, phraseolexemes, polylexical expressions [5]. Not all these names are fully equivalent but they have something in common: the fact that they are concerned with groups of words that must always be considered as a whole. The words that compose a MWE must have a representation that can indicate the fact that in an MWE instance into a text they can have eventually different forms (can be inflected) or even they can be replaced by other words that belong to some lexical classes. The MWE representation is specific to each grammar type: HPSG [5], Lexicon Grammar [7], Tree Adjoining Grammar [18] etc.

The most important problems of the MWE are followings:

a) The means of the MWE can be very different from the sense of each word of the MWE (the so called compositionality [1] or idiomaticity problem [16]). *Example:* John *kicked the proverbial bucket.*

b) MWE can appear with its word on different inflected forms (morphological variation [16] [17]). *Example:* John *turned on* the light. John *will turn on* the light.

J. L. Vicedo et al. (Eds.): EsTAL 2004, LNAI 3230, pp. 243–254, 2004.

c) MWE appears under different form by passivization, topicalization, scrambling, etc. (syntactic modification [1] or structural variation [17] [18]). *Example:* He *turned the tables on* me, and then I *turned them on* him. [13]

d) MWE appears with different extensions attached to some words of the expression (modifications [18]). Exemple: Il *est à bout des nerfs.*(He is exhausted.)) Il *est à bout maladif des nerfs.* (He is illy exhausted.)

e) MWE appears with different inserted word that some times are not directly linked with the expression words. *Example:* He *moved* John *to tears.* He *moved* a lot of people *to tears.*

f) MWE appears with different words that have similar sense (lexical variation [17] [18]). *Example:* John *sweep the dust under the carpet (rug, mat)* [13].

Solutions for these problems are not easy to find and perhaps, the great number of names of MWE are due (partially) to the fact that each sort of representation solves some aspects of the problems.

In this paper we will show a very general method to MWE representation based on Generation Dependency Grammar with Feature (GDGF) [2] [3] that solves many of these problems and can be used in machine translation (MT).

2 Representation of MWE in GDGF

We will show in an informal manner how MWE can be represented in GDGF. A more formal definition of GDGF can be found in [2] [3]. Let us have E_s a source expression from a text (phrase) T_s in the language with a lexicon L_s and E_t a target expression (equivalent with E_s) in the translation T_t (of the text T_s) in the language with the lexicon L_t. E_s and E_t can have a different number of words and sometimes with different senses (if we take the words one by one). In a bilingual phraseological dictionary (or MWE dictionary) that contains the correspondences between the expressions belonging to two languages L_s and L_t, ED_s and ED_t are the expressions in a basic form ("lemmatized form") corresponding to E_s and E_t. E_s is different from ED_s (it can be inflected or can have some insertions of other words, linked or not with the words of E_s by dependency relations. We will note E_x the extension of the ED_s in E_s. E_x will contain all the words that have dependency relations with the word from E_s. In the translation process E_s must be searched in the MWE dictionary (though it is not identical with ED_s) and the extension E_x must also be considered in order to create a similar extension for E_t.

The texts T_s (and E_s) and the entry ED_s (with its equivalence ED_t) in MWE dictionary will be represented in GDGF.

A GDGF is a rule collection. Each rule has in the left hand a non terminal and in right hand a syntactic part and a dependency part. The syntactic part is a sequence of non-terminals/terminals/pseudo-terminals/procedural-actions (*ntpa*). Each *ntpa* from the syntactic part have associated an Attribute Value Tree (AVT) that describes the syntactical/lexical categories and their values. The dependency part is a dependency tree (dependencies between the *ntpa*-s from the syntactic part). Terminals are words that belongs to the lexicon (L_s or

L_t in our case). Non-terminals are labels (symbols) for grammar categories (and are considered to not belonging to the lexicons L_s or L_t). Each non-terminal appears at least one time in the left side of a rule (with the exception of one symbol named root symbol). A pseudo-terminal is a sort of non-terminal that does not appear in the left side of a rule but it can be replaced directly by a word from the lexicon. A procedural-action (or action) is a routine that must be executed in order to identify the symbols from the text (for example a routine that identify a number).

In the MWE dictionary, an E_s (and the corresponding E_t) is represented only by one rule so it will not contain *ntpa* but only terminals, pseudo-terminals, actions (*tpa*). The left part of the right side of this rule will contain only *tpa*-s and the right part of the right side (the dependency tree) will be a final tree.

Until now all the GDGF description is conform to [2] [3]. We will introduce now something that is specific to the MWE treatment.

Each *tpa* from ED_s will have associated a "type of variability". There are three types of variability: invariable, partial variable and total variable.

a) Invariable *tpa*. A *tpa* is invariable, if it appears always in any context in the same form (so it will have associated always the same AVT or an AVT that subsumes the corresponding AVT from the MWE dictionary).

b) Partial variable *tpa*. A *tpa* is partial variable, if it has the same lemma (and lexical class) in all the apparitions of the expression in different contexts, and it has different lexical categories (it can be inflected).

c) Total variable *tpa*. A *tpa* is total variable, if it is any word (accepted by the grammar in the corresponding position), in all the apparitions of the expression in different contexts. More of this, in the source text, this *tpa* can be also a coordinate relation.

Example

Let us have the Romanian expression "*a abate pe cineva de la calea cea dreapta*" and an English equivalent "*to lead somebody astray*". The grammar rule for the Romanian expression is the following (we will do not indicate completely the AVTs):

<ED_s> -> ("*a abate*" [class = verb] "*pe*" [class = preposition] "*cineva*" [class = pronoun] [pronoun type = indefinite] "*de la*" [class = preposition] "*calea*" [class = noun] [gender = feminine] "*cel*" [class = pronoun] [pronoun type = demonstrative] [gender = feminine] [gender = feminine] "*dreapta*" [class = adjective] [gender = feminine], "*a abate*" (@r_1@("*pe*"(@r_2@("*cineva*"()))), @r_4@("*de la*"(@r_5@("*calea*"(@r_6@("*dreapta*"()), @r_7@("*cel*"())))))))

(Observations: In the rule, the terminals are lemmas. The inflected form is indicated by AVT. That is why the word "*cea*" from expression appears as "*cel*".)

The relations can have more intuitive names like "relations between noun and attribute" but we used only generic names like r_1, r_2, etc.

The grammar rule for the corresponding English expression is:

<ED_t> -> ("*to lead*" [class = verb] "*somebody*" [class = pronoun] [pronoun type = indefinite] "*astray*" [class = adverb], "*to lead*"(@r_8@("*somebody*"()), @r_9@("*astray*" ())))

We will define a correspondence between *cineva*() and *somebody*(), both being of total variable type:

Correspondence *cineva*() / *somebody*()

The Romanian expression can appear in a context like: "... *au abatut pe Ion si Maria de la calea cea dreapta* ...". The corresponding final rule will be:

<T_s> = (..."*a abate*" [class = verb] [mode = indicative] [person = III] [number = present] [time = perfect] "*pe*" [class = preposition] "*Ion*" [class = noun] [noun type = proper] "*si*" [class = conjunction] "*Maria*" [class = noun] [noun type = proper] "*de la*" [class = preposition] "*calea*" [class = noun] [number = singular] "*cel*" [class = pronoun] [pronoun type = demonstrative] [gender = feminine] [number = singular] "*dreapta*" [class = adjective] [number = singular] [gender = feminine] ..., ..."*a abate*"(@r$_1$@("*pe*"(@r$_2$@(@r$_3$@("*Ion*"(), "*Maria*"() /)))), @r$_4$@("*de la*"(@r$_5$@("*calea*"(@r$_6$@("*dreapta*"()), @r$_7$@("*cel*"()))))))...)

In order to find the expression "*a abate pe cineva de la calea cea dreapta*" in the source text we must make an equivalence between "*cineva*"() and @r$_3$@ ("*Ion*"(), "*Maria*"() /) that is a conjunctive relation represented as a coordinate relation. This is possible if we declare "*cineva*"() as "total variable". In the target expression, the terminal somebody() will be substituted by the coordinate relation @r$_3$@("*Ion*" ()," *Maria*" () /).

3 Transformation Rules

Between the nodes (of type terminal / pseudo-terminal / action / relation - *tpar*) from the two expressions ED_s and ED_t we will indicate some transformation rules. There are two types of transformation rules (see figure 1):

a) Transformation rule of type "correspondence" between two nodes indicates that the two *tpar*-s are relatively equivalent in the two expressions. This means that *tpar* from ED_t, during the translation process, will take over all the links (with their descendants) corresponding to *tpar* from Es (that contains the links from ED_s but also the links from the extension E_x of ED_s in T_s). We will consider the following convention: if between two *tpar*-s from the two expressions ED_s and ED_t exists a correspondence, then they are of the same invariable, partial variable or total variable type. A source *tpar* or a target *tpar* can appear at most in a transformation of type correspondence.

b) Transformation rule of type "transfer" between tpa_1 from ED_s and tpa_2 from ED_t indicates the fact that the two *tpa*-s are not equivalent in the two expressions but, if tpa_1 from ED_s has some links that goes to the extension E_x of the expression E_s (that corresponds to ED_s), then all these links with their descendents will be taken over by tpa_2 from ED_t (in order to obtain E_t). A transfer can not be defined between two relations.

A source *tpa* that appears in correspondences or transfers is said to have nonexclusive relationships, i.e. it can have in T_s some links that go to the extension E_x of E_s.

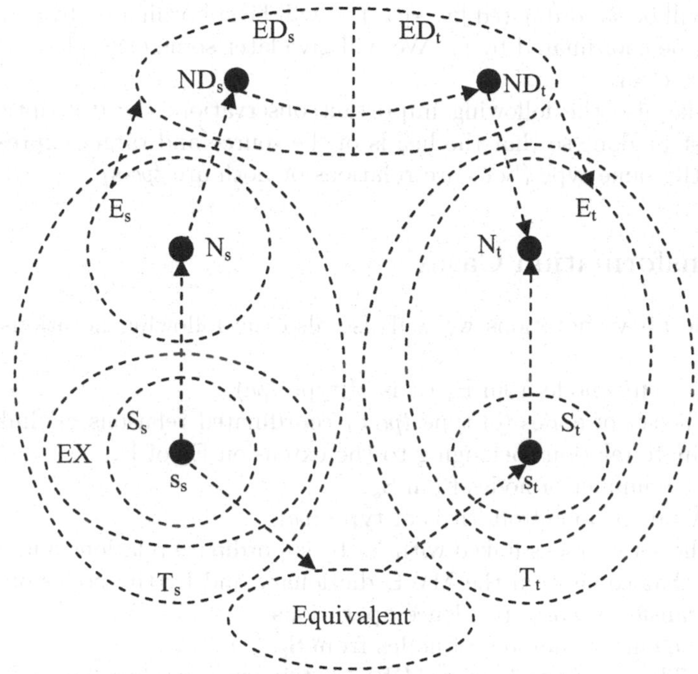

Fig. 1. Correspondences and transfers treatment

A source *tpa* that do not appear in correspondences or transfers is said to have exclusive relationships, i.e. it can not have links in T_s that go to the extension E_x. These names are explained by the followings:

– If a source *tpa* is nonexclusive then it can have some descendents in the extension of the expression and these descendents must be attached (by correspondence or transfer) to a target *tpa* from the target expression, so, in this case, *tpa* must have a correspondence or a transfer.

– If a source *tpa* is exclusive, then it can not have descendents in the extension of the expression and it is not useful to put it in a correspondence or a transfer.

Not always is possible to transfer the elements from an extension of the source expression to others nodes of the target expression. An important feature that we can associate to the *tpa* that is the target of a correspondence or transfer is the *combination feature*. Let us have a coordinate relation r_x = @relation name@ (a conjunction relation "and" for example) and a *tpa* s_t from target expression subordinated to another *tpa* t_t by the relation r_t. We consider now the *tpa* s_s from the extension of the source expression subordinate by the relation r_s so that $eq(r_s) = r_t$ (the equivalent of r_s from the source language is r_t in the target language) to another *tpa* t_s from source expression. We suppose that between t_s and t_t was defined a "correspondence" or a "transfer". We suppose also that the equivalent of t_s from the source expression is $eq(t_s)$ in the target expression. In this case the translation of the source expression together with its extension using the MWE dictionary will be made as follows: r_x will be subordinated to

t_t, eq(s_s) will be subordinated by eq(r_s), s_t will be subordinated by r_t and eq(r_s) and r_t will be coordinated by r_x. We will give later some examples to make the things more clear.

We make also the following important observation: the description in the MWE must be done so that the heads of the source and target expressions are always of the same type (both are relations or both are *tpa*-s).

4 Transformation Cases

Besides the above notations we will use also the following notations too (see figure 1):

N_s = A source node from E_s (it is of type *tpa*).

S_s = The set of nodes (of type *tpa* or coordinated relations *cr*) linked to N_s by subordinate relations belonging to the extension E_x of E_s.

n_s = The number of nodes from S_s.

N_t = A target node from (it is of type *tpa*).

S_t = The set of nodes linked with N_t by subordinate relations and formed by the nodes that come from the MWE dictionary and by the nodes obtained by previous transfer or correspondence operations.

n_t = The current number of nodes from S_t.

ND_s = The source node from MWE dictionary corresponding to N_s.

ND_t = The target node associated by correspondence or transfer to ND_t.

r_x = A relation defined for a combination.

type(s) = The type of s (where s is a *tpa* node) i. e. the tuple formed by lexical class of s and the relation by which it is subordinated to another node.

sr = Subordinate relation.

cr = Coordinate relation.

We will have type(s_s) = type(s_t) if:

– eq(s_s) has the same lexical class with s_t;

– if s_s is subordinated by r_s and s_t is subordinated by r_t then eq(r_s) = r_t.

We will have type(s_s) # type(s_t) (# means not equal) if:

– eq(s_s) has the same lexical class with s_t;

– if s_s is subordinated by r_s and s_t is subordinated by r_t then eq(r_s) # r_t.

We will have s_s ~ s_t if:

– eq(s_s) = s_t

– if s_s is subordinated by r_s and s_t is subordinated by r_t , then eq(r_s) = r_t.

Using these notations we will present some transformation cases.

The transformations by correspondences or transfers using eventually the combination feature are used in order to recognize in the source text not only the MWE but also the MWE that have different extensions and in order to translate these extended MWE more appropriately. For example the expression "*în toiul noptii*" in Romanian language that has the English equivalent "*in the dead night*" will be recognized also under the form "*în toiul noptii negre*" and translated under the form "*in the dead black night*" if between "*noapte*" and "*night*" will be indicated a correspondence.

The correspondence, transfers and combinations can be defined only for *tpa* and not for relations.

A source element of a correspondence or a transfer can be:
- *tpa* with *sr* descendents;
- *tpa* with *cr* descendents;
- *tpa* without descendents.

A subordinate relation *sr* can be:
- *sr* with *tpa* descendents;
- *sr* with *cr* descendents.

A coordinate relation *cr* can be:
- *cr* with only *cr* descendents;
- *cr* with only *tpa* descendents;
- *cr* with *tpa* and *cr* descendents.

By combining these possibilities for the source and for the target element we will have a lot of situations. Not all of these situations are useful in practical cases.

When an element A of a source expression is in a correspondence or a transfer relation with an element B of an equivalent target expression, the descendents of A that go to the extension of the expression in which A appears must be attached as descendents of B (by its equivalents). But B can have also some descendents. In this case we must establish a method to put together the descendents of A and the descendents of B.

We will consider the next transformation cases:

a) Both A and B have descendents. There are many situations:

Transformation Case a1: The node s_s is of type *tpa* and is linked with the node N_s by subordinate relation r_s. For each s_s belonging to S_s that have an s_t belonging to S_t so type(s_s) = type(s_t) but eq(s_s) # s_t we will do the followings:
- Create a new coordinate relation r_x with two entries r_x (1) and r_x (2).
- Mark that the equivalent of s_s is coordinated by r_x (1).
- Mark that s_t is coordinated by r_x (2).
- Mark that r_x is linked with N_t.

This type of treatment is named *attachment by coordination.*

The equivalences of the node s_s and of its eventual descendents will be transferred in the target language one by one.

Transformation Case a2: The node s_s is of type *tpa* and is linked with the node N_s by subordinate relation r_s. For each s_s belonging to S_s so there is not an s_t belonging to S_t and type(s_s) = type(s_t) we will mark the fact that eq(s_s) is subordinated by eq(r_s) to N_t.

This type of treatment is named *attachment without coordination.*

Transformation Case a3: The node s_s is of type *tpa* and is linked with the node N_s by subordinate relation r_s. For each s_s belonging to S_s so there is not an s_t belonging to S_t and s_s ˜ s_t we will do the followings:
- s_s is subsumed by s_t and it will be ignored.
- r_s is subsumed by r_s and it will be ignored.

This type of treatment is named *attachment by subsumption.*

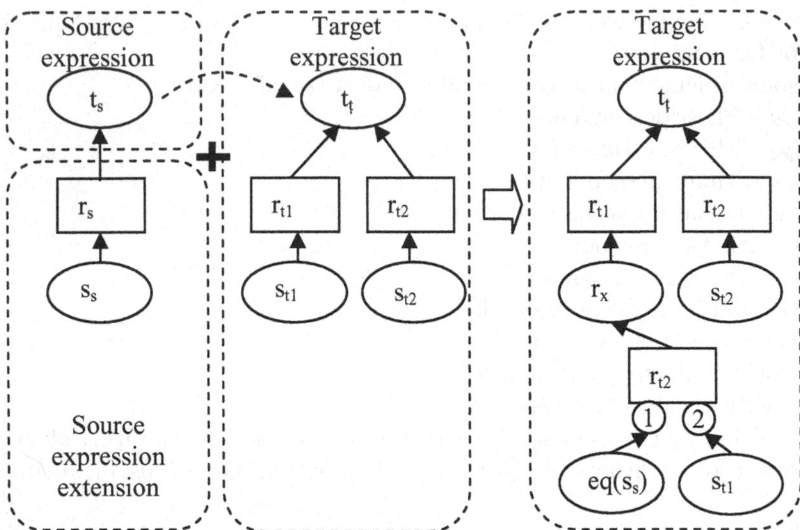

Fig. 2. Example of MWE dictionary entry

Transformation Case a4: The node s_s is of type coordinate relation and is linked with the node N_s by a subordinate relation. For each s_s belonging to S_s we will mark that eq(s_s) is subordinated by eq(r_s) to N_t. It is as in case (a2) an *attachment without coordination.*

b) A have descendents but B has not descendents. In this case the A descendents will be passed to B without conflicts.

c) A has not descendents but B has descendents. In this case the problem disappears because we have nothing to pass from A to B. B will remain with its descendents.

d) Neither A nor B have descendents. In this case the problem disappears.

This cases cover if not all the situations but a very large number of possible situations.

Example

Let us have the expression "*a fi în gratiile cuiva*" in Romanian language and the equivalent expression "*être dans des bonnes grâces de qn.*" in French language ("to be liked by someone" or literally "to be in the graces of someone").

The grammar rule for the Romanian expression is (we will do not indicate completely the AVTs) (remember that the terminals are lemmas):

<ED_s> -> ("*a fi*" [class = verb] "*în*" [class = preposition] "*gratie*" [class = nom] [gender = feminine] [article = articled] [article type = definite] "*cineva*" [class = pronoun] [pronoun type = indefinite] [case = genitive], "*a fi*"(@r_1@ ("*în*"(@r_2@("*gratie*"(@$_3$@("*cineva*"())))))))

The grammar rule for the corresponding French expression is:

<ED_t> -> ("*être*" [class = verb] "*dans*" [class = preposition] "*le*" [class = article] [article type = definite] [gender = feminine] [number = plural] "*bon*" [class = adjective] [gender = feminine] [number = plural] "*grâce*" [class = nom]

[gender = feminine] "*de*" [class = preposition] "*qn.*" [class = pronoun] [pronoun type = indefinite], "*être*"(@r_4@("*dans*"(@r_5@(("grâce"(@r_7@("*le*"()), @r_6@ ("*bon*"()), @r_8@("*de*" (@r_9@("*qn.*"( )))))))))

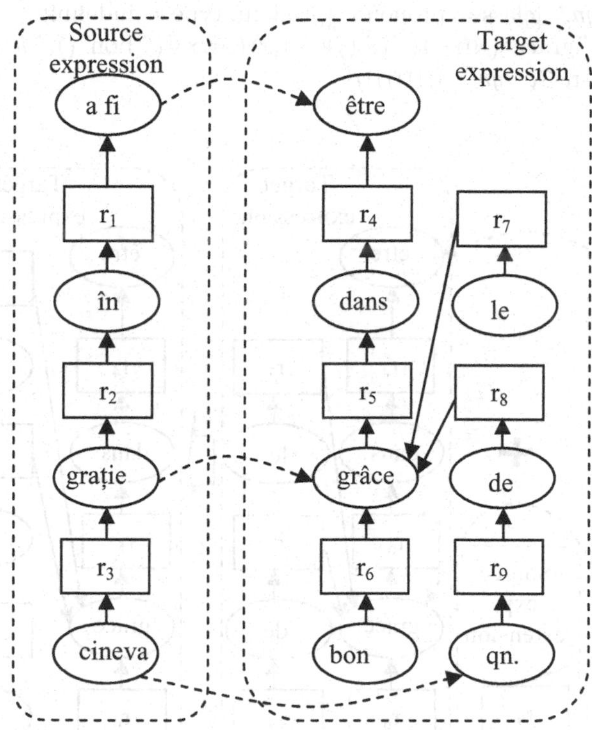

Fig. 3. Example - principle

In the MWE dictionary something like in the figure 2 will appear. A correspondence will be defined in MWE dictionary between "*a fi*" (to be) and "*être*"and between "*gratiile*" (grace) and "*grâce*". A combination with the relation "*et*" (and) will be associated with the target "*grâce*".

Let us have now an expression with an extension "*a fi în gratiile languroase ale cuiva*" (literally "to be in the languishing graces of someone").The grammar rule for this expression is the following:

<Exp> -> ("*a fi*" [class = verb] "*în*" [class = preposition] "*gratie*" [class = nom] [gender = feminine] [number = plural] [article = articled] [article type = definite] [number = plural] "*languros*" [class = adjective] [gender feminine] [number = plural] "cineva" [class = pronoun] [pronoun type = indefinite] [case = genitive], "*a fi*"(@r_1@("*în*"(@r_2@("*gratie*"(@r_0@("*languros*"()), @r_3@ ("*cineva*"())))))))

The general transformation case (of type (a1)) can be represented as in the figure 3. By applying this transformation case we will obtain the final translated rule (see figure 2):

<Exp.'> -> ("*être*" [class = verb] "dans" [class = preposition] "*le*" [class = article] [article type = definite] [gender = feminine] "*bon*" [class adjective] [gender = feminine] [number = plural] "*et*" [class = conjunction] "*langoureux*" [class = adjective] [gender = feminine] "*grâce*" [class = nom] [gender = feminine] "*de*" [preposition] "*qn.*" [class = pronoun] [pronoun type = indefinite], "*être*"(@r_4@("*dans*"(@r_5@("grâce"(@r_7@("*le*"()), @r_6@(@rx@("bon"(), "*langoureux*"())), @r_8@("*de*" (@r_9@("*qn.*"()))))))))

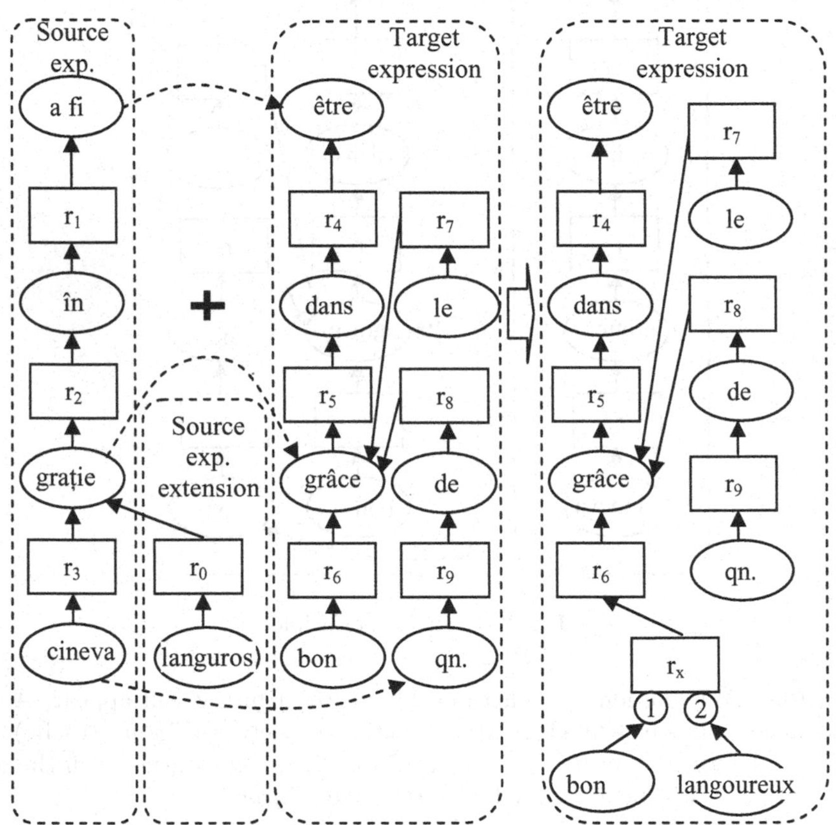

Fig. 4. Example - result

The reconstruction of the surface text "*être dans les bonnes et langoureuses grâce de qn.*" will be done using a GDGF grammar (that is a reversible grammar [2]) of the target language and a mechanism to force the agreement between a subordinate and a terminal to which the subordination is realized [4]. This mechanism says the followings: if the node B is subordinated by a relation to the node A, then the attribute values of B will be forced accordingly with the attribute values of A as described in the agreement sections of the grammar rules.

5 Conclusions

We presented how GDGF solve some problems of MWE treatment. We added to the GDGF formalism the notions of correspondence, transfer, combination and variability of MWE components (invariable, partial variable, total variable) that allow the MWE description and the MWE dictionary construction. Using partial variability and the total variability, the method is important not only for MWE but also it can be used to create a sort of dictionary of grammatical structures. So, we can put in correspondence some specific structures of the source language and the target language. The ideas presented in the paper were introduced in a language GRAALAN (Grammar Abstract Language) that contains many other features, all of them based on GDGF. This language is designated to describe pair of languages in order to make possible the machine translation between them. GRAALAN is now used to describe Romanian language and the correspondences with French and English language.

References

1. Chang, N., Fischer, I. (2000) Understanding Idioms, in KONVENS 2000 / SPRACHKOMMUNIKATION, Konferenz zur Verarbeitung natrlicher Sprache - ITG-Fachtagung "SPRACHKOMMUNIKATION", Technische Universitt Ilmenau.
2. Diaconescu, Stefan (2003) Morphological Categorization Attribute Value Tree and XML, in Mieczyslav A. Klopotek, Slawomir T. Wierzchon, Krzysztof Trojanowski (Eds), Intelligent Infrmation Processing and Web Mining, Proceedings of the International IIS: IIPWM'03 Conference, Zakopane, Poland, June 2-5, Springer 131-138.
3. Diaconescu, Stefan (2002) Natural Language Understanding Using Generative Dependency Grammar, in Max Bramer, Alun Preece and Frans Coenen (Eds), in Proceedings of ES2002, the 21-nd SGAI International Conference on Knowledge Based Systems and Applied Artificial Intelligence, Cambridge UK, Springer, 439-452
4. Diaconescu, Stefan (2003) Natural Language Agreement Description for Reversible Grammars, in Proceedings of 16th Australian Joint Conference on Artificial Intelligence University of Western Australia, Perth 2-5 December , in print.
5. Erbach, G. (1992) Head-Driven Lexical representation of Idioms in HPSG, in Proceedings of the International Conference on Idioms,Tilburg (NL)
6. Fellbaum, C. (1998) Towards a Representation of Idioms in WordNet, in Proceedings of the Workshop on Usage of WordNet in Natural Language Processing Systems, COLING/ACL. Montreal, Canada, 52-57
7. Gross, M. (1986) Lexicon-Grammar - The Representation of Compound words, in Proceedings of COOLING
8. Jurafsky, D. (1933) A Cognitive Model of Sentence Interpretation: the Construction Grammar approach, University of California at Berkley, TR-93-077
9. Matiasek, J. (1996) The Generation of Idiomatic and Collocational Expressions, in Trappl R. (ed), Cybernetics and Systems '96, "Osterreichische Studiengesellschaft fur Kybernetik, Wien 1201-1205
10. McKeown K.R., Radev D.R. (1998) Collocations, in Robert Dale, Hermann Moisl, and Harold Somers (eds), A Handbook of Natural Language Processing Marcel Dekker

11. Pedrazzini S. (1999) Treating Terms As Idioms, in Proceedings of the Sixth nternational Symposium on Communication and Applied Linguistics, Santiago de Cuba, Editorial Oriente, Santiago de Cuba
12. Poibeau, T. (1999) Parsing Natural Language Idioms with Bidirectional Finite-State Machines, in Jean-Marc Champarnaud, Denis Maurel, Djelloul Ziadi (eds.) Automata Implementation, Third International Workshop on Implementing Automata, WIA'98, Rouen, France, Lecture Notes in Computer Science 1660 Springer
13. Pulman, S.G. (1993) The recognition and interpretation of idioms, in C. Cacciari and P. Tabossi (eds.) 'Idioms: Processing, Structure, and Interpretation', New Jersey: Laurence Earlbaum Cognitive Science Monographs, 249-270.
14. Riehemann, S. (1997) Idiomatic Construction in HPSG, Stanford University
15. Riehemann, S., Bender, E. (1999) Absolute Constructions: On the Distribution of Predicative Idioms, in Sonya Bird, Andrew Carnie, Jason D. Haugen, and Peter Norquest (eds.) WCCFL 18: Proceedings of the 18th West Coast Conference on Formal Linguistics
16. Sag, I., Baldwin, T., Bond, F., Copestake, A., Flickinger, D. (2002) Multiword Expressions: Pain in the Neck for NLP, in Alexander Gelbukh, ed., Proceedings of CICLING-2002, Springer
17. Segond, F., Tapanainen P. (1995) Using a finite-state based formalism to identify and generate multiword expressions, Rank Xerox Research Center Technical Report, MLTT, 19
18. Segond, F., Valetto, G., Breidt, E. (1995) IDAREX: Formal Description of Multi-Word Lexemes with Regular Expressions, Meylan Tubingen

Named Entity Recognition Through Corpus Transformation and System Combination

José A. Troyano, Vicente Carrillo, Fernando Enríquez, and Francisco J. Galán

Department of Languages and Computer Systems
University of Seville
Av. Reina Mercedes s/n 41012, Sevilla (Spain)
troyano@lsi.us.es

Abstract. In this paper we investigate the way of combining different taggers to improve their performance in the named entity recognition task. The main resources used in our experiments are the publicly available taggers TnT and TBL and a corpus of Spanish texts in which named entities occurrences are tagged with BIO tags. We have defined three transformations that provide us three additional versions of the training corpus. The transformations change either the words or the tags, and the three of them improve the results of TnT and TBL when they are trained with the original version of the corpus. With the four versions of the corpus and the two taggers, we have eight different models that can be combined with several techniques. The experiments carried out show that using machine learning techniques to combine them the performance improves considerably. We improve the baselines for TnT ($F_{\beta=1}$ value of 85.25) and TBL ($F_{\beta=1}$ value of 87.45) up to a value of 90.90 in the best of our experiments.

1 Introduction

Named Entity Extraction (NEE) is a subtask of Information Extraction (IE). It involves 1) the identification of words, or sequences of words, that make up the name of an entity and 2) the classification of this name into a set of categories. These categories are predefined and they conform what we call the domain taxonomy. For example, if the domain taxonomy contains the categories PER (people), ORG (organizations), LOC (places) and MISC (rest of entities), in the following text we find an example of each one of them:

> El presidente del *COI*, *Juan Antonio Samaranch*, se sumó hoy a las alabanzas vertidas por otros dirigentes deportivos en *Río de Janeiro* sobre la capacidad de esta ciudad para acoger a medio plazo unos *Juegos Olímpicos*.

The words "Juan Antonio Samaranch" conform the name of a person, the word "COI" is an organization name, "Río de Janeiro" is the name of place and, finally, "Juegos Olímpicos" is an event name classified into the category MISC.

J. L. Vicedo et al. (Eds.): EsTAL 2004, LNAI 3230, pp. 255–266, 2004.

If we want to implement a system that extracts named entities from plain text we would meet with two different problems, the recognition of named entities and their classification:

– Named Entity Recognition (NER) is the identification of the word sequence that conforms the name of an entity.
– Named Entity Classification (NEC) is the subtask in charge of deciding which is the category assigned to a previously recognized entity.

There are systems that perform both subtasks at once. Other systems, however, make use of two independent subsystems to carry out each subtask sequentially. The second architecture allows us to choose the most suitable technique to each subtask. Named entity recognition is a typical grouping task (or chunking) while choosing its category is a classification problem. Therefore, chunking tools can be used to perform the first task, and classification tools for the second one. In practice, it has been shown [4] that the division into two separate subtasks is a very good option.

Our approach to the NEE problem is based on the separate architecture. We have focused the work presented in this paper on improving the performance of the first subtask of the architecture, the NER module. We have applied two main techniques:

– Corpus transformation: that allows us to train the taggers with different views of the original corpus, taking more advantage of the information contained in it.
– System combination: that takes into account the tags proposed by several systems to decide if a given word is part of a named entity.

The organization of the rest of the paper is as follows. The second section presents the resources, measures and baselines used in our experiments. In section three we describe the transformations that we have applied to obtain three additional versions of the training corpus. Section four describes the different methods that we have used to combine the tags proposed by each model. In section five we draw the final conclusions and point out some future work.

2 Resources and Baselines

In this section we describe the main resources used: CoNLL-02 corpus, TnT and TBL. We also define the baselines for our experiments with the results of TnT and TBL trained with the original corpus.

2.1 Corpus CoNLL-02

This corpus provides a wide set of named entity examples in Spanish. It was used in the Named Entity Recognition shared task of CoNLL-02 [13]. The distribution is composed of three different files:

– Training corpus with 264715 tokens and 18794 entities.
– Test-A corpus with 52923 tokens and 4315 entities. We have used this corpus as additional training material to estimate the parameters of some of the systems developed.
– Test-B corpus with 51533 tokens and 3558 entities. We have used it only to obtain the final experimental results.

The BIO notation is used to denote the limits of a named entity. The initial word of a named entity is tagged with a B tag, and the rest of words of a named entity are tagged with I tags. Words outside an entity are denoted with an O tag. There are four categories: PER (people), LOC (places), ORG (organizations) and MISC (rest of entities), so the complete set of tags is {B-LOC, I-LOC, B-PER, I-PER, B-ORG, I-ORG, B-MISC, I-MISC, O}. We do not need the information about the category for recognition purposes, so we have simplified the tag set by removing the category information from the tags. Figure 1 shows a fragment of the original corpus, and its simplified version.

Word	Tag
El	O
presidente	O
del	O
COI	B-ORG
,	O
Juan	B-PER
Antonio	I-PER
Samaranch	I-PER
...	...

Word	Tag
El	O
presidente	O
del	O
COI	B
,	O
Juan	B
Antonio	I
Samaranch	I
...	...

Fig. 1. Original corpus and corpus tagged only for the recognition subtask

2.2 Taggers

In order to have views as different as possible of the NER task we have chosen two taggers based upon radically different concepts, TnT and TBL. Both are publicly available and re-trainable.

TBL [3] is a transformation based learning technique that makes use of the knowledge provided by tagging errors. The basic idea of TBL consists of obtaining a set of rules that can transform an imperfect tagging into one with fewer errors. To achieve this goal, TBL implements an iterative process that starts with a naive tagging. This tagging is improved at each iteration learning rules that transform it into another one closer to the correct tagging. TBL has been successfully used in several Natural Language Processing (NLP) tasks like shallow parsing, POS tagging, text chunking or prepositional phrase attachment.

TnT [1] is one of the most widely used re-trainable tagger in NLP tasks. It is based upon second order Markov Models, consisting of word emission probabilities and tag transition probabilities computed from trigrams of tags. As a first step it computes the probabilities from a tagged corpus through maximum likelihood estimation, then it implements a linear interpolation smoothing method to manage the sparse data problem. It also incorporates a suffix analysis for dealing with unknown words, assigning tag probabilities according to the word ending.

2.3 Measures

The measures used in our experiments are, *precision*, *recall* and the overall performance measure $F_{\beta=1}$. These measures were originally used for Information Retrieval (IR) evaluation purposes, but they have been adapted to many NLP tasks. Precision is computed according to the number of correctly recognized entities, and recall is defined as the proportion of the actual entities that the system has been able to recognize:

$$Precision = \frac{\text{correct entities}}{\text{all recognized entities}} \qquad Recall = \frac{\text{correct entities}}{\text{actual entities}}$$

Finally, $F_{\beta=1}$ combines recall and precision in a single measure, giving to both the same relevance:

$$F_{\beta=1} = \frac{2\, Precision\, Recall}{Precision + Recall}$$

We will trust in $F_{\beta=1}$ measure for analyzing the results of our experiments. It is a good performance indicator of a system and it is usually used as comparison criterion.

2.4 Baselines

Table 1 shows the NER results obtained when TBL and TnT are trained with the CoNLL-02 corpus, we will adopt these results as baselines for the rest of experiments in this paper. TBL presents better results than TnT in the three measures, this will be a constant in the rest of experiments. In contrast, TBL is slower than TnT, while TnT trains in few seconds TBL needs several minutes to process the entire corpus.

Table 1. Baselines. NER results for TnT y TBL trained with the original version of CoNLL-02 corpus

	Precision	Recall	$F_{\beta=1}$
TnT	84.39%	86.12%	85.25
TBL	85.34%	89.66%	87.45

3 Corpus Transformations

It seems logical to think that if we have more information before taking a decision we have more possibilities of choosing the best option. For this reason we have decided to increase the number of models.

There are two obvious ways of building new models: using new training corpora or training other taggers with the same corpus. We have tried a different approach, defining three transformations that applied to the original corpus give us three additional versions of it. With four different views of the same information, the taggers learn in a different way and the resulting models can specialize in the recognition of named entities of different nature. Transformations can be defined to simplify the original corpus or to add new information to it. If we simplify the corpus we reduce the number of possible examples and the sparse data problem will be smoothed. On the other hand if we enrich the corpus the model can use the added information to identify new examples not recognized in the original model. In the following subsection we describe the transformation explored in our experiments. Figure 2 show the results of applying these transformations to the example of Figure 1.

Word	Tag
El	O
presidente	O
del	O
_all_cap_	B
,	O
_starts_cap_	B
_starts_cap_	I
_starts_cap_	I
...	...

a) Vocabulary reduction.

Word	Tag
El	O
presidente	O
del	O
COI	BE
,	O
Juan	B
Antonio	I
Samaranch	E
...	...

b) Change of tag set.

Word	Tag
El_det_	O
presidente_noun_	O
del_prep_	O
_all_cap__noun_	B
,_punt_	O
_cap__noun_	B
_cap__noun_	I
_cap__noun_	I
...	...

c) Addition of POS information.

Fig. 2. Result of applying transformations to the corpus fragment showed in Figure 1

3.1 Vocabulary Reduction

This transformation discards most of the information given by words in the corpus, emphasizing the most useful features for the recognition of named entities. We employ a technique similar to that used in [11] replacing the words in the corpus with tokens that contain relevant information for recognition.

One of the problems that we try to solve with this transformation is the treatment of unknown words. These are the words that do not appear in the training corpus, and therefore the tagger can not make any assumption about them. Handling unknown words is a typical problem in almost all corpus based applications, in the case of named entity recognition is even more important because unknown words are good candidates to be part of an entity. The lack of information of an unknown word can be mitigated with its typographic information, because in Spanish (like many other languages) capitalization is used when writing named entities.

Apart from typographic information there are other features that can be useful in the identification of entities, for example non-capitalized words that frequently appear before, after or inside named entities. We call them trigger words and they are of great help in the identification of entity boundaries.

Both pieces of information, trigger words and typographic clues, are extracted from the original corpus through the application of the following rules:

– Each word is replaced by a representative token, for example, it _starts_cap_ for words that start with capital letters, *_lower_* for words that are written in lower case letter, *_all_cap_* if the whole word is upper case, etc. These word patterns are identified using a small set of regular expressions.
– Not all words are replaced with its corresponding token, the trigger words remain as they appear in the original corpus. The list of trigger words is computed automatically counting the words that most frequently appear around or inside an entity.

Vocabulary reduction leads to an improvement in the performance of TnT and TBL. The results of the experiments (*TnT-V* and *TBL-V*) are presented in Table 2. TnT improves from 85.25 to 86.63 and TBL improves from 87.45 to 88.10.

3.2 Change of Tag Set

This transformation does not affect to words but to tags. The basic idea is to replace the original BIO notation with a more expressive one that includes information about the words that usually end a named entity. The new tag set have five tags, the three original (although two of them change slightly their semantic) plus two new tags:

– B, that denotes the beginning of a named entity with more than one word.
– BE, that is assigned to a single-word named entity.
– I, that is assigned to words that are inside of a multiple-word named entity, except to the last word.
– E, assigned to the last word of a multiple-word named entity
– O, that preserves its original meaning: words outside a named entity.

This new tag set give more relevance to the position of a word, forcing the taggers to learn which words appear more frequently at the beginning, at the end or inside a named entity.

Changing the tag set also leads to better results than those obtained with the original corpus. The results of the experiments (*TnT-N* and *TBL-N*) are showed in Table 2. TBL improves from 87.45 to 87.61 and TnT improves from 85.25 to 86.83, the best result achieved with TnT (with an error reduction of over 10%).

3.3 Addition of Part-of-Speech Information

Unlike the previous corpus transformations, in this case we will make use of external knowledge to add new information to the original corpus. Each word will be replaced with a compound tag that integrates two pieces of information:

- The result of applying the first transformation (vocabulary reduction).
- The part of speech (POS) tag of the word.

To obtain the POS tag of a word we have trained TnT with the Spanish corpus CLiC-TALP [5]. This corpus is a one hundred thousand word collection of samples of written language, it includes extracts from newspapers, journals, academic books and novels. It is completely tagged, each word has a lemma and a tag that indicates its part of speech and additional information like number, tense or gender. In our experiments we only have used the part of speech information.

We make use of a compound tag in the substitution because the POS tag does not provide enough information to recognize an entity. We would miss the knowledge given by typographical features. For this reason we decided to combine the POS tag with the tag resulting of the application of the vocabulary reduction transformation. The size of the new vocabulary is greater than the obtained with the first transformation, but it is still smaller than the size of the original vocabulary. So, besides the incorporation of the POS tag information, we still take advantage of the reduction of vocabulary in dealing with the unknown word and sparse data problems.

Adding part of speech information also implies an improvement in the performance of TBL and TnT. Table 2 presents the results of the experiments *TnT-P* and *TBL-P*. TnT improves from 85.25 to 86.69 and TBL improves from 87.45 to 89.22, the best result achieved with TBL (an error reduction of over 14%).

Table 2. Results of transformation experiments

	Precision	Recall	$F_{\beta=1}$
TnT	84.39%	86.12%	85.25
TnT-V	85.19%	88.11%	86.63
TnT-N	86.21%	87.47%	86.83
TnT-P	85.33%	88.09%	86.69
TBL	85.34%	89.66%	87.45
TBL-V	87.72%	88.48%	88.10
TBL-N	86.78%	89.07%	87.91
TBL-P	89.14%	89.29%	89.22

4 System Combination

The three transformations studied cause an improvement in the performance of the NER task. This proves that the two techniques employed, adding information and removing information, can produce good versions of the original corpus through different views of the same text.

But we still have room for improvement if instead of applying the transformations separately we make them work together. We can take advantage of discrepancies among models to choose the most suitable tag for a given word. In the following sections we present the experiments carried out by combining the results of the eight models using different combination schemas. All of these schemas achieve better values for $F_{\beta=1}$ than the best of the participant models in isolation.

System combination is not a new approach in NPL tasks, it has been used in several problems like part of speech tagging [7], word sense disambiguation [9], parsing [8], noun phrase identification [12] and even in named entity extraction [6]. The most popular techniques are voting and stacking (machine learning methods), and the different views of the problem are usually obtained using several taggers or several training corpora. In this paper, however, we are interested in investigate how these methods behave when the combined systems are obtained with transformed versions of the same training corpus.

4.1 Voting

The most obvious way of combining different opinions about the same task is voting. Surprisingly, and despite its simplicity, voting gives very good results, better even than some of the more sophisticated methods that we will present in further subsections. We have carried out two experiments based on this combination scheme:

- *Voting*: one model, one vote. The opinion of each model participant in the combination is equally important.
- *Voting-W*: giving more importance to the opinion of better models. The vote of a model is weighted according to its performance in a previous evaluation.

Table 3 shows the results for these experiments, both achieved better values for $F_{\beta=1}$ than the best of the participant models (*TBL-P* with 89.22). *Voting* reached 89.97 and *Voting-W* 90.02.

4.2 Stacking

Stacking consists in applying machine learning techniques for combining the results of different models. The main idea is to build a system that learns the way in which each model is right or makes a mistake. In this way the final decision is taken according to a pattern of correct and wrong answers.

In order to be able to learn the way in which every model is right or wrong, we need a set of examples, known as *training database* in machine learning terminology. Each example in the training database includes the eight tags proposed by the models for a given word (we call them features) and the actual tag (we call it class). From this point of view, deciding the tag given the tags proposed by several models is a typical classification problem.

Figure 3 shows a small database written in "arff" format, the notation employed by *weka* [14] to represent training databases. *Weka* is a collection of machine learning algorithms for data mining tasks, and is the tool that we have used in our stacking experiments.

```
@relation colaboration
@attribute TnT             {O, B, I}
@attribute TnT-VOC-RED     {O, B, I}
@attribute TnT-NEW-TAGS    {O, B, I}
@attribute TnT-POS         {O, B, I}
@attribute TBL             {O, B, I}
@attribute TBL-VOC-RED     {O, B, I}
@attribute TBL-NEW-TAGS    {O, B, I}
@attribute TBL-POS         {O, B, I}
@attribute ACTUAL-TAG      {O, B, I}
@data
I, I, I, B, B, B, I, I,      I
O, O, O, O, O, O, O, O,      O
B, B, B, B, B, B, B, B,      B
I, I, I, I, I, I, I, I,      I
O, I, I, I, I, I, O, O,      I
B, I, I, I, I, I, B, B,      I
O, O, O, O, O, O, O, O,      O
O, O, O, O, O, O, O, O,      O
B, B, B, O, O, B, B, B,      O
```

Fig. 3. A training data base. Each register corresponds to a word

Most of the examples in figure 3 can be resolved with a voting scheme, because the majority opinion agrees with the actual tag. However the last example presents a different situation, six of the eight models assign the tag B to the word in question, while only two (TnT-POS and TBL) assign the correct tag O. If this example is not an isolated one, it would be interesting to learn it and assign the tag O to those words that present this answer pattern.

The number of examples in the training database has a considerable influence in the learning process, using more examples usually leads to a better performance of the classifier. We have used the other evaluation corpus (test A) to generate them, it is independent of the models and it is also independent of the evaluation process. This corpus, with 52923 tokens, provides enough examples to learn a good classifier.

Table 3 shows the results of the experiment *Tree*, carried out using a decision tree [10] as stacking technique. The $F_{\beta=1}$ measure is 89.72, better than the best of participant models (*TBL-P* with 89.22) but worse than the value obtained by voting (90.02). This does not mean that stacking is a worse technique than voting, we will see in the following experiments that stacking achieves better results than voting. The fact is that the generalization process carried out to induce the tree does not cover all the examples, but there is still a feature of stacking that can compensate this phenomenon, the possibility of merging heterogeneous information.

4.3 Adding Contextual Information

As we have mentioned before one of the advantages of machine learning techniques is that they can make use of information of different nature. While in the voting scheme we only can take into account the tags proposed by the eight models, in a training database we can include as many features as we consider important for taking the correct decision.

One of the most valuable information is the knowledge of the tags assigned to the words around the word in question. To add this information we only have to extend the number of features of each example in the database. Now, besides the tags assigned by each model to a word we will include in the database the tags assigned by the models to the surrounding words. We have carried out two experiments varying the number of words included in the context:

- Tree-1: We only include the tags of the previous and the following words. So each example has twenty four features.
- Tree-2: The tags of the two previous words and the two following words are included. So each example has now, forty features.

In both experiments decision tree is the technique employed to learn the classifier. Table 3 shows the results of the experiments *Tree-1* and *Tree-2*, both improve the results of voting and stacking without contextual information. *Tree-1* got a value of 90.23 in $F_{\beta=1}$ measure, and *Tree-2* got 90.48.

Bigger values of the context increase considerably the number of features in the database and do not lead to better results.

4.4 Bagging

Apart from allowing the use of heterogeneous information, machine learning have another important advantage over voting: it is possible to choose among a great variety of schemes and techniques to find the most suitable one to each problem. *Bagging* [2] is one of this schemas, it provides a good way of handling the possible bias of the model towards some of the examples of the training database.

Bagging is based on the generation of several training data sets taking as base a unique data set. Each new version is obtained by sampling with replacement the original database. Each new data set can be used to train a model and the answers of all the models can be combined to obtain a joint answer. Generally, bagging leads to better results than those obtained with a single classifier. The price to pay is that this kind of combination methods increase the computational cost associated to learning.

Table 3 shows the results of the experiment *Bagging*. In this experiment we apply this scheme using a decision tree as base learner. With this method we obtain the best result (90.90), with an error reduction of over 38% and 27% with respect to the baselines given, respectively, by *TnT* and *TBL* experiments.

Table 3. Results of combination experiments

	Precision	Recall	$F_{\beta=1}$
Voting	89.67%	90.28%	89.97
Voting-W	89.43%	90.62%	90.02
Tree	88.93%	90.53%	89.72
Tree-1	89.54%	90.92%	90.23
Tree-2	90.18%	90.78%	90.48
Bagging	90.69%	91.12%	90.90

5 Conclusions and Future Work

In this paper we have shown that the combination of several taggers is an effective technique for named entity recognition. Taking as baselines the results obtained when TnT and TBL are trained with a corpus annotated with named entity tags, we have investigate alternative methods for taking more advantage of the knowledge provided by the corpus. We have experimented with three corpus transformations, adding or removing information to the corpus. The three of them improve the results obtained with the original version of the corpus.

The four versions of the corpus, and the two different taggers allow us to build eight models that can be combined using several techniques. All the proposed combination techniques improve the results of the best of the participant models in isolation. We have experimented with voting, stacking using a decision tree as learning technique, and stacking using bagging as learning scheme. Our best experiment achieved an $F_{\beta=1}$ measure of 90.90 what means an error reduction of 38.30% and 27.49% in relation to the baselines given by TnT and TBL. This performance is similar to state of the art NER systems, with comparable results to those obtained by the best system in the CoNLL-02 competition [4] that achieved an $F_{\beta=1}$ value of 91.66 in the recognition task.

We have developed our systems for recognizing named entities in Spanish texts because we are specially interested in this language, but it would be easy to reproduce the experiments in other languages having the corresponding corpus.

Much future work remains. We are interested in applying the ideas of this paper in the recognition of entities in specific domains. In this kind of tasks the knowledge about the domain could be incorporated to the system via new transformations. We also plan to take advantage of system combination to help in the construction of annotated corpus, using the jointly assigned tag as agreement criterion in co-training or active learning schemes.

Acknowledgments

We would like to thank the groups CLiC of the University of Barcelona, and TALP of the Polytechnic University of Cataluña, for letting us use the corpus CLiC-TALP.

References

1. Brants, T.: TnT. A statistical part-of-speech tagger. In *Proceedings of the 6th Applied NLP Conference (ANLP00)*. USA (2000) 224–231
2. Breiman, L.: Bagging predictors. In *Machine Learning Journal* 24 (1996) 123–140
3. Brill, E.: Transformation-based Error-Driven Learning and Natural Language Processing: A Case Study in Part-of-Speech Tagging. *Computational Linguistics 21* (1995) 543–565
4. Carreras, X., L. Màrquez y L. Padró: Named Entity Extraction using AdaBoost. In *CoNLL02 Computational Natural Language Learning*. Taiwan (2002) 167–170
5. Civit, M.: Guía para la anotación morfosintáctica del corpus CLiC-TALP. *X-TRACT Working Paper WP-00/06*. (2000)
6. Florian, R., Ittycheriah, A., Jing, H., Zhang, T.: Named Entity Recognition through Classifier Combination. In *Proceedings of CoNLL-2003*. Canada (2003) 168–171
7. Halteren, v. H., Zavrel, J. , Daelemans, W.: Improving accuracy in word class tagging through the combination of machine learning systems. *Computational Linguistics 27* (2001) 199–230
8. Henderson, J. C., Brill, E.: Exploiting diversity in natural language processing. Combining parsers. In *1999 Joint Sigdat Conference on Empirical Methods in Natural Language Processing and Very Large Corpora. ACL*. USA (1999) 187–194
9. Pedersen, T.: A simple approach to building ensembles of naive bayesian classifiers for word sense disambiguation. In *Proceedings of NAACL00*. USA (2000) 63–69
10. Quinlan, J.R.: Induction of decision trees. In *Machine Learning* 1 (1986) 81–106.
11. Rössler, M.: Using Markov Models for Named Entity recognition in German newspapers. In *Proceedings of the Workshop on Machine Learning Approaches in Computational Linguistics*. Italy (2002) 29–37
12. Tjong Kim Sang, E.F., Daelemans, W., Dejean, H., Koeling, R., Krymolowsky, Y., Punyakanok, V., Roth, D.: Applying system combination to base noun phrase identification. In *Proceedings of COLING00*. Germany (2000) 857–863
13. Tjong Kim Sang, E.F.: Introduction to the CoNLL-2002 Shared Task: Language-Independent Named Entity Recognition. In *Proceedings of CoNLL-2002*. Taiwan (2002) 155–158
14. Witten, I.H., Frank, E.: Data Mining. Machine Learning Algorithms in Java. Morgan Kaufmann Publishers (2000)

One Size Fits All? A Simple Technique to Perform Several NLP Tasks

Daniel Gayo-Avello, Darío Álvarez-Gutiérrez, and José Gayo-Avello

Department of Informatics, University of Oviedo, Calvo Sotelo s/n 33007 Oviedo (SPAIN)
dani@lsi.uniovi.es

Abstract. Word fragments or *n*-grams have been widely used to perform different Natural Language Processing tasks such as information retrieval [1] [2], document categorization [3], automatic summarization [4] or, even, genetic classification of languages [5]. All these techniques share some common aspects such as: (1) documents are mapped to a vector space where *n*-grams are used as coordinates and their relative frequencies as vector weights, (2) many of them compute a context which plays a role similar to stop-word lists, and (3) cosine distance is commonly used for document-to-document and query-to-document comparisons. blindLight is a new approach related to these classical *n*-gram techniques although it introduces two major differences: (1) Relative frequencies are no more used as vector weights but replaced by *n*-gram significances, and (2) cosine distance is abandoned in favor of a new metric inspired by sequence alignment techniques although not so computationally expensive. This new approach can be simultaneously used to perform document categorization and clustering, information retrieval, and text summarization. In this paper we will describe the foundations of such a technique and its application to both a particular categorization problem (i.e., language identification) and information retrieval tasks.

1 Introduction

N-grams are simply text sequences consisting of *n* items, not necessarily contiguous, which can be either words or characters. Frequently, the term *n*-gram refers to slices of adjoining *n* characters including blanks and running over different words. These character *n*-grams are well suited to support a vector space model to map documents. In such a model each document can be considered a *D* dimensional vector of weights, where *D* is the number of unique *n*-grams in the document set while the *i*-th weight in the vector is the relative frequency, within the document to be mapped, for the *i*-th *n*-gram. Thus, having two documents (or a query and a document) a simple similarity measure can be computed as the cosine of the angle between both vectors, this measure is especially interesting because it is not affected by length differences between the compared documents. This approach, exemplified in classical works such as [6] or [7], provides several advantages: it is language independent, quite robust in the face of typographical or grammatical errors and it does not require word-stemming or stop-word removal.

Nevertheless, the *n*-gram vector model has more applications besides information retrieval (i.e., comparing a query with a document). By using the same cosine distance as similarity measure, the model can be applied to document clustering and

J. L. Vicedo et al. (Eds.): EsTAL 2004, LNAI 3230, pp. 267–278, 2004.

categorization [3] [8]. In addition to this, document vectors from similar documents (a cluster or a human-made document set) can be used to obtain a centroid vector [8]. Within this centroid, each *i*-th weight is just the average of the *i*-th weights from all vectors in the set. Such a centroid provides a "context" where performing document comparisons given that it must be subtracted from the document vectors involved in the process. An especially interesting application of *n*-grams where a context had to be provided was Highlights [4] which used vectors to model both documents and these document's "background"[1]. Highlights extracted keywords automatically from a document with regards to its particular background.

Such classical approaches show two major drawbacks: (1) since documents are represented by *D* dimensional vectors of weights, where *D* is the total amount of different *n*-grams in the whole document set, such vectors are not document representations by themselves but representations according to a bigger "contextual" corpus, and (2) cosine similarities between high dimensional vectors tend to be 0 (i.e., two random documents have a high probability of being orthogonal to each other), so, to avoid this "curse of dimensionality" problem it is necessary to reduce the number of features (i.e. *n*-grams), which is usually done by setting arbitrary weight thresholds.

blindLight is a new approach related to those described before and so, applicable to the tasks mentioned above (i.e., document categorization and clustering, information retrieval, keyword extraction or automatic summarization [9]) however it takes into account some important requisites to avoid the problems in previous solutions: First, every document must have assigned a unique document vector with no regards to any corpus and, second, another measure, apart from cosine similarity, has to be used.

2 Foundations of the blindLight Approach

blindLight, as other *n*-gram vector space solutions, maps every document to a vector of weights; however, such document vectors are rather different from classical ones. On one hand, any two document vectors obtained through this technique are not necessarily of equal dimensions, thus, there is no actual "vector space" in this proposal. On the other hand, weights used in these vectors are not relative frequencies but the significance of each *n*-gram within the document.

Computing a measure of the relation between elements inside *n*-grams, and thus the importance of the whole *n*-gram, is a problem with a long history of research, however, we will focus in just a few references. In 1993 Dunning described a method based on likelihood ratio tests to detect keywords and domain-specific terms [10]. However, his technique worked only for word bigrams and were Ferreira da Silva and Pereira Lopes [11] the ones who presented a generalization of different statistical measures so these could be applied to arbitrary length word *n*-grams. In addition to this, they also introduced a new measure, Symmetrical Conditional Probability [12], which overcomes other statistics-based measures. According to Pereira Lopes, their approach obtains better results than those achieved by Dunning.

blindLight implements the technique described by da Silva and Lopes although applied to character *n*-grams rather than word *n*-grams. Thus, it measures the relation among characters inside each *n*-gram and, so, the significance of every *n*-gram, or what is the same, the weight for the components in a document vector.

---

[1] This background was not a centroid but built using the dataset as just one long document.

With regards to comparisons between vectors, a simple similarity measure such as the cosine distance cannot be straightforward applied when using vectors of different dimension. Of course, it could be considered a temporary vector space of dimension d_1+d_2, being d_1 and d_2 the respective dimensions of the document vectors to be compared, assigning a null weight to one vector's *n*-grams not present in the other and vice versa. However, we consider the absence of a particular *n*-gram within a document rather distinct from its presence with null significance.

Eventually, comparing two vectors with different dimensions can be seen as a pairwise alignment problem. There are two sequences with different lengths and some (or none) elements in common that must be aligned, that is, the highest number of columns of identical pairs must be obtained by only inserting gaps, changing or deleting elements in both sequences.

One of the simplest models of distance for pairwise alignment is the so-called Levenshtein or edit distance [13] which can be defined as the smallest number of insertions, deletions, and substitutions required to change one string into another (e.g. the distance between "`accommodate`" and "`aconmodate`" is 2).

However, there are two noticeable differences between pairwise-alignning text strings and comparing different length vectors, no matter the previous ones can be seen as vectors of characters. First difference is rather important, namely, the order of components is central in pairwise alignment (e.g., DNA analysis or spell checking) while unsuitable within a vector-space model. Second one is also highly significant: although not taking into account the order of the components, "weights" in pairwise alignment are integer values while in vector-space models they are real.

Thus, distance functions for pairwise alignment, although inspiring, cannot be applied to the concerned problem. Instead, a new distance measure is needed and, in fact, two are provided. Classical vector-space based approaches assume that the distance, and so the similarity, between two document vectors is commutative (e.g., cosine distance). blindLight, however, proposes two similarity measures when comparing document vectors. For the sake of clarity, we will called those two documents query (Q) and target (T) although these similarity functions can be equally applied to any pair of documents, not only for information retrieval purposes.

Let Q and T be two blindLight document vectors with dimensions m and n:

$$Q=\{(k_{1Q},w_{1Q})\ (k_{2Q},w_{2Q})\ \dots\ (k_{mQ},w_{mQ})\} \tag{1}$$

$$T=\{(k_{1T},w_{1T})\ (k_{2T},w_{2T})\ \dots\ (k_{nT},w_{nT})\} \tag{2}$$

k_{ij} is the i-th n-gram in document j while w_{ij} is the significance (computed using SCP [12]) for the n-gram k_{ij} within the same document j.

We define the total significance for document vectors Q and T, S_Q and S_T respectively, as:

$$S_Q=\sum_{i=1}^{m} w_{iQ} \tag{3}$$

$$S_T=\sum_{i=1}^{n} w_{iT} \tag{4}$$

Then, the pseudo-alignment operator, Ω, is defined as follows:

$$Q\Omega T = \left\{ (k_x, w_x) \middle/ \begin{array}{l} (k_x = k_{iQ} = k_{jT}) \wedge (w_x = \min(w_{iQ}, w_{jT})), \\ (k_{iQ}, w_{iQ}) \in Q, 0 \le i < m, \\ (k_{jT}, w_{jT}) \in T, 0 \le j < n \end{array} \right\} \quad (5)$$

Similarly to equations 3 and 4 we can define the total significance for $Q\Omega T$:

$$S_{Q\Omega T} = \sum w_{iQ\Omega T} \quad (6)$$

Finally, we can define two similarity measures, one to compare Q vs. T, Π (uppercase Pi), and a second one to compare T vs. Q, P (uppercase Rho), which can be seen analogous to precision and recall measures:

$$\Pi = S_{Q\Omega T} / S_Q \quad (7)$$

$$\mathrm{P} = S_{Q\Omega T} / S_T \quad (8)$$

To clarify these concepts we will show a simple example based on (one of) the shortest stories ever written. We will compare original version of Monterroso's Dinosaur with a Portuguese translation; the first one will play the query role and the second one the target, the *n*-grams will be quad-grams.

Cuando despertó, el dinosaurio todavía estaba allí. (Query)

Quando acordou, o dinossauro ainda estava lá. (Target)

Fig. 1. "El dinosaurio" by Augusto Monterroso, Spanish original and Portuguese translation

In summary, the blindLight technique, although vector-based, does not need a predefined document set where performing NLP tasks and so, such tasks can be achieved over ever-growing document sets or, just the opposite, over just one single document [9]. Relative frequencies are abandoned as vector weights in favor of a measure of the importance of each *n*-gram. In addition to this, similarity measures are analogous to those used in pairwise-alignment although computationally inexpensive and, also, non commutative which allows us to combine both measures, Π and P, into any linear combination to tune it to each NLP task.

The rest of the paper will describe some test bed experiments to evaluate our prototypes at different tasks, namely, language identification, genetic classification of languages, and document retrieval.

3 Language Identification and Genetic Classification of Languages Using blindLight

Natural language identification from digital text has a long tradition and many techniques have been proposed: for instance, looking within the text for particular

Q vector (45 elements)

Cuan	2.489
I_di	2.392
stab	2.392
...	
saur	2.313
desp	2.313
...	
ndo_	2.137
nosa	2.137
...	
ando	2.012
avía	1.945
_all	1.915

T vector (39 elements)

va_l	2.545
rdou	2.323
stav	2.323
...	
saur	2.244
noss	2.177
...	
a_lá	2.022
o_ac	2.022
...	
auro	1.908
ando	1.876
do_a	1.767

QΩT (10 elements)

saur	2.244
inos	2.177
uand	2.119
_est	2.091
dino	2.022
_din	2.022
esta	2.012
ndo_	1.981
a_es	1.943
ando	1.876

Π: 0.209 P: 0.253

Fig. 2. blindLight document vectors for both documents in Fig. 1 (truncated to show ten elements, blanks have been replaced by underscores). QΩT intersection vector is shown plus Π and P values indicating the similarities between both documents

characters [14], words [15], and, of course, *n*-grams [16] or [17]. Techniques based on *n*-gram vectors using the cosine distance perform quite well in this task. Such techniques usually follow these steps: (1) For each document in the corpus they create an *n*-gram vector, (2) while creating document vectors a centroid vector is also computed, and (3) when an unknown text sample is presented to the system it is (3-a) mapped into the vector space, (3-b) the centroid is subtracted from the sample, and (3-c) compared, by means of the cosine distance, with all the reference documents in the set (which also have had the centroid subtracted). Finally, the reference document found most similar to the sample is used to inform the user in which language the sample is probably written.

The application of blindLight to the construction of a language identifier supposes some subtle differences to previous approaches. On one hand, it is not necessary to subtract any centroid neither from reference documents or the text sample. On the other hand, our language identifier does not need to compare the sample vector to every reference language in the database because a language tree is prepared in advance in order to take the number of comparisons to a minimum.

The language identifier to be described is able to distinguish the following European languages: Basque, Catalan, Danish, Dutch, English, Faroese, Finnish, French, German, Italian, Norwegian, Portuguese, Spanish and Swedish. To assure that the identification is solely made on the basis of the language and is not biased by the contents of the reference documents the whole database consists of literal translations of the same document: the first three chapters of the Book of Genesis.

To build the first version of the language identifier was pretty simple. First, an *n*-gram vector was obtained for every translation of the Genesis. Afterwards, a similarity measure, based on Π and P, was defined, being eventually just Π (being the submitted sample the query). Finally, the identifier only needs to receive a sample of text, to create an *n*-gram vector for that sample and to compute the Π similarity between the sample and each reference document. The highest the value of Π, the most likely the language in the reference to be the one used in the sample.

The second version of the language identifier was inspired by the appealing idea of performing genetic classification of languages (i.e., determining how different human languages relate to each other) by automatic means. Of course, this idea has yet been explored (e.g., [5], [18], or [19]). However, many of these approaches employ either classical vector-space techniques or Levenshtein distance rightly applied to character or phoneme sequences, so, we found rather challenging the application of blindLight to this problem.

The genetic classification of languages using blindLight was performed over two different linguistic data. The first experiment was conducted on the vectors obtained from the text of the Book of Genesis and, so, produced a tree with 14 languages (Fig. 3). The second experiment, involved vectors computed from phonetic transcriptions of the fable "The North Wind and the Sun" which were mainly obtained from the Handbook of the International Phonetic Association [20]. The languages that took part in this second experiment were: Catalan, Dutch, English, French, Galician, German, Portuguese, Spanish, and Swedish. This task produced a tree with 9 languages (Fig. 4), from which 8 were also present in the results from the first experiment. Both experiments used as similarity measure the expression $0.5\Pi+0.5P$, thus, establishing a commutative similarity measure when comparing languages. A technique similar to Jarvis-Patrick clustering [21] was used to build the dendrograms (Figures 4 and 5), however, describing this technique is out of the scope of this paper.

We are not linguists so we will not attempt to conclude anything from both experiments. Nevertheless, not only both trees are coherent to each other but most of the relations shown in them are also consistent, to the best of our knowledge, with linguistics theories. Even the close relation shown between Catalan and French, both lexically and phonetically, finds support in some authors (e.g., Pere Verdaguer [22]), although it contrasts with those classifications which consider Catalan an Ibero Romance language rather distant from Oïl family (to which French belongs).

The data obtained from the lexical comparison of languages was used to prepare a set of artificial mixed vectors[2], namely, `Catalan-French`, `Danish-Swedish`, `Dutch-German`, `Portuguese-Spanish`, `Italic`, `northGermanic`, and `westGermanic`. Such vectors are simply the Ω-intersection of the different reference vectors belonging to each category (e.g., `westGermanic` involves `Dutch`, `English`, and `German` vectors).

To determine the language in which a sample is written two steps are followed: First, the sample is discriminated against `Basque`, `Finnish`, `Italic`, `northGermanic` and `westGermanic`. Then, depending in the broad category obtained, a second phase of comparisons may be needed. Once these two phases have been completed the system informs the user both about the language and the family to which it belongs.

Although the language identifier needs thorough testing, an extremely simple experiment was performed to get some feedback about its accuracy. 1,500 posts were downloaded from five `soc.culture.*` newsgroups, namely, `basque`, `catalan`, `french`, `galiza`, and `german`.

[2] It can be argued that the described language classification experiments were not needed given that actual language classifications are well-known, at least not to build the language identifier. Nevertheless, such experiments were, in fact, essential because it could not be assumed that artificial language vectors built using blindLight would work as expected by only taking into account data provided by non computational classifications.

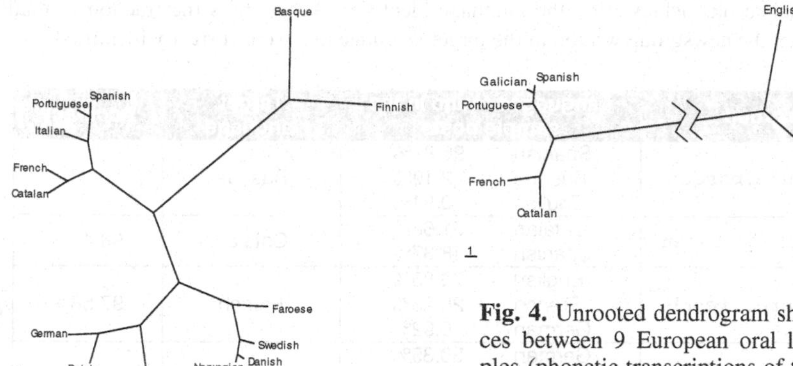

Fig. 3. Unrooted dendrogram showing distances between 14 European written language samples (three first chapters of the Book of Genesis)

Fig. 4. Unrooted dendrogram showing distances between 9 European oral language samples (phonetic transcriptions of the fable "The North Wind and the Sun"). Distance between Gallo-Iberian (on the left) and Germanic subtrees is 23.985, more than twice the distance shown in the picture

We included, posts from `soc.culture.galiza` to test the system with unknown languages. It must be said that really few posts in that group are actually written in Galician. From those which were actually Galician language samples 63.48% were classified as Portuguese and 36.52% as Spanish, which seems quite reasonable.

Each raw post, without stripping any header information[3], was submitted to the language identifier. Then, if the language assigned by the prototype did not match the supposed language for that post (according to its origin newsgroup) it was human reviewed to check if it was either a system's fault (e.g., assigning English to a post written in any other language), or an actual negative (e.g., a German document posted to `soc.culture.french`). Each fault was added to the count of positives to obtain the total amount of documents written in the target language within its newsgroup and, thus, to compute the language identifier accuracy for that language. Eventually, this was a daunting task because many of these newsgroups suffer from heavy spam and cross-posting problems. The results obtained with this experiment are shown in the following table.

4 Information Retrieval Using blindLight

An information retrieval prototype built upon this approach is participating at the CLEF[4] 2004 campaign at the moment of writing this paper. As with any other application of blindLight, a similarity measure to compare queries and documents is needed. At this moment just two have been tested: Π and a more complex one (see equation 9) which provides rather satisfactory results.

[3] Not stripping the header was done in order to check the system's tolerance to "noise" (i.e., the presence of many English-like text). It was founded that documents with an actual language sample of around 200 characters could be correctly classified in spite of being attached to quite lengthy headers (from 500 to more than 900 characters).

[4] Cross Language Evaluation Forum (`http://www.clef-campaign.org`).

Table 1. Partial results achieved by the language identifier. Accuracy is the fraction of total documents from the newsgroup written in the target language that were correctly identified

Newsgroup	Languages found in the sample posts		Target language	Accuracy
soc.culture.basque	Spanish Basque English	96.87% 2.19% 0.94%	Basque	100%
soc.culture.catalan	Catalan Spanish	51.63% 48.37%	Catalan	98.44%
soc.culture.french	English French German	73.85% 25.23% 0.92%	French	97.56%
soc.culture.german	German English French	50.35% 48.94% 0.71%	German	97.18%

$$\frac{\Pi + norm(\Pi \mathrm{P})}{2} \tag{9}$$

The goal of the *norm* function shown in previous equation is just translate the range of Π·P values into the range of Π values, making thus possible a comprehensive combination of both (otherwise, P, and thus Π·P values, are negligible when compared to Π).

The operation of the blindLight IR system is really simple:

- For each document in the database an *n*-gram vector is obtained and stored, just in the same way it can be computed to obtain a summary, a list of keyphrases or to determine the language in which it is written.
- When a query is submitted to the system this computes an *n*-gram vector and compares it with every document obtaining Π and P values.
- From these values a ranking measure is worked out, and a reverse ordered list of documents is returned as a response to the query.

This way of operation supposes both advantages and disadvantages: documents may be added to the database at any moment because there is no indexing process; however, comparing a query with every document in the database can be rather time consuming and not feasible with very large datasets. In order to reduce the number of document-to-query comparisons a clustering phase may be done in advance, in a similar way to the language tree used within the language identifier. Of course, by doing this the working over ever-growing datasets is no more possible because the system should be shut down periodically to perform indexing. Thorough performance analysis is needed to determine what database size requires this previous clustering.

There are no yet results about this system's performance at CLEF experiments, however, it was tested on two very small standard collections with promising results. These collections were CACM (3204 documents and 64 queries) and CISI (1460 documents and 112 queries). Both were originally provided with the SMART system[5]

[5] Available at `ftp://ftp.cs.cornell.edu/pub/smart`

and have become a widely used benchmark, thus, enabling comparisons between different IR systems.

Figure 6 shows the interpolated precision-recall graphs for both collections and ranking measures (namely, `pi` and `piro`). Such results are similar to those reached by several systems but not as good as those achieved by other ones; for instance, 11-pt. average precision was 16.73% and 13.41% for CACM and CISI, respectively, while the SMART IR system achieves 37.78% and 19.45% for the same collections. However, it must be said that these experiments were performed over the documents and the queries just as they are, that is, common techniques such as stop-word removal, stemming, or weighting of the query terms (all used by SMART) were not applied to the document set and the queries were provided to the system in a literal fashion[6], as if they were actually submitted by the original users. By avoiding such techniques, the system is totally language independent, at least for non ideographic languages, although performance must be improved.

In addition to this, it was really simple to evolve this system towards cross-language retrieval (i.e., a query written in one language retrieves documents written in another one). This was done without performing machine translation by taking advantage of a sentence aligned corpus of languages source (S) and target (T).

The query written in the source language, Q_S, is splitted in word chunks (from one word to the whole query). The S corpus is gathered looking for sentences containing any of these chunks. Every sentence found in S is replaced by its counterpart in the T corpus. All sentences from T corresponding to each chunk within the original query are Ω-intersected. Since such sentences contain, allegedly, the translation of some words from language S into language T, it can be supposed that the Ω-intersection of their vectors would contain a kind of "translated" n-grams (see Fig. 6).

Thus, it is obtained a vector similar, in theory, to that which could be compute from a real translation from the original query. To build this pseudo-translator within the blindLight IR prototype the European Parliament Proceedings Parallel Corpus 1996-2003 [23] has been used obtaining interesting results: in average terms, 38.59% of the n-grams from pseudo-translated query vectors are present within the vectors from actual translated queries and, in turn, 28.31% of the n-grams from the actual translated query vectors correspond to n-grams within the pseudo-translated ones.

5 Conclusions and Future Work

Gayo et al. [9] introduced a new technique, blindLight, claiming it could be used to perform several NLP tasks, such as document clustering and categorization, language identification, information retrieval, keyphrase extraction and automatic summarization from single documents, showing results for these two last tasks.

In this paper the vector model used within blindLight has been refined and the similarity measures used to perform document comparisons have been formalized. In addition to this it has been shown that such a technique can be really applied to language identification, genetic classification of languages and cross-language IR.

---

[6] Just an example query from the CACM collection: `#64 List all articles on EL1 and ECL (EL1 may be given as EL/1; I don't remember how they did it.` The blindLight IR prototype processes queries like this one in an "as is" manner.

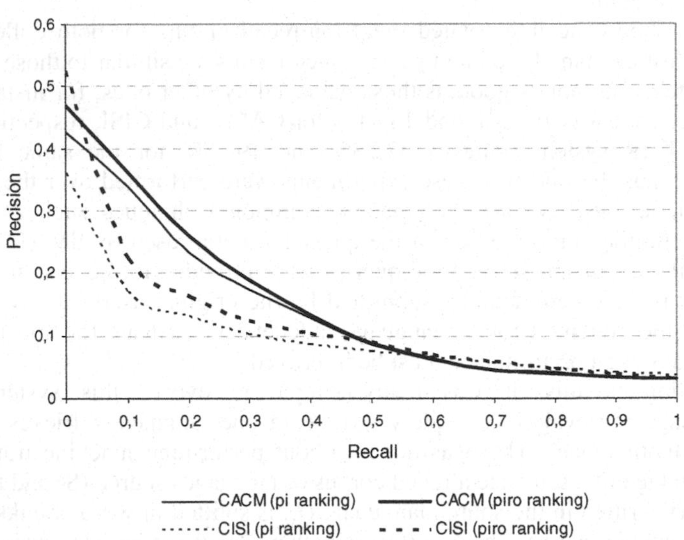

Fig. 5. Interpolated precision-recall graphs for the blindLight IR system applied to CACM and CISI test collections. Top-10 average precision for CACM and CISI was 19.8% and 19.6% respectively, in both cases using `piro` ranking

Query written in language S (from CLEF 2004 French topic list)

Trouver des documents évoquant des discussions sur la réforme des institutions financières, en particulier la Banque Mondiale et le Fond Monétaire International, lors du sommet du G7 qui a eu lieu à Halifax en 1995.

Some sentences from corpus S (Europarl French)

(0861) ...la Conférence intergouvernementale sur la réforme des institutions européennes...
(1104) ...l'état des travaux concernant la réforme des institutions, réforme qui...
(5116) ...le seul grand défi qui se pose à l'Union est la réforme des institutions de l'UE...

Counterpart sentences from corpus T (Europarl English)

(0861) ...The Intergov. Conferenc. to address [...] the reform of the European institutions...
(1104) ...the state of progress in the reform of the institutions, which is...
(5116) ...the single greatest challenge facing the Union is the reform of the EU institutions...

Pseudo-translated query vector (Ω-intersection of previous T sentences)

(..., _ins, _ref, _the, efor, form, inst, itut, nsti, orm_, refo, stit, the_, tion, titu, tuti, utio, ...)

Fig. 6. Procedure to pseudo-translate a query written originally in a source language (in this case French) onto a vector containing appropriate n-grams from the target language (English in this example). Blanks have been replaced by underscores, just one chunk from the query has been pseudo-translated

The partial results obtained for language identification prove that it is a robust technique, showing an accuracy higher than 97% with an information-to-noise ratio around 2/7.

The application of this approach to automatic genetic classification of languages, both to lexical and phonological input, produced data coherent to most of linguistics theories and, besides this, useful to improve the operation of a language identifier built using the very same technique.

The performance achieved when applying blindLight to IR is not as good as some IR systems but close to many others. However, it must be noticed that common techniques such as stop-word removal or stemming are not used. This surely has impacted on performance but, this way, the approach is totally language independent. On the other hand, it has been shown how easily cross-language IR can be implemented by performing pseudo-translation of queries (i.e., queries are not actually translated but parallel corpora is used to obtain a vector containing *n*-grams highly alike to be present in actual translations).

Therefore, an extremely simple technique relying on the mapping of documents to *n*-gram vectors in addition to a metric able to compare different length vectors appears to be flexible enough to be applied to a wide range of NLP tasks showing in all of them adequate performance.

References

1. D'Amore, R., Mah, C.P.: One-time complete indexing of text: Theory and practice. Proc. of SIGIR 1985, pp. 155-164 (1985)
2. Kimbrell, R.E.: Searching for text? Send an n-gram! Byte, 13(5), pp. 297-312 (1988)
3. Damashek, M.: Gauging similarity with n-grams: Language-independent categorization of text. Science, 267, pp. 843-848 (1995)
4. Cohen, J.D.: Highlights: Language and Domain-Independent Automatic Indexing Terms for Abstracting. JASIS, 46(3), pp. 162-174 (1995)
5. Huffman, S.: The Genetic Classification of Languages by n-gram Analysis: A Computational Technique, Ph. D. thesis, Georgetown University (1998)
6. Thomas, T.R.: Document retrieval from a large dataset of free-text descriptions of physician-patient encounters via n-gram analysis. Technical Report LA-UR-93-0020, Los Alamos National Laboratory, Los Alamos, NM (1993)
7. Cavnar, W.B.: Using an n-gram-based document representation with a vector processing retrieval model. In Proc. of TREC-3, pp. 269-277 (1994)
8. Huffman, S.: Acquaintance: Language-Independent Document Categorization by N-Grams. In Proceedings of The Fourth Text REtrieval Conference (1995)
9. Gayo-Avello, D., Álvarez-Gutiérrez, D., Gayo-Avello, J.: Naive Algorithms for Key-phrase Extraction and Text Summarization from a Single Document inspired by the Protein Biosynthesis Process. Proc. of Bio-ADIT 2004, LNCS (2004) In press.
10. Dunning, T.: Accurate methods for the statistics of surprise and coincidence. Computational Linguistics, 19(1), pp. 61-74 (1993)
11. Ferreira da Silva, J., Pereira Lopes, G.: A Local Maxima method and a Fair Dispersion Normalization for extracting multi-word units from corpora. In Proc. of MOL6 (1999)
12. Ferreira da Silva, J., Pereira Lopes, G.: Extracting Multiword Terms from Document Collections. Proc. of VExTAL, Venice, Italy (1999)
13. Levenshtein, V.I.: Binary codes capable of correcting deletions, insertions, and reversals, (English translation from Russian), Soviet Physics Doklady, 10(8), pp. 707-710 (1966).
14. Ziegler, D.: The Automatic Identification of Languages Using Linguistic Recognition Signals. PhD Thesis, State University of New York, Buffalo (1991)

15. Souter, C., Churcher, G., Hayes, J., Johnson, S.: Natural Language Identification using Corpus-based Models. Hermes Journal of Linguistics, Vol. 13, pp. 183-203, Faculty of Modern Languages, Aarhus School of Business, Denmark (1994)
16. Beesley, K.R.: Language Identifier: A Computer Program for Automatic Natural-Language Identification of Online Text. In Language at Crossroads: Proceedings of the 19th Annual Conference of the American Translators Association, pp. 47-54 (1988)
17. Dunning, T.: Statistical identification of language. Technical Report MCCS 94-273, New Mexico State University (1994)
18. Kessler, B.: Computational Dialectology in Irish Gaelic. Dublin: EACL. In: Proceedings of the European Association for Computational Linguistics, pp. 60-67 (1995)
19. Nerbonne, J., Heeringa, W.: Measuring Dialect Distance Phonetically, In John Coleman (ed.) Proceedings of the Third Meeting of the ACL Special Interest Group in Computational Phonology, pp.11-18 (1997)
20. Handbook of the International Phonetic Association: A Guide to the Use of the International Phonetic Alphabet, Cambridge University Press (1999)
21. Jarvis, R.A., Patrick, E.A.: Clustering Using a Similarity Measure Based on Shared Near Neighbors, IEEE Transactions on Computers, 22(11), pp. 1025-1034 (1973)
22. Verdaguer, P.: Grammaire de la langue catalane. Les origines de la langue, Curial (1999)
23. Koehn, P.: Europarl: A Multilingual Corpus for Evaluation of Machine Translation, Draft, Unpublished, `http://www.isi.edu/~koehn/publications/europarl.ps`

Ontology-Based Feature Transformations: A Data-Driven Approach

Filip Ginter, Sampo Pyysalo, Jorma Boberg, Jouni Järvinen, and Tapio Salakoski

Turku Centre for Computer Science and Department of Information Technology, University of Turku, Lemminkäisenkatu 14, 20520 Turku, Finland
firstname.lastname@it.utu.fi

Abstract. We present a novel approach to incorporating semantic information to the problems of natural language processing, in particular to the document classification task. The approach builds on the intuition that semantic relatedness of words can be viewed as a non-static property of the words that depends on the particular task at hand. The semantic relatedness information is incorporated using feature transformations, where the transformations are based on a feature ontology and on the particular classification task and data. We demonstrate the approach on the problem of classifying MEDLINE-indexed documents using the MeSH ontology. The results suggest that the method is capable of improving the classification performance on most of the datasets.

1 Introduction

Many natural language processing tasks can benefit from information about semantic relatedness of words. For example, the methods for information retrieval and text classification tasks can be extended to capture information about words that are lexically distinct but semantically related. This is in contrast with the common bag-of-words representation of text where no semantic relatedness information is captured. Information on semantic relatedness of words can be beneficial in at least two practical ways. Combining the related cases that would be distinct in the standard bag-of-words representation may result in a better predictor, for example, by yielding more accurate maximum-likelihood estimates in probabilistic methods such as the naive Bayes classifier. Further, words that are very rare or even unseen during training, but are closely semantically related to some more frequent word, can be used as a source of information.

Semantic networks such as WordNet[1] and UMLS[2] are obvious sources of semantic knowledge about words. The semantic networks are usually represented as graphs with nodes representing words and edges representing semantic relationships such as synonymy, hypernymy, and meronymy, for example.

One way to incorporate the information on semantic relatedness of words is to define a quantitative measure that can be used in various classification and

[1] http://www.cogsci.princeton.edu/~wn/
[2] http://www.nlm.nih.gov/research/umls/

J. L. Vicedo et al. (Eds.): EsTAL 2004, LNAI 3230, pp. 279–290, 2004.

clustering techniques. The need for such a quantitative measure has given rise to various techniques that measure pairwise word semantic relatedness based on semantic networks.

The approach of Rada and Bicknell ([1]) defines the strength of the relationship between two words in terms of the minimum number of edges connecting the words in the semantic network graph. Resnik ([2]) argues that the semantic distance covered by single edges varies and employs a corpus-based method for estimating the distance of related concepts. Budanitsky ([3]) presents an application-oriented evaluation of these two and three other methods. It should be noted that these methods aim to measure the strength of the pairwise word relationship as a static property of the words, that is, the strength of the relationship is defined independently of the task at hand.

In this paper, we devise and investigate techniques that are based on the intuition that an optimal measure of semantic relatedness is not a static property of words, but depends also on the problem at hand. To illustrate the intuition, let us consider the task of text classification and the two words "mouse" and "human". For many text classification tasks, it would be beneficial to consider "mouse" and "human" to be relatively distant, but in case of the hypothetical classification task where the goal is to distinguish between documents about eucaryotes and procaryotes, it might be beneficial to consider "mouse" and "human" similar or even synonymous. Conversely, the two words "wheat" and "oat" would typically be considered closely related, but, for example, in the Reuters-21578 classification dataset,[3] where the two words define distinct classes, it would be beneficial to consider the words unrelated. Relating features in a task-specific manner has also been considered by Baker and McCallum ([4]), who introduce a feature clustering method with a primary focus on dimensionality reduction. However, their method is not governed by semantic networks, but it is based on the distribution of class labels associated with each feature.

Instead of defining a quantitative measure of the strength of semantic relationship between words, we incorporate the semantic information in the form of transformations based on the hierarchical ontology that underlies the words. The relations encoded in the hierarchy are the starting point of the proposed method. The method then operates on a given training set for a given problem, and it attempts to identify elementary transformations of the features that are beneficial to the performance of a machine learning method for the problem. Roughly, each transformation decides on the relatedness or unrelatedness of a set of words. In the mouse vs. human example above, the method would be expected to relate the words "mouse" and "human" only if such a step improves the performance of the machine learning method on the task.

We apply the method to a classification of MEDLINE-indexed[4] documents, where each document is annotated with a set of terms from the MeSH

[3] http://www.daviddlewis.com/resources/testcollections/reuters21578/

[4] http://www.nlm.nih.gov/

ontology[5]. However, the method is applicable to any problem where the features are organized in a hierarchy and a measure of performance can be defined.

The paper is organized as follows. In Section 2 we define the necessary concepts and describe the method. Section 3 describes an application of the method to biomedical literature mining based on the MeSH ontology. The empirical results and possible future directions are discussed in Section 4, and Section 5 concludes the paper.

2 Feature Transformations

In this section we define a feature hierarchy in the form of a tree and present some of the possible elementary feature mappings based on the hierarchy.

2.1 Feature Hierarchy

Let F be a finite set of possible features that are organized into a "is a" concept hierarchy in the form of a tree. Let $a, b \in F$ be features. If a is a child of b, denoted as $a \prec b$, we say that a is a *direct specialization* of b and b is a *direct generalization* of a. If a is a descendant of b, denoted as $a \prec^* b$, we say that a is a *specialization* of b and b is a *generalization* of a.

Let further $\mathcal{G}(b) = \{a \mid b \prec^* a\}$ be the set of all generalizations of b. Similarly, let $\mathcal{S}(a) = \{b \mid b \prec^* a\}$ be the set of all specializations of a. We say that a is *most general* if it is the root of the hierarchy, that is, $\mathcal{G}(a) = \emptyset$. Similarly, we say that b is *most specific* if it is a leaf of the hierarchy, that is, $\mathcal{S}(b) = \emptyset$.

2.2 Elementary Transformations of Feature Multisets

Each document is represented as a multiset $X \subseteq F$ of features extracted from the document. Before X is passed to a text classifier, it undergoes a transformation, which may remove some features from the multiset, or replace some features with a multiset of (possibly different) features. The feature multiset transformations are independent of the classification method used for the data, since the classifier is applied only after the features were transformed.

In order to search through the space of possible feature multiset transformations, we define a set of elementary transformations, where each elementary transformation is a feature multiset mapping $2^F \rightarrow 2^F$. A locally optimal transformation is obtained as a composition of several elementary transformations. In the following, we consider some of the possible elementary transformations.

Generalization to a Feature. The generalization to a feature transformation is parametrized by a feature $a \in F$ and it causes all features belonging to $\mathcal{S}(a)$ (that is, features more specific than a) to be replaced by the feature a, in other words, the whole subtree under the feature a is "folded" up to the feature a.

[5] http://www.nlm.nih.gov/mesh/meshhome.html

The transformation causes all features belonging to $\mathcal{S}(a)$ to be treated as full synonyms of a:

$$G_a(X) = \bigcup_{x \in X} g_a(x)\,, \text{ where} \tag{1}$$

$$g_a(x) = \begin{cases} \{a\} & \text{if } x \prec^* a \\ \{x\} & \text{otherwise.} \end{cases} \tag{2}$$

Generalization to a Level. The generalization to a level transformation is parametrized by a level of generality $n \in \mathbb{N}$. The level n_x is defined inductively for all $x \in F$ as follows. Let $n_x = 0$ for the most general feature x. Let $a, b \in F$. Then $n_b = n_a + 1$ for all b such that $b \prec a$. The transformation causes all features $x \in F$ with level of generality $n_x > n$ to be mapped to their generalization $a \in F$ such that $n_a = n$. This transformation is achieved by the mapping

$$L_n(X) = \bigcup_{x \in X} l_n(x)\,, \text{ where} \tag{3}$$

$$l_n(x) = \begin{cases} \{a\}\,,\ n_a = n,\ x \prec^* a & \text{if } n_x > n \\ \{x\} & \text{if } n_x \leq n. \end{cases} \tag{4}$$

The transformation is closely related to the *heights of generalization* concept introduced by Scott and Matwin ([5]). Note that every L_n-transformation can be performed as a composition of G_a-transformations for all features a such that $n_a = n$. However, the expression power of the G_a-transformation is bigger than that of the L_n-transformation.

Omitting a Feature. The transformation causes the feature a, which is the parameter of this transformation, to be omitted from the feature multiset, including all specializations of a:

$$O_a(X) = \bigcup_{x \in X} o_a(x)\,, \text{ where} \tag{5}$$

$$o_a(x) = \begin{cases} \emptyset & \text{if } x \in \mathcal{S}(a) \bigcup \{a\} \\ \{x\} & \text{otherwise.} \end{cases} \tag{6}$$

The use of this transformation is related to the "wrapper" approach to feature selection (John et al., [6]), where a set of relevant features is chosen iteratively, by greedily adding or removing a single feature until significant decrease in the classification performance is observed. This greedy algorithm yields a locally minimal set of features that maintain the classification performance of the full set of features.

2.3 The Algorithm

We apply here a greedy approach to search for the locally optimal transformation. The algorithm assumes the existence of a target function $E\colon \mathcal{M} \rightarrow \mathbb{R}$, where $\mathcal{M}$ is the set of all possible feature mappings. The function E evaluates the goodness of feature mappings $M \in \mathcal{M}$ and can be used to compare two mappings with respect to a criteria represented by the function E. Let further $\Lambda \subseteq \mathcal{M}$ be the set of all defined elementary transformations with all possible parameter combinations, let $\theta \in \mathbb{R}$ be a small threshold constant, and let $I \in \mathcal{M}$ be the identity mapping. The greedy algorithm that returns a locally optimal transformation is presented in Figure 1.

input: Λ, E
output: a mapping $M \in \mathcal{M}$
$i \leftarrow 0$, $M_0 \leftarrow I$, $\Gamma \leftarrow \Lambda$
while $|\Gamma| > 0$
  $i \leftarrow i+1$
  $M_i^\star \leftarrow \arg\max_{M\in\Gamma} E(M \circ M_{i-1})$
  $M_i \leftarrow M_i^\star \circ M_{i-1}$
  $\Gamma \leftarrow \Gamma \setminus \{M_i^\star\}$
  if $E(M_i) - E(M_{i-1}) < \theta$ **then**
    return M_{i-1}
  end if
end while
return M_i

Fig. 1. A greedy algorithm to compute a locally optimal transformation as the composition of several elementary transformations drawn from the set Λ

Example 1. Let us consider the task introduced in Section 1, i.e., classification between documents about eucaryotes and procaryotes. Let F be the terms of the MeSH hierarchy and E be a function that evaluates how well a feature mapping M helps some classifier to separate the two classes. The set Λ contains all defined elementary transformations, that is, Λ contains all transformations that generalize up to a MeSH term $\bigcup_{x\in F} G_x$, all transformations that omit a MeSH term $\bigcup_{x\in F} O_x$, and all transformations that generalize to a level $\bigcup_{n=1}^{N} L_n$ where N is the depth of the MeSH hierarchy tree.

The set Λ contains, among others, also the transformations $G_{Organisms}$, $G_{Animals}$, and $G_{Bacteria}$. The transformation $G_{Organisms}$ is obviously harmful, as it suppresses the distinction between eucaryotes and procaryotes. The other two transformations are probably beneficial for any classifier, given the eucaryote vs. procaryote classification problem, since there is no need to distinguish between individual members of the *Bacteria* or *Animal* groups: all animals are eucaryotes and all bacteria are procaryotes. The transformation could, for example, be $G_{Animals} \circ G_{Bacteria} \circ G_{Plants} \circ G_{Fungi} \circ \ldots$ resulting in combining all the various direct specializations of *Organisms*, but never combining all the organisms.

The transformation in this example will affect the classification in at least two ways. Every feature that is a member of, for example, the *Animals* subtree is replaced with the feature *Animals*. Considering, for example, the maximum-likelihood probability estimate of the naive Bayes classifier, the replacement alleviates the data sparseness problem, because the classifier no longer needs to estimate the class-wise probabilities separately for every individual *Animals* feature. Further, when a document instance is being classified and its feature multiset contains some animal feature, but the particular animal was not encountered during the training of the classifier, the unknown feature can be used in the classification, because due to the transformation $G_{Animals}$ it "inherits" the class-wise characteristics of the feature *Animals*.

2.4 Evaluation Function E

The greedy algorithm introduced in Section 2.3 assumes an evaluation function E which can be used to evaluate how well a mapping fulfills the criteria represented by the function E. Here we define the function E in terms of cross-validated classification performance of a classifier using the mapped features on some text classification problem.

Let R be a set of labeled training examples, and let $r \in R$ be a training example. Let further $X_r \subseteq F$ be a multiset of features associated with the example r. Let us assume a classifier $\mathcal{C}\colon 2^F \to \mathbb{N}$ that assigns a class label to the instance r, based on its associated feature multiset X_r. Then, for each feature transformation mapping M, we can define $E(M)$ to be, for example, the average accuracy of $\mathcal{C}$ when performing a 10-fold cross-validation experiment using the set R. For each instance r and its associated feature multiset X_r, the class is computed as $\mathcal{C}(M(X_r))$.

3 Application to a Document Classification Problem

We apply the method to the problem of classifying MEDLINE-indexed documents. The set of transformations Λ is thus instantiated on the MeSH ontology. The evaluation function E is defined in terms of the naive Bayes classifier.

3.1 The MeSH Ontology

The MeSH (Medical Subject Headings) is the National Library of Medicine's (NLM) controlled vocabulary of medical and biological terms. MeSH terms are organized in a hierarchy that contains the most general terms (such as *Chemicals and Drugs*) at the top and the most specific terms (such as *Aspirin*) at the bottom. There are 21,973 main headings, termed *descriptors*, in the MeSH.

Publications in the MEDLINE database are manually indexed by NLM using MeSH terms, with typically 10–12 descriptors assigned to each publication. Hence, the MeSH annotation defines for each publication a highly descriptive set of features. Of the over 7 million MEDLINE publications that contain abstracts, more than 96% are currently indexed.

3.2 Feature Extraction from MeSH-Annotated MEDLINE Documents

An occurrence of a term in the MeSH hierarchy is not unique: a term may appear more than once in the hierarchy, as a member of different subtrees. For example the term *Neurons* appears in the subtrees *Cells* and *Nervous system*. The MEDLINE documents are annotated using MeSH terms, rather than their unique subtree numbers, and thus it is not possible to distinguish between the possible instances of the term in the MeSH hierarchy. We separate the ambiguous term occurrences by renaming them, for example, to *Neurons1* and *Neurons2*. When extracting the features (MeSH terms) of a MEDLINE document, we include all possible instances of the ambiguous term occurrence. Thus, a document annotated with the MeSH term *Neurons* will be represented as having two features: *Neurons1* and *Neurons2*. In the following, we will consider the MeSH hierarchy where all ambiguous occurrences of terms have been renamed and thus a term occurrence in this modified MeSH hierarchy is unique. The modified MeSH hierarchy contains 39,853 descriptors. Since the MeSH hierarchy consists of 15 separate trees, we also introduce a single root for the hierarchy.

3.3 Experimental Setup

In the empirical evaluation of the method, we consider the following classification problem. We randomly select 10 journals that have at least 2000 documents indexed in the MEDLINE database. For each of these 10 journals, 2000 random documents were retrieved from MEDLINE. The classification task is to assign a document to the correct journal, that is, to the journal in which the document was published. The 10 journals form 10 classification datasets, each having 2000 positive examples and 18000 negative examples formed by the documents belonging to the other 9 journals. The proportion of positive and negative examples is thus 1:9 in each of the datasets.

From the possible elementary transformations presented in Section 2.2, we only consider the generalization to a feature presented in Section 2.2, since the transformation that omits a feature is closely related to a standard and well researched feature-selection technique. The generalization up to a level was tested in our early experiments, but it proved out to be clearly less effective than the generalization to a feature transformation. This is in agreement with the findings of Scott and Matwin ([5]). However, note that the MeSH hierarchy requires 10 L-transformations only, whereas up to 11,335 G-transformations need to be evaluated in each step of the greedy algorithm.[6] Adopting the generalization to a feature transformations thus increases the computational requirements significantly.

We use the area under the precision-recall curve (AUC) induced by a leave-one-out cross-validation experiment using the naive Bayes classifier as the value of the evaluation function E. The area under the precision-recall curve is the average precision over the whole recall range. The AUC is directly related to

[6] The modified MeSH tree has depth 10 and 11,335 non-leaf nodes.

the well-known 11-point average precision (see, e.g., Witten and Frank ([7])). To avoid the variance at the extremities of the curve, we use a trimmed AUC only considering the area from 10% recall to 90% recall. We construct the curve by ordering the classified documents in descending order by the positive vs. negative class probability ratio of the naive Bayes classifier and computing the precision and recall values at each of the documents. An important property of the naive Bayes classifier is that it allows implementation of an $O(n)$ complexity leave-one-out cross-validation. A fast implementation of the leave-one-out cross-validation is necessary, since it is performed in each round of the greedy algorithm for each possible elementary transformation. We chose the leave-one-out cross-validation scheme to ensure high stability of the function E, avoiding the variance induced by the random dataset split in, for example, 10-fold cross-validation. Since most of the individual elementary transformations have only a very small effect on the performance, it is important to obtain an accurate and stable measure of the performance in order to distinguish even small gain from noise. The stopping criteria parameter θ is set $\theta = 10^{-4}$.

We cross-validate the results for each of the 10 journal datasets separately, using the 5×2cv cross-validation methodology introduced by Dietterich ([8]). The 5×2cv test performs five replications of a 2-fold cross-validation. In each fold, we use the training set data to build the transformation mapping, as described in Section 2.4, and then, using the transformation mapping and the training set data, we estimate the performance of the classifier on the test set data. The test set data is not used during the search for the mapping nor during the training of the classifier. Each of the 5 cross-validation replications consists of two folds. For each fold we measure the standard untrimmed AUC, unlike in the case of the function E, and then average the AUC of the two folds. The performance of the 5 replications is then averaged to obtain the final cross-validated measure of the classification performance for one dataset. To test for statistical significance, we use the robust 5x2cv test (Alpaydın, [9]), since the standard t-test would give misleading results due to the dependency problem of cross-validation.

As the baseline, we use the naive Bayes classifier with no feature transformation applied. In both cases the method introduced by Ng ([10]) was used to smooth the maximum-likelihood estimate of the probabilities for the naive Bayes classifier. The Ng's method is commonly applied in text classification tasks and it does not interfere with the $O(n)$ implementation of leave-one-out cross-validation for the naive Bayes classifier.

3.4 Empirical Results

The results for the 10 datasets are presented in Table 1.

For 6 datasets, the transformed feature hierarchy results in a statistically significant ($p < 0.05$) increase of the classification performance. Note that for two of the other datasets (datasets 2 and 5) the baseline performance is very close to 100% leaving little room for significant improvement. For the dataset 2, the transformed feature hierarchy results in a negligible decrease of the classification performance.

Table 1. The classification performance of the naive Bayes classifier. First, the untrimmed AUC percentages are given for the baseline and transformed features. The column denoted Δ is the improvement over the baseline. The column p is the p-value of the 5×2cv statistical significance test. Statistical significance ($p < 0.05$) is denoted in bold face. The column *rnds* is the average number of elementary transformations applied by the greedy algorithm, and the column *TS* is the average size of the transformed MeSH tree as a percentage of the original size of 39,853 nodes (see Section 3.4 for discussion)

#	Journal ID	AUC [%] Baseline	AUC [%] Transf.	Δ [%]	p	rnds	*TS* [%]
1	ActaAnatBasel	87.15	88.05	0.90	**0.043**	9.0	76.5
2	ApplEnvironMicrobiol	98.28	98.26	-0.02	0.535	0.2	99.7
3	BiolPsychiatry	95.14	95.70	0.56	**0.001**	5.0	80.3
4	EurJObstetGynecol.	91.21	92.31	1.10	**0.006**	8.7	73.0
5	FedRegist	99.48	99.48	0.00	undef.	0.0	100.0
6	JPathol	81.71	82.94	1.23	**0.003**	13.3	84.2
7	NipponRinsho	65.41	67.24	1.83	**0.017**	30.4	75.6
8	PresseMed	51.06	51.38	0.32	0.503	31.4	79.3
9	SchweizRundschMedPrax	58.95	61.53	2.58	**0.029**	25.8	68.4
10	ToxicolLett	88.93	89.12	0.19	0.403	5.5	92.0

Depending primarily on the number of transformations taken, the processing time varies from 3 minutes (no transformations taken) to 1 hour 45 minutes (44 transformations taken) for each fold, using a 2.8GHz processor.

The G-transformation used in the experimental evaluation can also be considered in terms of dimensionality reduction, since a G_a-transformation causes all features in $\mathcal{S}(a)$ to be replaced with a, hence the classifier never encounters any feature $f \in \mathcal{S}(a)$. The column TS of Table 1 presents the size of the tree when the features f are considered as removed. A reduction to about 80% of the tree size can be typically observed.

4 Discussion

To study the effect of dataset size on the performance of the method, we repeated the experiment for several smaller datasets. We observed, however, no systematic behavior of the 10 datasets with respect to dataset size.

Figure 2 demonstrates a rather good outcome of a classification experiment[7] for a single dataset, where the precision of the classifier with the transformed features is higher than the baseline over the whole recall range. In the experiments, however, it was often the case that the two curves crossed in at least one point, meaning that the transformed features increase the precision only on certain intervals of the recall range, while on other intervals the precision decreases. In such a case, the AUC values of the two curves are roughly similar,

[7] The curves represent a real experiment, however.

yielding a more conservative estimate of the performance than the accuracy at any single point on the curve. A full evaluation of the performance of the method for a single dataset thus ideally requires an analysis of the full precision-recall characteristic of the classifier.

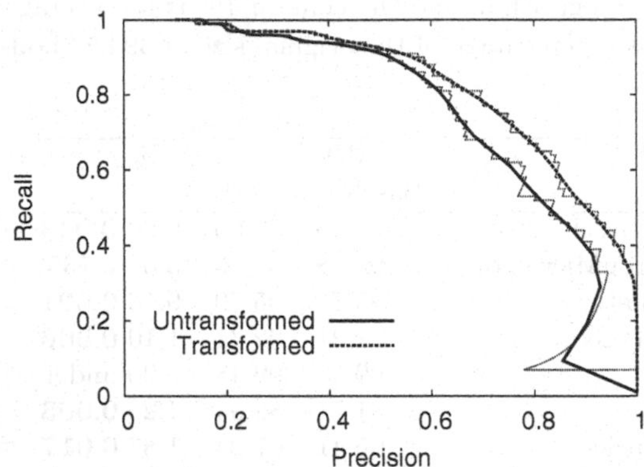

Fig. 2. An example of precision-recall curves of a classifier with transformed and untransformed features. The data is smoothed with a Bézier curve

The proposed method assumes that the features are organized in some hierarchical ontology. This, however, is not a prohibitive restriction, since any natural language text can be mapped to a general ontology such as WordNet. There also exists a biomedical ontology, the UMLS, which is provided with a tool for mapping unannotated text to the ontology, the MetaMap program. Such a mapping involves several issues, such as ambiguities in the text or the ontology, that can introduce errors into the feature extraction process. A further evaluation of the method on classification tasks involving features obtained by automatic mapping of a free text to an ontology is thus necessary.

The G-transformation used in the empirical evaluation of the method can be viewed as a binary semantic similarity measure, that is, two words can be either synonymous or semantically unrelated. This binary approach can be seen as a special case of a weighted approach, where the weights expressing the strength of a relationship between two words are 1 or 0. Future research can thus be directed to devise methods that compute finer-grained similarity representation tailored to the problem at hand.

5 Conclusions

In this paper we present a novel approach to incorporate semantic information to the problems of natural language processing, in particular to the document classification task. We devise a theoretical framework in which the semantic information is incorporated in the form of ontology-based feature transformations. We introduce several elementary transformations and an algorithm that identifies a beneficial transformation as a composition of elementary transformations. In order to obtain a feature transformation that is optimized both for the data and the classification method used, we define an evaluation function E that directs the greedy search in terms of the same classification method that is applied to the classification task. This is analogous to the wrapper approach of John et al. ([6]).

To test the method empirically, we apply it to a classification problem on MeSH-annotated documents. The empirical results show that the method is capable of statistically significant improvement of performance in 6 out of 10 datasets. In two datasets the improvement was not statistically significant, and for the remaining two datasets no significant improvement can be expected due to the very high baseline performance.

While the results indicate that the presented greedy algorithm is sufficient to validate the concept of feature transformations, it must repeatedly evaluate a potentially large number of elementary transformations, which makes it computationally expensive relative to the baseline method. Further research should thus be directed to devise better search strategies that result in a more efficient algorithm. For example, the search space could be reduced by exploiting the fact that the features are organized in a hierarchy. The search should also attempt to avoid stopping in local optima. Various forms of elementary transformations and evaluation functions E can also be studied. The results show that some datasets benefit more from the method than others. Further work should therefore be directed to study the properties of the data that determine whether a beneficial transformation can be found and how big an improvement can be achieved for the given dataset.

6 Acknowledgments

This work has been supported by Tekes, the Finnish National Technology Agency.

References

1. Rada, R., Bicknell, E.: Ranking documents with a thesaurus. Journal of the American Society for Information Science **40** (1989) 304–310
2. Resnik, P.: Using information content to evaluate semantic similarity in a taxonomy. In Mellish, C., ed.: Proceedings of the 14th International Joint Conference on Artificial Intelligence, Morgan Kaufmann, San Francisco (1995) 448–453
3. Budanitsky, A.: Lexical semantic relatedness and its application in natural language processing. Technical Report CSRG390, University of Toronto (1999)
4. Baker, D., McCallum, A.: Distributional clustering of words for text classification. In Croft, W.B., Moffat, A., van Rijsbergen, C.J., Wilkinson, R., Zobel, J., eds.: Proceedings of the 21st Annual International ACM SIGIR Conference on Research and Development in Information Retrieval, ACM Press, New York (1998) 96–103

5. Scott, S., Matwin, S.: Text classification using WordNet hypernyms. In Harabagiu, S., ed.: Use of WordNet in Natural Language Processing Systems: Proceedings of the Conference. Association for Computational Linguistics, Somerset, New Jersey (1998) 38–44
6. John, G.H., Kohavi, R., Pfleger, K.: Irrelevant features and the subset selection problem. In Cohen, W.W., Hirsh, H., eds.: Proceedings of the 11th International Conference on Machine Learning, Morgan Kaufmann, San Francisco (1994) 121–129
7. Witten, I.H., Frank E.: Data Mining. Morgan Kauffman, San Francisco (2000)
8. Dietterich, T.G.: Approximate statistical test for comparing supervised classification learning algorithms. Neural Computation **10** (1998) 1895–1923
9. Alpaydm, E.: Combined 5 × 2 cv F test for comparing supervised classification learning algorithms. Neural Computation **11** (1999) 1885–1892
10. Ng, H.T.: Exemplar-based word sense disambiguation: Some recent improvements. In Cardie, C., Weischedel, R., eds.: Proceedings of the Second Conference on Empirical Methods in Natural Language Processing, Association for Computational Linguistics, Somerset, New Jersey (1997) 208–213

On the Quality of Lexical Resources for Word Sense Disambiguation

Lluís Màrquez[1], Mariona Taulé[2], Lluís Padró[1],
Luis Villarejo[1], and Maria Antònia Martí[2]

[1] TALP Research Center, LSI Department
Universitat Politècnica de Catalunya
{lluism,padro,luisv}@lsi.upc.es
[2] Centre de Llenguatge i Computació (CLiC)
Universitat de Barcelona
{mtaule,amarti}@ub.edu

Abstract. Word Sense Disambiguation (WSD) systems are usually evaluated by comparing their absolute performance, in a fixed experimental setting, to other alternative algorithms and methods. However, little attention has been paid to analyze the lexical resources and the corpora defining the experimental settings and their possible interactions with the overall results obtained. In this paper we present some experiments supporting the hypothesis that the quality of lexical resources used for tagging the training corpora of WSD systems partly determines the quality of the results. In order to verify this initial hypothesis we have developed two kinds of experiments. At the linguistic level, we have tested the quality of lexical resources in terms of the annotators' agreement degree. From the computational point of view, we have evaluated how those different lexical resources affect the accuracy of the resulting WSD classifiers. We have carried out these experiments using three different lexical resources as sense inventories and a fixed WSD system based on Support Vector Machines.

1 Introduction

Natural Language Processing applications have to face ambiguity resolution problems at many levels of the linguistic processing. Among them, semantic (or lexical) ambiguity resolution is a currently open challenge, which would be potentially very beneficial for many NLP applications requiring some kind of *language understanding*, e.g., Machine Translation and Information Extraction/Retrieval systems [1].

The goal of WSD systems is to assign the correct semantic interpretation to each word in a text, which basically implies the automatic identification of its sense. In order to be able to address the WSD task, electronic dictionaries and lexicons, and semantically tagged corpora are needed. We assume that these linguistic resources are fundamental to successfully carry out WSD.

One of the approaches to WSD is the *supervised*, in which statistical or Machine Learning (ML) techniques are applied to automatically induce, from se-

J. L. Vicedo et al. (Eds.): EsTAL 2004, LNAI 3230, pp. 291–302, 2004.

mantically annotated corpora, a classification model for sense disambiguation. This approach is typically confronted with the *knowledge-based* approach (also referred sometimes as *unsupervised*[1]) in which some external knowledge sources (e.g., WordNet, dictionaries, parallel corpora, etc.) are used to devise some heuristic rules to perform sense disambiguation, avoiding the use of a manually annotated corpus. Despite the appeal of the unsupervised approach, it has been observed through a substantial body of comparative work, carried out mainly in the Senseval exercises[2], that the ML-based supervised techniques tend to overcome the results of the knowledge–based approach when enough training examples are available. In this paper we will concentrate on the quality of the resources needed to train supervised systems.

We consider that there are two critical points in the supervised WSD process which have been neglected, and are determinant when good results want to be reached: first, the quality of the lexical sources and, second, the quality of the manually tagged corpora. Moreover, the quality of these corpora is determined, to a large extent, by the quality of the lexical source used for carry out the tagging process. Our research has focused both on the evaluation of three different lexical sources: *Diccionario de la Real Academia Española* (DRAE, [2]), MiniDir (MD, [3]), and Spanish WordNet (SWN, [4]), and on how these resources determine the results of the machine learning-based methods for word sense disambiguation.

The methodology followed for the evaluation of the lexical sources is based on the parallel tagging of a single corpus by three different annotators for each lexical source. The annotators' agreement degree will be used for measuring the lexical source quality: the more agreement there is, the more quality the source will have. Thus, a high agreement would indicate that the senses in the lexical source are clearly defined and have a wide coverage. This methodology guarantees objectivity in the treatment of senses.

For measuring the influence of lexical sources in supervised WSD systems, we trained and tested a system based on Support Vector Machines (SVM, [5, 6]) using each of the lexical resources. Results are compared both straightforwardly and after a sense clustering process which intends to compensate for the advantage of disambiguating against a fine-grained resource such as WordNet lexical database or DRAE dictionary.

The rest of the paper is divided into two main parts. The first one is devoted to the analysis of the quality of lexical sources (section 2) and the second one aims at testing whether the best results in the first phase correlate with the best results obtained by the supervised word sense disambiguation system (section 3).

---

[1] This term is rather confusing since in machine learning terminology, *unsupervised* refers to a learning scenario from unnanotated examples (in which the class labels are omitted). In that case, the goal is to induce clusters of examples, representing the underlying classes.

[2] Senseval is a series of evaluation exercises for Word Sense Disambiguation organized by the ACL-SIGLEX. See `http://www.senseval.org` for more information.

Finally, in section 4 we present the main conclusions drawn and some lines for future work.

2 Lexical Resources Evaluation

Several authors have carried out studies with the aim of proposing specific models and methodologies for the elaboration of lexical sources oriented to WSD tasks. A very outstanding proposal is that of Véronis [7], in which the validity of traditional lexical representation of senses is questioned. This author proposes a model of lexical source suitable for WSD based mainly on syntactic criteria. Kilgarriff [8] developed an experiment on semantic tagging, with the aim to define the upper-bound in manual tagging. In that paper, the upper bound was established at 95% of annotators' agreement. Krishnamurthy and Nichols [9] analyze the process of the gold-standard corpus tagging for Senseval-2, highlighting the most common inconsistencies of dictionaries: incorrect sense division, definition errors, etc. Fellbaum et al. [10] analyze the process of semantic tagging with a lexical resource such as WordNet, but focusing on those features they consider as a source of difficulty: the lexical category, the order of the senses in the lexical source, and the annotators' profile. All the authors highlight the importance of the lexical source as an essential factor in order to obtain quality results. The aim of our research has been to evaluate the quality of lexical resources and test its influence in the quality of results of WSD based on machine learning techniques.

The methodology followed in this work for the evaluation of the lexical resources consists in the manual semantic tagging of a single corpus with three different lexical sources: DRAE, MiniDir, and Spanish WordNet. The tagging process has been carried out by different annotators. This methodology allows us to analyze comparatively the results obtained for each of the lexical sources and, therefore, to determine which of them is the most suitable for WSD tasks. Our starting point is the hypothesis that the annotator agreement degree is proportional to the quality level of the lexical resource: the more agreement there is the more quality has the lexical source.

The evaluated lexical sources present very different characteristics and have been selected for different reasons. Firstly, we have used the *Diccionario de la Real Academia Española*, as it is the reference and normative dictionary of Spanish language. Secondly, *MiniDir-2.1* is a lexicon designed specifically for automatic WSD. This lexical source contains a limited number of entries (50) which have been elaborated specifically as a resource for the Senseval-3 Spanish Lexical Sample Task[3]. Finally, we have also used *Spanish WordNet* as sense repository, since WordNet is one of the most used lexical resources for WSD.

We have performed all the evaluation and comparative experiments using the following subset of ten lexical entries (see the most common translations into English between parentheses). Four nouns: *columna* (column), *corazón* (heart),

[3] See `www.lsi.upc.es/~nlp/senseval-3/Spanish.html` for more information.

SOURCE:MiniDir-2.1; LEMMA:*columna*; POS:ncmfs; SENSE:**1**; DEFINITION:*figura arquitectónica de forma cilíndrica que sirve como soporte o elemento decorativo*; EXAMPLE:*una gran columna de hormigón; una antigua columna del tiempo de los romanos*; SYNONYMS:*manejar*; COLLOCATIONS: *columna_corintia, columna_de_bronce, columna_de_mármol, columna_de_piedra, columna_dórica, columna_griega, columna_jónica*; SYNSETS:02326166n/02326665n/02881716n; DRAE:1

SOURCE:MiniDir-2.1; LEMMA:*columna*; POS:ncmfs; SENSE:**4**; DEFINITION:*forma cilíndrica que toman algunos fluidos o gases cuando ascienden o cuando están contenidos en un cilindro*; EXAMPLE:*una densa columna de humo*; SYNONYMS:?; COLLOCATIONS:*columna_de_agua, columna_de_humo*; SYNSETS: 08508248n; DRAE:3/5

Fig. 1. Example of two Minidir-2.1 lexical entries for *columna*

letra (letter), and *pasaje* (passage). Two adjectives: *ciego* (blind) and *natural* (natural). Four verbs: *apoyar* (to lean/rest; to rely on), *apuntar* (to point/aim; to indicate; to make a note), *explotar* (to exploit; to explode), and *volar* (to fly; to blow up). See more information on these words in table 2.

2.1 The Lexical Sources

In the development of MiniDir-2.1 we have basically taken into account information extracted from corpora. We have used the corpora from the newspapers *El Periódico* and *La Vanguardia*, with a total of 3.5 million and 12.5 million words, respectively, and also Lexesp [11]. The latter is a balanced corpus of 5.5 million words, which includes texts on different topics (science, economics, justice, literature, etc.), written in different styles (essay, novel, etc.) and different language registers (standard, technical, etc.). The corpora provide quantitative and qualitative information which is essential to differentiate senses and to determine the degree of lexicalization. As regards the information of the entries of the dictionary, every sense is organized into the nine following lexical fields: LEMMA, POS CATEGORY[4], SENSE, DEFINITION, EXAMPLE, SYNONYMS (plus ANTONYMS in the case of adjectives), COLLOCATIONS, SYNSETS, DRAE. Figure 1 shows an example of the first and fourth senses of the lexical entry *columna* (column) in MiniDir-2.1. As Minidir-2.1 has a low granularity, in general, its senses correspond to multiple senses in Spanish WordNet. For instance, we can observe that the sense *columna_1* corresponds to three Spanish WordNet synsets (02326166n, 02326665n, and 02881716n).

Because of MiniDir2.1 is a lexical resource build up taking into account WSD, it includes additional information like examples and collocations. Such information, which is not present in the other sources, is potentially very useful for performing word sense disambiguation.

[4] The lexical category is represented by the Eagle tags (Eureka 1989-1995) which have been abridged.

SOURCE:DRAE; LEMMA:*columna*; POS:ncmfs; SENSE:**3**; DEFINITION:*forma que toman algunos fluidos, en su movimiento ascendente. Columna de fuego, de humo*; ... SYNSETS:08508248n; MiniDir-2.1:4

SOURCE:DRAE; LEMMA:*columna*; POS:ncmfs; SENSE:**5**; DEFINITION:*porción de fluido contenido en un cilindro*; ... SYNSETS:08508248n; MiniDir-2.1:4

Fig. 2. Two simplified DRAE lexical entries for the word *columna*

DRAE is a normative dictionary of Spanish language which has not been designed for the computational treatment of language nor word sense disambiguation. Entries have been adapted to the format required by the semantic tagging editor [12] used in the manually semantic tagging. DRAE presents also a high level of granularity and overlapping among definitions. Many senses belong to specific domains and it is also frequent to find outdated senses. Figure 2 contains an example of DRAE entries for senses 3 and 5 of the word *columna* (columna).

The third lexical source we have used is the Spanish WordNet lexical database. It was developed inside the framework of EuroWordNet [4] and includes paradigmatic information (hyperonymy, hyponymy, synonymy, and meronymy). As it is well known, this lexical knowledge base is characterized by its fine granularity and the overlapping of senses, which makes more difficult the annotation process. Spanish WordNet was developed following a semiautomatic methodology [4], which took as reference the English version (WordNet 1.5). Since there is not a one to one correspondence between the senses of both languages, some mismatches appeared in the mapping process. In spite of Spanish WordNet has been checked many times, some mismatches remain and this explains the lack of some senses in Spanish and the excessive granularity for others.

2.2 The Tagging Process

The annotated corpus used for evaluating the different lexical sources (DRAE, MiniDir 2.1 and Spanish WordNet) is the subset of the MiniCors [13] corpus corresponding to the ten selected words. MiniCors was compiled from the corpus of the EFE Spanish News Agency, which includes 289,066 news spanning from January to December of 2000[5], and it has been used as source for the Senseval-3 Spanish Lexical Sample task [14]. The MiniCors corpus contains a minimum of 200 examples for each of the represented words. The context considered for each word is larger than a sentence, as the previous and the following sentences were also included. For each word, the goal was to collect a minimum of 15 occurrences per sense from available corpora, which was not always possible. At the end, only the senses with a sufficient number of examples were included in the final version of the corpus.

The tagging process was carried out by experienced lexicographers and it was developed individually, so as to avoid interferences. Also, the authors of the

[5] The size of the complete EFE corpus is 2,814,291 sentences, 95,344,946 words, with an average of 33.8 words per sentence.

dictionary did not participate in the tagging process. In order to systematize and simplify the annotation process to the utmost, a tagging handbook specifying annotation criteria was designed in an initial phase [12], and a graphical Perl-Tk interface was programmed in order to assist the tagging process. See [14] for more details on the construction and annotation of the MiniCors corpus.

The 10–word subset of MiniCors treated in this paper has been annotated with the senses of DRAE and Spanish WordNet, in addition to the MiniDir-2.1 original annotations. Again, each word has been annotated by three different expert lexicographers in order to facilitate the manual arbitration phase, which was reduced only to cases of disagreement. The annotators could assign more than one tag to the same occurrence in order to reflect more precisely the different agreement degrees.

2.3 Evaluation and Arbitration

Once the corpus has been tagged, we have carried out a comparative study among the different annotations and the subsequent evaluation of the results in order to obtain a disambiguated corpus to begin with the evaluation of the lexical sources. Since each word has been tagged three times for each lexical source, the subsequent process of arbitration has been reduced to those cases of disagreement among the three annotators.

We distinguish 4 different situations of agreement/disagreement between annotators: *total agreement*, *partial agreement*, *minimum agreement*, and *disagreement*. Total agreement takes place when the three annotations completely match (e.g.: 1, 1, 1 ⇒ 1). When not all the annotations match but there is a individual sense assigned by all annotators we get partial agreement (e.g.: 1, 1, 1/2 ⇒ 1; 1/2, 1/2, 1 ⇒ 1). Minimum agreement occurs when two annotations match but the other one is different (e.g.: 1, 1, 2 ⇒ 1). Finally, disagreement is produced when none of the annotations match. These agreement cases, either total, partial or minimum, are validated automatically according to the pattern we have previously defined. Only cases of disagreement undergo a manual arbitration phase. We have considered also the pairwise agreements between annotators for the analysis of results. The measure Pairwise Agreement counts the average of the agreement levels between each pair of annotators. In this case, we distinguish among *Minimum Pairwise Agreement* (cases of total agreement among every pair of annotators) and *Maximum Pairwise Agreement* (cases of partial agreement among each pair of annotators).

Table 1 shows the results obtained on each of the previous measures for each sense repository and for each POS category. *NumSenses* is the average number of senses assigned by the annotators.

2.4 Analysis of the Results

The tagging experiments presented in table 1 show that the lexical source which has been designed with specific criteria for WSD, MiniDir-2.1, reaches much higher Total Agreement levels in the manual tagging of corpus than Spanish

Table 1. Per POS category and global annotation agreements using Spanish WordNet, MiniDir-2.1, and DRAE sources

Nouns	SWN	MD-2.1	DRAE	**Adjectives**	SWN	MD-2.1	DRAE
TotAgr	0.64	0.83	0.57	TotAgr	0.15	0.67	0.24
PartAgr	0.12	0.03	0.18	PartAgr	0.42	0.06	0.51
MinAgr	0.20	0.14	0.23	MinAgr	0.33	0.26	0.23
DisAgr	0.04	0.00	0.02	DisAgr	0.10	0.01	0.02
MaxPairAgr	0.83	0.90	0.83	MaxPairAgr	0.70	0.81	0.84
MinPairAgr	0.72	0.88	0.70	MinPairAgr	0.32	0.77	0.69
NumSenses	1.10	1.02	1.08	NumSenses	1.56	1.03	1.12

Verbs	SWN	MD-2.1	DRAE	**Overall**	SWN	MD-2.1	DRAE
TotAgr	0,34	0,66	0,53	TotAgr	0,42	0,72	0,45
PartAgr	0,30	0,08	0,08	PartAgr	0,25	0,06	0,25
MinAgr	0,34	0,25	0,36	MinAgr	0,28	0,21	0,28
DisAgr	0,02	0,01	0,03	DisAgr	0,05	0,01	0,02
MaxPairAgr	0,78	0,83	0,74	MaxPairAgr	0,77	0,85	0,80
MinPairAgr	0,47	0,76	0,67	MinPairAgr	0,50	0,80	0,69
NumSenses	1,53	1,03	1,05	NumSenses	1,39	1,03	1,08

WordNet or DRAE, which stand for lexical sources of common use. The worst results have been obtained by Spanish WordNet, being slightly worse than those of DRAE. We can also analyze the results obtained through three related dimensions: the disagreement measure, the overlapping degree between senses, and the number of senses per entry.

Regarding the disagreement measure, Spanish WordNet has the highest score, 0.05, in front of the 0.02 from DRAE and 0.01 from MiniDir-2.1. That means that the arbitration phase in MiniDir-2.1 and DRAE has been done almost automatically, whereas in the case of Spanish WordNet more manual intervention has been applied. In Spanish WordNet and DRAE we find a high level of overlapping between senses because these dictionaries are very fine grained. These characteristics are reflected in the high numbers for the Partial Agreement measure (compared to MiniDir-2.1) and in the big differences between Maximum and Minimum Pairwise Agreement. This is partially a consequence of the fact that the 1.39 average number of senses assigned to each example in Spanish WordNet is the highest one compared to 1.08 from DRAE and 1.03 from MiniDir-2.1.

If we evaluate the results according to lexical categories, nouns achieve the highest levels of agreement probably because of their referents are more stable and clearly identifiable. As regards adjectives and verbs, the levels of agreement are lower, specially in Spanish WordNet.

The annotation with MiniDir-2.1 reaches results considerably acceptable (with an overall agreement higher than 80% if we sum Total and Partial Agreement cases) that prove their adequacy for WSD tasks. Among the MiniDir-2.1 characteristics that could explain the better results in the annotators agreement degree we should point out the fact that it contains both syntagmatic and co-occurrence information, that constitute determining factors in order to help annotators to decide the correct sense, as it can be seen in the entries for *columna* presented in figure 1.

3 Automatic Disambiguation Experiments

A supervised word sense disambiguation system based on Support Vector Machines has been trained and tested using each of the three lexical resources. This system is the core learning component of two participant systems to the Senseval-3 English Allwords and Lexical Sample tasks, which obtained very competitive results [6, 15].

Support Vector Machines is a learning algorithm for training linear classifiers. Among all possible separating hyperplanes, SVM selects the hyperplane that separates with maximal distance the positive examples from the negatives, i.e., the maximal margin hyperplane. By using kernel functions SVMs can be used also to efficiently work in a high dimensional feature space and learn non-linear classification functions. In our WSD setting, we simply used a linear separator, since some experiments on using polynomial kernels did not provide better results. We used the SVM^{light} freely available implementation by Joachims [5] and a simple one–vs–all binarization scheme to deal with the multiclass classification WSD problem.

Regarding feature representation of the training examples, we used the Feature Extraction module of the TALP team in the Senseval-3 English Lexical Sample task. The feature set includes the classic window–based pattern features extracted from a ±3-token local context and the "bag–of–words" type of features taken from a broader context. It also contains a set of features representing the syntactic relations involving the target word, and some semantic features of the surrounding words extracted from the Multilingual Central Repository of the Meaning project. See [15, 6] for more details about the learning algorithm and the feature engineering used.

We have been working with a total of 1,536 examples, which are the examples in the intersection of the three annotation sources. That means that some examples had to be eliminated from the original Senseval-3 sets, since they could not be assigned to any sense either in the DRAE or Spanish WordNet sense repositories. The training and test partitions have been obtained by randomly selecting 2/3 and 1/3 of the total number of examples, respectively. The total number of training examples is 1,094, while the number of test examples is 543. The number of observed senses for these 10 words (ambiguity rate) range from 3 to 13 depending on the lexical source. Note that, though the DRAE and Spanish WordNet are much more fine-grained than MiniDir-2.1, the difference in the number of senses actually observed in the examples is not dramatic (7.9 and 7.8 versus 5.7). Moreover, the average number of senses according to DRAE and Spanish WordNet are almost identical. See more information about the individual words in table 2.

Table 2. Basic information about the 10 selected words for training and evaluating the SVM-based WSD system

		Number of senses			examples	
word	POS	DRAE	MD-2.1	SWN	#train	#test
apoyar	v	5	3	6	140	51
apuntar	v	8	9	7	124	54
ciego	a	8	5	7	83	49
columna	n	7	8	9	127	63
corazón	n	8	6	8	113	58
explotar	v	6	5	7	131	53
letra	n	10	5	7	92	63
natural	a	9	6	13	92	46
pasaje	n	11	4	7	87	53
volar	v	7	6	7	105	53
avg./total	-	7.9	5.7	7.8	1,094	543

The multiplicity of labels in examples (see the 'NumSenses' row in table 1) has been addressed in the following way. When training, the examples have been replicated, one for each sense label. When testing, we have considered a correct prediction whenever the proposed label is any of the example labels.

The overall and per-word accuracy results obtained are presented in table 3. For each lexical source we include also the results of the baseline Most Frequent Sense classifier (MFS). It can be seen that the MFS results are fairly similar for all three annotation sources (from 46.78% to 47.88%), while the SVM-based systems clearly outperforms the MFS classifier in all three cases. The best results are obtained when using the MiniDir-2.1 lexical source (70.90%), followed by DRAE (67.22%) and Spanish WordNet (66.67%). This accuracy represents an increase of 24.12 percentage points over MFS and an error reduction of 45.32%.

Table 3. WSD results using all three sense repositories: DRAE, MD-2.1, and SWN. Columns 3, 5, and 7 contain the results of the MFS baseline (mosty-frequent sense classifier). Columns 4, 6, and 8 contain the results of the SVM–based system

		DRAE		MD-2.1		SWN	
word	POS	MFS	%ACC.	MFS	%ACC.	MFS	%ACC.
apoyar	v	92.16%	92.16%	88.24%	84.31%	80.39%	68.63%
apuntar	v	55.56%	66.67%	46.30%	68.52%	59.26%	85.19%
ciego	a	57.14%	71.43%	61.22%	75.51%	48.98%	71.43%
columna	n	22.22%	74.60%	20.63%	79.37%	38.10%	74.60%
corazón	n	37.93%	58.62%	43.10%	67.24%	46.55%	65.52%
explotar	v	43.40%	50.94%	43.40%	69.81%	41.51%	64.15%
letra	n	39.68%	61.90%	34.92%	60.32%	41.27%	53.97%
natural	a	58.70%	73.91%	47.83%	65.22%	34.78%	50.00%
pasaje	n	35.85%	60.38%	39.62%	77.36%	37.74%	64.15%
volar	v	47.17%	64.15%	52.83%	62.26%	41.51%	67.92%
average	-	47.88%	67.22%	46.78%	70.90%	46.78%	66.67%

Compared to the other lexical sources, the differences in favor of MiniDir-2.1 are statistically significant with a confidence level of 90% (using a z–test for the difference of two proportions). The difference between MiniDir-2.1 and Spanish WordNet is also significant at 95%. These results provide some empirical evidence which complements the one presented in the previous section. Not only human annotators achieve a higher agreement when using MiniDir, but also a supervised WSD system obtains better results when using this source for training.

Nevertheless, the advantage could be due to the fact that MiniDir-2.1 (5.7 senses/word in average) is a bit coarser grained than DRAE (7.9 senses/word) and WordNet (7.8) on the ten considered words. To compare the lexical resources on a more fair basis, it seems that a new evaluation metric is needed able to compensate for the difference on the number of senses. As a first approach, we clustered together the senses from all lexical sources, following the coarsest of the three (MiniDir-2.1). That is, each DRAE and Spanish WordNet sense was mapped to a MiniDir-2.1 sense, and any answer inside the same cluster was considered correct. This procedure required some manual work in the generation of the mappings between lexical sources. Some ad-hoc decisions were taken in order to correct inconsistencies induced by the more natural mappings between the three sources.

The evaluation according to the sense clusters leaded to some disappointing results. The best overall accuracy results were obtained by DRAE (72.62%), followed by Spanish WordNet (71.19%) and MiniDir-2.1 (70.48%). However, it is worth noting that none of this differences is statistically significant (at a confidence level of 90%). It remains to be studied if this lack of actual differences is due to the small number of examples used in our experiments, or to the fact that the dictionary used is not really affecting very much the achievable performance of supervised machine learning WSD systems. The way in which we addressed the problem of the multiple sense labels per example (see table 1 and above) may tend to favor the evaluation of the most fine-grained lexical sources (Spanish WordNet and DRAE), and partly explaining the lack of differences observed. We think that the design of other evaluation measures, independent of the number of senses and able to isolate the contribution of the lexical sources, deserves also further investigation.

4 Conclusions

In this study we have evaluated different lexical sources in order to determine the most adequate one for WSD tasks. The evaluation has consisted of the tagging of a single corpus with three different dictionaries and different annotators. The agreement degree among the annotators has been the determining criteria to establish the quality of the lexical source.

According to our experiments, MiniDir-2.1, the lexical source designed with specific criteria for WSD, reaches much higher agreement levels (above 80%) in the manual tagging of the corpus than Spanish WordNet or DRAE. The MiniDir-2.1 specific features that help explaining these differences are the following: 1) MiniDir-2.1 is coarser grained than DRAE and Spanish WordNet, avoiding to some extent the overlapping of senses; 2) It contains both syntagmatic and co-occurrence information, which help the annotators to decide the correct senses.

The evaluation of a SVM–based WSD classifier, trained on the three different lexical resources, seems to indicate that a reference dictionary with a higher agreement degree produces also better results for automatic disambiguation.

We also provide results of a first attempt in trying to evaluate the WSD systems with independence of the average number of senses per word, by means of a sense mapping and clustering across lexical sources. Unfortunately, these results showed no significant differences among lexical sources. Up to now, it remains unclear whether the increase in performance produced by the use of a lexical source specifically designed for WSD is mainly explained by the the higher quality of the lexical source or by the decrease on sense granularity. This is an issue that requires further research, including experiments on bigger corpora to produce statistically significant results and a careful design of the evaluation metrics used.

Acknowledgments

This research has been possible thanks to the support of Spanish and European research projects: BFF2002-04226-C03 (X-TRACT2), TIC2000-0335-C03-02 (Hermes), and IST-2001-34460 (Meaning). The team of annotators was composed by members of the research group CLiC of the *Universitat de Barcelona* (UB) and by members of Natural Language Group of the *Universidad Nacional de Educación a Distancia* (UNED).

References

1. Ide, N., Véronis, J.: Introduction to the special issue on word sense disambiguation: the state of the art. Computational Linguistics, Special issue on Word Sense Disambiguation **24** (1998) 1–40
2. Real Academia Española: *Diccionario de la lengua española*, 22nd edition, Madrid, Spain (2001)
3. Artigas, N., García, M., Martí, M., Taulé, M.: *Diccionario MiniDir-2.1.* Technical Report XTRACT2-WP-03/08, Centre de Llenguatge i Computaci (CLiC), Universitat de Barcelona (2003)
4. Vossen, P., ed.: EuroWordNet: A Multilingual Database with Lexical Semantic Networks. Kluwer Academic Publishers, Dordrecht (1999)
5. Joachims, T.: Making large–scale SVM learning practical. In Schölkopf, B., Burges, C.J.C., Smola, A.J., eds.: Advances in Kernel Methods — Support Vector Learning. MIT Press, Cambridge, MA (1999) 169–184
6. Villarejo, L., Màrquez, L., Agirre, E., Martínez, D., Magnini, B., Strapparava, C., McCarthy, D., Montoyo, A., Suárez, A.: The “Meaning” system on the english all-words task. In: Proceedings of the Senseval-3 ACL-SIGLEX Workshop, Barcelona, Spain (2004)
7. Véronis, J.: Sense tagging: does it make sense? In: Proceedings of the Corpus Linguistics’2001 Conference, Lancaster, U.K. (2001)

8. Kilgarriff, A.: 95% replicability for manual word sense tagging. In: Proceedings of the 9th Conference of the European Chapter of the Association for Computational Linguistics, EACL'99, Bergen, Norway (1999)
9. Krishnamurthy, R., Nicholls, D.: Peeling an onion: The lexicographer's experience of manual sense-tagging. Computers and the Humanities. Special Issue on Evaluating Word Sense Disambiguation Programs **34** (2000) 85–97
10. Fellbaum, C., Grabowsky, J., Landes, S.: Analysis of a hand-tagging task. In: Proceedings of the ANLP-97 Workshop on Tagging Text with Lexical Semantics: Why, What, and How?, Washington D.C., USA (1997)
11. Sebastián, N., Martí, M.A., Carreiras, M.F., Gómez, F.C.: *Lexesp, léxico informatizado del español.* Edicions de la Universitat de Barcelona, Barcelona (2000)
12. Artigas, N., García, M., Martí, M., Taulé, M.: *Manual de anotacin semántica.* Technical Report XTRACT2-WP-03/03, Centre de Llenguatge i Computaci (CLiC), Universitat de Barcelona (2003)
13. Taulé, M., Civit, M., Artigas, N., García, M., Màrquez, L., Martí, M., Navarro, B.: Minicors and cast3lb: Two semantically tagged soanish corpora. In: Proceedings of the 4th International Conference on Language Resources and Evaluation, LREC-2004, Lisbon, Portugal (2004)
14. Màrquez, L., Taulé, M., Martí, M.A., García, M., Artigas, N., Real, F., Ferrés, D.: Senseval-3: The spanish lexical sample task. In: Proceedings of the Senseval-3 ACL Workshop, Barcelona, Spain (2004)
15. Escudero, G., Màrquez, L., Rigau, G.: TALP system for the english lexical sample task. In: Proceedings of the Senseval-3 ACL Workshop, Barcelona, Spain (2004)

Reuse of Free Online MT Engines to Develop a Meta-system of Multilingual Machine Translation

Vo Trung Hung

Institut National Polytechnique de Grenoble
GETA-CLIPS-IMAG
385, rue de la Bibliothèque, 38041 Grenoble cedex 9, France
Hung.Vo-Trung@imag.fr

Abstract. We propose a method to develop a meta system of multilingual machine translation by reusing free online automatic translation engines. This system can process and translate a homogeneous or heterogeneous document (multilingual and multicoding). This system's purpose is to identify the language(s) and the coding(s) of the input text, to segment a heterogeneous text into several homogeneous zones, and to call a better MT engine for the target and source language pair and to retrieve the translated results in the desired language. This system can be used in several different applications, such as multilingual research, translation of the electronic mails, construction of multilingual Web sites, etc.

1 Introduction

Currently, there are several free online MT engines, like Systran, WorldLingo, Reverso... but these free versions limit the length of the entry text to less than 50-150 words. These engines only allow translating the monolinguals and monocoding texts or Web pages with a language pair determined in advance.

With the widespread use of Internet, we can receive the information written in several different languages (electronic mails, technical catalogues, notes, Web sites, and etc.) and the need for the translation of these texts in the mother tongues of users naturally arises. We can also receive information of which we don't know the language used in the text.

Moreover, the translation quality is a problem which users concern [3], [13]. To translate an English document into French, one can choose either Systran or the other engines (Reverso, WorldLingo, etc). How do we choose from the existing MT engines for our document?

Our principal idea is to construct a system which uses free online translation engines and to add on this system necessary functions such as, the identification of the language and the coding of the entry text, the segmentation of a heterogeneous text into homogeneous zones, the choice of a better translation engine for a language pair determined in advance and the parameterization in calling the translation engines.

We here present a method to develop a meta system of multilingual machine translation by reusing the free online automatic translation systems [15]. In the first part,

J. L. Vicedo et al. (Eds.): EsTAL 2004, LNAI 3230, pp. 303–313, 2004.

we present the general architecture of our system to translate automatically online documents. Next, we present an N-grams method of automatic identification of the language and coding of a text, and then the method of segmentation of a heterogeneous text in homogeneous zones. Furthermore we present a solution to choose a better MT engine for a source and target language pair based on the evaluation of the engines by the methods BLEU and NIST. Finally, we present a method to parameterize the MT engines and to retrieve the results. We also combine several MT engines and use English as pivot language to obtain a maximum number of language pairs. This system was adapted for several different systems of coding like BIG-5 (traditional Chinese), GB-2312 (simplified Chinese), Shift-JIS (Japanese), EUC-Kr (Korean), KOI-8, CP-1251 (Russian), etc. We can apply this system in several different domains such as multilingual research, the translation of the electronic mails, the construction of the multilingual Web sites, etc.

2 Objectives

Our first objective is to construct a tool to call these translation engines and to retrieve their results. We can use the parameters such as: language (source and target), coding, name of the translation engine to obtain different translation results of the same entry text. The second objective is to use the translation engines to develop multilingual applications. We can integrate these engines in a multilingual systems to translate texts, messages by executing out programs. We developed a Web site to translate the heterogeneous texts (containing multilingual and multilicoding segments) into the target language, even we don't know the language of the entry text. This tool makes it possible to translate any text into the desired language. If this text is heterogeneous, the system will segment the text and identify the language and the coding of each segment. For example, we can copy/paste a text containing several languages (English, Chinese, Japanese, etc.) and choose, for example, French as the target language. Or, we can look up sites containing a given word (in particular, technical terms) for example, if we enter the word "segment" as our keyword of research on Google, the result could contain the Web sites in several languages, such as French, English, German, etc, simply because they all happened to have used this word somewhere in their Web page. We can use this tool to read the results in the same language. We can also integrate this tool in several different applications such as the translation from the electronic mails, the generation of a message in several languages, the evaluation of quality of the MT engines, etc.

3 Free Online MT Engines

In this section we present some recent machine translation engines. We can access the systems to translate texts.

3.1 Systran

Currently, SYSTRAN is a well known translation engine and its technology ranges from the solutions of translation for Internet, PC and infrastructures of network with 36 language pairs and 20 different specialized fields. Systran is a translation engine used by European Community or NASA since long time, more recently, by some important Internet entry gates, such as AltaVista or Google. The online version can translate for 34 language pairs. It can be accessed at the address http://www.systranbox.com/.

3.2 Gist-in-Time

This is a tool developed by Alis Technologies Inc., for the Web environment and online companies. The users of Gist-In-Time benefit from the most level of comprehension available in Internet at present. It provide 17 language pairs (English <> French, English <> German, English <> Spanish, etc). We can access this translation system on the site of Gist-In-Time: http://www.teletranslator.com:8100/cgi-bin/transint.Fr.pl?AlisTargetHost=localhost.

3.3 Reverso

This tool can function in PC environment, Internet, Intranet, either as an autonomous application (for example, text processing) or as a translation engine directly integrated in an application (for example, in Word or Excel). The address of the site of Reverso is http://www.reverso.net/textonly/default.asp.

3.4 FreeTranslation

FreeTranslation is a product of SDL International, which provides the service of translation and localization of the applications. The translation server of SDL provides 15 language pairs on the site http://www.freetranslation.com/.

3.5 IBM Alphaworks

Alphaworks is an online automatic translation system, that dedicates its service in online Web page translation. The input data is actually the URL of the Web page starting with: http://www. It can translate Web pages into 12 language pairs and the address of the site of translation of Alphaworks is http://www.alphaworks.IBM.com/aw.nsf/html/m.

4 System Description

4.1 Structure of the System

We developed a tool to automatically translate texts (multilingual or monolingual) using the existing online translation engines. The architecture of the system is as follows:

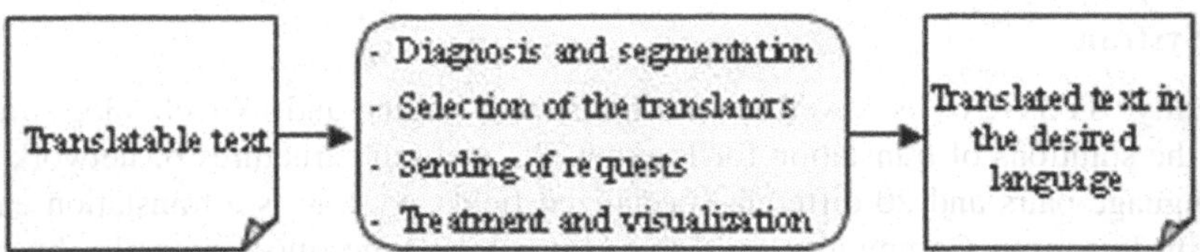

Fig. 1. Meta-system of multilingual machine translation

The input text can be a multilingual text or multicoding (one can copy/paste input data from several different Web sites, or the received texts can be heterogeneous). We extract each paragraph to diagnose the language and coding, and to send to the translation servers since these servers often accept only the text no longer than 150 words. If the paragraph is monolingual, we immediately send it to the servers, otherwise it is necessary to segment it in monolingual zones, each one corresponding to one or more sentences.

4.2 Diagnostic and Segmentation

We developed a tool SANDOH (System of Analysis of the Heterogeneous Documents) [14] to analyze a heterogeneous text by using the method of N-grams and method of the progressive segmentation to segment a heterogeneous text in homogeneous zones. The result of the analysis is the couple <language, coding> if this document is homogeneous, otherwise, the zones and the couple <language, coding> used in each zone {zone-1, language-1, coding-1}, {zone-2, language-2, coding-2},..., {zone-n, language-n, coding-n}. A demonstration of this tool is accessible online at the following address http://www-clips.imag.fr/geta/User/hung.vo-trung/id_langue/web_fr/index.htm. To segment a text, we use a technique of progressive segmentation based on the punctuation marks. Normally, the parts written in different languages are separated by punctuation marks such as the period, the indent, the colons, the bracket, the quotation mark, the point of exclamation, the semicolon, etc. The idea here is that after having evaluated a zone, if it is heterogeneous, one continues to separate this zone into smaller zones and to further evaluate these zones. But it should be made sure that these zones will not be too short for the identification. Initially, we evaluate each paragraph (the termination of each paragraph is the sign of End of Line "EOL") to detect whether the paragraph is homogeneous or heterogeneous. If it is homogeneous, one continues analyzing next paragraph, if not, it is necessary to segment this paragraph into two zones. It is enough to separate the text in the medium and then to test what happens when one moves of a word towards the left or the right-hand side until obtaining that each zone contains a whole of sentences. We continue to evaluate and separate this zone in smaller zones and to evaluate until we obtain a homogeneous zone. The identification of the language and coding is carried out as the diagram below shows [12]:

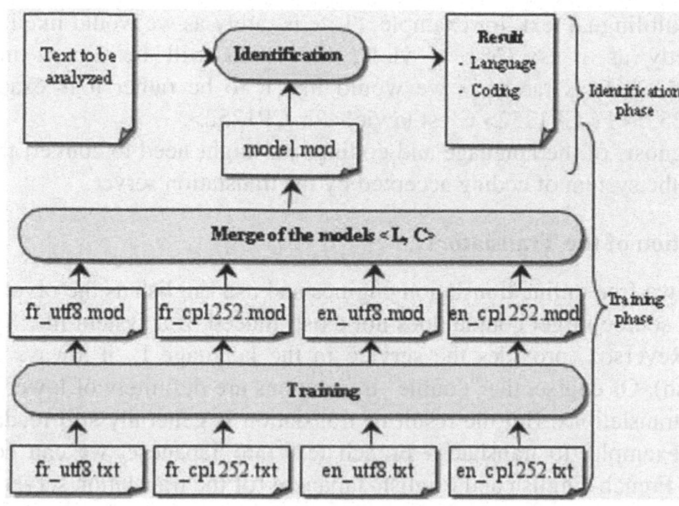

Fig. 2. General architecture of an identifier of language and coding

The phase of training is built on the basis of statistical model. At the beginning, one must have files annotated by beacons <language, coding>. The module of training then creates the "models" corresponding to each couple <language, coding>. These models are built based on the frequency of the sequences, which one counted in the file of training. Then we can fusion all these model files into a unified file that contains all the language and coding distribution models. This file will be used to identify the other texts in the future. The phase of identification will determine in which language a text is written and with which coding. It uses the same method by comparing segments in the text to be analyzed with sequences of the model of languages to evaluate the text to be analyzed. Here is an example of diagnostic result (table of scores) of a French text *"les chiens et les chats sont des animaux"* and a Chinese text 地是空虚混沌。渊面黑暗。神的灵运行在水面上 with the 10 highest scores:

Table 1. Scores of diagnostic result

French text		**Chinese text**	
Language-encoding	Score	Language-encoding	Score
French	255.8934	Chinese-gb2312	344.3639
Catalan	236.9501	Chinese-big5	234.7359
English	231.5291	Korean	222.3591
Breton	211.8286	Arab-windows1256	170.5808
Latin	195.9060	Tamoul	169.7671
Slovenian-iso8859_2	195.1329	Arab-iso8859_6	140.7884
Irish	183.8261	Ukrainian-koi8_r	135.7941
Quechua	167.9354	Japanese-shift_jis	128.0966
Slovak-windows1250	167.8815	Thai	119.0824
…	…	…	…

For a multilingual text, for example, “Life is rarely as we would like it to be rather it is exactly as it is: Cest la vie!”, the result will be a text in the form: <En-CP1252>Life is rarely as we would like it to be rather it is exactly as it is: </En-CP1252><Fr-CP1252> C’est la vie!</Fr-CP1252>.

For diagnosis of the language and coding, we might need to convert the coding of the text to the system of coding accepted by the translation server.

4.3 Selection of the Translators

We reuse two free online translation engines and use English as the pivot if the direct translation source-target couple does not exist. Indeed, if a system like Systran, Gist-in-Time, Reverso... provides the service in the language L, it always has the pair (L , English). Of course, the "double" translations are definitely of lower quality than the direct translations. But the result of translation is generally still readable and usable. For example, to translate a French text into Japanese, we can compose two translators French-English and English-Japanese (of the translation server Systran). In the same way, to translate an Arabic text into French, we can compose the bilingual engine Arab-English (FreeLanguageTranslation) and English-French (Systran).

In order to choose a better translation engine for a source and target language pair, we evaluated the translation quality of the engines of each language pair. Then we use the results obtained of the evaluation as a reference of choice of an engine for a language pair to translate [5]. For evaluation of the translation engine, we use two well known methods: BLEU and NIST [10]. BLEU is a technique to evaluate MT engines, which was introduced by IBM at July 2001 in Philadelphia [9]. The principal idea is to compare the result of MT engines with the expert translations of reference in terms of statistics of the short orders of the words (N-grams of word) [4]. It showed a strong correlation between these automatic generated scores and human judgments for the quality of translation. The evaluation employs statistics of co-occurrence of N-grams requires a corpus to be evaluated and translations of reference of high quality [8]. The algorithm of IBM marks the quality of MT in terms of nap of matched N-grams and also includes a comparison length of translations and that of reference. The score of co-occurrence of N-gram is typically carried out segment-by-segment, where a segment is the minimum unit of the agreement of translation, usually one or several sentences. The statistics of co-occurrence of N-grams, based on the sets of N-grams for the segments of translation and reference, are calculated for each one of these segments and then accumulated up to all the segments [10], [16]. Method NIST is derived from the criterion of evaluation of BLEU but differs in a fundamental aspect: instead of the precision of N-grams, the profit of the information of each N-gram is taken into account [7]. The idea is to give more credit, if a system obtains an agreement of one N-gram. This makes the scores also sensitive to the differences proportional in the co-occurrence for all the N-grams. Consequently, there exists the potential of the against-productive dissension due to low co-occurrences for the larger values of N-grams. An alternative should employ an arithmetic mean of accounts of N-grams.

We developed a tool to automatically evaluate the translation engines on the basis of available corpus like the Bible and BTEC [1].

The evaluation of the translation engines is carried out as shows the following diagram:

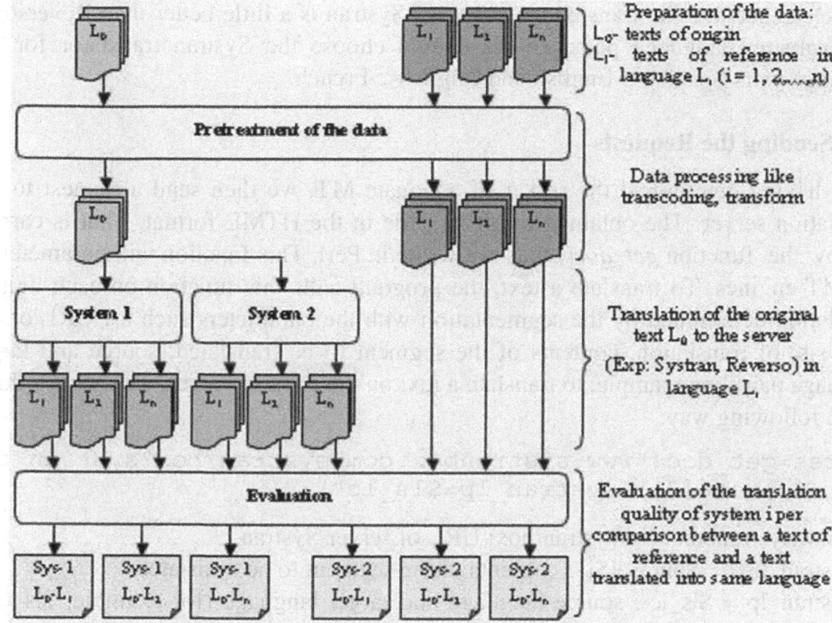

Fig. 3. Diagram of evaluation of the translation engines

Here is an example of the result of evaluation of two MT engines Systran and Reverso on the corpus Bible [11]:

Table 2. Scores of the evaluation of the online translation engines

Couple of languages	Systran		Reverso	
	BLEU	NIST	BLEU	NIST
Spanish→ English	0,1322	3,5117	0,1257	3,3567
English → Spanish	0,0962	3,2985		
French → English	0,1277	3,4968	0,1276	3,4010
English → French	0,1163	3,1208	0,0996	3,1349

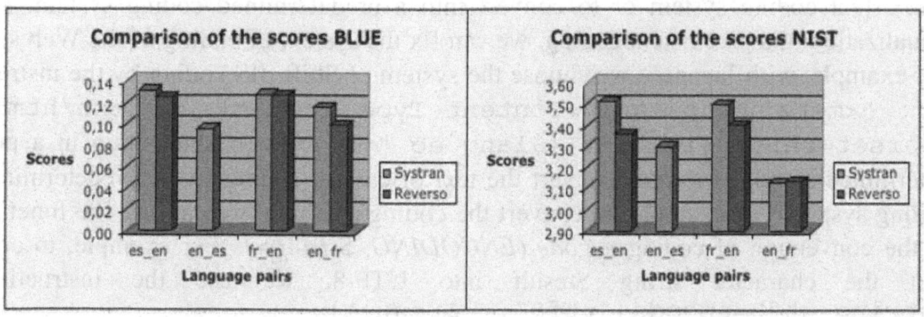

Fig. 4. Comparison chart of the scores of NIST and BLEU

We can see that the translation quality of Systran is a little better than Reverso on the evaluated language pairs, so we should choose the Systran translator for the language pairs Spanish<>English and English<>French.

4.4 Sending the Requests

After having determined the server of adequate MT, we then send a request to the translation server. The obtained result is a file in the HTML format. That is carried out by the function *get_doc()* that we wrote in Perl. This function will parameterize the MT engines. To translate a text, the program calls this function on each unit of translation determined by the segmentation with the parameters such as: URL of the Web site of translation, contents of the segment to be translated, source and target language pair. For example, to translate a text on the Systran server, we call get_doc() in the following way:

```
@res=get_doc("www.systranbox.com/systran/box?systran_te
xt=$phrase[$j]&systran_lp=$ls_lc");
```

- www.systranbox.com/systran/box: URL of server Systran
- systran_text = $phrase[$j] : contents of the segment to be translated
- systran_lp = $ls_lc : source language and target language (for example, $ls_lc = "fr_en" to translate a French text into English).

The servers of MT often accept different coding for the same language (for example, EUC_jp or Shift-JIS for Japanese, ISO-8958-1 or Unicode for French). It is necessary to convert the coding of the text into the accepted coding of the server before sending a request.

4.5 Treatment of the Results

The result obtained after the server processed a request is generally an HTML file. We must further process this file to extract a true result from translation. For this process, we use HTML tags to identify the position of the translated text. The result obtained is a string in target language. The coding applied to this text depends on the language. For example, the system of coding GB-2312 for simplified Chinese, Shift-JIS for Japanese, EUC-Kr for Korean, CP 1251 for Russian, etc. To visualize this text correctly, we can choose one of the following solutions: to visualize of the text in the preexistent coding system or to convert into a predetermined coding system. For visualization in a preexistent coding, we can fix the system of coding of the Web site. For example, with Japanese we choose the system of Shift_JIS coding by the instruction: "<meta http-equiv=Content-Type Content = text/html; charset=shift_jis>" if ($lang eq "ja"). For visualization in a predetermined coding, we must convert the text of current coding to the predetermined coding system. For example, to convert the coding of a text, we can use the function of the conversion of coding *encode (ENCODING, $string>)*. For example, to convert the character string $result into UTF-8, we use the instruction: $string_utf8=encode("utf8", $result);

5 Experimentation

We built a Web site which could automatically translate 11 languages with 55 different language pairs into simple translation. We can enter the text directly in a textbox to be translated, or open the text in the files stored on the local disk. The length of the text for translation is not limited. This text can be monolingual or multilingual. For example, after searching for the word "segment" on Google, we receive the results and use them as input data of our Web site to obtain a multilingual text and choose the language: For example, here are two URL's (one is for a Web site in Russia, the other is in English):

www.segment.ru/ База данных производителей и поставщиков канцелярских,...

www.segpub.com.au/ Segment Publishing is a Sydney, Australia-based company who specialise in standards-compliant Web development and FreeBSD-powered Web hosting...

After we pass the two URL's to our system and the system translates these text into French (by calling other MT engines) the result is as follows:

www.segment.ru/ La base des données des producteurs et des fournisseurs du bureau,...

www.segpub.com.au/ L'édition de segment est Sydney, compagnie Australie-basée qui se spécialise dans le développement norme-conforme de site Web et l'accueil FreeBSD-actionné de site Web.

We are now writing a program to process the format of the file before translating it. This function will allow preprocessed corpora using several different formats (rtf, HTML, xhtml, xml...). This module will transform all these files into a single format (a class of documents XML) for translation.

6 Applications

We can apply this system in several different fields such as: multilingual information retrieval, the translation of the electronic mails, the construction of multilingual Web sites, etc. For us, this system has been applied in the internationalization of the applications with three following principal aspects:

Localization of the Software. We are thinking to apply these systems to two levels. On the first level, it can be the issue of translating messages, files of messages, menus, help files, documents in localization of the software (for example, to transcribe the files of messages in ARIANE G5). On the second level, one can use it as an internal module in multilingual systems, to directly translate the execution messages from a language to another. The application of the translators to the second level will make the management of the user interface easier. We will then be able to build a multilingual software, which includes only one code of program, the catalogues of messages in only language (for example in English), a module of translator and sources linguistic (for the local languages).

Integration in the Communication Systems on Internet. We also envisage to use this tool in the systems of electronic mail (to automatically translate the received mails into the language of the user), the systems of online multilingual dialogue (the dialogue in several languages), the systems of electronic trade, etc.

Treatment of Multilingual Corpora. This tool can be used to produce corpora in a new language (or at least to produce a first jet, as in the TraCorpEx project), to evaluate corpora, etc.

7 Conclusion

We have proposed a method of construction of a meta-system of machine multilingual translation. This system integrates the existing online translation systems. The advantages of this system are: no limitation on the length of the text for translation, automatic identification of the language of the text for translation, automatic identification and conversion of the coding of the text to adapt to servers, the choice a better translator in existing translation engines for a determined language pair, increase in the number of the language pairs of translation, and especially, parameterization of the existing translation engines to be able to easily integrate in systems which need texts translation. In the near future, we will extend our system by an interface allowing "to self-describe" the MT engines available on the Web, with all information necessary (language pairs, codings, formats, etc). We will also extend the function getdoc() to enable it to call the local MT engines (installed on local machine or local server) because they are faster and more stable to access.

References

1. Boitet C. (2003). Approaches to enlarge bilingual corpora of example sentences to more languages. Papillon-03 seminar, Saporo.
2. Culy C., Riehemann S.S (2003). The limits of N-gram translation evaluation metrics. Proceedings of the Ninth Machine Translation Summit. New Orleans, Louisiana, USA.
3. Hutchins J. (2001). Machine Translation Over Fifty Years. Revue HEL (Histoire Epistemologies Langage), Vol. 23, published by the "Société d'Histoire et d'Epistémologie des Sciences du Langage" (SHESL), University of Paris VII.
4. Hovy E.H. (1999). Toward finely differentiated evaluation metrics for machine translation. Proceedings of the Eagles Workshop on Standards and Evaluation, Pisa, Italy.
5. Larosse L. (1998). Méthodologie de l'évaluation des traductions. Meta, Vol. 43, N° 2, Presses de l'Université de Montréal.
7. NIST report (2002). Automatic evaluation of machine translation quality using N-gram co-occurrence statistics. http://www.nist.gov/speech/tests/mt/doc/n-gram-study.pdf
8. Popescu-Belis A. (2003). An experiment in comparative evaluation: Humans vs. Computers. Proceedings of the Ninth Machine Translation Summit. New Orleans, Louisiana, USA.
9. Papineni K., Roukos S., Ward T., Zhu Z-J. (July 2001). BLEU: a method for Automatic Evaluation of Machine Translation. Proceedings of the 20th Annual Meeting of the Association for Computational Linguistics (ACL), Philadelphia, p.p 311-318.

10. Ramaswany G.N., Navratil J., Chaudhari U.V., Zilca R.D (Avril 2003). The IBM system for the NIST 2002 cellular speaker verification evaluation. ICASSP-2003, Hong Kong, http://www.reseach.ibm.com/CGB/jiri_pub.html.
11. Resnik P., Olsen M.B, Diab M. (2000). The Bible as a parallel corpus: annotating the "Book off 2000 Tongues". Computers and the Humanities, N°33, pp 129-153.
12. Russell G., Lapalme G., Plamondon P. (2003). Automatic Identification of Language and Encoding. Rapport Scientifique. Laboratoire de Recherche Appliquée en Linguistique Informatique (RALI), Université de Montréal, Canada, 7-2003.
13. Van Slype G. (1979). Critical study of methods for evaluating the quality of machine translation. BR 19142, http://issco-www.unige.ch/projects/isle/van-slype.pdf
14. Vo-Trung H. (2004). SANDOH - un système d'analyse de documents hétérogènes. Proceedings of the conference JADT 2004 (Journées internationales d'Analyse statistique des Données Textuelles), University of Louvain-la-Neuve, Belgium, Vol. 2, p.p 1177-1184.
15. Vo-Trung H. (2004). Réutilisation de traducteurs gratuits pour développer des systèmes multilingues. Proceedings of the conference RECITAL 2004, Fès, Maroc, p.p 111-117.
16. White J.S, T. O'Connell (1994). The ARPA MT evaluation methodologies : evolution, lessons, and future approaches. Proceedings of the first conference of the association for machine translation in the Americas, p.p 193-205, Columbia, Maryland.

Semantic-Aided Anaphora Resolution in Large Corpora Development

Maximiliano Saiz-Noeda, Borja Navarro, and Rubén Izquierdo

Departamento de Lenguajes y Sistemas Informáticos.
University of Alicante. Spain
{max,borja,ruben}@dlsi.ua.es

Abstract. This paper presents a novel approach to the development of anaphoric annotation of large corpora based on the use of semantic information to help the annotation process. The anaphora annotation scheme has been developed from a multilingual point of view in order to annotate three corpora: one for Catalan, one for Basque and one for Spanish. An anaphora resolution system based on restrictions and preferences has been used to aid the manual annotation process. Together with morpho-syntactic information, the system exploits the semantic relation between the anaphora and its antecedent.

1 Introduction

Anaphora and coreference resolution has been during last decades one of the most prolific research areas in Natural Language Processing. Nevertheless, it seems that this research is in a kind of impasse probably due to the lack of large manually annotated corpora. According to [1], the anaphora annotation is a "indispensable, albeit time-consuming, preliminary to anaphora resolution, since the data they provide are critical to the development, optimization and evaluation of new approaches". For the development of robust anaphora resolution systems, it is necessary to build large corpora annotated with anaphora units and their antecedents, essential for system training and evaluation.

In this paper we will present a manual anaphora annotation process based on the use of semantic information: the process is aided with an anaphora resolution system that finds each anaphora and suggests its possible antecedent. One of the special features of this system is the use of enriched syntactic and semantic information.

The method has been developed within the 3LB project[1]. The objective of this project is to develop three large annotated corpora: one for Catalan (Cat3LB), one for Basque (Eus3LB) and one for Spanish (Cast3LB). These corpus are annotated at four linguistics levels: morphological, syntactic (complete), semantic and discourse. In the latter, anaphora and coreferencial chains are annotated. Due to the corpus (and specifically the Spanish corpus Cast3LB) has

[1] Project partially funded by Spanish Government FIT-150-500-2002-244.

J. L. Vicedo et al. (Eds.): EsTAL 2004, LNAI 3230, pp. 314–327, 2004.

been previously annotated with syntactic and semantic information, it is possible to exploit this information in the anaphoric annotation phase (in fact, the proposed AR method make use of these kinds of linguistic information).

In order to test the usability of this method in the manual annotation process, an experiment about the correctness of the system is necessary, together with the annotation agreement measure. In this paper this experiments will be presented, in order to specify its real improvement.

Next section presents the anaphora resolution method enriched with semantic information. Then, the corpus annotation scheme is presented. The paper will conclude with the evaluation data regarding the system's accuracy and the annotation agreement.

2 Semantic-Aided Anaphora Resolution

Anaphora resolution (AR) has worried linguists and computer scientists during last two decades. This task, considered as one of the most important within the ambiguity treatment in Natural Language Processing, has been tackled from different points of view and by a wide variety of systems.

It's difficult to make an universal classification of AR methods, due to a lot of them have developed combined strategies to improve the results, but having in mind the interest of this paper to show the relevance of semantic information in anaphora resolution we could make the following classification:

- *Limited Knowledge Methods*: approaches that solve the anaphora using just morphological and syntactic information. These are the most prolific methods due to their low computational requirements. From first methods [2, 3], a lot authors have proposed different approaches [4, 5, 6, 7, 8, 9, 10, 11, 12, 13, 14] that have demonstrated the high resolution level that can be reached only applying basic morphological and syntactic knowledge, in most cases, to restricted domain corpora.
- *Enriched Methods*: strategies that add, to the previous ones, additional sources such as the semantic (based in semantic tagging or in use of ontologies) or the pragmatic (through the discourse analysis or world knowledge). Although limited knowledge methods provide good computational results in AR, their own creators [3] accept the general idea of improving the results with enriched knowledge. Although inicial methods [15, 16] have been tested on small data sets (mostly manually treated), due to the absence of big enough resources, the birth and development of lexical resources like WordNet [17] or EuroWordNet [18] and ontologies such as Mikrokosmos [19] provide new perspectives in this kind of methods [20, 21, 22, 23]. Discourse based theories like centering [24] has given inspiration to several authors in AR methods [25, 12].
- *Alternative Methods*: this group integrates those methods not included in the previous ones. They use techniques based on statistics [26, 27, 13] or artificial intelligence models [28, 11].

We would like to remark that most of the methods previously reviewed deal with AR problem for English, but none of them deal with the problem using enriched strategies for Spanish.

Furthermore, as mentioned before, one of the most important problems in the improvement of AR methods is the lack of resources that integrates linguistic information enough to cope with possible enriched approaches.

2.1 ERA Method

Enriched Resolution of Anaphora (ERA) method [29] can be included among the group of enriched methods. It is the result of adding new information sources to a review of a classical AR method based on restrictions and preferences [14]. These new information sources come from, on the one hand, the enrichment of the syntactic analysis of the text and, on the other hand, the use of semantic information both applied to the pronoun resolution (personal, omitted, reflexive and demonstrative).

The enrichment of the syntactic analysis is based on an additional set of labels that mark syntactic roles. This labels will allow to redefine the original restrictions and avoid different guesses based on syntactic roles that sometimes fail due to the free order of the Spanish language[2].

Semantic information is added through a set of labels that indicates the correct sense of each word in the text. These correct senses have been selected using Spanish WordNet synset identifiers [30] [18]. The method elaborates the semantic information using two techniques:

- *Corpus-Based Semantic*: ontological concepts of anaphoric candidates will be related to the verb of the anaphora. The semantic features of the lexical words have been extracted form the ontological concepts of EuroWorNet, that is, the Top Ontology[3] With this, and the enriched syntactic information, subject-verb,verb-direct object and verb-indirect object semantic patterns are extracted. This way, a set of semantic (or ontological) patterns will give a measure of semantic compatibility for the preference phase in order to score the candidates in the resolution process.
- *Knowledge-Based Semantic*: two sets of semantic compatibility rules will be defined:

[2] The original method which is enriched in ERA is based only in basic syntactic information and is able to use only the relative position of a noun and a verb, supposing that this position reveals the syntactic role of the former regarding the latter.

[3] All the synsets in EuroWordnet are semantically described through a set of base concepts (the more general concepts). In the EuroWorNet's Top Ontology, these base concepts are classified in the three orders of Lyons [31], according to basic semantic distinctions. So through the top ontology, all the synsets of EuroWordNet are semantically described with concepts like "human", "animal", "artifact", ... However, [32] reports some inconsistences in the process of inheriting semantic properties from WordNet hierarchy. At this stage of the project, these inconsistences have not been taken into account.

- "NO" rules: NO(v#sense,c,r) defines the incompatibility between the verb v (and it sense) and any name which contains 'c' in its ontological concept list, being 'r' the syntactic function that relates them.
- "MUST" rules: MUST(v#sense,c,r) defines the incompatibility between the verb v (and its sense) and all the names that don't contain 'c' in their ontological concept list, being 'r' the syntactic function that relates them.

These rules will be applied in the restriction phase in order to delete incompatible candidates.

Therefore, the specific use of semantic information is related to the sematic compatibility (or incompatibility) between the possible antecedent (a noun) and the verb of the sentence in which the anaphoric pronoun appears. Due to the pronoun replaces a lexical word (the antecedent), the semantic information of the antecedent must be compatible with the semantic restrictions of the verb. In other words, the anaphoric expression takes the semantic features of the antecedent, so they must be compatible with the semantic restrictions of the verb. In this way, verbs like "eat" or "drink" should be specially compatible with animal subjects and eatable and drinkable objects than others.

ERA method applies first a set of restrictions based on morphological, syntactic and semantic information in order to reject all the candidates clearly incompatible with the pronoun. Restrictions in ERA mixes classical morphological and syntactic information with the semantic one in order to state the next set of restrictions:

- Morpho-semantic restriction: based in the agreement and specific kinds of ontological concepts combination.
- Syntactic-semantic restrictions: based in syntactic roles of the candidates related to the anaphoric verb and their ontological features.
- Syntactic restrictions: based on the classical positional restrictions but enriched with the specific syntactic roles. These restriction varies from the type of pronoun will be solved.
- Semantic restrictions: based on the semantic rules previously defined (*NO* and *MUST*).

Once the incompatible candidates have been rejected, ERA applies a set of preferences to get a score of each candidate in order to select the best scored one as the correct antecedent of the anaphora. These preferences are based on morphological, syntactic, semantic and structural criteria and have variations among the different types of treated pronouns. If the preference phase doesn't give a unique candidate as antecedent, a final common preference set is applied in order to decide (including the selection, in case of draw, of the candidate closest to the pronoun).

Figure 1 shows the application algorithm defined for the previously defined Enriched Resolution of Anaphora (ERA) method.

```
--------------------------------------------------------------------------------
For each sentence S
  L = L + Store NPs with their enrichment data
  Compatibility patterns acquisition with the NPs in L
  For each pronoun P in S
    Identify pronoun P type
    Restriction application to L according to pronoun P type
      L'=Application of morpho-semantic restrictions to L
        L'=Application of syntactic-semantic restrictions to L
        L'=Application of syntactic restrictions to L
        L'=Application of incompatibility rules to L
    If |L'| = 0 then P is not anaphoric
    If |L'| = 1 then L[1] is the antecedent of P
    If |L'| > 1 then
      Preference application to L' according to pronoun P type
        L' = Application of structural and semantic-structural preferences to L'
        L' = Application of morphological preferences to L'
        L' = Application of syntactic preferences to L'
        L' = Application of semantic preferences to L'
      L'' = Best(L')
      If |L''| = 1 then L[1] in the antecedent of P
      If |L''| > 1 then
        L' = Application of common preferences
        Best(L') is the antecedent of P
      endIf
    endIf
  endFor
endFor
--------------------------------------------------------------------------------
```

Fig. 1. ERA method algorithm application

According to all said before, the application of this method requires a corpus tagged not only with basic morphological and shallow syntactic information but enriched with complete syntactic analysis and sense disambiguation. Thanks to the 3LB project (that will be described bellow), this resource will be a reality soon and allows, by know, to make basic evaluations of his kind of enriched corpus-based approaches. 3LB annotation schema will be described in next section.

3 Annotation Schema: 3LB Project

Cast3Lb project is part of the general project 3LB[4]. As we said before, the main objective of this general project is to develop three corpora annotated with syntactic, semantic and pragmatic/coreferential information: one for Catalan (Cat3LB), one for Basque (Eus3LB) and one for Spanish (Cast3LB).

The Spanish corpus Cast3LB is a part of the CLIC-TALP corpus, which is made up of 100.000 words from LexEsp [33] plus 25.000 words coming from the EFE Spanish Corpus, given by the Agencia EFE (the official news agency)

[4] Project partially funded by Spanish Government FIT-150-500-2002-244.

for research purposes. The EFE corpus is a comparable fragment to the other corpora involved in the general project (Catalan and Basque).

3.1 Morpho-Syntactic Annotation

At morphological level, this corpus was automatically annotated and manually checked in previous projects [34]. At the syntactic level, the corpus have been annotated following the constituency annotation scheme. The main principles of syntactic annotation are the following [35]:

- only the explicit elements are annotated (except for elliptical subjects);
- the surface word order of the elements is not altered;
- any specific theoretical framework is followed;
- the verbal phrase is not taken into account, rather, the main constituents of the sentence become the daughters of the root node;
- the syntactic information is enriched by the functional information of the main phrases, but we have not taken into account the possibility of double functions.

3.2 Semantic Annotation

At the semantic level, the correct sense of nouns, verbs and adjectives has been annotated following an all-words approach. The specific sense (or senses) of each word is made by means of the EuroWordNet offset number [18], that is, the identification number of the sense (synset) in the InterLingua Index of EuroWordNet. The corpus has 42291 lexical words, where 20461 are nouns, 13471 are verbs and 8543 are adjectives. Also, due to some words are not available in EuroWordNet or do not have the suitable sense, we have created two new tags to mark this special cases.

Our proposal is based on the SemCor corpus [36], that is formed by approximately 250000 words. All nouns, verbs, adjectives and adverbs have been annotated manually with WordNet senses [36].

We have decided to use Spanish WordNet for several reasons. First of all, Spanish WordNet is, up to now, the more commonly used lexical resource in Word Sense Disambiguation tasks. Secondly, it is one of the most complete lexical resources currently available for Spanish. Finally, as part of EuroWordNet, the lexical structure of Spanish and the lexical structure of Catalan and Basque are related. Therefore, the annotated senses of the three corpora of 3LB project are related too.

We have followed a transversal (or "lexical") semantic annotation method [37]. In this method, the human annotator marks word-type by word-type, all the occurrences of each word in the corpus one by one. With this method, the annotator must read and analyze all the senses of a word only once.

The main advantage of this method is that the annotator can focus the attention over the sense structure of one word and deal with its specific semantic problems: its main sense or senses, its specific senses, ... Then, checks the context of the single word each time it appears and selects the corresponding sense.

Through this approach, semantic features of each word is taken into consideration only once, and the whole corpus achieves greater consistency.

For the semantic annotation process, a Semantic Annotation Tool (3LB-SAT) has been developed [38]. The main features of this tool are:

- it is word-oriented,
- it allows different format for input corpus; basically, the main formats used in corpus annotation: treebank format (TBF) and XML format;
- it uses EuroWordNet as a lexical resource.

In the annotation process, monosemic words are annotated automatically. So the tools itself is used to annotate polysemic words, and to check if monosemic words do not have the suitable sense.

3.3 Discourse Annotation: Anaphora and Coreference

At the discourse level, the coreference of nominal phrases and some elliptical elements are marked. The coreference expressions taken into account are personal pronouns, clitic pronouns, elliptical subjects and some elliptical nominal heads (with an adjective as explicit element[5].). The possible antecedents considered are the nominal phrases or other coreferential expressions.

Specifically, in each kind of anaphoric expression, we mark:

- Anaphoric ellipsis:
  - The elliptical subject, made explicit in the syntactic annotation step. Being a noun phrase, it could also be an antecedent too.
    Unlike English, where it is possible an expletive pronoun as subject, in Spanish it is very common an elliptical nominal phrase as subject of the sentence. This is why we have decide to include this kind of anaphora in the annotation process.
  - Elliptical head of nominal phrases with an adjective complement. In English, this construction is the "one anaphora". In Spanish, however, the anaphoric construction is made up by an elliptical head noun and an adjective complement.
- Anaphoric pronouns:
  - The tonic personal pronouns in the third person. They can appear in subject function or in object function.
  - The atonic pronouns, specifically the clitic pronouns that appear in the subcategorization frame of the main verb.
- Finally, there are sets of anaphoric and elliptical units that corefer to the same entity. These units form coreferential chains. They must be marked in order to show the cohesion and coherence of the text. They are annotated by means of the identification of the same antecedent.

[5] This kind of anaphora corresponds with the English "one" anaphora.

Definite descriptions are not annotated in this project. They consist of nominal phrases that can refer (or not) to an antecedent. We do not mark them because they outline specific problems that make this task very difficult: firstly, there are not clear criteria that allow us to distinguish between coreferential and not coreferential nominal phrases; secondly, there are not a clear typology for definite descriptions; and finally, there are not a clear typology of relationships between the definite description and their antecedents. These problems could further increase the time-consuming in the annotation process and widen the gap of disagreement between the human annotators.

This proposal of annotation scheme is based on the one used in the MUC (Message Understanding Conference) [39] as well as in the works of [40] and [41]: this is the mostly used scheme in coreferential annotation [1].

In the coreference annotation, two linguistic elements must be marked: the coreferential expression and its antecedent. In the antecedent we annotate the following information:

– A reference tag that shows the presence of an antecedent ("REF"),
– An identification number ("ID"),
– The minimum continuous substring that could be considerer correct ("MIN").

In the coreferential expression, we annotate:

– The presence of a coreferential expression ("COREF"),
– An identification number ("ID"),
– The type of coreferential expression: elliptical noun phrase, coreferential adjective, tonic pronoun or atonic pronoun ("TYPE"),
– The antecedent, through its identification number ("REF"),
– Finally, a status tag where the annotators shows their confidence in the annotation ("STATUS").

For the anaphoric and coreferential annotation, a Reference Annotation Tool (3LB-RAT) has been developed. This tool provides to the annotator three ways of work: manual, semiautomatic and automatic. In the first one, the tool locates and shows all possible anaphoric and coreference elements and their possible antecedents. The annotator chooses one of these possible antecedents and indicates the certainty degree on this selection (standby, certain or uncertain).

There are some exceptional cases that the tool always offers:

– cases of cataphora
– possible syntactic mistakes (that will be used to review and to correct the syntactic annotation)
– the possibility of a non-located antecedent
– the possibility that an antecedent do not appear explicitly in the text
– the possibility of non-anaphora, that is, the application has no located correctly an anaphoric expression

In the semiautomatic way, the tool solves each coreference by means of the enriched resolution anaphora method previously explained. So the system proposes and shows the most suitable candidate to the annotator. The annotator can choose the solution that the resolution method offers in all cases, or choose an other solution (manually).

The automatic process doesn't give the annotator the chance of select any option and simply solves all the pronouns according to the system's parameters.

As we said before, the tool uses syntactic, morphologic and semantic information for the specification of an anaphora and its antecedent. The semantic information used by the tool is limited to ontology concepts and synonymous. All these data have been indexed. From the semantically annotated text, three tables are created, one for each syntactic function: subject, direct object and indirect object. In these tables the frequency of appearance of words with verbs (with their correct senses) is reflected. These tables are the base to construct the semantic compatibility patterns, which indicate the compatibility between the ontological concept related with the possible antecedent and the verb of the sentence where the anaphoric expression appears. In order to calculate this information, the occurrence frequency and the conceptual generality degree in the ontology are considered. In this case, a higher punctuation is given to the most concrete concepts.

For example, "Human" concept gives us further information than "Natural" concept. These patterns are used in the semantic preferences application. For a specific candidate, its semantic compatibility is calculated from the compatible ontological concepts on the patterns. The candidates with greater compatibility are preferred.

4 Enriched Anaphora Resolution System in Annotation Process. Evaluation Data

According to the specifications described in section 2.1 related to the application of the enriched anaphora resolution method, it is necessary to count on specific information that is provided by the corpus annotation schema. Due to the corpus has been annotated with syntactic information, and the sense of each word is marked with the offset number of EuroWordNet, it is possible to extract semantic features of each verb and noun through the ontological concepts of the EuroWordNet's Top Ontology. Furthermore, the corpus has been annotated with syntactic roles, so it is possible to extract syntactic patterns formed by the verb and its main complements: subject-verb, verb-direct objects, verb-indirect objects.

What we try to test is if the AR interactive process improves the single manual annotation and makes it faster, less tedious, and more consistent through the improvement of the annotation agreement.

The speed of the process lies in the fact that the annotator doesn't need to locate the anaphoric element (pronoun or elliptical in this case) and go back in the text in order to search all possible candidates to be the antecedent. The system simplifies and makes the process faster and less tedious by the automatic detection of the anaphora and the collection of the candidates in a unique list based on the space search criteria.

Furthermore, as it has been said, the system provides the annotator with a possible solution, it means, a suggestion of the correct antecedent. This methodology can contribute to the consistence of the annotation decision, converting a completely free process in a guided one.

In order to test if the AR system (enriched with semantic information) is really useful, we have selected the passage with the highest amount of different anaphoric elements. The passage have been marked by two annotators using the semantic aided AR method (through the 3LB-RAP), and we have calculated, on the one hand, the agreement between the annotator and the system (through the system's accuracy) and, on the other hand, the agreement between the annotators.

4.1 AR System's Accuracy

One of the main obstacles found in the evaluation proccess has been the selected fragment itself. Unfortunately, according to the highest-number-of-anaphoras criterion, the selected fragment turned out to be one of the most complex in the corpus. This fragment belongs to a novelistic text and has a set of features that make really difficult to proccess with the AR system.

The passage has 36 possible anaphoric expressions that must be annotated: 23 elliptical subjects, 12 atonic pronouns and 1 tonic pronoun.

However, only the half (18 units) are anaphoric expressions. The rest of the cases correspond:

- Cataphoras: Although the system is not designed to solve cataphora, as mentioned in the algorithm in section 2.1 it returns no antecedent, suggesting the possibility of a cathaphoric expression. This can be considered as a system success.
- Pronominal verbs: in Spanish, some verbs can be accompanied by pronoun particles that modified it but without reference function. The system cannot distinguish them unless they have different tags (it does not occur in this corpus).
- Elliptical subject with a verb in first or second person: these elliptical subjects are not anaphoric but deictic expressions. System does not deal with first or second pronouns.
- Not explicit antecedent: finally, some anaphoric expressions have not an explicit antecedent in the previous text. Of course, it is not possible to find the antecedent if it does not exist in the text.

From this 18 anaphoric expressions, the system has correctly located and solved the half. Although this can be considered too low according to the results provided by the classical AR approaches, it is fundamental (and very interesting) to have in mind the kind of problems detected in the resolution process:

1. Positional criterion: the selected fragment changes sometimes from direct to indirect style due to the existence of dialogues. It is well-known that approaches to solve dialogues have to use different solving strategies (e.g. based in discourse theories) than the monologue texts (that is the case of

ERA method). For example, the simple selection of the closest candidate fails due to changes in the direct-indirect style.
2. Sentence window: the own features of the text makes that the standard search space to look for the solution (established in three sentences) might be extended to seven in order to include the correct antecedent in the candidate list. Unfortunately, this search window is too big and introduce too much noise (the number of candidates are more than the triple) in the resolution process.

To summarize, although the system provides a low accuracy result, it is more that justified bearing in mind the special characteristics of the text selected. Although another "easier" fragment could have been selected for the evaluation, we believe that these kinds of texts can help to better improve the AR methods.

We are sure (based on the evaluation of the ERA method in other corpora) that the advances in the 3LB corpus tagging and, therefore, the availability of a bigger set of texts, will provide the opportunity of demonstrate a much better system capability in a more varied domain corpus.

4.2 Human Annotation Agreement

One of the most important problems in manual annotation is the agreement between two or more human annotators, and this situation is specially critical in coreference annotation [1]. In order to calculate the annotation agreement, the work of two annotators has been compared and the kappa measure [42] [43] has been calculated[6].

The annotation process has been guided by the ERA method through the 3LB-RAT tool. Five possible cases of agreement have been defined:

a) the annotator selects the antecedent suggested by the system
b) the annotator selects the second antecedent suggested by the system
c) the annotator selects the third antecedent suggested by the system
d) the annotator selects other antecedent
e) other cases (no anaphora, no explicit antecedent, etc.).

According to these cases, the results show an agreement of $k = 0.84$. According to [44], a kappa measure higher than k = 0.8 is a good agreement, so we can consider the AR system as a good consensus tool to guide the annotation process.

5 Conclusions

In this paper we have presented a coreference annotation scheme supported by a semantic-aided anaphora resolution method. We have tried to evaluate

[6] Kappa measure is calculated according to the well-known $k = \frac{P_A - P_E}{1 - P_E}$ where P_A represents the annotation agreement percentage and P_E the agreement expected by coincidence.

the way and the grade the use of an AR system helps annotators in their job. Furthermore, it has been presented as an interesting agreement tool. Problems detected in the resolution process can be used to improve the system and to consider new viewpoints in the definition of tagging strategies.

Acknowledgements

The authors would like to thank Belén and Raquel for their hard work in the supervised annotation process.

References

1. Mitkov, R.: Anaphora resolution. Longman, London. UK (2002)
2. Hobbs, J.R.: Pronoun resolution. Research report # 76-1, Department of Computer Sciences. City College. City University of New York, New York, USA (1976)
3. Hobbs, J.R.: Resolving pronoun references. Lingua **44** (1978) 311–338
4. Walker, M.A.: 4. In: Centering, anaphora resolution and discourse structure. Oxford University Press, Oxford, UK (1998)
5. Dagan, I., Itai, A.: A statistical filter for resolving pronoun references. Artificial Intelligence and Computer Vision (1991) 125–135
6. Lappin, S., Leass, H.: An algorithm for pronominal anaphora resolution. Computational Linguistics **20** (1994) 535–561
7. Kennedy, C., Boguraev, B.: Anaphora for everyone: pronominal anaphora resolution without a parser. In: Proceedings of 16th International Conference on Computational Linguistics. Volume I., Copenhagen, Denmark (1996) 113–118
8. Baldwin, B.: CogNIAC: high precision coreference with limited knowledge and linguistic resources. In: Proceedings of the ACL'97/EACL'97 workshop on Operational Factors in Practical, Robust Anaphor Resolution, Madrid, Spain (1997) 38–45
9. Mitkov, R.: Robust pronoun resolution with limited knowledge. In: Proceedings of the 36th Annual Meeting of the Association for Computational Linguistics and 17th International Conference on Computational Linguistics (COLING-ACL'98), Montreal, Canada (1998) 869–875
10. Ge, N., Hale, J., Charniak, E.: A statistical approach to anaphora resolution. In Charniak, E., ed.: Proceedings of Sixth WorkShop on Very Large Corpora, Montreal, Canada (1998) 161–170
11. Byron, D.K., Allen, J.F.: Applying Genetic Algorithms to Pronoun Resolution. In: Proceedings of the Sixteenth National Conference on Artificial Intelligence (AAAI'99), Orlando, Florida (1999) 957
12. Tetreault, J.R.: Analysis of Syntax-Based Pronoun Resolution Methods. In: Proceedings of the 37th Annual Meeting of the Association for Computational Linguistics (ACL'99), Maryland, USA (1999) 602–605
13. Ge, N.: An approach to anaphoric pronouns. PhD thesis, Department of Computer Sicence. Brown University, Providence. Rhode Island. USA (2000)
14. Palomar, M., Ferrández, A., Moreno, L., Martínez-Barco, P., Peral, J., Saiz-Noeda, M., Muoz, R.: An algorithm for Anaphora Resolution in Spanish Texts. Computational Linguistics **27** (2001) 545–567

15. Carbonell, J.G., Brown, R.D.: Anaphora resolution: a multi-strategy approach. In: Proceedings of 12th International Conference on Computational Linguistics (COLING'88), Budapest, Hungary (1988) 96–101
16. Rich, E., Luperfoy, S.: An Architecture for Anaphora Resolution. In: Proceedings of the Second Conference on Applied Natural Language Processing, Austin, Texas (1998) 18–24
17. Miller, G.A., Beckwith, R., Fellbaum, C., Gross, D., Miller, K.J.: Five Papers on WordNet. Special Issue of the International Journal of Lexicography **3** (1993) 235–312
18. Vossen, P.: EuroWordNet: Building a Multilingual Database with WordNets for European Languages. The ELRA Newsletter **3** (1998)
19. O'Hara, T., Mahesh, K., Niremburg, S.: Lexical Acquisition with WordNet and the Mikrokosmos Ontology. In: Proceedings of the WorkShop on Usage of WordNet in the 36th Annual Meeting of the Association for Computational Linguistics and 17th International Conference on Computational Linguistics (COLING-ACL'98), Montreal, Canada (1998)
20. Mitkov, R.: Anaphora resolution: a combination of linguistic and statistical approaches. In: Proceedings of the Discourse Anaphora and Anaphor Resolution Colloquium (DAARC'96), Lancaster, UK (1996)
21. Azzam, S., Humphreys, K., Gaizauskas, R.: Coreference Resolution in a Multilingual Information Extraction System. In: Proceedings of the Workshop on Linguistic Coreference. First Language Resources and Evaluation Conference (LREC'98)., Granada, Spain (1998) 74–78
22. Harabagiu, S., Maiorano, S.: Knowledge-lean coreference resolution and its relation to textual cohesion and coreference. In Cristea, D., Ide, N., Marcu, D., eds.: The Relation of Discourse/Dialogue Structure and Reference. Association for Computational Linguistics, New Brunswick, New Jersey (1999) 29–38
23. Saiz-Noeda, M., Palomar, M.: Semantic Knowledge-driven Method to Solve Pronominal Anaphora in Spanish. In: NLP'2000 Filling the gap between theory and practice. Lecture Notes In Artificial Intelligence. Springer-Verlag, Patras, Greece (2000) 204–211
24. Grosz, B., Joshi, A., Weinstein, S.: Centering: a framework for modeling the local coherence of discourse. Computational Linguistics **21** (1995) 203–225
25. Brennan, S., Friedman, M., Pollard, C.: A centering approach to pronouns. In: Proceedings of the 25st Annual Meeting of the Association for Computational Linguistics (ACL'87), Stanford, California. USA (1987) 155–162
26. Dagan, I., Justeson, J., Lappin, S., Leass, H., Ribak, A.: Syntax and lexical statistics in anaphora resolution. Applied Artificial Intelligence **9** (1995) 633–644
27. Cardie, C., Wagstaff, K.: Noun Phrase Coreference as Clustering. In: Proceedings of the Joint SIGDAT Conference on Empirical Methods in NLP and Very Large Corpora, Maryland, USA (1999) 82–89
28. Aone, C., Bennett, S.W.: Evaluating automated and manual acquisition of anaphora resolution strategies. In Publishers, M.K., ed.: Proceedings of the 33th Annual Meeting of the Association for Computational Linguistics (ACL'95), Cambridge, Massachusetts (1995) 122–129
29. Saiz-Noeda, M.: Influencia y aplicación de papeles sintácticos e información semántica en la resolución de la anáfora pronominal en español. PhD thesis, Universidad de Alicante, Alicante (2002)
30. Atserias, J., Villarejo, L., Rigau, G.: Spanish WordNet 1.6: Porting the Spansih WordNet across Princeton versions. In: 4th International Conference on Language Resources and Evaluation, LREC04, Lisbon, Portugal (2004)

31. Lyons, J.: Semantics. Cambridge University Press, London (1977)
32. Atserias, J., Climent, S., Rigau, G.: Towards the MEANING Top Ontology: Sources of Ontological Meaning. In: 4th International Conference on Language Resources and Evaluation, LREC04, Lisbon, Portugal (2004)
33. Sebastián, N., Martí, M.A., Carreiras, M.F., Cuetos, F.: 2000 LEXESP: Léxico Informatizado del Español. Edicions de la Universitat de Barcelona, Barcelona (2000)
34. Civit, M.: Criterios de etiquetación y desambiguación morfosintáctica de corpus en Español. Sociedad Espaola para el Procesamiento del Lenguaje Natural, Alicante (2003)
35. Civit, M., Martí, M.A., Navarro, B., Bufí, N., Fernández, B., Marcos, R.: Issues in the Syntactic Annotation of Cast3LB. In: 4th International Workshop on Linguistically Interpreted Corpora (LINC03), EACL03, Budapest (2003)
36. Miller, G.A.: Wordnet: An on-line lexical database. Intenational Journal of Lexicography **3** (1990) 235–312
37. Kilgarriff, A.: Gold standard datasets for evaluating word sense disambiguation programs. Computer Speech and Language. Special Use on Evaluation **12** (1998) 453–472
38. Bisbal, E., Molina, A., Moreno, L., Pla, F., Saiz-Noeda, M., Sanchís, E.: 3LB-SAT: una herramienta de anotación semántica. Procesamiento del Lenguaje Natural **31** (2003) 193–200
39. Hirschman, L.: MUC-7 coreference task definition Message Understanding Conference Proceedings (1997)
40. Gaizauskas, R., Humphreys, K.: Quantitative evaluation of coreference algorithms in an information extraction system. In Botley, S.P., McEnery, A.M., eds.: Corpus-based and Computational Approaches to Discourse Anaphora. John Benjamins, Amsterdam (1996) 143–167
41. Mitkov, R., Evans, R., Orasan, C., Barbu, C., Jones, L., V.Sotirova: Coreference and anaphora: developing annotating tools, annotated resources and annotation strategies. In: Proceedings of the Discourse, Anaphora and Reference Resolution Conference (DAARC 2000), Lancaster, UK (2002)
42. Carletta, J.: Assessing agreement on classification tasks: the kappa statistics. Computational Linguistics **22** (1996) 249–254
43. Vieira, R.: How to evaluate systems against human judgement on the presence of sidagreement? Encontro Preparatrio de Avaliao Conjunta do Processamento Computacional do Portugus (2002) http://acdc.linguateca.pt/aval_conjunta/Faro2002/Renata_Vieira.pdf.
44. Kripperdorff, K.: Content Analysis. Sage Publications, London (1985)

SemRol: Recognition of Semantic Roles

P. Moreda, M. Palomar, and A. Suárez

Grupo de investigación del Procesamiento del Lenguaje y Sistemas de Información.
Departamento de Lenguajes y Sistemas Informáticos. Universidad de Alicante.
Alicante, Spain
{moreda,mpalomar,armando}@dlsi.ua.es

Abstract. In order to achieve high precision Question Answering Systems or Information Retrieval Systems, the incorporation of Natural Language Processing techniques are needed. For this reason, in this paper a method that can be integrated in these kinds of systems, is presented. The aim of this method, based on maximum entropy conditional probability models, is semantic role labelling. The method, named SemRol, consists of three modules. First, the sense of the verb is disambiguated. Then, the argument boundaries of the verb are determined. Finally, the semantic roles that fill these arguments are obtained.

1 Introduction

One of the challenges of applications such as Information Retrieval (IR) or Question Answering (QA), is to develop high quality systems (high precision IR/QA). In order to do this, it is necessary to involve Natural Language Processing (NLP) techniques in this kind of systems. Among the different NLP techniques which would improve Information Retrieval or Question Answering systems it is found Word Sense Disambiguation (WSD) and Semantic Role Labelling (SRL). In this paper a method of Semantic Role Labelling using Word Sense Disambiguation is presented. This research is integrated in the project R2D2[1].

A semantic role is the relationship that a syntactic constituent has with a predicate. For instance, in the next sentence

(E0) The executives gave the chefs a standing ovation

The executives has the Agent role, *the chefs* the Recipient role and *a standing ovation* the Theme role.

The problem of the Semantic Role Labeling is not trivial. In order to identify the semantic role of the arguments of a verb, two phases have to be solved. Firstly, the sense of the verb is disambiguated. Secondly, the argument boundaries of the disambiguated verb are identified.

[1] This paper has been supported by the Spanish Government under project "R2D2: Recuperación de Respuestas de Documentos Digitalizados" (TIC2003-07158-C04-01).

J. L. Vicedo et al. (Eds.): EsTAL 2004, LNAI 3230, pp. 328–339, 2004.

(E1) John gives out lots of candy on Halloween to the kids on his block

(E2) The radiator gives off a lot of heat

Depending on the sense of the verb a different set of roles must be considered. For instance, Figure 1 shows three senses of verb *give* and the set of roles of each sense. So, sentence (E0) matches with sense 01. Therefore, roles *giver*, *thing given* and *entity given to* are considered. Nevertheless, sentence (E1) matches with sense 06 and sentence (E2) matches with sense 04. Then, the sets of roles are (*distributor, thing distributed, distributed*) and (*emitter, thing emitted*), respectively. In sentence (E1), *John* has the distributor role, *lots of candy* the thing distributed role, *the kids on his block* the distributed role and *on Halloween* the temporal role. In sentence (E2), *the radiator* has the emitter role and *a lot of heat* the thing emitted role.

```
<roleset id="give.01" name="transfer"> <roles>
  <role n="0"  descr="giver"  vntheta="Agent"/>
  <role n="1"  descr="thing given"  vntheta="Theme"/>
  <role n="2"  descr="entity given  vntheta="Recipient""/>
</roles>
```

```
<roleset id="give.04" name="emit">
<roles>
  <role n="0"  descr="emitter"/>
  <role n="1"  descr="thing emitted"/>
</roles>
```

```
<roleset id="give.06" name="transfer">
<roles>
  <role n="0"  descr="distributor"/>
  <role n="1"  descr="thing distributed"/>
  <role n="2"  descr="distributed"/>
</roles>
```

Fig. 1. Some senses and roles of the frame *give* in PropBank [18]

To achieve high precision IR/QA systems, recognizing and labelling semantic arguments is a key task for answering "Who", "When", "What", "Where", "Why", etc. For instance, the following questions could be answered with the sentence (E0). The Agent role answers the question (E3) and the Theme role answers the question (E4).

(E3) Who gave the chefs a standing ovation?

(E4) What did the executives give the chefs?

Currently, several works have used WSD or Semantic Role Labeling in IR or QA systems, unsuccessfully. Mainly, it is due to two reasons:

1. The lower precision achieved in these tasks.
2. The lower portability of these methods.

It is easy to find methods of WSD and Semantic Role Labeling that work with high precision for a specific task or specific domain. Nevertheless, this precision drops when the domain or the task are changed. For these reasons, this paper is about the problem of a Semantic Role Labeling integrated with WSD system. A method based on a corpus approach is presented and several experiments about both, WSD and Semantic Role Labeling modules, are shown. Shortly, a QA system with this Semantic Role Labeling module using WSD will be developed in the R2D2 framework.

The remaining paper is organized as follows: section 2 gives an idea about the state-of-art in automatic Semantic Role Labeling systems in the subsection 2.1. Besides, subsection 2.2 summarizes Maximum Entropy Models as the approach used. Afterwards, the maximum entropy-based method is presented in subsection 2.3. Then, some comments about experimental data, and an evaluation of our results using the method, are presented in sections 3 and 4, respectively. Finally, section 5 concludes.

2 The SemRol Method

The method, named SemRol, presented in this section consists of three main modules: i) Word Sense Disambiguation Module, ii) Module of Heuristics, and iii) Semantic Role Disambiguation Module. Both Word Sense Disambiguation Module and Semantic Role Disambiguation Module are based on Maximum Entropy Models. Module of Heuristics and Semantic Role Disambiguation modules take care of recognition and labeling of arguments, respectively. WSD module means a new phase in the task. It disambiguates the sense of the target verbs. So, the task turns more straightforward because semantic roles are assigned to sense level.

In order to build this three-phase learning system, training and development data ser are used. It is used PropBank corpus [18], which is the Penn Treebank corpus [17] enriched with predicate-argument structures. It addresses predicates expressed by verbs and labels core arguments with consecutive numbers (A0 to A5), trying to maintain coherence along different predicates. A number of adjuncts, derived from the Treebank functional tags, are also included in PropBank annotations.

2.1 Background

Several approaches [3] have been proposed to identify semantic roles or to build semantic classifier. The task has been usually approached as a two phase procedure consisting of recognition and labeling arguments.

Regarding the learning component of the systems, we find pure probabilistic models ([8]; [9]; [7]), Maximum Entropy ([6]; [2]; [15]), generative models [26], Decision Trees ([25]; [5]), Brill's Transformation-based Error-driven Learning ([13]; [28]), Memory-based Learning ([27]; [14]), and vector-based linear classifiers of different types: Support Vector Machines (SVM) ([12]; [20]; [21]), SVM with polynomial kernels ([11]; [19]), and Voted Perceptrons also with polynomial kernels [4], and finally, SNoW, a Winnow-based network of linear separators [22].

There have also been some attempts at relaxing the necessity of using syntactic information derived from full parse trees. For instance, in ([20]; [12]), only shallow syntactic information at the level of phrase chunk is used; or in the systems presented in the CoNLL-2004 shared task only partial syntactic information, i.e., words, part-of-speech (PoS) tags, base chunks, clauses and named entities, is used.

Regarding the labeling strategy, it can be distinguished at least three different strategies. The first one consists of performing role identification directly by a IOB-type[2] sequence tagging. The second approach consists of dividing the problem into two independent phases: recognition, in which the arguments are recognized, and labeling, in which the already recognized arguments are assigned role labels. The third approach also proceeds in two phases: filtering, in which a set of argument candidates are decided and labeling, in which a set of optimal arguments is derived from the proposed candidates. As a variant of the first two-phase strategy, in [27] first is performed a direct classification of chunks into argument labels, and then the actual arguments are decided in a post-process by joining previously classified arguments fragments.

2.2 Maximum Entropy Models

Maximum Entropy (ME) modelling provides a framework to integrate information for classification from many heterogeneous information sources [16]. ME probability models have been successfully applied to some NLP tasks, such as PoS tagging or sentence boundary detection [23].

The method presented in this paper is based on conditional ME probability models. It has been implemented using a supervised learning method that consists of building classifiers using a tagged corpus. A classifier obtained by means of an ME technique consists of a set of parameters or coefficients which are estimated using an optimization procedure. Each coefficient is associated with one feature observed in the training data. The main purpose is to obtain the probability distribution that maximizes the entropy, that is, maximum ignorance is assumed and nothing apart from the training data is considered. Some advantages of using the ME framework are that even knowledge-poor features may be applied accurately; the ME framework thus allows a virtually unrestricted ability to represent problem-specific knowledge in the form of features [23].

Let us assume a set of contexts X and a set of classes C. The function $cl : X \rightarrow C$ chooses the class c with the highest conditional probability in the context x: $cl(x) = \arg\max_c p(c|x)$. Each feature is calculated by a function that is associated with a specific class c', and it takes the form of equation (1), where $cp(x)$ is some observable characteristic in the context[3]. The conditional probability $p(c|x)$ is defined by equation (2), where α_i is the parameter or weight of the feature i, K is the number of features defined, and $Z(x)$ is a constant to ensure that the sum of all conditional probabilities for this context is equal to 1.

---

[2] IOB format represents chunks which do not overlap nor embed. Words outside a chunk receive the tag O. For words forming a chunk of type k, the first word receives the B-k tag (Begin), and the remaining words receive the tag I-k (Inside).

[3] The ME approach is not limited to binary functions, but the optimization procedure used for the estimation of the parameters, the *Generalized Iterative Scaling* procedure, uses this feature.

$$f(x,c) = \begin{cases} 1 \text{ if } c' = c \text{ and } cp(x) = true \\ 0 \text{ otherwise} \end{cases} \quad (1)$$

$$p(c|x) = \frac{1}{Z(x)} \prod_{i=1}^{K} \alpha_i^{f_i(x,c)} \quad (2)$$

2.3 The Core of SemRol Method

The method consists of three main modules: i) Word Sense Disambiguation (WSD) Module, ii) Module of Heuristics, and iii) Semantic Role Disambiguation (SRD) Module.

Unlike the systems presented in section 2.1, first of all, the process to obtain the semantic role needs the sense of the target verb. After that, several heuristics are applied in order to obtain the arguments of the sentence. And finally, the semantic roles that fill these arguments are obtained.

Word Sense Disambiguation Module. This module is based on the WSD system developed by [24]. It is based on conditional ME probability models.

The learning module produces classifiers for each target verb. This module has two subsystems. The first subsystem consists of two component actions: in a first step, the module processes the learning corpus in order to define the functions that will apprise the linguistic features of each context; in a second step, the module then fills in the feature vectors. The second subsystem of the learning module performs the estimation of the coefficients and stores the classification functions.

The classification module carries out the disambiguation of new contexts using the previously stored classification functions. When ME does not have enough information about a specific context, several senses may achieve the same maximum probability and thus the classification cannot be done properly. In these cases, the most frequent sense in the corpus is assigned. However, this heuristic is only necessary for a minimum number of contexts or when the set of linguistic attributes processed is very small.

Description of Features. The set of features defined for the training of the system is described below (Figure 2) and depend on the data in the training corpus. These features are based on words, PoS tags, chunks and clauses in the local context.

SW **features**: content words in a sentence
CW **features**: content words in a clause
HP **features**: heads in syntactic phrases
HLRP **features**: heads in -1, +1 syntactic phrases

Fig. 2. List of types of features in WSD module

Content-words refer to words with PoS related to noun, adjective, adverb or verb. For instance, if the sentence

(E5) Confidence in the pound is widely expected to take another sharp dive if trade figures for September, due for release tomorrow, fail to show a substantial improvement from July and August's near-record deficits

is considered, the SW features is the set of words: *Confidence, pound, is, widely, expected, take, sharp, dive, trade, figures, September, due, release, tomorrow, show, substantial, improvement, July, August, near-record, deficits.*

Heads in syntactic phrases refer to words with PoS related to noun, in a noun phrase; or related to verb, in a verb phrase.

Module of Heuristics. After determining the sense for every target verb of the corpus, it is necessary to determine the argument boundaries of those verbs. In a first approach), two arguments, the left argument and the right argument, have been considered for each target verb. The left/right argument is made up of the words of the sentence at the left/right of the verbal phrase where the target verb is included. Besides, these words must belong to the same clause as the target verb. If the sentence (E5) is considered, where the target verb is *fail*, its left and right arguments are *trade figures for September, due for release tomorrow*, and *a substantial improvement from July and August's near-record deficits*, respectively.

In a second approach, left and right arguments have been also considered. However, in this case, the left argument is only the noun phrase at the left of the target verb, and the right argument is only the noun phrase at the right of the target verb. Besides, if exists a prepositional phrase close together the right noun phrase, it will be considered a second right argument. In any case, the phrases must belong to the same clause as the target verb. So, in the sentence

(E6) The current account deficit will narrow to only 1.8 billion in September

the target verb is *narrow*, the left argument is *the current account deficit* and right arguments are *only 1.8 billion* and *in September*.

Both approximation consider the verbal phrase of the target verb as the verb argument, and modal verbs and particles *not* and *n't* in the verbal phrase of the target verb, as arguments. For instances, in the previous sentence, *will* is considered an argument.

It is expected that the number of successes in left arguments, modal arguments and negative arguments, will be high and it will not account for much error. However, the results in right arguments will be probably lower. In future works we will take interest in determining the arguments of the verbs using a machine learning strategy, such as a maximum entropy conditional probability method, or a support vector machines method [10]. This strategy will allow us to determine the argument boundaries more accurately.

Semantic Role Disambiguation Module. Finally, the role for each target verb depending on sense will be determined. This task uses a conditional ME probability model. This one is like the method used in WSD task. In this case, features are extracted for each argument for every target verb. These features are used to classify those arguments. Instead of working with all roles [6], in this classification, the classes considered will be the roles of each sense of each verb. It increases the total number of the classes for the full task on SRD, but it reduces the partial number of classes that are taken into account in each argument, considerably. In the sentence (E5), the sense of fail is 01, so, the classes of the roles 0,1,2,3, of fail.01 have just been considered, however the roles 0,1 of fail.02 have not been considered. It is possible to do this because the sense of every target verb was determined in the WSD module. Figure 3 shows the roles of *fail* verb.

```
<roleset id="fail.01" name="not succeed"> <roles>
  <role n="0"  descr="assessor of not failing (professor)"/>
  <role n="1"  descr="thing failing"/>
  <role n="2"  descr="task"/>
  <role n="3"  descr="benefactive"/>
</roles>

<roleset id="fail.02" name="give failing grade"> <roles>
  <role n="0"  descr="teacher"/>
  <role n="1"  descr="student"/>
</roles>
```

Fig. 3. Senses and roles of the frame *fail* in PropBank

Description of Features. For each argument, the features are based on words and part of speech tags in the local context. The words in the arguments which part of speech tag is one of the following NN, NNS, NNP, NNPS, JJ, JJR, JJS, RB, RBR, RBS have been considered. That is, only nouns, adjectives or adverbs have been considered.

In addition, verbs (VB, VBD, VBG, VBN, VBP, VBZ, MD) have been considered whether they are target verbs or not. This set of features is named AW, content-words in the argument. In the (E5) instance, AW for left argument is the set of words *trade, figures, September, due, release, tomorrow*; and AW for right argument is the set of words *substantial, improvement, July, August, near-record, deficits*.

A straightforward classifier with just one set of features has been built. This is an attempt to evaluate the performance of the module with simple events and low computational cost.

3 Experimental Data

Our method has been trained and evaluated using the PropBank corpus [18], which is the Penn Treebank [17] corpus enriched with predicate-arguments structures. To be precise, the data consists of sections of the Wall Street Journal. Training set matches with sections 15-18 and development set matches with section 20.

PropBank annotates the Penn Treebank with arguments structures related to verbs. The semantic roles considered in PropBank are the following [3]:

- Numbered arguments (A0-A5, AA): Arguments defining verb-specific roles. Their semantic depends on the verb and the verb usage in a sentence, or verb sense. In general, A0 stands for the *agent* and A1 corresponds to the *patient* or *theme* of the proposition, and these two are the most frequent roles. However, no consistent generalization can be made across different verbs or different senses of the same verb. PropBank takes the definition of verb senses from VerbNet, and for each verb and each sense defines the set of possible roles for that verb usage, called roleset.
- Adjuncts (AM-): General arguments that any verb may take optionally. There are 13 types of adjuncts:
  - AM-LOC: location
  - AM-EXT: extent
  - AM-DIS: discourse marker
  - AM-ADV: general-porpouse
  - AM-NEC: negation marker
  - AM-MOD: modal verb
  - AM-CAU: cause
  - AM-TEMP: temporal
  - AM-PRP: purpose
  - AM-MNR: manner
  - AM-DIR: direction
- References (R-): Arguments representing arguments realized in other parts of the sentence. The role of a reference is the same than the role of the referenced argument. The label is an R-tag preceded to the label of the referent, e.g. R-A1.
- Verbs (V): Participant realizing the verb of the proposition.

Training data consists of 8936 sentences, with 50182 arguments and 1838 distinct target verbs. Development data consists of 2012 sentences, with 11121 arguments and 978 distinct target verbs.

Apart from the correct output, both datasets contain the input part of the data: PoS tags, chunks and clauses. Besides, the sense of verb is available if the word is a target verb.

4 Results and Discussion

Following, the results of the three modules are shown in Table 1. These results have been obtained on the development set. Modules have been evaluated based on precision, recall and F1 measure. In each case, precision is the proportion of senses, arguments or roles predicted by the system which are correct; and recall is the proportion of correct senses, correct arguments or correct roles which are predicted by each module. F1 computes the harmonic mean of precision and recall: $F_{\beta=1}=(2pr)/(p+r)$.

Table 1. Results on the development set

WSD	Successes	3650	Precision	**0.88**
	Fails	486	Recall	0.85
	No disambiguated	169	F1	0.86
MH	Successes	4426	Precision	**0.51**
	Fails	4201	Recall	0.40
	No detected	2494	F1	0.45
SRD	Successes	5085	Precision	**0.48**
	Fails	5464	Recall	0.46
	No disambiguated	572	F1	0.47

4.1 WSD Module Results

In this experiment one set of features have just been considered, features about *content word in a sentence.* Table 1 shows that 3650 verbs have been disambiguated successfully, and 655 unsuccessfully. From these, 169 are due to no disambiguated verbs and 486 to mistakes in the disambiguation process. As a result, a precision of 88% is obtained. Such precision has been calculated including all verbs, polysemic and monosemic verbs. These results show the goodness of the ME module and reveal that the ME module is correctly defined. Besides, it is expected that the tuning with the others set of features (see section 2.3) will improve the results.

4.2 MH Module Results

This module has been tested with two approaches described in section 2.3. Table 1 shows the result about the second one (see section 2.3). In this case, a total of 4426 arguments have been detected successfully, but 6695 have been erroneously detected or missing. Therefore, the precision of MH module is 51%. Other experiments carried out with the other approach drops the precision to 34%.

In any case, the experiments have been done assuming correct senses for target verbs. By means of this, the independence of MH module in relation to WSD module has been evaluated.

These results confirm the need for determining the arguments of the verbs by defining new heuristics or using a machine learning strategy.

4.3 SRD Module Results

In order to evaluate this module, correct senses of the verbs and correct argument boundaries have been presumed. So, SRD module has been tested independently of WSD and MH modules.

Table 1 shows a precision of 48%. For further details, the precision for each kind of argument is shown in Table 2. Besides, if verb argument is considered, precision goes up to 62%. These results show that the ME module is correctly defined. However, it is need a tuning phase in order to improve them. Besides, a precision of 0,00% in several *R-* arguments shows the need for a co-reference resolution module.

Table 2. Results on the development set. SRD module

	Precision	Recall	$F_{\beta=1}$		Precision	Recall	$F_{\beta=1}$
A0	47.22%	44.56%	45.85	AM-MNR	66.29%	17.66%	27.90
A1	44.99%	69.12%	54.50	AM-MOD	82.35%	39.59%	53.47
A2	52.26%	26.62%	35.28	AM-NEG	80.00%	64.12%	71.19
A3	30.16%	12.75%	17.92	AM-PNC	39.47%	15.00%	21.74
A4	64.52%	13.61%	22.47	AM-PRD	0.00%	0.00%	0.00
A5	100.00%	25.00%	40.00	AM-PRP	0.00%	0.00%	0.00
AM-ADV	21.93%	7.10%	10.73	AM-REC	0.00%	0.00%	0.00
AM-CAU	0.00%	0.00%	0.00	AM-TMP	61.98%	21.48%	31.90
AM-DIR	55.56%	8.33%	14.49	R-A0	0.00%	0.00%	0.00
AM-DIS	86.44%	25.00%	38.78	R-A1	0.00%	0.00%	0.00
AM-EXT	70.00%	14.29%	23.73	R-A2	0.00%	0.00%	0.00
AM-LOC	44.44%	22.61%	29.97	R-AM-LOC	100.00%	25.00%	40.00
R-AM-TMP	33.33%	33.33%	33.33	V	97.44%	97.44%	97.44
				all	**61.92%**	**59.62%**	**60.75**
				all–{V}	**47.42%**	**44.98%**	**46.17**

5 Conclusions and Working in Progress

In this paper, a Semantic Role Labeling method using a WSD module is presented. It is based on *maximum entropy conditional probability models.* The method presented consists of three sub-tasks. First of all, the process of obtaining the semantic role needs the sense of the target verb. After that, several heuristics are applied in order to obtain the arguments of the sentence. And finally, the semantic roles that fill these arguments are obtained. Training and development data are used to build this learning system.

Results about the WSD, MH and SRD modules have been shown. Currently, we are working on the definition of new features to the SRD modules. So, the re-definition of the heuristics is planned in order to improve the results. After that, we are going to work on the tuning phase in order to achieve an optimum identification of the semantic roles.

On the other hand, we are working in the integration of semantic aspects in Question Answering or Information Retrieval Systems, in order to obtain High Precision QA/IR Systems. Shortly, we will show results about this incorporations.

References

1. *Eighth Conference on Natural Language Learning (CoNLL-2004)*, Boston, MA, USA, Mayo 2004.
2. U. Baldewein, K. Erk, S. Padó, and D. Prescher. Semantic role labeling with chunk sequences. In *Proceedings of the Eighth Conference on Natural Language Learning (CoNLL-2004)* [1].

3. X. Carreras and L. Màrquez. Introduction to the CoNLL-2004 Shared Task: Semantic Role Labeling. In *Proceedings of the Eighth Conference on Natural Language Learning (CoNLL-2004)* [1].
4. X. Carreras, L. Màrquez, and G. Chrupala. Hierarchical Recognition of Propositional Arguments with Perceptrons. In *Proceedings of the Eighth Conference on Natural Language Learning (CoNLL-2004)* [1].
5. J. Chen and O. Rambow. Use of deep linguistic features for the recognition and labeling of semantic arguments. In *Proceedings of the Conference on Empirical Methods in Natural Language Processing (EMNLP2003)*, July 2003.
6. M. Fleischman, N. Kwon, and E. Hovy. Maximum Entropy Models for FrameNet Classification. In *Proceedings of the Conference on Empirical Methods in Natural Language Processing (EMNLP2003)*, July 2003.
7. D. Gildea and J. Hockenmaier. Identifying semantic roles using combinatory categorial grammar. In *Proceedings of the Conference on Empirical Methods in Natural Language Processing (EMNLP2003)*, July 2003.
8. D. Gildea and D. Jurafsky. Automatic labeling of semantic roles. *Computational Linguistics*, 28(3):245–288, 2002.
9. D. Gildea and M. Palmer. The necessity of parsing for predicate argument recognition. In *Proceedings of the 40th Annual Meeting of the Association for Computational Linguistic (ACL)*, Philadelphia, Julio 2002.
10. J. Giménez and L. Màrquez. Fast and Accurate Part-of-Speech Tagging: The SVM Approach Revisited. In *Proceedings of Recent Advances in Natural Language Processing 2003*, Borovets, Bulgaria, Septiembre 2003.
11. K. Hacioglu, S. Pradhan, W. Ward, J.H. Martin, and D. Jurafsky. Semantic Role Labeling by Tagging Syntactic Chunks. In *Proceedings of the Eighth Conference on Natural Language Learning (CoNLL-2004)* [1].
12. K. Hacioglu and W. Ward. Target word detection and semantic role chunking using support vector machines. In *Proceedings of the Human Language Technology Conference (HLT-NAACL)*, Edmonton, Canada, Junio 2003.
13. D. Higgins. A transformation-based approach to argument labeling. In *Proceedings of the Eighth Conference on Natural Language Learning (CoNLL-2004)* [1].
14. B. Kouchnir. A Memory-based Approach for Semantic Role Labeling. In *Proceedings of the Eighth Conference on Natural Language Learning (CoNLL-2004)* [1].
15. J. Lim, Y. Hwang, S. Park, and H. Rim. Semantic role labeling using maximum entropy model. In *Proceedings of the Eighth Conference on Natural Language Learning (CoNLL-2004)* [1].
16. C.D. Manning and H. Schütze. *Foundations of Statistical Natural Language Processing*. The MIT Press, Cambridge, Massachusetts, 1999.
17. M.P. Marcus, B. Santorini, and M.A. Marcinkiewicz. Building a large annotated corpus of english: the penn treebank. *Computational Linguistics*, (19), 1993.
18. M. Palmer, D. Gildea, and P. Kingsbury. The proposition bank: An annotated corpus of semantic roles. *Computational Linguistics*, 2004. Submitted.
19. K. Park, Y. Hwang, and H. Rim. Two-Phase Semantic Role Labeling bsed on Support Vector Machines. In *Proceedings of the Eighth Conference on Natural Language Learning (CoNLL-2004)* [1].
20. S. Pradhan, K. Hacioglu, V. Krugler, W. Ward, J.H. Martin, and D. Jurafsky. Support vector learning for semantic argument classification. Technical report, International Computer Science Institute, Center for Spoken Language Research, University of Colorado, 2003.

21. S. Pradhan, K. Hacioglu, W. Ward, J.H. Martin, and D.Jurafsky. Semantic role parsing: Adding semantic structure to unstructured text. In *Proceedings of the Third IEEE International Conference on Data Mining (ICDM)*, Melbourne, Florida, USA, Noviembre 2003.
22. V. Punyakanok, D. Roth, W. Yih, D. Zimak, and Y. Tu. Semantic Role Labeling Via Generalized Inference Over Classifiers. In *Proceedings of the Eighth Conference on Natural Language Learning (CoNLL-2004)* [1].
23. A. Ratnaparkhi. *Maximum Entropy Models for Natural Language Ambiguity Resolution.* PhD thesis, University of Pennsylvania, 1998.
24. A. Suárez and M. Palomar. A maximum entropy-based word sense disambiguation system. In *Proceedings of the 19th International Conference on Computational Linguistics (COLING)*, pages 960–966, Taipei, Taiwan, Agosto 2002.
25. M. Surdeanu, S. Harabagiu, J. Williams, and P. Aarseth. Using predicate-argument structures for information extraction. In *Proceedings of the 41st Annual Meeting of the Association for Computational Linguistics (ACL)*, Sapporo, Japan, Julio 2003.
26. A. Thompson, R. Levy, and C.D. Manning. A generative model for semantic role labeling. In *Proceedings of the 14th European Conference on Machine Learning (ECML)*, Cavtat-Dubrovnik, Croatia, Septiembre 2003.
27. A. van den Bosch, S. Canisius, I. Hendricks, W. Daelemans, and E.T.K. Sang. Memory-based semantic role labeling: Optimizing features, algorithm and output. In *Proceedings of the Eighth Conference on Natural Language Learning (CoNLL-2004)* [1].
28. K. Williams, C. Dozier, and A. McCulloh. Learning Transformation Rules for Semantic Role Labeling. In *Proceedings of the Eighth Conference on Natural Language Learning (CoNLL-2004)* [1].

Significance of Syntactic Features for Word Sense Disambiguation

Ala Sasi Kanth and Kavi Narayana Murthy

Department of Computer and Information Sciences
University of Hyderabad, India
sasi_kanth_a@yahoo.co.in, knmuh@yahoo.com

Abstract. In this paper[1] we explore the use of syntax in improving the performance of Word Sense Disambiguation(WSD) systems. We argue that not all words in a sentence are useful for disambiguating the senses of a target word and eliminating noise is important. Syntax can be used to identify related words and eliminating other words as noise actually improves performance significantly. CMU's Link Parser has been used for syntactic analysis. Supervised learning techniques have been applied to perform word sense disambiguation on selected target words. The Naive Bayes classifier has been used in all the experiments. All the major grammatical categories of words have been covered. Experiments conducted and results obtained have been described. Ten fold cross validation has been performed in all cases. The results we have obtained are better than the published results for the same data.

1 Introduction

A word can have more than one sense. The sense in which the word is used can be determined, most of the times, by the context in which the word occurs. The word *bank* has several senses out of which *bank* as a financial institution and *bank* as a sloping land bordering a river can be easily distinguished from the context. Distinguishing between the senses of *bank* as a financial institution and *bank* as a building housing such an institution is more difficult. The process of identifying the correct sense of words in context is called *Word Sense Disambiguation* (WSD). Homonymy and Polysemy must both be considered. Word sense disambiguation contributes significantly to many natural language processing tasks such as machine translation and information retrieval.

The focus of research in WSD is on distinguishing between senses of words within a given syntactic category, since senses across syntactic categories are better disambiguated through POS tagging techniques. Many researchers have focused on disambiguation of selected target words although there is some recent interest in unrestricted WSD [1, 2].

[1] The research reported here was supported in part by the University Grants Commission under the UPE scheme.

J. L. Vicedo et al. (Eds.): EsTAL 2004, LNAI 3230, pp. 340–348, 2004.

WSD systems often rely upon sense definitions in dictionaries, features of senses (for example, box-codes and subject categories present in Longman's Dictionary of Contemporary English (LDOCE)), entries in bilingual dictionaries, WordNet etc. Dictionaries and other sources do not always agree on the number and nature of senses for given words. For some tasks the fine granularity of senses as given in some dictionaries is not required or may even be counter productive and so methods to merge closely related senses have been explored by some researchers[3].

Both knowledge based and machine learning approaches have been applied for WSD. Lesk [4] used glossaries of senses present in dictionaries. The sense definition which has the maximum overlap with the definitions of the words in the context was taken as the correct sense. Lesk's algorithm uses the knowledge present in dictionaries and does not use any sense tagged corpus for training. On the other hand, machine learning methods require a training corpus. Yarowsky [5] devised an algorithm which takes some initial seed collocations for each sense and uses unsupervised techniques to produce decision lists for disambiguation. In supervised disambiguation, machine learning techniques are used to build a model from labeled training data. Some of the machine learning techniques used for WSD are - decision lists [6, 7], Naive Bayes classifier [8] and decision trees. In this work we have used the Naive Bayes Classifier.

It has been argued that the choice of the right features is more important than the choice of techniques for classification [9, 10]. A variety of features have been used, including bigrams, surface form of the target word, collocations, POS tags of target and neighboring words and syntactic features such as heads of phrases and categories of phrases in which the target word appears. Some researchers believe that lexical features are sufficient while others [11, 12] have argued for combining lexical features with syntactic features. In this paper we show that syntax can significantly improve the performance of WSD systems. We argue that elimination of noise is important - not all words in a given sentence are useful for disambiguating the sense of a target word. We have used CMU's Link parser to identify words that are syntactically related to the target word. Words which are not syntactically related to the target word are considered to be noise and eliminated. The results we get are comparable to, or better than, the best results obtained so far on the same data.

2 Role of Syntax in WSD

Not all words in the context are helpful for determining the sense of a target word. Syntax can help in identifying relevant parts of the context, thereby eliminating noise. Using syntactic features for WSD is not entirely new. Ng [13] used syntactic information such as verb-object and subject-verb relationships along with the basic lexical features. Yarowsky [14] also used similar syntactic information including verb-object, subject-verb and noun-modifier. Stetina [15] and some of the work presented in the Senseval-2 workshop [16] have also explored the possibility of combining lexical and syntactic features. Recently, Mohammad and Pedersen [11] have analyzed the role of various kinds of lexical and syntactic features in isolation as well as in various combinations. They also employ an ensemble technique to combine the results of classifiers using different sets of features. They propose a method to estimate the best possible performance through such an ensemble technique. They use a simple ensemble method and show that their results are comparable to the best published results and close to the optimal. However, the exact contribution of syntax is not very clear from these studies. David Martinez et al [12] have compared the performance obtained by using only basic (lexical and topical) features with the performance obtained by using basic features combined with syntactic features. They show a performance gain of 1% to 2% for the AdaBoost algorithm while there was no improvement for the Decision List method. In this paper we explore the role of syntactic features in WSD and show that syntax can in fact make a significant contribution to WSD. We have obtained 4% to 12% improvement in performance for various target words. The results we get are comparable to, or better than, the best published results on the same data.

We have used the Link parser developed by Carnegie-Mellon University. The link parser gives labeled links which connect pairs of words. We have found this representation more convenient than parse trees or other representations given by other parsers. Our studies have shown that eliminating noise and using only selected context words is the key to good performance. Syntax has been used only for identifying related words. In the next section we describe the experiments we have conducted and the results obtained.

3 Experimental Setup

Here we have applied supervised learning techniques to perform word sense disambiguation on selected target words. All the major grammatical categories of words have been covered. The Naive Bayes classifier has been used as the base. Ten fold cross validation has been performed in all cases. We give below the details of the corpora and syntactic parser used and the details of the experiments conducted.

3.1 Corpora

For our experiments we have used publicly available corpora converted into Senseval-2 data format by Ted Pedersen [2] We have chosen *interest*, *serve*, and *hard* as the target words, covering the major syntactic categories - noun, verb and adjective respectively.

In *interest* corpus each instance of the word *interest* is tagged with one of six possible LDOCE senses. There is a total of 2368 occurrences in the sense tagged corpus, where each occurrence is a single sentence that contains the word *interest*. The instances in the corpus are selected from Penn Treebank Wall Street Journal Corpus(ACL/DCI version). Sense tagging was done by Rebecca Bruce

[2] http://www.d.umn.edu/~tpederse/data.html

and Janyce Wiebe [17]. The sense tags used, frequency, and glosses of the senses are given in Table 1.

Table 1. Senses of the word *interest*, their distribution in the corpus and the gloss of senses

Sense Label	Frequency	Sense Definition
interest_1	361(15%)	readiness to give attention
interest_2	11(01%)	quality of causing attention to be given to
interest_3	66(03%)	activity, etc. that one gives attention to
interest_4	178(08%)	advantage, advancement or favor
interest_5	500(21%)	a share in a company or business
interest_6	1252(53%)	money paid for the use of money

The *hard* corpus contains the word *hard* with part of speech as adjective and is manually tagged with three senses in 4333 contexts. The *hard* data was created by Leacock, Chodorow and Miller [18]. The instances were picked from the San Jose Mercury News Corpus and manually annotated with one of three senses form WordNet. The sense tags used, frequency in the corpus, glosses of the senses and examples are given in Table 2.

Table 2. Senses of the word *hard*, their distribution in the corpus, glosses of senses and examples

Sense Label	Frequency	Sense Definition	Example
HARD1	3455(80%)	not easy - difficult	it's hard to be disciplined
HARD2	502(11%)	not soft - metaphoric	these are hard times
HARD3	376(9%)	not soft - physical	the hard crust

The *serve* corpus contains the word *serve* with part of speech as verb and is manually tagged in 4378 contexts. The *serve* data was created by Leacock, Chodorow and Miller [18]. The instances were picked from the Wall Street Journal Corpus(1987-89) and the American Printing House for the Blind (APHB) corpus. The sentences have been manually tagged with the four senses from WordNet. The sense tags used, frequency in the corpus, glosses of the senses and examples are given in Table 3.

3.2 Parser

For obtaining the syntactic information we have used the link parser from Carnegie-Mellon University[3]. Link parser is a syntactic parser based on link grammar, a theory of English syntax [19, 20]. It is a robust and broad coverage parser. If in case it is unable to parse the sentence fully, it tries to give a partial

[3] http://www.link.cs.cmu.edu/link/

Table 3. Senses of the word *serve*, their distribution in the corpus, and the gloss of senses

SenseLabel	Frequency	Sense Definition	Example
SERVE2	853(20%)	function as something	serves as yard stick to
SERVE6	439(10%)	provide a service	department will serve select few
SERVE10	1814(41%)	supply with food/means	serve dinner
SERVE12	1272(29%)	hold an office	served as head of department

structure to the sentence. Given a sentence, the parser assigns to it a syntactic structure, which consists of a set of labeled links connecting pairs of words. For example the parsed structure of the sentence

```
"The flight landed on rocky terrain"
```

is given by the link parser as

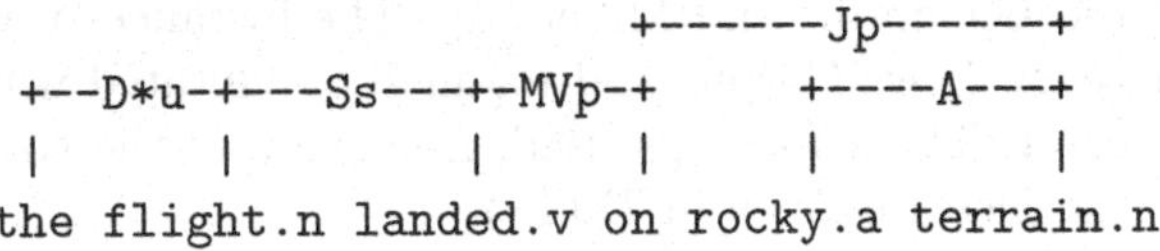


```
A4- connects attributive adjectives to following nouns
S - connects subject nouns to finite verbs
D - connects determiners to nouns
J - connects prepositions to their objects
MV- connects verbs and adjectives to modifying phrases that follow,
   like adverbs, prepositional phrases, subordinating conjunctions,
   comparatives and participle phrases with commas.
```

A word to be disambiguated may be connected directly to another word with a link or it can be indirectly connected with a series of links. Consider the target word *interest* in the context:

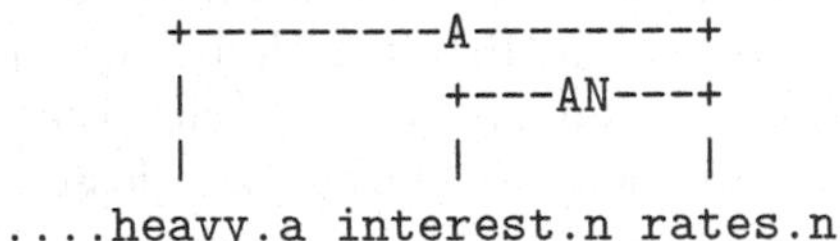


```
AN - connects noun-modifiers to
     following nouns
```

Here the word *rates* is directly linked with the word *interest*, and the word *heavy* is indirectly linked to *interest*. The words which are directly or indirectly

[4] The lower case letters in the label specify additional properties of the links. These are not used in our experiments.

connected to the target word can be taken as the values of the attribute labeled with the name or names of the links. An exclamation mark indicates a leftward link to the target word. The attribute and the value are represented as (attribute,value) pairs. See examples below.

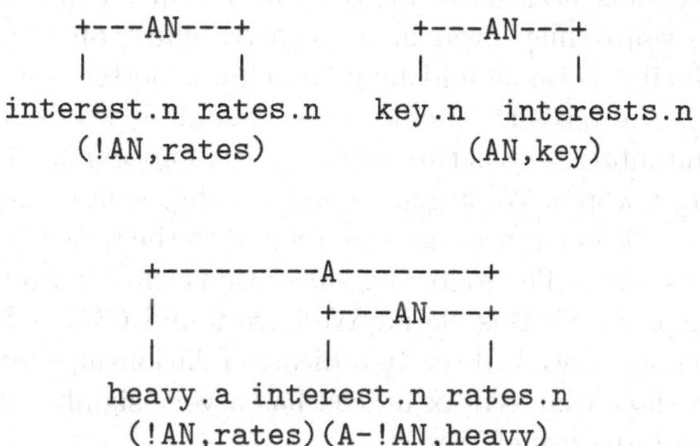

Alternatively, we can simply use the syntactically related words as features, without regard to the specific syntactic relationships. The Link parser employs a large number of different types of links and including the link labels greatly increases the space of possible feature values, thereby introducing sparseness in available data. In our experiments described here, we have used only words as features, not the link labels.

4 Experiments and Results

We give below the details of the experiments we have conducted. The results are summarized in the table 4 below.

4.1 Experiment A: Baseline

The baseline performance can be defined as the performance obtained when the most frequent sense in the corpus is assigned for the target word in all contexts. This can be viewed as a bottom-line for comparison of various techniques. The base line performance depends on the flatness of the distribution of the various senses for a given target word. If the senses are all more or less equally likely, the baseline would be low and if one of the senses is much more frequent than others, the baseline would be high. It can be seen that the baseline for *hard* is quite high.

4.2 Experiment B: NaiveBayes (All Words in the Context)

Here all the words in the context of the target word are taken as features. By context we mean the whole sentence in which the target word appears. The words in the context are considered as a bag of words without regard to word order or syntactic structure.

It may be noted that the performance is in general much better than the baseline. (There is, however, a small decrease in the case of the word *hard* - the distribution of senses of the word *hard* is quite peaked and the baseline itself is quite high.)

Not all words in the sentence are likely to be useful for disambiguating the target word. Some words may even have negative effect on the performance. Eliminating or reducing noise should help to achieve better results. The question that remains is the basis for including or excluding words in the context. Syntax captures the internal structure of sentences and explicates a variety of relationships amongst words. We argue, therefore, that syntax should be useful for deciding which words in the sentence are related to the target word and hence likely to influence its sense. The following subsections show various experiments we have carried out to verify this claim. We have found CMU's Link Parser to be an appropriate choice since it directly indicates relationships between pairs of words. Our studies show that syntax indeed has a very significant contribution in improving the performance of WSD.

4.3 Experiment C: NaiveBayes (Syntactically Relevant Words)

In this experiment, all the words which are linked directly or indirectly (up to two levels) to the target word, that is, a bag of selected words from the sentence, are taken as features. It may be seen from the table of results that performance has significantly improved. This vindicates our claim that not all words in context are useful and elimination of noise is important.

4.4 Experiment D: NaiveBayes (Words in a Window)

Our studies have shown that neighboring words often have a considerable influence on the sense of a target word. For example, adjectives and the nouns they modify occur close together and tend to influence one another. The object of a verb may appear close to the verb and have a say in the sense of the verb. Our results for a window of ± 2 words around the target word validate this point. The results also confirm our claim that not all words in the sentence are relevant and eliminating noise helps.

We have conducted experiments with various sizes of windows around the target word. The best results are obtained for a window size of 2 to 3. As the window size gets larger, more and more noise words will start getting in and the performance drops.

4.5 Experiment E: NaiveBayes (Syntactically Related and Neighborhood Words)

Here we try to combine syntactically linked words and words in the neighborhood of the target word for feature selection. Note that neighboring words may not always be linked syntactically. In this study words syntactically related to the target word either directly or through one level of intermediate link have been included. Also, words in a neighborhood of ± 2 are included. All other words in the sentence are treated as noise and ignored. It may be seen that this combination generally outperforms the other schemes. In fact the results obtained here are better than the best published results [11]. It may be noted that we have actually used only lexical features, not any syntactic features directly. Syntax has been used only to identify related words and remove other words as noise.

We have also conducted experiments where the features included not just the related words but also the specific syntactic relations as expressed by the links in the Link parser. This greatly enlarges the feature space as there are several hundred different types of links. The sparseness of training data under this expanded feature space will limit the performance obtainable. Our experiments have shown that not much improvement in performance is possible with the available data.

4.6 Results

Table 4 shows the results of our experiments:

Table 4. Table showing the accuracy (in %) for the three words

words	Experiment				
	A: Baseline	B: All words in sentence	C: Only syntactically related words	D: Neighboring words	E: Selected words
interest(n)	52.87	85.66	86.14	87.94	89.39
hard(ad)	79.73	78.22	90.59	91.53	90.91
serve(v)	41.43	76.88	81.93	81.23	85.25

5 Conclusions

In this paper we have explored the contribution of syntax for word sense disambiguation. Not all words in a sentence are helpful for identifying the intended sense of a given target word. Syntactic information can be used to identify useful parts of the context and thereby reduce noise. We have not directly used any syntactic features. Syntax helps in the selection of the right lexical features and our experiments show that elimination of noise can significantly improve the performance of WSD. Improvement in performance ranges from about 4 % to about 12 %. Overall performance achieved ranges from about 85 % to about 90 % and is comparable to, or better than, the best results published on similar data.

References

1. Mihalcea, R., Moldovan, D.: A method for word sense disambiguation of unrestricted text. In: Proceedings of the 37th Annual Meeting of the Association for Computational Linguistics (ACL-99), Maryland, NY (1999)
2. Wilks, Y., Stevenson, M.: Word sense disambiguation using optimized combinations of knowledge sources. In: Proceedings of ACL 36/Coling 17. (1998) 1398–1402

3. Dolan, W.B.: Word sense ambiguation: Clustering related senses. Technical Report MSR-TR-94-18, Microsoft Corporation, Redmond, WA (1994)
4. Lesk, M.: Automated sense disambiguation using machine-readable dictionaries: How to tell a pine cone from a ice cream cone. In: proceedings of the SIGDOC Conference, Toronto, Canada (1986) 24–26
5. Yarowsky, D.: Unsupervised word sense disambiguation rivaling supervised methods. In: Meeting of the Association for Computational Linguistics. (1995) 189–196
6. Rivest, R.: Learning decision lists. Machine Learning **2** (1987) 229–246
7. Yarowsky, D.: Decision lists for lexical ambiguity resolution: application to accent restoration in spanish and french. In: Proceedings of ACL '94. (1994) 88–95
8. Gale, W.A., Church, K.W., Yarowsky, D.: Estimating upper and lower bounds on the performance of word-sense disambiguation programs. In: Proceedings of the 30th Annual Meeting of the Association for Computational Linguistics, University of Delaware, Newark, Delaware (1992) 249–256
9. Pedersen, T.: A decision tree of bigrams is an accurate predictor of word sense. In: Proceedings of the Second Annual Meeting of the North American Chapter of the Association for Computational Linguistics. (2001) 79–86
10. Ng, H.T., Lee, K.L.: An empirical evaluation of knowledge sources and learning algirithms for word sense disambiguation. In: Proceedings of the Conference on Empirical Methods in Natural Language Processing. (2002) 41–48
11. Mohammad, S., Pedersen, T.: Combining lexical and syntactic features for supervised word sense disambiguation. In: Proceedings of CoNLL-2004, Boston, MA, USA (2004) 25–32
12. Martínez, D., Agirre, E., Màrquez, L.: Syntactic features for high precision word sense disambiguation. In: Coling. (2002)
13. Ng, H.T., Lee, H.B.: Integrating multiple knowledge sources to disambiguate word sense: An exemplar-based approach. In: Proceedings of the Thirty-Fourth Annual Meeting of the Association for Computational Linguistics, San Francisco, Morgan Kaufmann Publishers (1996) 40–47
14. Yarowsky, D.: Hierarchical decision lists for word sense disambiguation. Computers and the Humanities **34** (2000)
15. Stetina, J., Kurohashi, S., Nagao, M.: General word sense disambiguation method based on a full sentential context. In: Usage of WordNet in Natural Language Processing, Proceedings of COLING-ACL Workshop, Montreal, Canada. (1998)
16. J, P., Yarowsky, D. In: Proceedings of the Second International Workshop on Evaluating Word Sense Disambiguation Systems (Senseval 2). In conjunction with ACL2001EACL2001, Toulouse, France. (2001)
17. Bruce, R., Wiebe, J.: Word-sense disambiguation using decomposable models. In: Proceedings of the 32nd Annual Meeting of the Association for Computational Linguistics. (1994) 139–146
18. Leacock, Chodorow, Miller: Using corpus statistics and wordnet relations for sense identification. In: Computational Linguistics. Volume 24(1). (1998)
19. Sleator, D., Temperley, D.: Parsing english with a link grammar. Technical Report CMU-CS-91-196, Carnegie Mellon University (1991)
20. Sleator, D.D., Temperley, D.: Parsing English with a link grammar. In: Third International Workshop on Parsing Technologies. (1993)

SisHiTra*: A Hybrid Machine Translation System from Spanish to Catalan

José R. Navarro[†], Jorge González[†], David Picó[†], Francisco Casacuberta[†], Joan M. de Val[‡], Ferran Fabregat[‡], Ferran Pla[+], and Jesús Tomás[*]

[†]Instituto Tecnológico de Informática
Universidad Politécnica de Valencia
{jonacer, jgonza, dpico, fcn}@iti.upv.es
[‡]Servei de Normalització Lingüística
Universitat de València
{Joan.M.Val, Ferran.Fabregat}@uv.es
[+]Departamento de Sistemas Informáticos y Computación
Universidad Politécnica de Valencia
fpla@dsic.upv.es
[*]Departamento de Comunicaciones
Universidad Politécnica de Valencia
jtomas@dcom.upv.es

Abstract. In the current European scenario, characterized by the coexistence of communities writing and speaking a great variety of languages, machine translation has become a technology of capital importance. In areas of Spain and of other countries, coofficiality of several languages implies producing several versions of public information. Machine translation between all the languages of the Iberian Peninsula and from them into English will allow for a better integration of Iberian linguistic communities among them and inside Europe. The purpose of this paper is to show a machine translation system from Spanish to Catalan that deals with text input. In our approach, both deductive (linguistic) and inductive (corpus-based) methodologies are combined in an homogeneous and efficient framework: finite-state transducers. Some preliminary results show the interest of the proposed architecture.

1 Introduction

Machine translation and natural computer interaction are questions that engineers and scientists have been interested in for decades. In addition to their importance for the study of human speech characteristics, these applications have social and economic interests because their development would allow for a reduction of the linguistic barriers that prevent us to make with confidence activities as, for example, travelling to other countries or the access to some computer science services (foreign websites and so on).

* Work partially supported by the Spanish CICYT under grants TIC 2000-1599-C02-01 and TIC 2003-08681-C02-02 and by the Research Supporting Program from the Univ. Pol. of Valencia.

J. L. Vicedo et al. (Eds.): EsTAL 2004, LNAI 3230, pp. 349–359, 2004.

Machine translation has received an increasing attention in the last decades due to its commercial interest and to the availability of large linguistic and computational resources. These resources are allowing machine translation systems to leave the academic scope to become more useful tools for professionals and general users.

Nevertheless, natural language complexity creates too many difficulties to develop high quality systems. This opens multiple investigation lines in which researchers work hard to improve translation results. The three most important machine translation problems are:

- PoS[1] tagging, whose objective is to identify the lexical category that a word has in a sentence [1, 2, 3].
- Semantic disambiguation, that decides which is the right sense of a word in a text [4, 5].
- Reordering, which can appear quite often when translating between different family languages.

The approaches that have been traditionally used to face these problems can be classified into two big families: *knowledge-based* and *corpus-based* methods. Knowledge-based techniques formalize expert linguistic knowledge, in form of rules, dictionaries, etc., in a computable way. Corpus-based methods use statistical pattern recognition techniques to automatically infer models from text samples without necessarily using a-priori linguistic knowledge.

SisHiTra (Hybrid Translation System) project tries to combine knowledge-based and corpus-based techniques to produce a Spanish-to-Catalan machine translation system with no semantic constraints. Spanish and Catalan are languages belonging to the Romance language family and have a lot of characteristics in common. SisHiTra makes use of their similarities to simplify the translation process. A SisHiTra future perspective is the extension to other language pairs (Portuguese, French, Italian, etc.).

Knowledge-based techniques are classical approaches to tackle general scope machine translation systems. Nevertheless, inductive methods have shown competitive results dealing with semantically constrained tasks.

Moreover, finite-state transducers [6, 7, 8] have been successfully used to implement both rule-based and corpus-based machine translation systems. Techniques based on finite-state models have also allowed for the development of useful tools for natural language processing [9, 10, 11, 3] that are interesting because of their simplicity and their adequate temporal complexity.

With the experience acquired in InterNOSTRUM [12] and TAVAL [13], *SisHiTra* project was proposed. SisHiTra system is able to deal with both eastern and western Catalan dialectal varieties, because the dictionary, which is its main database, establishes explicitely such distinction.

SisHiTra prototype has been thought to be a serial process where every module performs a specific task. In the next section we will explain the different parts in which SisHiTra system is divided.

---

[1] Parts of Speech.

2 Implementation

The methodologies that are going to be used to represent the different knowledge sources (dictionary, module interfaces, etc.) are based on finite-state machines: Hidden Markov Models (HMM) are applied in disambiguation modules [13], and stochastic transducers are used as data structures for dictionary requests as well as for inter-module communication. Reasons for using finite-state methodology are as following:

- Finite-state machines are easily represented in a computer, which facilitates their exploitation, visualization and transference.
- There are algorithms that allow for their manipulation in an efficient way (Viterbi, beam search, etc.).
- There are algorithms for their automatic inference (both their topology and their associated probability distributions) from examples.
- Linguistic knowledge incorporation can be adequately carried out.
- It allows for both serial or integrated use of the different knowledge sources.
- More powerful models can be used, such as context-free grammars, by means of a finite-state approach.

2.1 System Architecture

The system developed in SisHiTra project translates from Spanish to Catalan. It is a general scope translator with a wide vocabulary recall, so it is able to deal with all kind of sentences.

As previously commented, translation prototype modules are based on finite-state machines. This provides an homogeneous and efficient framework. Engine modules process input text in Spanish by means of a cascade of finite-state models that represent both linguistic and statistical knowledge. As an example, PoS tagging of input sentences is done by means of a serial process that requires the use of two finite-state machines: first of them represents a knowledge-based dictionary and the second one defines a corpus-based disambiguation model. Finite-state models are also used to represent partial information during translation stages (e.g. lexically ambiguous sentences).

SisHiTra and lots of other systems need, somehow, to semantically disambiguate words before turning them into target language items. Semantic disambiguation methods try to find out the implicit meaning of a word in a surrounding context.

SisHiTra is designed to make semantic disambiguation in two steps: first, a rule-based module solves some ambiguities according to certain well-known linguistic information and, afterwards, a second module ends the job by means of corpus-based inductive methods. Statistical models are receiving more interest every day for several reasons. The most important one is that they are cheaper and faster to generate than knowledge-based systems. Statistical techniques learn automatically from corpora, without the process of producing linguistic knowledge. Of course, obtaining corpora for model training is not a task free of effort. Models for semantic disambiguation in SisHiTra need parallel corpora, that is, corpora where text segments (as sentences or paragraphs) in a language are matched with their corresponding translations in the other language. These corpora have been obtained from different bilingual electronic publications (newspapers, official texts, etc.) and they have been paralleled through different alignment algorithms.

SisHiTra system is structured in the following modules:

- **Fragmenter module:** It divides the original text into sentences.
- **Labeler module:** A dictionary request produces a syntactic graph that represents all the possible analyses over the input sentence.
- **Syntactic disambiguation module:** By means of statistical models, it finds the most likely syntactic analysis between all those that labeler module produces.
- **Nominal phrase agreement module:** Every phrase element must agree in gender and number with each other.
- **Localizer module:** Another dictionary request produces a lemma-graph that represents all the possible translations for the previously analyzed and disambiguated sentence.
- **Semantic disambiguation module:** Here, a prototype in which disambiguation is carried out according only to the dictionary is presented, but we are testing some beta-systems that consider statistical models to make this decision.
- **Inflection module:** Lemmas are turned into their corresponding inflected words from the morphological information previously analyzed.
- **Formatting module:** Contraction and apostrophization are applied in order to respect the Catalan ortographic rules.
- **Integration module:** Compilation of translations, according to the original text format, is finally done.

In the following section, examples are used in order to show the functionality of each module in a more concrete way.

3 Modules

3.1 Fragmenter Module

Input text must be segmented into sentences so that translation can be carried out. By means of rules, this module is able to do it.

Input: Input to this module is Spanish text to be translated.

La estudiante atendió.

Output: Output from this module expresses the whole text in a *xml* format, in which every paragraph, sentence, translation unit (*ut*) and upper character has been detected.

<doc> <p> <o> <ut ort="M">la</ut> <ut>estudiante</ut> <ut>atendió</ut> </o> </p> </doc>

3.2 Labeler Module

This module outputs a graph that represents all the syntactic analysis possibilities for the input sentence. The applied method consists of a full search of translation units (words or compound expressions) through a finite-state network representing the dictionary.

Input: Input to this module are fragmented sentences.

<doc> <p> <o> <ut ort="M">la</ut> <ut>estudiante</ut> <ut>atendió</ut> </o> </p> </doc>

Output: Output from this module is a finite-state transducer in which each edge associates translation units and lexical categories[2] according to the dictionary. Note that each translation unit, represented as a conection between states, can be referred to both a word or a compound expression, since TAVAL dictionary stores lexical labels for single words as well as for phrases.

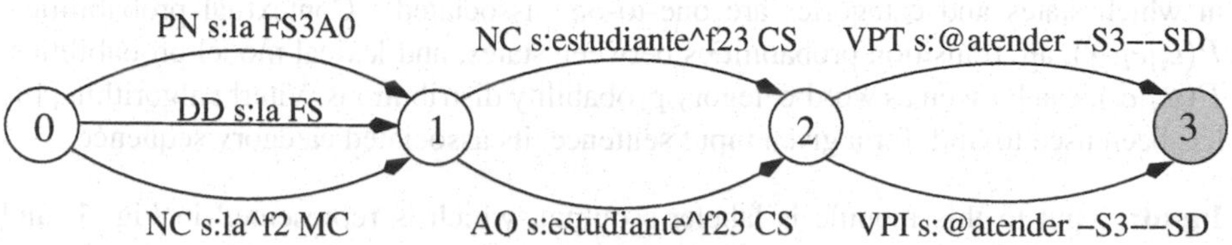

Fig. 1. Labeler's output

Fig. 1 shows all the possible PoS-tags for the example sentence, together with some linguistic information. In concrete, word *la* can be a pronoun, an article or a noun. Word *estudiante* can be an adjective or a noun; it is a singular word (S) and its gender depends on some issues that are implemented in Nominal phrase agreement module (C). PoS-tags for word *atendió* are VPT and VPI, both corresponding to an inflected form[3] from verb *atender*.

3.3 Syntactic Disambiguation Module

Syntactic disambiguation aims to decide the lexical category that a word has in a context. To do this, both rule-based and corpus-based techniques are applied.

Statistical disambiguation can be defined as a maximization problem. Let $\mathcal{W} = \{w_1, w_2, \ldots, w_N\}$ be the source language vocabulary and let $\mathcal{C} = \{c_1, c_2, \ldots, c_m\}$ be all the possible categories. Given an input sentence $w = w_1, \ldots, w_L$, the process can be accomplished by searching the category sequence $\widetilde{c} = c_1, \ldots, c_L$ that maximizes:

$$\widetilde{c} = \arg\max_{c \in \mathcal{C}^L} P(c|w) \tag{1}$$

Using Bayes rule and given that the maximization process is independent on the input sentence w, equation (1) can be rewritten as:

$$\widetilde{c} = \arg\max_{c \in \mathcal{C}^L} P(c)P(w|c) \tag{2}$$

In this equation, contextual (or language model) probabilities, $P(c)$, represent all the possible category sequences, whereas emission (or lexical model) probabilities, $P(w|c)$, establish the relationship between words and categories.

---

[2] *PN*:Pronoun, *DD*:Article, *NC*:Noun, *AQ*:Adjective, *VPT*:Transitive verb, *VPI*:Intransitive verb.

[3] 3rd person singular (S3) from simple past (SD).

To solve this equation, certain Markov assumptions can be accepted to simplify the problem. First, contextual probabilities for one determined category are assumed to only depend on the immediately previous n categories. The second constraint consists of assuming that emission probabilities only depend on the category itself.

For 1st order Markov models (bigrams), problem is reduced to solve next equation:

$$\widetilde{c} = \underset{c_1,\ldots,c_L}{\arg\max} \left(\prod_{1\ldots L} P(c_i|c_{i-1}) P(w_i|c_i) \right) \tag{3}$$

Parameters from this equation can be represented as a Hidden Markov Model (HMM) in which states and categories are one-to-one associated. Contextual probabilities, $P(c_i|c_{i-1})$, are transition probabilities between states, and lexical model probabilities, $P(w_i|c_i)$, can be seen as word-category probability distributions. Viterbi algorithm [14] has been used to find, for a given input sentence, its associated category sequence.

Input: Input to this module is labeler's output, which is represented in Fig. 1, and models all the possible syntactic analyses for the input sentence.

Output: Output from this module is the linear graph corresponding to the most likely path through the input graph, according to the category-based models described before.

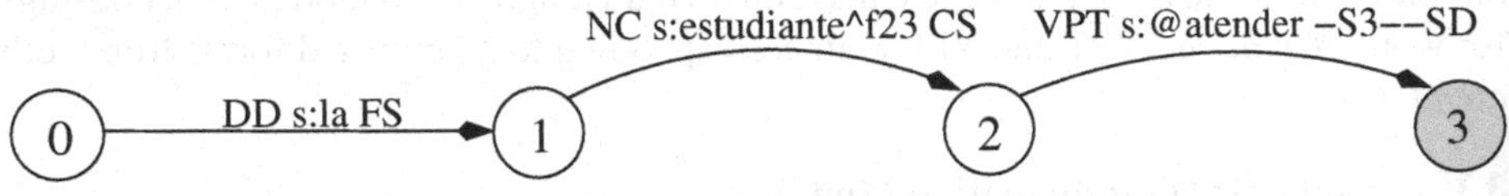

Fig. 2. Syntactic disambiguation output

Actually, some rules are used so as to reduce ambiguity, then the statistical disambiguation model presented here is applied.

3.4 Nominal Phrase Agreement Module

Due to the fact that training corpus for syntactic disambiguation does not include information about word gender or number, it is necessary to perform a subsequent process making agree all the words in each nominal phrase.

The followed method consists of nominal phrase localization inside a sentence by means of a knowledge-based nominal phrase codification in terms of category sequences [15].

Once a nominal phrase has been located, it is possible to make agree gender and number words inside it through the application of some hierarchical rules that depend on the kind of phrase detected.

Input: Input to this module is Syntactic disambiguation module's output. As Fig. 2 shows, it consists of a linear graph containing PoS-tag labelling.

Output: Output from this module offers sentences in which gender and number agreement has been made at a nominal phrase level. In Fig. 3, it is possible to see a nominal phrase detection (*la estudiante*) and, as a result, noun's gender has been agreed with article's.

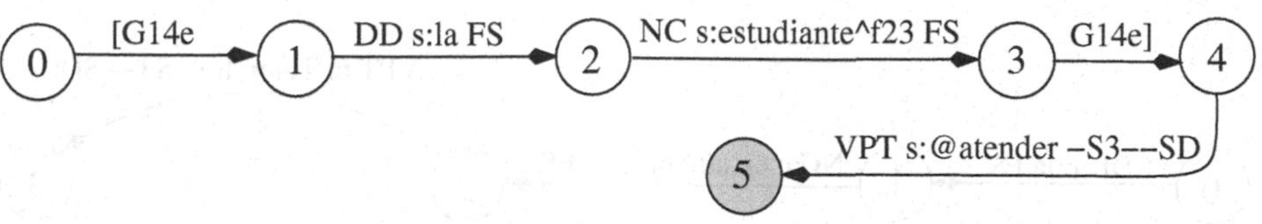

Fig. 3. Nominal phrase agreement output

3.5 Localizer Module

This module is dedicated to expand each *ut* into all its possible translations according to the dictionary.

Input: Input to this module is agreement module's output, where nominal phrase marks have been deleted.

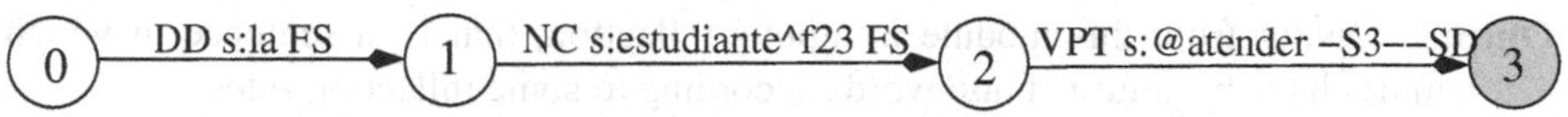

Fig. 4. Nominal phrase agreement output without phrase marks

Output: Output from this module is a lemma graph including every possible translation to the input graph, according to the dictionary.

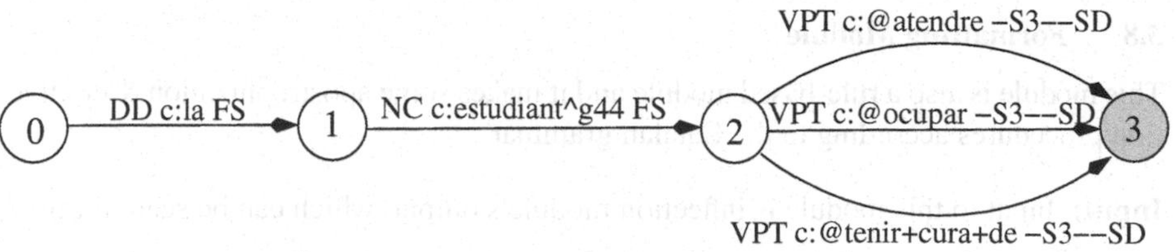

Fig. 5. Localizer's output

3.6 Semantic Disambiguation Module

Semantic disambiguation module tries to decide the right translation for a *ut* according to the input sentence context. In this paper, only the most likely translation for each dialectal variety is taken into account. Dictionary entries have their meanings manually scored. Therefore, for each ut, prototype chooses the best scored sense in a user-given dialectal variety. Corpus-based statistical models are planned to be working on future versions of this module.

Input: Input to this module is localizer's output. As Fig. 5 shows, every possible translation to each ut from Fig. 4 is represented.

Output: Output from this module is a linear graph which corresponds to the best scored path through the input graph.

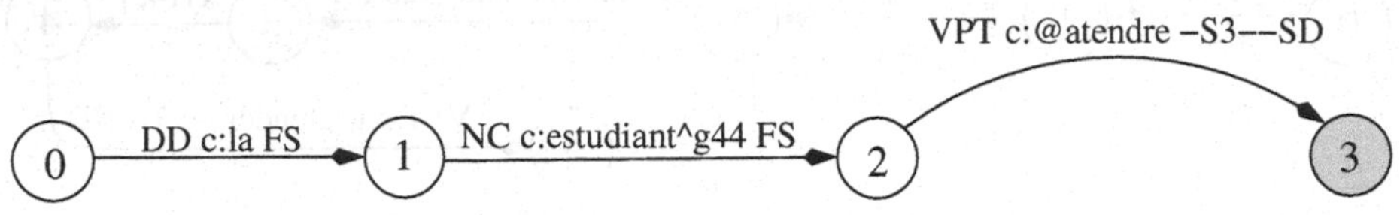

Fig. 6. Semantic disambiguation output

3.7 Inflection Module

This is a rule-based module which makes word inflection according to the Catalan inflection model.

Input: Input to this module is Semantic disambiguation module's output, which is shown in Fig. 6. It represents a Catalan lemma sentence to be inflected.

Output: Output from this module is input's inflection, that is, a sentence in which lemmas have been turned into words according to some inflection rules.

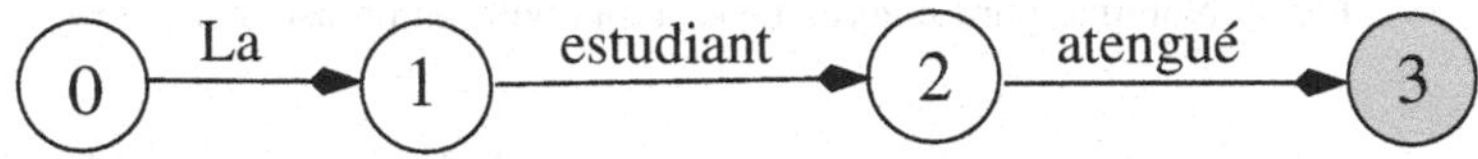

Fig. 7. Inflecter's output

3.8 Formatting Module

This module is also a rule-based module and it makes some apostrophization & contraction procedures according to the Catalan grammar.

Input: Input to this module is inflection module's output, which can be seen in Fig. 7.

Output: This module finally offers well-written sentences from an ortographic point of view. In Fig. 8, it is possible to see the transformation of *La estudiant* into *L'estudiant* as well as an alternative way of expressing past tenses, which tends to be more usual.

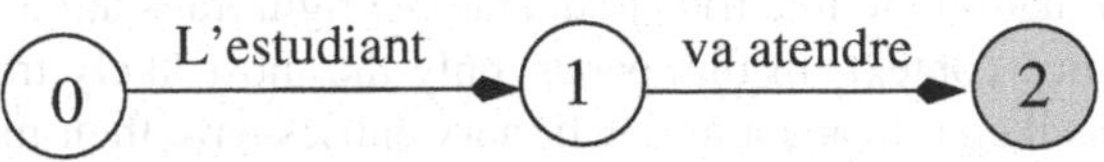

Fig. 8. Formatter's output

3.9 Integration Module

This module turns finite-state linear graphs into sentences, according to the original text format.

Input: Module's input is formatter's output, which Fig. 8 shows.

Output: Output from this module (or final output) is displayed as a Catalan text, which is a translation for the Spanish input text.

L'estudiant va atendre.

4 Experiments

4.1 Corpora

In order to be able to make a statistical estimation of the different models used in the implemented version of the prototype, diverse data corpora have been collected.

Specific tools were developed to look for information through the web. These tools were very useful, especially at the time of collecting the necessary corpora.

LexEsp corpus [16], with nearly 90.000 running words, was used to estimate *syntactic disambiguation* model parameters. A label, from a set of approximately 70 categories, was manually assigned to each word.

Other two corpora (*El periódico de Cataluña* and *Diari oficial de la Generalitat Valenciana*) were obtained by means of web tools. These corpora will be used in some system improvements such as training models for *semantic disambiguation*. These corpora consist of parallel texts, aligned at sentence level, in a Spanish-to-Catalan translation framework without semantic constraints.

In order to perform the system assessment, a bilingual corpus was created. This corpus is composed of 240 sentence pairs, extracted from different sources and published in both languages. Of course, they are not included in any training corpus.

- 120 sentence pairs from *El Periódico de Cataluña*, with no semantic constraints.
- 50 pairs from *Diari Oficial de la Generalitat Valenciana*, a official publication from the Valencian Community government.
- 50 pairs from technical software manuals.
- 20 pairs from websites (Valencia Polytechnical University, Valencia city council, etc.).

4.2 Results

Word error rate (WER[4]) is a translation quality measure that computes the edition distance between translation hypotheses and a predefined reference translation. The edition distance calculates the number of substitutions, insertions and deletions that are needed to turned a translation hypothesis into the reference translation. The accumulated number of errors for all the test sentences is then divided by the number of running words,

[4] Also known as Translation WER (TWER).

and the resulting percentage shows the average number of incorrect words. Since it can be automatically computed, it has become a very popular measure. WER results for SisHiTra system can be seen at Table 1.

Table 1. WER comparison for some machine translation systems

System	WER
InterNOSTRUM	11.9
SisHiTra	10.1
SALT	9.9

A disadvantage of WER is that it only compares the translation hypothesis with a fixed reference translation. This does not offer any margin to possible right translations, expressed in a different writing style. So, to avoid this problem, we used the WER with multireferences (MWER[5]) for evaluating the prototype. MWER considers several reference translations for a same test sentence, then computes the edition distance with all of them, returning the minimum value as the error corresponding to that sentence. MWER offers a more realistic measure than WER because it allows for more variability in translation style. MWER results for SisHiTra system are similar to the reached ones by other commercial systems (InterNOSTRUM[6] and SALT[7]), as it can be seen at Table 2.

Table 2. MWER comparison for some machine translation systems

System	MWER
InterNOSTRUM	8.4
SisHiTra	6.8
SALT	6.5

5 Conclusions and Future Work

In the framework of SisHiTra project, a general scope Spanish-to-Catalan translation prototype has been developed. The translation process is based on finite-state machines and statistical models, automatically inferred from parallel corpora. Translation results are promising enough, considering that there are still a lot of things to be done.

We hope to improve results through the correction of some mistakes, accidentally produced at some of the hand-made knowledge sources (dictionary, grammatical rules, etc.), as well as to prosper in the prototype modular development, including new processes to increase translation quality.

[5] Multi-reference Word Error Rate.

[6] See http://www.torsimany.ua.es

[7] See http://www.cult.gva.es/DGOIEPL/SALT/salt_programes_salt2.htm

The most relevant areas where the system could be improved are:

- Semantic disambiguation, where statistical models for ambiguous words could be trained in order to be able to choose the most appropriate context-dependent translations.
- Gender and number agreement between verbal phrases.
- Disambiguation in some verb pairs like: *ser* and *ir*, *creer* and *crear*, etc. since they have lexical forms in common.

Finally, a SisHiTra future perspective is the extension to other Romance languages (Portuguese, French, Italian, etc.).

References

1. Halteren, H.V., Zavrel, J., Daelemans, W.: Improving accuracy in word class tagging through the combination of machine learning systems. Computational Linguistics **27** (2001) 199–229
2. Pla, F., Molina, A.: Improving part-of-speech tagging using lexicalized hmms. Natural Language Engineering **10** (2004) 167–189
3. Roche, E., Schabes, Y.: Deterministic part-of-speech tagging with finite-state transducers. Computational Linguistics **21** (1995) 227–253
4. Aguirre, E., Rigau, G.: Word sense disambiguation using conceptual density. In: COLING. (1996)
5. Ide, N., Véronis, J.: Word sense disambiguation: The state of the art. Computational Linguistics **24** (1998) 1–40
6. Karttunen, L.: Finite-state lexicon compiler. Volume 1. (1994) 406–411
7. Roche, E.: Finite-state transducers: parsing fre and frozen sentences. In Kornai, A., ed.: Proceedings of the ECAI 96 Workshop on Extended Finite State Models of Language. (1996) 52–57
8. Roche, E., Schabes, Y.: Finite-state language processing. MIT Press, Cambridge, Mass. (1997) 1–65
9. Mohri, M.: Finite-state transducers in language and speech processing. Computational Linguistics **23** (1997)
10. Mohri, M., Pereira, F., Riley, M.: The design principles of a weighted finite-state transducer library. Theoretical Computer Science **231** (2000) 17–32
11. Oflazer, K.: Error-tolerant finite-state recognition with applications to morphological analysis and spelling correction. Computational Linguistics **22** (1996) 73–89
12. Canals, R., Esteve, A., Garrido, A., Guardiola, M., Iturraspe, A., Montserrat, S., Pastor, H., Pérez, P., Forcada, M.L.: The spanish-catalan machine translation system internostrum. In: MT Summit VIII: Machine Translation in the Information Age. (2001) 73–76
13. Sanchis, A., Picó, D., del Val, J., Fabregat, F., Tomás, J., Pastor, M., Casacuberta, F., Vidal, E.: A morphological analyser for machine translation based on finite-state transducers. In: MT Summit VIII: Machine Translation in the Information Age. (2001) 305–309
14. Viterbi, A.: Error bounds for convolutional codes and an asymtotically optimal decoding algorithm. IEEE Transactions on Information Theory (1967) 260–269
15. Molina, A., Pla, F., Moreno, L., Prieto, N.: Apoln: A partial parser of unrestricted text. In: Proceedings of 5th Conference on Computational Lexicography and Text Research COMPLEX-99, Pecs, Hungary (1999) 101–108
16. Carmona, J., Cervell, S., Màrquez, L., Martí, M., Padró, L., Placer, R., Rodríguez, H., Taulé, M., Turmo, J.: An environment for morphosyntactic processing of unrestricted spanish text. In: Proceedings of the 1st International Conference on Language Resources and Evaluation, LREC, Granada, Spain (1998) 915–922

Smoothing and Word Sense Disambiguation

Eneko Agirre and David Martinez

IXA NLP Group
University of the Basque Country
649 pk. 20.080 Donostia, Spain
{eneko,davidm}@si.ehu.es

Abstract. This paper presents an algorithm to apply the smoothing techniques described in [15] to three different Machine Learning (ML) methods for Word Sense Disambiguation (WSD). The method to obtain better estimations for the features is explained step by step, and applied to n-way ambiguities. The results obtained in the Senseval-2 framework show that the method can help improve the precision of some weak learners, and in combination attain the best results so far in this setting.

1 Introduction

Many current Natural Language Processing (NLP) systems rely on linguistic knowledge acquired from tagged text via Machine Learning (ML) methods. Statistical or alternative models are learned, and then applied to running text. The main problem faced by such systems is the sparse data problem, due to the small amount of training examples. Focusing on Word Sense Disambiguation (WSD), only a handful of occurrences with sense tags are available per word. For example, if we take the word *channel*, we see that it occurs 5 times in SemCor [10], the only all-words sense-tagged corpus publicly available: the first sense has four occurrences, the second a single occurrence, and the other 5 senses are not represented. For a few words, more extensive training data exists. Senseval-2 [4] provides 145 occurrences of *channel*, but still some of the senses are represented by only 3 or 5 occurrences.

It has to be noted that both in NLP and WSD, most of the events occur rarely, even when large quantities of training data are available. Besides, fine-grained analysis of the context requires that it is represented with many features, some of them rare, but which can be very informative. Therefore, the estimation of rare-occurring features might be crucial to have high performances.

Smoothing is the technique that tries to estimate the probability distribution that approximates the one we expect to find in held-out data. In WSD, if all occurrences of a feature for a given word occur in the same sense, Maximum Likelihood Estimation (MLE) would give a 0 probability to the other senses of the word given the feature, which is a severe underestimation. We will denote these cases as X/0, where X is the frequency of the majority sense, and zero is the frequency of the other senses.

For instance, if the word *Jerry* occurs in the context of *art* only once in the training data with a given sense, does it mean that the probability of other senses of *art* occurring in the context of *Jerry* is 0? We will see in Section 4.3 that this is not the case, and that

J. L. Vicedo et al. (Eds.): EsTAL 2004, LNAI 3230, pp. 360–371, 2004.

the other senses are nearly as probable. Our smoothing study will show for this feature of the word *art* that the smoothed ratio should be closer to 1/1.

In this paper, we follow the smoothing method proposed by Yarowsky in his PhD dissertation [15], and present a detailed algorithm of its implementation for the WSD problem, defining some of the parameters used, alongside the account of its use by three different ML algorithms: Decision Lists (DL), Naive Bayes (NB), and Vector Space Model (VSM). The impact of several smoothing strategies is also presented, and the results indicate that the smoothing method explored in this paper is able to make both statistically motivated methods (DL and NB) perform at very high precisions, comparable and in some cases superior to the best results attained in the Senseval-2 competition. We also show that a simple combination of the methods and a fourth system based on Support Vector Machines (SVM) attains the best result for the Senseval-2 competition reported so far.

An independent but related motivation for this work is the possibility to use smoothing techniques in bootstrapping approaches. Bootstrapping techniques such as [16] have shown that if we have good seeds, it could be possible to devise a method that could perform with quality similar to that of supervised systems. Smoothing techniques could help to detect rare but strong features which could be used as seeds for each of the target word senses.

The paper is organized as follows. Section 2 presents the experimental setting. Section 3 introduces smoothing of feature types and Section 4 presents the detailed algorithm with examples. Section 5 presents the results and comparison with other systems, and, finally, the last section draws some conclusions.

2 Experimental Setting

In this section we describe the target task and corpus used for evaluation, the type of features that represent the context of the target word, and the ML algorithms applied to the task.

2.1 Corpus

The experiments have been performed using the Senseval-2 English Lexical-Sample data [4]. This will allow us to compare our results with the systems in the competition and with other recent works that have focused on this dataset. The corpus consists on 73 target words (nouns, verbs, and adjectives), with 4,328 testing instances, and approximately twice as much training. We used the training corpus with cross-validation to estimate the C parameter for the SVM algorithm, and to obtain the smoothed frequencies for the features (see below). For the set of experiments in the last section, the systems were trained on the training part, and tested on the testing part.

A peculiarity of this hand-tagged corpus is that the examples for a given target word include multiword senses, phrasal verbs, and proper nouns. A separate preprocess is carried out in order to detect those cases with 96.7% recall.

2.2 Features

The feature types can be grouped in three main sets:
Local Collocations: bigrams and trigrams formed with the words around the target. These features are constituted by lemmas, word-forms, or PoS tags[1]. Other local features are those formed with the previous/posterior lemma/word-form in the context.
Syntactic Dependencies: syntactic dependencies were extracted using heuristic patterns, and regular expressions defined with the PoS tags around the target[2]. The following relations were used: object, subject, noun-modifier, preposition, and sibling.
Bag-of-words Features: we extract the lemmas of the content words in the whole context, and in a ± 4-word window around the target. We also obtain salient bigrams in the context, with the methods and the software described in [14].

2.3 ML Methods

Given an occurrence of a word, the ML methods below return a weight for each sense ($weight(s_k)$). The sense with maximum weight will be selected. The occurrences are represented by the features in the context (f_i).

The **Decision List (DL)** algorithm is described in [15]. In this algorithm the sense s_k with the highest weighted feature f is selected, as shown below. In order to avoid 0 probabilities in the divisor, we can use smoothing or discard the feature altogether.

$$weight(s_k) = \arg\max_f \log\left(\frac{P(s_k|f)}{\sum_{j \neq k} P(s_j|f)}\right) \quad (1)$$

The **Naive Bayes (NB)** method is based on the conditional probability of each sense s_k given the features f_i in the context. It requires smoothing in order to prevent the whole productory to return zero because of a single feature.

$$weight(s_k) = P(s_k) \prod_{i=1}^{m} P(f_i|s_k) \quad (2)$$

For the **Vector Space Model (VSM)** method, we represent each occurrence context as a vector, where each feature will have a 1 or 0 value to indicate the occurrence/absence of the feature. For each sense in training, one centroid vector is obtained ($\boldsymbol{C_{s_k}}$). These centroids are compared with the vectors that represent testing examples ($\boldsymbol{f}$), by means of the cosine similarity function. The closest centroid assigns its sense to the testing example. No smoothing is required to apply this algorithm, but it is possible to use smoothed values instead of 1s and 0s.

$$weight(s_k) = cos(\boldsymbol{C_{s_k}}, \boldsymbol{f}) = \frac{\boldsymbol{C_{s_k}} . \boldsymbol{f}}{|\boldsymbol{C_{s_k}}||\boldsymbol{f}|} \quad (3)$$

Regarding **Support Vector Machines (SVM)** we utilized SVM-Light, a public distribution of SVM by [8]. We estimated the soft margin (C) using a greedy process in cross-validation on the training data. The weight for each sense is given by the distance to the hyperplane that supports the classes, that is, the sense s_k versus the rest of senses.

[1] The PoS tagging was performed with the fnTBL toolkit [13].

[2] This software was kindly provided by David Yarowsky's group, from the Johns Hopkins University.

3 Feature-Type Smoothing

We have already seen in the introduction that estimating X/0 features with MLE would yield a probability $P(s|f) = 1$ for the majority sense and a probability $P(s|f) = 0$ for the minority senses, which is an underestimation. Features with X/0 counts are usual when the training data is sparse, and these values must be smoothed before they are fed to some learning algorithms, such as DL or NB, as they lead to undetermined values in their formulations.

Other distributions, such as X/1, X/2, ... can also be estimated using smoothing techniques. [15] argues that the probability of the second majority sense in X/1 distributions would be overestimated by MLE. For intermediate cases, such as X/2, X/3, etc. it is not clear whether the effort of modeling would be worth pursuing. For higher frequencies, using the raw frequency could be good enough. In this work we focused in X/0 and X/1 distributions.

The smoothing algorithm shown here (which we will call *feature-type smoothing*) follows the ideas of [15]. The main criteria to partition the training data has been to use raw frequencies and feature types (e.g. *prev_N_wf*, feature type that represents the first noun word-form to the left of the target). Raw frequency is the most important parameter when estimating the distribution, and joining features of the same type is a conservative approach to partition the data. Therefore we join all occurrences of the *prev_N_wf* feature type that have the same frequency distribution for the target word, e.g. 1/0. This way, we perform smoothing separately for each word.

We could use the smoothed values calculated in this manner directly, but many data points would still be missing. For instance, when studying *prev_N_wf* in the X/0 frequency case for *art*, we found occurrences of this feature type in held-out data in the 1/0, 2/0 and 3/0 cases, but not the rest (4/0 and higher). In this case it is necessary to use interpolation for the missing data points, and we applied log-linear interpolation. The interpolation also offers additional benefits. Firstly, using the slope of the interpolated line we can detect anomalous data (such as cases where 1/0 gets higher smoothed values than 5/0) as we always expect a positive slope, that is, higher ratios deserve higher smoothed values. Secondly, interpolation can be used to override a minority of data points which contradict the general trend. These points will be illustrated in the examples presented in Section 4.3.

However, when using interpolation, we need at least two or three data points for all feature types. For feature types with few points, we apply a back-off strategy: we join the available data for all words in the same Part of Speech. The rationale for this grouping is that strong features for a noun should be also strong for other nouns. In order to decide whether we have enough data for a feature type or not, we use the number of data points (minimum of three) available for interpolation. In order to check the validity of the interpolation, those cases where we get negative slope are discarded.

4 Feature-Type Smoothing Algorithm

There are two steps in the application of the smoothing algorithm to the disambiguation task. First, we use the available training data in cross-validation, with an interpolation method, in order to estimate the smoothing tables for each feature type with X/0 or X/1

Table 1. Smoothing table for the feature *prev_N_wf* and the word *art* (X/0 distribution)

Original	Held-out		Accumulated			Interpolated		
X Y	X' Y'	X'/Y'	X' Y'	X'/Y'	log(X'/Y')	X" Y"	X"/Y"	log(X"/Y")
1 0	4 4	1	4 4	1.00	0.00	1 0.91	1.10	0.09
2 0	6 1	6	10 5	2.00	0.69	2 1.18	1.69	0.52
3 0	2 0	∞	12 5	2.4	0.88	3 1.14	2.63	0.96
						4 0.98	4.08	1.40
						...		

raw frequency. Second, the interpolated tables are accessed on the disambiguation phase, when the WSD methods require them. Sections 4.1 and 4.2 present the algorithms, and Section 4.3 shows some illustrative examples.

4.1 Building Smoothing Tables

We build two kinds of smoothing tables. The first kind is the application of the grouping strategy based on feature types and frequency distributions. Two tables are produced: one at the word level, and another at the PoS level, which we will call *smoothed tables*. The second kind is the result of the interpolation method over the two aforementioned tables, which we will call *interpolated tables*. All in all, four tables are produced in two steps for each frequency distribution (X/0 and X/1).

1) Construct Smoothing Tables for Each Target Word and for Each PoS. For each feature type (e.g.: *prev_N_wf*), we identify the instances that have X/0 or X/1 distributions (e.g. *prev_N_wf Aboriginal*) and we count collectively their occurrences per sense. We obtain tables with (X',Y') values for each word, feature type and pair (X,Y); where (X,Y) indicate the values seen for each feature in the training part, and (X',Y') represent the counts for all the instances of the feature type with the same (X,Y) distribution in the held-out part.

We perform this step using 5-fold cross-validation on the training data. We separate in a stratified way[3] the training data in two parts: estimation-fold (4/5 of the data) and target-fold (1/5 of the data), which plays the role of the held-out data. We run the algorithm five times in turn, until each part has been used as target. The algorithm is described in detail in Figure 1 for the X/0 case (the X/1 case is similar). Note that the X count corresponds to the majority sense for the feature, and the Y count to all the rest of minority senses for the feature. For example, we can see in the held-out columns in Table 1 the (X',Y') counts obtained for the feature type *prev_N_wf* and the target word *art* in the Senseval-2 training data for the X/0 cases.

2) Create Interpolation Curves. From the smoothing tables, we interpolate curves for feature types that have at least 3 points. The process is described in detail in the second part of Figure 1. We first accumulate the counts in the smoothed table from the previous step. The “Accumulated” columns in Table 1 show these values, as well as the X/Y ratio

[3] By stratified, we mean that we try to keep the same proportion of word senses in each of the 5 folds.

```
1. Construct word smoothing tables for X/0 (X0)
- For each fold from training-data (5 folds)
  Build count(f, w, sense) for all senses from the estimation-folds (4 folds)
  For each word w, for each feature f in each occurrence in target-fold (1 fold)
     get count'(f, w, sense) for all senses of w in target-fold
     If distribution of count'(f, w, sense) is of kind X/0 (X0) then
        For each sense
           if sense = s. max_s count(f, w, s)
           then                          # sense is major sense in estimation-fold
              increment X' in table_word_X0(w,type(f),X)
           else
              increment Y' in table_word_X0(w,type(f),X)

- Normalize all tables: X' is set to X, and Y' := Y'X'/X
  Output (No need to keep X'): normtable_word_X0(w, type(f), X) := Y'

2. Log linear Interpolation
- Accumulate X' and Y' values
- Map into linear space:
  logtable_word_X0(w, type(f), X) :=
     log(acctable_word_X0(w, type(f), X).X'/acctable_word_X0(w, type(f), X).Y')
- Do linear interpolation of logtable: sourcepoint(w, type(f)) = a0,
     gradient(w, type(f)) = a1
- For each X from 1 to ∞
     interpolatedtable_word_X0(w, type(f), X) := X/(e^(a0+a1X))
```

Fig. 1. Construction of smoothing tables for X/0 features for words. The X/1 and PoS tables are built similarly

and its logarithm. The Y value is then normalized, and mapped into the logarithmic space. We apply a common linear interpolation algorithm called *least square method* [11], which yields the starting point and slopes for each interpolation table. If we get a negative slope, we discard this interpolation result. Otherwise, we can apply it to any X, and after mapping again into the original space we get the interpolated values of Y, which we denote Y". Table 1 shows the Y" values, the X"/Y" ratios, and the log values we finally obtain for the *prev_N_wf* example for *art* for $X = 1..4$ and $Y = 0$ ("Interpolated" columns). The X"/Y"ratios indicate that for X values lower than 4, the feature type is not reliable, but for $X >= 4$ and $Y = 0$, this feature type can be used with high confidence for *art*.

4.2 Using the Smoothed Values

The process to use the smoothed values in testing is described in Figure 2. There we see that when we find X/0 or X/1 distributions, the algorithm resorts to the *obtain_smoothed_value* function to access the smoothing tables. The four tables constructed in the previous section are all partial, i.e. in some cases there is no data available for some of the senses. The tables are consulted in a fixed order: we first check the interpolated table for the target word; if it is not available for the feature type, we access the interpolated table for the PoS of the target word. Otherwise, we resort to the non-interpolated smoothing table at the word level. Finally we access the non-interpolated smoothing table for the PoS.

In cases were the four tables fail to provide information, we can benefit from additional smoothing techniques. The three ML methods that we have applied have different smoothing requirements, and one of them (NB) does need a generally applicable smoothing technique:

```
Given an occurrence of a word w in testing, for each feature f in the context:
  Get count(f,w,sense) for all senses from all training (all 5 folds)
  If counts are not X/1 or X/0 then
    For each sense:
      count'(f,w,sense) := count(f,w,sense)

  Elseif count is X/Y (where Y is 1 or 0) then
    If Y' = obtain_smoothed_value(X,Y)
    Then
      For each sense
        If sense = s.max_s count(f,w,s) then                    #(MAJOR SENSE)
          count'(f,w,sense) = X
        Elsif sense = 2nd_sense then    #(ONLY IF Y=1, WHERE A MINORITY SENSE
                                                              OCCURS ONCE)
          count'(f,w,sense) := Y'               #(SECOND SENSE GETS MORE CREDIT)
        Else
          count'(f,w,sense) := Y'/|othersenses| # (DISTRIBUTE WEIGHT UNIFORMLY
                                                         AMONG MINOR SENSES)

    Else                          # (THERE IS NO SMOOTHING DATA FOR THIS X/Y)
      DISCARD                                   #(THIS IS POSSIBLE FOR DL)
      For each sense
        If sense = s.max_s count(f,w,s) then                   # (MAJOR SENSE)
          count'(f,w,sense) := X
        Elsif sense = 2nd_sense then    #(ONLY IF Y=1, WHERE A MINORITY SENSE
                                                              OCCURS ONCE)
          count'(f,w,sense) := 1              # (SECOND SENSE GETS MORE CREDIT)
```

Fig. 2. Application of Feature-type smoothing to DL, NB and VSM

DL: as it only uses the strongest piece of evidence, it can discard X/0 features. It does not require X/1 smoothing either.
NB: It needs to estimate all single probabilities, i.e. all features for all senses, therefore it needs smoothing in X/0, X/1 and even X/2 and larger values of Y. The reason is that in the case of polisemy degrees larger than 2, the rare senses might not occur for the target feature and could lead to infinite values in Equation (2).
VSM: it has no requirement for smoothing.

In order to check the impact of the various smoothing possibilities we have devised 6 smoothing algorithms to be applied with the 3 ML methods (DL, NB, and VSM). We want to note that not requiring smoothing does not mean that the method does not profit from the smoothing technique (as we shall see in the evaluation). For the baseline smoothing strategy we chose both "no smoothing", and "fixed smoothing"; we also tried a simple but competitive method from [12], denoted as "Ng smoothing" (methods to be described below). The other three possibilities consist on applying the Feature-Type method as in Figure 2, with two variants: use "Ng smoothing" for back-off (E), or in a combined fashion (F):

(A) No smoothing: Use raw frequencies directly.
(B) Fixed smoothing: Assign 0.1 raw frequency to each sense with a 0 value.
(Ng) Ng smoothing: This method is based on the global distribution of the senses in the training data. For each feature, each of the senses of the target word that has no occurrences in the training data gets the ratio between the probability of the sense occurring in the training data and the total number of examples: *Prob(sense)/Number_of_examples*.

Table 2. Smoothed values (interpolation per word) for the feature types *prev_N_wf*, *win_cont_lem_context* and *win_2gram_context* with the target word *art*

X Y	*prev_N_wf*				*win_cont_lem_context*				*win_2gram_context*			
	X'	Y'	X"	Y"	X'	Y'	X"	Y"	X'	Y'	X"	Y"
1 0	4	4	1	0.91	517	1187	1	2.24	63	150	1	2.31
2 0	6	1	2	1.18	82	125	2	4.45	8	4	2	4.37
3 0	2	0	3	1.14	13	22	3	6.62	2	1	3	6.48
...												

(Ft) Feature-type smoothing: The method described in this paper. In the case of DL, note that when no data is available the feature is just discarded. For NB, it is necessary to rely in back-off strategies (see E and F).
(E) Ft with Ng as back-off: When Ft does not provide smoothed values, Ng is applied.
(F) Ft and Ng combined: The smoothed values are obtained by multiplying Ft and Ng values. Thus, in Figure 2, the $count'(f, w, sense)$ values are multiplied by *Prob(sense)/Number_of_examples*.

The output of the smoothing algorithm is the list of counts that replace the original frequency counts when computing the probabilities. We tested all possible combinations, but notice that not all smoothing techniques can be used with all the methods (e.g. we cannot use NB with "no smoothing").

4.3 Application of Smoothing: An Example

We will focus on three feature types and the target word *art* in order to show how the smoothed values are computed. For *art*, the following features have a 1/0 distribution in the training data: *"prev_N_wf Aboriginal"*, *"win_cont_lem_context Jerry"*, and *"win_2gram_context collection owned"*[4]. The majority sense for the three cases is the first sense. If we find one of those features in a test occurrence of *art*, we would like to know whether they are good indicators of the first sense or not.

As all these features occur with frequency 1/0, we have collected all counts for the feature types (e.g. *prev_N_wf*) which also have 1/0 occurrences in the training data. Table 1 shows the counts for *prev_N_wf*; the (4,4) values that appear for (X',Y') indicate that the *prev_N_wf* features that have 1/0 distribution in the target-folds contribute 4 examples to the majority sense and 4 to the minority senses when looked up in the estimation-folds.

The data for *prev_N_wf* has at least 3 points, and therefore we use the accumulated frequencies to obtain an interpolation table. We see that the interpolated frequencies for the minority senses stay nearly constant when the X values go up. This would reflect that the probability of the minority senses would go down quickly for higher values of X. In fact, the interpolated table can be used for values of X greater that 3, which had not been attested in the training data.

[4] The first feature indicates that *Aboriginal* was the first noun to the left of *art*. The second that *Jerry* was found in the context window. The third that the bigram *collection owned* was found in the context window.

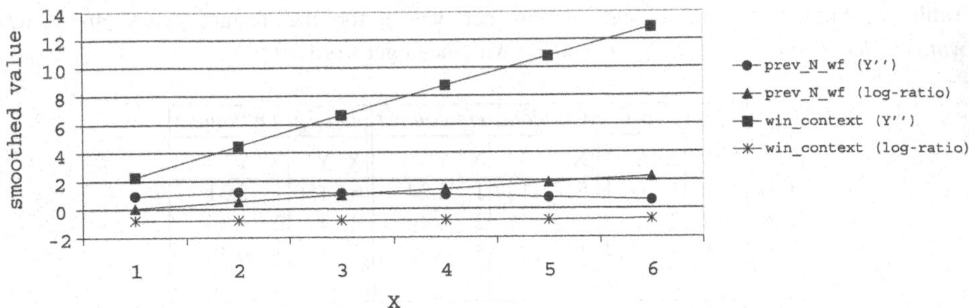

Fig. 3. Interpolation curves for the X/0 case (features *prev_N_wf* and *win_context*) with the target word *art*. The Y" estimation and the $log(X''/Y'')$ values are given for each X value and feature

The same process is followed for the other two feature types: *win_cont_lem_context* and *win_2gram_context*. Table 2 shows the smoothed values (X',Y') and the interpolated values (X",Y") for the three types studied. The values for Y are much higher in the latter two cases, indicating that there is a very low confidence for these features for the word *art*. In contrast, *prev_N_wf* can be a valuable feature if found in 4/0 or greater distributions.

Figure 3 shows this different behavior graphically for *win_cont_lem_context* and *prev_N_wf*. For each feature type, the estimated Y" values and the log-ratio of the majority sense are given: the higher the Y" the lower the confidence in the majority sense, and inversely for the log-ratio. We can see that the curve for the Y" values assigned to *prev_N_wf* get lower credit as X increases, and the log-ratio grows constantly. On the contrary, for *win_cont_lem_context* the values of Y" increase, and that the log-ratio remains below zero, indicating that this feature type is not informative.

5 Results

The main experiment is aimed at studying the performance of four ML methods with the different smoothing approaches (where applicable). The recall achieved on the Senseval-2 dataset is shown in Table 3, the best results per method marked in bold. We separated the results according to the type of smoothing: basic smoothing ("no smoothing" and "fixed smoothing"), and complex smoothing (techniques that rely on "Feature-type smoothing" and "Ng smoothing"). We can see that the results are different depending on the ML method, but the best results are achieved with complex smoothing for the 3 ML methods studied: DL (Ft and E), NB (F), and VSM (Ng). The best performance is attained by the VSM method, reaching 66.2%, which is one of the highest reported in this dataset. The other methods get more profit from the smoothing techniques, but their performance is clearly lower. McNemar's test[5] shows that the difference between the results of the best "basic smoothing" technique and the best "complex smoothing" technique is significant for DL and NB, but not for VSM.

All in all, we see that the performance of the statistically-based (DL, NB) methods improves significantly, making them comparable to the best single methods. In the next

[5] McNemar's significance test has been applied with a 95% confidence interval.

Table 3. ML methods and smoothing techniques: (A) no smoothing, (B) fixed smoothing, (Ng) Ng smoothing, (Ft) Feature-type smoothing, the method presented in this paper, (E) Ft with Ng as back-off, and (F) the combination of Ft and Ng

	Basic Smoothing		Complex Smoothing			
	A	B	Ng	Ft	E	F
DL		60.4	60.7	**64.4**	**64.4**	64.3
NB		62.9	63.5		61.8	**63.8**
VSM	65.9	65.6	**66.2**	64.0	64.2	65.2
SVM	**65.8**					

Table 4. Combination of systems with basic smoothing and complex smoothing. The rows show the recall achieved combining the 4 systems, and discarding one in turn

Systems	Basic smoothing	Complex smoothing
All methods	65.7	66.2
except SVM	64.9	66.2
except NB	**66.0**	**66.7**
except VSM	64.9	65.7
except DL	65.7	66.3

experiment, we tested a simple way to combine the output of the 4 systems: one system, one vote. The combination was tested on 2 types of systems: those that relied on "complex smoothing", and those that not. For each algorithm, the best smoothing technique for each type was chosen; e.g. the VSM algorithm would use the (A) approach for "simple smoothing", and (Ng) for "complex smoothing" (see Table 3). The performance of these systems is given in Table 4. The table also shows the results achieved discarding one system in turn.

The results show that we get an improvement over the best system (VSM) of 0.5% when combining it with DL and SVM. The table also illustrates that smoothing accounts for all the improvement, as the combination of methods with simple smoothing only reaches 66.0% in the best case, for 66.7% of the "complex smoothing" (difference statistically significant according to McNemar's test with 95% confidence interval).

As a reference, Table 5 shows the results reported for different groups and algorithms in the Senseval-2 competition and in more recent works. Our algorithms are identified by the "IXA" letters. "JHU - S2", corresponds to the Johns Hopkins University system in Senseval-2, which was the best performing system. "JHU" indicates the systems from the Johns Hopkins University implemented after Senseval-2 [3, 5]. Finally, "NUS" (National University of Singapore) stands for the systems presented in [9]. The Table is sorted by recall.

We can see that our systems achieve high performance, and that the combination of systems is able to beat the best results. However, we chose the best smoothing algorithm for the methods using the testing data (instead of using cross-validation on training, which would require to construct the smoothing tables for each fold). This fact makes the combined system not directly comparable. In any case, it seems clear that the system benefits from smoothing, and obtains results similar to the best figures reported to date.

Table 5. Comparison with the best systems in the Senseval-2 competition and the recent literature

Method	Group	Smoothing	Recall	
Combination	IXA	Complex (best)	66.7	
Combination	**JHU**		**66.5**	⇒ **Best result to date**
VSM	IXA	Ng	66.2	
Combination	IXA	Basic (best)	66.0	
SVM	IXA		65.8	
SVM	**NUS**		**65.4**	⇒ **2nd best result to date**
DL	IXA	Ft	64.4	
Combination	**JHU-S2**		**64.2**	⇒ **Senseval-2 winner**
NB	IXA	E	63.8	
NB	NUS	"Add one"	62.7	

6 Conclusions

In this work, we have studied the smoothing method proposed in [15], and we present a detailed algorithm for its application to WSD. We have described the parameters used, and we have applied the method on three different ML algorithms: Decision Lists (DL), Naive Bayes (NB), and Vector Space Model (VSM). We also analyzed the impact of several smoothing strategies. The results indicate that the smoothing method explored in this paper is able to make all three methods perform at very high precisions, comparable and in some cases superior to the best result attained in the Senseval-2 competition, which was a combination of several systems. We also show that a simple combination of the methods and a fourth system based on Support Vector Machines (SVM) attains the best result for the Senseval-2 competition reported so far (although only in its more successful configuration, as the system was not "frozen" using cross-validation). At present, this architecture has also been applied in the Senseval-3 competition, with good results, only 0.6% below the best system for English [1].

For the future, we would like to extend this work to X/Y features for Y greater than 1, and try other grouping criteria, e.g. taking into account the class of the word. We would also like to compare our results to other more general smoothing techniques [6, 7, 2].

Finally, we would like to apply the smoothing results to detect good features for bootstrapping, even in the case of low amounts of training data (as it is the case for most of the words in WSD). The DL method, which improves significantly with smoothing, may be well suited for this task, as it relies on one single piece of evidence (feature) to choose the correct sense.

References

1. Agirre A., Martinez D.: The Basque Country University system: English and Basque tasks. Proceedings on the 3rd ACL workshop on the Evaluation of Systems for the Semantic Analysis of Text (SENSEVAL). Barcelona, Spain (2004)
2. Chen S.F.: Building Probabilistic Models for Natural Language. Ph.D. Thesis, Harvard University (1996)

3. Cucerzan S., Yarowsky D.: Minimally Supervised Induction of Grammatical Gender. Proceedings of HLT/NAACL 2003. Edmonton, Canada (2003)
4. Edmonds P., Cotton S.: SENSEVAL-2: Overview. Proceedings of the Second International Workshop on evaluating Word Sense Disambiguation Systems. Toulouse, France (2001)
5. Florian R., Cucerzan S., Schafer C., Yarowsky D.: Combining Classifiers for Word Sense Disambiguation. Journal of Natural Language Engineering. Cambridge University Press (2002)
6. Good I.J.: The Population Frequencies of Species and the Estimation of Population Parameters. Biometrika, Vol. 40. (1953) 237–264
7. Jelinek F., Mercer R.: Interpolated estimation of Markov source parameters from sparse data. Pattern Recognition in Practice. Amsterdam : North Holland Publishing Co. (1980) 381–397
8. Joachims T.: Making Large-Scale SVM Learning Practical. Advances in Kernel Methods - Support Vector Learning. MIT Press. Cambridge, MA (1999) 169–184
9. Lee Y., Ng H.T.: An Empirical Evaluation of Knowledge Sources and Learning Algorithms for Word Sense Disambiguation. Proceedings of the 2002 Conference on Empirical Methods in Natural Language Processing (EMNLP-2002). Philadelphia, PA, USA (2002) 41–48.
10. Miller G.A., Leacock C., Tengi R., Bunker R.: A Semantic Concordance. Proceedings of the ARPA Human Language Technology Workshop. Distributed as *Human Language Technology* by San Mateo, CA: Morgan Kaufmann Publishers. Princeton, NJ (1993) 303–308
11. Neter J., Wasserman W., Kutner M. H.: Applied Linear Statistical Models. Irwin. Homewood, Illinois (1985)
12. Ng H.T.: Exemplar-Based Word Sense Disambiguation: Some Recent Improvements. Proceedings of the Second Conference on Empirical Methods in Natural Language Processing Somerset, New Jersey (1997) 208–213
13. Ngai G., Florian R.: Transformation-Based Learning in the Fast Lane. Proceedings of the Second Conference of the North American Chapter of the Association for Computational Linguistics. Pittsburgh, PA, USA (2001) 40–47
14. Pedersen T.: A Decision Tree of Bigrams is an Accurate Predictor of Word Sense. Proceedings of the Second Conference of the North American Chapter of the Association for Computational Linguistics. Pittsburgh, PA, USA (2001)
15. Yarowsky D.: Three Machine Learning Algorithms for Lexical Ambiguity Resolution. PhD thesis, Department of Computer and Information Sciences. University of Pennsylvania (1995)
16. Yarowsky D.: Unsupervised Word Sense Disambiguation Rivaling Supervised Methods. Proceedings of the 33rd Annual Meeting of the Association for Computational Linguistics. Cambridge, MA (1995) 189–196

Spelling Correction for Search Engine Queries

Bruno Martins and Mário J. Silva

Departamento de Informática
Faculdade de Ciências da Universidade de Lisboa
1749-016 Lisboa, Portugal
bmartins@xldb.di.fc.ul.pt,mjs@di.fc.ul.pt

Abstract. Search engines have become the primary means of accessing information on the Web. However, recent studies show misspelled words are very common in queries to these systems. When users misspell query, the results are incorrect or provide inconclusive information. In this work, we discuss the integration of a spelling correction component into tumba!, our community Web search engine. We present an algorithm that attempts to select the best choice among all possible corrections for a misspelled term, and discuss its implementation based on a ternary search tree data structure.

1 Introduction

Millions of people use the Web to obtain needed information, with search engines currently answering tens of millions of queries every day. However, with the increasing popularity of these tools, spelling errors are also increasingly more frequent. Between 10 to 12 percent of all query terms entered into Web search engines are misspelled [10]. A large number of Web pages also contain misspelled words. Web search is thus a task of information retrieval in an environment of faulty texts and queries. Even with misspelled terms in the queries, search engines often retrieve several matching documents – those containing spelling errors themselves. However, the best and most "authoritative" pages are often missed, as they are likely to contain only the correctly spelled forms. An interactive spelling facility that informs users of possible misspells and presents appropriate corrections to their queries could bring improvements in terms of precision, recall, and user effort. Google was the first major search engine to offer this facility [8].

One of the key requirements imposed by the Web environment on a spelling checker is that it should be capable of selecting the best choice among all possible corrections for a misspelled word, instead of giving a list of choices as in word processor spelling checking tools. Users of Web search systems already give little attention to query formulation, and we feel that overloading them with an interactive correction mechanism would not be well accepted. It is therefore important to make the right choice among all possible corrections autonomously.

This work presents the development of a spelling correction component for tumba!, our community search engine for the Portuguese Web [29]. In tumba! we check the query for misspelled terms while results are being retrieved. If errors are detected, we provide a suggestive link to a new "possibly correct" query, together with the search results for the original one.

J. L. Vicedo et al. (Eds.): EsTAL 2004, LNAI 3230, pp. 372–383, 2004.

The rest of this paper is organized as follows: the next section presents the terminology used throughout this work. Section 3 gives an overview on previous approaches to spelling correction. Section 4 presents the ternary search tree data structure, used in our system for storing the dictionary. Section 5 details our algorithm and the heuristics behind it. Section 6 describes the data sources used to build the dictionary. Section 7 describes experimental results. Finally, Section 8 points our conclusions and directions for future work.

2 Terminology

Information Retrieval (IR) concerns with the problem of providing relevant documents in response to a user's query [2]. The most commonly used IR tools are **Web search engines**, which have become a fact of life for most Internet users. Search engines use software robots to survey the Web, retrieving and indexing HTML documents. Queries are checked against the keyword indexes, and the best matches are returned.

Precision and **Recall** are the most popular metrics in evaluating IR systems. Precision is the percentage of retrieved documents that the searcher is actually interested on. Recall, on the other hand, is the percentage of relevant documents retrieved from the set of all documents, this way referring to how much information is retrieved by the search. The ultimate goal of an information retrieval system is to achieve recall with high precision.

Spelling has always been an issue in computer-based text tools. Two main problems can be identified in this context: **Error detection**, which is the process of finding misspelled words, and **Error correction**, which is the process of suggesting correct words to a misspelled one. Although other approaches exist, most spelling checking tools are based on a **dictionary** which contains a set of words which are considered to be correct. The problem of spelling correction can be defined abstractly as follows: Given an alphabet σ, a dictionary D consisting of strings in σ^* and a string s, where $s \notin D$ and $s \in \sigma^*$, find the word $w \in D$ that is most likely to have been erroneously input as s.

Spelling errors can be divided into two broad categories: **typographic errors**, which occur because the typist accidentally presses the wrong key, presses two keys, presses the keys in the wrong order, etc; and **phonetic errors**, where the misspelling is pronounced the same as the intended word but the spelling is wrong. Phonetic errors are harder to correct because they distort the word more than a single insertion, deletion or substitution. In this case, we want to be able to key in something that sounds like the misspelled word (a "phonetic code") and perform a "fuzzy" search for close matches. The search for candidate correct forms can be done at typographic level, and then refined using this method.

3 Related Work

Web information retrieval systems have been around for quite some time now, having become the primary means of accessing information the Web [1, 8]. Early systems engines did not check query spelling but since April 2001, several webwide search engines, including Excite and Google, provide dynamic spelling checking, while others such as Yahoo, simply tracked common misspellings of frequent queries, such as movie star names. Technical details for these systems are unavailable, but they seem to be based on spelling algorithms and statistical frequencies.

Algorithmic techniques for detecting and correcting spelling errors in text has also a long and robust history in computer science [20]. Previous studies have also addressed the use of spelling correctors in the context of user interfaces [13]. Spelling checkers (sometimes called "spell checkers" by people who need syntax checkers) are nowadays common tools for many languages, and many proposals can also be found on the literature. Proposed methods include edit distance [11, 31, 21], rule-based techniques [32], n-grams [25, 33]probabilistic techniques [18], neural nets [28, 6, 17], similarity key techniques [34, 23], or combinations [16, 22]. All of these methods can be thought of as calculating a distance between the misspelled word and each word in the dictionary. The shorter the distance, the higher the dictionary word is ranked as a good correction.

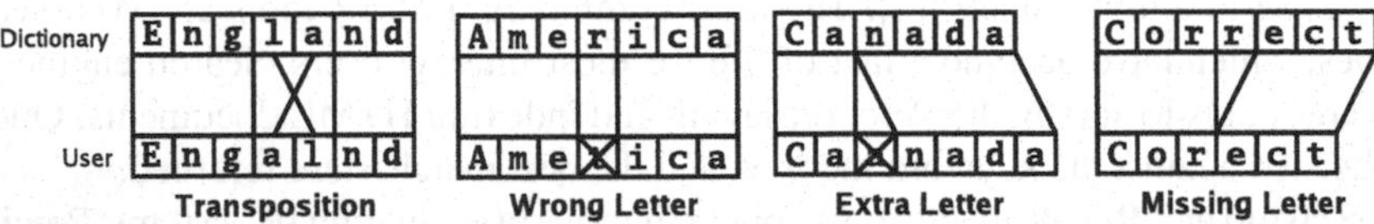

Fig. 1. The four most common spelling errors

Edit distance is a simple technique. The distance between two words is the number of editing operations required to transform one into another. Analysis of errors – mainly typing errors – in very large text files have found that the great majority of wrong spellings (80-95%) differ from the correct spellings in just one of the four ways described in Figure 1. The editing operations to consider should therefore correspond to these four errors, and candidate corrections include the words that differ from the original in a minimum number of editing operations [11]. Recent works are experimenting with modeling more powerful edit operations, allowing generic string-to-string edits [7]. Additional heuristics are also typically used to complement techniques based on edit distance. For instance, in the case of typographic errors, the keyboard layout is very important. It is much more usual to accidentally substitute a key by another if they are placed near each other on the keyboard.

Similarity key methods are based on transforming words into similarity keys that reflect their characteristics. The words in the dictionary and the words to test are both transformed into similarity keys. All words in the dictionary sharing the same key with a word being tested are candidates to return as corrections. An example of this method is the popular Soundex system. Soundex (the name stands for "Indexing on sound") was devised to help with the problem of phonetic errors [12, 19]. It takes an English word and produces a four digit representation, in a rough-and-ready way designed to preserve the salient features of the phonetic pronunciation of the word.

The metaphone algorithm is also a system for transforming words into codes based on phonetic properties [23, 24]. However, unlike Soundex, which operates on a letter-by-letter scheme, metaphone analyzes both single consonants and groups of letters called diphthongs, according to a set of rules for grouping consonants, and then mapping groups to metaphone codes. The disadvantage of this algorithm is that it is specific to the English language. A version of these rules for the Portuguese language has, to the best of our knowledge, not yet been proposed. Still, there has been recent research on machine learning methods for letter-to-phoneme conversion [15, 30]. Application of these techniques to Portuguese should be straightforward, providing he have enough training data.

More recent studies on error correction propose the use of context, attempting to detect words which are misused but spelled correctly [5, 14]. Spelling checkers based on isolated word methods would see the following sentence as correct: *a paragraph cud half mini flaws but wood bee past by the spill checker*. However, since in search engines users oddly type more than tree terms for a query, it would be a waste to make context dependent correction. Isolated word methods should prove sufficient for our task.

4 Ternary Search Trees

In this work, we use a ternary search tree (TST) data structure for storing the dictionary in memory. TSTs are a type of trie that is limited to three children per node [3, 4]. Trie is the common definition for a tree storing strings, in which there is one node for every common prefix and the strings are stored in extra leaf nodes. TSTs have been successfully used for several years in searching dictionaries. Search times in this structure are $O(log(n) + k)$ in the worst case, where n is the number of strings in the tree and k is the length of the string being searched for. In a detailed analysis of various implementations of trie structures, the authors concluded that "*Ternary Search Tries are an effective data structure from the information theoretic point of view since a search costs typically about* $log(n)$ *comparisons on real life textual data. [...] This justifies using ternary search tries as a method of choice for managing textual data*" [9].

Figure 2 illustrates a TST. The structure stores key-value pairs, where keys are the words and values are integers corresponding to the word frequency. As we can see, each node of the tree stores one letter and has three children. A search compares the current character in the search string with the character at the node. If the search character comes lexically first, the search goes to the left child; if the search character comes after, the search goes to the right child. When the search character is equal, the search goes to the middle child, and proceeds to the next character in the search string.

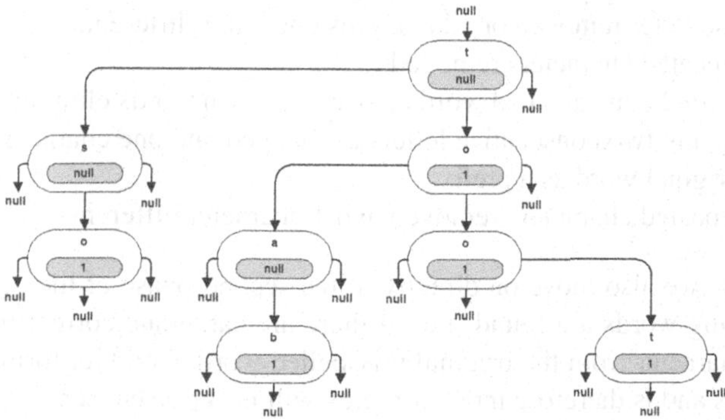

Fig. 2. A ternary search tree storing the words "to", "too", "toot", "tab" and "so", all with an associated frequency of 1

TSTs combine the time efficiency of tries with the space efficiency of binary search trees. They are faster than hashing for many typical search problems, and support a broad range of useful operations, like finding all keys having a given prefix, suffix, or infix, or finding those keys that closely match a given pattern.

5 Spelling Correction Algorithm

A TST data structure stores the dictionary. For each stored word, we also keep a frequency count, originally obtained from the analysis of a large corpora. To choose among possible corrections for a misspelled word, we use these word frequency counts as a popularity ranking, together with other information such as metaphone keys. Although we do not have a specific text-to-phoneme algorithm for the Portuguese language, using the standard metaphone algorithm yields in practice good results.

Queries entered in the search engine are parsed and the individual terms are extracted, with non word tokens ignored. Each word is then converted to lower case, and checked to see if it is correctly spelled. Correctly spelled words found in user queries are updated in the dictionary, by incrementing their frequency count. This way, we use the information in the queries as feedback to the system, and the spelling checker can adapt to the patterns in user's searches by adjusting its behavior. For the misspelled words, a correctly spelled form is generated. Finally, a new query is presented to the user as a suggestion, together with the results page for the original query. By clicking on the suggestion, the user can reformulate the query.

Our system integrates a wide range of heuristics and the algorithm used for making the suggestions for each misspelled word is divided in two phases. In the first, we generate a set of candidate suggestions. In the second, we select the best.

The first phase of the algorithm can be further decomposed into 9 steps. In each step, we look up the dictionary for words that relate to the original misspelling, under specific conditions:

1. Differ in one character from the original word.
2. Differ in two characters from the original word.
3. Differ in one letter removed or added.
4. Differ in one letter removed or added, plus one letter different.
5. Differ in repeated characters removed.
6. Correspond to 2 concatenated words (space between words eliminated).
7. Differ in having two consecutive letters exchanged and one character different.
8. Have the original word as a prefix.
9. Differ in repeated characters removed and 1 character different

In each step, we also move on directly to the second phase of the algorithm if one or more matching words are found (i.e., if there are candidate correct forms that only differ in one character from the original misspelled word, a correct form that differs in more characters and is therefore more complex will never be chosen).

In the second phase, we start with a list of possible corrections. We then try to select the best one, following these heuristics:

1. If there is one solution that differs only in accented characters, we automatically return it. Typing words without correct accents is a very common mistake in the Portuguese language (20% according to Medeiros [22]).
2. If there is one solution that differs only in one character, with the error corresponding to an adjacent letter in the same row of the keyboard (the QWERTY layout is assumed), we automatically return it.
3. If there are solutions that have the same metaphone key as the original string, we return the smallest one, that is, the one with less characters.
4. If there is one solution that differs only in one character, with the error corresponding to an adjacent letter in an adjacent row of the keyboard, we automatically return it.
5. In the last case, we return the smallest word.

We follow the list of heuristics sequentially, and only move to the next if no matching words are found. If there is more than one word satisfying the conditions for each heuristic, we first try to return the one where the first character is equal to the correctly spelled word. If there is still more than one word, we return the one that has the highest frequency count.

6 Data Sources and Associated Problems

The dictionary for the spelling checking system is a normal text file, where each line contains a term and its associated frequency. The sources of Portuguese words and word frequencies for the dictionary were the texts from the Natura-Publico and the Natura-Minho corpora [27, 26]. The first one is made of the two first paragraphs of news articles from *Publico* in the years of 1991, 1992, 1993 and 1994. The second, corresponds to the full articles in 86 days of editions of the newspaper *Diario do Minho*, spread across the years of 1998 and 1999.

The dictionary strongly affects the quality of a spelling checking system. If it is too small, not only will the candidate list for misspellings be severely limited, but the user will also be frustrated by too many false rejections of words that are correct. On the other hand, a lexicon that is too large may not detect misspellings when they occur, due to the dense "word space".

News articles capture the majority of the words commonly used, as well as technical terms, proper names, common foreign words, or references to entities. However, such large corpora often contain many spelling errors [26]. We use word frequencies to choose among possible corrections, which to some extent should deal with this problem. As misspelled terms are, in principle, less frequent over the corpus than their corresponding correct form, only on rare occasions should the spelling checker provide an erroneous suggestion.

The Web environment introduces difficulties. It is general in subject, as opposed to domain specific, and multilingualism issues are also common. While spelling checkers in text editors use standard and personal dictionaries, search engine spelling checkers should be more closely tied to the content they index, providing suggestions based on the content of the corpus. This would avoid the dead-end effect of suggesting a word that is correctly spelled but not included in any words on the site, and add access to names and codes which will not be in any dictionary. However, using a search engine's inverted index as the basis of the spelling dictionary only works well when the content has been copy edited, or when an editor is available to check the word list and reject misspellings.

7 Evaluation Experiments

Some experiments were performed in order to quantitatively evaluate our spelling correction mechanism.

We were first interested in evaluating the quality of the proposed suggestions. To achieve this, we compared the suggestions produced by our spelling checker against Aspell – see the project homepage at `http://aspell.sourceforge.net/`. Aspell is a popular interactive spelling checking program for Unix environments. Its strength comes from merging the metaphone algorithm with a near miss strategy, this way correcting phonetic errors and making better suggestions for seriously misspelled words. The algorithm behind Aspell is therefore quite similar to the one used in our work, and the quality of the results in both systems should be similar.

We used a hand-compiled list of 120 common misspellings, obtained from *CiberDúvidas da Lingua Portuguesa* (`http://ciberduvidas.sapo.pt/\-php/\-glossario.php`) and by inspecting the query logs for the search engine. The table below shows the list of misspelled terms used, the correctly spelled word, and the suggestions produced. In the table, a "*" means that the algorithm did not detect the misspelling and a "-" means the algorithm failed in returning a suggestion.

Correct Form	Spelling Error	Our Algorithm	ASpell
ameixial	ameixeal	ameixial	ameixial
artífice	artífece	artífice	artífice
camoniano	camoneano	camoniano	camoniano
definido	defenido	definido	defendo
lampião	lampeão	lampião	lampião
oficina	ofecina	oficina	oficina
acerca	àcerca	acerca	acerca
açoriano	açoreano	açoriano	coreano
alcoolémia	alcoolemia	*	*
antepor	antepôr	*	antepor
árctico	artico	artigo	aórtico
antárctico	antártico	catártico	antárctico
bainha	baínha	bainha	bainha
bebé	bébé	bebé	bebe
bege	beje	*	beije
bênção	benção	*	*
beneficência	beneficiência	beneficência	beneficência
biopsia	biópsia	*	*
burburinho	borborinho	burburinho	burburinho
caiem	caem	*	*
calvície	calvíce	calvície	calvície
campeão	campião	campeão	campeão
comboio	combóio	comboio	comboio
compor	compôr	*	compor
comummente	comumente	comovente	comummente
constituia	constituía	*	*
constituiu	constituíu	constituiu	constituiu
cor	côr	*	*
crânio	crâneo	crânio	cárneo
despretensioso	despretencioso	despretensioso	despretensioso
pretensioso	pretencioso	pretensioso	pretensioso
definição	defenição	definição	definição
			Continued on next page

Table 1. – Continued from previous page

Correct Form	Spelling Error	Our Algorithm	ASpell
definir	defenir	definir	definir
desiquilíbrio	desequilibrio	desequilíbrio	desequilíbrio
dispender	despender	*	*
dignatários	dignitários	dignatários	digitarias
dispêndio	dispendio	*	dispêndio
ecrã	ecran	*	écran
emirados	emiratos	estratos	méritos
esquisito	esquesito	esquisito	esquisito
estratego	estratega	*	*
feminino	femenino	feminino	feminino
feminismo	femininismo	-	feminismo
fôr	for	*	*
gineceu	geneceu	gineceu	gineceu
gorjeta	gorgeta	gorjeta	gorjeta
granjear	grangear	granjear	granjear
guisar	guizar	guisar	gizar
hectare	hectar	*	*
halariedade	hilaridade	*	*
hiroshima	hiroxima	aproxima	próxima
ilacção	elação	ilação	ilação
indispensável	indespensável	indispensável	indispensável
inflacção	inflação	*	*
interveio	interviu	intervir	inter viu
intervindo	intervido	*	*
invocar	evocar	*	*
ípsilon	ipslon	ípsilon	ípsilon
irisar	irizar	irisar	razar
irupção	irrupção	*	*
esotérico	isotérico	*	*
jeropiga	geropiga	-	geórgia
juiz	juíz	*	juiz
lêem	lêm	lês	lema
linguista	linguísta	*	linguista
lisonjear	lisongear	lisonjear	lisonjear
logótipo	logotipo	logo tipo	logo tipo
saem	saiem	saiam	saem
saloiice	saloice	baloice	saloiice
sarjeta	sargeta	sarjeta	sarjeta
semear	semiar	semear	semear
suíça	suiça	suíça	suíça
supor	supôr	*	supor
rainha	raínha	rainha	rainha
raiz	raíz	*	raiz
raul	raúl	raul	raul
rédea	rédia	rédea	radia
regurgitar	regurjitar	regurgitar	regurgitar
rejeitar	regeitar	rejeitar	regatar
requeiro	requero	requere	requeiro
réstia	réstea	réstia	resta
rectaguarda	retaguarda	*	*
rubrica	rúbrica	*	*
quadricromia	quadricomia	-	quadriculai
quadruplicado	quadriplicado	quadruplicado	quadruplicado
quasímodo	quasimodo	-	quisido
quilo	kilo	*	Nilo
quilograma	kilograma	holograma	holograma
quilómetro	kilómetro	milímetro	milímetro
quis	quiz	quis	qui
paralisar	paralizar	paralisar	paralisar
perserverança	preseverança	perseverança	perseverança
persuasão	persuação	persuasão	persuasão
persuasão	presuasão	persuasão	persuasão
pirinéus	pirenéus	*	*
privilégio	previlégio	privilégio	privilegio

Continued on next page

Table 1. – Continued from previous page

Correct Form	Spelling Error	Our Algorithm	ASpell
oceânia	oceania	*	*
opróbrio	opróbio	aeróbio	proíbo
organograma	organigrama	*	*
nonagésimo	nonagessimo	nonagésimo	nonagésimo
maciço	massiço	mássico	mássico
majestade	magestade	majestade	majestade
manjerico	mangerico	manjerico	manjerico
manjerona	mangerona	tangerina	tangerina
meteorologia	metereologia	meteorologia	meteorologia
miscigenação	miscegenação	miscigenação	miscigenação
trânsfuga	transfuga	transfira	transfira
transpôr	transpor	*	*
urano	úrano	*	*
ventoinha	ventoínha	ventoinha	ventoinha
verosímil	verosímel	*	*
vigilante	vegilante	vigilante	vigilante
vôo	voo	*	*
vultuoso	vultoso	*	*
xadrez	xadrês	xadrez	ladres
xamã	chamã	chama	chama
xelindró	xilindró	cilindro	cilindro
chiita	xiita	*	xiitas
zângão	zangão	*	*
zepelin	zeppelin	-	zeplim
zoo	zoô	zoo	coo

48.33% of the correct forms were correctly guessed and our algorithm outperformed Aspell by a slight margin of 1.66%. On the 120 misspellings, our algorithm failed in detecting a spelling error 38 times, and it failed on providing a suggestion only 5 times. Note that the data source used to build the dictionary has itself spelling errors. A careful process of reviewing the dictionary could improve results in the future.

Kukich points out that most researchers report accuracy levels above 90% when the first three candidates are considered instead of the first guess [20]. Guessing the one right suggestion to present to the user is much harder than simply identifying misspelled words and present a list of possible corrections.

In the second experiment, we took some measures from the integration of our spelling checker with a search engine for the Portuguese Web. We tried to see if, by using the spelling correction component, there were improvements in terms of precision and recall in our system. Using a hand compiled list of misspelled queries, we measured the number of retrieved documents in the original query, and the number of retrieved documents in the transformed query. We also had an human evaluator accessing the quality of the first ten results returned by the search engine, that is, measuring how many documents in the first ten results were relevant to the query.

Results confirm our initial hypothesis that integrating spelling correction in Web search tools can bring substantial improvements. Although many pages were returned in response to misspelled queries (and in some cases all pages were indeed relevant), the results for the correctly spelled queries were always of better quality and more relevant.

Table 2. Results from the Integration of the Spelling Checker With Tumba!

Misspelled Query	# Relevant Results	Correct Query	# Relevant Results
camoneano	5	camoniano	10
açoreano	10	açoriano	10
calvíce	3	calvície	10
campião	9	campeão	10
femenino	9	feminino	10
guizar	6	guisar	10
raínha	10	rainha	10
regurjitar	0	regurgitar	10
magestade	9	majestade	10
mangerico	9	manjerico	10
metereologia	10	meteorologia	10
vegilante	0	vigilante	10
xadrês	9	xadrez	10
zôo	0	zoo	10

8 Conclusions and Future Work

This paper presented the integration of a spelling correction component into tumba!, a Portuguese community Web search engine. The key challenge in this work was determining how to pick the most appropriate spelling correction for a mistyped query from a number of possible candidates.

The spelling checker uses a ternary search tree data structure for storing the dictionary. As source data, we used a large textual corpus of from two popular Portuguese newspapers. The evaluation showed that our system gives results of acceptable quality, and that integrating spelling correction in Web search tools can be beneficial. However, the validation work could be improved with more test data to support our claims.

An important area for future work concerns phonetic error correction. We would like to experiment with machine learning text-to-phoneme techniques that could adapt to the Portuguese language, instead of using the standard metaphone algorithm [15, 30]. We also find that queries in our search engine often contain company names, acronyms, foreign words and names, etc. Having a dictionary that can account for all these cases is very hard, and large dictionaries may result in inability to detect misspellings due to the dense "word space". However, keeping two separate dictionaries, one in the TST used for correction and another in an hash-table used only for checking valid words, could yield interesting results. Studying ways of using the corpus of Web pages and the logs from our system, as the basis for the spelling checker, is also a strong objective for future work. Since our system imports dictionaries in the form of ASCII word lists, we do however have an infrastructure that facilitates lexicon management.

9 Acknowledgments

Special thanks to our colleagues and fellow members of the tumba! development, and to the various members of Linguateca, for their valuable insights and suggestions. This research was partially supported by the FCCN - Fundação para a Computação Científica Nacional, FCT - Fundação para a Ciência e Tecnologia, and FFCUL - Fundação da

Faculdade de Ciências da Universidade de Lisboa, under grants POSI/SRI/47071/2002- (project GREASE) and SFRH/BD/10757/2002 (FCT scholarship).

References

1. Arvind Arasu, Junghoo Cho, Hector Garcia-Molina, Andreas Paepcke, and Sriram Raghavan. Searching the web. *ACM Transactions on Internet Technology*, 1(1):2–43, 2001.
2. Ricardo Baeza-Yates and Berthier Ribeiro-Neto. *Modern Information Retrieval*. ACM Press, 1999.
3. Jon Bentley and Robert Sedgewick. Fast algorithms for sorting and searching strings. In *Proceedings of SODA-97, the 8th ACM-SIAM Symposium on Discrete Algorithms*, 1997.
4. Jon Bentley and Robert Sedgewick. Ternary search trees. *Dr. Dobb's Journal*, 23(4):20–25, April 1998.
5. Johnny Bigert. Probabilistic detection of context-sensitive spelling errors. In *Proceedings of LREC-2004, the 4th International Conference on Language Resources and Evaluation*, 2004.
6. Andréia Gentil Bonfante. Uso de redes neurais para correção gramatical do português: Um estudo de caso. Master's thesis, Instituto de Ciências Matemáticas e da Computação da Universidade de São Paulo, São Carlos, São Paulo, Brazil, 1997. Dissertação de Mestrado.
7. Eric Brill and Robert C. Moore. An improved error model for noisy channel spelling correction. In *Proceedings of ACL-2000, the 38th Annual Meeting of the Association for Computational Linguistics*, pages 286–293, 2000.
8. Sergey Brin and Lawrence Page. The anatomy of a large-scale hypertextual Web search engine. *Computer Networks and ISDN Systems*, 30(1–7):107–117, 1998.
9. Julien Clément, Philippe Flajolet, and Brigitte Vallée. The analysis of hybrid trie structures. In *Proceedings of DA-98, the 9th annual ACM-SIAM symposium on discrete algorithms*, pages 531–539. Society for Industrial and Applied Mathematics, 1998.
10. Hercules Dalianis. Evaluating a spelling support in a search engine. In *Proceedings of NLDB-2002, the 7th International Workshop on the Applications of Natural Language to Information Systems*, June 2002.
11. Fred J. Damerau. A technique for computer detection and correction of spelling errors. *Communications of the ACM*, 7(3):171–176, 1964.
12. Leon Davidson. Retrieval of mis-spelled names in an airline passenger record system. *Communications of the ACM*, 5(3):169–171, March 1962.
13. Ivor Durham, David A. Lamb, and James B. Saxe. Spelling correction in user interfaces. *Communications of the ACM*, 26(10):764–773, October 1983.
14. Mohammad Ali Elmi and Martha Evens. Spelling correction using context. In Christian Boitet and Pete Whitelock, editors, *Proceedings of the 26th Annual Meeting of the Association for Computational Linguistics and 17th International Conference on Computational Linguistics*, pages 360–364, San Francisco, California, 1998. Morgan Kaufmann Publishers.
15. William M. Fisher. A statistical text-to-phone function using n-grams and rules. In *Proceedings of ICASSP-99, the 1999 IEEE International Conference on Acoustics, Speech and Signal Processing*, volume 2, pages 649–652, March 1999.
16. Victoria J. Hodge and Jim Austin. An evaluation of phonetic spell checkers. Technical Report YCS 338, Department of Computer Science of the University of York, 2001.
17. Victoria J. Hodge and Jim Austin. A novel binary spell checker. In *Proceedings of ICANN-01, the 11th International Conference on Articial Neural Networks*, August 2001.
18. Rangasami L. Kashyap and John Oommen. Spelling correction using probabilistic methods. *Pattern Recognition Letters*, 1985.

19. Donald Erwin Knuth. *The Art of Computer Programming*, volume 3 / Sorting and Searching. Addison-Wesley Publishing Company, Reading, Massachusetts, 2nd edition, 1982.
20. Karen Kukich. Techniques for automatically correcting words in text. *ACM Computing Surveys*, 24(4):377–440, 1992.
21. Vladimir I. Levenshtein. Binary codes capable of correcting deletions, insertions and reversals. *Soviet Physics Doklady*, 10:707–710, 1966.
22. José Carlos Dinis Medeiros. Processamento morfológico e correcção ortográfica do português. Master's thesis, Instituto Superior Técnico, 1995.
23. Lawrence Philips. Hanging on the metaphone. *Computer Language*, 7(12):39–43, 1990.
24. Lawrence Philips. The double-metaphone search algorithm. *C/C++ User's Journal*, 18(6), June 2000.
25. Edward M. Riseman and Allen R. Hanson. A contextual postprocessing system for error correction using binary n-grams. *IEEE Transactions on Computer Systems*, C-23(5):480–493, May 1974.
26. Diana Santos and Paulo Rocha. Evaluating cetempúblico, a free resource for portuguese. In *Proceedings of ACL-2001, the 39th Annual Meeting of the Association for Computational Linguistics*, pages 442–449, July 2001.
27. Diana Santos and Luís Sarmento. O projecto AC/DC: acesso a corpora / disponibilização de corpora. In Amália Mendes and Tiago Freitas, editors, *Actas do XVIII Encontro da Associação Portuguesa de Linguística*, pages 705–717, October 2002.
28. Terrence J. Sejnowski and Charles R. Rosenberg. Parallel networks that learn to pronounce english text. *Complex Systems*, 1:145–168, 1987.
29. Mário J. Silva. The case for a portuguese Web search engine. DI/FCUL TR 03–03, Department of Informatics, University of Lisbon, March 2003.
30. Kristina Toutanova and Robert C. Moore. Pronunciation modeling for improved spelling correction, July 2002.
31. Robert A. Wagner and Michael J. Fischer. The string-to-string correction problem. *Communications of the ACM*, 1(21):168–173, 1974.
32. Emmanuel J. Yannakoudakis. Expert spelling error analysis and correction. In Kevin P. Jones, editor, *Proceedings of a Conference held by the Aslib Informatics Group and the Information Retrieval Group of the British Computer Society*, pages 39–52, March 1983.
33. E. M. Zamora, J. J. Pollock, and Antonio Zamora. The use of trigram analysis for spelling error detection. *Information Processing and Management*, 6(17):305–316, 1981.
34. Justin Zobel and Philip Dart. Phonetic string matching: Lessons from information retrieval. In *Proceedings of SIGIR-96, the 19th Annual International ACM SIGIR Conference on Research and Development in Information Retrieval*, pages 166–172, 1996.

A Statistical Study of the WPT-03 Corpus

Bruno Martins and Mário J. Silva

Departamento de Informática
Faculdade de Ciências da Universidade de Lisboa
1749-016 Lisboa, Portugal
bmartins@xldb.di.fc.ul.pt, mjs@di.fc.ul.pt

Abstract. This report presents a statistical study of WPT-03, a text corpus built from the pages of the "Portuguese Web" collected in the repository of the tumba! search engine. We give a statistical analysis of the textual contents available in the Portuguese Web, including size distributions, the language of the pages, and the terms they contain.

1 Introduction

This study provides a statistical analysis of the textual contents on the Web page repository of the tumba! search engine [15]. More specifically, the source of information is the text extracted from a collection of documents from the "Portuguese Web", during the first semester of 2003. This roughly comprises all the pages hosted under the .PT top level domain (TLD), and other pages written in Portuguese and hosted in other TLDs (excluding .BR because most of these pages are also written in the Portuguese language).

The information presented in this study is of interest for the characterization of the textual contents of the Portuguese Web, as well as for future work within the scope of project tumba!. It is complemented by another report which provides statistics on the structure of the Portuguese Web [6].

The textual corpus is named WPT-03 and it is distributed by Linguateca (a resource center for the the processing of the Portuguese language – `http://www.linguateca.pt`) to researchers in the area of Natural Language Processing (NLP). For more information about the availability WPT-03, see the corresponding Web page at `http://xldb.fc.ul.pt/linguateca/WPT_03.html`.

The rest of this report is organized as follows: The next Section describes the WPT-03 corpus. In Section 3, we give statistics of the data in the corpus of web documents. Finally, Section 4 presents some conclusions.

2 Contents of the WPT-03 Corpus

The source of information for our study is a corpus of Web pages retrieved by the crawler of the tumba! search engine [5]. This snapshot of the Portuguese Web includes, for the most part, documents of types HTML and PDF, hosted in the .PT domain or written in Portuguese and hosted in the .COM, .NET, .ORG, or .TV domains.

J. L. Vicedo et al. (Eds.): EsTAL 2004, LNAI 3230, pp. 384–394, 2004.

The data was harvested and processed using the components from the XMLBASE Web database software, which includes the crawler, a Web content analyzer and a repository – see the project Web page at `http://xldb.di.fc.ul.pt/index.php?page=XMLBase`.

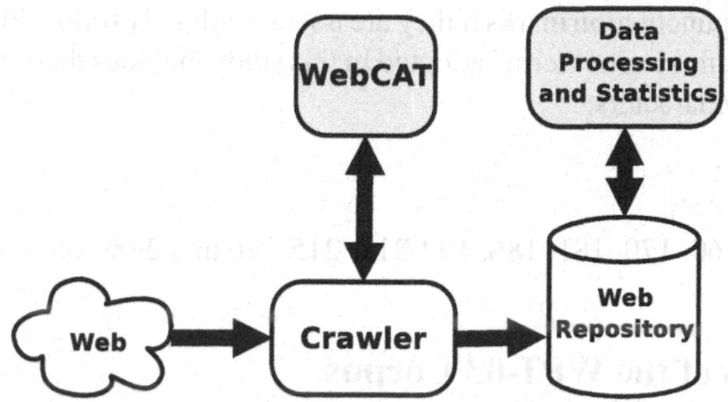

Fig. 1. Overview of the XMLBase Framework

WebCAT is the tool responsible for parsing and analyzing the Web contents [8]. Among other things, it performs document format conversion, text extraction, and meta-data extraction. Both the original documents and the corresponding "textual versions" are maintained in Versus, a data repository for Web information [3]. All statistics are based on the corpus formed by the text documents stored in Versus.

The repository also contains meta-information about the documents, including for example the size, storage date, and language properties. Since there is no way of knowing the language in which the documents extracted from the Web were written, an automatic tool to perform this task had to be developed. This language "guessing" component is based on a well-known n-gram analysis algorithm [4], together with heuristics for handling Dublin Core meta-data (which may or not be available in the documents). In a controlled study, the algorithm presented a precision of about 91% in discriminating among 11 different languages [7].

A problem we faced concerns files in the PDF format – although most of the documents can be converted into plain text, the conversion tool sometimes fails in extracting the text, producing garbage as output instead of terminating with an error. Filtering this situations can be very hard. We currently exclude most of the faulty documents using a simple filter, which looks at the first characters of the file. However, this is not a perfect solution and many "garbage" documents are still included in the corpus.

Many of the presented statistics count "terms". We adopted a definition of "term" similar to that given by the Berkeley elib project – see the corresponding Web page at `http://elib.cs.berkeley.edu/docfreq`. According to it, terms are the sequences of the characters:

- a-z, A-Z, 0-9
- ASCII 150-160, 170, 181, 186, 192-214, 215-246, and 248-255 (U, Ů, Ÿ, Ź, Ž, IJ, I, đ, §, ă, ł, ţ, ž, À, Á, Â, Ã, Ä, Å, Æ, Ç, È, É, Ê, Ë, Ì, Í, Î, Ï, Đ, Ñ, Ò, Ó, Ô, Õ, Ö, Œ, Ø, Ù, Ú, Û, Ü, Ý, Þ, SS, à, á, â, ã, ä, å, æ, ç, è, é, ê, ë, ì, í, î, ï, ð, ñ, ò, ó, ô, õ, ö, ø, ù, ú, û, ü, ý, þ, ß).

All other characters are regarded as term breaks. We differ from this definition in the way we handle hyphens. It is considered as a valid character of a term, when the next character is one of a-z or A-Z, in order to account that hyphens are essential characters in Portuguese, whereas in English they are mere punctuation marks (note that we still consider them as punctuation marks if they are not immediately followed by an alphabetic character). The definition of "term" adopted in this study includes therefore all sequences of the following characters:

- a-z, A-Z, 0-9;
- ASCII 45 (= "-");
- ASCII 150-160, 170, 181, 186, 192-214, 215-246 and 248-255.

3 Statistics of the WPT-03 Corpus

3.1 Document Statistics

The Portuguese Web snapshot analyzed in this study has 3775611 documents, collected between the 21st of March 2003 and the 26th of June 2003. Of these documents, about 68.6% (2590641 documents) are written in Portuguese.

Table 1 shows the average, median, and standard deviation of document sizes for WPT-03. Document size is measured in real size, text size and number of terms. Real size and text size are given in bytes, measuring the size of the document in the original format (HTML, PDF, etc.) and converted into plain text, respectively.

Table 1. Document size statistics

	Real size	Text size	Number of terms
Average	24461	2886	438
Median	14672	1336	188
Standard deviation	54191	8240	1327

Figure 2 shows the distribution of document sizes measured in the number of terms. As in other corpora, the number of small documents is much higher and we conjecture that the distribution is identical. The distribution naturally follows Zipf's law [17, 11], as shown by the displayed trend-line.

3.2 Term Statistics

Number and Frequency of Distinct Terms. Table 2 gives the total number of terms, the number of distinct terms, and the average and median number of occurrences of each distinct term. In order to abstract from differences in capitalization, all characters were converted into lower case before computing these statistics.

The document frequency for terms, i.e., the number of documents in which a certain term appears (disregarding the number of occurrences in the document) is another important statistic. Since a substantial part of the documents are written in foreign languages, it is interesting to get some statistics for the terms occurring only in documents

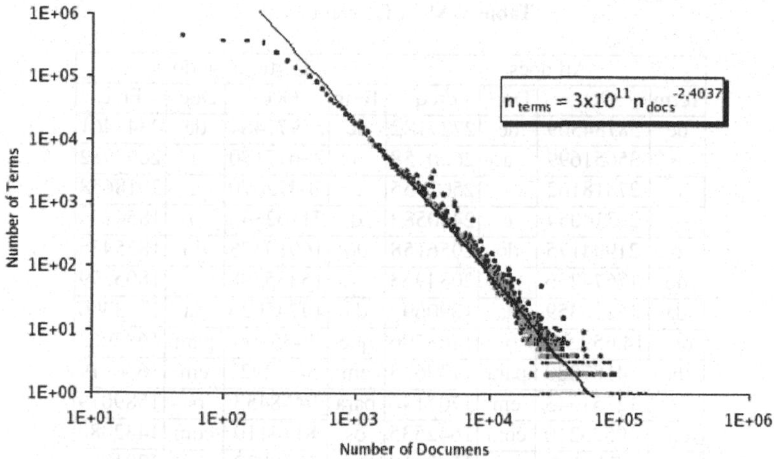

Fig. 2. Document sizes in terms per document

Table 2. Number of terms

	All Pages	Pages in Port. only
Total number of terms	1652645998	1208036873
Number of distinct terms	7880609	4066300
Average number of occurrences	210	297
Median number of occurrences	2	2
Standard deviation (# of occur.)	3428	42247
Average document frequency	865	128
Median document frequency	1	1
Standard deviation (doc. freq)	4496	5305

written in Portuguese. We therefore computed the frequencies considering both the full corpus and only the pages written in Portuguese.

Table 3 lists the 25 most frequent terms occurring in the corpus. Frequency is measured both in terms of the total number of term occurrences and document frequency, respectively. Most terms occurring in this list are candidate stop words in information retrieval systems for the Portuguese language.

Term Size. We analyzed the average number of characters per term, regarding all terms occurring in the corpora and regarding all distinct terms. Additionally, we give the median and standard deviation. Once again the analysis is two-fold, with respect to all documents in the corpus and restricted to documents written in Portuguese. Results are given in Table 4.

Figure 3 shows the distribution of term size (regarding all terms of the corpora). Approximately 99% of the terms are shorter than 15 characters, and a major part of those longer than 15 characters are due to "garbage" in the corpus and the problem of extracting the text from PDF files mentioned above.

Table 3. Most frequent terms

All docs				Portuguese docs			
Term	Occ.	Doc.	Freq.	Term	Occ.	Doc.	Freq
de	58734369	de	2727182	de	55977484	de	2344461
a	35651699	a	2600458	a	29617180	e	2093982
e	27818162	-	2502955	e	26472070	a	2018658
-	22314054	e	2400583	o	21162843	o	1854189
o	21994175	do	2056158	do	16919378	do	1825455
do	17674236	o	2034963	-	15435398	-	1805399
da	15196359	da	1890699	da	14745024	da	1733306
que	14,659,562	os	1865796	que	1435160	para	1632962
the	14187020	para	1747633	em	10302921	em	1606919
1	12251543	em	1707146	para	9468453	os	1589019
em	10523210	com	1642535	os	8114119	com	1442380
para	9742012	no	1572418	com	7678022	que	1291286
os	8692680	as	1477125	1	7532463	por	1260588
com	8345476	1	1446037	um	6755990	um	1256344
0	8114739	que	1371220	no	6412220	no	1243250
2	8026747	2	1363302	por	5630947	na	1174801
no	7140563	por	1349638	não	5534784	as	1123699
um	6845245	um	1294310	as	5383637	dos	1072318
as	6800040	na	1240599	dos	5363523	uma	1053919
of	6427217	3	1183339	uma	5339622	não	1040530
and	6085323	s	1152840	2	5080441	ao	1040371
to	5934084	dos	1132724	na	5041565	todos	1037091
por	5825647	pt	1106868	é	4630006	1	1007115
não	5608615	uma	1102931	se	4351434	ou	950273
dos	5497639	todos	1090087	ou	4284627	2	944924

E-mail Addresses, Numbers and Hyphen Statistics. To improve the search engine's handling of queries, it was interesting for us to analyze the frequency of things like e-mail addresses or numeric terms.

Numeric terms, as the name suggests, consist solely of numeric characters. As for e-mail addresses, they are of the form X@X.X, where X stands for a non-empty alphanumeric sequence plus the characters "-" and "_" (See the Internet RFC822 - Standard for the format of ARPA Internet text messages). Although each e-mail address counts as several terms in all other statistics (the separators are seen as punctuation), here they are seen as atomic units.

Finally, hyphenated words are terms where one character is a hyphen, as defined in Section 3.1. Counting hyphenated terms is important as, depending on their frequency, it may be more interesting for the search engine to consider them as separated sequences of terms.

Table 5 shows the total number of occurrences, the average number of occurrences for each distinct term in the collection, and the average size (in number of characters) of e-mail addresses, numeric terms and terms containing hyphens. The weighted av-

Table 4. Term size

	All terms		Distinct terms	
	all docs	only port.	all docs	only port.
average	4.8840	4.9680	8.9780	8.7400
standard deviation	4.4762	3.7930	39.6400	20.6860
median	4	4	7	8

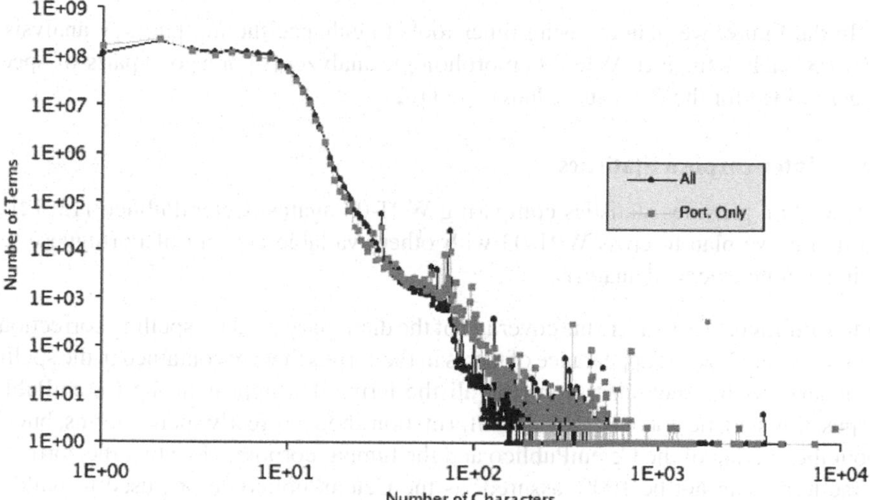

Fig. 3. Term size in characters per term

erage size also refers to the number of characters, but considering the number of all occurences, instead of only the distinct ones.

Morphology of the Terms. In order to get an idea of the morphology of the terms occurring in the corpus, we used the jspell [16] morphologic analyzer. This allowed us to relate base forms of words to inflected variants, and find out which syntactic categories the terms in the corpus belong to.

After excluding all terms containing numeric characters, we obtained 1884932 distinct terms (regarding only the Portuguese documents). 429937 of these can be analyzed morphologically using jspell. To reduce ambiguity, we only accept a solution if the lemma resulting from undoing inflection is contained either in the WPT-03 corpus itself, or in the CetemPublico corpus (see Section 3.3).

Of the 429937 terms that can be analyzed, 179778 (41.81%) are unambiguously analyzed as both nouns and adjectives, 137270 (31.93%) as verbs, 13932 (3.24%) as adjectives and 10322 (2.40%) as nouns. Furthermore, 71321 (16.59%) terms are ambiguous between verb and noun/adjective, 7117 (1.66%) between just noun and noun/adjective and 2342 (0.54%) between adjective and noun/adjective. 7855 (1.83 %) terms are ambiguous in other respects.

Table 5. Special terms

	E-mail addresses	Numeric terms	Terms with hyphens
Number of All Occ.	1264939	146136400	52499281
Number of Dif. Occ.	203638	570406	1510253
Average of occ.	6.21	256.20	34.76
Average term size	21.48	7.44	11.76
Average term size (weighted)	20.44	2.13	5.87

In the future, we plan on using other tools to enhance the morphology analysis in WPT-03, such as the PALAVROSO morphologic analyzer [9] or a good parts-of-speech tagger trained for the Portuguese language [1, 2].

3.3 Inter-corpora Statistics

This Section provides statistics comparing WPT-03 against CetemPublico [13, 12]. In the future, we plan to cross WPT-03 with other available corpora of Portuguese text, giving a more extended analysis.

CetemPublico. To measure the coverage of the dictionary used for spelling correction in tumba!, we analyze the appearance of terms in the corpus that are contained in the spelling dictionary. As the dictionary contains all the terms that appear in the CetemPublico corpus, this statistic not only provides information about correctly spelled terms, but also about the overlap of the CetemPublico and the tumba! corpora. Note that the correction of the terms can not be 100% assured, as the CetemPublico corpus used to build the spelling dictionary contains itself errors.

A substantial part of the terms differ only by the use of accents (i. e., replacing for example *á* by *a*). For that reason, in the statistics that compare these corpora, we provide on Tables 6 and 7 two result sets: one considering accented characters, and the other ignoring them. The meaning of each line on both tables is as follows:

#WPT-03 terms in CP (distinct) indicates the number of distinct terms in the WPT-03 corpus that also occur in the CetemPublico corpus; the percentage represents how many of the distinct terms of WPT-03 also appear inside the CetemPublico corpus.

 # CP terms in WPT-03 (distinct) indicates the number of distinct terms in CetemPublico that also occur inside the WPT-03 corpus; this is the same number as above, but the percentage is slightly different.

 # WPT-03 terms in CP (total) indicates the total number of terms in the WPT-03 corpus that also occur in CetemPublico; the percentage represents how many of all the terms in WPT-03 also occur inside the CetemPublico corpus.

 # CP terms in WPT-03 (total) indicates the total number of terms in the CetemPublico corpus that also occur in WPT-03; the percentage represents how many of all the terms in CetemPublico also occur inside the WPT-03 corpus.

Note that whereas almost all of the terms in CetemPublico also occur in the WPT-03 corpus, only 60% of the terms from WPT-03 appear in the CetemPublico corpus.

Table 6. Overlap with CetemPublico (counting all characters)

	All docs	Only port.
#WPT-03 terms in CP (distinct)	153729 (1.95%)	152641 (3.75%)
# CP terms in WPT-03 (distinct)	153729 (3.46%)	152641 (3.43%)
# WPT-03 terms in CP (total)	4213578 (94.77%)	4212486 (94.74%)
# CP terms in WPT-03 (total)	984033934 (59.54%)	897616340 (74.30%)

Table 7. Overlap with CetemPublico (ignoring accentuated characters)

	All docs	Only Port.
#WPT-03 terms in CP (distinct)	150157 (1.91%)	148913 (3.66%)
# CP terms in WPT-03 (distinct)	150157 (38.89%)	148913 (38.57%)
# WPT-03 terms in CP (total)	4221291 (94.94%)	4219958 (94.91%)
# CP terms in WPT-03 (total)	1003575179 (60.73%)	907834378 (54.93%)

This is, at least partly, due to the amount of documents written in languages other than Portuguese, and also to CetemPublico being much "cleaner", i.e., it contains less terms including numeric characters or "garbage" text. Previous studies have already indicated that while Web corpora have advantages in quantity (more "live" language information, more words and case-frames that newspaper corpus, etc.), they are usually noisier [14].

Postal Codes. Having an idea of the amount of geographic entities that are present in the WPT-03 corpus would be very interesting for us in the context of project tumba!. We used a list of Portuguese postal codes to find out which and how many "geographic" names appear in the text. The list is provided by CTT (Portuguese Post Office) and can be downloaded from `http://codigopostal.ctt.pt/pdcp-files/todos_cp.zip`. It contains not only postal codes, but also city, street and district names (277980 names of geographic entities overall).

Table 8. Postal Codes found in tumba! and in CTT list

	All Postal Codes	Distinct Postal Codes
WPT-03	683458	33799
CTT	236924	170549

Table 9. Statistics of Postal Code occurrences

	All Docs
CTT Postal codes in WPT-03 (distinct)	27695 (81,94%)
WPT-03 Postal Codes in CTT (distinct)	27695 (16,24%)
CTT Postal codes in WPT-03 (total)	567326 (83,01%)
WPT-03 Postal Codes in CTT (total)	60885 (25,70%)
Average of occ.	2,20

In the analysis, we considered all terms in the form XXXX-XXX as postal codes, with X being a numeric character. Tables 3.3 and 3.3 show the statistics for postal codes occurrences. Near 1/6 of all Portuguese Postal Codes appear in the WPT-03. We can speculate that these are the Postal Codes for areas where many business and commercial entities are located. The amount of CTT postal codes in the WPT-03 that also occur in the CTT database should be 100%, but 17-19% of the Postal Codes in WPT-03 are infact invalid.

Geographic Entities. To have an idea of the richness of WPT-03 on geographical references, we searched the corpus for such information. For this purpose, we did a case-insensitive search on the 308 Portuguese municipalities.

As many Portuguese geographic names consist of more than one word, we need to group individual terms, in order to provide statistics on the geographic entities identified in the corpus. To locate these entities, we use a simple algorithm that looks at all matches of those geographic names in the "word-grams" from WPT-03.

The total number of geographic entities identified in the corpus using this method is 8147120. The ten most frequent are given in Table 10, along with the overall number of occurrences.

Table 10. Most Frequent geographic names

Geographic Name	Number of Occurrences
lisboa	1034268
porto	651108
coimbra	307881
guarda	198436
aveiro	192804
braga	186410
almeida	142591
leiria	121280
faro	111028

This was only a crude approach to measure the amount of geographic references, and the results are not conclusive. For instance many Portuguese proper names (especially people's names) are also geographic names, and they were identified in this study as geographic references. In the future, we plan on conducting a much more accurate analysis of the occurrence of this information on WPT-03, using specific software for accurate named entity recognition.

4 Conclusions

We used the tumba! repository to construct a textual corpus from the pages of the "Portuguese Web", denominated WPT-03. The corpus was then analyzed using common statistical techniques from corpus linguistics [10].

This study was motivated by our interest in finding more about the textual contents of the tumba! repository, including both information about the documents (their size, language, etc.) and the terms contained in the documents. With this data we can better model the capacity and the algorithms of the tumba! search engine, and in tandem provide insights to a large corpus in natural language that are of interest to other researchers.

Specially interesting is comparing WPT-03 with several other corpora made available through Linguateca. WPT-03 contains the more or less colloquial language found on Web pages, whereas the Linguateca corpora have mostly the more formal language found in newspaper articles.

It will also be interesting to repeat this study regularly and track the evolution of the data – most probably the most frequent terms (apart from function words, of course) will change over time. The study could also be carried out using different sub-corpora, in order to find differences and similarities for different Web "communities".

Finally, a complementary study on the logs for the queries submitted to tumba! would also be very useful, in order to understand the way Portuguese users search for information on the Web, and if the information they are looking for is widely available or not.

5 Acknowledgments

We wish to thank Ruth Fuchss, for developing the initial scripts to compute statistics over the corpus, and Daniel Gomes for doing most of the work in harvesting WPT-03. Nuno Cardoso did several optimizations on the original scripts, and also helped on reviewing early drafts of this paper. Finally, a special thanks goes also to Diana Santos, for providing us with valuable insights and suggestions.

References

1. Thorsten Brants. TnT – a statistical part-of-speech tagger. In *Proceedings of ANLP-00, the 6th Conference on Applied Natural Language Processing*, 2000.
2. Eric Brill. A simple rule-based part-of-speech tagger. In *Proceedings of ANLP-92, the 3rd Conference on Applied Natural Language Processing*, pages 152–155, Trento, Italy, 1992.
3. João P. Campos. Versus: a web data repository with time support. DI/FCUL TR 03–08, Department of Informatics, University of Lisbon, May 2003. Masters thesis.
4. William B. Cavnar and John M. Trenkle. N-gram-based text categorization. In *Proceedings of SDAIR-94, the 3rd Annual Symposium on Document Analysis and Information Retrieval*, pages 161–175, Las Vegas, Nevada, U.S.A, 1994.
5. Daniel Gomes. Tarântula – sistema de recolha de documentos da Web. Technical report, Departamento de Informática da Faculdade de Ciências da Universidade de Lisboa, August 2001. Report of the traineeship done by the author at the LaSIGE `http://lasige.di.fc.ul.pt`. In portuguese.
6. Daniel Gomes and Mário J. Silva. A characterization of the Portuguese Web. In *Proceedings of the 3rd ECDL Workshop on Web Archives*, Trondheim, Norway, August 2003.
7. Bruno Martins and Mário Silva. Language identification in Web pages, 2004. (To appear).
8. Bruno Martins and Mário Silva. WebCAT: A Web content analysis tool for IR applications, 2004. (To appear).
9. José Carlos Dinis Medeiros. Processamento morfológico e correcção ortográfica do português. Master's thesis, Instituto Superior Técnico, 1995.

10. Michael P. Oakes. *Statistics For Corpus Linguistics*. Edinburgh University Press, February 1998.
11. Viswanath Poosala. Zipf's law. Technical Report 900 839 0750, Bell Laboratories, 1997.
12. Diana Santos and Paulo Rocha. Evaluating cetempúblico, a free resource for portuguese. In *Proceedings of ACL-2001, the 39th Annual Meeting of the Association for Computational Linguistics*, pages 442–449, July 2001.
13. Diana Santos and Luís Sarmento. O projecto AC/DC: acesso a corpora / disponibilização de corpora. In Amália Mendes and Tiago Freitas, editors, *Actas do XVIII Encontro da Associação Portuguesa de Linguística*, pages 705–717, October 2002.
14. Youichi Sekiguchi and Kazuhide Yamamoto. Web corpus construction with quality improvement. In *Proceedings of IJCNLP-04, the 1st International Joint Conference on Natural Language Processing*, pages 201–206, 2004.
15. Mário J. Silva. The case for a portuguese web search engine. In *Proceedings of ICWI-2003, the IADIS International Conference WWW/Internet 2003*, November 2003.
16. Alberto Manuel Simões and José João Almeida. `jspell.pm` – um módulo de análise morfológica para uso em processamento de linguagem natural. In *Actas da Associação Portuguêsa de Linguística*, pages 485–495, 2001.
17. George Kingsley Zipf. *Human Behaviour and the Principle of Least Effort*. Addison-Wesley, Reading, Massachussets, U.S.A., 1949.

A Study of Chunk-Based and Keyword-Based Approaches for Generating Headlines*

Enrique Alfonseca[1], José María Guirao[2], and Antonio Moreno-Sandoval[3]

[1] Computer Science Dep., Universidad Autonoma de Madrid, 28049 Madrid, Spain
Enrique.Alfonseca@ii.uam.es

[2] Department of Computer Science, Universidad de Granada, 18071 Granada, Spain
jmguirao@ugr.es

[3] Department of Linguistics, Universidad Autonoma de Madrid, 28049 Madrid, Spain
sandoval@maria.lllf.uam.es

Abstract. This paper describes two procedures for generating very short summaries for documents from the DUC-2003 competition: a chunk extraction method based on syntactic dependences, and a simple keyword-based extraction. We explore different techniques for extraction and weighting chunks from the texts, and we draw conclusions on the evaluation metric used and the kind of features that are more useful. Two preliminary versions of this procedure ranked in the 12th and 13th positions with respect to unigram recall (ROUGE-1) at DUC-2004 (out of 39 runs submitted).

1 Introduction

Headline generation is the problem of generating a very short summary of a document, which condenses the main ideas discussed in it. This paper describes two different procedures tested on the collection provided for the 2003 Document Understanding Conference (DUC-2003), and a hybrid approach that combines them. In all the experiments described here, we can identify two separate steps: firstly, an identification and extraction of the most important sentences from the document. Secondly, the extraction of relevant keywords and phrases from those sentences. The purpose of the first step is to restrict as much as possible the search space for the second step, thereby simplifying the selection of fragments for the headline. We have evaluated the procedures using the ROUGE-1 score [1], and we also explore some of the characteristics of this metric. The words *summary* and *headline* will be used indistinctly throughout this paper.

A popular approach for generating headlines consists in first identifying the most relevant sentences, and then applying a compaction procedure. Sentence-extraction procedures are already well-studied [2], so we shall focus on the differences in the compaction step. Some of the techniques are (a) deletion of all subordinate clauses; (b) deletion of stopwords (determiners, auxiliary verbs, etc.) [3–5]; (c) extracting fragments from the sentences using syntactic information, e.g. the verb and some kind of arguments, such as subject, objects or negative particles [6–9]; and (d) using pre-defined templates [10]. A

* This work has been sponsored by CICYT, project number TIC2001-0685-C02-01.

J. L. Vicedo et al. (Eds.): EsTAL 2004, LNAI 3230, pp. 395–406, 2004.

different approach consists in extracting, from the document, a list of topical keywords, collocations, noun phrases [3, 11–13]. Using this procedure, the resulting headline will not be grammatical, but it may provide a useful description of the topic of the article.

In Section 2 we describe the experimental settings for evaluating the system, and Section 3 briefly summarises the general architecture of the system. Next, Section 4 describes the procedures for sentence selection, and Sections 5, 6 and 7 describe all the experiments performed for generating headlines. Finally, Section 8 describes the conclusions we can draw from the results obtained, and discusses possible lines for future work.

2 Experimental Settings

The purpose of the work is to generate very short headlines from documents. We can describe this task using Mani's classification of automatic summarisation systems [2], which takes into account the following characteristics: **compression rate** is typically very high (a few words or bytes); the **audience** is generic, as the headlines do not depend on the user; the **function** is indicative, as it must suggest the contents of the original document without giving away details; and they should be coherent, and generated from single documents. In the experiments, the genre used is newswire articles, written in a single language (English).

All the experiments have been tested on the data provided for task 1 in DUC-2003. It is a set of 624 documents, grouped in sixty collections about some topics, such as schizophrenia or floodings in the Yangtze river. For each of the documents, NIST has provided four hand-written summaries to be used as gold standard. Throughout this work, we use a 75-byte limit, but we apply it in a lenient way: if a word or a chunk selected for a summary exceeds the limit, it will not be truncated.

2.1 ROUGE as Evaluation Metric

ROUGE [1, 14] is a method to automatically rank summaries by comparing them to other summaries written by humans. The original idea for the ROUGE-N metric is basically an n-gram recall metric, which calculates the percentage of n-grams from the reference summaries appear in the candidate summary:

$$\frac{\sum_{S \epsilon Refs} \sum_{gram_n \epsilon S} |\{gram_n : gram_n \epsilon Cand\}|}{\sum_{S \epsilon Refs} \sum_{gram_n \epsilon S} |\{gram_n\}|}$$

Note that if an n-gram appears in several references at the same time, it is counted as many times, which makes sense because an n-gram for which there is consensus between the humans should receive a higher weight. The procedure has been extended with additional calculations in order to improve its accuracy [14].

Lin and Hovy's experiments [1] indicate that ROUGE-1 correlates well with human evaluations of automatic headlines. In fact, given the availability of four hand-written summaries for each document, ROUGE has been used for evaluating the summaries produced by the participant teams in DUC-2004. Therefore, we have chosen to evaluate our system with the ROUGE-1 metric.

Table 1. Example of the procedure for finding the combination of words for which the unigram recall is maximised

	Document 1					
Words	w_1	w_2	w_3	w_4	w_5	w_6
Model 1	1	0	1	1	0	0
Model 2	0	0	1	1	1	1
Model 3	0	0	1	1	0	0
Model 4	2	1	0	1	0	1
Frequency	3	1	3	4	1	2

	Genotype						Score
Words	w_1	w_2	w_3	w_4	w_5	w_6	
Candidate 1	1	0	1	1	0	1	0.8571
Candidate 2	1	0	1	0	0	1	0.5714
Candidate 3	1	0	0	0	0	1	0.3571
Candidate 4	0	0	0	0	1	0	0.0714
Candidate 5	1	1	1	1	1	1	0

2.2 Upper Bound of ROUGE-1 Score in 75-Bytes Summaries

Before using ROUGE-1 to evaluate the summaries, it would be interesting to discover which is the range of scores that a system can obtain in this particular task. ROUGE-1 has been used to rank existing summarisation systems in the DUC-2004 competition. Although we know the score obtained by human summarisers, between 0.25017 and 0.31478 in DUC-2004 for 75-byte summaries, to our knowledge, we are not aware of the highest score that can possibly be obtained with this score.

In a first experiment, we study which is the range of values that can be obtained using ROUGE-1 when comparing a candidate summary to four manual headlines.

We shall use, as in DUC, four reference summaries for each documents. When evaluating a candidate headline, ROUGE-1 can be considered as the unigram recall of the candidate. If the candidate and all the references have the same length, it is obvious that, unless all the references have the same words, a candidate summary will never contain every word from every reference (which would mean a recall of 1).

The experiment for discovering the highest possible score has been designed in the following way:

A. For each document,
   1. Take its four hand-written headlines.
   2. Collect all the words that appear in them, excluding closed-class words.
   3. Count the frequency of each word.
   4. Look for the combination of words that maximises the ROUGE-1 score and has less than 75 bytes altogether.

B. Calculate the average of this score for all the documents.

Step 4 is the most costly step. A good approximation can be obtained by choosing the words with the highest frequencies in the model summaries. Still, that does not guarantee that the obtained summary will be the best one, as it may be better to substitute a long word with a large frequency for two short words which altogether have a higher frequency. A brute force approach would require too much computational time, and therefore we opted for a genetic algorithm to find the combination of words that maximises the unigram recall. Table 1 illustrates how the search is performed:

- The upper part of the table represents the reference headlines (the models) for a couple of documents, and the frequency of each word in each model. For instance, the fourth model contains w_1 twice, and w_2, w_4 and w_6 once.

find babies may be more schizophrenia possibly brain development dopamine
cesarean babies be more schizophrenia possibly brain development dopamine
1. Researchers find Cesarean babies may be more susceptible to schizophrenia.
2. Natural childbirth possibly instrumental in brain development. Cesareans associated with schizophrenia
3. Canadian rat research links caesarean birth with schizophrenic dopamine reactions.
4. Cesarean, babies, susceptible, schizophrenia, Boksa, El-Khodor, dopamine, amphetamines, brain, development

Fig. 1. Two of the best scoring summaries for a document from collection d100 (DUC-2003 data), and the four gold-standard headlines

- The next line, labelled *Frequency*, contains the sum of frequencies of each word in all the models, for each of the documents.
- We encode a candidate summary, shown below in the table, as a boolean vector of a length equal to the total number of words in all the models.
- The fitness function for the genetic algorithm is 0 if any summary has more than 75 bytes (e.g. Candidate 5), and the ROUGE-1 metric otherwise (all the others).
- The genetic algorithm evolves a population of boolean vectors, using the mutation and crossover operators, until for a large number of generations there is no improvement in the fitness of the population.

The summaries obtained with this procedure are simply a list of keywords. Figure 1 shows a couple of keyword choices that produce the best ROUGE-1 scores for a document in collection d100, and the four gold-standards used.

The best choice of keywords for the 624 documents in the data set has produced a mean ROUGE-1 score of 0.48735. Therefore, we may take it as the upper bound that can be obtained using this evaluation procedure with this data collection. This result is consistent to the evaluation done in DUC-2004, where the test set is very similar: newswire articles and four manual summaries for each one. In this case, all the human-made models have received a ROUGE-1 score between 0.25017 and 0.31478, which represents nearly 65% of the upper bound. Constraints such as grammaticality and the fact that the same idea can be expressed in many ways probably make it difficult to reach a higher score.

3 Our Approach

Our system has been divided into two main steps:

1. Firstly, we select a few sentences from the document, so that there is much less information from where to extract the headline.
2. Secondly, from those sentences, we extract and rank either keywords or phrases.
3. The headline is finally built by concatenating the keywords or chunks extracted in the previous step, until we reach the length limit. As said before, if the last keyword exceeds the limit, we do not truncate the summaries.

The following three sections further elaborate these steps.

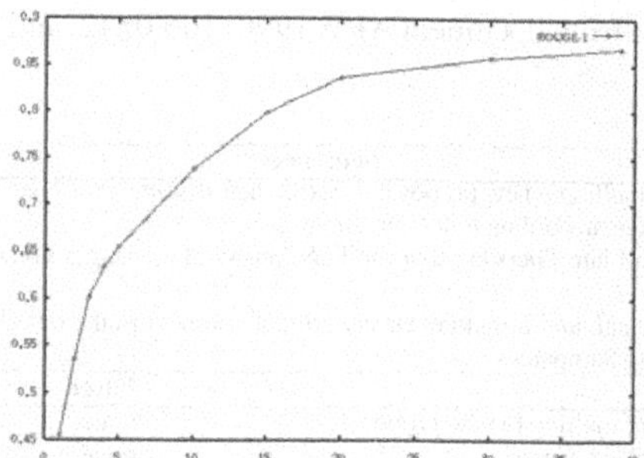

Fig. 2. ROUGE-1 results for a different number of sentences selected

4 Selection of Sentences

The first step of our system is the selection of the most relevant sentences. This is done to reduce the search space for finding the best chunks of texts with which to construct the headline. The sentence-extraction procedure we use is based on the Edmundsonian paradigm: as a linear combination of the value of several features. The features used are, among others, the sentence length, the position of the sentence in the paragraph, the position of the paragraph in the document, and the word overlapping between the sentences selected for the summary. Although some related work indicates that just by choosing the first sentences from the document can be equally useful for headline extraction [9, 15], we have opted to continue using this paradigm.

In previous work we described a procedure for acquiring the weights for the linear combination [7, 16]. It uses genetic algorithms, in a way which is very similar to the procedure used in the previous section: for each possible set of weights, we calculate the summary produced from those weights and evaluate it against the model headlines. The unigram recall of the summary is the fitness function of the set of weights. Finally, we keep the weights which select the summaries that maximise the unigram recall. The use of genetic algorithms for summarisation had been used previously by Jaoua and Ben Hamadou [17].

The hypothesis that is the basis for every sentence-extraction procedure is that there are a few sentences which hold the most relevant information, and a large number of sentences which elaborate those main ideas. Figure 2 shows the ROUGE-1 score of a summary in function of the number of sentences selected. As can be seen, with just the top three sentences, the ROUGE-1 score reaches around 0.60, using the same reference headlines as in the previous experiment. From that point onward, the slope of the curve slows down. The maximum score attained is around 0.87, when the complete documents are selected.

This indicates that just a few sentences have enough information for generating the summaries. The next step will be to reduce those sentences to no more than 75 bytes, trying to keep the ROUGE-1 score as near 0.35 as possible.

Table 2. Sentences selected from document APW19981106.0542, and verb phrases obtained from them

Sentences	
Portugal and Indonesia are mulling a new proposal to settle their dispute over East Timor, and talks between the two sides are at a crucial stage, according to a U.N. envoy.	
Envoy Jamsheed Marker said late Thursday that the U.N. proposal envisages broad autonomy for the disputed Southeast Asian territory.	
We've reached a very important, and I might even say critical, moment in the talks,", Marker told reporters after a dinner with President Jorge Sampaio.	
Verb phrases	**Filter**
[Portugal and Indonesia] are mulling [a new proposal]	none.
to settle [their dispute over East Timor]	none.
are	1
[Envoy Jamsheed Marker] said [autonomy]	2
[We] 've reached [a very important]	3
[I] might even say	2
[Marker] told [reporters]	2

5 Chunk-Based Headline Extraction

Most newswire articles describe events, which are usually (but not always) expressed with verbs. Therefore, we thought that a good idea for generating the headline was to select the most relevant verbs from the selected sentences, together with their arguments. The process is divided in three steps: verb extraction, verb-phrase ranking and headline generation.

To this aim, we process all the documents using a syntax analyser. The parser used is the wraetlic tools [18][1]. These include a Java PoS tagger based on TnT [19], a stemmer based on the LaSIE morphological analyser, [20], three chunkers written in C++ and Java (with ~94.5% accuracy when evaluated on the WSJ corpus), and a subject-verb and verb-object detector, written in Java *ad hoc* with hand-crafted rules. Multiword expressions have also been identified automatically with the following procedure: (a) eliminate stop-words and verbs from the text; (b) Collect bigrams and trigrams whose frequency is above a threshold (e.g. three times); (c) put again stopwords where necessary (e.g. in *"President of the United States"*). All the experiments reported in this section were evaluated on the whole DUC-2003 corpus for Task 1 (headline generation).

5.1 Verb-Phrase Extraction

Verbs are extracted in the following way: using our PoS tagger, we first obtain all the verbs from the document. With the partial parser, we markup each verb with its subject and arguments. Table 2 shows the sentences obtained from a document, and the verb phrases extracted from them. Note that the parser is not perfect: sometimes it cannot identify the arguments of a verb. Some errors are due to a poor grammar coverage, and others are due to mistakes in the PoS tagging. However, in many cases the arguments found are correct.

Filtering Heuristics. A manual revision of the verb phrases showed that many of them contained information that most probably was not relevant enough as to be included in the headline. Some of these cases include the following:

[1] Available at www.ii.uam.es/~ealfon/eng/download.html

Table 3. ROUGE-1 score obtained (a) by selecting sentences from the document; (b) by extracting the verb phrases (with their arguments) from them; and (c) after filtering

	All sentences		**All VPs**		**Kept VPs**	
No. of sentences	**Mean length**	**ROUGE-1**	**Mean length**	**ROUGE-1**	**Mean length**	**ROUGE-1**
1	198	0.44155	113	0.24635	73	0.20851
2	364	0.53025	194	0.30725	102	0.23756
3	527	0.59137	277	0.35974	129	0.26616
4	723	0.63480	333	0.38579	145	0.28082

1. If the parser has not been able to identify any argument of the verb phrase.
2. If the verb, in WordNet, is a hyponym of *communicate*, *utter*, or *judge*, because in many cases the information that was communicated is more relevant than the name of the person who stated it.
3. If the subject is in first or second person.
4. If the verb is either in passive form or a past participle, and the parser did not find its subject nor its agent. This is because in most of these cases the verb is functioning as an adjective and it was wrongly tagged by the PoS tagger.

The right column of Table 2 shows, for each verb, either the number of the filter because of which it was ruled out, or *none*, in the case that it passed all filters. As can be seen, only two verb phrases from this document have passed the set of filters.

Information Kept in the VPs. By extracting the verbs, the sentences selected in the previous step are reduced to a small set of verbs and their arguments. After applying the filters, this set is reduced even further, as in the example above. In Figure 2 we studied the amount of information, expressed with the ROUGE-1 score, that we still kept by selecting just two or three sentences from a document. We can do the same experiment now to see how large is the decrease in the ROUGE-1 score if we substitute the selected sentences with the list of verb phrases, and if we substitute this list with just the verb phrases that have passed all the filters.

The results are shown in Table 3. The first column shows the number of sentences that have been selected from the original document. The second column shows the ROUGE-1 score if the summary contains the complete sentences selected. These are the same values used for plotting Figure 2. The third column shows the ROUGE-1 score if we score not the complete sentences, but the list of verbs and their arguments, as printed in Table 2. Finally, the fourth column shows the score if we list the verb phrases after applying all the filters. It can be seen that the score decreases in the last two columns. However, the decrease is not proportional to the compaction level performed in each of these steps. Therefore, we know that we are removing mostly words that do not appear in the reference summaries.

5.2 Verb-Phrase Ranking

We have now extracted a list of verbs from the selected sentences. In order to generate the headline, we would like to rank them according to some metric of relevance. Lin and Hovy [21] describe how topic signatures can be built automatically from collections, and shows an application to text summarisation. We have followed the same approach, but we have calculated the topic signatures both for collections and for single documents. The procedure is the following:

1. Collect all the words and their frequencies for each document or collection.
2. Collect all the words from the rest of the documents or collections. Consider this as the contrast set.
3. Calculate the weight of each of the words using a weight function.

There are several parameters whose values we can vary. There are many weight functions that we can apply. We have tried with the *likelihood ratio* [22], which was the one used by Lin and Hovy [21]; and the tf.idf, χ^2, Mutual Information and t-score metrics. Furthermore, as indicated above, the signatures may be calculated either for each document separately, or for each collection.

With this procedure, for all the words in each document or collection, we can calculate their weight, which is a measure of the relevance of that word in the scope of the document or collection. The verb phrases that we had extracted and filtered can be weighted using the values from the topic signatures: each verb phrase may receive as weight the sum of the weights of all the words in the verb and its arguments.

5.3 Headline Generation and Results

To generate the headline, while the summary has a length lower than 75 bytes, we add the next verb phrase with the highest score . To keep the grammaticality, we do not truncate the summaries if they exceed the limit in a few bytes. In the example above, only two verb phrases remain after the filtering:

[Portugal and Indonesia] are mulling [a new proposal]
to settle [their dispute over East Timor]

These will be weighted and ranked next using a topic signature. The headline will be generated in the following way:

1. Firstly, the system chooses the most weighty verb phrases until their total length limit exceeds 75 bytes. Note that, if the limit is exceeded by a few bytes, we do not truncate the summaries, so as to keep them grammatical. In this example, both VPs will be selected.
2. Secondly, they will be put together in the order in which they appeared in the original document. If there was any conjunction linking them, it will be added to the summary so as to improve the readability.

The resulting summary in the example will be:

Portugal and Indonesia are mulling a new proposal to settle their dispute over East Timor.

We have evaluated the ten different configurations (choice of weight function and topic signatures for either documents and collections) using the ROUGE-1 score. We saw, at the beginning, that by choosing just three sentences from the original document we could reach a very high ROUGE-1 score, and the slope of the curve in Figure 2 slows

Table 4. (a) Effect of using a different weight function for calculating the topic signatures in the final ROUGE-1 score. (b) Effect of selecting a different number of sentences for each document or for each collection in the final ROUGE-1 score

(a)

Function	Docs	Cols.
Likelihood ratio	0.18298	0.19726
tf.idf	0.18910	0.19231
χ^2	0.19753	**0.20105**
Mutual Information	0.18458	0.17933
t-score	0.18599	0.19011

(b)

No. of sentences	ROUGE-1 score
1	0.19363
2	0.19956
3	**0.20105**
4	0.19972

down from that point onward, this experiment was done using three sentences from each document.

Table 4(a) shows the results. The best score is the one obtained with the χ^2 function and for collections; while the likelihood ratio for collections has attained the second best score (not statistically significant). Apart from tf.idf, the other weight functions have lower results, statistically significant at 0.95 confidence.

It can be observed here that the likelihood ratio needs a larger set of examples, because it is the one that scored worse if the signatures are obtained for single documents, but reaches the second place if we consider documents. Furthermore, when we calculate the signatures for each collection the results are slightly better than when we select the words that are more representative just for each document.

In order to check whether the choice of selecting three sentences at the beginning of the process was correct, we tried yet another experiment. We may think that the more sentences selected, the more verb phrases we have for generating the headline. On the other hand, if we have too many verb phrases, it will be more difficult to identify those that are more informative. Table 4(b) shows the results obtained by selecting a different number of sentences from each document in the sentence extraction step. This result also suggests that three sentences is a good choice, although the difference is not statistically significant.

Finally, Figure 3 shows the headlines obtained for the documents in the collection about East Timor. It can be seen that most of them are grammatical and easy to read, although the context of the news does not appear in the headlines, so it is not possible to know for most of them that the events occurred in East Timor.

Indonesia 's National Commission will investigate accusations.
the documents show a total, of Indonesian troops assigned the number.
to extradite former President Suharto; Suharto be extradited.
Stray bullets killed two villagers and police.
Habibie put an end.
Rebels were holding two soldiers; Three soldiers and one activist were killed.
Jakarta does not let six East Timorese asylum-seekers.
Portugal and Indonesia are mulling a new proposal; to settle their dispute over East Timor.
who to break the long-standing deadlock over East Timor
Assailants killed three soldiers and a civilian.

Fig. 3. Summaries generated for the documents in the collection about East Timor

6 Keyword-Based Headline Extraction

After selecting the most relevant sentences from a document, at the beginning of the process, we can follow a completely different approach for headline generation which consists in extracting keywords about the topic discussed in the document. These headlines will not be grammatical, but they may also be informative for a reader.

In our experiments, the keyword-based headlines have been generated in six ways:

1. By collecting the highest frequency words in the document.
2. By collecting the highest frequency words in the collection.
3. By alternating high frequency words from the document and its collection, i.e. we start with the highest-frequency word in the collection; next the highest-frequency word in the document, next the 2nd. highest-frequency word in the collection, etc.
4. By collecting the words with the highest χ^2 weights in the document.
5. By collecting the words with the highest χ^2 weights in the collection.
6. By alternating the highest weight words from the document and from its collection.

Table 5 shows the results obtained with each approach. As can be seen, using just the collections is not very useful, because all the documents from the same collection will have the same headline. As expected, the best results have been obtained with a combination of the words with the highest frequencies or weights from the document and its collection. In general, we can see that using weights is better than using frequencies. Finally, Figure 4 shows some headlines obtained for the collection about East Timor. From them, a reader can guess the topic of the document, but it is still difficult to grasp the main idea. However, the ROUGE-1 score is surprisingly high (approaching 0.30).

Table 5. ROUGE-1 score for the several keyword selection strategies

Setting no.	Doc.	Col.	ROUGE-1 score
1	freq	-	0.25997
2	-	freq	0.21689
3	freq	freq	0.27255
4	wei.	-	0.26810
5	-	wei.	0.20724
6	wei.	wei.	**0.29643**

pro-independence, troops, portuguese, timorese, indonesian, timor, east, carrascalao
territory, timorese, portuguese, autonomy, indonesian, timor, east, document
affair, timorese, portugal, timor, indonesian, portuguese, east, extradite
marker, jakarta, pro-independence, timorese, portuguese, be, east, indonesian
timorese, protester, portuguese, activist, indonesian, timor, east, habibie

Fig. 4. Keyword-based summaries generated for the first five documents in the collection about East Timor

timorese, east, timor, Indonesia 's National Commission will investigate accusations.
timor, the documents show a total, of Indonesian troops assigned the number.
portuguese, east, timor, to extradite former President Suharto; Suharto be extradited.
indonesian, east, timor, be, said Yacob Hamzah , a lawyer; is a Muslim province.
group, portuguese, activist, indonesian, east, timor, xanana, Habibie put an end.
timor, Rebels were holding two soldiers; Three soldiers and one activist were killed.
pro-independence, indonesian, Jakarta does not let six East Timorese asylum-seekers.
marker, Portugal and Indonesia are mulling a new proposal; to settle their dispute over East Timor.
have, say, indonesian, who to break the long-standing deadlock over East Timor.
portuguese, east, timor, indonesian, Assailants killed three soldiers and a civilian.

Fig. 5. Summaries generated for the documents in the collection about East Timor

7 Mixed Approach

We have seen that a keyword-based approach produces headlines difficult to read, but which are highly informative, as they receive very high ROUGE-1 scores. On the other hand, using the verb phrases produces grammatical headlines, but it is difficult to place the contents of the headline in context, as most of the times there are no topical keywords. A mixed approach can combine the strongest points of both.

Our final approach consists of generating the headlines from the verb phrases of the documents, weighted with the χ^2 weight function. Most of these summaries have far less than 75 bytes, so we can complete them with other information in the following way:

- While the length of the summary is lower than 75,
  - Add the next word, from the document and the collection alternatively.

Furthermore, to check the impact of the keywords, we always add at least one keyword to the VP-based summary. When tested on the DUC-2003 data, this configuration attains a ROUGE-1 score of 0.28270, which is a large improvement from the highest score obtained by the verb phrases alone (0.20105). It is lower than the best mark obtained with only keywords, but the headlines are easier to read as a large part of the headline is formed with complete sentences. The summaries obtained for the collection on East Timor are shown in Table 5.

8 Conclusions and Future Work

We have developed a method for headline generation that combines a verb-phrase extraction phase and a keyword-extraction procedure. In general, we have observed that the keywords can be very useful for identifying the topic of the text. In fact, the addition of a few keywords boost the ROUGE-1 score from around 0.20 up to around 0.28. On the other hand, the verb phrases not only usually provide the main idea of the document, but also give the headline a more natural and readable shape than headlines formed of just keywords.

Another conclusion that we can draw from the results is that it is equally important to study both the separate documents alone, and the documents inside their collection. A combination of the topic signatures from the documents and from their collections is the one that has produced the best results. It can be argued that having the documents organised in collections is not natural. However, if we have a single document, this problem can in theory be overcome by automatically downloading similar documents from the Internet, or by clustering them to form automatically the collections. Future work includes a deeper understanding of the meaning of ROUGE-1 and other possible metrics for evaluating automatic summaries.

References

1. Lin, C.Y., Hovy, E.H.: Automatic evaluation of summaries using n-gram co-occurrence statistics. In: Proceedings of HLT-NAACL 2003. (2003)
2. Mani, I.: Automatic Summarization. John Benjamins Publishing Company (2001)
3. Angheluta, R., Moens, M.F., Busser, R.D.: K. u. leuven summarization system - DUC 2003. In: Proceedings of DUC-2003. (2003)
4. Zhou, L., Hovy, E.: Headline summarization at ISI. In: Proceedings of DUC-2003. (2003)
5. Liang, S.F., Devlin, S., Tait, J.: Feature selection for summarising: The sunderland duc 2004 experience. In: Proceedings of DUC-2004, Boston, MA (2004)
6. Fuentes, M., Massot, M., Rodríguez, H., Alonso, L.: Mixed approach to headline extraction for DUC 2003. In: Proceedings of DUC-2003. (2003)
7. Alfonseca, E., Rodríguez, P.: Description of the UAM system for generating very short summaries at DUC-2003. In: Proceedings of the DUC-2003. (2003)
8. Dorr, B., Zajic, D., Schwartz, R.: Hedge Trimmer: A parse-and-trim approach to headline generation. In: Proceedings of Workshop on Automatic Summarization, Edmonton (2003)
9. Zajic, D., Dorr, B.J., Schwartz, R.R.: Bbn/umd at duc-2004: Topiary. In: DUC-2004. (2004)
10. Daumé III, H., Echihabi, A., Marcu, D., Munteanu, D., Soricut, R.: GLEANS: A generator of logical extracts and abstracts for nice summaries. In: Proceedings of DUC-2003. (2003)
11. Bergler, S., Witte, R., Khalife, M., Li, Z., Rudzickz, F.: Using knowledge-poor coreference resolution for text summarization. In: Proceedings of DUC-2003. (2003)
12. Kraaij, W., Spitters, M., Hulth, A.: Headline extraction based on a combination of uni- and multidocument summarization techniques. In: Proceedings of DUC-2003. (2003)
13. Witte, R., Bergler, A., Li, Z., Khalifé, M.: Multi-erss and erss 2004. In: DUC-2004. (2004)
14. Lin, C.Y.: Rouge working note v. 1.3.1 (2004)
15. Erkan, G., Radev, D.R.: The university of michigan at duc 2004. In: DUC-2004. (2004)
16. Alfonseca, E., Guirao, J.M., Moreno-Sandoval, A.: Description of the UAM system for generating very short summaries at DUC-2004. In: Proceedings DUC-2004. (2004)
17. Jaoua, M., Hamadou, A.B.: Automatic text summarization of scientific articles based on classification of extract's population. In: Proceedings of CICLING-2003. (2003)
18. Alfonseca, E.: Wraetlic user guide version 1.0 (2003)
19. Brants, T.: Tnt – a statistical part-of-speech tagger. In: Proceedings of the 6th Applied NLP Conference, ANLP-2000, Seattle, WA, U.S.A (2000)
20. Gaizauskas, R., Wakao, T., Humphreys, K., Cunningham, H., Wilks, Y.: University of sheffield: Description of the lasie system as used for MUC-6. In: Proceedings of the Sixth Message Understanding Conference (MUC-6), Morgan Kauffmann (1995) 207–220
21. Lin, C.Y., Hovy, E.: The automated acquisition of topic signatures for text summarization. In: Proceedings of the COLING conference. (2000)
22. Dunning, T.E.: Accurate methods for the statistics of surprise and coincidence. Computational Linguistics **19** (1993) 61–74

Suffixal and Prefixal Morpholexical Relationships of the Spanish

Octavio Santana, José Pérez, Francisco Carreras, and Gustavo Rodríguez

Departamento de Informática y Sistemas, Universidad de Las Palmas de Gran Canaria, 35017 Las Palmas de Gran Canaria, Spain
{OSantana, JPerez, Fcarreras, GRodriguez}@dis.ulpgc.es
http://www.gedlc.ulpgc.es

Abstract. This work is about derivational suffixes, endings and prefixes of the Spanish language, which are useful for the establishment of about 70 000 suffixal and 11 000 prefixal extended morpholexical relationships deduced from a corpus of 134 109 canonical forms. A computational tool is developed capable of solving and answering to any morphological aspect of a Spanish word. The tool encompasses everything related with derivation, prefixation and other nearby aspects. It allows the recognition, the generation and the manipulation of morpholexical relationships of any word and of its related words, includes the recovery of all its lexicogenetical information until arriving at a primitive, the management and the control of the affixes in the treatment of its relationships, as well as the regularity in the established relationship.

1 Introduction

This work aims at obtaining a set of extended morpholexical relationships between Spanish words useful for automatic applications in natural language processing —in a synchronous study with automation on mind, formal or theoretical aspects may do not coincide with those strictly linguistic. There are Spanish words maintaining a strong functional and semantic relationship —the same appearing at the derivational or prefixal level—, that can not be taken as derivation or prefixation, although there is a formal relationship through other stages in the evolution of the languages, so it is indeed considered necessary to include them —*agua* with *acuoso*, *vejiga* with *vesical*, *conejo* with *cunicular*. This concept must be restricted to avoid arriving to the concept of related idea —which exceeds the objectives of this work, *blanco* with *albura*, *sólido* with *endurecer*, *niño* with *pueril*—, therefore a historic-etymological meeting criterion is applied. It is obvious that for the speaker *acuario*, *portuario* and *campanario* are all places equally related with *agua*, *puerto* and *campana* —it must also be so for the automatic data processing—; in order to solve the linguistic boundaries preventing to treat relationships beyond the strict derivation or prefixation, it is necessary to be located at a different level from the morphological level; thus the concept of morpholexical relationship is extended.

J. L. Vicedo et al. (Eds.): EsTAL 2004, LNAI 3230, pp. 407–418, 2004.

2 Lexicon

The corpus handled in this work has been created from: the *Diccionario de la Lengua Española* (DRAE), the *Diccionario General de la Lengua Española* (VOX), the *Diccionario de Uso del Español* (María Moliner), the *Gran Diccionario de la Lengua Española* (LAROUSSE), the *Diccionario de Uso del Español Actual* (Clave SM), the *Diccionario de Sinónimos y Antónimos* (Espasa Calpe), the *Diccionario Ideológico de la Lengua Española* (Julio Casares) and the *Diccionario de Voces de Uso Actual* (Manuel Alvar Ezquerra).

A canonical form is defined as any word with its own identity susceptible of enduring derivational processes to form other words. Such a word could be formed from another by similar processes. In the reference corpus a canonical form is any entry word of consulted sources having own meaning —those entries that are appreciative forms of others and do not add any substantial meaning variation are discarded. The universe of words analyzed in this work is composed of 148 798 canonical forms.

3 Suffixal Relationships

Spanish derivational processes consist fundamentally of suffixal modifications and usually, but not always, it implies a change of the derivative grammatical category with respect to its primitive canonical form.

Frequently, there are pairs of primitive forms in Spanish coming from a same mother tongue in which they went through a derivational process. The current relationship between the members of such pairs is considered as suffixal alteration, since in the current state of the Spanish language the existing relationship between them presents a strong parallelism with the derivational processes between Spanish forms, in its morphological aspects as well as in the semantic and grammatical aspects: for the verb *multiplicar* and the adjective *multiplicable* —both Spanish primitive words derived directly from the Latin— it is commendable to consider *multiplicable* as a deverbal adjetivation of *multiplicar*.

There are many words in Spanish which come from a same mother tongue, where they suffered a derivational process from a common element that was never consolidate in the current Spanish; thus, they are etymologically related and are considered derivatives from a non-existent Spanish form, since they show a high similarity in the morphological, semantic and grammatical aspects with analogous Spanish derivatives from an existing form: between the forms *concupiscente* and *concupiscible* —both Spanish primitive words derived directly from the Latin— results feasible to consider an analogous relationships to those between any pair of Spanish deverbal adjetivations formed from a common primitive with the same endings, like *dirigente* and *dirigible* from *dirigir*.

Other important aspect about the formation of Spanish words is to decide what words must be considered as primitives and what as derivatives —temporary line of appearance of the words must be maintained. The main difficulty appears when there is ambiguity between two morpholexically related primitives about their diachronic formation; in such case, and for synchronous treatment of the Spanish purpose, the verb, if any, is designed as primitive; when there is not a verb involved, the primitive is selected using the Spanish word formation rules supposing that words are morpholexically related in equality terms: *lamento* is considered a deverbal sustantivation of *lamentar* knowingly of the fact that both are primitive.

It is necessary to emphasize that there are Spanish words with a close functional and semantic relationship that cannot be directly established through a process classified within the derivational morphology. So, the concept of extended morpholexical relationship is incorporated and encompasses, in addition to the relationships produced by derivation, other characterized by having a meeting point in their etymological record and by incorporating an ending with the adequate semantic and functional contribution: *audición* is considered suffixaly related with *oír*, although *audición* is primitive and possesses a different root from *oír*.

The extended morpholexical relationship includes to relate words through an ending graphically coinciding with a suffix if having the semantics and functionality corresponding to that suffix: that is the relationship between *miel* and *melaza* ('sediments of honey'), whose ending coincides with the suffix *-azo/a*, in spite of the different formative process; as in *seise* of *seis*, through the ending *-e*, being aware of the fact that it is regressive of the plural *seises* —in definitive, it is a noun closely related to the adjective *seis*.

The extended relationships also includes those cases in which the only impediment to establish it are some characters of the ending: between *diez* and *décimo* —by analogy to the relationship between *mil* and *milésimo*, among others, through the numerical ending *-ésimo*.

Although both the inflection and the appreciative derivation constitute suffixal morphological processes of interest for the development of automatic natural language processors, neither of this aspects will be dealt here, since it have been settled in FLANOM[1].

A suffix is "a phonic sequence added to the end of a word stem, prior to the desinences, if any, that lacks self existence outside the word system, it can not to be joined to other morpheme to form a derivative, it is interchangeable with other suffixes and it can be added to other stems" [2]. Basing on the previous definition, the set of suffixes considered in this work to establish relationships can be enumerated — a sequence is considered as suffix if appears in three or more different words. Thus, endings like *-arra*, *-aste*, *-ello*, *-ingo*, *-uz* fulfil the described suffix definition although theirs suffixal condition in the grammatical sense is questionable.

An original word can be any Spanish word with self identity that admits suffixes addition to obtain another related word. Deverbal regressions with addition to the endings *-a*, *-e*, *-o* and zero-suffix or empty suffix, as well as plurals and appreciative suffixes with consolidated meaning are also considered in this work. Suffixal elements —

---

[1] *FLANOM: Flexionador y Lematizador Automático de Formas Nominales*. Developed by the Grupo de Estructuras de Datos y Lingüística Computacional of the Las Palmas de Gran Canaria University, available on Internet.

suffixes with a strong semantic load on the original word or those possessing self existence— are left for another work, since they are part of the research of composition.

Even though it is true that most of the relationships between words coincide with a formal derivation —mainly the regulars—, the spelling coincidence with a concrete suffix can lead to of relationships detached from such linguistic concept, at least by means of that suffix, but covering the proposed objective. For example, the words *psiquiatra* and *psiquiátrico* are related to *psiquiatría* through the endings *-a* and *-'ico*, in spite of being aware of the existence of *-iatría* and *-iatra*, the relationship is intended to be established between previously mentioned words and not with a possible root *psiqui-*.

A related word can also be original to another by adding a new suffix: *quej-a* → *quej-ica* → *quejic-oso*. The arrow must not to be interpreted as derivation in a strict sense, but as a extended morpholexical relationship between two words: **original** and **related**.

Changes affecting the root such as erudite words relationships or foreign languages influences, among other, are considered irregularities, although they are not pure linguistic derivation, since it notably enriches computer applications. The possible suffix combinations which lead to a relationship are also considered as irregularities, as long as the previously explained continuity criterion cannot be established due to the nonconsolidation or nonexistence of the intermediate form in the corpus. Appearances of interffixes and infixes are considered irregularities.

Now the alphabetical list of studied suffixes is presented together with their corresponding number of extended morpholexical relationship: *-a* (1419), *-áceo/a* (190), *-acho/a* (35), *-aco/a* (27), *-'ada, -'ade* (9), *-'ago/a* (11), *-aino/a* (16), *-aje* (315), *-ajo/a* (65), *-al* (1574), *-ales* (6), *-allo/a, -alle* (36), *-amen* (34), *-án/a* (38), *-áneo/a* (18), *-ano/a, -iano/a* (732), *-año/a* (36), *-anza, -enza* (127), verbalizer *-ar* (2635), *-ar* (407), *-ario/a* (532), *-astro/a, -astre* (27), *-atario/a* (36), *-ate* (33), *-átil* (16), *-ato/a* (294), *-avo/a* (29), *-az* (22), *-azgo/a, -adgo/a* (100), *-azo/a* (562), *-azón* (75), *-bilidad* (263), *-able, -ible* (1088), *-abundo, -ebundo, -ibundo,* (13), *-ación, -ición* (2637), *-'culo/a, -áculo/a, -ículo/a* (41), *-dad, -edad, -idad* (1095), *-adero/a, -edero/a, -idero/a,* (650), *-adizo/a, -edizo/a, -idizo/a* (118), *-ado/a, -ido/a* (16320), *-ador/a, -edor/a, -idor/a,* (3034), *-edumbre, -idumbre* (19), *-adura, -edura, -idura* (789), *-aduría, -eduría, -iduría* (42), *-e* (542), *-ear* (1786), *-eser* (102), *-eco/a* (32), *-edo/a* (62), *-ego/a, -iego/a* (68), *-ejo/a* (86), *-el* (57), *-elo/a* (63), *-én* (17), *-enco/a, -engo/a* (30), *-eno/a* (84), *-eño/a* (381), *-ense, -iense* (417), *-enta* (16), *-ento/a, -iento/a, -ulento/a, -olento/a* (125), *-eo/a* (152), *-'eo/a* (128), *-er, -ier* (29), *-ería* (881), *-erio* (24), *-erío* (55), *-erizo/a* (23), *-erno/a* (12), *-ero/a* (3151), *-és/a* (207), *-esa* (29), *-ésimo/a* (36), *-ete, -eto/a* (394), *-euta* (14), *-ez/a* (374), *-ezno/a* (13), *-grama* (51), *-í* (49), *-íaco/a, -iaco/a* (72), *-icio/a, -icie* (78), *-ico/a* (35), *-'ico/a* (1690), *-'ide* (18), *-'ido/a* (156), *-ificar* (135), *-'igo/a* (18), *-iguar* (4), *-ijo/a* (59), *-'il* (16), *-il* (155), *-illo/a* (797), *-imonio/a* (6), *-ín/a* (241), *-ina* (174), *-íneo/a* (26), *-ing* (15), *-ingo/a* (13), *-ino/a* (526), *-iño/a* (16), *-'io/a* (499), *-ío/a* (629), *-ión* (279), *-ir* (25), *-is* (9), *-ismo* (1365), *-ista* (1325), *-ístico/a* (122), *-ita* (66), *-ita* (83), *-ito/a* (258), *-'ito/a* (18), *-itud* (57), *-ivo/a, -ativo/a, -itivo/a,* (692), *-izar* (554), *-izo/a* (95), *-ma, -ema* (20), *-ambre, -imbre, -umbre* (23), *-mente* (2432), *-amento, -imento, -amiento, -imiento* (1876), *-ancia, -encia* (532), *-ander/a, -endero/a* (28), *-ando/a,*

-endo/a, -iendo/a, -ondo/a, -iondo/a (87), *-ante, -ente, -iente* (1 617), *-o* (2 740), *-ol* (17), *-olo/a, -ol* (73), *-ón/a* (1 334), *-ongo/a* (15), *-or/a* (286), *-'ora* (4), *-orio/a* (89), *-oso/a* (1 286), *-ote/a, -oto* (125), *-arro/a, -orro/a, -arrio/a, -orrio/a* (55), *-s* (46), *-asco/a, -esco/a, -isco/a, -usco/a* (213), *-tano/a, -itano/a, -etano/a* (44), *-aticio/a, -iticio/a* (15), *-'tico/a, -ático/a, -ético/a, -ítico/a, -ótico/a* (382), *-atorio/a, -itorio/a* (298), *-triz* (28), *-ucho/a* (23), *-uco/a* (17), *-udo/a* (238), *-uelo/a* (134), *-ujo/a* (17), *-'ulo/a* (45), *-uno/a* (60), *-ura* (202), *-uro* (22), *-uto/a* (33) and other lower frequency endings.

4 Prefixal Relationships

Prefixation does not produce grammatical category change; normally, it shades, amends, modifies, in short, it guides the meaning of the word. In addition to the prefixation through traditional elements, there is the certain composition through prefixal elements, among other forms of composition —these elements will not be taken into account in this work due to the strong semantic load they provide.

A prefixal morpholexical relationship between a pair of primitive forms is established when, formally, one could be obtained by prefixation from the other and it shows semantic relationship inherent in the prefix —*culpar* and *inculpar* came directly from the Latin *culpare* and *inculpare* but one can be obtained from the other by adding the prefix *in-*.

Independently from the existing suffixal morpholexical relationships, a prefixal relationship between two original words is projected to the corresponding derived pairs —the prefixal relationship between *amortizar* and *desamortizar* is applied to *amortización* with *desamortización* and to *amortizable* with *desamortizable*.

Apart from the prefixal morpholexical relationships, the suffixal morpholexical relationships of a word are projected to their corresponding prefixed forms, since their mutual morphological, semantic and grammatical relationships are equivalent —*sobrecalentamiento* and *sobrecalentar* are prefixal forms between which the same suffixal morpholexical relationship existing between *calentamiento* and *calentar* is established.

The same considerations as in the suffixal alterations are applied to extend the concept of prefixal morpholexical relationship: *coepíscopo* is considered to be prefixaly related with *obispo*, though *coepíscopo* is primitive and, from a synchronic perspective, it possesses a different base from that of *obispo*.

Extended morpholexical relationship includes to relate words through a start graphically coinciding with a prefix if having the semantics and functionality corresponding to that prefix: a relationship is established between *eficiente* and *deficiente*, because the initials of the second word coincide with the prefix *de-* and it verifies with the rest of the criterion with respect to the first one.

Also, other graphic elements providing some type of relationship between words are studied, such is the case of the article of Arabic origin *al-* that permits to establish extended morpholexical relationship between *juba* and *aljuba* as variants one from the other.

The relationship between an original word and a prefixed form is semantic, functional and formal. In the semantic aspect, the prefix incorporates its own specific nuance, but the main semantic load corresponds to the original word. Syntactic and grammatical functions tend to be maintained in the prefixed form, though eventually it might produce a grammatical category change, due more to use than to the prefixational process. The formal differences are adjusted to the general rules of prefixation and to those which are specific to each prefix, and, though irregularities exist, they have a much lower incidence than that of alterations in other positions of the lexical base.

Prefixal element, henceforth prefix, can be defined as an affix attached to the front of the original word. This definition is so wide that produces two problems when delimiting what prefixes must be considered in this work without approaching composition.

Some prefixes have their own functional identity in Spanish —generally prepositions and some adverbs—, they are called vulgar prefixes and some authors consider them compositional elements. However, a prefix coming from one preposition can be detached from this since it does not fulfil the same grammatical function, though sometimes they agree in meaning. The semantic contribution of prepositions is a nominal subordination and that of prefix is a semantic addition and the similarity between them is reduced at present, and in a synchronic study, to a phonetic issue. In this work, all prefixes of this type are treated in a similar way —each them is accompanied with the cardinality of its extended morpholexical relationships—: *a-* (615), *ab-* (29), *ad-* (52), *al-* (58), *ana-* (14), *ante-* (106), *con-* (516), *contra-* (313), *cuasi-* (6), *de-* (287), *des-* (1 815), *e-* (50), *en-* (228), *entre-* (136), *ex-* (85), *extra-* (64), *in-* (1 317), *para-* (61), *por-* (3), *post-* (89), *pro-* (102), *sin-* (28), *so-* (91), *sobre-* (254), *sota-* (14), *sub-* (249), *ultra-* (64).

The second issue under discussion is what prefixes of the erudite prefixes, prefixoids, prefixal elements or compositive elements should be included. It is opted for generously studying those changing the meaning of the term to which they are joined, in an objective or subjective way, and those providing a pronominal or adverbial sense to the base. They do not appear as independent terms, and their semantic value are generic and applicable to any grammatical category. The prefixes of this type are: *abiso-* (2), *acro-* (4), *ambi-* (4), *anfi-* (6), *auto-* (185), *bar-* (7), *bati-* (5), *bi-* (111), *circa-* (0), *circun-* (16), *di-* (87), *diali-* (3), *ecto-* (3), *endo-* (27), *equi-* (14), *eu-* (3), *exo-* (18), *hemi-* (7), *hetero-* (32), *hiper-* (97), *hipo-* (72), *infra-* (21), *iso-* (28), *macro-* (44), *maxi-* (3), *mega-* (24), *meso-* (15), *meta-* (33), *micro-* (116), *mini-* (58), *mono-* (64), *multi-* (54), *omni-* (10), *opisto-* (1), *pan-* (44), *pen-* (4), *pluri-* (11), *plus-* (4), *poli-* (49), *preter-* (5), *proto-* (23), *retro-* (33), *semi-* (159), *super-* (220), *supra-* (21), *tele-* (70), *uni-* (23), *vice-* (42), *yuxta-* (3). Erudite prefixes whose semantic contribution is strong are discarded: *bio-* (life), *foto-* (light), *metro-* (measure), among other, and apocopes acting as prefixal elements, like *auto-* (of *automóvil*), *tele-* (of *televisión*) among other.

Of course, prefixes that the employed sources define as such are considered too: *anti-* (416), *apo-* (12), *archi-* (44), *cachi-* (10), *cata-* (8), *cis-* (6), *citra-* (1), *dia-* (21), *dis-* (86), *epi-* (36), *es-* (82), *inter-* (161), *intra-* (35), *ob-* (20), *per-* (74), *peri-* (20), *pre-* (243), *re-* (995), *requete-* (3), *res-* (9), *tatara-* (3), *trans-* (258), *za-* (7).

A related word can be original to another by adding a new prefix: *emitir* → *ransmitir* → *retransmitir*. The arrow must not to be interpreted as prefixation in a strict sense, but as a extended morpholexical relationship between two words: **original** and **related**.

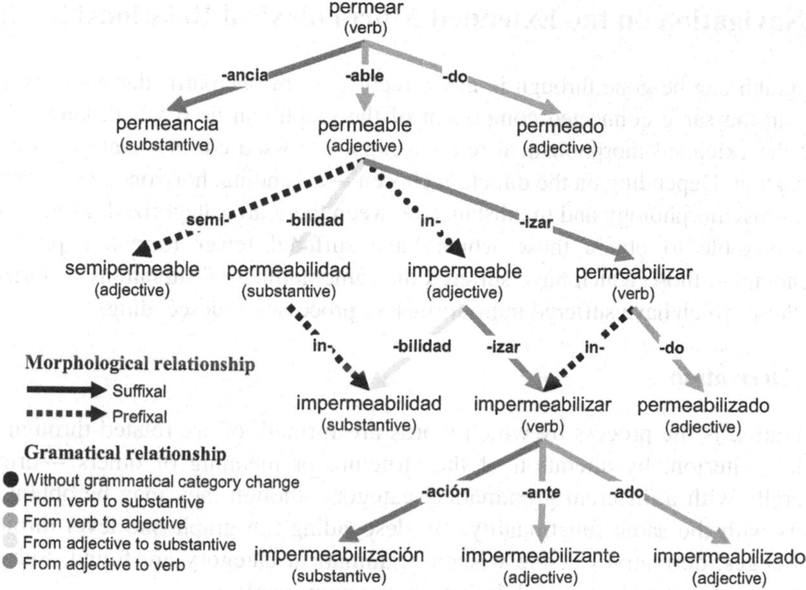

Fig. 1. Extended morpholexical relationships clan of permear

Changes affecting the root such as erudite words relationships or foreign languages influences, among other, are considered irregularities, although they are not pure linguistic prefixations, since they notably enrich computer applications. They are also treated as irregularities the prefix combinations causing a relationship, when the previously explained continuity criterion cannot be established due to the nonconsolidation or nonexistence of the intermediate form in the corpus.

5 Extended Morpholexical Relationships Organization

The joint formed by an original word and all its morpholexically related words is designated as **family**. Since a word can be related to an original word and at the same time to be original word in relationships linked with other words, kinship relationships between different families are established through this word. All the families related in this way compose a **clan**.

In order to represent the different types of relationships produced by the rules to form Spanish words and by the applied extended criteria, a directed graph has been chosen; nodes identify the Spanish words, edges express existence of extended morpholexical relationships, the direction of each edge determines the relationship between the nodes and the edge labels classify the type of extended morpholexical relationship. Spanish words become grouped into disjoint sets of mutually related elements —connected components of the graph, or clans—, Figure 1.

6 Navigation on the Extended Morpholexical Relationship Graph

The graph can be gone through in any direction: from one particular node, every other node in the same connected component of the graph can be reached, knowing at any time the extended morpholexical relationships —crossed edges— until arriving at the destination. Depending on the direction chosen —ascending, horizontal or descending— the words' morphology and the distance between them are categorized. From one word, it is possible to obtain those which have suffered fewer formative processes —ascending—, those which have suffered the same number of alterations —horizontal— and those which have suffered more formative processes —descending.

6.1 Derivation

Derivation is the process by which words are formed, or are related through the extended criterion, by alteration of the structure or meaning of others —original—, generally with a different grammatical category, though they may be obtained from others with the same functionality. By descending the graph one level through suffixal edges, derivatives of the wished grammatical category are found. Substantive, adjective, verbal and adverbial derivation are envisaged.

6.2 Direct Ancestry

Direct ancestry permits to obtain the original word with which a concrete word has been related —the inverse to derivation or prefixation. Ancestors are found ascending the graph one level. Thus, the direct ancestry of the verb *tutear* is the personal pronoun *tú*, that of verb *preconcebir* is the verb *concebir* and in the clan of *permear*, the direct ancestry of the substantive *permeabilidad* would be the adjective *permeable*. If the direct ancestry process is applied twice, the original from the original from the current node is obtained; so, the direct ancestor in two levels of the verb *permeabilizar* is *permear*; on the other hand, the verb *tutear* has not this option because the pronoun *tú* is the root of the graph.

6.3 Indirect Ancestry

Indirect ancestry gets the morpholexically related words with the direct ancestors and that are found at the same level on the graph. Words of the clan having suffered one alteration less than the current word can be obtained in this way. In the clan of *permear*, the indirect ancestors of the adjective *impermeable* are the adjective *permeado* and the substantive *permeancia*. As occurs with direct ancestry, it is possible to navigate other levels of morpholexical relationships: second level indirect ancestors of *permeabilizado* are the substantive *permeancia* and the adjective *permeado*, the same results as with only one level for *permeabilidad*.

6.4 Horizontality

Words morpholexically related with the same original word constitute the horizontal direction —they are words with the same number of alterations. They are achieved recovering the direct ancestors and descending one level through all the edges of that node. This option recovers all members of a family from one of them —it does not include the original word. From the adjective *impermeabilizante*, the adjective *impermeabilizado* and the substantive *impermeabilización* are obtained.

6.5 Descendents

Descendents from a word are the other members of the family for which it is the original word. The level two descendents are the descendent family of each one of the members of the family of the original word. In the clan of *permear*, the descendents from the adjective *permeable* are the substantive *permeabilidad*, the verb *permeabilizar* and the adjectives *impermeable* and *semipermeable*. The level two descendents from the adjective *permeable* are the adjective *permeabilizado*, the substantive *impermeabilidad* and the verb *impermeabilizar*.

7 Filters

Filters in the extended morpholexical relationships permit selective discrimination of navigation response. Results of different types of navigation are susceptible of being submitted to various diverse nature filters —functional, regularity and by affixes.

7.1 Functional

It consists of accomplishing a selection by grammatical category. Thus, in the clan of *permear*, the only one substantive descendent from the adjective *permeable* is *permeabilidad*.

7.2 Regularity

It consists of selecting the regular morpholexical relationships or the irregular morpholexical relationships that maintain the words with respect to the original word. If wanting to explore the irregular horizontal relationships of one word, horizontal navigation and the irregular filter are applied.

7.3 Affixal

The affixal filter makes the selection according to the affixes establishing the morpholexical relationships —discrimination by one or more affixes can be applied.

8 Application

The application interprets and handles with versatility the most relevant aspects of the extended morpholexical relationships. It represents a form of showing the system power, without damage of its integration in other useful natural language processing tools. The interface of *RELACIONES*, Figure 2, facilitates exploration of the extended

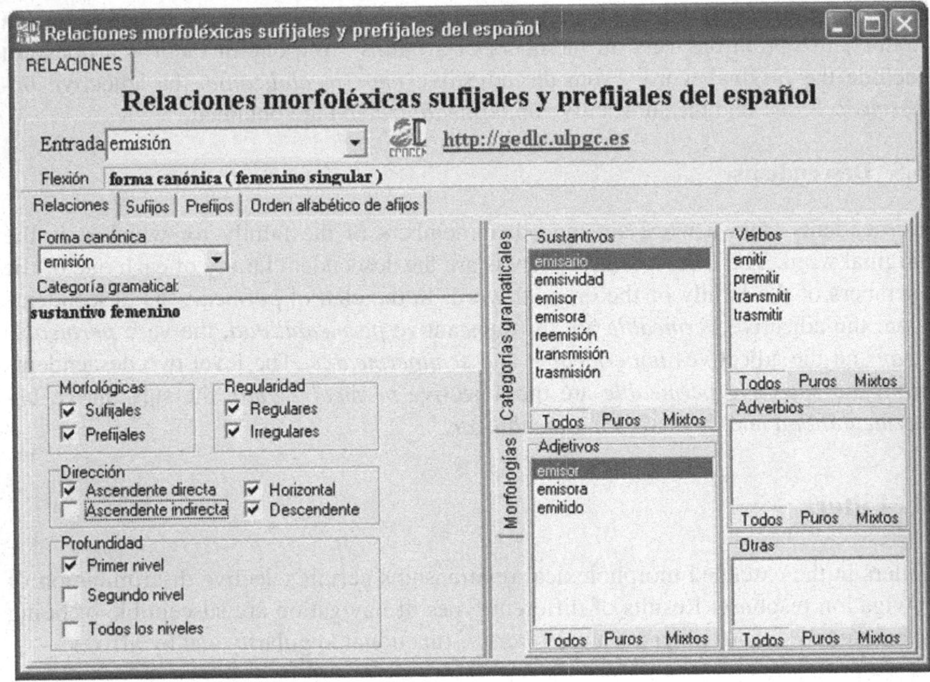

Fig. 2. Extended morpholexical relationships interface

morpholexical relationships of a canonical form of any Spanish word. The *Entrada* permits the user to introduce any word. As a result of recognition, only canonical forms that possess extended morpholexical relationships are located in the *Forma canónica* combo box —it permits to request its relationships.

A set of check boxes permits navigation by the clan of related words while filtering the results. The related words are shown on the list boxes located on the right of the interface which are organized by grammatical category.

Check boxes grouped under *Regularidad* filter the response according to the regularity: regular relationships, irregular relationships or both.

Dirección and *Profundidad* check boxes establish which words morphologically related with the canonical form are shown. These two check boxes groups are linked since when establishing the search direction on the graph, it is needed to specify its depth level. The result shows the union of all related words for each one of the indicated directions with each one of the depth levels chosen —they are classified in list boxes by grammatical categories.

Three buttons appear under each grammatical category list box —*Todos*, *Puros* and *Mixtos*— which permit to select the words of that list only by the list grammatical function —*Puros*— or those having another grammatical function in addition to the one defines by the list —*Mixtos*—, or well to show all words having at least the grammatical function defined by the list —*Todos*.

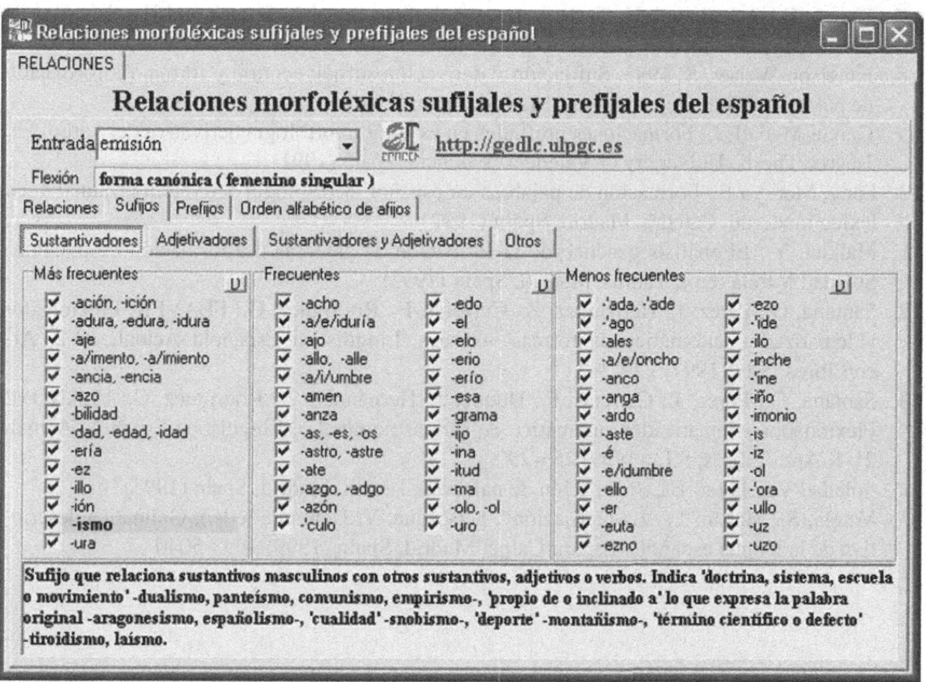

Fig. 3. The interface of extended morpholexical relationships: Suffix

In the interface of *RELACIONES*, Figure 3, appears the *Sufijos* tab sheet —it permits to configure suffixal filter. The considered suffixes are shown classified by the grammatical category that they produce and by its appearance frequency. Each group appears alphabetically ordered to facilitate location. The *Otros* tab sheet collects the verbalizer suffixes, adverbializer suffixes and others not easily classifiable irregular suffixes —they do not appear by appearance frequency. The *Prefijos* tab sheet permits to configure prefixal filter the prefixes are shown classified by its appearance frequency.

References

1. Alarcos Llorach, E.: Gramática de la Lengua Española. Espasa-Calpe, Madrid, Spain (1995)
2. Almela Pérez, R.: Procedimientos de formación de palabras en español. Ariel, Barcelona, Spain (1999)
3. Alvar Ezquerra, M.: La formación de las palabras en español. Cuadernos de lengua española. Arco/Libros, Madrid, Spain (1993)
4. Bajo Pérez, E.: La derivación nominal en español. Arco/Libros, Madrid, Spain (1997)
5. Bosque, I., Demonte, V., Lázaro Carreter, F.: Gramática descriptiva de la lengua española. Espasa, Madrid, Spain (1999)
6. Dee, J. H.: A lexicon of latin derivatives in Italian, Spanish, French and English, Vol. I Introduction and Lexicon. Olms-Weidmann, New York, USA (1997)

7. Dee, J. H.: A lexicon of latin derivatives in Italian, Spanish, French and English, Vol. II Index. Olms-Weidmann, New York, USA (1997)
8. Faitelson-Weiser, S. 1993. Sufijación y derivación sufijal: sentido y forma. La formación de palabras. Varela (ed.), Taurus, Madrid, Spain (1993)
9. García-Medall, J.: Formaciones prefijales en español: morfología derivativa del verbo. Ph. Degree Thesis. University of Valencia, Valencia, Spain (1991)
10. Lang, Mervyn F.: Formacion de palabras en español. Morfología derivativa productiva en léxico moderno. Cátedra, Madrid, Spain (1992)
11. Malkiel, Y.: El análisis genético de la formación de palabras. La formación de palabras. Soledad Varela (ed.), Taurus, Madrid, Spain (1993)
12. Santana, O., Pérez, J., Hernández, Z., Carreras, F., Rodríguez, G.: FLAVER: Flexionador y lematizador automático de formas verbales. Lingüística Española Actual, 19-2, Arco/Libros, S.L. (1997) 229-282
13. Santana, O., Pérez, J., Carreras, F., Duque, J., Hernández, Z., Rodríguez, G.: FLANOM: Flexionador y lematizador automático de formas nominales. Lingüística Española Actual. 21-1, Arco/Libros, S.L. (1999) 253-297
14. Soledad Varela (ed.): La formación de palabras. Taurus, Madrid, Spain (1993)
15. Varela, S., Martín, J.: "La prefijación", I. Bosque, V. Demonte (eds.), Gramática descriptiva de la lengua española. Espasa-Calpe, Madrid, Spain (1999) 4993-5040

SuPor: An Environment for AS of Texts in Brazilian Portuguese

Lucia Helena Machado Rino[+] and Marcelo Módolo[*]

[+]Departamento de Computação – Universidade Federal de São Carlos (UFSCar)
lucia@dc.ufscar.br
[*]Coordenação de Sistemas de Informação – Faculdade Seama
mmodolo@seama.edu.br
Núcleo Interinstitucional de Lingüística Computacional (NILC/São Carlos)

Abstract. This paper presents SuPor, an environment for extractive Automatic Summarization of texts written in Brazilian Portuguese, which can be explored by a specialist on AS to select promising strategic features for extraction. By combining any number of features, SuPor actually entitles one to investigate the performance of distinct AS systems and identify which groups of features are more adequate for Brazilian Portuguese. One of its systems has outperformed six other extractive summarizers, signaling a significant grouping of features, as shown in this paper.

1 Introduction

The present work combines classical (e.g., [14]; [5]) and novel approaches (e.g., [2]) to AS of English texts, in order to investigate which features can contribute best to summarize texts in BP. Specific BP resources were used, namely, electronic dictionaries, a lexicon, and a thesaurus (see, for example, [20], [6], and [4]), added to BP-driven tools, such as a parser [17], a part-of-speech tagger [1], a stemmer [3], and a sentencer. These allowed us to devise AS extractive systems to explore more thoroughly the AS of texts in BP. So far, texts under consideration are genre-specific. Summarization strategies focus upon both linguistic and non-linguistic constraints, in a multifaceted environment that allows the user to choose distinct summarization features. Once customized, the environment, hereafter named SuPor (an environment for automatic **SU**mmarization of texts in **POR**tuguese) [19], is ready to produce as many extracts to the same input as the user wishes, through distinct compression rates. By diversifying the groups of selected features, distinct AS strategies may be considered, which allow analyzing which features grouping apply better to the extraction of text units from texts in Brazilian Portuguese. Like other proposed methodologies, SuPor aims at identifying text units that are sufficiently relevant to compose an extract. Unlike them, it allows the user to quite freely set which combination of features s/he intends to explore for AS. Henceforth, summaries automatically generated are named extracts after the extractive methodology, i.e., the copy-and-paste of text units considered relevant to include in a summary [16].

In Section 2 we briefly describe the approaches for English that have been incorporated into SuPor. The distinctive ways to generate extracts are described in

J. L. Vicedo et al. (Eds.): EsTAL 2004, LNAI 3230, pp. 419–430, 2004.

Section 3. Preliminary evaluations, described in Section 4, indicate promising combinations of features to summarize texts in BP. Final remarks are presented in Section 5.

2 Extractive Approaches Incorporated to SuPor

SuPor considers four extractive methods explored for the English language, hereafter named the 'Classifier' [11], which combines corpora-based features, the 'Lexical Chains Method' [2], which computes connectedness between words, the 'Relationship Map Method' [29], which performs similarly to the previous one, but considering paragraphs instead, and the 'Importance of Topics Method' [12], which identifies important topics of a source text.

The Classifier Method uses a Bayesian classifier to train the system in recognizing relevant features. These include the sentence length, limited to 5 words the minimum; the words frequency; signaling nouns; sentence or paragraph location; and the occurrence of proper nouns. The last three features have been firstly addressed by Edmundson [5]. As a result of the training phase, a probabilistic distribution is produced to allow the automatic summarizer to select sentences through the certified features.

The Lexical Chains Method computes lexical cohesion through several maps of word correlations, considering only nouns as basic significant units of a source text. They follow [9, 7] in that strong lexical chains are those whose semantic relationship is more expressive. To compute lexical chaining, an ontology and the WordNet [18] are used to identify the lexical chaining mechanisms of cohesion (synonymy/antonym, hiperonimy/hiponimy, etc.), resulting in a set of strongly correlated words. Three diverse summarization heuristics may be applied to select sentences to include in an extract based on lexical chaining. The 1st heuristics selects every sentence S of the source text based upon each member M of every strong lexical chain of the set formerly computed. S is the sentence that contains the 1st occurrence of M. The 2nd heuristics applies the former one only to representative members of a strong lexical chain. A representative member of a lexical chain is that whose frequency is greater than the average frequency of all the words in the chain. Finally, the 3rd heuristics is based upon the representativeness of a given strong lexical chain in every topic of the source text.

The Relationship Map Method focuses on three distinct ways of interconnecting paragraphs, to build maps of correlated text units, yielding the following paths: the dense or bushy, the deep, and the segmented ones. Dense paths are those with more connections in the map. To build them, top-ranked paragraphs are chosen totally independent from each other. Because of this, texture (i.e., cohesion and coherence) is not guaranteed. Trying to overcome this, the deep path focuses on paragraphs that are semantically inter-related. However, a unique topic may be conveyed in the extract which may not be the main topic of the source text. The segmented bushy path aims at overcoming the bottlenecks of the former methods by addressing distinct topics of the source text.

Finally, the Importance of Topics Method is based upon the so-called TF-ISF, or Term Frequency-Inverse Sentence Frequency measure, which identifies sentences that may uniquely convey relevant topics to include in the extract. Topics are delimited by the Text Tiling algorithm [8].

Besides the methods variations themselves, the following differences are observed: (a) the Classifier is the only one that depends on genre and domain, because it requires training on corpora of texts; (b) the Lexical Chains one is the only one that does not allow a compression rate to be specified, because it is the heuristic that determines the number of extract sentences and not the user; (c) the Relationship Map method is the only one that deals with paragraphs, instead of sentences, as minimal units. Preprocessing applies to all of them, aiming at producing the source texts internal representation. However, distinct tools are used, as follows (methods that embed them are pinpointed between brackets): stopwords removal (all but Lexical Chaining), stemming (Relationship Map and Importance of Topics), segmenting (all), tagging and parsing (only Lexical Chaining), and 4-grams extraction (only Importance of Topics). This is used for Romance languages, if no stemming is available.

The Lexical Chains Method is the most costly, since it depends on sophisticated linguistic resources. Actually, this is the only method that has been significantly modified for Brazilian Portuguese: for the lack of an ontology and a WordNet for BP, its implementation to BP in SuPor uses a thesaurus instead [4]. Other minor adaptations of the referred methods to SuPor have been made, which are detailed in Section 3.

Our selection of these models has been limited, on one hand, to the already available linguistic resources at NILC[1] and, on the other hand, to their portability to BP. Promising aspects of such methods included the following: a) in the Classifier Method, metrics for AS can be made available through training and the automatic summarizer may be modeled upon relevant corpora-based features; b) focusing on expressive relationships between lexical items, the Lexical Chains Method increases the chance of selecting sentences better; c) similarly to the previous one, both the Relationship Map and Importance of Topics methods target more coherence in focusing upon the interconnectedness of the topics of a source text. However, the latter innovates in using text tiling to determine the relevant ones.

Problematic aspects of those approaches are still common to most of the existing AS proposals. They refer, for example, to a) the need to have a corpus of ideal summaries[2] for training the Classifier; b) the need to provide specific, domain-dependent, information repositories, such as the list of signaling and proper nouns for the Classifier or the lexicon and the ontology for the Lexical Chains Method, added to taggers and parsers; c) the costly implementation of sophisticated methods, such as the Lexical Chains one. However struggling those aspects may be, SuPor ultimately aims at certifying that linguistic information helps producing more satisfactory output extracts with respect to both, information reproduction and coherence. We should notice, though, that the only property addressed in this paper is content selection, and not coherence.

3 SuPor Architecture

SuPor comprises training (Figure 1) and extraction (Figure 2)[3]. During training, each feature is weighed by measuring its representativeness in both the source texts and

[1] Núcleo Interinstitucional de Lingüística Computacional (http://www.nilc.icmc.usp.br).

[2] As defined by Teufel and Moens [31], ideal summaries are well-formed and satisfactorily corresponding to their respective source texts and, thus, can be considered guidelines.

[3] Dotted frames signal NILC knowledge repositories for BP.

their corresponding ideal extracts. These have been built by correlating each sentence of authentic, manually produced, summaries with those sentences of the corresponding source texts. The manual summaries have been built by a professional summarizer. Correlations are based on the cosine similarity measure [30]. Relevant features for AS are pointed out through training, yielding a probabilistic distribution. This signals the probability of a given feature to occur in both texts, as in Kupiec et al.'s approach [11].

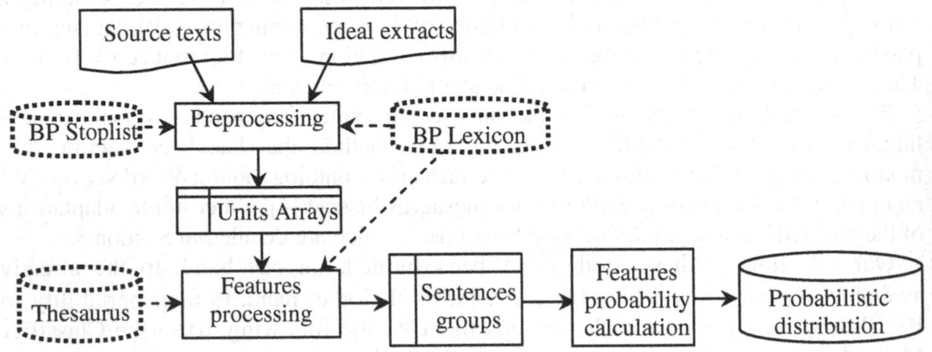

Fig. 1. SuPor training module

After training, the specialized user can customize SuPor to summarize any source text by (a) pinpointing the way the source text must be preprocessed (either removing stopwords and stemming what remains, or producing a 4-gram distribution); (b) selecting the group of features that will drive summarization; and (c) specifying the compression rate. These options are indicated in the user interface in Figure 2. The main features of the extraction module are detailed below.

3.1 Features Selection

Features selection is actually at the core of SuPor, since it allows for distinct AS strategies to be used. Through them, the strategies may address either non-linguistic or linguistic knowledge. The former includes those used in the Classifier Method, i.e., sentence length, proper names, location of sentences in a paragraph and location of a paragraph in the text, and keywords (i.e., the words frequency). As originally proposed in that method for texts in English, only initial and final paragraphs of a source text and sentences of a paragraph (with a minimum of 2 sentences) are selected by SuPor.

Linguistic knowledge is embedded in SuPor through the manipulation of surface indicators of linguistically related information, such as those that link paragraphs, lexical chaining, or determining topics. Trying to overcome the connectedness problems introduced by the reused methods, in some cases we introduce some changes on them. For example, for the Relationship Map method, all the paths are calculated and all the resulting paragraphs are incorporated in just one extract. Oppositely, the Importance of Topics method has been fully embedded in SuPor. Similarly to the Lexical Chains Method, SuPor focuses on a single, or on the most nuclear, noun, when a noun compound is focused upon. However, differently from English, the corresponding Brazilian Portuguese chains to the noun compounds are actually chains of adjectives as modifiers of only one noun. So, determining their nuclei is simpler than it is in English: it is enough to use NILC's tagger [1]. Strong lexical chains are determined by counting the number of words and the number of their repetitions in the source text. The heuristics of the original method have also been incorporated in SuPor, to build just one extract.

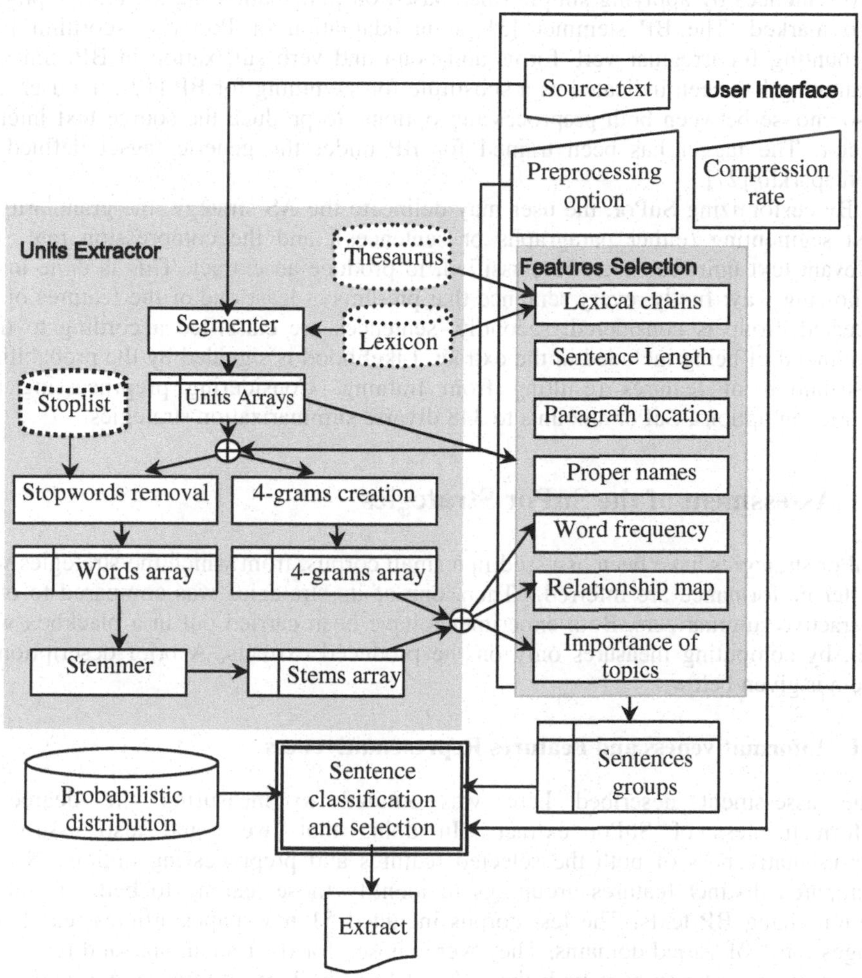

Fig. 2. SuPor extraction module

The Classifier Method is not explicit in Figure 2. Instead, it is depicted by selecting features 2 to 5. In all, SuPor embeds the seven features outlined in the box 'Feature selection' in Figure 2.

3.2 Linguistic and Empirical Resources

SuPor BP-oriented linguistic resources include a stoplist, a lexicon [20], and a thesaurus [4]. Added to these, the probabilistic distribution resulting from training is the most important empirical resource in SuPor. As mentioned before, SuPor generic tools (i.e., the text segmenter, the stemmer, and the tagger) do not necessarily run altogether. Their activation depends on the preprocessing option and on the group of features selected by the user. Text segmentation focuses on splitting the source text into sentences by applying simple rules based on punctuation marks. Paragraphs are also marked. The BP stemmer [3] is an adaptation of Porter's algorithm [25], accounting for irregular verb forms and noun and verb suffixation in BP. Since 4-gramming has been indicated as a substitute for stemming for BP [12], the user may also choose between both preprocessing options, to produce the source text internal vector. The tagger has been trained for BP under the generic tagset defined by Ratnaparkhi [27].

By customizing SuPor, the user may delineate the AS strategy, the granularity of text segmenting (either paragraphs or sentences), and the compression rate. The relevant text units can then be classified, to produce an extract. This is done in the following way: firstly, every sentence that presents at least one of the features of the selected group is considered; secondly, sentences are classified according to their likelihood of being included in the extract. Likelihood is signaled by the probabilistic distribution of features resulting from training. Considering preprocessing and extraction options, SuPor amounts to 348 diverse summarization strategies.

4 Assessment of the SuPor Strategies

SuPor strategies have been assessed in a small corpus, from which the strategies with better performance are inferred. Then, one of its strategies was compared to other extractive summarizers. Both experiments have been carried out in a blackbox way, i.e., by computing measures only on the produced extracts. A brief description of them is given below.

4.1 Informativeness and Features Representativeness

The assessment described here was limited to measuring the degree of informativeness of SuPor extracts. In doing that, we could also assess the representativeness of both the selected features and preprocessing options. So, we compared distinct features groupings to identify those leading to better results in summarizing BP texts. The test corpus included 51 newspaper articles (ca. 1 to 3 pages long) of varied domains. They were chosen for their small size and readership coverage, in order to ease both the tasks of hand-building reference summaries and evaluating the output extracts. The test corpus was also used for training. For this reason, 5-fold cross-validation was used.

Two experiments were carried out for similarity: in the first, the output extracts were compared with *ideal extracts*; in the second, they were compared with *ideal summaries* instead. Every condensed text was obtained on a ca. 28% compression rate (and is, therefore, ca. 8 sentences long). Ideal extracts are those automatically generated by an automatic generator of ideal extracts.[4] Ideal summaries are those hand-built by BP fluent writers and, thus, result from a rewriting task. Only co-selection measures [26] were used, namely, precision (P), recall (R), and the balanced F-measure (F). P is the ratio between the number of relevant sentences included in the output extract and its total number of sentences. R is the ratio between the same number of relevant sentences and the total number of sentences in the ideal reference (either extracts or summaries). In the first experiment, those measures were computed in a Boolean fashion (i.e., presence or absence of sentences of the output extract in the corresponding ideal extract). Hereafter, this procedure is named *sentence co-selection*. In the second, they were calculated through a comparison of the output extract and its corresponding ideal summary. This procedure is named *content-based similarity*.

To overcome the impossibility of pairing sentences in the second experiment, each sentence of the output extract was compared with all the sentences of the ideal summary, as suggested by Mani [15], through a variation of the cosine similarity measure.

Finally, to compute P and R for content-based similarity, the obtained values were normalized to the interval [0,1] (most similar equals 1). After computing those for the full collection of extracts, average measures were produced for the 348 features groupings (FGs) provided by SuPor (amounting to 17.748 extracts). The most significant figures are shown in Table 1, along with their rankings in the whole collection.

Table 1. Average F-measures for both procedures

Features grouping	**Sentence co-selection**		**Content-based similarity**	
	F-measure	Ranking	F-measure	Ranking
FG_1	0.40	1°.	0.42	2°.
FG_2	0.40	1°.	0.39	25°.
FG_3	0.38	12°.	0.43	1°.

The features groupings with the biggest, and equal, F-measures in the sentence co-selection procedure are FG1=[lexical chaining, sentence length, proper nouns] and FG2=[lexical chaining, sentence length, words frequency], both running under the 4-grams preprocessing option. In the content-based similarity procedure, the best grouping was FG3=[lexical chaining, relationship map], signaling that the combination of the two full methods, Lexical Chaining and the Relationship Map one, applied better to the test corpus. In this case, preprocessing options differed: Lexical Chaining ran on text tiling and the Relationship Map Method, on 4-gramming.

By comparing FG1 with FG2, we can see that extracting sentences based upon proper nouns or words frequency makes no difference in content selection. However, performance based upon proper nouns was slightly better in the second procedure. This may indicate that SuPor performs closer to ideal summaries when proper nouns are focused upon, instead of words frequency. With respect to using any of the varied features along lexical chaining, the comparison between FG1 and FG3 shows that the Relationship Map Method still outperforms them in the second experiment. After all, it is worth noticing that both the Lexical Chains and Relationship Map methods use

[4] This is also based upon the cosine similarity measure [30] and can be found in http://www.nilc.icmc.usp.br/~thiago.

the connectedness between text units to indicate the relevant ones. The fact that the latter uses paragraphs instead of sentences may be significant in improving performance. Overall, it is noticeable that, although 7 features were available in SuPor, the inclusion of other features to any of the topmost groupings did not provide a significant performance improvement. Additionally, it did not deteriorate the results either. So, the best results indicate that those strategies that comprised only 3 out of 7 features should be better explored.

In both experiments lexical chaining was based on text tiling at the preprocessing stage. It was also the commonest feature in the great majority of the topmost features groupings and the least common in those groupings with the smallest F-measures. The least representative feature was 'Importance of topics': it appears in most of the worst figures and is absent in the best ones. This lack of representativeness may be due to the size of the source texts: for being small, proper identification of their topics could have been damaged. In other words, just one topic may be chosen, which does not convey the important ones. The fluency of news texts may also imply that topic change is too subtle for automatic detection.

Preprocessing by paragraphing or text tiling evenly influenced the figures in both experiments. However, text tiling showed a slight improvement in SuPor performance. Input stemming or 4-gramming resulted differently, though: in sentence co-selection, the preprocessing mode is not relevant; in content-based similarity, 4-gramming yielded better results for BP. Recall measures are smaller than precision ones in both experiments, but in the second one, they slightly outperform the first. This may indicate that, in comparing output extracts with ideal summaries, instead of comparing them with ideal extracts, more sentences are considered similar. However, more experiments are needed to confirm this finding.

4.2 Comparing Just One Strategy with Other Extractive Summarizers

Based on the former experiment, only one strategy of SuPor was chosen for a more thorough comparison with other six systems, as reported in [28], combining the following features: location (of sentences in a paragraph and of a paragraph in the text), words frequency, sentence length, proper nouns, and lexical chaining.. The systems considered are the following (a brief description on how they identify sentences to include in an extract is given): (1) TF-ISF-Summ (**T**erm **F**requency-**I**nverse **S**entence **F**requency-based **Summ**arizer) [12], which mirrors Salton's TF-IDF information retrieval measure [30] in its pulling out documents from a collection, but correspondingly considering sentences from a single source text; (2) NeuralSumm (**Neural Summ**arizer) [23], which is driven by an unsupervised neural network for sentence determination, based on a self-organizing map (SOM) [10]; (3) GistSumm (**Gist Summ**arizer) [22], which matches lexical items of the source text against lexical items of its gist sentence; finally, (4) ClassSumm [13], which is also a classification-based summarizer, like Kupiec et al.'s one, which is embedded in SuPor. Added to those, the baseline from-top sentences and random-based systems were used.

Location was the only feature included in SuPor summarizer that was not representative in the former evaluation. It was considered because it is a common feature to 3 out of the 6 other systems. The experiment was carried out in a blackbox fashion on a single, distinct from the former, test corpus [24]. This comprises 100 newspaper texts, paired with hand-produced summaries written by a consultant on the

Brazilian Portuguese language. For this reason, they were considered our corpus of ideal summaries. Similarly to the former experiment, a 10-fold cross validation was used, under a 30% compression rate (approximated to the ideal summaries and extracts).

Run independently, the systems performances were also assessed similarly to the former experiment: average precision, recall and F-measures were obtained automatically. As shown in Table 2, SuPor summarizer outperformed the other systems, having a ca. 0.38 f-measure over the baseline random and a 0.43 f-measure when comparing absolute average performances.

Although a distinct, and bigger, test corpus was used in this experiment and location was considered, there was no improvement in SuPor performance, when compared to the former experiment. However, the figures show that the selected features make it close to the performance of ClassSumm, which is also a classification system. This may not be surprising, because both systems are based on a Bayesian classifier. However, ClassSumm uses a total of 16 features associated to each sentence. It should be interesting to investigate, thus, if SuPor performance is representative enough of the lack of improvement of AS strategies when more features are added.

Table 2. Systems performance (in %)

Systems	Avg. P	Avg. R	Avg. F	Avg. F over random
SuPor	44.9	40.8	42.8	38
ClassSumm	45.6	39.7	42.4	37
From-top	42.9	32.6	37.0	19
TF-ISF-Summ	39.6	34.3	36.8	19
GistSumm	49.9	25.6	33.8	9
NeuralSumm	36.0	29.5	32.4	5
Random order	34.0	28.5	31.0	0

5 Final Remarks

The reported experiment showed that, of the five features, SuPor summarizer is distinctive on its lexical chaining (this is the only feature that differentiates it from the other systems). This confirms the first experiment. However, the features grouping, itself, should be better analyzed, for results may improve because of the combination of each component of such a grouping. With respect to combining features, SuPor provides a meaningful environment for the user to explore empirical measures to determine the relevance of text units, as both experiments show. Although the Bayesian classifier by Kupiec et al. also incorporates a combination of features, SuPor goes one step further in allowing any number of features to be chosen out of the seven largely considered in the field nowadays. However, SuPor usability has not yet been assessed. One of the reasons is that it offers too many summarizing possibilities. A more productive strategy is to limit it to just the most promising features groupings, in order to carry out more comprehensive tests. Besides, to make better use of SuPor, more people should be available to work with it. There should be no trouble in this, from the user viewpoint, for it runs in a pretty friendly, Windows-based platform. The problem rests in the expertise level of the user: the more specialist the user on AS features, the more directly or deeply s/he could assess the influence of linguistic features in the production of the extracts. This is one of the most interesting aspects provided by SuPor: to select, for example, only non-linguistic features and run it. Then, running it only on the linguistic ones, in order to compare the results obtained through both groups of features. Actually, our preliminary assessments showed that considering linguistic features (such as lexical chaining and relationships mapping) outperforms the results produced when considering only non-linguistic ones.

Even though the comparative analysis has been made on a very small corpus, the results are promising. SuPor exploration may well end up as a means to specify a useful benchmark comparison to the field. So far, we have no knowledge of the existence of similar environments. CAST [21] seems to be the closer to SuPor one can get: it also considers a set of features, including lexical cohesion [9], but it aims at giving support to human summarizers instead of providing the means to deeply explore distinct summarizing strategies and their potential combinations. Clearly, CAST writers could not assess AS strategies from the viewpoint of research and development of AS systems, as it is intended in SuPor. So, it would be interesting to put together CAST and SuPor environments, to complement each other: CAST allows registering feedback from the writer, annotating important sentences signaled by its distinct summarization methods, and comparing results. By running SuPor on common corpora to CAST, its results could be thus compared to information obtained through CAST registers. Also, similar experiments to the ones reported above could be carried out involving both CAST and SuPor. In order to do so, CAST should be also assessed as a summarizing tool. To our knowledge, this has not been done so far, which makes SuPor assessment yet more useful. However, in considering CAST and SuPor altogether, common NL-dependent resources must be provided.

Acknowledgments

This work has been partly supported by the Brazilian agency FAPESP.

References

[1] Aires, R.V.X.; Aluísio, S.M.; Kuhn, D.C.S.; Andreeta, M.L.B.; Oliveira Jr., O.N. (2000). Combining Multiple Classifiers to Improve Part of Speech Tagging: A Case Study for Brazilian Portuguese. In the *Proc. of the Brazilian Symposium on Artificial Intelligence*. Atibaia – SP, Brasil.

[2] Barzilay, R. and Elhadad, M. (1997). Using Lexical Chains for Text Summarization. In the Proc. of the Intelligent Scalable Text Summarization Workshop, Madri, Spain. Also In I. Mani and M.T. Maybury (eds.), Advances in Automatic Text Summarization. MIT Press, pp. 111-121, 1999.

[3] Caldas Junior, J.; Imamura, C.Y.M.; Rezende, S.O. (2001). Avaliação de um algoritmo de Stemming para a Língua Portuguesa. In Proceedings of the 2nd Congress of Logic Applied to Technology – LABTEC'2001, Vol. II, pp. 267-274. Faculdade SENAC de Ciências Exatas e Tecnologia, São Paulo, Brasil.

[4] Dias-da-Silva, B.C.; Oliveira, M.F.; Moraes, H. R.; Paschoalino, C.; Hasegawa, R.; Amorin, D.; Nascimento, A. C. (2000). Construção de um Thesaurus Eletrônico para o Português do Brasil. In Proceedings of the V Encontro para o Processamento Computacional da Língua Portuguesa Escrita e Falada (PROPOR 2000), pp. 1-11. Atibaia – SP.

[5] Edmundson, H.P. (1969). New Methods in Automatic Extracting. Journal for Computing Machinery 16(2), pp. 264-285.
[6] Greghi, J.G.; Martins, R.T.; Nunes, M.G.V. (2002). Diadorim: a Lexical database for Brazilian Portuguese In Manuel G. Rodríguez and Carmem P. S. Araujo (Eds.), Proceedings of the Third International Conference on Language Resources and Evaluation LREC 2002, Vol. IV, pp. 1346-1350. Las Palmas.
[7] Halliday, M. A.K.; Hasan, R. (1976). Cohesion in English. Longman.
[8] Hearst, M.A. (1993). TextTiling: A Quantitative Approach to Discourse Segmentation. Technical Report 93/24. University of California, Berkeley.
[9] Hoey, M. (1991). Patterns of Lexis in Text. Oxford University Press.
[10] Kohonen, T. (1982). Self-organized formation of topologically correct feature maps. *Biological Cybernetics*, Vol. 43, pp. 59-69.
[11] Kupiec, J.; Petersen, J.; Chen, F. (1995). A trainable document summarizer. In Edward A. Fox, Peter Ingwersen, and Raya Fidel (Eds.), Proceedings of the 18th Annual International ACM-SIGIR Conference on Research and Development in Information Retrieval, pp. 68-73, Seattle, WA. EUA. July.
[12] Larocca Neto, J.; Santos, A.D.; Kaestner, A.A.; Freitas, A.A. (2000). Document clustering and text summarization. In the Proceedings of the 4th Int. Conf. on Practical Applications of Knowledge Discovery and Data Mining (PADD-2000), pp. 41-55. London.
[13] Larocca Neto, J.; Freitas, A.A.; Kaestner, C.A. (2002). Automatic Text Summarization using a ML Approach. In the Proc. of the XVI Brazilian Symposium on Artificial Intelligence, Lecture Notes on Compute Science, No. 2507, pp. 205-215.
[14] Luhn, H.P. (1958). The Automatic Creation of Literature Abstracts. IBM Journal of Research and Development 2(2), pp. 159-165.
[15] Mani, I. (2001). Automatic Summarization. John Benjamin's Publishing Company. USA.
[16] Mani, I.; Maybury, M.T. (1999), eds., Advances in automatic text summarization. MIT Press, Cambridge, MA.
[17] Martins, R.T.; Hasegawa, R.; Nunes, M.G.V. (2002). Curupira: um Parser Funcional para o Português. Relatório Técnico do NILC, NILC-TR-02-26. São Carlos, Dezembro, 43p.
[18] Miller, G.A.; Beckwith, R.; Fellbaum, C.; Gross, D.; Miller, K. (1993). Introduction to WordNet: An On-line Lexical Database. [ftp://www.cogsci.princeton.edu/pub/wordnet/5papers.ps]. Abril/2003.
[19] Módolo, M. (2003). SuPor: an Environment for Exploration of Extractive Methods for Automatic Text Summarization for Portuguese (in Portuguese). MSc. Dissertation. Departamento de Computação, UFSCar.
[20] Nunes, M.G.V.; Vieira, F.M.C.; Zavaglia, C.; Sossolote, C.R.C.; Hernandez, J. (1996). A Construção de um Léxico da Língua Portuguesa do Brasil para suporte à Correção Automática de Textos. Relatórios Técnicos do ICMC-USP, Nro. 42. Setembro, 36p.
[21] Orasan, C.; Mitkov, R.; Hasler, L. (2003). CAST: a Computer-Aided Summarisation Tool. In the Proceedings of the 10th Conference of The European Chapter of the Association for Computational Linguistics (EACL2003), Budapest, Hungary.
[22] Pardo, T.A.S.; Rino, L.H.M.; Nunes, M.G.V. (2003a). GistSumm: A Summarization Tool Based on a New Extractive Method. In N.J. Mamede, J. Baptista, I. Trancoso, M.G.V. Nunes (eds.), 6th Workshop on Computational Processing of the Portuguese Language - Written and Spoken, pp. 210-218 (Lecture Notes in Artificial Intelligence 2721). Springer-Verlag, Germany.
[23] Pardo, T.A.S; Rino, L.H.M.; Nunes, M.G.V. (2003b). NeuralSumm: A Connexionist Approach to Automatic Text Summarization (in Portuguese). In Anais do IV Encontro Nacional de Inteligência Artificial – ENIA'2003. XXII Cong. Nac.da SBC. Campinas – SP.
[24] Pardo, T.A.S. e Rino, L.H.M. (2003). TeMário: A Corpus for Automatic Text Summarization (in Portuguese). NILC Tech. Report. NILC-TR-03-09. São Carlos, Outubro, 12p.

[25] Porter, M. F. (1980). An Algorithm for Suffix Stripping. Program, 14 (3), pp 130-137, July.

[26] Radev, D.; Teufel, S.; Saggion, H.; Lam, W.; Blitzer, J.; Qi, H.; Çelebi, A.; Liu, D.; Drabek, E. (2003). Evaluation challenges in large-scale document summarization. In the Proc. of the 41st Annual Meeting of the Association for Computational Linguistics, pp. 375-382. July.

[27] Ratnaparkhi, A. (1996). A Maximum Entropy Part-Of-Speech Tagger. In Proceedings of the Empirical Methods in Natural Language Processing Conference, May 17-18. University of Pennsylvania, USA.

[28] Rino, L.H.M.; Pardo, T.A.S; Silla Jr., C.N.; Kaestner, C.A.; Pombo, M. A Comparison of Automatic Summarization Systems for Brazilian Portuguese Texts. XVII Brazilian Symposium on Artificial Intelligence - SBIA'04. September 29-October 1. São Luís, Maranhão, Brazil.

[29] Salton, G.; Singhal, A.; Mitra, M.; Buckley, C. (1997). Automatic Text Structuring and Summarization. Information Processing & Management 33(2), pp. 193-207.

[30] Salton, G.; Buckley, C. (1988). Term-weighting approaches in automatic text retrieval. Information Processing & Management 24, 513-523. 1988. Reprinted in: K. Sparck-Jones; P. Willet (eds.), Readings in Information Retrieval, pp. 323-328. Morgan Kaufmann. 1997.

[31] Teufel, S.; Moens, M. (1999). Argumentative Classification of Extracted Sentences as a First Step Towards Flexible Abstracting. In Inderjeet Mani and Mark T. Maybury (Eds.), Advances in Automatic Text Summarization, pp. 155-175. MIT Press, Cambridge, MA.

Systemic Analysis Applied to Problem Solving: The Case of the Past Participle in French

Séverine Vienney, Sylviane Cardey, and Peter Greenfield

Centre de recherche en linguistique Lucien Tesnière
Université de Franche-Comté, France

Abstract. In segmenting a given language or languages in general in a systemic manner, we show how it is possible to effect computations which lead to reliable human language technology applications. Some problems have not yet been solved in language processing; we will show how in applying the theory "systemic analysis" and the calculus of "SyGuLAC" (Systemic Grammar using a Linguistically motivated Algebra and Calculus), we can solve difficult problems. Systems such as the ones outlined in the paper can be created whenever there is a need. The only requirements are that such systems can be manipulated, and that they be verifiable and above all traceable. A system ought to be computable and be able to be represented in its entirety; if not it cannot be verified.

Keywords: human language technology, language calculability, system, systemic analysis, agreement of French participle.

1 Introduction

The intention of this paper is to show how by segmenting a language in a systemic manner it is possible to obtain human language technology applications which give reliable results. We will show firstly with an example why systemic analysis is useful and secondly the results of an application of systemic analysis knowing that complementary processes have to be done at the level of the sentence.

2 Systemic Analysis

Whether one examines a language from the point of view of its components (signifiers) in the Saussurian sense or of its organisation (syntax), languages fortunately present regularities which ought to be systematically brought into prominence. Grammarians have always studied the problem of language description, and regularities and rules have been discerned as much for syntax as for lexis at least for the teaching or the comparison of languages. With the advent of the digital computer, we are now confronted with problems concerning language analysis, recognition and generation by machine.

Systemic analysis [1], [4] is based on the postulate that a language or indeed languages (as in translation) can be segmented into individual systems based on the observation that such systems influence each other.

J. L. Vicedo et al. (Eds.): EsTAL 2004, LNAI 3230, pp. 431–441, 2004.

The systems that we are talking about have to be sufficiently small so as to be humanly prehensile and subsequently be able to be processed by machine, but also sufficiently large so as to function formally as a whole. Each such system may be a component of a larger system to which the system's properties can be extended.

Furthermore it must also be possible to create links between the component systems of a system in order to obtain a complete formal description of the system. The component systems of such a system may be nested, have common parts or function in identical and identifiable manners. All levels of language analysis can be described in this way (lexis, syntax, morpho-syntax, semantics, morpho-semantics and others). Because of this, what must then be done is to describe the invariant part of a system as well as its variant parts and to state formally the reason for the variations.

The advantage of this systemic analysis model is that it is reliable and finely grained. Systemic analysis is conducive to mathematical modelling by means of mathematical structures which place language first and incorporate constraints such as to maximise the coverage. Such modelling involves for example the modelling of grammatical classifications (by means nested partitioning and thus the use of equivalence relations) and modelling for computational ends (entailing model theoretical and proof theoretical approaches) including the benefits provided by normalising (supported by means of lattice theory) such as algebraic and calculational operations on analyses [6], [7]. A systemic analysis can be viewed as a *grammatical* concordance for the specific linguistic phenomenon treated in which each case (equivalence class) is treated. With systemic linguistics, one can, amongst other things, verify that a system of relations is well formed in terms of strict nesting constraints [5], [8]. Furthermore systemic analysis allows tracing of operations done by machine and thus omissions can be easily added. The methodology is suited as much to lexis as to syntax, to semantics or to their intersections (morpho-syntax etc.)[2].

A properly conducted analysis incorporates for each case a justification, from which benchmarks can be constructed. Furthermore, systemic analysis is neutral in marrying linguistic performance and linguistic competence where both empiricism and thesis are admitted. The evaluation of a given systemic analysis is in reality a clear matter. One has to ensure that the analysis is sufficiently fine (are there still further cases?) and that each case revealed in the analysis is accompanied with a justification (with the nature of the justification itself justified). Justifications and their nature can depend on the application. For example there are applications such as controlled languages used in safety critical systems that demand a corpus based and indeed experimental based approach (and thus are performance based) together with provenance information, these providing a static reproducible trace for each case. In this matter systemic linguistics with its inherent traceability marries well with systemic quality. By default the justification is synthetic, devised by the linguist and depending thus on his or her competence. We see too that in terms of scientific method systemic linguistics methodology accommodates to theoretical and intuitional approaches as well as to empirical and experimental approaches. Indeed, in Centre Tesnière we use systemic analysis itself as a meta analysis tool for producing linguistic systemic analyses.

In this paper we give an example of the application of the "systemic theory" of French lexico-morpho-syntax for the agreement of the French past participle. We thus will also see that syntax cannot be in reality separated from lexis and from morphology. We show how such a system can be represented so that it can be processed by machine.

Because in general the different systems influence each other, what has to be done is to describe for each system its invariant part, which allows us to find and indeed discover the system, to name it and to give it prominence as a system in its own right. The variant parts of a system need also to be described, these parts being due to the system being put into relation with other systems of the language system, this in the knowledge that a system can be related with several systems which in their turn can influence one another. Thus to begin with we have a recognizable "invariant" system which is necessarily canonical and another system representing its variant parts. However, we are missing the system which relates these two systems, this being a system of relationships. It is these systems of relationships which allow us to organize system 1 (canonical) according to the systems 2 (variations).

3 Methodology

To illustrate the systemic modeling approach, we take as an example one which is indeed quite complex, and this is the agreement of the French past participle followed by an infinitive [1]. We have here three systems:

- System 1: the past participles (represented below by a.,b.,...,h.)
- System 2: their inflexions (represented below by I, A)
- System 3: the relationship that structures the past participle system 1 according to the inflexional system 2 (represented by what is between a. and I, for example)

What is in fact going to be the most difficult thing to do is not so much describing the first two systems, which involves finding for system 1 all the French past participles as well as for system 2 all their inflected forms, but it is rather how to describe system 3 which links systems 1 and 2. In creating this relationship, it is necessary to say when a link can exist and when not. Furthermore, the representation used for system 3 will depend on whether we envisage use by humans or automatic processing by machine, but in both cases an algorithm [9] is necessary (this being the <u>C</u>alculus in SyGuLA<u>C</u>). In the former case the algorithm could take the following form:

Algorithm

- a. the past participle is preceded by **"en"** → **I**
- b. the past participle of the verb **faire** is immediately followed by an infinitive → **I**

– c. the past participle of the verb **laisser** is immediately followed by an infinitive → **I** or **A**
– d. **eu, donné, laissé** are followed by "à" and the direct object refers to the infinitive → **I**
– e. the verb (past participle) marks an opinion or a declaration **(List)** → **I**
– f. the direct object performs the **action** of the **infinitive** → **A**
– g. the direct object **refers** to the **past participle** → **A**
– h. the direct object **refers** to the **infinitive** → **I**

List: affirmé, assuré, cru, dit, espéré, estimé, nié, pensé, prétendu, promis, reconnu, voulu
Operators: **I** : invariable **A** : agreement

Agreement of the French Past Participle: Interactive Algorithm

whilst in the latter case, that of automatic processing, the representation of the algorithm could take the following form:

– a'. P1(,)(adv)**en**(P3)(adv)(P4)(adv)avoir(adj)(P3)(P4)(adv)p.p.(adv)(prep)(P5)inf(P5) → **I**
– b'. P1(,)(adv)(P2)(adv)(P3)(adv)**en**(adv)avoir(adj)(P3)(adv)p.p.(adv)(prep)(P5)inf(P5) → **I**
– c'. P1(,)(adv)P2(adv)(I')(P3)(adv)(P4)(adv)avoir(adj)(P3)(P4)(adv)**fait**(adv)(P5)inf(P5) → **I**
– d'. P1(,)(adv)P2(adv)(I')(P3)(adv)(P4)(adv)avoir(adj)(P3)(P4)(adv)**List**(adv)(prep)(P5)inf(P5) → **I**
– k'. P1(,)(adv)P2(adv)(I')(P3)(adv)(P4)(adv)avoir(adj)(p3)(P4)(adv)p.p.(adv)(prep)**P5**(adv)inf → **I**
  • u'. P5 is the direct object → **agreement with P2**
    ∗ g'. P2 = "que" → **agreement with Pl**
    ∗ h'. if P3 exists → **agreement with Pl**
– j'. P1(,)(adv)P2(adv)(I')(P3)(adv)(P4)(adv)avoir(adj)(P3)(P4)(adv)p.p.(adv)(prep)inf(adv)P5 → **I**
  • u'. P5 is the direct object → **agreement with P2**
    ∗ g'. P2 = "que" → **agreement with Pl**
    ∗ h'. if P3 exists → **agreement with Pl**

Agreement of the French Past Participle: Automatic Algorithm

The execution of such algorithms is performed in the following manner. Taking for example the automatic algorithm:

If **a'** is true then the past participle is **invariable** (operator **I**);

If **a', b', c', d'** are false and **k'** true then if **u'** is true then if **g'** is true then make the agreement with **Pl**; otherwise, **g'** being false then if **h'** is false apply the operator of the last true condition, **u'**, that is to say, make the agreement with **P2**.

With the algorithm (or super-system) which incorporates these three systems, we can, for example, obtain the correct response (agreement or no agreement) for a sentence such as:

Ces bûcherons, je les ai fait? sortir
P1 , P2 P3 avoir p.p. inf
(These lumberjacks, I have made them leave)

If we examine the automatic algorithm, we find that the structure shown at condition c' is the appropriate one:

- c'. P1(,)(adv)P2(adv)(I')(P3)(adv)(P4)(adv)avoir(adj)(P3)(P4)(adv) **fait**(adv)(P5)inf(P5) $\rightarrow$ **I**

which provides the correct response, operator **I**, this being that there is no agreement of the past participle.

We can see that all the parts or layers (lexis, syntax, morphology, and semantics) of linguistic analysis are involved together in an organized system.

4 Application

Now, let us take a text representing all the cases of agreement of the past participle of pronominal verbs in French. We see here the concern for exhaustive analyses in systemic linguistics. The text can be the basis of a bench mark, and for the automatic algorithm, an automatic test data set (thus enabling regression testing). It is for this reason that we reproduce the text in full.

4.1 Text

(due to Yves Gentilhomme)
Les amours de Jeanneton et Jeannot

Jeanneton s'est blessé()1, elle s'est entaillé()2 profondément deux phalangettes avec une faucille. C'est à sa main gauche qu'elle s'est coupé()3 pendant qu'elle s'était penché()4 sur un tas de joncs. S'étant vu()5 saigner abondamment - sa robe, d'ailleurs, s'en était trouvé()6 toute tâché()7 et fripé()8, elle s'était cru()9 mourir, mais elle s'est ressaisi()10 et s'est comporté()11 courageusement. Elle s'est souvenu()12 de son ami Jeannot, s'est mis()13 à l'appeler, puis s'est laissé()14 transporter par lui à la clinique.

Elle s'en est tiré()15 à bon compte, s'était-il entendu()16 dire par les infirmiers auprès desquels elle s'est fait()17 soigner.

Par la suite les mauvaises langues se sont délié()18. Bien des histoires se sont raconté()19. Il s'en serait passé()20 des choses ! Nous, ses copines, on s'est cru()21 en plein délire et moi, je ne m'en suis pas encore remi()22, à parler franc.

De bon matin, Jeanneton et Jeannot se seraient levé()23, puis après s'être trop coquettement habillé()24, lavé()25, coiffé()26 et enfin, chacun de son côté, dirigé()27 vers le marais, où la veille ils se seraient entendu()28 pour se revoir, ils s'y seraient secrètement retrouvé()29.

Par de vilaines mégères, ne s'était-il pas dit()30 que ces blancs-becs se seraient ri()31 des conseils qu'ils s'étaient entendu()32 prodiguer ? Hélas, ils se seraient complu()33 dans leur entêtement, ils se seraient amusé()34, se seraient joué()35 de tous et se seraient plu()36 à contredire leurs parents. Comment ces commères s'y sont-elles pris()37 pour s'en être persuadé()38 jusqu'à s'être adonné()39 à de telles calomnies ? D'ailleurs personne, pas même la femme du garde champêtre, ne s'est aperu()40 de rien, laquelle pourtant ne s'est jamais ni privé()41 de médire, ni gêné()42 de faire courir des ragots.

D'aucuns se seraient fait()43 confirmer qu'après s'être bien conté()44 fleurettes, les deux se seraient fait()45 pincer s'ils ne s'taient pas douté() 46 du danger. Bref ils se sont méfié()47 et se sont esquivé()48 à temps. Aussi personne ne les a vus ni s'être dissipé()49, encore moins s'être enlacé()50 ou s'être abandonné()51 à des actes coupables.

Après ces émotions l'un comme l'autre se sont retrouvé()52 assez fatigué()53, s'étant beaucoup dépensé()54 et même un peu énervé()55 sans cependant s'être querellé()56 ni grossièrement insulté()57.

L'aventure finie, des retombées, ne s'en serait-il ensuivi()58 ?

Bien que la morale de l'histoire ne se soit prononc()59 que sur le fait que les joncs se sont raréfié()60, je me suis cru()61 obligé()62 de conclure que les deux jouvenceaux se sont dûment marié()63 et même se sont perpétué()64 par de nombreux héritiers.

Ah, que d'émotions !

Son amie Larirette

4.2 Formal Representation

Following our representation of the solution of this second problem, the agreement of the past participle of pronominal verbs in French by a second algorithm, we show how to perform automatically, with an example, the agreement of a past participle in the text given above. This second algorithm could take the following form :

Algorithm

- a. the subject is the impersonal pronoun "il" → **I**
- b. the verb is se plaire, se déplaire, se complaire, se rire → **I**
- c. the past participle of the verb is followed by an infinitive → **I**
  - d. the subject of the past participle performs the action of the infinitive → **A with the direct object**
- e. "se" is the indirect object or the second object → **I**
  - f. the direct object precedes the past particple → **A with the direct object**

For the other cases, the general rules is: **A with the subject**
Operators: I: invariable **A**: agreement

Agreement of the French Past Participle: Interactive Algorithm

We do not present the methodology or the calculus; these would be organized in the same manner as in the first example given above, that of the agreement of the French past participle followed by an infinitive. The only thing to be noticed is that when the object is *se* and it is *se* that governs the agreement, in fact we have to refer to the subject to do the agreement (see P1 below).

4.3 Analysis

Let us take the first sentence of our text to check automatically its past participles:

(1) *Jeanneton s'est blessé()1, elle s'est entaillé()2 profondément deux phalangettes avec une faucille.*

The first step of our grammar checker is the tagging of each unit of the sentence, this is performed by a morpho-syntactic analysis.

We use the automatic morphological disambiguated tagging of texts system, Labelgram [2], [5], which has been developed in the L. Tesniere Research Centre (see http://www.labelgram.com). This system is also based on systemic linguistics and as such serves as an evaluation of the methodology. In Labelgram, the overall systemic grammars are 'super' systems modelling the relationship between texts and morphologically disambiguated tagged texts.

One of the strengths of this system is its intentionally driven approach. This approach is inherent to systemic linguistics in which the methodology captures the grammarian's concern with language description, the regularities present in languages and their exceptions. This intentionally driven approach leads not only to representations which are efficient in terms of size [3] but which accept for example, in the case of word dictionaries, neologisms "obeying the rules for French word formation". For example in Labelgram's French raw grammatical category tagger, the context rule which recognises and tags word forms ending in at least: **-er** has 579 entries whilst the electronic Robert dictionary of French, an extensional dictionary, has 6666 entries. The overall default context tags (perhaps new) words in -er as Verbe inf. (verb infinitives).

Moreover, Labelgram disambiguates each unit of the sentence; a first super-system finds all grammatical categories of each unit and a second super-system calculates the right category in the given context; the complete system being the forward relational composition of these two systems (an example of the Algebra in SyGuLAC).

For example, the unit *"blessé"* in our sentence can be:

- a **Substantive**: *Le* ***blessé*** *est conduit à l'hôpital.* (The hurt man is led to the hospital.)
- a **Past participle**: *Le chasseur a* ***blessé*** *l'animal.* (The hunter hurt the animal.)
- an **Adjective**: *L'homme* ***blessé*** *et fatigué ne peut pas courir.* (The hurt and tired man cannot run.)

Using context rules (our ambiguous unit follows a verb and precedes a comma), the second super-system of Labelgram detects that in this case the unit *"blessé"* is a Past Participle.

The system correctly tags each unit of our sentence and gives the following result:

Table 1. Result of the Labelgram analysis - http://www.labelgram.com

Mot	Catégories	Catégorie
jeanneton	[Nom]	Nom
s	[Pro. pers.]	Pro. pers.
est	[Nom, Verbe conj.]	Verbe conj.
blessé	[Nom, Ppa., Adj.]	Ppa.
,	[virgule]	virgule
elle	[Pro. pers.]	Pro. pers.
s	[Pro. pers.]	Pro. pers.
est	[Nom, Verbe conj.]	Verbe conj.
entaillé	[Ppa., Adj.]	Ppa.
profondément	[Adv.]	Adv.
deux	[Adj. num. car.]	Adj. num. car.
phalangettes	[Nom]	Nom
avec	[Adv., Prp.]	Prp.
une	[Art. ind., Adj. num. car., Adj. num. ord., Nom]	Art. ind.
faucille	[Nom]	Nom

A second major strength of Labelgram which it owes to systemic analysis is that it can treat sequences of units with grammatical category ambiguities, and this is indeed the case in our sentence as is shown above.

This tagging is essential for the second step of our checking system. Indeed, in order to simplify the syntactic analysis for the automatic checking of the agreement of the past participle, our methodology consists in the reduction of the sentence to its "minimum", analysing the parts of speech of each unit of the sentence [10]. The aim is to keep only the elements necessary for our application; this means the sentence's subject and verb, and sometimes its objects.

For our example sentence, the system detects two past participles (Ppa.) to check : *blessé* et *entaillé*. It should thus find two structures.

The "superficial" units of the sentence correspond to the elements in parentheses in the algorithm of our system 3: the adjectives, the adverbs, but also the incidental complements, the complements of the name, etc. In reality, none of these elements has any influence on the agreement of the past participle. Their role is to specify variously the place, the manner and the time of the action. These are semantic elements which are not relevant for this application. This is the reason why they can be separated out and removed by our grammar correcting system.

Thus, for our start sentence:

(1) *Jeanneton s'est blessé()1, elle s'est entaillé()2* ***profondément*** *deux phalangettes* ***avec une faucille.***

we obtain after the simplification system, the following two "sub-sentences":

(1a) *Jeanneton s'est blessé*
(1b) *elle s'est entaillé deux phalangettes*

These two sub-sentences correspond to the following two syntactic structures respectively:

(1a) P1 (Pro.pers.) (Verbe conj.) (Ppa.)
(1b) P1 (Pro. Pers.) (Verbe conj.) (Ppa.) P2

Our system 3 then applies the agreement rule linked to each of the obtained structures in order to check the past participle and correct it if need be.

For the first structure:

(1a) *Jeanneton s'est blessé*
(1a) P1 (Pro.pers.) (Verbe conj.) (Ppa.)

system 3 contains the rule:

– P1 Pro.pers. être Ppa. → **Agreement with P1**

Thus, the system checks that the past participle *blessé* is in correct agreement in gender and number with the subject P1 *Jeanneton*:

- *Jeanneton*
  - gender: **feminine**
  - number: singular
- *blessé*
  - gender: **masculine**
  - number : singular

The system detects an error and corrects it automatically:

(1aCorrected) *Jeanneton s'est blessée*

As we have argued elsewhere [2], in some cases we need a semantic or pragmatic analysis to complete the syntactic analysis.

For the second structure:

(1b) *elle s'est entaillé deux phalangettes*
(1b) P1 (Pro. Pers.) (Verbe conj.) (Ppa.) P2

System 3 contains the rule:

– P1 Pro. pers. être Ppa. P2 (and P2 is the direct object) → **I**

In order to know if P2 is the direct object, we need to identify some semantic information contained in the syntagm P2 and which it is necessary for checking the agreement of the past participle. Indeed, P2 could be "la nuit", for example, which would not be a direct object. However, in this case, our simplification system would have detected that "la nuit" corresponds to an incidental complement of time and would have deleted it from the structure to keep only the minimal structure (1a): P1 (Pro.pers.) (Verbe conj.) (Ppa.)

Thus, in our example, P2 "*deux phalangettes*" is the direct object and consequently the rule 'e.' of our algorithm is applied. The system checks that the past participle *entaillé* is in the invariable form (operator **I**), which means masculine, singular:

- *entaillé*
  - gender: masculine
  - number: singular

Thus the past participle does not need to be corrected.

Let us take another sentence from our text:

(2) *De bon matin, Jeanneton et Jeannot se seraient levé()23, puis après s'être trop coquettement habillé()24, lavé()25, coiffé()26 et enfin, chacun de son côté, dirigé()27 vers le marais, où la veille ils se seraient entendu()28 pour se revoir, ils s'y seraient secrètement retrouvé()29.*

After applying the simplification system, we obtain the seven sub-sentences to be checked and these are:

(2a) *Jeanneton et Jeannot se seraient levé()23*
(2b) *Jeanneton et Jeannot s'être habillé()24*
(2c) *Jeanneton et Jeannot s'être lavé()25*
(2d) *Jeanneton et Jeannot s'être coiffé()26*
(2e) *Jeanneton et Jeannot s'être dirigé()27*
(2f) *ils se seraient entendu()28*
(2g) *ils s' seraient retrouvé()29*

For all these similar sub-sentences we have the same structure P1 (Pro. Pers.) (Verbe conj.) (Ppa.) which corresponds to the general rule, where in fact *se* is the direct object of the verb, and in consequence the system checks the agreement of the past participle with the subject *Jeanneton et Jeannot.* Thus, our second example will be corrected to give:

(2Corrected) *De bon matin, Jeanneton et Jeannot se seraient levé**s**, puis après s'être trop coquettement habillé**s**, lavé**s**, coiffé**s** et enfin, chacun de son côté, dirigé**s** vers le marais, où la veille ils se seraient entendu**s** pour se revoir, ils s'y seraient secrètement retrouvé**s**.*

With these results provided by our application, we see that systemic analysis is an efficacious methodology for solving difficult problems such as the automatic agreement of the French past participle, a problem that no other current checking system succeeds in correcting.

5 Conclusion

Systemic analysis is useful because the decompositions to be done are not definitely imposed by systemic analysis itself, whether from the beginning or subsequently. On the contrary the different systems are decomposed (and thus built) according to the problems to be solved during the analysis. What systemic analysis does provide is the structuring in terms of Super-system, System 1, System 2, System 3. In our example, we have shown that the usual decomposition in terms of syntax, lexis, morphology is not really what is needed to solve problems in language processing but on the contrary we have designed systems which include data from all these "layers" and only as and when needed.

References

1. Cardey, S.: Traitement algorithmique de la grammaire normative du franais pour une utilisation automatique et didactique. Thèse de Doctorat d'Etat, Université de Franche-Comté, France. (June 1987)
2. Cardey, S., Greenfield, P.: Peut-on séparer lexique, syntaxe, sémantique en traitement automatique des langues? In Cahiers de lexicologie 71. (1997) ISSN 007-9871, 37-51.
3. Cardey, S., El Harouchy, Z., Greenfield, P.: La forme des mots nous renseigne-t-elle sur leur nature? In Actes des 5èmes journées scientifiques, Réseau Lexicologie, Terminologie, Traduction, LA MEMOIRE DES MOTS, Tunis, 22-23 septembre 1997. Collection "actualité scientifique" de l'AUPELF-UREF. (1997)
4. Cardey, S., Greenfield, P.: Systemic Language Analysis and Processing. To appear in the Proceedings of the International Conference on Language, Brain and Computation, Venice, Italy. (October 3-5, 2002) Benjamins (2004).
5. Cardey, S., Greenfield, P.: Disambiguating and Tagging Using Systemic Grammar. Proceedings of the 8th International Symposium on Social Communication, Santiago de Cuba. (January 20-24, 2003) 559–564.
6. Greenfield, P.: Exploiting the Model Theory and Proof Theory of Propositional Logic in the Microsystem Approach to Natural Language Processing In BULAG 22. (1997) ISSN07586787, 325-346.
7. Greenfield, P.: An initial study concerning the basis for the computational modelling of Systemic Grammar. In BULAG 28. (2003) ISSN07586787, 83-95.
8. Robardet, G.: Vrification automatise des rgles de contexte du Logiciel Labelgram Mmoire de Matrise, Universit de Franche-Comt. (2003)
9. Trakhtenbrot, B.A.: Algorithms and Automatic Computing Machines. D.C. Heath and Company, Lexington, Massachusetts. (1963)
10. Vienney, S.: Analyse et syntaxe pour la correction grammaticale automatique. To appear in the Proceedings of "Les 18èmes journées de linguistique", Québec, Canada. (March 11-12, 2004) Editions du Centre Interdisciplinaire de Recherches sur les Activités Langagières. (2004)

The Merging Problem in Distributed Information Retrieval and the 2-Step RSV Merging Algorithm

Fernando Martínez-Santiago, Miguel Angel García Cumbreras, and L. Alfonso Ureña López

Department of Computer Science, University of Jaén, Jaén, Spain

Abstract. This paper[1] presents the application of the 2-step RSV (retrieval status value) merging algorithm to DIR environments. The reported experiment shows that the proposed algorithm is scalable and stable. In addition, it obtains a precision measure higher than the well known CORI algorithm.

1 Introduction

Usually, a Distributed Information Retrieval (DIR) system must rank document collections by query relevance, selecting the best set of collections from a ranked list, and merging the document rankings that are returned from a set of collections. This last issue is the so-called "collection fusion problem" [8, 9], and it is the topic of this work. We propose an algorithm called 2-Step RSV [3, 4]. This algorithm works well in Cross Language Information Retrieval (CLIR) systems based on query translation, but the application of 2-Step RSV in DIR environments requires an additional effort: learning of collection issues such as document frequency, collection size and so on. On the other hand, since 2-Step RSV makes up a new global index based on query terms and the whole of retrieved documents, it makes possible the application of blind feedback at a global level by means of the DIR monitor, rather than a local level by means of each individual Information Retrieval (IR) engine. Previous works have researched into the application of Pseudo-Relevance Feedback (PRF) to improve the selection process of the best set of collections from a ranked list [5]. This work emphasizes the effectiveness of PRF applied to the collection fusion problem. Finally, a second objective is to study the stability of 2-Step RSV against weighting function variances in the local indices.

The rest of the paper is organized as follows. Firstly, we present a brief revision of DIR problems. Section 2 describes our proposed method which is integrated into CORI model[1]. In section 3, we detail the experiments carried out and the results obtained. Finally, we present our conclusions and future lines of work.

[1] This work has been supported by Spanish Government (MCYT) with grant TIC2003-07158-C04-04.

J. L. Vicedo et al. (Eds.): EsTAL 2004, LNAI 3230, pp. 442–453, 2004.

2 The 2-Step RSV Algorithm

The basic 2-step RSV idea is straightforward: given a query term distributed over several selected collections, their document frequencies are grouped together. In this way, the method recalculates the document score by changing the document frequency of each query term. Given a query term, the new document frequency will be calculated by means of the sum of the local document frequency of the term for each selected collection. Given a user query, the two steps are:

1. The document pre-selection phase consists of searching relevant documents locally for each selected collection. The result of this previous task is a single collection of preselected documents (I' collection) as result of the union of the top retrieved documents for each collection.
2. The re-indexing phase consists of re-indexing the global collection I', but considering solely the query vocabulary. Only the query terms are re-indexed: given a term, its document frequency is the result of grouping together the document frequency of each term from each selected collection. Finally, a new index is created by using the global document frequency, and the query is carried out against the new index. Thus for example, if two collections are selected, I_1 and I_2, and the term "government" is part of the query, then the new global frequency is $df_{I_1}(government) + df_{I_2}(government)$.

In this work, we have used OKAPI BM-25 [6] to create the global index for the second step of the 2-step RSV approach. The collection size, the average document length, the term frequency and the document frequency are required elements in order to calculate OKAPI BM-25. These elements -except the term frequency- are learned by means of *Capture-recapture* [2] and *sample-resample* [7] algorithms. Term frequency requires the document to be downloaded before 2- step RSV creates the index at query time. Note that the merging process is created step by step. For example, the DIR monitor downloads two or three documents per selected collection, it applies 2-step RSV and shows the result to the user. If more documents are required by the user, then the DIR monitor downloads the next two or three documents per selected collection and so on. After some documents (no more than 10 or 20) have been downloaded and reindexed, the application of blind feedback is easy. Given the R top-ranked documents at global level, the Robertson-Spark Jones PRF approach [6]] is applied. In this work, PRF is applied by expanding the original query using the top ten terms obtained from the top ten documents. Then, the expanded-query is applied to reweigh every downloaded document. Note that the expanded query is only applied at a global and not a local level.

3 Experiments and Results

3.1 Experimental Methods

The steps to run each experiment are the followings:

1. Create one index for each collection (OKAPI or a random index).
2. Use CORI to score each collection for that query.
3. When all collections have been scored, choose the most relevant using a *clustering* algorithm or by selecting the N best scored.
4. Run the query using the selected indices.
5. In some experiments, apply pseudo-relevance feedback in each collection, running each expanded query against its index.
6. Merge the document rankings using CORI or 2-Step RSV .
7. In some experiments, apply again pseudo-relevance feedback using the *on-line* index created by 2-Step RSV .
8. Evaluate the quality of the results in terms of precision and recall. The precision measure used is the average precision at 5,10,20 and 100 documents, and the average precision at eleven coverage points.

The parameters of each experiment are the set of queries used, whether or no we have used feedback and the fusion strategy. Another variable is the weighting function used with each index (always OKAPI in the multilingual scene). This means that there are some experiments where we have only used OKAPI, but in others we have used mixed indices since this scene shows in a real manner a distributed system: two collections that belong to the same distributed system cannot use the same weighting function.

3.2 Test Collection Description

The experiments are carried out using three partitions of the conferences TREC1 and TREC2 and two sets of queries for the queries 51-100 and 101-150 of the TREC collections. The TREC1 and TREC2 collections belong to the text published between 1987 and 1990 in various newspapers, news agencies and editorials. They contain more than two gigabytes of data, divided into 740.000 documents. Over these thirteen collections we have made three tests, described in the 1:

- **TREC-1**. The thirteen collections indexed with only one index. It shows the best case.
- **TREC-13**. Each collection of the thirteen has been indexed separately.
- **TREC-80**. The original thirteen collections have been divided into eighty collections, and indexed separately. The procedure to create these eighty collections is the following:
  1. Each source (AP,DOE,FR,WSJ,ZIFF) has a number of subcollections, according to its size. Therefore, AP has 19 subcollections, DOE has 7, FR has 18, WSJ has 20 and ZIFF has 16.
  2. With a random value and according to its source each document has been copied in one of its subcollections.

The queries used appear in the first two editions of the TREC conferences, 100 queries, in total. We have used, in the experiments, only the title and description fields.

Table 1. Description of the collections sets

	# of docs.			Size (in MB)		
	Min.	Avg.	Max.	Min.	Avg.	Max.
TREC-1	741.991	741.991	741.991	2168	2168	2168
TREC-13	10.163	57.066	226.087	33	159.23	260
TREC-80	2473	9273	32.401	23	25,81	30

3.3 Experiments Description

Using the sets of indices, TREC-1, TREC-13 and TREC-80, we have run some experiments, according to the following parameters:

- Weighting functions used in the indices. We decided to measure the stability of the proposed model, and for this purpose we have worked with two index sets, *OKAPI* and *random*. With the first, all collections have been indexed with *OKAPI* weighting method. In the second case we have chosen a random weighting function from those of the ZPRISE system. The TREC-1 collection has been indexed using only OKAPI.
- Collection selection method. In a distributed system it is necessary to weight each collection for a given query, and choose the most relevant. CORI allows us to value each collection, but does not say which judgement we should follow to choose more or fewer collections. [1] suggests using cluster methods or setting a fixed value of recovery collections. We have applied both; we have used clustering and also a fixed value N (with N=5,10,15 and 20).
- Application of local pseudo-relevance feedback. Each librarian can expand automatically the query, with the increase of the local results in mind. Nonetheless, since the added terms are local, these are not known by the receptionist or the central system, so CORI and also 2-step RSV lose some of the possible local increase. Even so, it is very important to study how this popular method can affect in the final result [5]. The expansion has been made by adding the most relevant ten terms of the ten first documents to the original query.
- Application of global pseudo-relevance feedback. Since the estimation of the 2- step RSV generates a new index in a query time, it is possible to use this new index to apply PRF, although it is necessary to download the first N documents, to analyze them and to extract the terms with the most relevant power of these N documents. In this work we use the first ten documents. Therefore, this method introduces a low cost.

Experiments without Query Expansion and Homogeneous Indices. In this section CORI and 2-step RSV are compared. All collections have been indexed using the same weighting method, OKAPI. We have applied neither local nor global query expansion.

Tables 2 and 3 show the results obtained. The best results are from 2-step RSV, whose increase is better, in average precision terms, between 19,4%,

Table 2. DIR experiments without feedback and homogeneous indices (set TREC-13, queries 101-150)

Fusion	5-prec	10-prec	20-prec	100-prec	Avg-prec
Top-10					
CORI	0,484	0,416	0,360	0,268	0,134
2-Step RSV	0,492	0,478	0,445	0,348	0,199
Centralized	0,492	0,492	0,444	0,346	0,194

Table 3. DIR experiments without feedback and homogeneous indices (set TREC-80, queries 51-100)

Fusion	5-prec	10-prec	20-prec	100-prec	Avg-prec
Top-20					
CORI	0,261	0,263	0,293	0,210	0,071
2-Step RSV	0,488	0,460	0443	0,318	0,147
Centralized	*0,556*	*0,514*	*0,492*	*0,371*	*0,210*

if we use the five first documents over TREC-13, and 107% if we use the first twenty documents over TREC-80. In this last case, in absolute terms, 2-step RSV improves CORI in 7,6 points, but CORI starts from a low average precision (0,07), so the increase looks better than it actually is. CORI obtains its best results when the ten first collections are selected. However its performance suddenly drops if the twenty first collections are selected. In this point 2-step RSV is more stable, because the more selected collections, the better the precision. This aspect is shown in figure 1, which shows the performance of 2-step RSV in relation to CORI.

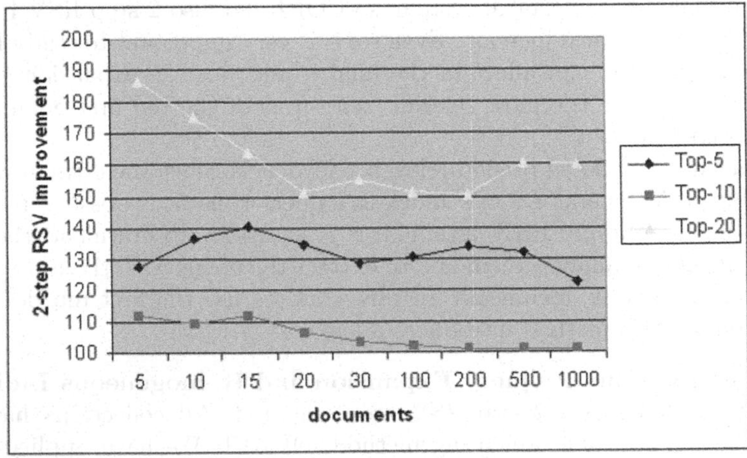

Fig. 1. Improvement of *2-step RSV* over CORI (coll. TREC-80,queries 51-100). The base case (100%) shows CORI precision

Finally, in the comparison between CORI and 2-step RSV, and a centralized model, an interesting result appears. The precision obtained with 2-step RSV over 13 subcollections, using $Top-10$, is better than the precision obtained with the centralized model, and therefore, it is proved that if the system does not use all collections, there is not always a loss of precision. The good performance and level obtained with TREC-13 is not the same with TREC-80. In this case the precision obtained is lower, although the most probable reason is that the ratio of the collections used is lower in comparison with the total available. In fact, if the twenty first collections are used, which represents 25% of the total, the average precision obtained is higher than 70% of the precision obtained with a centralized model.

Experiments without Query Expansion and Heterogeneous Indices. In this section we have studied how the use of a random weighting function can affect each subcollection. While in the last section all the subcollections have been indexed with the same weighting function OKAPI, in this one each subcollection has been indexed with a random function, available in the IR ZPrise system. Tables 4 and 5 show that the results obtained follow the same tendency as the previous section:

- Using the test set TREC-13, 2-step RSV almost doubles the average precision of CORI, over the run selection procedures (Top-5, Top-10 and *clustering*).
- Using TREC-80, this difference is not so important, except if we use the twenty first collections. In this last case, CORI drops again, and the performance obtained is not even the third part of the performance obtained with 2-Step RSV . In the other cases the increase of the performance is about 40%.

Table 4. DIR Experiments without feedback and heterogeneous indices (TREC-13 set, queries 101-150)

Fusion	5-prec	10-prec	20-prec	100-prec	Avg-prec
Top-10					
CORI	0,348	0,254	0,228	0,208	0,100
2-Step RSV	0,492	0,480	0,443	0,350	0,198
Centralized	*0,492*	*0,492*	*0,444*	*0,346*	*0,194*

Table 5. Experiments without feedback and heterogeneous indices (TREC-80 set, queries 51-100)

Fusion	5-prec	10-prec	20-prec	100-prec	Avg-prec
Top-20					
CORI	0,176	0,214	0,231	0,167	0,046
2-Step RSV	0,610	0,619	0,569	0,377	0,160
Centralized	*0,556*	*0,514*	*0,492*	*0,371*	*0,210*

2-step RSV and also CORI lose precision when a random method is introduced in the selection of the weighting function. This is almost inevitable because the local results obtained with each collection are in some experiments worse than with OKAPI. Nonetheless, this loss of precision is not the same with CORI as with 2-step RSV. If we focus on the results obtained over TREC-80, while 2- step RSV loses in general between 10% and 20%, CORI, with the inclusion of various weighting functions, loses more than 40%. This situation is shown in the figure 2, which shows the quotient between the precision obtained with OKAPI and with the random functions. Using *clustering* and also Top-10, while with 2-step RSV the performance is around 80% of the precision obtained with homogeneous indices, CORI is only around 60%. Therefore, it is possible to arm that 2-step RSV is a stable algorithm against the variation of the weighting functions used in each subcollection.

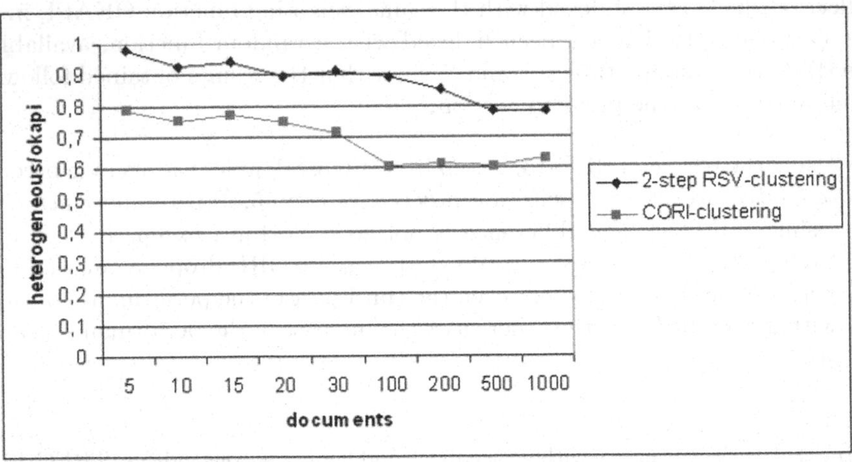

Fig. 2. Impact of the use of heterogeneous indices in the performance of CORI and 2-Step RSV (coll. TREC-80,queries 51-100,clustering). The base case (100%) shows the precision obtained with the algorithm using homogeneous indices (only OKAPI)

3.4 Experiments with Query Expansion

In this section we study the impact of the use of query expansion method based in local and global PRF:

- Local pseudo-relevance feedback. Each librarian applies PRF locally with the purpose of increasing the results obtained over this library.
- Global pseudo-relevance feedback. This case can only be applied to 2-step RSV. Since the receptionist generates a new global index, it is possible to apply PRF over this index.
- Local and global pseudo-relevance feedback. Finally, it is possible to apply PRF first for each librarian, and also for the receptionist later.

Local PRF Experiments. As figures 3 and 4 show, the local feedback does not provide an increase in the 2-step RSV case. If we use CORI the situation is a little better over 13 collections. The use of the PRF over 80 collections makes the results even worse, but this is not always so. In every case the differences are very small (not more than two points) and the conclusion is that it is possible to assume that the PRF does not affect the final result, with both CORI and with 2-step RSV.

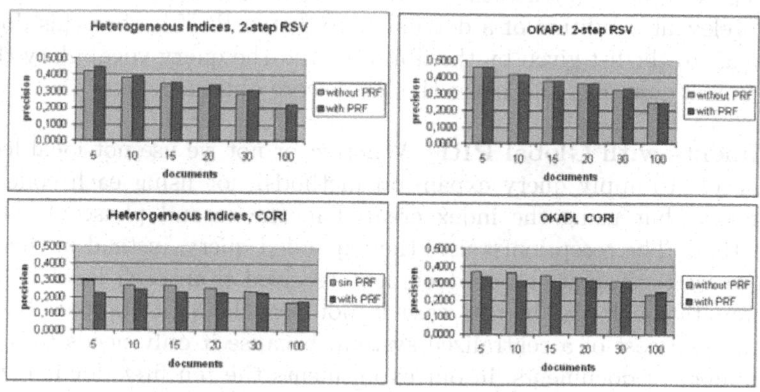

Fig. 3. Local feedback impact (TREC-13, Top-10)

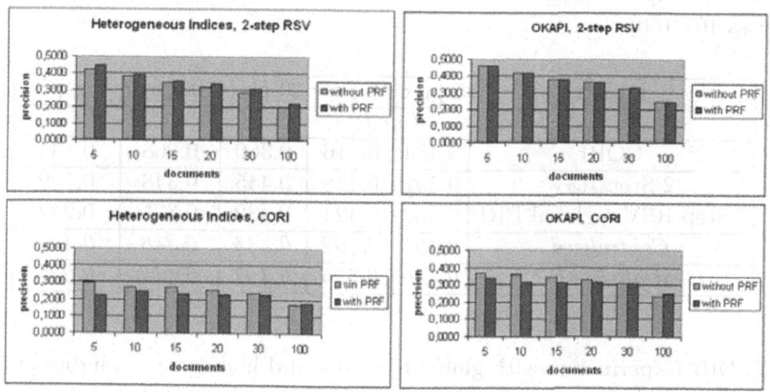

Fig. 4. Local feedback impact (TREC-80, clustering)

In systems that do not collaborate completely (the receptionist cannot access to the added terms of each librarian) this result was already known to CORI. [5] shows that the use of query expansion methods (in their case, *Local Context Analysis*) does not increase either the collections selection or the documents selection. A possible cause is the expanded query length, because this new length makes the score normalization difficult. This reason cannot be applied to 2-step RSV . Some experiments in the last section show that the performance of the 2-step RSV is not different if the length of the query is different. In the case of 2-step RSV there may be two causes:

- The receptionist only works with the original query vocabulary, so the documents that are now relevant because of the query expansion, are not selected.
- 2-step RSV does not use the local score obtained for each document. The sole relevant condition of a document to 2-step RSV is that this document belongs to the list given by the librarian and the query vocabulary that this document contains, and never the local score obtained.

Experiments with Global PRF. Whether or not we use not local feedback, it is possible to apply query expansion methods, not using each collection as a single unit but using the index created in the second phase of the 2-step RSV method. The receptionist uses the expanded query, instead of the original one, in order to evaluate every document received from each local IR system. The computational cost in this case is not very high, if compared with the computational cost of a centralized system, because it only needs to analyze a small number of documents, in our experiments the ten first documents, so in general it is only necessary to download two or three documents per selected collection, using any procedure like the ones described in section 4.

Table 6. DIR Experiments with global feedback and homogeneous indices (TREC-13 set, queries 101-150)

Fusion	5-prec	10-prec	20-prec	100-prec	Avg-prec
Top-10					
CORI	0,484	0,416	0,360	0,268	0,134
2-Step RSV	0,492	0,478	0,445	0,348	0,199
2-Step RSV +global PRF	0,432	0,424	0,432	0,375	0,232
Centralized	*0,492*	*0,492*	*0,444*	*0,346*	*0,194*
Centralized+PRF	*0,540*	*0,526*	*0,497*	*0,418*	*0,273*

Table 7. DIR Experiments with global feedback and homogeneous indices (TREC-80 set, queries 101-150)

Fusion	5-prec	10-prec	20-prec	100-prec	Avg-prec
Top-20					
CORI	0,274	0,259	0,272	0,192	0,067
2-Step RSV	0,488	0,446	0,408	0,289	0,131
2-Step RSV +global PRF	0,480	0,440	0,431	0,326	0,155
Centralized	*0,492*	*0,492*	*0,444*	*0,346*	*0,194*
Centralized+PRF	*0,540*	*0,526*	*0,497*	*0,418*	*0,273*

In tables 6 and 7 the results obtained for the query set 51-100 and homogeneous indices are shown.

The increase of the average precision introduced using global PRF in relation to the original 2-step RSV is quite signicant, around 15-20%. The lowest increase, TREC-13 case, is 16.6% (Top-10) and the highest is 21%, with TREC- 13 and *clustering.* In this way the results of the experiments with TREC-80 are between 17.4% (Top-5) and 20% (Top-20). The increase of the centralized model with PRF is 41%, much more than the 20% obtained with 2-step RSV . The reason is clear: the centralized model has access to *all* documents of *all* collections, so it is possible to include relevant documents which have not been selected previously. This is impossible with 2-step RSV , because this method only includes *some* documents and *some* collections, and only resorts documents selected previously, but never adds new documents. In any case, this situation could change if we run the expanded query over each selected collection, and then apply over these new results the original 2-step RSV algorithm.

It is clear that the global PRF increases the average precision, but it does not always increase the selection of the first documents, and it is frequent to obtain worse precisions with global PRF compared with the results without PRF, when only the five or ten first documents are considered. This conclusion is shown in figure 5.

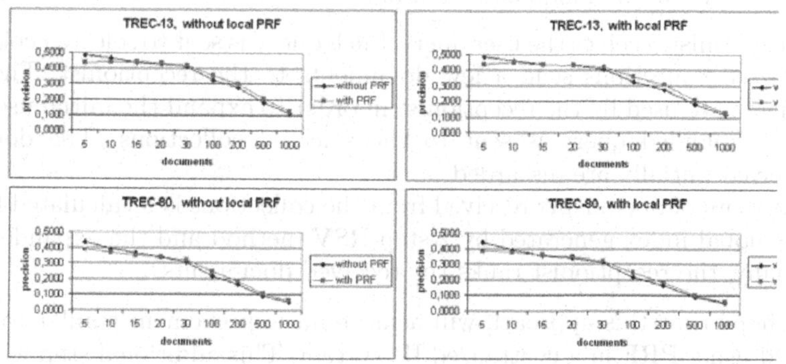

Fig. 5. Global feedback impact (random indices, clustering) (I)

The use of global PRF increases recall in general, because it introduces more relevant documents between the first thousands, but it does not increase the precision of the first documents. Is it always advisable to use global PRF?. As is usual in these cases, the answer depends on the user's needs. In general the application of PRF worsens a little the ranking of the first 10 or 15 documents, and from this number the result increases. On the other hand, the computational cost of applying PRF is moderate but not null, because it needs to analyze the first documents in the query time. It is possible that this computational cost will be the reason to apply or not this method: a little better results in general but the user has to wait some more seconds.

4 Conclusions and Future Work

This paper shows the application of 2-step RSV to DIR environments. We have focused on two questions:

1. Collections with different weighting functions and the improvement of blind feedback applied by the DIR monitor at global level. The experiments about the first question show that 2-step RSV is robust against weighting functions variances. 2-step RSV and also CORI lose precision when a random method is introduced into the selection of the weighting function. The loss of precision with CORI is more than 40%, while with 2-step RSV it is between 10% and 20%.
2. Blind feedback is a useful technique whenever it is applied at global level rather than individually for each IR system. Global PRF applied with 2-step RSV increases the average precision, but it does not always increase the selection of the first documents, and it is frequent to obtain worse precisions with global PRF compared with the results without PRF, when only the five or ten first documents are considered.

We can also test the improvement of the results using global PRF by sending expanded queries for each collection instead of recalculating the score of documents received by means of the original query. The steps of the proposal architecture would be modified as follows:

1. Receptionist receives the user query. Such query is sent to selected collections.
2. Selected collections send a few documents to the receptionist. These documents are used by the receptionist in order to expand the initial user query.
3. The expanded query is sent to the selected collections. The documents received initially are discarded.
4. The score of documents received from the collections is recalculated by using the global index generated by 2-step RSV method and the expanded query.
5. Finally, the receptionist ranks the received documents.

We hope that this approach will achieve an improvement similar to the one obtained using PRF in a centralized IR system. This additional step will have a computational cost that will be also studied.

References

1. J. P. Callan, Z. Lu, and W. B. Croft. Searching distributed collections with inference networks. In *Proceedings of the 18th International Conference of the ACM SIGIR'95*, pages 21–28, New York, 1995. The ACM Press.
2. K. Liu, C. Yu, W. Meng, A. Santos, and C. Zhang. Discovering the representative of a search engine. In *Proceedings of 10th ACM International Conference on Information and Knowledge Managemenet (CIKM)*, 2001.
3. F. Martínez-Santiago, M. Martín, and L. Ureña. SINAI at CLEF 2002: Experiments with merging strategies. *Advances in Cross-Language Information Retrieval. Lecture Notes in Computer Science. Springer Verlag*, pages 187–197, 2003.

4. F. Martínez-Santiago, A. Montejo-Ráez, L. Ureña, and M. Diaz. SINAI at CLEF 2003: Merging and decompounding. In C. Peters, M. Braschler, J. Gonzalo, and M. Kluck, editors, *Proceedings of the CLEF 2003 Cross-Language Text Retrieval System Evaluation Campaign*, pages 99–109, 2003.
5. P. Ogilve and J. Callan. The effectiveness of query expansion for distributed information retrieval. In *Proceedings of the Tenth International Conference on Information Knowledge Management (CIKM 2001)*, pages 193–190, 2001.
6. S. E. Robertson, S. Walker., and M. Beaulieu. Experimentation as a way of life: Okapi at TREC. *Information Processing and Management*, 1(36):95–108, 2000.
7. L. Si and J. Callan. Relevant document distribution estimation method for resource selection. In T. A. Press., editor, *Proc. of the 26 Annual Int'l ACM SIGIR Conference on Research and Development in Information Retrieval*, Toronto, 2003.
8. E. Voorhees, N. K. Gupta, and B. Johnson-Laird. The collection fusion problem. In D. K. Harman, editor, *Proceedings of the 3th Text Retrieval Conference TREC-3*, volume 500-225, pages 95–104, Gaithersburg, 1995. National Institute of Standards and Technology, Special Publication.
9. E. Voorhees, N. K. Gupta, and B. Johnson-Laird. Learning collection fusion strategies. In ACM, editor, *Proceedings of the Eighteenth Annual International ACM SIGIR Conference on Research and Development in Information Retrieval*, pages 172–179, Seattle, 1995.

Unsupervised Training of a Finite-State Sliding-Window Part-of-Speech Tagger*

Enrique Sánchez-Villamil, Mikel L. Forcada, and Rafael C. Carrasco

Transducens
Departament de Llenguatges i Sistemes Informàtics
Universitat d'Alacant
E-03071 Alacant

Abstract. A simple, robust sliding-window part-of-speech tagger is presented and a method is given to estimate its parameters from an untagged corpus. Its performance is compared to a standard Baum-Welch-trained hidden-Markov-model part-of-speech tagger. Transformation into a finite-state machine —behaving exactly as the tagger itself— is demonstrated.

1 Introduction

A large fraction (typically 30%, but varying from one language to another) of the words in natural language texts are words that, in isolation, may be assigned more than one morphological analysis and, in particular, more than one part of speech (PoS). The correct resolution of this kind of ambiguity for each occurrence of the word in the text is crucial in many natural language processing applications; for example, in machine translation, the correct equivalent of a word may be very different depending on its part of speech.

This paper presents a sliding-window PoS tagger (SWPoST), that is, a system which assigns the part of speech of a word based on the information provided by a fixed window of words around it. The SWPoST idea is not new; however, we are not aware of any SWPoST which, using reasonable approximations, may easily be trained in an unsupervised manner; that is, avoiding costly manual tagging of a corpus. Furthermore, as with any fixed-window SWPoST, and in contrast with more customary approaches such as hidden Markov models (HMM), the tagger may be implemented exactly as a finite-state machine (a Mealy machine).

The paper is organized as follows: section 2 gives some definitions, describes the notation that will be used throughout the paper, and compares the sliding-window approach to the customary (HMM) approach to part-of-speech tagging; section 3 describes the approximations that allow a SWPoST to be trained in an unsupervised manner and describes the training process itself; section 4 describes how the tagger may be used on new text and how it may be turned into a finite-state tagger; section 5 describes a series of experiments performed to compare

* Work funded by the Spanish Government through grant TIC2003-08681-C02-01.

J. L. Vicedo et al. (Eds.): EsTAL 2004, LNAI 3230, pp. 454–463, 2004.

the performance of a SWPoST to that of a HMM tagger and to explore the size of the resulting finite state taggers (after minimization); and, finally, concluding remarks are given in section 6.

2 Preliminaries

Let $\Gamma = \{\gamma_1, \gamma_2, \ldots, \gamma_{|\Gamma|}\}$ be the *tagset* for the task, that is, the set of PoS tags a word may receive and $W = \{w_1, w_2, \ldots\}$ be the vocabulary of the task. A partition of W is established so that $w_i \equiv w_j$ if and only if both are assigned the same subset of tags. Each of the classes of this partition is usually called an *ambiguity class*. It is usual [1] to refine this partition so that, for high-frequency words, each word class contains just one word whereas, for lower-frequency words, word classes are made to correspond exactly to ambiguity classes (although it is also possible to use one-word classes for all words or to use only ambiguity classes), which allows for improved performance on very frequent ambiguous words while keeping the number of parameters of the tagger under control.

Any such refinement will be denoted as $\Sigma = \{\sigma_1, \sigma_2, \ldots, \sigma_{|\Sigma|}\}$ where σ_i are word classes. In this paper, word classes will simply be ambiguity classes, without any refinement. We will call $T : \Sigma \to 2^\Gamma$ the function returning the set $T(\sigma)$ of PoS tags for each word class σ.

The part-of-speech tagging problem may be formulated as follows: given a text $w[1]w[2]\ldots w[L] \in W^+$, each word $w[t]$ is assigned (using a lexicon, a morphological analyser, or a guesser) a word class $\sigma[t] \in \Sigma$ to obtain an *ambiguously tagged* text $\sigma[1]\sigma[2]\ldots\sigma[L] \in \Sigma^+$; the task of the PoS tagger is to obtain a tagged text $\gamma[1]\gamma[2]\ldots\gamma[L] \in \Gamma^+$ (with $\gamma[t] \in T(\sigma[t])$) as correct as possible.

Statistical part-of-speech tagging looks for the *most likely* tagging of an ambiguously tagged text $\sigma[1]\sigma[2]\ldots\sigma[L]$:

$$\gamma^*[1]\ldots\gamma^*[L] = \operatorname*{argmax}_{\gamma[t]\in T(\sigma[t])} P(\gamma[1]\ldots\gamma[L]|\sigma[1]\ldots\sigma[L]) \qquad (1)$$

which, using Bayes' formula, becomes equivalent to:

$$\gamma^*[1]\ldots\gamma^*[L] = \operatorname*{argmax}_{\gamma[t]\in T(\sigma[t])} P_S(\gamma[1]\ldots\gamma[L])P_L(\sigma[1]\ldots\sigma[L]|\gamma[1]\ldots\gamma[L])) \qquad (2)$$

where $P_S(\gamma[1]\ldots\gamma[L])$ is the probability of a particular tagging (syntactical probability) and $P_L(\sigma[1]\ldots\sigma[L]|\gamma[1]\ldots\gamma[L])$ is the probability of that particular tagging generating the text $\sigma[1]\ldots\sigma[L]$ (lexical probability). In hidden Markov models (HMM) [5], these probabilities are approximated as products; the syntactical probabilities are modeled by a first-order Markov process:

$$P_S(\gamma[1]\gamma[2]\ldots\gamma[L]) = \prod_{t=0}^{t=L} p_S(\gamma[t+1]|\gamma[t]) \qquad (3)$$

where $\gamma[0]$ and $\gamma[L+1]$ are fixed delimiting tags (which we will denote as $\gamma_\#$ and will usually correspond to sentence boundaries); lexical probabilities are made independent of context:

$$P_L(\sigma[1]\sigma[2]\ldots\sigma[L]|\gamma[1]\gamma[2]\ldots\gamma[L]) = \prod_{t=1}^{t=L} p_L(\sigma[t]|\gamma[t]). \quad (4)$$

The number of trainable parameters for such a tagger is $(|\Gamma| + |\Sigma|)|\Gamma|$. Tagging (searching for the optimal $\gamma^*[1]\gamma^*[2]\ldots\gamma^*[L]$) is implemented using a very efficient, left-to-right algorithm usually known as Viterbi's algorithm [1, 5]. If conveniently implemented, Viterbi's algorithm can output a partial tagging each time a nonambiguous word is seen, but maintains multiple hypotheses when reading ambiguous words. HMMs may be trained either from tagged text (simply by counting and taking probabilities to be equal to frequencies) or from untagged text, using the well-known expectation-maximization backward-forward Baum-Welch algorithm [5, 1].

In this paper we look at tagging from a completely different perspective. Instead of using the inverted formulation in eq. (2) we approximate the probability in eq. (1) directly as:

$$P(\gamma[1]\gamma[2]\ldots\gamma[L]|\sigma[1]\sigma[2]\ldots\sigma[L]) = \prod_{t=1}^{t=L} p(\gamma[t]|C_{(-)}[t]\sigma[t]C_{(+)}[t]) \quad (5)$$

where

$$C_{(-)}[t] = \sigma[t - N_{(-)}]\sigma[t - N_{(-)} + 1]\cdots\sigma[t-1]$$

is a *left context* of size $N_{(-)}$,

$$C_{(+)}[t] = \sigma[t+1]\sigma[t+2]\cdots\sigma[t + N_{(+)}]$$

is a *right context* of size $N_{(+)}$, and $\sigma[-N_{(-)} + 1], \sigma[-N_{(-)} + 2], \ldots, \sigma[0]$ and $\sigma[L+1], \sigma[L+2], \ldots \sigma[L + N_{(+)}]$ are all set to a special delimiting word class $\sigma_\#$ such that $T(\sigma_\#) = \{\gamma_\#\}$, e.g., one containing the sentence-boundary marker tag $\gamma_\# \in \Gamma$. This *sliding window* method is local in nature; it does not consider any context beyond the window of $N_{(-)} + N_{(+)} + 1$ words; its implementation is straightforward, even more that of Viterbi's algorithm. The main problem is the estimation of the probabilities $p(\gamma[t]|C_{(-)}[t]\sigma[t]C_{(+)}[t])$. From a tagged corpus, these probabilities may be easily counted; in this paper, however, we propose a way of estimating them from an untagged corpus. Another problem is the large number of parameters of the model (worst case $O(|\Sigma|^{N_{(+)}+N_{(-)}+1}|\Gamma|)$); we will discuss a way to reduce the number of parameters to just $O(|\Sigma|^{N_{(+)}+N_{(-)}}|\Gamma|)$ and show that, for many applications, $N_{(-)} = N_{(+)} = 1$ is an adequate choice.

3 Training from an Untagged Corpus

The main approximation in this model is the following: we will assume that the probability of finding a certain tag $\gamma[t]$ in the center of the window depends only on the preceding context $C_{(-)}[t]$ and the succeeding context $C_{(+)}[t]$ but not on the particular word class at position t, $\sigma[t]$; that is, the probability that a word receives a certain label depends only *selectionally* on the word (the context determines the probabilities of each label, whereas the word just selects labels among those in $T(\sigma[t])$). We will denote this probability as $p_{C_{(-)}\gamma C_{(+)}}$ for short (with the position index $[t]$ dropped because of the invariance). The most probable tag $\gamma^*[t]$ is then

$$\gamma^*[t] = \underset{\gamma \in T(\sigma[t])}{\mathrm{argmax}}\ p_{C_{(-)}[t]\gamma C_{(+)}[t]}, \tag{6}$$

that is, the most probable tag in that context among those corresponding to the current word class. The probabilities $p_{C_{(-)}\gamma C_{(+)}}$ are easily estimated from a tagged corpus (e.g., by counting) but estimating them from an untagged corpus involves an iterative process; instead of estimating the probability we will estimate the count $\tilde{n}_{C_{(-)}\gamma C_{(+)}}$ which can be interpreted as the effective number of times that label γ would appear in the text between contexts $C_{(-)}$ and $C_{(+)}$.

Therefore,

$$p(\gamma|C_{(-)}\sigma C_{(+)}) = \begin{cases} k_{\sigma_{(-)}\sigma\sigma_{(+)}}\tilde{n}_{C_{(-)}\gamma C_{(+)}} & \text{if } \gamma \in T(\sigma) \\ 0 & \text{otherwise} \end{cases}, \tag{7}$$

where $k_{\sigma_{(-)}\sigma\sigma_{(+)}}$ is a normalization factor

$$k_{\sigma_{(-)}\sigma\sigma_{(+)}} = \left(\sum_{\gamma' \in T(\sigma)} \tilde{n}_{C_{(-)}\gamma' C_{(+)}} \right)^{-1}. \tag{8}$$

Now, how can the counts $\tilde{n}_{C_{(-)}[t]\gamma C_{(+)}[t]}$ be estimated? If the window probabilities $p(\gamma|C_{(-)}[t]\sigma C_{(+)}[t])$ were known, they could be easily obtained from the text itself as follows:

$$\tilde{n}_{C_{(-)}\gamma C_{(+)}} = \sum_{\sigma:\gamma \in T(\sigma)} n_{C_{(-)}\sigma C_{(+)}} p(\gamma|C_{(-)}\sigma C_{(+)}), \tag{9}$$

where $n_{C_{(-)}\sigma C_{(+)}}$ is the number of times that label σ appears between contexts $C_{(-)}$ and $C_{(+)}$; that is, one would add $p(\gamma|C_{(-)}\sigma C_{(+)})$ each time a word class σ containing tag γ appears between $C_{(-)}$ and $C_{(+)}$. Equations (7) and (9) may be iteratively solved until the $\tilde{n}_{C_{(-)}\gamma C_{(+)}}$ converge. For the computation to be more efficient, one can avoid storing the probabilities $p(\gamma|C_{(-)}\sigma C_{(+)})$ by organizing the iterations around the $\tilde{n}_{C_{(-)}\gamma C_{(+)}}$ as follows, by combining eqs. (7), (8), and (9) and using an iteration index denoted with a superscript $[k]$,

$$\tilde{n}^{[k]}_{C_{(-)}\gamma C_{(+)}} = \tilde{n}^{[k-1]}_{C_{(-)}\gamma C_{(+)}} \sum_{\sigma:\gamma \in T(\sigma)} n_{C_{(-)}\sigma C_{(+)}} \left(\sum_{\gamma' \in T(\sigma)} \tilde{n}^{[k-1]}_{C_{(-)}\gamma' C_{(+)}} \right)^{-1}, \tag{10}$$

where the iteration may be easily seen as a process of successive corrections to the effective counts $\tilde{n}_{C_{(-)}\gamma C_{(+)}}$. A possible initial value is given by

$$\tilde{n}^{[0]}_{C_{(-)}\gamma C_{(+)}} = \sum_{\sigma:\gamma \in T(\sigma)} n_{C_{(-)}\sigma C_{(+)}} \frac{1}{|T(\sigma)|}, \tag{11}$$

that is, assuming that, initially, all possible tags are equally probable for each word class.

Equations (10) and (11) contain the counts $n_{C_{(-)}\sigma C_{(+)}}$ which depend on $N_{(+)} + N_{(-)} + 1$ word classes; if memory is at a premium, instead of reading the text once to count these and then iterating, the text may be read in each iteration to avoid storing the $n_{C_{(-)}\sigma C_{(+)}}$, and the $\tilde{n}^{[k]}_{C_{(-)}\gamma C_{(+)}}$ may be computed *on the fly*. Iterations proceed until a selected convergence condition has been met (e.g. a comparison of the $\tilde{n}^{[k]}_{C_{(-)}\gamma C_{(+)}}$ with respect to the $\tilde{n}^{[k-1]}_{C_{(-)}\gamma C_{(+)}}$, or the completion of a predetermined number of iterations).

4 Tagging Text: A Finite-State Tagger

Once the $\tilde{n}_{C_{(-)}\gamma C_{(+)}}$ have been computed, the winning tag for class σ in context $C_{(-)} \cdots C_{(+)}$, eq. (6), may be easily computed for all of the words in a text. Unlike with HMM [2], a sliding window PoS tagger may be turned exactly into a finite-state transducer [6]; in particular, into a Mealy machine with transitions having the form

$$\sigma[t - N_{(-)}]\sigma[t - N_{(-)} + 1] \cdots \sigma[t + N_{(+)} - 1] \stackrel{\sigma[t+N_{(+)}]:\gamma^*}{\longrightarrow}$$
$$\sigma[t - N_{(-)} + 1]\sigma[t - N_{(-)} + 2] \cdots \sigma[t + N_{(+)}]$$

This Mealy machine reads a text $\sigma[1] \ldots \sigma[L]$ word by word and outputs the winner tag sequence $\gamma^*[1] \ldots \gamma^*[L]$ with a delay of $N_{(+)}$ words. The resulting transducer has, in the worst case, $O(|\Sigma|^{N_{(+)}+N_{(-)}})$ states and $O(|\Sigma|^{N_{(+)}+N_{(-)}+1})$ transitions, but it may be minimized using traditional methods for finite-state transducers into a compact version of the sliding window PoS tagger, which takes into account the fact that different contexts may actually be grouped because they lead to the same disambiguation results.

5 Experiments

This section reports experiments to assess the performance of sliding-window part-of-speech using different amounts of context, compares it with that of customary Baum-Welch-trained HMM taggers [1], and describes the conversion of the resulting SWPoST taggers into finite-state machines.

The corpora we have used for training and testing is the Penn Treebank, version 3 [4, 3], which has more than one million PoS-tagged words (1014377) of English text taken from *The Wall Street Journal*. The word classes Σ of the Treebank will be taken simply to be ambiguity classes, that is, subsets of the collection of different part-of-speech tags (Γ). The Treebank has 45 different part-of-speech tags; 244261 words are ambiguous (24.08%).

The experiments use a lexicon extracted from the Penn Treebank, that is, a list of words with all the possible parts of speech observed. The exact tag given in the Treebank for each occurrence of each word is taken into account for testing but not for training. However, to simulate the effect of using a real, limited morphological analyser, we have filtered the resulting lexicon as follows:

- only the 14276 most frequent words have been kept, which ensures a 95% text coverage (i.e, 5% of the words are unknown).
- for each word, any part-of-speech tag occuring less than 5% of the time has been removed.

Using this simplified lexicon, texts in the Penn Treebank show 219 ambiguity classes. Words which are not included in our lexicon are assigned to a special ambiguity class (the *open* class) containing all tags representing parts of speech that can grow (i.e. a new word can be a noun or a verb but hardly ever a preposition).[1]

In order to train the taggers we have applied the following strategy, so that we can use as much text as possible for training: the Treebank is divided into 20 similarly-sized sections; a leaving-one-out procedure is applied, using 19 sections for training and the remaining one for testing, so that our results are the average of all 20 different train–test configurations. Figures show the average correct-tag rate only over ambiguous words (non-ambiguous words are not counted as successful disambiguations).

5.1 Effect of the Amount of Context

First of all, we show the results of a SWPoST using no context ($N_{(-)} = N_{(+)} = 0$) as a baseline, and compare them to those of a Baum-Welch-trained HMM tagger and to random tagging. As can be seen in figure 1, the performance of the SWPoST without context is not much better than random tagging. This happens because without context the SWPoST simply delivers an estimate of the most likely tag in each class. We can also observe that the HMM has an accuracy of around 61% of ambiguous words.

In order to improve the results one obviously needs to increase the context (i.e., widen the sliding window). As a first step we show the results of using a reduced context of only one word either before ($N_{(-)} = 1, N_{(+)} = 0$) or after ($N_{(-)} = 0, N_{(+)} = 1$) the current word. Figure 2 shows how that even using such a limited context the performance is more adequate. The number or trainable parameters of the SWPoST in this case is $O(|\Sigma||\Gamma|)$, slightly less than the $O(|\Sigma||\Gamma| + |\Gamma|^2)$ of the HMM tagger.

There is a significant difference between using as context the preceding ($N_{(-)} = 1$ and $N_{(+)} = 0$) or the succeeding ($N_{(-)} = 0$ and $N_{(+)} = 1$) word. The cognitive origin of this difference could be due to the fact that when people process language they tend to build hyphotheses based on what they have already heard or read which are used to reduce the ambiguity of words as they arrive.

[1] Our open class contains the tags `CD`, `JJ`, `JJR`, `JJS`, `NN`, `NNP`, `NNPS`, `RB`, `RBR`, `RBS`, `UH`, `VB`, `VBD`, `VBG`, `VBN`, `VBP`, and `VBZ`.

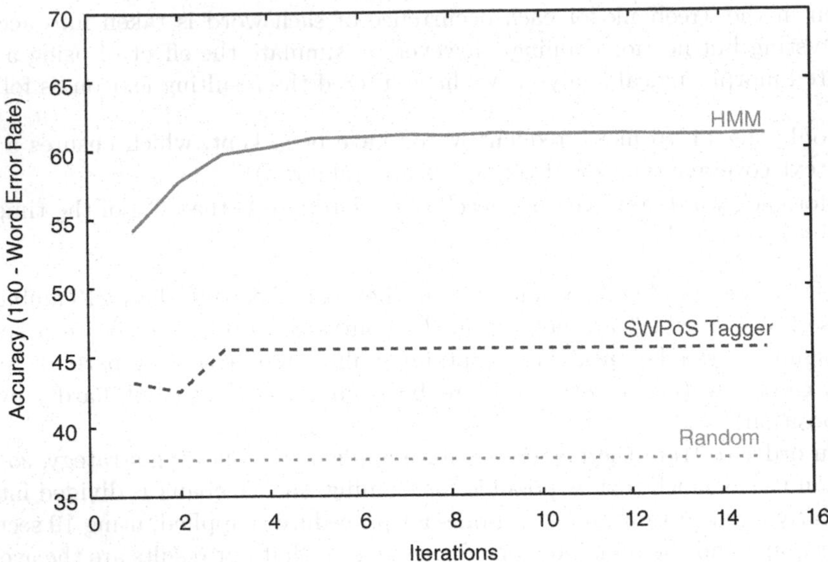

Fig. 1. Comparison between an HMM tagger, the SWPoST with no context ($N_{(-)} = N_{(+)} = 0$) and a random tagger

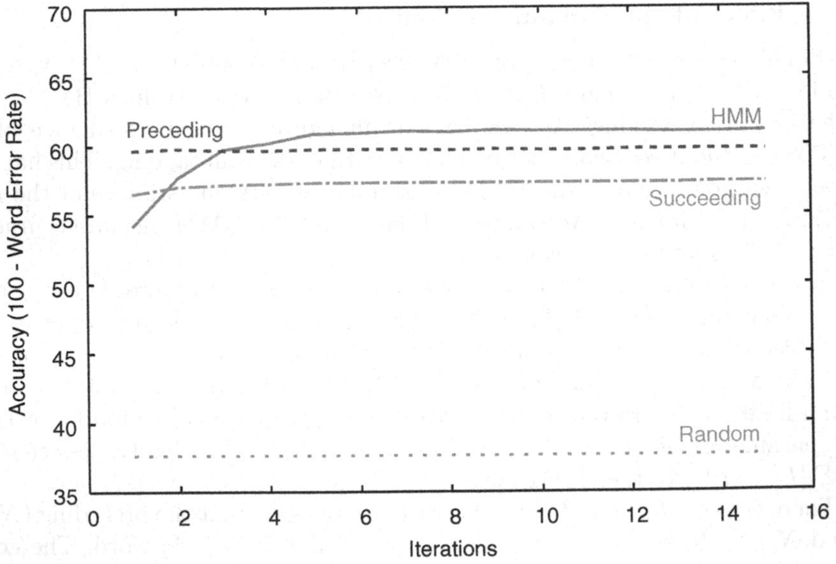

Fig. 2. Comparison between an HMM tagger and the SWPoST using $N_{(-)} = 1$ and $N_{(+)}$=0 (preceding) and using $N_{(-)}$=0 and $N_{(+)}$=1 (succeeding)

The next step is increasing a bit more the size of the context until having two context words. In this case we have three different possibilities: using the two immediately preceding words ($N_{(-)} = 2$ and $N_{(+)} = 0$), using one preceeding and one succeeding word ($N_{(-)} = 1$ and $N_{(+)} = 1$), and using two succeeding words ($N_{(-)} = 0$ and $N_{(+)} = 2$). We can see the results in figure 3. The performance of the SWPoST is now much better than the HMM tagger when using a context of $N_{(-)}$=1 and $N_{(+)}$=1. However when using the two succeeding words the results are worse than with the HMM tagger, and the performance of the SWPoST with $N_{(-)}$=2 and $N_{(+)}$=0 is about as good as that of an HMM tagger.

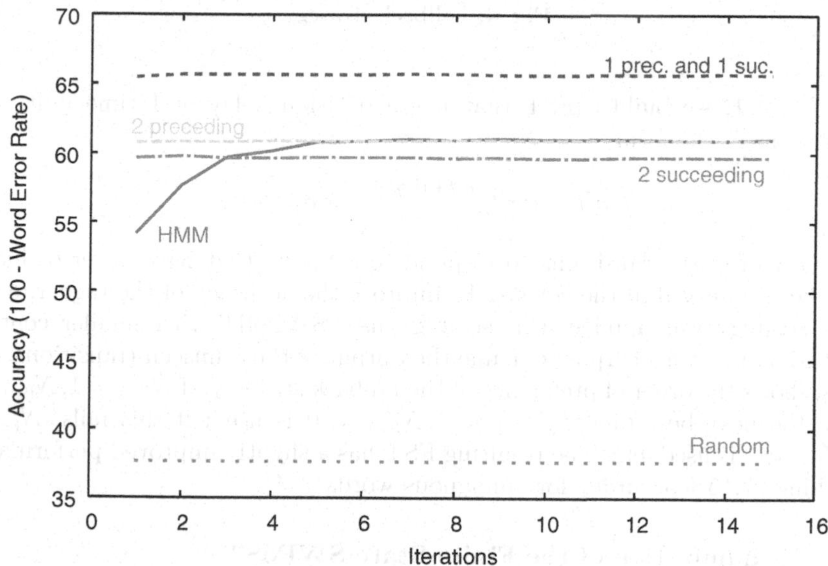

Fig. 3. Comparison between an HMM tagger and the SWPoST with using $N_{(-)}$=2 and $N_{(+)}$=0 (2 preceding) and using $N_{(-)}$=1 and $N_{(+)}$=1 (1 prec. and 1 suc.) and $N_{(-)}$=0 and $N_{(+)}$=2 (2 succeeding)

Finally, we tried increasing the context a bit more, until using three context words in all possible geometries, but the results were not as good as we expected (actually worse) due to the fact that the corpus is not large enough to allow the estimation of $O|\Gamma||\Sigma|^3)$ parameters.

The whole set of figures shows that SWPoST training usually converges after three or four iterations, which makes training very efficient in terms of time.

5.2 Finite-State Sliding-Window PoS Tagger

Once we have analysed the performance of the SWPoST we study its transformation into an equivalent finite-state transducer (FST). Given that the best results reported in the previous section correspond to using the context $N_{(-)}$=1

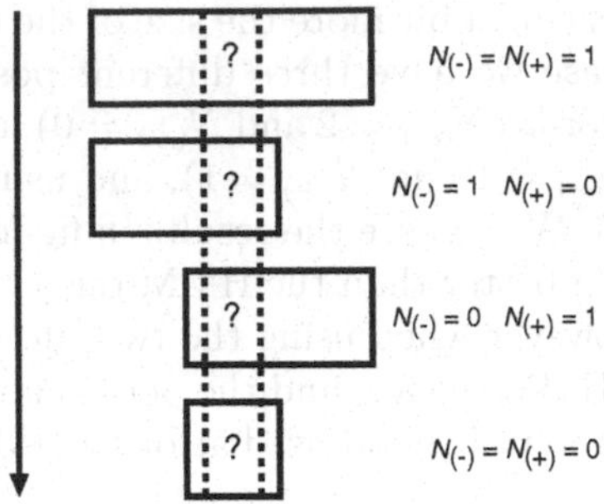

Fig. 4. Fallback strategy

and $N_{(+)}$=1, we build a FST that has a decision delay of 1 time unit, with transitions of the form

$$\sigma[t-1]\sigma[t] \overset{\sigma[t+1]:\gamma^*[t]}{\longrightarrow} \sigma[t]\sigma[t+1].$$

Many of these transitions correspond to contexts that have never or hardly ever been observed in the corpus. To improve the accuracy of the tagger, a fallback strategy was applied; this strategy uses SWPoST with smaller contexts trained on the same corpus to define the output of these unseen transitions. Figure 4 shows the order of preference of the fallback strategy: if $N_{(-)} = 1, N_{(+)} = 1$ fails, the next best tagger $N_{(-)} = 1, N_{(+)} = 0$ is used; if this fails, $N_{(-)} = 0, N_{(+)} = 1$ is used, etc. The resulting FST has a slightly improved performance, reaching 67.15% accuracy for ambiguous words.

5.3 Minimization of the Finite-State SWPoST

The FST created in this way has a large number of states; customary finite-state minimization may be expected to reduce the number of states and therefore reduce memory requirements. The algorithm to build the FST generates in our case 48400 states ($|\Sigma|^2$) and 10648000 ($|\Sigma|^3$) transitions. After minimization the FST is reduced to 22137 states and 4870140 transitions. Given the large amount of ambiguity classes, minimizing to about half the size is not far from what we expected.

6 Concluding Remarks

We have shown that, as commonly-used HMM taggers, simple and intuitive sliding-window part-of-speech taggers (SWPoST) may be iteratively trained in an unsupervised manner using reasonable approximations to reduce the number of trainable parameters. The number of trainable parameters depends on the size of the sliding window. Experimental results with the Penn Treebank show that the performance of SWPoST and HMM taggers having a similar number of trainable parameters is comparable. The best results, better than those of HMM taggers, are obtained using a SWPoST using a context of one preceding and one succeeding word, for a worst-case total of 2178000 parameters (with the HMM tagger having only 11925). The SWPoST can be exactly implemented as a finite-state transducer which, after minimization, has 22137 states and 4870140 transitions. Furthermore, the functioning of SWPoST is simple and intuitive, which allows for simple implementation and maintenance; for instance, if a training error is found it is easy to manually correct a transition in the resulting FST.

We are currently studying ways to reduce further the number of states and transitions at a small price in tagging accuracy, by using probabilistic criteria to prune uncommon contexts which do not contribute significantly to the overall accuracy.

References

1. D. Cutting, J. Kupiec, J. Pedersen, and P. Sibun. A practical part-of-speech tagger. In *Third Conference on Applied Natural Language Processing. Association for Computational Linguistics. Proceedings of the Conference*, pages 133–140, Trento, Italia, 31 marzo–3 abril 1992.
2. André Kempe. Finite state transducers approximating hidden Markov models. In Philip R. Cohen and Wolfgang Wahlster, editors, *Proceedings of the Thirty-Fifth Annual Meeting of the Association for Computational Linguistics and Eighth Conference of the European Chapter of the Association for Computational Linguistics*, pages 460–467, Somerset, New Jersey, 1997.
3. Mitchell Marcus, Grace Kim, Mary Ann Marcinkiewicz, Robert MacIntyre, Ann Bies, Mark Ferguson, Karen Katz, and Britta Schasberger. The Penn Treebank: Annotating predicate argument structure. In *Proc. ARPA Human Language Technology Workshop*, pages 110–115, 1994.
4. Mitchell P. Marcus, Beatrice Santorini, and Mary Ann Marcinkiewicz. Building a large annotated corpus of english: the Penn Treebank. *Computational linguistics*, 19:313–330, 1993. Reprinted in Susan Armstrong, ed. 1994, *Using large corpora*, Cambridge, MA: MIT Press, 273–290.
5. Lawrence R. Rabiner. A tutorial on hidden Markov models and selected applications in speech recognition. *Proceedings of the IEEE*, 77(2):257–286, 1989.
6. E. Roche and Y. Schabes. Introduction. In E. Roche and Y. Schabes, editors, *Finite-State Language Processing*, pages 1–65. MIT Press, Cambridge, Mass., 1997.

Using Seed Words to Learn to Categorize Chinese Text

Jingbo Zhu, Wenliang Chen, and Tianshun Yao

Natural Language Processing Lab
Institute of Computer Software & Theory
Northeastern University, Shenyang, P.R.China, 110004
{zhujingbo,chenwl,tsyao}@mail.neu.edu.cn

Abstract. In this paper, we focus on text categorization model by unsupervised learning techniques that do not require labeled data. We propose a feature learning bootstrapping algorithm (FLB) using a small number of seed words, in that features for each of categories could be automatically learned from a large amount of unlabeled documents. Using these learned features we develop a new Naïve Bayes classifier named NB_FLB. Experimental results show that the NB_FLB classifier performs better than other Naïve Bayes classifiers by supervised learning in small number of features cases.

1 Introduction

A growing number of statistical classification methods and machine learning techniques have been applied to text categorization in recent years, such as Rocchio[1,2], SVM[3], Decision Tree[4], Maximum Entropy model[5], Naïve Bayes[6]. Most categorization systems make use of a training collection of documents to predict the assignment of new documents to pre-defined categories. However, when applied to complex domains with many classes, these methods often require extremely large training collection to achieve better accuracy. But creating these labeled data is very tedious and expensive, because labeled documents should be labeled by hand. In other words, obtaining labeled data is difficult to the contrary unlabeled data is readily available and plentiful.

In this paper, we mainly focus on using unsupervised learning technique in text categorization that does not require labeled data. This work is organized as follows. In section 2, we introduce the scheme of the unsupervised text categorization classifier. And a feature learning algorithm based on bootstrapping is proposed. In section 3, using these learned features we develop a new Naïve Bayes classifier. And evaluation environment and experiments are given.

2 Unsupervised Text Categorization Scheme

In the machine learning literature, a large number of clustering algorithms have been extensively studied to handle the classification task, either directly or after minor modification. These include SOM-based models such as WEBSOM[7] and LabelSOM[8], the ART-based models such as ARTMAP[9] and ARAM[10], as well as various hybrid models.

J. L. Vicedo et al. (Eds.): EsTAL 2004, LNAI 3230, pp. 464–473, 2004.

Castelli and Cover[11] showed in the theoretical framework that unlabeled data can be used in some settings to improve classification, although it is exponentially less valuable than labeled data. Youngjoong Ko and Jungyun Sco[12] proposed a text categorization method based on unsupervised learning. The method divides the documents into sentences, and categorizes each sentence using keyword lists of each category and sentence similarity measure. In essence, most unsupervised learning algorithms applied to classification form a hybrid model. The hybrid involves the topology-preserving approximation of the primitive training domain via unsupervised learning, followed with the nearest-neighbor-like predictions of the testing inputs.

In this paper, we propose a new text categorization method by unsupervised learning. Without creating training labeled documents by hand, it automatically learns some features for each category using a small set of seed words and a large amount of unlabeled documents. Using these features a new Naïve Bayes classifier is developed.

In this scheme our proposed system consists of three modules as shown in figure 1: a module to preprocess collected unlabeled documents, a module to learn features for each category, and a module to classify text documents.

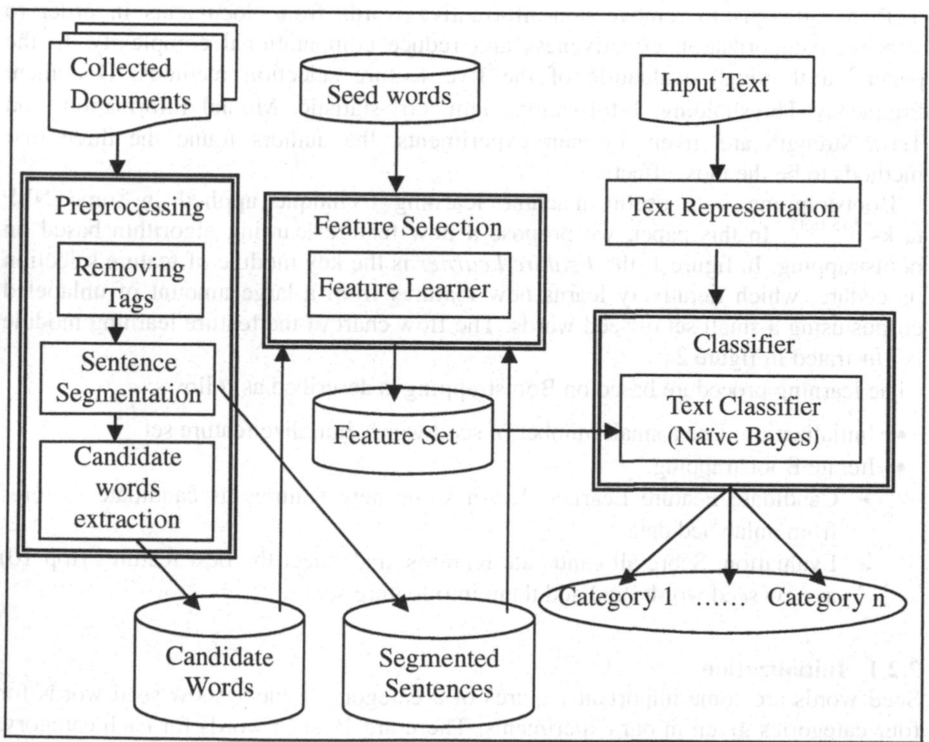

Fig. 1. Architecture for the unsupervised text categorization system

2.1 Preprocessing

The first step in text categorization and feature learning is to transform collected documents into a representation suitable for the feature learning algorithm and the classification task. The preprocessing procedure consists of the following steps:

- Remove all HTML tags and special characters in the collected documents.
- Segment the contents of the documents into sentences, and the sentences are segmented into words.
- Remove stopwords from sentences. The stopwords are frequent words that carry no content information, such as pronouns, prepositions, conjunctions.
- Extract the rest words as candidate words.

2.2 Feature Learning Algorithm

The other central problem in statistical text categorization is the high dimensionality of the feature space. Standard categorization techniques can not deal with such a large feature set, since processing is extremely costly in computational terms, and the results become unreliable due to the lack of sufficient training data. Hence, we need feature selection techniques to reduce the original feature set. Feature selection methods attempts to remove non-informative words from documents in order to improve categorization effectiveness and reduce computational complexity. In the paper[13] a thorough evaluation of the five feature selection methods: Document Frequency Thresholding, Information Gain, CHI-statistic, Mutual Information, and Term Strength are given. In their experiments, the authors found the three first methods to be the most effective.

Bootstrapping is a useful machine learning technique applied in some NLP tasks[14,15,16,17]. In this paper, we propose a new feature learning algorithm based on bootstrapping. In figure 1, the *Feature Learner* is the key module of feature selection procedure, which iteratively learns new features from a large amount of unlabeled corpus using a small set of seed words. The flow chart of the feature learning module is illustrated in figure 2.

The learning procedure based on Bootstrapping is described as follows:

- Initialization: Use a small number of seed words initialize feature set
- Iterate Bootstrapping:
  - ➢ Candidate Feature Learner: Learn some new features as candidate features from unlabeled data
  - ➢ Evaluation: Score all candidate features, and select the best features (top 10) as new seed words, and add them into feature set.

2.2.1 Initialization

Seed words are some important features of a category. Table 1 show seed words for four categories given in our experiments. There are 10 seed words for each category. In initialization procedure, seed words of each category are added into the feature set of corresponding category.

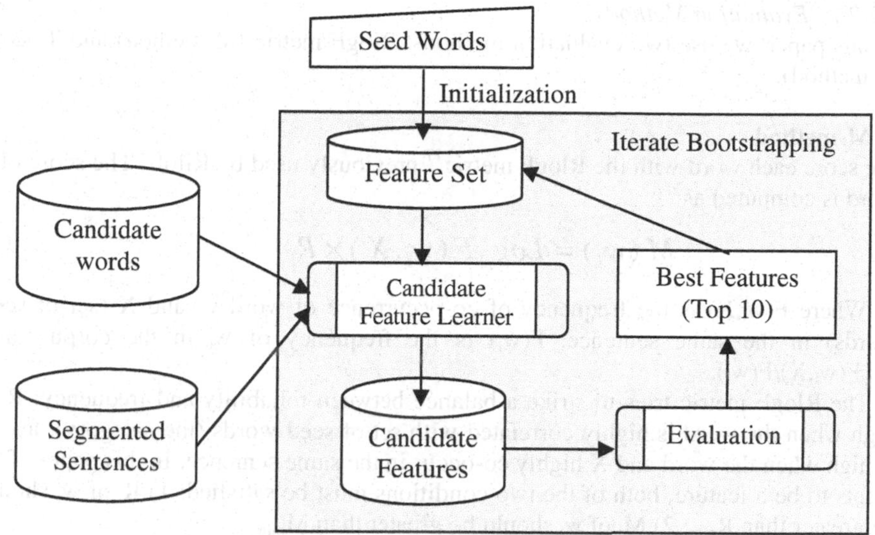

Fig. 2. Flow chart of the feature learning module

Table 1. Seed words for four categories

Category	Seed words
金融 (*finance*)	股票(*stock*) 金融(*finance*) 贷款(*loan*) 证券(*stock*) 财经(*finance and economics*) 银行(*bank*) 税收(*tax*) 外汇(*foreign exchange*) 投资(*investment*) 股市(*stock market*)
军事 (*military*)	军事(*military*) 武器(*weaponry*) 军队(*army*) 战争(*war*) 部队(*army*) 枪炮(*firearm*) 军人(*army-man*) 军区(*military area*) 核试验(*nuclear tests*) 核裁军(*nuclear disarmament*)
体育 (*sports*)	体育(*sports*) 选手(*player*) 足球(*football*) 联赛(*league*) 运动(*athletics*) 中国队(*China team*)锦标赛(*tournament*) 运动员(*player*)决赛(*final*) 教练(*coach*)
法律 (*law*)	法律(*law*) 法院(*court*) 律师(*lawyer*) 诉讼(*lawsuit*) 案件(*low case*) 犯罪(*crime*) 执法(*execute the law*) 法制(*legal system*) 违法(*transgress*) 检察官(*law officer*)

2.2.2 Iterate Bootstrapping

We can regard bootstrapping as iterative clustering. Our bootstrapping algorithm begins with some seed words for a category. From the set of candidate words, we can learn some candidate features using these seed words. These learned features are of the same category as the seed words. We score all the candidate features, and the best of the features are then added into the feature set that are used to learn new candidate features, and the process repeats.

2.2.2.1 *Evaluation Methods*

In this paper, we use two evaluation methods: RlogF metric (M-method) and T score (T-method).

1) M-method

We score each word with the RlogF metric[17] previously used by Riloff. The score of a word is computed as:

$$M(w_i) = Log_2 F(w_i, X) \times R_i \tag{1}$$

Where $F(w_i,X)$ is the frequency of co-occurrence of word w_i and X (set of seed words) in the same sentence, $F(w_i)$ is the frequency of w_i in the corpus, and $R_i=F(w_i,X)/F(w_i)$.

The RlogF metric tries to strike a balance between reliability and frequency: R is high when the word is highly correlated with set of seed words (the category), and F is high when the word and X highly co-occur in the same sentence. In this paper, if w_i wants to be a feature, both of the two conditions must be satisfied: 1) R_i of w_i should be greater than R_{min}; 2) M_i of w_i should be greater than M_{min}.

2) T-method

In this paper, we define a computation formula for T score evaluation method (T-method) described as:

$$T(w_i) = \frac{P(w_i, X) - P(w_i)P(X)}{\sqrt{\frac{P(w_i, X)}{N}}} \tag{2}$$

Where $P(w_i,X)$ is the probability of co-occurrence of word w_i and X (set of seed words) in the same sentence, $P(w_i)$ is the probability of occurrence of w_i, P(X) is the probability of occurrence of X as a class. N is the total number of sentences in corpus. More higher $T(w_i)$ of word w_i, the more relevant it is to corresponding category.

2.2.2.2 *Feature Learning Bootstrapping Algorithm*

Figure 3 outlines our feature learning bootstrapping algorithm (FLB), which iteratively learns features from a large amount of unlabeled documents when some seed words are given. And the new features are identified as new seed words by *Feature Learner* based on both the original seed words and the new seed words. These new learned features are added into the feature set. Then the iteratively learning process repeats.

In Figure 3, we define that C denotes a large size of unlabeled data (segmented sentences), W is a set of candidate words, W_1 is a set of candidate feature, K is a set of hand-selected seed words as showed in Table 1. F denotes the feature set. E denotes score of a candidate feature using M-method or T-method.

2.2.3 Experiments of Feature Learning Bootstrapping Algorithm

We use the corpus from 1996-1998 *People's Daily* (includes articles of 30 months) as unlabeled data. We name the corpus as PDC. The data set contains 1,630,000 sentences. We use the toolkit *CipSegSDK*[18] for text segmentation. In the experiments,

---

Input: C, W, K
Initialization:
Put all k in K into F
R_{min} = R_Init_Value;
Features Learner Bootstrapping:
a) Select w whose R(w) > R_{min} from W, and add w to W_1
b) If $W_1 \subset \Phi$, R_{min} -=R_Step, go to a)
c) Score all words in W_1
d) F_New = the words whose E is greater than E_{min}
e) Put all f in F_New into S
f) F_Best = the top 10 scoring words from S not already in F
g) Put all f in F_Best into F, and remove all f from W
h) If total number of learned features is larger than predefined number, then STOP, otherwise Go to a) continue.
Output: F

Fig. 3. FLB Algorithm

to evaluate performance of feature learning based on two evaluation methods, we select four categories to be tested, including finance, military, sports and law. Ten seed words for each category are showed in Table 1. In this experiment we use the following setting:

$$F_{min}=10,\ R\_Init\_Value=0.5,\ R\_Step=0.05,\ M_{min}=log_2(10)*0.5,\ T_{min}=2.576,$$

At each iteration, we select 10 new seed words. According to human judgments, figure 4 shows relationship between loop number of iterative learning and average precision of features for four categories using M-method and T-method.

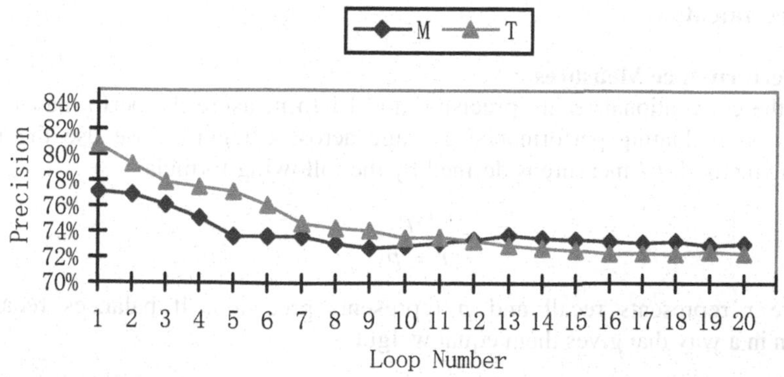

Fig. 4. Relationship between loop number and average precision

Experiment results show that M-method is better than T-method once the number of learned features is larger than 120. So we use M-method as the evaluation method for feature learning technique in our text categorization system.

3 Text Classifier

3.1 Modification of the Multinomial Naïve Bayes Classifier

We use naïve Bayes for classifying documents. We only describe multinomial naïve Bayes briefly since full details have been presented in the paper[6]. The basic idea in naïve Bayes approaches is to use the joint probabilities of words and categories to estimate the probabilities of categories when a document is given. Given a document *d* for classification, we calculate the probabilities of each category *c* as follows:

$$P(c \mid d) = \frac{P(c)P(d \mid c)}{P(d)} = P(c)\prod_{i=1}^{|T|} \frac{P(t_i \mid c)^{N(t_i|d)}}{N(t_i \mid d)!} \tag{3}$$

Where $N(t_i|d)$ is the frequency of word t_i in document *d,* T is the vocabulary and |T| is the size of T, t_i is the ith word in the vocabulary, and $P(t_i|c)$ thus represents the probability that a randomly drawn word from a randomly drawn document in category *c* will be the word t_i. In our naïve Bayes classifier, the probability $P(t_i|c)$ is estimated as:

$$P(t_i \mid c) = \frac{M(t_i, X_c) + 0.1}{\sum_{j=1}^{|T|} M(t_j, X_c) + 0.1|T|} \tag{4}$$

Where X_c denotes the set of seed words for category *c*. $M(t_i, X_c)$ denotes value of RlogF between t_i and X_c. Because we have not labeled training collection, so we suppose that for all categories probability P(c) in formula (3) is given equal value.

3.2 Experiments

3.2.1 Performance Measures

We use the conventional recall, precision and F1 to measure the performance of the system. For evaluating performance average across categories, we use the micro-averaging method. *F1* measure is defined by the following formula:

$$F_1 = \frac{2rp}{r+p} \tag{5}$$

Where *r* represents recall and *p* represents precision. It balances recall and precision in a way that gives them equal weight.

3.2.2 Experimental Setting

The NEU_TC data set contains web pages collected from web sites. The pages are divided into 10 categories: IT, finance, military, education, sports, recreation, house, law, profession and tour, which consists of 14,405 documents. In the experiments, we use 3000 documents (300 documents for each category) for training NB by supervised learning. The rest of data set is used to test, and it consists of 11,405 documents. We construct three text categorization models. The first model is *naïve Bayes by supervised learning* named **NB_SL** in which Features is selected by ranking features according to their information gain (IG) with respect to the category. The second model is *naïve Bayes by unsupervised feature learning algorithm* as **NB_FLB** which does not require labeled training documents, and uses formula (4) to estimate the probability $P(t_i|c)$ in the formula (3). The third model is *naïve Bayes by unsupervised feature learning algorithm as* **NB_FLB_SL** which uses learned features same as in NB_FLB, and uses all labeled training collection to estimate the probability $P(t_i|c)$.

3.2.3 Experimental Results

In our experiments, we compare the performance of NB_FLB with NB_SL and NB_FLB_SL. We use all the sentences to learn new features and train NB_FLB and NB_FLB_SL classifier, and vary number of labeled documents to train NB_SL classifier. In the figure 5, NB_SL100, NB_SL200, NB_SL300, NB_SL500 and NB_SL3000 refer to number of labeled training documents for NB_SL classifier are 100, 200, 300, 500, 3000, respectively. We use 3000 training documents to estimate the probability P(ti|c) for NB_FLB_SL classifier.

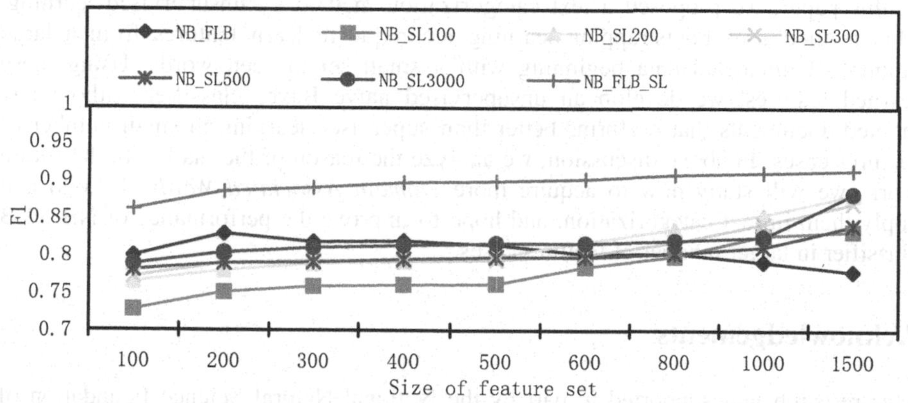

Fig. 5. Experimental Results of NB_FLB, NB_SL and NB_FLB_SL classifier

It is interesting to note that in small number of features cases, NB_FLB classifier always performs better than NB_SL classifier with IG. Even using 3000 documents for training, NB_SL with IG provides a F1 of 2.5% lower than NB_FLB when the number of features is 200. However, Figure 5 shows that once increasing the number of features, the performance of NB_FLB starts to decline and the performance of NB_SL with IG increases continually. The performance of NB_FLB_SL classifier using labeled training data is better than other models.

3.2.4 Discussion

First, we investigate the reason why adding more features the performance of NB_FLB classifier is declined. Because the set of later learned features include more "irrelevant words" than in the set of previous learned features. Here "relevant words" for each category refer to the words that are strongly indicative to the category on the basis of human judgments. For iterative learning based on unreliable learned features, more and more irrelevant words will be learned as features for the category later. And these words hurt performance of NB_FLB classifier.

Second, we investigate the reason why NB_FLB outperforms NB_SL in small number of features cases. We collect the features for each category in both NB_FLB and NB_SL classifiers, and sort them by their score. We find NB_FLB obviously has more relevant words than NB_SL with IG in top 200 feature set by human judgment.

Third, we investigate the reason why the performance of NB_FLB_SL classifier is better than other models. There are two reasons. 1) Parameters of naïve Bayes model estimated by labeled training collection are better than by unlabeled collection. 2) As above mentioned, according to human judgments, these features learned by FLB algorithm are more relevant to categories than by IG in small number of features cases. We find that some learned features could be considered as *Domain Associated Words* (DAWs). We believe DAWs are very useful to text categorization.

4 Conclusion

In this paper, we proposed a text categorization method by unsupervised learning. This method uses bootstrapping learning technique to learn features from a large amount of unlabeled data beginning with a small set of seed words. Using these learned features, we develop an unsupervised naïve Bayes classifier without any labeled documents that performs better than supervised learning in small number of features cases. In above discussion, we analyze the reason of the matter. In the future work, we will study how to acquire more *Domain Associated Words* (DAWs) and apply them in text categorization, and hope to improve the performance of NB_FLB classifier in larger number of features cases.

Acknowledgements

This research was supported in part by the National Natural Science Foundation of China & Microsoft Asia Research (No. 60203019) and the Key Project of Chinese Ministry of Education (No. 104065).

References

1. David J. Ittner, David D. Lewis, and David D. Ahn, Text categorization of low quality images. In Symposium on Document Analysis and Information Retrieval, Las Vegas, Las Vegas(1995)
2. D. Lewis, R. Schapire, J. Callan, and R. Papka, Training Algorithms for Linear Text Classifiers, Proceedings of ACM SIGIR (1996)298-306
3. T. Joachims, Text categorization with Support Vector Machines: Learning with many relevant features. In Machine Learning: ECML-98, Tenth European Conference on Machine Learning (1998)137-142
4. D. Lewis, A Comparison of Two Learning Algorithms for Text Categorization, Symposium on Document Analysis and IR(1994)

5. K. Nigam, John Lafferty, and Andrew McCallum, Using maximum entropy for text classification. In IJCAI-99 Workshop on Machine Learning for Information Filtering(1999)61-67
6. A. McCallum and K. Nigam, A Comparison of Event Models for naïve Bayes Text Classification, In AAAI-98 Workshop on Learning for Text Categorization(1998)
7. T. Kohonen, S. Kaski, K. Lagus, J. Salojarvi, J. Honkela, V. Paatero, and A. Saarela. Self organization of a massive document collection. IEEE Transactions on Neural Networks, 11(3), (2000)574–585
8. A. Rauber, E. Schweighofer, and D. Merkl. Text classification and labelling of document clusters with self-organising maps. Journal of the Austrian Society for Artificial Intelligence, 19(3),(2000)17–23
9. G.A. Carpenter, S. Grossberg, and J.H. Reynolds. ARTMAP: Supervised realtime learning and classification of nonstationary data by self-organizing neural network. Neural Networks, vol.4(1991)565–588
10. A.H. Tan. Adaptive resonance associative map. Neural Networks, 8(3)(1995)437–446
11. V. Castelli and T. M. Cover. The relative value of labeled and unlabeled samples in pattern recognition with unknown mixing parameter. IEEE Transactions on Information Theory, November(1996)
12. Youngjoong Ko and Jungyun Sco, Automatic Text Categorization by Unsupervised Learning, COLING02(2002)
13. Y. Yang and J.P. Pedersen, Feature selection in statistical learning of text categorization, In the 14th Int. Conf. on Machine Learning (1997)412-420
14. Steven Abney, Bootstrapping, Proceedings of the 40th Annual Meeting of the Association for Computational Linguistics (ACL-02) (2002)
15. A. Blum and T. Mitchell, Combining labeled and unlabeled data with co-training. In COLT: Proceedings of the Workshop on Computational Learning Theory(1998)
16. Cong Li and Hang Li, Word Translation Disambiguation Using Bilingual Bootstrapping. Proceedings of the 40th Annual Meeting of Association for Computational Linguistics (ACL'02)(2002)
17. Ellen Riloff, Rosie Jones, Learning Dictionaries for Information Extraction by Multi-Level Bootstrapping, Proceedings of the Sixteenth National Conference on Artificial Intelligence(AAAI-99)(1999)
18. T.S. Yao, et al, Natural Language Processing-research on making computers understand human languages, Tsinghua University Press(2002)(In Chinese).

On Word Frequency Information and Negative Evidence in Naive Bayes Text Classification

Karl-Michael Schneider

Department of General Linguistics
University of Passau, Germany
schneide@phil.uni-passau.de

Abstract. The Naive Bayes classifier exists in different versions. One version, called multi-variate Bernoulli or binary independence model, uses binary word occurrence vectors, while the multinomial model uses word frequency counts. Many publications cite this difference as the main reason for the superior performance of the multinomial Naive Bayes classifier. We argue that this is not true. We show that when all word frequency information is eliminated from the document vectors, the multinomial Naive Bayes model performs even better. Moreover, we argue that the main reason for the difference in performance is the way that negative evidence, i.e. evidence from words that do not occur in a document, is incorporated in the model. Therefore, this paper aims at a better understanding and a clarification of the difference between the two probabilistic models of Naive Bayes.

1 Introduction

Naive Bayes is a popular machine learning technique for text classification because it performs well despite its simplicity [1, 2]. Naive Bayes comes in different versions, depending on how text documents are represented [3, 4]. In one version, a document is represented as a binary vector of word occurrences: Each component of a document vector corresponds to a word from a fixed vocabulary, and the component is one if the word occurs in the document and zero otherwise. This is called multi-variate Bernoulli model (aka binary independence model) because a document vector can be regarded as the outcome of multiple independent Bernoulli experiments. In another version, a document is represented as a vector of word counts: Each component indicates the number of occurrences of the corresponding word in the document. This is called multinomial Naive Bayes model because the probability of a document vector is given by a multinomial distribution.

Previous studies have found that the multinomial version of Naive Bayes usually gives higher classification accuracy than the multi-variate Bernoulli version [3, 4]. Many people who use multinomial Naive Bayes, even the authors of these studies, attribute its superior performance to the fact that the document representation captures word frequency information in documents, whereas the multi-variate Bernoulli version does not.

J. L. Vicedo et al. (Eds.): EsTAL 2004, LNAI 3230, pp. 474–485, 2004.

This paper argues that word frequency information is not what makes the multinomial Naive Bayes classifier superior in the first place. We show that removal of the word frequency information results in increased, rather than decreased performance. Furthermore, we argue that the difference in performance between the two versions of Naive Bayes should be attributed to the way the two models treat negative evidence, i.e. evidence from words that do *not* occur in a document.

The rest of the paper is structured as follows. In Sect. 2 we review the two versions of the Naive Bayes classifier. Sections 3 and 4 are concerned with the role that word frequency information and negative evidence play in the Naive Bayes models. In Sect. 5 we discuss our results and show relations to other work. Finally, in Sect. 6 we draw some conclusions.

2 Naive Bayes

All Naive Bayes classifiers are based on the assumption that documents are generated by a parametric mixture model, where the mixture components correspond to the possible classes [3]. A document is created by choosing a class and then letting the corresponding mixture component create the document according to its parameters. The total probability, or likelihood, of d is

$$p(d) = \sum_{j=1}^{|C|} p(c_j)p(d|c_j) \tag{1}$$

where $p(c_j)$ is the prior probability that class c_j is chosen, and $p(d|c_j)$ is the probability that the mixture component c_j generates document d. Using Bayes' rule, the model can be inverted to get the posterior probability that d was generated by the mixture component c_j:

$$p(c_j|d) = \frac{p(c_j)p(d|c_j)}{p(d)} \tag{2}$$

To classify a document, choose the class with maximum posterior probability, given the document:

$$c^*(d) = \operatorname*{argmax}_j p(c_j)p(d|c_j) \tag{3}$$

Note that we have ignored $p(d)$ in (3) because it does not depend on the class. The prior probabilities $p(c_j)$ are estimated from a training corpus by counting the number of training documents in class c_j and dividing by the total number of training documents.

The distribution of documents in each class, $p(d|c_j)$, cannot be estimated directly. Rather, it is assumed that documents are composed from smaller units, usually words or word stems. To make the estimation of parameters tractable, we make the Naive Bayes assumption: that the basic units are distributed independently. The different versions of Naive Bayes make different assumptions to model the composition of documents from the basic units.

2.1 Multi-variate Bernoulli Model

In this version, each word w_t in a fixed vocabulary V is modeled by a random variable $W_t \in \{0, 1\}$ with distribution $p(w_t|c_j) = p(W_t = 1|c_j)$. w_t is included in a document if and only if the outcome of W_t is one. Thus a document is represented as a binary vector $d = \langle x_t \rangle_{t=1\ldots|V|}$. The distribution of documents, assuming independence, is then given by the formula:

$$p(d|c_j) = \prod_{t=1}^{|V|} p(w_t|c_j)^{x_t}(1 - p(w_t|c_j))^{(1-x_t)} \tag{4}$$

The parameters $p(w_t|c_j)$ are estimated from labeled training documents using maximum likelihood estimation with a Laplacean prior, as the fraction of training documents in class c_j that contain the word w_t:

$$p(w_t|c_j) = \frac{1 + B_{jt}}{2 + |c_j|} \tag{5}$$

where B_{jt} is the number of training documents in c_j that contain w_t.

2.2 Multinomial Model

In the multinomial version, a document d is modeled as the outcome of $|d|$ independent trials on a single random variable W that takes on values $w_t \in V$ with probabilities $p(w_t|c_j)$ and $\sum_{t=1}^{|V|} p(w_t|c_j) = 1$. Each trial with outcome w_t yields an independent occurrence of w_t in d. Thus a document is represented as a vector of word counts $d = \langle x_t \rangle_{t=1\ldots|V|}$ where each x_t is the number of trials with outcome w_t, i.e. the number of times w_t occurs in d. The probability of d is given by the multinomial distribution:

$$p(d|c_j) = p(|d|)|d|! \prod_{t=1}^{|V|} \frac{p(w_t|c_j)^{x_t}}{x_t!} \tag{6}$$

Here we assume that the length of a document is chosen according to some length distribution, independently of the class.

The parameters $p(w_t|c_j)$ are estimated by counting the occurrences of w_t in all training documents in c_j, using a Laplacean prior:

$$p(w_t|c_j) = \frac{1 + N_{jt}}{|V| + N_j} \tag{7}$$

where N_{jt} is the number of occurrences of w_t in the training documents in c_j and N_j is the total number of word occurrences in c_j.

3 Word Frequency Information

In [3] it was found that the multinomial model outperformed the multi-variate Bernoulli model consistently on five text categorization datasets, especially for larger vocabulary sizes. In [4] it was found that the multinomial model performed best among four probabilistic models, including the multi-variate Bernoulli model, on three text categorization datasets. Both studies point out as the main distinguishing factor of the two models the fact that the multinomial model takes the frequency of appearance of a word into account. Although [4] also study the different forms of independence assumptions the two models make, many authors refer only to this point and attribute the superior performance of the multinomial Naive Bayes classifier solely to the word frequency information.

We argue that capturing word frequency information is not the main factor that distinguishes the multinomial model from the multi-variate Bernoulli model. In this section we show that word frequency information does not account for the superior performance of the multinomial model, while the next section suggests that the way in which negative evidence is incorporated is more important.

We perform classification experiments on three publicly available datasets: 20 Newsgroups, WebKB and ling-spam (see the appendix for a description). To see the influence of term frequency on classification, we apply a simple transformation to the documents in the training and test set: $x'_t = \min\{x_t, 1\}$. This has the effect of replacing multiple occurrences of the same word in a document with a single occurrence. Figure 3 shows classification accuracy on the 20 Newsgroups dataset. Figure 2 shows classification accuracy on the ling-spam corpus. Figure 3 shows classification accuracy on the WebKB dataset. In all three experiments we used a multinomial Naive Bayes classifier, applied to the raw data and to

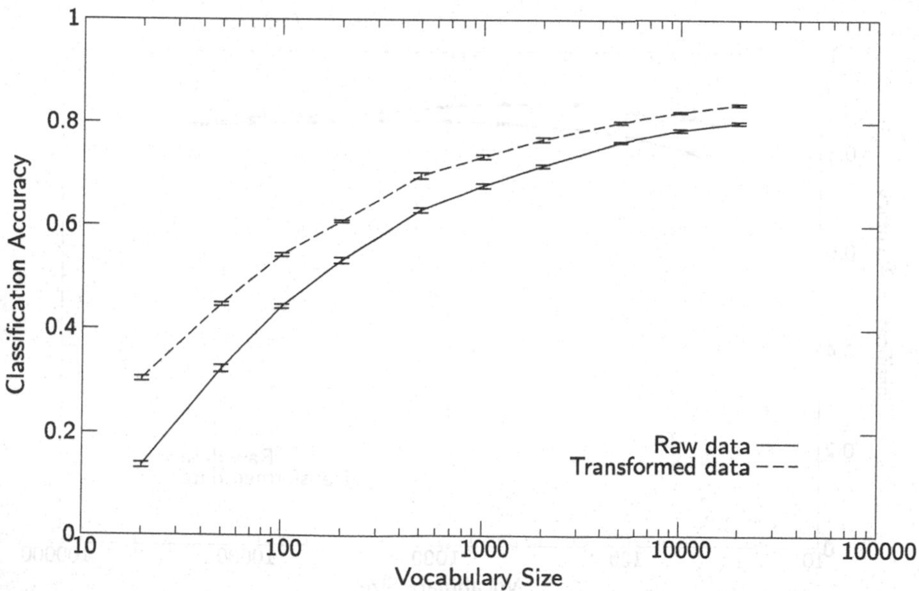

Fig. 1. Classification accuracy for multinomial Naive Bayes on the 20 Newsgroups dataset with raw and transformed word counts. Results are averaged over five cross-validation trials, with small error bars shown. The number of selected features varies from 20 to 20000

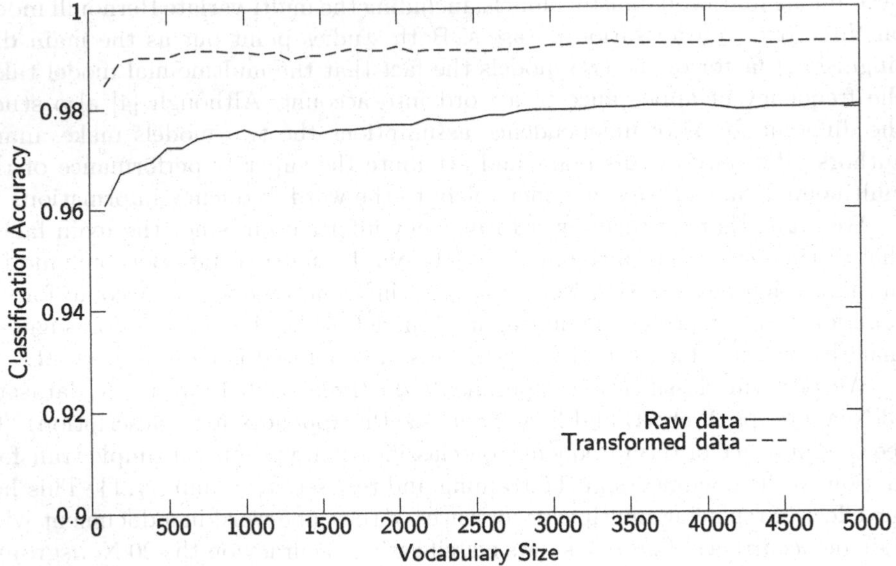

Fig. 2. Classification accuracy for multinomial Naive Bayes on the ling-spam corpus with raw and transformed word counts. Results are averaged over ten cross-validation trials

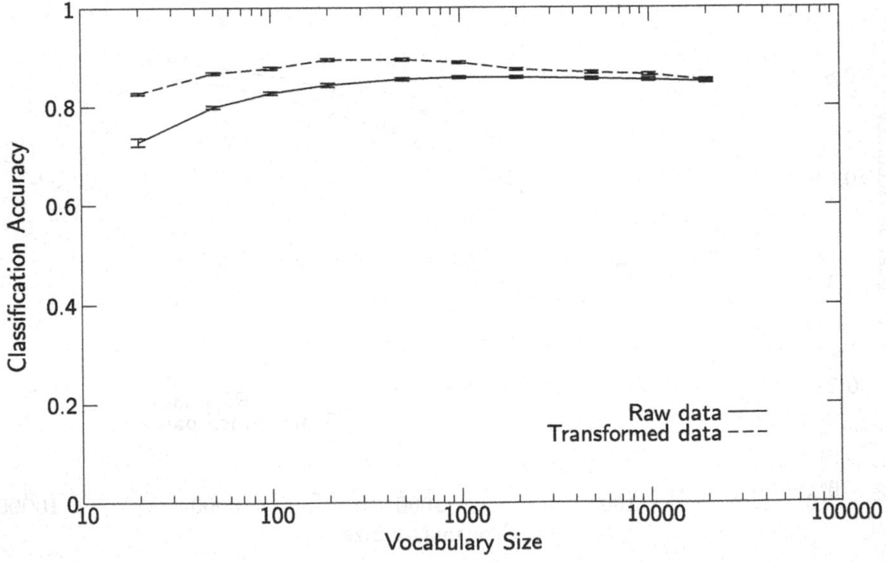

Fig. 3. Classification accuracy for multinomial Naive Bayes on the WebKB dataset with raw and transformed word counts. Results are averaged over ten cross-validation trials with random splits, using 70% of the data for training and 30% for testing. Small error bars are shown

the transformed documents. We reduced the vocabulary size by selecting the words with the highest mutual information [5] with the class variable (see [3] for details). Using the transformed word counts (i.e. with the word frequency removed) leads to higher classification accuracy on all three datasets. For WebKB the improvement is significant up to 5000 words at the 0.99 confidence level using a two-tailed paired t-test. For the other datasets, the improvement is significant over the full range at the 0.99 confidence level. The difference is more pronounced for smaller vocabulary sizes.

4 Negative Evidence

Why does the multinomial Naive Bayes model perform better than the multivariate Bernoulli model? We use the ling-spam corpus as a case study. To get a clue, we plot separate recall curves for the ling class and spam class (Fig. 4 and 5). The multi-variate Bernoulli model has high ling recall but poor spam recall, whereas recall in the multinomial model is much more balanced. This bias in recall is somehow caused by the particular properties of the ling-spam corpus. Table 1 shows some statistics of the ling-spam corpus. Note that 8.3% of the words do *not* occur in ling documents while 81.2% of the words do *not* occur in spam documents.

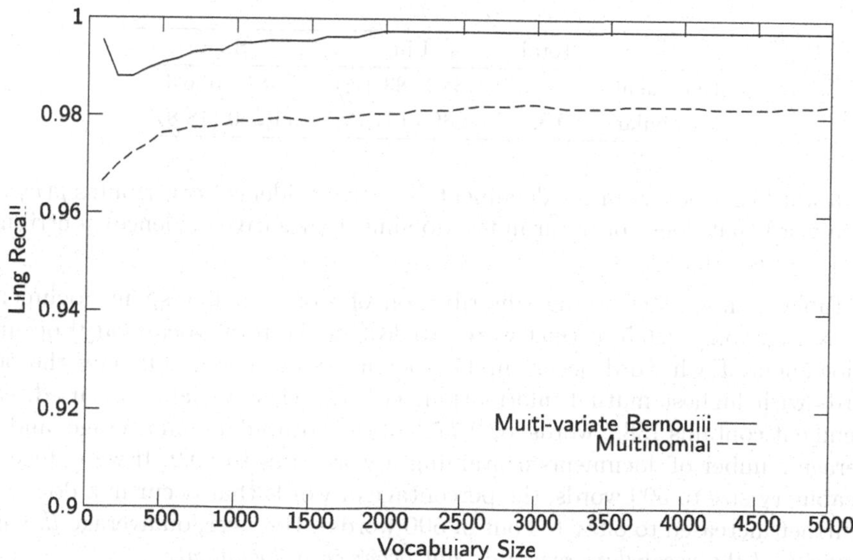

Fig. 4. Ling recall for multi-variate Bernoulli and multinomial Naive Bayes on the ling-spam corpus, with 10-fold cross validation

Consider the multi-variate Bernoulli distribution (4): Each word in the vocabulary contributes to the probability of a document in one of two ways, depending on whether it occurs in the document or not:

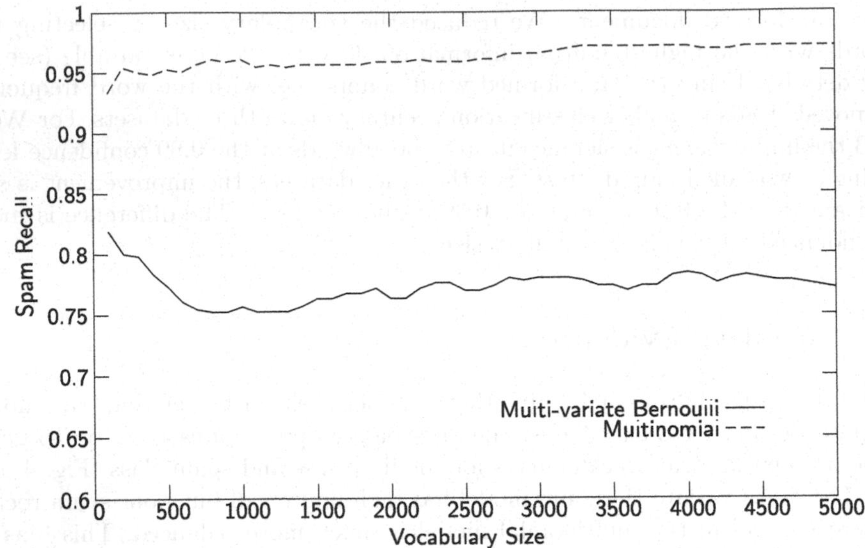

Fig. 5. Spam recall for multi-variate Bernoulli and multinomial Naive Bayes on the ling-spam corpus, with 10-fold cross validation

Table 1. Statistics of the ling-spam corpus

	Total	Ling	Spam
Documents	2893	2412 (83.4%)	481 (16.6%)
Vocabulary	59,829	54,860 (91.7%)	11,250 (18.8%)

– a word that occurs in the document (positive evidence) contributes $p(w_t|c_j)$.
– a word that does not occur in the document (negative evidence) contributes $1 - p(w_t|c_j)$.

Table 2 shows the average distribution of words in ling-spam documents. On average, only 226.5 distinct words (0.38% of the total vocabulary) occur in a document. Each word occurs in 11 documents on average. If only the 5000 words with highest mutual information with the class variable are used, each document contains 138.5 words, or 2.77% of the vocabulary, on average, and the average number of documents containing a word rises to 80.2. If we reduce the vocabulary size to 500 words, the percentage of words that occur in a document is further increased to 8.8% (44 out of 500 words). However, on average *the large majority of the vocabulary words do not occur in a document.*

This observation implies that the probability of a document is mostly determined on the basis of words that do not occur in the document, i.e. *the classification of documents is heavily dominated by negative evidence.* Table 3 shows the probability of an empty document according to the multi-variate Bernoulli distribution in the ling-spam corpus. An empty document is always classified as a ling document. This can be explained as follows: First, note that there are much

Table 2. Average distribution of vocabulary words in the ling-spam corpus for three different vocabulary sizes. Shown are the average number of distinct words per document and the average number of1 documents in which a word occurs

Vocabulary	Total		Ling		Spam	
	Words	Documents	Words	Documents	Words	Documents
Full	226.5	11.0	226.9	9.1	224.5	1.8
MI 5000	138.5	80.2	133.8	64.5	162.5	15.6
MI 500	44.0	254.5	39.6	190.9	66.2	63.7

Table 3. Probability of an empty document in the ling-spam corpus, for three different vocabulary sizes. Parameters are estimated according to (5) using the full corpus

Vocabulary	Total	Ling	Spam
Full	3.21e-137	1.29e-131	5.2e-174
MI 5000	6.44e-78	8.4e-76	1.45e-96
MI 500	5.21e-24	1.41e-22	3.59e-37

more ling words than spam words (cf. Table 1). However, the number of distinct words in ling documents is not higher than in spam documents (cf. Table 2), especially when the full vocabulary is not used. Therefore, the probability of each word in the ling class is lower than in the spam class. According to Table 2, when a document is classified most of the words are counted as negative evidence (in an empty document, all words are counted as negative evidence). Therefore their contribution to the probability of a document is higher in the ling class than in the spam class, because their conditional probability is lower in the ling class. Note that the impact of the prior probabilities in (4) is negligible.

The impact of negative evidence on classification can be visualized using the *weight of evidence* of a word for each of the two classes. In Fig. 6 and 7 we plot the weight of evidence of a word for the spam class in the ling-spam corpus against the weight of evidence for the ling class when the word is *not* in the document, for each of the 500, respectively 5000, words with highest mutual information. This plot visualizes how much weight the multi-variate Bernoulli model gives to each word as an indicator for the class of a document when that word is *not* in the document. One can see that all of the selected words occur more frequently in one class than the other (all words are either above or below the diagonal), but a larger number of words is used as evidence for the ling class when they do not appear in a document.

5 Discussion

In [4] it was shown that the multinomial model defined in (6) is a modified Naive Bayes Poisson model that assumes independence of document length and document class. In the Naive Bayes Poisson model, each word w_t is modeled as a

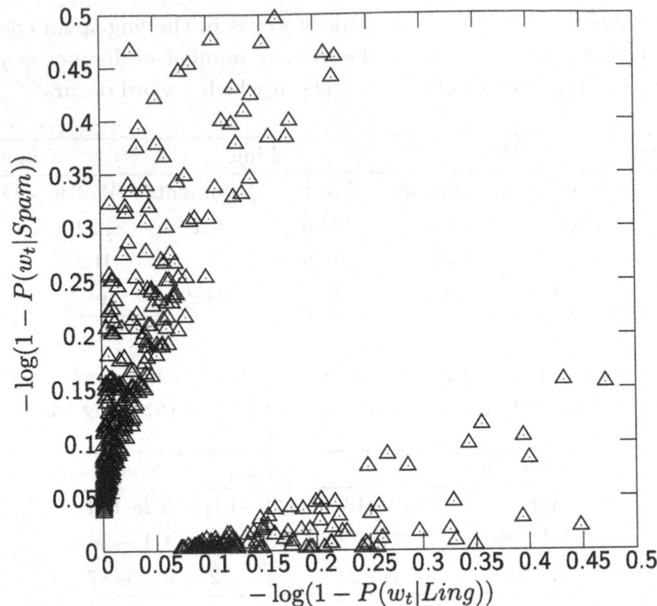

Fig. 6. Weight of evidence of words that do not appear in a document for the 500 words in the ling-spam corpus with highest mutual information with the class variable. Lower values mean stronger evidence. For example, a word in the upper left region of the scatter plot means evidence for the ling class when that word does not appear in a document. Probabilities are estimated according to (5) using the full corpus

random variable W_t that takes on non-negative values representing the number of occurrences in a document, thus incorporating word frequencies directly. The variables W_t have a Poisson distribution, and the Naive Bayes Poisson model assumes independence between the variables W_t. Note that in this model the length of a document is dependent on the class. However, in [4] it was found that the Poisson model was not superior to the multinomial model. The multinomial Naive Bayes model also assumes that the word counts in a document vector have a Poisson distribution.

Why is the performance of the multinomial Naive Bayes classifier improved when the word frequency information is eliminated in the documents? In [6] and [7] the distribution of terms in documents was studied. It was found that terms often exhibit *burstiness*: the probability that a term appears a second time in a document is much larger than the probability that it appears at all in a document. The Poisson distribution does not fit this behaviour well. In [6, 7] more sophisticated distributions (mixtures of Poisson distributions) were employed to model the distribution of terms in documents more accurately. However, in [8] it was found that changing the word counts in the document vectors with a simple transformation like $x'_t = \log(d + x_t)$ is sufficient to improve the performance of the multinomial Naive Bayes classifier. This transformation has the effect of pushing down larger word counts, thus giving documents with multiple occurrences of the same word a higher probability in the multinomial model.

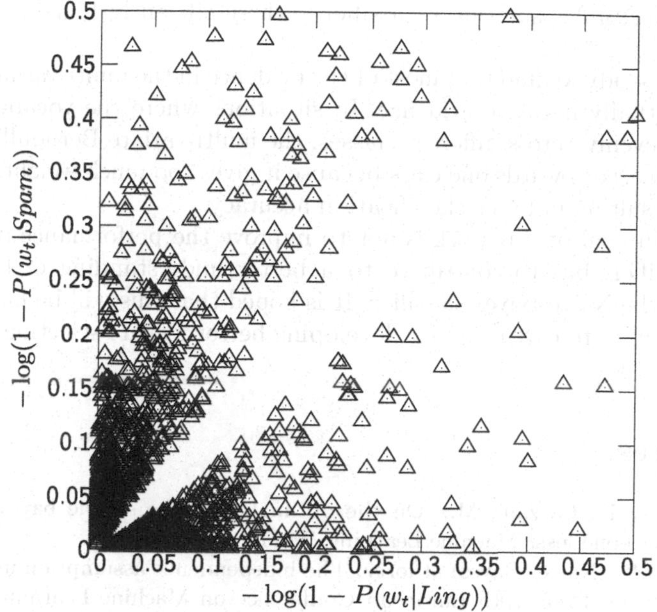

Fig. 7. Weight of evidence of words that do not appear in a document for the 5000 words in the ling-spam corpus with highest mutual information with the class variable

The transformation that we used in our experiments (Sect. 3) eliminates the word frequency information in the document vectors completely, reducing it to binary word occurrence information, while also improving classification accuracy.

Then what is the difference between the multi-variate Bernoulli and the multinomial Naive Bayes classifier? The multi-variate Bernoulli distribution (4) gives equal weight to positive and negative evidence, whereas in the multinomial model (6) each word $w_t \in V$ contributes to $p(d|c_j)$ according to the number of times w_t occurs in d. In [3] it was noted that words that do not occur in d contribute to $p(d|c_j)$ indirectly because the relative frequency of these words is encoded in the class-conditional probabilities $p(w_t|c_j)$. When a word appears more frequently in the training documents, it gets a higher probability, and the probability of the other words will be lower. However, this impact of negative evidence is much lower than in the multi-variate Bernoulli model.

6 Conclusions

The multinomial Naive Bayes classifier outperforms the multi-variate Bernoulli model in the domain of text classification, not because it uses word frequency information, but because of the different ways the two models incorporate negative evidence from documents, i.e. words that do not occur in a document. In fact, eliminating all word frequency information (by a simple transformation of the document vectors) results in a classifier with significantly higher classification accuracy.

In a case study we find that most of the evidence in the multi-variate Bernoulli model is actually negative evidence. In situations where the vocabulary is distributed unevenly across different classes, the multi-variate Bernoulli model can be heavily biased towards one class because it gives too much weight to negative evidence, resulting in lower classification accuracy.

The main goal of this work is not to improve the performance of the Naive Bayes classifier, but to contribute to a better understanding of the different versions of the Naive Bayes classifier. It is hoped that this will be beneficial also for other lines of research, e.g. for developing better feature selection techniques.

References

1. Domingos, P., Pazzani, M.: On the optimality of the simple bayesian classifier under zero-one loss. Machine Learning **29** (1997) 103–130
2. Lewis, D.D.: Naive (Bayes) at forty: The independence assumption in information retrieval. In: Proc. 10th European Conference on Machine Learning (ECML98). Volume 1398 of Lecture Notes in Computer Science., Heidelberg, Springer (1998) 4–15
3. McCallum, A., Nigam, K.: A comparison of event models for Naive Bayes text classification. In: Learning for Text Categorization: Papers from the AAAI Workshop, AAAI Press (1998) 41–48 Technical Report WS-98-05.
4. Eyheramendy, S., Lewis, D.D., Madigan, D.: On the Naive Bayes model for text categorization. In Bishop, C.M., Frey, B.J., eds.: AI & Statistics 2003: Proceedings of the Ninth International Workshop on Artificial Intelligence and Statistics. (2003) 332–339
5. Cover, T.M., Thomas, J.A.: Elements of Information Theory. John Wiley, New York (1991)
6. Church, K.W., Gale, W.A.: Poisson mixtures. Natural Language Engineering **1** (1995) 163–190
7. Katz, S.M.: Distribution of content words and phrases in text and language modelling. Natural Language Engineering **2** (1996) 15–59
8. Rennie, J.D.M., Shih, L., Teevan, J., Karger, D.: Tackling the poor assumptions of Naive Bayes text classifiers. In Fawcett, T., Mishra, N., eds.: Proceedings of the Twentieth International Conference on Machine Learning (ICML-2003), Washington, D.C., AAAI Press (2003) 616–623
9. Androutsopoulos, I., Paliouras, G., Karkaletsis, V., Sakkis, G., Spyropoulos, C.D., Stamatopoulos, P.: Learning to filter spam e-mail: A comparison of a Naive Bayesian and a memory-based approach. In Zaragoza, H., Gallinari, P., Rajman, M., eds.: Proc. Workshop on Machine Learning and Textual Information Access, 4th European Conference on Principles and Practice of Knowledge Discovery in Databases (PKDD 2000), Lyon, France (2000) 1–13
10. Craven, M., DiPasquo, D., Freitag, D., McCallum, A., Mitchell, T., Nigam, K., Slattery, S.: Learning to extract symbolic knowledge from the world wide web. In: Proc. 15th Conference of the American Association for Artificial Intelligence (AAAI-98), Madison, WI, AAAI Press (1998) 509–516

A Datasets

The 20 Newsgroups dataset consists of 19,997 documents distributed evenly across 20 different newsgroups. It is available from http://people.csail.mit.edu/people/jrennie/20Newsgroups/. We removed all newsgroup headers and used only words consisting of alphabetic characters as tokens, after applying a stoplist and converting to lower case.

The ling-spam corpus consists of messages from a linguistics mailing list and spam messages [9]. It is available from the publications section of http://www.aueb.gr/users/ion/. The messages have been tokenized and lemmatized, with all attachments, HTML tags and E-mail headers (except the subject) removed.

The WebKB dataset contains web pages gathered from computer science departments [10]. It is available from http://www.cs.cmu.edu/afs/cs.cmu.edu/project/theo-20/www/data/. We use only the four most populous classes *course*, *faculty*, *project* and *student*. We stripped all HTML tags and used only words and numbers as tokens, after converting to lower case.

Author Index

Lecture Notes in Artificial Intelligence (LNAI)

Vol. 3265: R.E. Frederking, K.B. Taylor (Eds.), Machine Translation: From Real Users to Research. XI, 392 pages. 2004.

Vol. 3264: G. Paliouras, Y. Sakakibara (Eds.), Grammatical Inference: Algorithms and Applications. XI, 291 pages. 2004.

Vol. 3257: E. Motta, N.R. Shadbolt, A. Stutt, N. Gibbins (Eds.), Engineering Knowledge in the Age of the Semantic Web. XVII, 517 pages. 2004.

Vol. 3249: B. Buchberger, J.A. Campbell (Eds.), Artificial Intelligence and Symbolic Computation. X, 285 pages. 2004.

Vol. 3245: E. Suzuki, S. Arikawa (Eds.), Discovery Science. XIV, 430 pages. 2004.

Vol. 3244: S. Ben-David, J. Case, A. Maruoka (Eds.), Algorithmic Learning Theory. XIV, 505 pages. 2004.

Vol. 3238: S. Biundo, T. Frühwirth, G. Palm (Eds.), KI 2004: Advances in Artificial Intelligence. XI, 467 pages. 2004.

Vol. 3230: J.L. Vicedo, P. Martínez-Barco, R. Muñoz, M.Saiz Noeda (Eds.), Advances in Natural Language Processing. XII, 488 pages. 2004.

Vol. 3229: J.J. Alferes, J. Leite (Eds.), Logics in Artificial Intelligence. XIV, 744 pages. 2004.

Vol. 3215: M.G.. Negoita, R.J. Howlett, L.C. Jain (Eds.), Knowledge-Based Intelligent Information and Engineering Systems. LVII, 906 pages. 2004.

Vol. 3214: M.G.. Negoita, R.J. Howlett, L.C. Jain (Eds.), Knowledge-Based Intelligent Information and Engineering Systems. LVIII, 1302 pages. 2004.

Vol. 3213: M.G.. Negoita, R.J. Howlett, L.C. Jain (Eds.), Knowledge-Based Intelligent Information and Engineering Systems. LVIII, 1280 pages. 2004.

Vol. 3209: B. Berendt, A. Hotho, D. Mladenic, M. van Someren, M. Spiliopoulou, G. Stumme (Eds.), Web Mining: From Web to Semantic Web. IX, 201 pages. 2004.

Vol. 3206: P. Sojka, I. Kopecek, K. Pala (Eds.), Text, Speech and Dialogue. XIII, 667 pages. 2004.

Vol. 3202: J.-F. Boulicaut, F. Esposito, F. Giannotti, D. Pedreschi (Eds.), Knowledge Discovery in Databases: PKDD 2004. XIX, 560 pages. 2004.

Vol. 3201: J.-F. Boulicaut, F. Esposito, F. Giannotti, D. Pedreschi (Eds.), Machine Learning: ECML 2004. XVIII, 580 pages. 2004.

Vol. 3194: R. Camacho, R. King, A. Srinivasan (Eds.), Inductive Logic Programming. XI, 361 pages. 2004.

Vol. 3192: C. Bussler, D. Fensel (Eds.), Artificial Intelligence: Methodology, Systems, and Applications. XIII, 522 pages. 2004.

Vol. 3191: M. Klusch, S. Ossowski, V. Kashyap, R. Unland (Eds.), Cooperative Information Agents VIII. XI, 303 pages. 2004.

Vol. 3187: G. Lindemann, J. Denzinger, I.J. Timm, R. Unland (Eds.), Multiagent System Technologies. XIII, 341 pages. 2004.

Vol. 3176: O. Bousquet, U. von Luxburg, G. Rätsch (Eds.), Advanced Lectures on Machine Learning. IX, 241 pages. 2004.

Vol. 3171: A.L.C. Bazzan, S. Labidi (Eds.), Advances in Artificial Intelligence – SBIA 2004. XVII, 548 pages. 2004.

Vol. 3159: U. Visser, Intelligent Information Integration for the Semantic Web. XIV, 150 pages. 2004.

Vol. 3157: C. Zhang, H. W. Guesgen, W.K. Yeap (Eds.), PRICAI 2004: Trends in Artificial Intelligence. XX, 1023 pages. 2004.

Vol. 3155: P. Funk, P.A. González Calero (Eds.), Advances in Case-Based Reasoning. XIII, 822 pages. 2004.

Vol. 3139: F. Iida, R. Pfeifer, L. Steels, Y. Kuniyoshi (Eds.), Embodied Artificial Intelligence. IX, 331 pages. 2004.

Vol. 3131: V. Torra, Y. Narukawa (Eds.), Modeling Decisions for Artificial Intelligence. XI, 327 pages. 2004.

Vol. 3127: K.E. Wolff, H.D. Pfeiffer, H.S. Delugach (Eds.), Conceptual Structures at Work. XI, 403 pages. 2004.

Vol. 3123: A. Belz, R. Evans, P. Piwek (Eds.), Natural Language Generation. X, 219 pages. 2004.

Vol. 3120: J. Shawe-Taylor, Y. Singer (Eds.), Learning Theory. X, 648 pages. 2004.

Vol. 3097: D. Basin, M. Rusinowitch (Eds.), Automated Reasoning. XII, 493 pages. 2004.

Vol. 3071: A. Omicini, P. Petta, J. Pitt (Eds.), Engineering Societies in the Agents World. XIII, 409 pages. 2004.

Vol. 3070: L. Rutkowski, J. Siekmann, R. Tadeusiewicz, L.A. Zadeh (Eds.), Artificial Intelligence and Soft Computing - ICAISC 2004. XXV, 1208 pages. 2004.

Vol. 3068: E. André, L. Dybkjær, W. Minker, P. Heisterkamp (Eds.), Affective Dialogue Systems. XII, 324 pages. 2004.

Vol. 3067: M. Dastani, J. Dix, A. El Fallah-Seghrouchni (Eds.), Programming Multi-Agent Systems. X, 221 pages. 2004.

Vol. 3066: S. Tsumoto, R. Słowiński, J. Komorowski, J.W. Grzymała-Busse (Eds.), Rough Sets and Current Trends in Computing. XX, 853 pages. 2004.

Vol. 3065: A. Lomuscio, D. Nute (Eds.), Deontic Logic in Computer Science. X, 275 pages. 2004.

Vol. 3060: A.Y. Tawfik, S.D. Goodwin (Eds.), Advances in Artificial Intelligence. XIII, 582 pages. 2004.

Vol. 3056: H. Dai, R. Srikant, C. Zhang (Eds.), Advances in Knowledge Discovery and Data Mining. XIX, 713 pages. 2004.

Vol. 3055: H. Christiansen, M.-S. Hacid, T. Andreasen, H.L. Larsen (Eds.), Flexible Query Answering Systems. X, 500 pages. 2004.

Vol. 3048: P. Faratin, D.C. Parkes, J.A. Rodríguez-Aguilar, W.E. Walsh (Eds.), Agent-Mediated Electronic Commerce V. XI, 155 pages. 2004.

Vol. 3040: R. Conejo, M. Urretavizcaya, J.-L. Pérez-de-la-Cruz (Eds.), Current Topics in Artificial Intelligence. XIV, 689 pages. 2004.

Vol. 3035: M.A. Wimmer (Ed.), Knowledge Management in Electronic Government. XII, 326 pages. 2004.

Vol. 3034: J. Favela, E. Menasalvas, E. Chávez (Eds.), Advances in Web Intelligence. XIII, 227 pages. 2004.

Vol. 3030: P. Giorgini, B. Henderson-Sellers, M. Winikoff (Eds.), Agent-Oriented Information Systems. XIV, 207 pages. 2004.

Vol. 3029: B. Orchard, C. Yang, M. Ali (Eds.), Innovations in Applied Artificial Intelligence. XXI, 1272 pages. 2004.

Vol. 3025: G.A. Vouros, T. Panayiotopoulos (Eds.), Methods and Applications of Artificial Intelligence. XV, 546 pages. 2004.

Vol. 3020: D. Polani, B. Browning, A. Bonarini, K. Yoshida (Eds.), RoboCup 2003: Robot Soccer World Cup VII. XVI, 767 pages. 2004.

Vol. 3012: K. Kurumatani, S.-H. Chen, A. Ohuchi (Eds.), Multi-Agents for Mass User Support. X, 217 pages. 2004.

Vol. 3010: K.R. Apt, F. Fages, F. Rossi, P. Szeredi, J. Váncza (Eds.), Recent Advances in Constraints. VIII, 285 pages. 2004.

Vol. 2990: J. Leite, A. Omicini, L. Sterling, P. Torroni (Eds.), Declarative Agent Languages and Technologies. XII, 281 pages. 2004.

Vol. 2980: A. Blackwell, K. Marriott, A. Shimojima (Eds.), Diagrammatic Representation and Inference. XV, 448 pages. 2004.

Vol. 2977: G. Di Marzo Serugendo, A. Karageorgos, O.F. Rana, F. Zambonelli (Eds.), Engineering Self-Organising Systems. X, 299 pages. 2004.

Vol. 2972: R. Monroy, G. Arroyo-Figueroa, L.E. Sucar, H. Sossa (Eds.), MICAI 2004: Advances in Artificial Intelligence. XVII, 923 pages. 2004.

Vol. 2969: M. Nickles, M. Rovatsos, G. Weiss (Eds.), Agents and Computational Autonomy. X, 275 pages. 2004.

Vol. 2961: P. Eklund (Ed.), Concept Lattices. IX, 411 pages. 2004.

Vol. 2953: K. Konrad, Model Generation for Natural Language Interpretation and Analysis. XIII, 166 pages. 2004.

Vol. 2934: G. Lindemann, D. Moldt, M. Paolucci (Eds.), Regulated Agent-Based Social Systems. X, 301 pages. 2004.

Vol. 2930: F. Winkler (Ed.), Automated Deduction in Geometry. VII, 231 pages. 2004.

Vol. 2926: L. van Elst, V. Dignum, A. Abecker (Eds.), Agent-Mediated Knowledge Management. XI, 428 pages. 2004.

Vol. 2923: V. Lifschitz, I. Niemelä (Eds.), Logic Programming and Nonmonotonic Reasoning. IX, 365 pages. 2004.

Vol. 2915: A. Camurri, G. Volpe (Eds.), Gesture-Based Communication in Human-Computer Interaction. XIII, 558 pages. 2004.

Vol. 2913: T.M. Pinkston, V.K. Prasanna (Eds.), High Performance Computing - HiPC 2003. XX, 512 pages. 2003.

Vol. 2903: T.D. Gedeon, L.C.C. Fung (Eds.), AI 2003: Advances in Artificial Intelligence. XVI, 1075 pages. 2003.

Vol. 2902: F.M. Pires, S.P. Abreu (Eds.), Progress in Artificial Intelligence. XV, 504 pages. 2003.

Vol. 2892: F. Dau, The Logic System of Concept Graphs with Negation. XI, 213 pages. 2003.

Vol. 2891: J. Lee, M. Barley (Eds.), Intelligent Agents and Multi-Agent Systems. X, 215 pages. 2003.

Vol. 2882: D. Veit, Matchmaking in Electronic Markets. XV, 180 pages. 2003.

Vol. 2871: N. Zhong, Z.W. Raś, S. Tsumoto, E. Suzuki (Eds.), Foundations of Intelligent Systems. XV, 697 pages. 2003.

Vol. 2854: J. Hoffmann, Utilizing Problem Structure in Planing. XIII, 251 pages. 2003.

Vol. 2843: G. Grieser, Y. Tanaka, A. Yamamoto (Eds.), Discovery Science. XII, 504 pages. 2003.

Vol. 2842: R. Gavaldá, K.P. Jantke, E. Takimoto (Eds.), Algorithmic Learning Theory. XI, 313 pages. 2003.

Vol. 2838: N. Lavrač, D. Gamberger, L. Todorovski, H. Blockeel (Eds.), Knowledge Discovery in Databases: PKDD 2003. XVI, 508 pages. 2003.

Vol. 2837: N. Lavrač, D. Gamberger, L. Todorovski, H. Blockeel (Eds.), Machine Learning: ECML 2003. XVI, 504 pages. 2003.

Vol. 2835: T. Horváth, A. Yamamoto (Eds.), Inductive Logic Programming. X, 401 pages. 2003.

Vol. 2821: A. Günter, R. Kruse, B. Neumann (Eds.), KI 2003: Advances in Artificial Intelligence. XII, 662 pages. 2003.

Vol. 2807: V. Matoušek, P. Mautner (Eds.), Text, Speech and Dialogue. XIII, 426 pages. 2003.

Vol. 2801: W. Banzhaf, J. Ziegler, T. Christaller, P. Dittrich, J.T. Kim (Eds.), Advances in Artificial Life. XVI, 905 pages. 2003.

Vol. 2797: O.R. Zaïane, S.J. Simoff, C. Djeraba (Eds.), Mining Multimedia and Complex Data. XII, 281 pages. 2003.

Vol. 2792: T. Rist, R.S. Aylett, D. Ballin, J. Rickel (Eds.), Intelligent Virtual Agents. XV, 364 pages. 2003.

Vol. 2782: M. Klusch, A. Omicini, S. Ossowski, H. Laamanen (Eds.), Cooperative Information Agents VII. XI, 345 pages. 2003.

Vol. 2780: M. Dojat, E. Keravnou, P. Barahona (Eds.), Artificial Intelligence in Medicine. XIII, 388 pages. 2003.

Vol. 2777: B. Schölkopf, M.K. Warmuth (Eds.), Learning Theory and Kernel Machines. XIV, 746 pages. 2003.

Vol. 2752: G.A. Kaminka, P.U. Lima, R. Rojas (Eds.), RoboCup 2002: Robot Soccer World Cup VI. XVI, 498 pages. 2003.